THE ILLUSTRATED ENCYCLOPAEDIA OF
FAIRIES

THE ILLUSTRATED ENCYCLOPAEDIA OF
FAIRIES

ANNA FRANKLIN

Illustrated by
PAUL MASON and HELEN FIELD

vega

First published in 2002 by
Vega
64 Brewery Road
London N7 9NT

A member of **Chrysalis** Books plc

www.chrysalisbooks.co.uk

Text © 2000 Anna Franklin
Illustrations © 2002
Paul Mason and Helen Field
(from photographs by Paul Mason
and Anna Franklin)

The moral right of Anna Franklin as author and
Paul Mason and Helen Field as illustrators of this
work have been asserted in accordance with the
UK Copyrights Designs and Patent Act 1988

Design © 2002 Vega

A CIP catalogue record for this book is available
from the British Library

ISBN 1-84333-624-3

Editor and project manager: Stuart Booth
Designer: Justina Leitão
Production: Susan Sutterby

Printed in Slovenia by Mladinska Knjiga

ACKNOWLEDGEMENTS

*My thanks to Nigel Pennick who helped me out with the
German and Dutch portions of the book, and who shared many
useful insights with me. Also to Dr. Craig Brandist who helped
me with the Slavonic languages; and to Sue Phillips who helped
me with the French and German translations, and who gave
invaluable help in reading the text and making useful
suggestions. Any mistakes are entirely my own.*

*Gratitude must go to Paul Mason and Helen Field for their
inspiring illustrations and to Justina Leitão for her expertise in
designing the finished book. Also, to Will Steeds at Chrysalis
Books for the Vega team there and the enthusiasm and
commitment to the project.*

*Finally, grateful thanks to Stuart Booth, whose faith in this
project kept it alive, and who also proved to be a great editor.
Without him, this book would not exist.*

FOREWORD

TO OPEN THIS BOOK IS TO ENTER THE WORLD OF
MAGIC, FILLED WITH MYSTICAL CREATURES AND
STRANGE FAIRY REALMS, WHERE NOTHING IS QUITE AS IT
SEEMS AND WHERE EVEN THE SIMPLE ACT OF UTTERING
A NAME IS FRAUGHT WITH DANGER.

Yet, what are fairies? Do they really exist, or are they just figments of our
imagination? Hardly - for belief in fairies goes back to the dawn of time and is
a worldwide phenomenon. It is possible to find parallels in the traditions of
peoples from as far apart as Africa, New Zealand and Britain. As an example of
this universality and interconnection, consider the metal iron. This has always
been a potent protection against British fairies stealing away babies, where an
iron key or a pair of iron scissors was once hidden in or beneath their cradles.
Similarly, the African Dahomean tribes protect their children from being stolen
by a forest spirit called the Abiku by giving them iron bracelets to wear.

Most of us have a stylized idea of what a fairy should look like, that idea
being something that we inherited from the Victorians. However, if you think all
fairies are little girls in ballerina costumes with gossamer wings and long flowing
hair, or tiny sparkling points of light like Tinkerbell in J. M. Barrie's classic
children's tale *Peter Pan*, it's time to think again. Many of the creatures we now
call fairies began their existence as gods and goddesses who were demoted by
subsequent religions to fairies and nature spirits. Others are, and always have
been creatures of other realms that wander into our world on occasion.

Fairies come in all shapes and sizes from the monstrous Formorians of
Ireland to the tiny South African Abatwa. Some do resemble humans and have
been known to live with, and even marry, mortals, passing on their special gifts
and attributes to future generations; but one can never be sure of them.

Worryingly, malevolent fairies are rather more common than friendly ones
and some are very frightening indeed. You certainly wouldn't want to meet a
Fachan on a dark night. Shabbily dressed house fairies known as Brownies are
somewhat less than beautiful, but are generally benevolent. They'll happily
work from dusk till dawn helping with the housework or even outside tasks in
exchange for a nightly dish of cream, yet if you upset it even the friendliest
Brownie can become a Boggart - mischievous and sometimes downright

malicious. Angering a fairy is dangerously easy. In the case of a Brownie, all you need to do is give it decent clothing or fail to leave that bowl of cream. Others may be angered by the mention of their names, which is why so many are called euphemistically: the fair folk, the kindly ones, or simply them. In general the more flattering the description, the more dangerous the creature - would you want to offend something that could swallow you whole and still have room for more?

Returning to Peter Pan for a moment, do you remember when Peter Pan lost his shadow and had to have it sewn back on by Wendy? Perhaps his caution was justified. English fairies have a reputation for stealing people's shadows with dire consequences for their victims. Fairy thieves abound, mostly stealing animals or children, though since they take only the substance or spirit, it isn't immediately obvious what has happened. When a cow is elf-taken, it appears to be struck down by some disease. Though it eats as usual, it produces no milk and will turn into a block of wood when it dies. It's said, however, that fairies only take away what selfish humans deserve to lose. They have a reputation for scrupulous fairness. You'll never catch a fairy breaking a promise.

Fairies also keep animals of their own: and it is said that the first ever pigs came from fairy stock. In addition, there are fairy cows, dogs, cats, horses, seals, birds and butterflies. Some are good, others extremely dangerous.

Fairies love music and their tunes are reputed to be far more beautiful than any created by humankind. Many old Irish tunes such as The Pretty Girl Milking the Cow and The Londonderry Air are said to be fairy songs that should not be sung or whistled near a fairy mound. It might annoy the inhabitants to hear their music on mortal lips and as we've already established, angry fairies are best avoided. Traditionally, fairy music is irresistible to mortals and tales abound of people being drawn down into the world of fairies when they heard the call of fairy PIPES. The most famous example is the tale of the children of Hamlin lured into a mountain by a mysterious piper who had been swindled by the town's mayor. Some fairies have sweet voices that will lure people to their doom. There can be few sailors who have not heard of the MERMAIDS who call out from treacherous rocks. Not all mortals have lost their lives to fairy music. Renowned poets and bards of ancient times like Thomas the Rhymer and the blind harpist O'Carolan learned their craft from the fairies and lived long into old age because they knew the rules and followed them unerringly.

When Anna Franklin told me that she intended to write an illustrated fairy encyclopaedia, I expected a slender volume with perhaps a hundred or so entries and a dozen illustrations. I'd reckoned without her vast knowledge and ability to sift and organize information from around the globe. I'd also underestimated the artistic abilities and enthusiasm of Paul Mason and Helen Field. Anna invited me to help her proof-read the first draft, which contained several hundred entries. She then spent the better part of two years adding to and refining this data, until it became the book you are holding in your hand with nearly 3000 and a collection of dazzlingly beautiful illustrations.

Beautiful as it is to look at, this is a book that is also designed to be used. Whether you are a serious student or simply have an interest in the subject, there is no better starting point. Each entry provides insights into specific aspects of fairy lore. These are the main entries in bold **CAPITALS**, which will lead you on to other related entries in CAPITALS. In this way, the book can be used almost like a thesaurus and with the same ease. All entries are in alphabetical order and include a wide variety of alternative spellings of traditional and ethnic names; so finding even the most obscure reference is fast and simple – provided that you can resist being side-tracked by the intriguing details waiting to be discovered.

If you are not quite sure of the correct name, just think of a word related to the subject that interests you and look it up. You will find capitalized words within the entry that will help you find what you are looking for, together with annotated book references for further reading. If all else fails, you could do worse than leaf through the beautiful illustrations to find a particular detail of appearance or dress.

Just for fun try looking up one of the fairies in this introduction and see where it leads you. However, remember not to eat any fairy food whilst you are exploring. You may never find your way home!

SUE PHILLIPS
Spring 2002

Words in CAPITALS within an entry are cross-references to other main entries

ABAPANSI or **Amatongo** are fairies of the Amazulu tribe of southern Africa. They share many characteristics with their Celtic cousins, being spirits of the DEAD, and often appear as FETCHES to lead people into the OTHERWORLD. Some say they can only be seen by WITCHES.

ABARTA ('Performer of Feats') is a trickster of the Irish fairies, the TUATHA DÉ DANAAN. He captured some of the Fianna, the ancient heroes, and took them to the OTHERWORLD.

ABATWA are tiny South African fairies that live peacefully with the ants in anthills. They are very shy, only revealing themselves occasionally - to wizards, young children and pregnant women. If a woman in the seventh month of her pregnancy should see one, she will have a boy child. *See also* MURYAN.

ABHAC ('River') or **Abac** is an Irish DWARF or WATER FAIRY; equivalent to the Welsh AFRANC.

ABHEAN is the harper of the TUATHA DÉ DANAAN.

ABIKU is a forest spirit known to the African Dahomean tribe, which seeks to steal human children. To prevent this, children are ritually scarred or dressed in the CLOTHES of the opposite sex, which fools the spirits; or they are given protective IRON

bracelets. The Yoruba of Nigeria view the Abiku as an evil DEMON that eats or tries to possess children. It has no stomach and therefore is always hungry.

ABRUZZO MAZZAMARELLE is an Italian wind fairy, one of the FOLLETTO, about 60 cm (two feet) tall and wearing a fancy silk hat covered with flowers. He also appears as a grasshopper.

ABUNDIA, **Habundia** or **Wandering Dame Abonde** is Queen of the Normandy fairies of northern France, called the FÉE – though some say she is queen of the Normandy WHITE LADIES. She appears as a lovely woman with dark hair, wearing a circlet with a star on her forehead. She was mentioned in documents of the Middle Ages as a Fairy Queen and as an Italian WITCH goddess with a following of female dancers.

ACHACILA are Bolivian WEATHER FAIRIES from South America who live underground and control the hail, rain and frost. They occasionally appear to humans as little old men.

ACHERI is an Indian spirit, said to be the GHOST of a little girl, who brings disease in her shadow. She lives in the mountains and her singing is an OMEN OF DEATH and sickness. A protection against her attentions is to wear a RED THREAD about the neck.

ACORN LADY is an English fairy who appears as a DWARF woman dressed in peasant clothing. She loves nuts and will punish, with bloating and cramps, anyone who takes acorns from her tree.

She hates lazy humans and will pinch them into activity.

ADACHIGAHARA is a Japanese OGRESS who attacks travellers and children with her sharp knife in order to kill and eat them.

ADAMASTOR is the spirit of the Cape of Good Hope. It is said to have appeared to Vasco de Gama and prophesied disaster for anyone attempting to sail to India round that tip of southern Africa.

ADARO are the Pacific MERMEN of the Solomon Isles. They have single horns, gills and webbed feet. They live in the sun, travel to earth on RAINBOWS, and are always active when the sun shines during a storm. They dislike humans and shoot them with ARROWS, causing paralysis and death.

ADDER is a poisonous SNAKE, which in Scottish folklore, often represents the power of the CAILLEACH or fairy HAG of winter. At the Celtic celebration of IMBOLC (2nd February), it is defeated by the lamb of the maiden BRIGHID.

ADDLERS is an English designation for fairies in the county of Yorkshire.

ADH SIDHE are Irish fairies who pursue wrongdoers and drive them insane. They usually appear as HAGS who rend their victims' flesh with their sharp teeth. However, they sometimes manifest themselves as lovely young women or even as black HORSES.

AD-HENE ('Themselves') is a Manx euphemism for the fairies. The people of the ISLE OF MAN take care to keep on the right side of these little people, as they can be very malicious when angered.

AEDA is an Irish DWARF, the size of a three-year-old human child. He went to Faylinn (a fairy realm) where he caused great panic, as he seemed like a GIANT to the inhabitants.

AEDH is the son of the King of Leinster who was enticed into a fairy MOUND by the Irish fairies. After many years, he managed to escape with fifty other human captives. Immediately, they encountered St. Patrick who had recently arrived in Ireland. Aedh converted to Christianity on the spot and declared that thenceforth the TUATHA DÉ DANAAN had no more power over him.

AEGLE is one of the HESPERIDES.

AELF is a Scandinavian ELF, the name meaning something like 'white spirit', or 'shining spirit'. Aelfs were originally nature or fertility spirits, with a great many varieties such as the *dunaelfen* or hill elves, *wyldaelfen* or wild-elves; plus field elves, mountain elves, sea elves, wood elves and water elves.

Aelf or *elf* appears as a component of many human names including Aelfgar ('elf-spear'), Aelfhelm ('elf-helmet') Elfrida ('threatening elf'), Alvin ('elf

NEWGRANGE See AENGUS

friend') and Aelfric ('elf king'), which survives as Aubrey.

The most famous elf name belongs to King Aelfred - better known as Alfred the Great - meaning 'elf-counsel'. This famous early English king's name indicates that he was cunning in council, or as crafty as a supernatural being. One Archbishop of Canterbury was called Aelfhaeg, meaning 'high as an elf'. The significance of his name doesn't seem to have escaped the church, which Latinized it as Alphaegius. Such names began to disappear from England after the Norman invasion.

Elves were thought to cause sicknesses such as the *aelfsogotha* or 'elf disease' which made a human's eyes go yellow (possibly jaundice), or 'elf cake' consisting of a hardness in the side (maybe hernia) and the *waeteraelf-adl* or 'water-elf disease' (possibly

chicken pox, still known in Germany as waterpox or *wasserpocken*). The Scottish word eldritch (or in its older spelling 'elriche'), meaning uncanny, is either formed from the Anglo-Saxon *aelf* and *ric* referring to a place rich in spirits, or *elfrice* meaning the fairy kingdom, or FAIRYLAND.

AELFTHONE is the plant Enchanter's Nightshade (*Circaea lutetiana*), used by Anglo Saxon leeches, or doctors, to counteract the powers of evil elves. It grew in the places they frequented, such as shady, moist spots, but had greater power than they did. In Germany, it was associated with WITCHES and called *Hexenkraut* or 'witches herb'.

AENGUS, Aonghus Og, Oenghus Og or Angus Og is one of the Irish fairies the TUATHA DÉ DANAAN, though

he was originally the god of love and youth, the son of the DAGDA and the river goddess Boann. He is called *Mac Og*, which means 'young son', as he is said to be beautiful. He is accompanied by four birds that hover around his head and represent his kisses. He lives in a MOUND called Bruig na Boinne, the prehistoric site of Newgrange in Co. Meath.

The most famous story about him tells of how, in a dream, he was visited by a fairy maiden called CAER and fell in love with her.[1] He set out to find her and eventually discovered her one SAMHAIN Eve, one of a hundred and fifty SWAN MAIDENS bound together in pairs with silver chains. Aengus turned himself into a swan and away they flew together, THREE times around the lake, singing a magical song that put all the local people to sleep for three days and nights.

AËRICO are Albanian TREE FAIRIES who haunt old and barren cherry trees. They are malicious, and anyone who even steps into the shadow of one of their trees will be afflicted with swellings and pains in the hands and feet.

AES SIDHE ('People of the Hills') are Irish fairies who live in the ancient hills and burial MOUNDS. They leave their mounds on SAMHAIN Eve, IMBOLC Eve, BELTANE Eve, and LUGHNASA Eve to move amongst humans.

AFRANC or **Addanc** is a Welsh WATER FAIRY, or primeval water spirit, with claws and able to throw spears. King ARTHUR fought an afranc in Llyn Barfog; and another was dragged from its lair in the River Conway by a giant ox and dropped into Glaslyn, the 'bottomless' lake on Mount Snowdon. Afranc is equivalent to the Irish ABHAC, a type of DWARF or river spirit. The word is derived from the word *abha*, meaning 'river'.

AFREET or **Ifrit** (*f.* Afreeta; *m.* Afreet) are a type of DJINN generally thought of as evil.

AGOGWE are Tanzanian fairies that appear as tiny, hairy RED men.

AGUANE/AGUANA is a female fairy of Northern Italy and of the Austrian and southern Slavonic borders. These fairies are able to SHAPESHIFT, but generally appear as beautiful, long-haired women, of human size or smaller, and dressed in furs. They possess lovely voices but have the FEET of GOATS or horses. Sometimes they appear as old HAGS. As they are the

guardians of streams and mountains, you must ask the Aguana's permission before bathing in mountain waters. If an Aguana comes upon a man muddying the water she will wrap her hair round his feet and drag him beneath the surface to drown him, or take him into her CAVE to sexually molest him; or she may even eat him. However, Aguane appear to be particularly fond of small children whom they carry around on their backs, tossing one of their long breasts over their shoulders to suckle them. Their husbands are known as the SILVANI.

AHES, Dahut or **Ahes Dahut** was the daughter of King Gradlon of the land of Ys in Celtic lore. Each night she took a new lover, until a strange prince appeared with eyes of fire, entirely clad in RED. As the price of his love, he demanded the keys that opened the floodgates of the city. (Some say that her lover was the Black Prince and her father's enemy). With these keys, the prince opened the sluices and drowned the city. As a punishment, she became a MORGEN, a sea fairy with a woman's body and fish tail. She is sometimes seen sitting on a rock combing her hair. The legend has evolved from the mythology of A Hes, a British sea goddess.

AHL AL-TRAB are tiny, mischievous fairies of Arabic folklore, that live beneath the sands of the Sahara and emerge to plague wayfarers in the desert, annoying camels, raising sand storms, and drinking the pools of water in oases just before thirsty travellers arrive.

AHUIZOTL is an Aztec WATER FAIRY from Mexico who resembles a cross between a DOG and a monkey - but with a human hand at the end of its tail. It lures people into water, where it devours their eyes, teeth and nails.

AIGAMUXO are the Hottentot OGRES of southern Africa who have long teeth and eyes in their heels. They like to catch people and eat them.

AIKEN DRUM is a BROWNIE known in Galloway, Scotland.

AILLEANN is a fairy woman who often turned herself into a deer, in Irish romance. In one story, she married King ARTHUR, while his men married other fairy women.

AILLEN MAC MIDHNA travelled to the court of the Irish High King in Tara every SAMHAIN. His magical MUSIC lulled all the inhabitants to sleep, so that he was able to destroy the castle with THREE fiery breaths. This happened every year for twenty-three years until the mortal hero Finn Mac Cumhal was able to resist the spell of the music, and succeeded in beheading the fairy musician.

AINE or Ainé was sitting one day by Lough Gur in Ireland when the Earl of Desmond (Gearoid Iarla 1338-98) chanced to see her combing her hair. Thereupon, he instantly fell in love with her and in one version of the tale, made her his wife by seizing her CLOTHES. In another, she agreed to marry him on the condition that he was never surprised by anything that their children did. Unfortunately, when their son, the Earl of Fitzgerald, jumped in and out of a bottle he couldn't hide his amazement. Poor Fitzgerald turned into a wild goose and flew away, while Aine fled into the MOUND still known as CNOC Aine in Co. Limerick. She is sometimes seen in the middle of a lake, her body only half out of the water, combing her hair. Gearoid Iarla lives underneath the lake, and once every SEVEN years he rides out from it on a white HORSE.

In Co. Derry, people say that Aine was a mortal women taken away to become Queen of the Fairies. The local O'Corra family claim descent from her and Aine is also said to live at Dunany (Dun Aine) Point in Co. Louth.

Originally a deity of the TUATHA DÉ DANAAN, Aine was a MOON goddess, the patroness of crops and COWS, demoted to the status of a fairy. The older legends are less attractive in nature and relate how she revenged her rape by the King of Munster by slaying him with MAGIC. Her feast day is MIDSUMMER Eve when she appears at Cnoc Aine, surrounded by maidens. Local people once gathered there to hold processions, carrying torches (cliars) of straw and hay on poles through the fields of ripening crops and cattle folds. Sometimes Aine herself leads the train. The first Friday, Saturday and Sunday after LUGHNASA (August 1st) are also sacred to her. It

was said that she would claim a human life on those days.

AINSEL is a Scottish fairy who appeared one night to a little boy who stayed up too late. As soon as his mother had put out the candle, the little fairy began to dance in front of the boy. He asked the fairy its name, and she replied 'Ainsel' and in turn asked him his. Cunningly, he replied: 'My ainsel' (my own self). They began to play together until the boy stirred up the fire so that a spark shot out and burned the foot of the fairy, who set up a yowl. Then a big voice boomed down the chimney asking what the matter was, and the fairy mother appeared. The little fairy replied that it was burned on the foot. 'Who did it?', asked the mother. 'My Ainsel', she replied. 'Well, what's all the fuss about, if no one else is to blame!', exclaimed the mother, and kicked Ainsel up the chimney. Variations on the tale are told the world over.

AIRI is a WILD HUNTSMAN of India who may show travellers the TREASURE that is concealed in his UNDERWORLD caves, but is more likely to hunt them with his DOGS.

AITVARAS are Lithuanian HOUSE FAIRIES who supply their adopted human home and family with stolen grain and money, thereby often getting them into trouble. They appear as cockerels inside the house and DRAGONS outside. You can purchase one from the DEVIL for the price of your soul.

AJATAR is a Finnish forest DEMON that causes sickness and plagues. She appears as a DRAGON.

AKAKOSAH is one of the NATS, or Burmese NATURE FAIRIES.

AKUMA is an evil Japanese fairy with a fiery head, burning eyes, and who carries a threatening sword. When it appears it is a very bad OMEN.

AL is an evil Persian fairy who devours the spirits of UNBORN CHILDREN. A mother and child must be protected by surrounding the birthing bed with IRON implements. Als are humanoid, but are covered in hair, have burning eyes, iron teeth and a single tusk. They live in boggy places, or may take up residence in any area of a house or stable that is not properly cleaned.

ALAKA is the magical kingdom ruled by KUBERA, king of the YAKSHAS, the Himalayan fairies.

ALAN are mischievous but benign Philippine fairies that have toes instead of fingers, and fingers instead of toes. Half-bird and half-human, they hang from forest trees.

ALB is a German term for a DWARF. In the Nibelungen the king of the dwarfs is ALBERICH, and an alternative - possibly earlier - spelling of OBERON is Alberon.

ALBA or Turanna is the queen of the Tuscan fairies in central Italy. The latter name may be the older one and of Etruscan origin.

ALBERICH is a famous DWARF and the guardian of the TREASURE Hoard that the hero Siegfied won from the Nibelungen.

ALBION is an ancient name for Britain and is used to denote the magical, OTHERWORLD aspects of the land. It is said to have been the name of Britain before Brutus landed there from Troy. William Blake used the name for a GIANT equated with the TITAN Cronos.

ALCHERINGA are fairies known to the Arunta tribes of central Australia. They are a spirit race, usually invisible, living in trees and stones. SHAMANS and WITCHES can see them and describe the creatures as thin and shadowy, but always youthful in appearance. These spirits must be placated if their good will is to be maintained. Some may attach themselves to favoured individuals as guardian spirits.

ALCINA or **Fata Alcina** is one of the sisters of MORGAN LE FAY. She appears in Italian Renaissance poetry, described as particularly vengeful towards her former lovers, turning them into animals, trees and stones rather than the traditional FROG. She lives in a palace in the straits of Messina. Sailors sometimes glimpse it, but if they try to reach it, they will drown.

ALDEGANNO is an ivy fairy from Tuscany in Italy.

ALDER (*Alnus glutinosa*) is a tree species which grows near water and it is said to be under the protection of WATER FAIRIES. It yields three dyes; RED from the bark, GREEN from the flowers and brown from the twigs. These are taken to represent fire, water and earth. The GREEN dye is also associated with fairy CLOTHES. In Ireland, a branch of alder was tied over the cradle of a newborn boy to prevent the fairies from KIDNAPPING him. In medieval German legend, it is the tree of the ERLKING.

ALECTO is one of the ERINNYES.

ÁLF (*pl.* **Álfar**) is an ELF in Scandinavian mythology, half-DWARF, and half-divine. In folklore, it is also a DEMON that causes NIGHTMARES.

ÁLFABLÓT ('Elves' Sacrifice') is a ritual described in early Scandinavian sagas, designed to appease harmful ELVES or beg assistance from them. For example, a person seeking healing would redden the outside of a MOUND with the blood of a sacrificed bull, then offer the meat as a meal to the elves.

ÁLFHEIM ('Elf Home') is the home of the Light ELVES, the LIOSÁLFAR, in Scandinavian folklore. It exists in a mysterious realm between heaven and earth and is ruled by the god FREY.

ALLERÜNKEN is a type of south German KOBOLD which inhabits a carved figurine.

ALMAS are creatures of China and Mongolia that are similar to SASQUATCH or WILD MEN. They are tall and covered with shaggy hair, have naked hands and faces and were first mentioned in a journal of the 1420s.

ALP or **Trud** (*pl.* **Alpe**) is a German fairy that causes nightmares by sitting on a sleeper's chest and pressing down on him. The word is related to the word ELF.

During the night, Alpe try to get into houses to play their tricks. They are able to enter through the smallest hole and if they get in, you should plug the hole so that they cannot escape and you will be able to force them to promise never to bother you again. Some say that IRON will keep them away, while others swear that placing your shoes at the side of the bed with the toes pointing outwards will deter them. If an alp is pressing down on you, put your thumb into your palm and he will have to let go. Alpe may also mess up your hair during the night by sucking on it and knotting it. These knots are called 'mare braids'.

Sorcerers can send alpe to plague people they dislike. Such a magician will have eyebrows that meet in the middle. The alp emerges from the eyebrows in the form of a small BUTTERFLY.

A German carpenter encountered an ALP in the shape of a CAT. He was accustomed to sleeping in his workshop but all one week he felt something pressing so hard on his chest each night that he was almost suffocated. Then a cat crept into the room through a small hole. The carpenter quickly jumped up, stopped the opening, and nailed one of the cat's paws to the floor. For the first time in days he lay down and slept peacefully. The next morning he was astonished to discover a lovely, naked woman with her hand nailed to the floor. He was so taken with her that he married her and she bore him three children over the course of the next few years. One day she was with him in the workshop when he forgot himself and pointed out to her the hole where she had first entered. She suddenly turned into a cat and ran out through the hole, never to be seen again.[2]

Alpe are very interested in HORSES. They will ride unprotected horses during the night, leaving them exhausted in the morning. They will even ride chairs unless you move them each night at bedtime. Alpe attack unprotected farm animals, crushing them to death. A BROOM placed in the pen will protect the beasts.

ALP-DRÜCKEN ('Elf Pressure') is a German expression for a NIGHTMARE.

ALP-LUACHA or **Joint Eater** is an Irish fairy who sits by a person and shares his food, drawing away all the goodness and substance from it, so that no matter how much the man eats he becomes lean and wasted, and always hungry. One man got rid of his Alp-Luacha by eating huge quantities of salted meat without taking any water. He then lay beside a stream and fell asleep with his mouth open, whereupon the desperate

Alp-Luacha jumped into the water to quench its thirst.

ALRAUNE is a type of KOBOLD which inhabits a figurine carved from a mandrake root.

ALUX are little people who have magical powers and dwell in the vicinity of the ancient temples, according to the Mayan folklore of Central America.

ALVEN or **Ottermaaner** are Dutch WATER FAIRIES who live in barren ponds or small hills called Alvinnen Hills. They are so slight and insubstantial that they are almost transparent, which enables them to rise into the air in water bubbles, and to travel on the wind or in EGGSHELLS. Occasionally, they become visible when they don otter skins; or when they SHAPESHIFT from tiny creatures into massive beings that cover half the sky. Despite their fragile appearance, they are very powerful, controlling rivers such as the Elbe, coming out at night to care for their flowers, and punishing any human who touches their favourite blossoms such as night wort and elf leaf.

ALVE is sometimes given as an alternative to ÁLF or ELF. These elves are the EARTH-FAIRIES of Norse folklore who live in MOUNDS. In earlier tales, they were the spirits of the DEAD dwelling in the burial chambers, to which sacrifices had to be made.

ALVGEST ('Elf Wind') is the breath of ELVES, feared by people in Norway, which covers the body of a person with blisters. To cure it, a BIBLE must be opened and the pages brushed over the sufferer several times.

AMADÁN ('Fool') is a fairy fool or jester, in Irish folklore, though his tricks are not funny. His touch will cause a STROKE, making a person crippled or paralysed permanently down one side. He attacks those who linger in fairy haunts at night, especially during the month of June.

AMADÁN DUBH ('Dark Fool') is an Irish trickster who brings madness or oblivion. He haunts the hills after sunset, playing REED pipes to work his MAGIC.

AMADÁN MÓR 'Great Fool' is a fairy jester in Irish tales.

AMADÁN-NA-BRIONA is an Irish fairy, also called 'The Fool of the Forth', who changes his shape every two days. When he appears as a man he is very, very wide and wears a high hat and a RED scarf - though he has been known to appear as a beast and even a sheep with a beard. If you meet him you should say: 'The Lord be between us and harm', because if he touches you he will inflict an incurable madness or even death. He is most often at his tricks during the month of June, knocking on doors late at night, throwing basins after people, or popping up from behind hedges.

The Irish say: 'To meet the Amadán is to be in prison forever'.

AMFORTAS

AMADÁN-NA-BRUIDNE ('The Fool of the Fairy MOUNDS') is another Irish trickster fairy.

AMATHAON is a WILD MAN in Welsh folklore and probably an ancient god of agriculture. He is a son of DÔN and fought ARAWN, the king of ANNWN.

AMATSU-OTOME are female Japanese mountain spirits or FALLEN ANGELS. The name is also applied to WITCHES.

AMFORTAS is the name of the Fisher King in Arthurian lore, the fairy guardian of the Holy Grail. He was wounded in the scrotum by a poisoned lance and had to await the coming of the Grail Knight to restore him to health. Ancient tales contains a number of kings so wounded, and it is possible that the scrotum or thigh wound symbolises a loss of virility and capability on the part of the king. The King was once associated with the land itself. If he were fit and strong, it was believed the land would be bountiful. If he were ill or dishonourable, the gods would punish the whole land by making it barren.

AMMAZZAMAREDDU, also called Mazzamarieddu, are Italian FOLLETTI who travel only when they have seen the blood of a murdered man. They cause earthquakes, wind and snow storms. Every year they fight the saints Fillippo and Giacomo. If the wind blows on these days, the farmers know that the fairies are victorious, and chew copious amounts of garlic to keep them away.

ANA (Sanskrit for 'Nourishment') is the Romany gypsy queen of the KESHALYI fairies. She lived in a palace in the mountains until she was forced to marry the king of the LOÇOLICO, the DEMONS of the UNDERWORLD. She bore him many monstrous children until finally their son PORESKORO was so hideous that he even horrified her demon husband.

Thereupon, he granted Ana her freedom on condition that all female keshalyi should be sent to the demons at the age of 999. Ana now lives in an inaccessible castle and only shows herself on rare occasions, and then only in the form of a golden TOAD.

ANCHANCHU is a VAMPIRE fairy of the Aymará Indians of Peru. He travels in whirlwinds and seduces his victims with pleasant smiles before draining their strength and blood.

ANCHO is a Spanish HOUSE FAIRY who will perform small tasks in return for a modest reward. He is very friendly and loquacious towards his adopted human family though he dislikes the sound of church BELLS, which drive him away.

ANDVARI ('Watcher') is a DWARF mentioned in Icelandic literature. He was a son of the chief god Odin and was condemned by the NORNS to spend his life as a fish. The trickster god Loki caught him and forced him to hand over all of his TREASURE.

ANGELS are, according to a branch of modern Theosophy, what fairies (designated nature spirits or DEVAS) evolve into as they gain experience and knowledge. The process runs as follows: ELEMENTAL to GNOME, to ELF, to FAUN, to cherub, to seraph and to angel.[3] Some early folklorists stated that fairies were FALLEN ANGELS.

ANGIAK is a spirit created from the soul of a baby deliberately killed by exposure in the snow according to Inuit folklore. Unless the tribe moves after such a death, they will be haunted by its wailing cries.

ANHANGA is an evil spirit who roams the forests of Brazil. His appearance is unknown, but he often haunts the dreams of travellers, and sometimes prevents hunters going about their business. He occasionally KIDNAPS unprotected children.

ANIMA is a form of soul. Many early religions were animistic in nature, sharing a belief that humans, animals, trees, plants, rocks, streams, rivers and places have anima or soul. As long as certain offerings were made and particular procedures followed, the spirits would remain friendly and beneficent. If they were neglected or offended, they would take their revenge. A river spirit might rise up and drown humans crossing his domain. The spirit of the corn might cause the crops to fail; an apple tree might refuse to be fruitful.

The animistic origins of some fairy beliefs are easily traced. The classical Greeks and Romans believed in DRYADS and HAMADRYADS as well as NYMPHS of meadows, mountains, streams, woods, the sea, lakes, pools, and valleys. The Celts and Teutons held trees and groves to be sacred to the spirits that inhabited them. The ancient Japanese believed that trees had souls, especially very old and gnarled trees: the woodcutter saw a spirit in every knotted trunk. The natives of Tasmania believed in DEMONS that resided in trees. Various WATER FAIRIES have to be placated or they will drown travellers. WHITE LADIES may represent the GENII LOCI or spirits of place. See also TREE FAIRIES and VEGETATION SPIRITS.

ANKOU is a Breton fairy who collects the souls of the dead. He wears a black hooded costume and drives a black cart drawn by four coal-black HORSES, or appears as a skeleton in a white shroud driving a cart with squeaky wheels. Like other fairies, he and his retinue follow straight paths in sacred processions (see LEY LINES). No one has ever seen his gaunt face and lived. He is derived from an ancient Celtic death god called Ankeu, known as 'Master of the World'. Every village in Brittany has its own Ankou - the last man in the parish to die each year. Each King of the DEAD therefore holds his office for no more than twelve months. Sometimes the Ankou may be seen entering a house where a person is about to die, sometimes only his knocking or mournful cries are heard. In Wales, GWYN AP NUDD plays a parallel role. The Irish say that when Ankou comes, he will not go away empty handed.

ANNA is the full sister of ARTHUR, according to Geoffrey of Monmouth.[4] She may be identified with ANU or ANNIS.

ANNEQUINS are French WILL O'THE WISPS.

ANNIS *See* BLACK ANNIS.

ANNWN or **Annwfn** is the enchanted OTHERWORLD or fairyland of Brythonic Celtic myth, comparable to the Gaelic TIR NAN OG. It is an UNDERWORLD realm to which human souls travel at death. In Annwn the fountains run with wine, while old age and sickness are unknown. Its inhabitants spend their days feasting and drinking. It is ruled over by ARAWN, the LORD OF THE DEAD, and is a place of ancestral knowledge and power, which may occasionally be accessed by living mortals. The WILD HUNT rides out from its portals.

ANTHROPOPHAGI ('Man Eating') are strange fairies mentioned in Shakespeare's *Merry Wives of Windsor* and in *Othello*. They have no heads, their brains are near their sexual organs, their eyes appear on their shoulders and their mouths are in the centres of their chests. They have no noses at all. They are cannibals and eat human beings, afterwards using the bones for tools and the skulls for cups.

ANU is the mother of the Irish fairies, possibly identical with AINE and BLACK ANNIS. Sometimes she is made cognate with DANU, though Anu was an earth and fertility goddess, while Danu was a water goddess. The twin hills near Killarney are called The Paps of Anu.

ANUANIMA is the ruler of a race of fairies that live in the airy realms above the sky, according to Arawak (Caribbean) legend. The fairies sometimes descend to earth in the guise of birds.

AOIBHILL, **Aoibheall**, **Aoibhell** or **Aoibheal** is a Fairy Queen who appears in Ireland as a BANSHEE to herald the deaths of members of the Dalcassian family of North Munster. When a member of the O'Brien family hears the music of her magical HARP, he will not long survive the experience. Other tales describe her as a SIDHE woman of Co. Clare who appeared to Brian Ború to predict that the first of his sons he should see thereafter would succeed him as High King of Ireland. She rules the Craig Liath ('Grey Rock') in Co. Clare.

AONBARR is the magical fairy HORSE of the Isle of Man ridden by MANANNAN. It could travel with equal ease over either land or sea.

APC'LNIC are small fairies of the Montagnais Indians of Canada. They appear and disappear magically. They often KIDNAP human children.

APPEARANCE and DRESS Fairies come in all shapes and sizes. Some are as tiny as insects, others as large as GIANTS. Some are very beautiful, others incredibly ugly. Some look human, others like monsters or animals. Some are invisible and most can change shape at will. Many fairies go naked, and these are often covered in hair, particularly RED HAIR. Some are very smartly dressed while others go about in rags and are offended by gifts of CLOTHES. Fairies usually dress in WHITE, RED and GREEN or in earthy colours to blend in with the landscape they inhabit. Those associated with the fog dress in grey. Few fairies have wings.

APPLE (*Malus sp.*) is a tree sacred to fairies. In the west of England the small apples left on the trees are called 'the pixies' harvest' and children used to be allowed to scrump them, even being encouraged with pennies or bread and cheese by the farmer's wife to do so. Grafted apple trees, called 'ymp trees' (IMP trees) in old English, fall under the dominion of the fairies, and anyone sleeping under one is liable to be abducted by them.

Eating a fairy apple (one that grows in the OTHERWORLD) confers eternal youth, immortality, or rebirth. However, gaining the fruit is fraught with danger. The tree is always guarded, usually by a SNAKE or DRAGON. Once the fruit has been eaten, the partaker can never return to being what he or she was before. The Fairy Queen warned THOMAS THE RHYMER about eating the apples in her garden. She said that to share the food of the DEAD is to know no return to the land of the living.

In European mythology, legendary fairy isles of apples - such as AVALON - are common, and always lie in the west, the place of the dying sun. NEOLITHIC and Bronze Age paradises were orchards. Indeed 'paradise' means 'orchard'. In ancient Pagan myth, the round, RED apple is a symbol of the sun or sun god who dies each night to enter the UNDERWORLD, or Land of Youth, travelling through the realms of the DEAD to the east and rebirth with each dawn.

APPLE TREE MAN dwells in one particular tree in every English apple orchard, though he is best known in Somerset.[5] His tree is always the oldest, or the one bearing the heaviest crop. He can grant a good harvest for the whole orchard, and other benefits besides. The last of the crop should be left on the ground for him, and his tree should be wassailed at YULE.

APSARI are little Javanese fairies.

APUKU are forest fairies of the native Indian tribes of Surinam.

ARAIGNÉES LUTINS are French country dwelling LUTINS.

ÀRÀK is a Cambodian HOUSE FAIRY who adopts a family and then either dwells in the house with them or in a nearby tree.

ARAWN is ancient Welsh god of the UNDERWORLD sometimes said to be the King of the Fairies, like his counterpart in south Wales, GWYN AP NUDD. In one story, he appeared chasing a FAIRY HART, accompanied by a pack of white DOGS with red ears. In another, he changed places with the human King Pwyll for a time. When he returned to his own land, he rewarded Pwyll with a herd of PIGS. This seems to be a symbolic tale of the seasonal battle or exchange between the forces of winter and summer.

ARGANTE ('Silver') is the Fairy Queen of AVALON in some Arthurian tales. She may be derived from the Welsh goddess of the moon ARIANRHOD ('Silver Wheel') or the name may be a corruption of *Morgante*, i.e. MORGAN LE FAY.

ARIANRHOD is a MOON and SPINNING goddess in Welsh mythology, perhaps akin to the Greek FATES and the prototype of various fate or spinning fairies. She is the mistress of the OTHERWORLD tower CAER SIDDI or Caer Arianrhod - where the DEAD go between incarnations, which poets visit in dreams to gain inspiration, and where magicians go to be initiated. The Corona Borealis is known in Welsh as *Caer Arianrhod*, paralleling its association with the spinner/weaver goddess Ariadne in Greek myth.

ARIEL is an ELEMENTAL fairy of the air, immortalised by Shakespeare in *The Tempest*. He had been a servant of Sycorax, the WITCH. With his song he could bind or loose the winds, enchant men, or drive them mad. He eventually passed entirely into the element of air and was never seen again. The name is sometimes used as a generic term for supernatural beings. According to neo-Platonists and magicians, Ariel is a SYLPH, sometimes said to be the ruler of Africa. Alexander Pope used the name Ariel for a sylph in *The Rape of the Lock*.

ARIMASPEANS ('One-eyed') are strange beings who lived near the route along which votive offerings were sent to the Greek god Apollo's shrine. Their 'one-eyed' name may be a code for MUSHROOMS, perhaps FLY AGARIC mushrooms, used shamanically. There are many one-eyed spirits and fairies.

ARKAN SONNEY are fairy PIGS from the ISLE OF MAN who bring great good fortune if they can be captured.

ARROWS and bows are used by a variety of fairies. These include the English ROBIN GOODFELLOW, PUCK, GREEN MEN and SPRIGGANS, the Slavonic VILE, the American BAYKOK, the Sioux LITTLE FAIRIES, the Cambodian PRÄY, the Scottish UNSEELIE COURT, ADARO from the Soloman Isles, the German PILWIZ, the Hawaiian MENAHUNE and the Welsh Y GWYLLIED COCHION, to name but a few.

When Stone Age flint arrowheads were found they were often called fairy arrows or ELF BOLTS and attributed to fairy manufacture. Welsh legends tell of people being found dead in the forest shot with numerous tiny arrows. Fairy archers were much feared in Scotland, according to an old poem, which states:
'We dare not go a-hunting
For fear of little men!'.
Anyone who went near the fairy mounds was likely to be struck with a fairy arrow. Attack by an evil spirit must have seemed the only explanation for the sudden one-sided paralysis of a stroke.

This association of arrows and the spirit world is very ancient. Supernatural or divine bowmen appear in many mythologies. In Indian legend there is the god Rama; in English folklore the tales of ROBIN HOOD; and in classical mythology, the arrows of Eros never miss their mark, tipped with gold to cause love, and with lead to extinguish passion. In the Bible, we read of the mighty hunter Nimrod; and the Persian god Mithras was a divine archer who shot an arrow into a rock from which water then sprang. Similarly, Apollo is the Greek god of the sun with attributes of bow and lyre.

The only straight thing in nature is the shaft of sunlight piercing the clouds. These shafts are spoken of as the 'fiery arrows of the sun' or 'darts of the sun'.[6] The sun-arrows touch the earth and thus link the earth and the heavens as a kind of divine *axis mundi*. Another archer associated with the sun is the zodiac sign of Sagittarius, the archer who precedes the house of Capricorn in which the GOAT gives birth to the sun or Sun God in December.

Apollo's sister is the MOON goddess Artemis. She too has a bow and arrows. Her bow is the crescent of the moon and her arrows the shafts of moonbeams. Like many moon goddesses she is the patroness of the hunt, sudden death, and the wild goddess of the woods who brings prosperity to those who honour her. Artemis is later identified with the Roman goddess Diana whose name is found as a component of many fairy names. In Romania, she became Dziana. Among the Slavs she was Diiwica (Lusatia), Devana (Western Slavonic) and Dziewona among the Poles.

Our ancestors were hunter-gatherers prowling through the dark forests in search of game. To them, the bow was important, and the sound of the bowstring is often considered magical, attracting game. It is the precursor of such musical instruments such as the HARP or lyre. The bowshot was a unit of length used to define boundaries and limits. It is also straight and straight lines were considered sacred (*See* LEY LINES).

ARSILE is a FAIRY GODMOTHER, one of the French BONNES DAMES.

ARTHUR ('Bear-Man') has many associations with the realm of the fairy. He was educated by the half-fairy

MERLIN, and was given his magical sword by the LADY OF THE LAKE. After his death, four fairy queens, including MORGAN LE FAY, carried King Arthur to the mystical Isle of AVALON. He now sleeps beneath a fairy MOUND to await the time when Britain shall need him once more.

Though Arthur is most familiar as the knight-king of the medieval romances, he is a very ancient figure. The clues to his real identity lie in his name, and in the idea that he lies beneath a mound to await a new day. The Celtic word for bear was *arth* or *arthe*, Latinized as *Artos*. Arthur may be translated as 'bear-man'. The constellation of the Great Bear is known in Wales as 'Arthur's Wain' while YULE was called *Alban Arthur* or 'Arthur's Time'. The bear retreats into a CAVE in the winter in order to hibernate, emerging renewed with the spring, often walking on his hind legs like a man. This made the bear a symbol of renewal, especially as an emblem of the rebirth of the sun from the UNDERWORLD at midwinter. Many sun gods are reborn from a cave or mound at the winter solstice - Arthur's Time.

Arthur's Bosom is a name sometimes given to the OTHERWORLD place where the spirits of DEAD warriors rest.

ASH (*Fraxinus sp.*) is a tree commonly associated with fairies. In Ireland, some solitary ashes are sacred to them and cannot be cut down. In Somerset, England, ash gads are used to protect cattle against fairy mischief, while ash buds placed in the cradle prevent fairies exchanging a CHANGELING for the child.

In Greek myth, the chief god Zeus was nursed in childhood by an ash NYMPH. He fashioned the first bronze race from ash, whereas OAK trees are the mothers of the present race of humankind. In Scandinavian lore, the first man Askr was made from ash, while the first woman Embla was made from ALDER.

The ancients observed that the ash tree was often struck by lightening and seemed to channel the fertilizing lightening flash of the sky god into the belly of the Mother Earth. Therefore they viewed it as an *axis mundi* or World Tree, linking all the planes of existence - sky, earth and UNDERWORLD. According to Norse mythology, the chief god Odin created Yggdrasil, a massive ash tree that linked all the realms of creation. It had three roots in the primal source of being: one in Nifl-heim, the underworld of the cold north; one in Midgard, or the Earth, being the home of mankind; and the third root in Asgard, the home of the gods. One of the daily duties of the NORNS was to sprinkle the sacred tree with water from the Urdar fountain and put fresh clay around its roots.

ASHES from the hearth FIRE form a protective barrier against invasion by evil fairies.

ASKAFROA ('Wife of the Ash') is a Scandinavian DRYAD or ASH tree fairy who had to be propitiated with a sacrifice every Ash Wednesday. She was generally thought to be an evil spirit.

ASOOM JAN TANUSHI was the first DJINN, according to North African folklore.

ASPARAS or Sky Dancers are NYMPHS of Hindu folklore. They live in fig trees and are sent by the gods to deflect pious men from their meditations and prevent them reaching godhead. They offer blessings at weddings, or comfort the dying on battlefields by showing themselves as lovely courtesans, hinting at the delights of heaven.

ASRAI are the small and delicate English WATER FAIRIES of Cheshire and Shropshire, who melt into a pool of water when captured or exposed to sunlight. When you see the tendrils of mist that drift upwards from a body of water as the sun starts to rise, these are the asrai. They melt as the sun climbs in the sky, but they also come out on the nights of the full moon to gaze at its luminous face. Such nights are called Asrai Nights. Each asrai only comes to the surface once a century. They are always female, lovely with long green hair and webbed feet.

A fisherman once caught an asrai with the idea of selling it to the rich people at the castle. Though the fairy begged for her freedom the man hardened his heart. She touched his arm and it felt like ice, but still he rowed on, covering her with rushes. The sun had risen by the time he reached the shore and when he lifted the rushes his net was empty and all that remained was a damp patch. But the arm she had touched was paralysed the rest of his life, and nothing could warm it.[7]

ASRAIS or ASHRAYS are Scottish WATER FAIRIES with pale, ghost-like bodies. They cannot live on land or appear in the sunlight, which makes them melt away, leaving nothing but an iridescent pool.

ASTRAL FAIRIES are creatures of the Astral Plane which Irish occultists have described as being some 2 – 2.5 metres (seven to eight feet) tall with rays of coloured light streaming from them.

ATHACH is a Scots Highland term for a monster or GIANT, used to describe the various unpleasant fairies that haunt lonely lochs and mountains.

ATHAIR-LUZZ is ground ivy (*Glechoma hederacea*) and a MAGIC charm against the unwanted attentions of fairies. One young girl was seized by fairies who tried to get her to join them in their revels and drink their wine. She was saved by a RED HAIRED MAN who led her out of the FAIRY RING and gave her a branch of *athair-luzz,* advising her to hold it in her hand till she got safely home. She took it and ran, followed by the sound of pursuing footsteps. When she reached home she dashed inside and bolted the door behind her, but heard voices saying: 'The power we had over you is gone through the magic of the herb - but when you dance again with us on the hill, you will stay with us forever more, and none shall hinder.' She kept the herb safe and the fairies troubled her no more, but for a long time she heard the FAIRY MUSIC.

ATLANTIS is maintained by some to have been a corporeal realm that sank beneath the oceans. Others think of it as an OTHERWORLD place, a FAIRY ISLAND, that can sink beneath the waves and rise again. Some say MERLIN came out of Atlantis and that he and the other survivors became the Druid priests of ancient Britain.

ATROPOS ('She Who Cannot Be Avoided') is one of the FATES, the HAG who cuts the thread of life, or, in other words, death.

ATTILIO is an Italian HOUSE FAIRY who lives near the HEARTH and who may be a latter day version of the LARE.

ATTORCROPPE ('Little Poison Head') is a fairy of Saxony and a very curious creature. It looks like a small, upright SNAKE with arms and legs. It is known to dislike humans intensely and will do them harm whenever possible.

ATUA or **Nuku Mai Tore** ('People of the Otherworld') are Polynesian fairies who fly and live in the trees. They are nature fairies, or NYMPHS, manifest in animals, plants and the weather though they sometimes marry humans and act like HOUSE FAIRIES. The atua are highly honoured and it is not permitted to speak their names.

AUGHISKY or **Augh-Iska** is a ghoulish Irish WATER HORSE that inhabits streams and lochs, luring its human victims into the water. There, it tears them to pieces and devours them, leaving only their livers. It comes ashore in November and, if you can catch one, saddle and bridle it, then it will make a fine horse. But you must never ride it near the water or it will return to its origins and highly unpleasant habits.

AUKI is a Peruvian mountain fairy, who lives in the Andes complete with his household. He sometimes helps SHAMANS with healing and predicting the future.

AURVANGAR ('Wet Gravel Plains') is the home of the DWARFS, according to the Scandinavian Eddic poems.

AUSTRI ('East') is one of the four DWARFS of Icelandic legend who hold up the sky.

AVAIKI is the UNDERWORLD realm of the Pacific island water NYMPHS, the TAPAIRU, and is accessed through pools.

AVALLOC lived in AVALON with his daughters and according to William of Malmesbury, was its king and the father of Modron.

AVALON ('Isle of Apples'), **Avallach, Avallo** or **Avilion** is a magical fairy island or Land of the DEAD, which exists outside time and space, and where illness, old age and death are unknown. Its name is derived from the Welsh *afall* meaning APPLE (*aball* in Irish, *avallenn* in Breton), since the island is covered in apple orchards. It is also sometimes called The Fortunate Isle, and may be compared with the Irish TIR NAN OG and even the Norse Valhalla. The island is inhabited by nine sisters of which MORGAN LE FAY is the most beautiful and powerful. She has knowledge of SHAPESHIFTING, can turn herself into any animal or bird, and knows the properties of all plants for healing and MAGIC.

According to other sources, Avalon is ruled by AVALLOC, GUINGAMUER, or BANGON.

The fifteenth-century poet Lydgate described King ARTHUR as: 'a king crowned in the land of the fairy'. He goes on to say that he was taken by four fairy queens, one of which was Morgan, to Avalon. There he still lies with his knights, under a fairy hill, until Britain shall need him again.

Some associate Avalon with modern day Somerset town of Glastonbury in south-western England. However, the island existed in legend long before the familiar Arthurian tales. In early Celtic legend, the island could only be reached on a boat guided by the sea god Barinthus, and was a place fit only for the bravest and best.

AWAY is a description in Ireland of any person who has been kidnapped by the fairies. They may have had a CHANGELING or a STOCK OF WOOD substituted for them or their spirit may have been taken, leaving behind a passive body as in the case of Ethna, kidnapped by the Fairy King FINVARRA. Alternatively, a person may have voluntarily entered a FAIRY RING or MOUND. People who are *away* sometimes return after SEVEN years, though many never return at all. Those who do are greatly changed, and often soon pine away and die, longing for the delights of FAIRYLAND.[8]

AWD GOGGIE is a BOGIE who haunts the forests and orchards of Scotland and the north of England. He guards unripe gooseberries (colloquially called 'goosegogs'). Children are advised to stay away from gooseberry bushes lest he should kidnap them.

AYANA are Ethiopian spirits who live in a paradisiacal OTHERWORLD.

AYNIA is the Fairy Queen of Tyrone in Ireland, possibly synonymous with the goddess ANU or DANU, mother of the TUATHA DÉ DANAAN.

AZÂZEL was a DJINN of Arabian legend who was captured by the angels and who became an angel himself. However, he refused to worship Adam and was banished from heaven to become the father of all SHAITAN or DEVILS.

AZEMAN is a VAMPIRE fairy of South America who appears as a woman by day and a bat by night, seeking the blood of humans.

AZIZA are benevolent forest fairies of the Dahomey of West Africa who teach humans practical skills, particularly the craft of hunting.

BABA ('Grandmother') is a Slavonic OGRE who eats humans and has the power to turn men to stone.

BABA YAGA ('Grandmother Bony-shanks') is the noted Russian HAG fairy sometimes said to be a WITCH or OGRESS. She lives in a magical house which moves about from place to place on chicken legs. It is fenced around with human bones. She also flies about in a CAULDRON, obliterating her tracks with a BROOM, calls up storms, and guards the Fountain of Life. She helps those who are pure of heart, but eats the flesh of

those who displease her, tearing her victims apart with her stone teeth.

BABOUSHKA or **BABUSHKA** ('Grandmother' or 'Peasant Woman') is a Russian fairy similar to the Italian BEFANA. She began as a human who failed to give hospitality to the Magi on their journey to witness the birth of Jesus. Now, she roams the land, searching for the Christ Child, as she delivers presents to children at Christmas.

BABCI ('Grandmothers') are Polish fairies or WITCHES.

BAC ('Barrier') is a bank of sand or earth where fairies dwell in Gaelic folklore.

BACHUNTHA is one of the names given to the BANSHEE.

BADBA ('Furies') are supernatural spirits invoked by the Irish TUATHA DÉ DANAAN, employed in the battle of Magh Tuiredh.

BADBH, Badb or **Bahbh** ('Raven' or 'Scald-crow') is a generic term in Ireland for a bad fairy, a WITCH or type of BANSHEE that appears as a CROW or RAVEN to presage death. The term is probably derived from the name of the Celtic war goddess Badbh who appears in triad with NEMAIN and MACHA under the collective, triumverate name of MORRIGAN. She sometimes appears as a lovely maiden, at other times as an ugly HAG or bird. She presides over the battlefield and is seen before a battle washing the armour of those about to die. She manifested as a WASHER AT THE FORD to the hero Cuchulain. She may be one of the origins of the BANSHEE, since a common form of a banshee is a crow, perching on the house of one about to die.

BADHBH CHAOINTE ('Wailing Crow') is another name for the BANSHEE.

BADI are offspring of the DJINN in Malayan lore. They are bad fairies who can take possession of people or objects.

BAGAN (pl. Bagany) is a Russian fairy who looks after livestock, especially GOATS and HORSES. He lives in the barn or behind the stove, but is only visible on Holy Thursday and Easter Sunday. If he doesn't like an animal you have acquired, particularly its colour, he will torture it to within an inch of its life. If he likes the beast, he will lavish attention on it until it grows sleek and fat. To find out what colour he approves of, take a piece of cake and wrap it in a cloth. On Easter Sunday, hang it in the stable and leave it there for six weeks, until it is full of maggots. If they are red, then the bagan favours red, if they are white, you had better buy white animals from now on.

BAGINIS are rapacious aboriginal Australian fairies who have the faces of lovely women, but the FEET and claws of beasts. They capture and ravish human men.

BAGNICA (from *bagnu* meaning 'swamp') is a female Polish fairy who lives in bogs and swamps.

BAJANG is a Malaysian fairy who appears as a polecat to presage sickness and other evils. It is the spirit of a stillborn child and powerful magicians may be able to capture one to act as a FAMILIAR, feeding it on milk and eggs. *See also* UNBORN CHILDREN.

BAKEMONO are Japanese GOBLINS with long straight hair and no FEET.

BAKRU are South American fairies created by MAGIC to act as FAMILIARS. In appearance, they are the size of human children, but are composed partly of wood. They may be purchased from magicians, one pair at a time; but generally, they turn out to be more trouble than they are worth.

BAKU, the Eater of Dreams, causes NIGHTMARES in Japan. It has the

BANSHEE

head of a lion, the body of a HORSE, the tail of a COW, and the feet of a tiger.

BALLYBOGS are Irish BOGGANS who dwell in the peat bogs. They have spherical bodies, spindly arms and legs, all of which are entirely covered in mud. They are thought to be very stupid, and certainly, they cannot speak intelligibly, only grunting and dribbling instead.

BALOR is a one-eyed GIANT in Irish legend, the king of the FORMORIANS.

BANÁNACHS are shrieking spirits of Irish myth. They flew around the hero Cuchulain when he fought his enemy Ferdia. They may be the progenitors of the BANSHEE.

BANGON is an obscure character who is said by some to be the ruler of AVALON. He may be a later form of BARINTHUS, a Welsh sea deity.

BANNAFEET ('Bannock Feet') is one of the Orkney TROWS.

BANNIK (*pl.* **Banniki**) is a Russian HOUSE FAIRY who looks after freshwater ponds and bath-houses. You should leave out your bath water or a special pail of water for him, or he will become very annoyed. An upset bannik might use his sharp claws to flay a victim alive. Every third firing of the heating for the bath should be for him alone, and not used by humans. He creeps under the benches in the bath-house, giggling or making hissing sounds. If he caresses your back while you bathe, this is a good OMEN; but if he scratches you, this is very bad luck. Banniks are sometimes also glimpsed through the steam of saunas and may take on the appearance of a relative or family friend.

In Slavonic countries, the bath-house was often used by a woman in which to give birth, though the newborn babies were rarely left there long as the fairies would KIDNAP them. It was also associated with healing.

The bannik is a creature to be encouraged, and no crosses or other Christian symbols should be placed in the bath-house in case they should frighten him away. He is given offerings of fir tree branches, soap and hot water.

BANSHEE, Bean Sidhe or **Ban Sith** ('Woman Fairy' or 'Woman of the Mound') has the plural form **Banshees**, or, more correctly **Mna' Sidhe** or **Mna' Sige**. The Banshee attaches herself to Irish and Scottish families of pure Milesian descent, or to families particularly gifted with music and song. Their banshee follows even those families that have emigrated abroad. Some families know the name of their banshee: AIOBHILL appears for the Dalcassians of North Munster, and CLIODNA for the McCarthys and other families of South Munster.

Although banshees sometimes seem to give advice, more often they appear to foretell a tragedy and their wailing is an OMEN OF DEATH. The funeral keen of the peasants (*caoine*) is said to be an imitation of a banshee wail and reputed to be a combination of a wild goose's screech, a wolf's howl and the cry of an abandoned child. In Galway, the banshee is said to be the spirit of a DEAD friend or family member. Sometimes the banshee assumes the form of a sweet singing virgin of the family. More usually, she is seen at night as a shrouded woman, crouched beneath the trees, or flying past in the moonlight, lamenting with a veiled face, or combing her long flowing hair while sitting in a tree. If one of her hairs should fall on you, it is a very bad portent. (Conversely, the Love family of Co. Wexford takes it to mean that you will be blessed with riches).[9] A banshee's eyes are always red from weeping. In Donegal, the banshee adopts a GREEN dress and grey cloak, while in Co. Mayo she dresses in black. Sometimes she is accompanied by the omen of the COISTE-BODHAR, an immense black coach with a coffin on it. Several banshees might wail in

chorus at the death of an important or very holy person.

There are several possible mythological sources for the banshee. In Irish legend, shrieking fairies called Banánachs flew around the hero Cuchulain when he fought Ferdia, accompanied by fury-type fairies called Bocánachs. The banshee is also sometimes called a BADBH, which was the name of an Irish death and battle goddess, part of the MORRIGAN triad. The Morrigan herself appeared as a death omen, washing the entrails of those about to die in a stream. Those warriors who heard the songs of the Morrigan were destined to die in battle, while those who did not might have wit enough to live. Thus, her song is a herald of death, like the wail of the banshee. In folk tales, she is said to choose the loveliest maidens to become banshees.

In the Scottish Highlands, the banshee, or *ban sith,* has only one nostril, a long front tooth and pendulous breasts.

BAPTISM is a protection against unwanted fairy attentions. Fairies have the power to KIDNAP human babies until they are baptised. On the ISLE OF MAN, the fairies would sometimes act out a mock baptism of a human baby, in order to have power over it.

BARABO or **BARABAO** is a small SHAPESHIFTING Venetian fairy, which generally appears as a small, fat man in a RED CAP. He loves human women and will change himself into a thread to nestle between their breasts, crying out with pleasure. When the woman looks down to see where the voice is coming from he will already have moved on to his next victim. He has a sense of humour and delights in stealing bread from the bakery or pulling washing from the lines. He squeezes in through keyholes to watch couples making love and impersonates humans to take gondola rides for which he refuses to pay. The basic concept of this character is a part of the famous scary film *'Don't Look Now'*.

BARBEGAZI ('Frozen Beards') are male Alpine fairies who hibernate in the summer and only come out when the temperature drops below freezing point. Then, they entertain themselves by riding along on avalanches. Occasionally, they have been captured by mountaineers but are said to have survived for only a few hours when transported below the tree line. They have large FEET, which serve as snowshoes, and their hair and beards look like icicles. Sometimes, they will help stranded mountaineers or warn them of avalanches by hooting loudly.

BARBOUE, LÉ (from *barbe-blue*, possibly meaning 'blue-beard') is a Guernsey BOGEYMAN used to threaten children into good behaviour.

BARGUEST is a fairy of northern England, possessing horns, claws, teeth and fiery eyes. He usually appears as a BLACK DOG - the Great Dog-Fiend - with glowing eyes, horns and clanking chains. However, he has also been spotted in the guise of a headless man or woman, a white CAT, or even in full human form. The appearance of the barguest is an OMEN OF DEATH or disaster. When an important person dies, he rounds all the dogs in the town up, and leads them howling through the streets, uttering horrible cries. He sometimes shrieks to frighten young girls who are out of bed and shouldn't be.

One barguest haunts the North Yorkshire gorge of Trollers Ghyll. He manifests as a black dog with huge saucer eyes, a shaggy coat and drags clanking chains behind him. An 1881 record recounts how a foolish local man ventured there at midnight. Shepherds found his mutilated corpse the next day, with marks on him not made by any human hand.

Barguests also wander around the fells of Cumberland, wailing and preying on the unwary traveller. The early Christians erected a cross on Cross Fell, the highest point on the Pennines, to protect people from them, though all that is left of the site now is a cairn.

Its name is something of a puzzle. It may be derived from the German *bargeist*, making it the spirit of the funeral bier; or the German *Bär*, 'bear'; or *berg-gheist*, meaning mountain spirit. Others say it is because the creature often appears at styles, which are called 'bars' in Yorkshire. Or perhaps the 'bar' comes from *burg*, meaning a town, since it usually haunts towns. Yet again, Keightley called it Barn-ghaist ('barn-ghost') as it takes the form of a domestic animal.

BARINTHUS is a fairy boatman, designated 'the navigator', who ferried the dying King ARTHUR to the Isle of AVALON. He also guided MERLIN and Taliesin on their voyage to the OTHERWORLD. He was a Welsh sea deity, who was also a god of the DEAD in the ferryman tradition. He was Christianised as St. Barrind and in this guise was responsible for starting St. Brendan on his voyages.

BARROW is a burial chamber or tomb surmounted with stones or earth, also called a MOUND. Barrows are associated with fairies who are said to live inside them.

BARROW-WIGHT is an English fairy that haunts BARROWS or burial MOUNDS. The term is derived from the Norse *haugbui* ('barrow spirit'). A barrow-wight looks like a rock with matted hair all over it and has pale, flat eyes. *See also* WIGHT.

BARSTUKKEN is a German or Prussian TREE FAIRY who lives in the roots of a tree, under the supervision of the PUSCHKAIT.

BASADONE ('Woman Kisser') is a fairy of northern Italy who travels on the noonday breeze and steals kisses from women as he passes. He is a lord among the fairies, ruling the little eddies of

WEST KENNET LONGBARROW

whirling dust that are his subject spirits. A basadone is a type of FOLLETTO.

BAUCHAN, **Bogan** or **Bocan** is a sort of Scottish HOBGOBLIN, who is very fond of tricks. Bauchans may be helpful or threatening as they choose. One followed its human master when he emigrated to America.

BAUMESEL ('Ass of the Trees') is an evil German forest fairy or DEMON.

BAYKOK is an evil fairy of the American Chippewa people. It attacks warriors, shooting invisible ARROWS at them, or hits them with an equally invisible club. It appears at night as a skeleton with burning red eyes and its bones can be heard creaking.

BÉ FIND ('White Lady') is an ancient Irish term for the female WATER FAIRIES of lakes, streams and fountains.

BEAN CHAOINTE ('Wailing Woman') is another name for the Irish or Scottish BANSHEE.

BEAN RIGHEAN NA BRUGH ('Fairy Queen of the Palace') is one of the several Irish Fairy Queens mentioned in legends, including AINE and CLIODNA. They are often the guardians of particular clans and were probably once their tutelary deities.

BEAN FIONN or **Bean Fhionn** ('White Lady') is a white-robed fairy woman who lives beneath the waters of Irish lakes and streams. She rises to drag children playing near her domain into the water where she drowns them. One lives in Loch Gur and will take the life of a human being every SEVEN years. *See also* WATER FAIRIES, WHITE LADIES.

BEAN-NIGHE ('Washer-Woman'), **Ban Nighechain** or **Nigheag Na H'ath** is a type of BANSHEE that haunts the streams of Scotland and Ireland. Washing the bloodstained clothes of those about to die, it sings: *Se do leine,*

se do leine ga mi nigheadh ('It is your shirt I am washing, your shirt I am washing'). Some say the bean-nighe are the GHOSTS of murdered women, or women who have died in CHILDBIRTH leaving behind unwashed clothes, and who are doomed to wash until the day they would have died naturally. Seeing one is a sure sign that a death is near. If you can catch one unawares, you will be safe, but if she sees you first you will lose the power of your limbs.

The appearance of the bean nighe varies in different parts of Scotland. In Mull, she is said to have very long breasts, which get in the way of her washing. She throws them over her shoulders and they hang down her back. Whoever sees her must attempt to approach her without her being aware of their presence. When he is near enough he must catch one of her breasts and call upon her to witness that she is his first foster mother. She will then tell him whatever he needs to know. If the shirt she is washing belongs to one of his enemies he can allow the washing to continue, if it is his own or one of his friends' he can prevail on her to stop.

In Skye, she is said to be small and squat and if she can be caught will answer any question, but the captor must also answer hers. In Perthshire, the washing women are said to be small, round, and dressed in pretty GREEN, but with red webbed-feet. In the moonlight, they spread out the linen winding sheets of those soon to die. They can be made to communicate at the point of a sword. The Caointeach of Islay is very fierce. If anyone interrupts her washing she will strike at his legs with a wet sheet and he will lose the use of his limbs.

BEAN-TIGHE ('Woman of the House') is an Irish HOUSE FAIRY who looks like a kindly faced old peasant woman. Although these fairies are rarely seen, they perform household tasks for their adopted human families in return for a small reward, such as a bowl of cream. One of them looks after the enchanted

underwater castle that is the home of the Earl of Desmond, AINE's son. She appears on Knock Adoon on a formation called the 'Housekeeper's Little Seat' (*Suidheachan*), which juts out into the Lough. She fell asleep there one day and the BUACHAILLEEN appeared and stole her golden comb. When she woke, she realised what had happened and cursed all of the Little Herd Boy's cattle. They all died, followed soon after by the boy himself, but not before he cast the comb into the Lough, where it still lies.

BEBEL was a LEPRECHAUN who visited the Winter family of Blarney in Cork. He told the family that fairies like to ride the backs of hens but are afraid of DOGS, and that the Winter holding was a traditional home of leprechauns, ruled by Queen Picel, who flew on a dragonfly, while PIXIES lived in the nearby ruined fort.

BEBO is a Fairy Queen of the realm of the Faylinn and the wife of IUBDAN in ancient Irish legend. She visited humans in Ulster, though they seemed to be giants to her.

BECUMA is a fairy woman who married King Conn Catchatach in an Irish legend. However, the union was ill-fated and the land began to suffer. The cattle produced no milk and the ears of corn would not mature. She forced the king to banish his son Art, who eventually returned and defeated Becuma in a game of CHESS, and thus banished her from Tara.

BEDIADARI or **Bidadari** ('Good People') are little Malaysian fairies who have much in common with their European cousins, including being called the 'good people'.

BEER may be a very common and ancient beverage, but it was once thought that the yeast which causes

fermentation was magical, and could be spoiled by the attentions of malicious fairies. A heart or CROSS was drawn on the mash or a live coal thrown into the vat in order to deter them.

BEFANA is an Italian crone fairy who travels around on the Eve of the Epiphany (January 6th) placing gifts and toys in the stockings or shoes of good children, but leaving only pebbles and coal for naughty ones (shops sell *carbone,* a sweet that looks like coal). Children leave notes for her in the chimney. After her visit, people will hold parties or go visiting friends and relatives. Befana dolls are placed in windows during the festivities, and afterwards burned in token of the passing of the old year and beginning of the new. 'Befana' may be a corruption of *Epifania* (Epiphany). The Magi were said to have invited her to journey with them to see the new-born Christ child, but she was too busy with housework.

She is often depicted with a BROOM, on which she can fly. She is known as *La Strega* (The WITCH). She appears in street parades as a masked figure accompanied by her consort BEFANO. She is a complex figure, undoubtedly the survival of an ancient goddess, associated with the HEARTH, like BERCHTE, and a witch, like Hecate.

As a winter HAG an image of her is burned during the New Year celebrations, as are images of the Winter Witch in Germany. If the smoke blows towards the east, it is an OMEN that the harvest will be good. If the smoke blows towards the west, it will be poor. Befana herself is sometimes depicted with grain, fruit, and nuts. The rites of the Epiphany signal that the dark time has ended with the rebirth of the sun at the solstice. They include purification ceremonies with sprinkled water. Befana's visit to the HEARTH reaffirms the bond between the spirit world and the human one at this traditionally dangerous time of year.

Sometimes, she appears as part of a triad with Rododsa and Maratega to weave the destinies of humankind, a version of the FATES. She is associated with SPINNING and her symbol is the woven stocking. Children hang these from the hearth at the Epiphany for her to fill with gifts.

BEFANO is an Italian fairy with a humped back who carries a staff, and appears with his wife BEFANA on January 6th. They are represented in a street procession, accompanied by musicians, people dressed in rags with blackened faces, and a live HORSE. They stop at houses where they dance and call out to the children, before being rewarded with a glass of wine or some money.

BÉFIND ('White Lady') is an Irish FAIRY GODMOTHER who attends the birth of a child, along with two other fairies, to predict its future and bestow it with fairy gifts. It was also MIDIR's name for Etain when she dwelt in the land of the SIDHE.

BEITHIR is a destructive male spirit of the Scottish Highlands who haunts CAVES and corries.

BELA are Indonesian DRYADS, or TREE FAIRIES. If a person wishes to cut down a tree, they must offer food to the Bela and ask it, politely, to move to another tree. Should these precautions not be taken, the Bela can cause NIGHTMARES or illness.

BELAGOG was a GIANT who guarded ARTHUR's Castle which was in the form of a sacred grotto.

BELLARIE are the ELEMENTAL spirits of the east and air in Italian occult lore.

BELLS are known to scare away fairies. The ringing of church bells drove the TROLLS, DWARFS and fairies out of Germany. In Europe, after HALLOWEEN, any crops remaining in the fields belong to the fairies. Consequently, bells used to be tolled all day on October 30th in order to make sure the little folk did not pre-empt their prerogative as the harvesters hurried to finish their work. The bells on the dancing costumes of English Morris Men are often said to offer them protection from evil fairies and other spirits. However, it is possible that good fairies like the sound of bells (as long as they are not church bells), since they decorate their horses with jingling harnesses.

BELTANE, Beltaine or Bealtinne was the ancient Celtic festival that celebrated the start of summer and which we know today as May Day. The festival may have been dedicated to the sun god Bel, or to Beltené, the god of the DEAD. For the ancient Celts there were only two seasons: summer, which began at Beltane, and winter, which began at SAMHAIN (October 31st). Western European fairies also observe this division of the year. Good fairies are most active from Beltane to Samhain and bad fairies from Samhain to Beltane.

At Beltane, the winter fairies, represented by various HAGs and UNSEELIE creatures, give up their dominion over the land. All fairies hold great festivals at Beltane and try to steal the ritual fire and fresh butter made by humans.

The Lunatishee, the Irish blackthorn Fairies, guard the sacred thorn and will not allow it to be cut on May 11th (Old Beltane). Every seventh year on May Eve fairies fight for the rights to the harvest, for the best ears of grain belong to them.[10]

BÉLUN is a Belarussian fairy who looks like an old man with a long white beard, dressed in a white robe. He helps harvesters and rewards them with gifts. He appears only during the daylight hours and sets lost travellers back upon their paths.

BEN BAYNAC is an evil Scots fairy that haunted the region of Craig

Aulnaic. He beat his wife, Clashnichd Aulnaic, every night until her screams woke up the entire neighbourhood. The farmer James Grey berated the fairy woman for keeping everyone awake, whereupon she told the man that she cried out because of the ill treatment of her husband. The outraged farmer determined to put a stop to this and shot the wicked Ben through the bonnet-sized mole in his breast - the only vulnerable spot on his body. Clashnichd was so grateful that she began appearing at various houses around the district, but as she stole any food she found, she proved a great nuisance. Eventually, the miller's wife became so annoyed that she poured boiling water over the fairy who ran off howling and was never seen again.

BEN SOCIA ('Good Neighbour') is flattering French/Breton for the fairies.

BEN VARREY is a MERMAID from the ISLE OF MAN who is generally friendly towards the islanders, warning its sailors about coming storms - although she also occasionally lures men to their deaths with her seductive songs.

BENDITH Y MAMAU ('Mother's Blessing') is a somewhat flattering Glamorganshire term for these ugly Welsh creatures that are the result of the interbreeding of GOBLINS and fairies. They live underground in tribes and hate humans, killing their farm animals, breaking their tools, and stealing COWS. The Mother's Blessing will also steal human children and leave one of their own children, the CRIMBILS, as CHANGELINGS in their place. The help of a WITCH must be sought in order to recover the real child. The returning child will remember nothing of its time among the fairies, except the lovely FAIRY MUSIC.

BERCHTE or **Berchta** ('The Bright One' or 'White Lady') also **Butzenbrecht** ('Bringer of Gifts') and

Perchta ('Shining') is a German fairy with many aspects. One of these is a BOGEY WOMAN invoked to threaten naughty children into good behaviour. She is also a HAG fairy with a splayfoot, an IRON nose, long grey hair and beady eyes. She carries a distaff and will blind anyone who spies on her activities, or some say, anyone who gets in her way on Twelfth Night will fall into a trance. When he wakes, he will be able to foretell how next year's crops will turn out.

As Butzenbrecht, she is busiest at between Christmas and New Year, destroying any SPINNING that is unfinished by the time the Old Year is over. In her honour, houses are decorated with evergreens and food must be left out for her on Twelfth Night – Epiphany - or she will cut some from a living human stomach. However, she also has a good side; cakes are baked in the shape of slippers and she will fill these with small presents and treats for good children. The Feast of the Epiphany was originally known as Perchtun Night, since she is also Perchta who takes the souls of dead children into her care.

She is the guardian of fields and livestock, and anyone who neglects their work will be punished. Performers called *Perchten*, dressed to represent spirits of goodness and blight, dance in the fields to drive out bad spirits.

Berchte also appears as an OMEN OF DEATH. In parts of Germany, she is the leader of the WILD HUNT, accompanied by fairies and the ghosts of UNBAPTISED CHILDREN, whom she takes into her care. In the spring, she is a lovely maiden with long flaxen hair and a sprig of HAWTHORN flowers in her hand.

She was once a goddess similar to or identical with HOLDA, a deity of fertility and marriage; she is sometimes called 'Holdaberta' a combination of the names Holda and Berchte. In addition, she was almost certainly the chief goddess of the

HEARTH and home, and in Pagan days was honoured at YULE in every home with a flat stone altar on which a fire of fragrant evergreens burned. She was invoked to foretell the future of everyone present.

BEREGUN (*pl.* **Bereguny**) also given as **Bereginy** or **Bereguini** ('Bank Spirits'), are Russian bog fairies who steal newborn babies and leave behind instead ugly CHANGELINGS called Oborotni ('Changed Ones').

BERGFOLK ('Mound People') are Danish fairies who live in MOUNDS, like many of their cousins around the world. A young girl once saw one of their mounds teeming with green beetles, and when she took two home, they turned into gold coins.

BERGMANLI ('Mountain Man') is a male fairy of the ERDLUITLE.

BERGMONCKS or **BERG-MÖNCHE** ('Mountain Monks) are German fairies who appear as pale monks to chase travellers away from gold mines. Some say that they are the GHOSTS of monks who have hidden church candlesticks and plate in the mines.

BERTILAK is name of the GREEN KNIGHT, a seasonal fairy fought by Sir Gawain in an Arthurian tale.

BETIKHAN is a forest fairy with the appearance of a FAUN who resides in the Neilgherry Hills and hunts wild beasts.

BEU, LÉ is a solitary Guernsey fairy or GOBLIN with an evil reputation. When a person wants to startle someone he will creep up behind him or her and cry 'Beu!' just as an English person might cry 'Boo!'

BHRINGI is a three legged Hindu dwarf and an attendant of Shiva. His natural advantages make him a very good dancer.

BHUTA are Hindu GOBLINS who live in graveyards and eat the flesh of the living. They cast no shadow and can be repulsed by incense of turmeric.

BIASD BEALACH ODAIL is a monstrous Scottish fairy of the Isle of Skye.

BIASD BHEULACH is a wicked fairy of Odail Pass on the Isle of Skye and is sometimes said to be the GHOST of a human man, hungry for revenge.

BIBLE According to popular folklore, the physical presence of a Bible can break fairy spells or prevent fairies from entering a house. Brushing the pages of an open Bible over an afflicted body will cure certain skin conditions caused by ELVES, while pages of the Bible torn out and rolled into pellets can be fed to cattle that have been struck by ELF BOLTS. Similar beliefs were held in all Christian countries.

BIERSAL is a German HOUSE FAIRY who looks after the beer cellar, keeping everything in good order as long as he is given a jug of BEER every day. Otherwise, he will make a nuisance of himself.

BIG EARS is the king of the Cait Sith or fairy CATS. He appears when any of his brethren are in danger.

BIL ('Vision') is a henbane fairy, a later form of the Scandinavian goddess Bil who is associated with the RAINBOW bridge which led to Asgard, the home of the gods. The association probably arises because henbane is a powerful, if poisonous, hallucinogenic.

BILBERRY-MAN lives in the forests of Franconia, where he attacks passing travellers. To propitiate him and prevent the assault, bread and fruit must be placed on a stone before entering the forest.

BILDUKKA is a noisy Eastern European HOUSE FAIRY.

BILE is the LORD OF THE DEAD, in Irish legend. He comes from Spain (in this case, a term for the Land of the Dead). He is sometimes said to be the husband of DANU, and is paralleled in British legend by Bel or Belinus.

BILLY BLIND, Billy Blen, Belly Blin or **Blind Barlow** is a famous English HOUSE FAIRY who often appeared in old folk ballads as a generous figure who protected his chosen family and gave them helpful advice. According to one ballad, he warned Burd Isbel of Bekie's inconstancy.

BILLY WI'T'WISP from West Yorkshire is a north of England version of WILL O'THE WISP.

BILLY WINKER is an English fairy from Lancashire who appears at bedtime to bring sleep to children. He is comparable to the SANDMAN.

BILSENSCHNITTER ('Henbane Cutter') is a German fairy, possibly synonymous with the PILWIZ, who damages the corn as it stands in the fields, ready to be harvested.

BINDICA or **Binidica** is a Sicilian fairy who is very beautiful and kind, though it is usually invisible.

BINDWEED (*Convulvulus sp.*) is used in a charm to prevent a baby being kidnapped by fairies. An Irish mother might take some bindweed, burn the ends and place it over the cradle, in order that the fairies will have no power over the child.

BIRCH (*Betula alba*) is a tree with many associations with the fairy folk. In south-west England, a female fairy called the One with the White Hand flickers from birch copses in Somerset, pale and gaunt as the trees, to ambush young men. In Scotland, the Ghillie Dhu lives in birch copses. In some other parts of England and Scotland, a birch was hung with RED and white rags and set against stable doors at

BELTANE (May Day) to prevent horses being 'hag-ridden', i.e. being taken out by fairies or WITCHES and ridden to the point of exhaustion.

The hallucinogenic mushroom the FLY AGARIC grows beneath the birch. This may be why the birch constitutes the shaman's seven-stepped pole, which enables him to ascend and visit FAIRYLAND in trance. In Russia, the forest fairies called LIESCHI were considered to be always present in clumps of trees, particularly the tops of birch trees.

BISIMBI or **Kisimbi** are the female WATER FAIRIES of the Congo.

BITARR are Australian Aboriginal spirits who appear as little old men to play tricks on children. One may appear as a stranger child on the edge of games.

BJERGFOLK ('Hill Folk') *See* TROLL.

BLACK ANGUS is a large BLACK DOG with glowing yellow eyes and horns. He roams the north of England and the Scottish borders looking for victims. Those he growls at will be dead within the fortnight.

BLACK ANNIS is a blue-faced storm or winter HAG who haunts the Dane Hills of Leicestershire in the English East Midlands. She has tattered hair, long, yellow fangs and lives in a CAVE called Black Annis' Bower, which she has scraped out of the rock with her own sharp fingernails.[11] In front of the cave is an OAK tree, in which she hides in order to dash out and ambush lambs and young children who wander too far from home. She will drink their blood, eat their flesh and hang their skins up in her cave to dry. Black Annis may be a debased form or alter ego of the Celtic goddess ANU or DANU, the mother of the gods.

BLACK DOGS or phantom hounds are found all over Britain and Europe. They appear in lonely places: CROSSROADS, bridges, old roads, deserted country lanes, churchyards, burial MOUNDS, wells and bridges. They linger near field stiles and gates and also seem to guard man-made structures, particularly borders of various kinds. Some people even speculate on a connection between black dogs and LEY LINES.

They are usually slightly larger than mortal dogs, have red, green or burning eyes, or merely a single eye. Some are headless and have their saucer eyes floating before them. In England, East Anglia, Essex and Buckinghamshire all have instances of spectral dogs that vanished in sensational flashes, in one case burning to death a farmer, his horse and wagon.[12]

The black dog is an object of fear and terror. Its appearance is usually an ill omen, portending death for the one that sees it or a member of their family. Charles Walton met a black dog on his way home to Alveston, on NINE successive evenings. On the ninth night, a headless dog charged past him and the succeeding day, he heard of his sister's death.[13] In East Anglia, when a man is dying, it is said that 'the Black Dog is at his heels'. Some black dogs will commit murder and mutilation and the inspiration for the death-hound of Arthur Conan Doyle's *The Hound of the Baskervilles* was the tale of a Dartmoor black dog.

There are hundreds of accounts of black dogs all over England (some forty in the county of Wiltshire alone), and they often have local names. In East Anglia, the dog is BLACK SHUCK or Old Shuck; in Suffolk, Old Shock; in Somerset, the Gurt Dog. In the North of England we find the BARGUEST, Black Shag, Padfoot and Hooter, Gytrash and Trash or Skriker. On the Isle of Man is the MODDEY DHOO.

In addition to single black dogs, there are packs of spectral hounds, some of which are accompanied by WILD HUNTSMEN. These are seen all over Europe and include the British GABRIEL HOUNDS, Gabble Retchets, Dandy Dogs, Yeff Hounds, Wisht Hounds, and the Cwm Annwn, the WILD HUNT and Woden's Hunt in Scandinavia. All are a warning of death or disaster.

BLACK DWARFS or **DWARVES** is a term for Scottish KNOCKERS or MINE FAIRIES.

BLACK ELVES is an alternative term for the DARK ELVES or DWARFS in Scandinavian myth. They live underground and are darker than pitch.

BLACK ERIC is an evil fairy who lived in a CAVE at Fitful Head in the Shetland Isles. He would steal sheep and ride about the island on a demon HORSE called TANGIE. Eventually, a brave crofter called Sandy Breamer cornered Black Eric and threw him off the Head, but Tangie continues to plague the district and harass young women in an attempt to steal a mortal bride. Eric's cave is still called the Thief's House.

BLACK JINN are evil spirits who can possess people, according to Malaysian folklore.

BLACK SHAG is a fearful BLACK DOG whose appearance is an OMEN OF DEATH.

BLACKBERRY

BLACK SHUCK or **Old Shuck** is a phantom dog that haunts the mud flats of East Anglia, particularly the area around Devil's Ditch. The name is derived from the Saxon word for an evil spirit, *scucca*. Grendel, the monster of the Old English epic poem *Beowulf,* was described as a *scucca* and 'from his eyes shone a fire-like, baleful light'.

Black Shuck is variously described as having a single eye set in the centre of his head, or having glowing red eyes, or even as being headless, yet having glowing red or green fiery eyes suspended in front of him. He emerges from his lair at dusk and haunts riverbanks and lonely roads, sometimes vanishing in churchyards.

When a Black Shuck appears in these parts of eastern England, it is generally an OMEN OF DEATH. In Norfolk, it is said that no one can see a Black Shuck and live. People in lonely places have sometimes felt its icy breath on their necks, and in East Anglia, when people are dying, it is said that 'the BLACK DOG is at his heels'. The Essex Shuck is kindlier and protects travellers in lonely places. In Suffolk, the Black Shuck is believed to be harmless if left alone, but if challenged will strike and kill the aggressor. The Norfolk Shuck is a terrifying, ebony creature whose fiendish howls can be heard above the wildest gales. The Cambridgeshire Shuck is sinister and may be seen between Wicken and the marshes of Spinney Abbey. His appearance warns of a death in the family.

BLACKBERRY (*Rubus fructicosus*) has an odd place in folklore and a taboo on eating blackberries exists in Celtic countries. In Brittany and Cornwall, the reason given is that the blackberry belongs to the fairy folk. In France, some people still will not eat them, as they are associated with the DEVIL who enters into them after November 11th (Old SAMHAIN). The bramble was a sacred plant of the Celts; in Scotland, the bramble, along with the ROWAN and the yew, constituted the sacred fire.

BLACKBIRDS are called the Birds of RHIANNON in Welsh folklore and can enchant the hearer and lead him or her into the fairy OTHERWORLD.

BLACKTHORN (*Prunus spinosa*) is a tree associated with fairies that appears in a variety of tales, forming magical obstacles that have to be overcome, or which protect the heroine. A popular English fairy story concerns a GIANT's daughter who fled with a prince, the giant in pursuit. The prince threw a thorn behind him and from it sprang a thicket so dense that scarcely a weasel could slip through and the giant had to give up the pursuit.

Similarly, in the tale of Sleeping Beauty, a hedge of blackthorns grew up around the castle, but opened to allow the prince to pass. In the story of Rapunzel, the WITCH who had imprisoned her threw her suitor from the high tower. He fell onto a blackthorn and was blinded. He wandered for two years until Rapunzel, who had by that time escaped from the tower, found him. Finding him blind she wept, but when her tears fell onto his eyes, he was instantly cured.

November 11th (Old SAMHAIN) is recognised in Ireland as the day of the blackthorn sprites, the Lunantishees, the Otherworldly beings who guard the sacred blackthorn from any human foolhardy enough to profane the sacred tree by cutting the wood at this time. In Ogham, the druidic tree alphabet, the blackthorn was *straif*, which translates as 'strife'. The words 'slay' and 'sloe' (the fruit of the blackthorn) are also closely linked.

BLANCHARD is the fairy HORSE of the knight Lanval, given to him by the fairy TRYAMOUR.

BLANQUETTES are a type of French FÉE, small and lovely fairies who always dressed in white.

BLATHNAT is a lovely fairy maiden captured by the Irish hero Cuchulain when he raided the OTHERWORLD.

However, she became the object of a dispute between him and Cu Roi Mac Dairi, who seized and married the girl. Cuchulain planned his revenge, conspiring with Blathnat, and on the feast of SAMHAIN they murdered her husband. The unfortunate fairy did not survive long after the event, but was pushed over a cliff by a former servant of Cu Roi Mac Dairi.

BLESSED COURT *See* SEELIE COURT.

BLIGHT/BLIGHTS and ills and diseases were believed, all over the world to be the fault of spirits. Deaths and paralysis are attributed to their use of ELF BOLTS; the origin of the word 'stroke' for paralysis is derived from 'elf-stroke'. Fairy darts may be aimed at the fingers, causing the joints to swell, and become red and inflamed with rheumatism and arthritis. Paralysis is also caused by the invisible presence of a fairy market. Cramps are a punishment for annoying the fairies. Tuberculosis is caused by eating FAIRY FOOD or by visiting a fairy hill at night. Fairies can impose cramps, bruising, impetigo and lice. Infantile paralysis indicates that the baby is a CHANGELING, while if a baby is left unattended bad fairies will appear and give its limbs a twist, causing childhood deformities. Fairies steal horses at night and tangle their manes into elflocks. English fairies can steal your shadow, which will eventually cause you to fade away and die. In Norway, the breath of elves covers the body of a person with blisters.

Fairies that cause blight are more common in the winter, indicating that they may be associated with the ancient spirits which bring in the winter, the powers of decline, disease and death. *See* HAG and FAIRY FESTIVALS.

BLODEUWEDD ('Flower Face') is a fairy woman created from NINE types of blossom in Welsh myth. She was made as a bride for Llew, as his mother ARIANRHOD had laid a taboo on him that he should never marry a mortal woman. However, Blodeuwedd fell in love with another man, Gronw Pebyr, and plotted with him to kill her husband, according to the only conditions that would achieve his death. However, the magician Gwydion found Llew and restored him, turning Blodeuwedd into an OWL as a punishment.

At first the story seems to be merely the tale of an unfaithful wife, but it is an ancient tale of the changing roles of the gods and goddesses of the seasons. Llew means 'Bright One' and is the summer sun god. His bride Blodeuwedd ('Flower Face') is the flowering summer goddess. Gronw is Lord of Pebyr ('Lord of the Lake'), a rival of Llew with water/autumn associations. Blodeuwedd becomes the HAG goddess in the form of an owl (Some say the face of an owl resembles a flower.) The story of the rebellious bride is also echoed in the stories of GUINEVERE and ARTHUR, and BLATHNAT and Cuchulain.

BLOOD is something the Irish believe that fairies have an antipathy to the sight of. In former times the peasants had an aversion to being bled (an old cure for many ills) lest the good folk be angry. Some say that fairies have thin white blood, like MILK, and this may be the reason that they like to interbreed with humans, to strengthen their bloodlines. Any whitish substance found on the ground in the morning was said to be the blood of fairies, the product of night-time battles. However, there are a large number of fairies that like to suck human blood (*see* VAMPIRES). On the ISLE OF MAN, it is thought that if water is not left out at night for fairies to drink they will suck human blood.

BLOODY BONES, Rawhead-and-Bloody-Bones or **Tommy Rawhead** is an evil English GOBLIN who eats naughty children in Somerset. He lives in a cupboard, usually under the stairs. If you peer through a crack you will see him crouching inside, with blood running down his face, crouched on a pile of lying or foul mouthed children's bones. He has no skin and walks about as raw as if he has just been flayed. If you peek through the keyhole at him, he will get you!

BLOODY CAP *See* RED CAPS.

BLUE BEN is a fiery English fairy DRAGON who lives in Putsham Hill in Somerset. He cools himself by swimming in the sea. Locals claimed that a fossilised ichthyosaur on display in Taunton museum was the remains of Blue Ben.

BLUE BURCHES is an English fairy who once lived at a cobbler's house on the Blackdown Hills in Somerset. He usually appeared as an old man wearing blue trousers, though he could SHAPESHIFT.

BLUE HAG *See* CAILLEACH BHEUR.

BLUE MEN OF THE MINCH or **Blue Men of the Muir** inhabit the Minch, a channel dividing the Outer Hebrides from the mainland. In the channel are the Shiant ('Charmed') Islands, surrounded by turbulent waters which are churned up by WATER FAIRIES known as the Blue Men of the Minch. The tideway between the islands and Lewis is called *Sruth nan Fear Gorma* or 'Stream of the Blue Men'. The fairies attack any vessel whose captain cannot answer their riddles and then lure the unfortunate sailors or fishermen down to their undersea CAVES. The Blue Men are a shiny blue and grey in appearance, with bearded faces, and may be seen bobbing up and down in the waves. They are ruled by a chieftain.

BLUEBELL woods are places of fairy spells and enchantments, especially in England. The ringing of the bluebell summons fairies to their moonlit revels. The presence of bluebells in OAK copses is a sure sign that those mischievous creatures called OAKMEN are present and mortals should be wary. In Somerset, it is believed that you should never go into the woods to pick bluebells, as it will anger the fairies. If you are a child you will never be seen again, as the fairies will take you away, but if you are an adult you will be PIXY-LED and will not be able to find your way out of the woods until someone rescues you. WITCHES often grow bluebells to attract fairies, and at one time their presence in a garden was a damning piece of evidence in a witch trial.

BO MEN or **Bo** are nasty Irish fairies who live in the marshes of Co. Down and entice unwary travellers to their deaths. They may be driven away by being slapped by a type of seaweed.

BOABHAN SITH or **Baoban Sith** ('Wicked Woman Fairy') are Scottish Highland fairies who look like beautiful women but who are really VAMPIRES thirsty for the blood of young men. They appear first as crows or RAVENS, then as lovely girls in white or green dresses with plaid sashes, but with hooves instead of FEET. Their wails can be heard for miles around. A Boabhan Sith may be a sinister form of the WHITE LADY type of fairy. The name boabhan also denotes a scald crow. It is derived from the Irish Badhbh or Badba, the sinister war goddess, whose name is also used to denote a fairy, WITCH or hoodie crow.

BOAG is a WATER FAIRY who haunts an old mill and bridge across the River Biss, a tributary of the Avon in the south west of Engalnd. He is only 30 cm tall (twelve inches) and has a red nose, perhaps explained by his penchant for cider. He used to lurk under the bridge and imitate the screams of young girls in order to lure men down to his lair. Once he had captured them he would wrap them in spiders' webs and drown them. His antics were eventually brought to an end when all the drowned spirits sent up such a cry that another fairy rode up on a white horse, tied Boag up in a rope and dropped him over the bridge. The spirits of the drowned imprisoned him in a GOSSAMER cage on the riverbed, and torment him there still.

BÓANN or **Boanna** ('She of the White Cows') is a Fairy Queen of the TUATHA DÉ DANAAN, and the mother of AENGUS OG by the DAGDA. She once boasted that she could look into the well that was forbidden to all but the god Nechtan, but was drowned when the waters arose from it and formed the river that now bears her name, the Boyne.

BOCAN is an unpleasant fairy who lives on the Isle of Skye and attacks unwary travellers; sometimes leaving them horribly mutilated.

BOCÁNACHS are shrieking spirits in Irish legend. They flew around the hero Cuchulain when he fought Ferdia, accompanied by fury-type spirits called Bocánachs. They may be the origin of the well-known death omen, the BANSHEE.

BOCKLE (*pl.* **Bockles**) is a Cornish fairy mentioned by Hunt as being a fairy of the same category as the BUCCA, and seems to be related to the Scottish BOGIE or the English BUG.

BOCKMANN ('Man-Goat') is an evil German forest fairy, half GOAT in appearance, who frightens children that go into the forest.

BODACH ('Old Man') is a nasty fairy or BUGBEAR of the Scottish Highlands. These fairies come down the chimney to KIDNAP naughty children or punish them by pinching them or inflicting NIGHTMARES. In some areas their appearance is an OMEN OF DEATH. They look like shrivelled old men, and can be kept at bay by a sprinkle of SALT in the fire.

BODACH GLAS ('Dark Grey Man') is a grey fairy of the Scottish Highlands whose appearance is an OMEN OF DEATH for the person that sees it.

BODACH NA CROIBHE MOIRE is an Irish oak TREE FAIRY, usually depicted as a strong looking, small old man.

BODACHAN SABHAILL ('The Little Old Men of the Barn') are Scots Highland HOUSE FAIRIES who work at night threshing corn and keeping everything in order for the elderly men they take pity on. They are very wise and look like old men themselves.

BODB or **Bodb Derg** is a hero of the Irish fairies the TUATHA DÉ DANAAN. He was chosen as their king after the battle of Tailtiu. In folklore he is known as the Fairy King of Munster.

BODCA-AN-DUN is an OMEN OF DEATH that appears to the Rothmurchus family.

BOGIE or **Bogey** (*pl.* **Bogies** or **Bogeys**) is a type of English fairy related to the BUGBEAR or BOGGART and the Scottish BOGLE. The term was formerly used for the DEVIL and some say that bogies steal children for the devil to torment in hell, though since the nineteenth century bogies have become spirits invoked to frighten naughty children. The word is probably derived from the Middle English *bogey* meaning to bluster or to brag. They sometimes appear as shadowy black humanoids, but can change shape to appear as BLACK DOGS, tree trunks, or beings with icy fingers and glowing yellow eyes. They live in cellars, attics, cupboards, CAVES, hollow trees and anywhere dark and dank. At Worthen in Shropshire, the Reynolds family was driven from their home by two bogies looking like a little old man and a little old woman. Unfortunately, the bogies followed them to their new house.

BOGEY BEAST is a British term for a mischievous HOBGOBLIN.

BOGEY WOMAN are almost as numerous as BOGEYMEN and include BERCHTE and LA LLORONA.

BOGEYHOLE is the dwelling place of those evil fairies the BOGEYMEN and is often the cupboard under the stairs.

BOGEYMAN is a nasty BOGIE that unscrupulous parents invoke to threaten naughty children: 'If you don't behave, the bogeyman will get you'. Bogeymen live in the bogeyhole, the cupboard under the stairs, or in cellars, barns, old houses, mines, and CAVES. They lurk behind people, causing an uneasy feeling, or pull the bedclothes off sleepers. They steal away naughty children. If you look through a keyhole, you might catch sight of a bogeyman's eye looking back at you. Usually though, the only sight of a bogeyman is as a cloud of dust.

Bogeyman is also a general term for a frightening, supernatural being, a monster used to frighten the weak or superstitious. When, in 1890 a certain Major Wellman was introduced by Great Yarmouth Golf Club in Norfolk` to the idea of playing against a ground score, he exclaimed that this well nigh invincible opponent was a regular bogeyman. The term caught on and playing against the bogey (or number of strokes a reasonable player takes for each hole) caught on and remains popular golfing parlance today.

BOGGARD is a local English term for a BOGGART in Lincolnshire.

BOGGART, **Boggard** or **Boogart** is a type of BOGLE more common in the north of England, especially Lancashire and Yorkshire; while in Lincolnshire it is usually called a boggard. It is also called a TRASH or a SHRIKER, the latter name earned from its horrible cries, and often confused with BARGUEST. It may appear as a white COW or HORSE, a white or BLACK DOG or in human form. In their natural state, boggarts are dark and hairy, with long yellow teeth. Their appearance is often an OMEN OF DEATH. They only appear on very

dark nights; in Lancashire there was a rhyme:

'Stars is shining, moon is breet;
Boggard woant cum oot toneet.'

On the moor were dark black holes where the boggarts lived, and where mothers threatened to throw their naughty children.

Some say that boggarts are HOUSE FAIRIES who have turned evil. They may wreck houses, steal children's suppers, and knock things on the floor. They can terrorise a whole district. They eat wood and are able to consume a whole house. If a family tries to move away from them they will climb into the crocks and butter churns and travel with the unfortunate people to their new home.

A boggart haunted the country lanes around Longridge in Lancashire. From behind it looked like an old woman in a fringed shawl and poke bonnet, but when she turned around, she would reveal that the bonnet was empty and her head was in the basket she carried. The head would shriek with laughter and snap at the unfortunate observer.

BOGGART OF THE BROOK haunted a bridge near Garstang. It appeared wrapped in a cloak and hood and would often beg rides from passing horsemen. When it was safely up behind the rider, it would reveal its hideous skeletal form, and whip up the HORSE to a wild gallop until the human rider was thrown.

BOGGE is a German BOGLE.

BOGGELMANN is a BOGEYMAN.

BOGGLE-BO, Boggle Boo, Bogglebo, Boggy-Bo, Bugleboo, Bogill-Bo or **Bogil-Bo** is a form of BUG-A-BOO, perhaps a fairy or sometimes a WITCH in Scotland and the English North Country. The Scots commented that someone 'was taking the bogil-bo' when they meant he had gone into a huff.

One itinerant old woman from Hylton was called Old Bogglebo and was a witch. She asked Jock the keelman to take her over the water to Sunderland, despite the stormy weather that threatened. Quelling his protests she assured him that the voices that whispered in the wind promised it would be quite safe. The superstitious sailor dared not refuse and the two took to the water in the teeth of the storm. The wind howled and the sea moaned and raged about them, but the boat cut a clean swathe through the water, while Old Bogglebo sat in the stern shrieking with laughter. At last the shore was reached, but when Jock turned to the old woman she was no where to be seen; instead a black CAT leaped from the boat.

BÓGINKI ('Little Goddess') is a Polish riverbank WATER FAIRY who steals newborn children and leaves CHANGELINGS called Odmience in their place.

BOGLE is a GOBLIN of the Scottish borders, the English North Country and Lincolnshire, a version of the BUG. It is rarely visible but nevertheless, its presence causes a sense of dread. To see one might be mind *boggling* indeed! It performs evil deeds, but only at the expense of liars and murderers, who might be said to deserve them. To paraphrase William Henderson the bogles are a better kind of spirit and meddle with none but the guilty; the murderer, the forsworn, and the cheaters of the widows and fatherless.[14] He relates the story of a man who stole some candles from a poor neighbour woman. The next night he was in the barn when a dark figure appeared in the garden. He fired his gun at it but the figure exclaimed that it was neither flesh nor blood and could not be harmed. The next night it appeared to him and demanded that he return the candles. The man handed them over but the bogle punished him by plucking out one of his eyelashes. This might not seem much but the eye twitched forever afterwards.

A bogle is generally said to have a very dark, unpleasant appearance.

Bogles were greatly feared by the fenmen of East Anglia who at darkling bore lights in their hands to circle their houses, chanting word charms to keep them off. They also smeared blood on the doorstep to scare away the horrors and put bread and SALT on flat stones to solicit a good harvest.

BOH is an old Anglo-Saxon word meaning DEMON; *boh* or *bo* is a component in many fairy names. It is also a prankster's custom to creep up behind people and scare them by suddenly crying 'Boh!' or 'Boo!' meaning 'The devil is behind you!'

BÖHLERS-MÄNNCHEN are small and gentle German fairies.

BOHYNIA ('Goddess') is a Ukrainian WATER FAIRY cognate with the RUSALKA.

BOKWUS is a North American fairy of the spruce and fir forests. He has a war-painted face and likes to push anglers off the banks to drown so he can capture their souls, which he takes to live with him.

BOLLA is an Albanian fairy who appears in the form of a DRAGON on St George's Day (April 23rd). After twelve years it transforms into a huge HAG called Kulshedra with pendulous breasts and a hairy body.

BOLOTNYI (*boloto* meaning 'swamp') is a Slavonic female swamp or bog spirit.

BOM NOZ is a French HOUSE FAIRY, one of the LUTIN.

BONNES DAMES ('Beautiful Ladies') is a general term for lovely female French fairies, but sometimes used to categorise those related to FATES and FAIRY GODMOTHERS. They preside over the childbed and confer good and bad qualities on the newborn baby. A thirteenth-century *trouvère* called Adam de Halle named them as Morgue, Arsile and Maglore. In his tale, Maglore is offended as no place is laid for her at the table and curses the family. Texts from the Middle Ages mention female dancers called Bonnes Dames who follow the fairy queen ABUNDIA.

BONNEFÜHRLEIN is a fairy of the RUMPELSTILTSKIN type, whose name has to be guessed.

BONNES MÈRES LES FÉES ('Our Good Mothers the Fairies') is a name for fairies on the Brittany coast. They are spoken of with a great deal of respect.

BORUTA

BOOBRIE is a gigantic Scottish fairy water bird with black feathers and a huge three-foot long bill. It attacks ships carrying cattle and sheep, imitating the cries of calves and lambs to lure the animals over the side and into the water, where it devours them. The boobrie can also transform itself into a WATER HORSE, which gallops along the top of the waves.

BOOMAN is a type of HOBGOBLIN in Orkney and the Shetland islands.

BOOYAN is a magical OTHERWORLD island in Russian folklore, peopled by healers and situated in the middle of the ocean.

BORROWING can be a strange activity where fairies are involved. Should a mortal borrow fairy utensils or food, he or she will cause offence if they try to return more than what was borrowed, while fairies always return favours with a bonus. Fairies always return two measures of barleymeal for one of oatmeal, and if this is kept in a place by itself it proves an inexhaustible supply, providing the bottom of the vessel is never made to appear, no questions asked, and no blessing pronounced over it.

At the thirteenth-century church at Frensham in Surrey, England, there is a huge CAULDRON which local people say was borrowed from the fairies, but never returned. For this reason, the fairies would never lend the village anything again.

BORUTA is a female Polish TREE FAIRY who inhabits fir trees.

BOTTLE IMP is an IMP or DJINN that is captured in a bottle or some such container (e.g. Aladdin's lamp) and forced to serve a human master.

BOUDIGUETS are a type of KORRED.

BÔV THE RED is the king of the TUATHA DÉ DANAAN of Munster. He is the brother of the DAGDA.

BOWA is an East Munster BANSHEE.

BRAGS are Scottish and Northern English HOBGOBLINS. The name may be derived from the Celtic *breugach,* implying a deceitful female. Brags can appear in a variety of forms including HORSES, COWS with white sheets around their necks, asses, GIANTS, singing white CATS, crooning girls or naked men flapping white sheets. They live in rivers and lakes and try to lure people into the water with their tricks in order to drown them.

BRASH is a grotesque north of England BOGIE.

BREAD can be a safeguard. If you must go to a place haunted by evil fairies, place a piece of dry bread in your pocket as a protection.

BREGOSTANI are Alpine fairies, cognate with the SALVANI and mates of the BREGOSTÉNE. They protect the lower slopes of the Alps and their trees.

BREGOSTÉNE are Italian fairies, cognate with the AGUANE and mates of the BREGOSTANI. They protect the lower slopes of the Alps and their meadows.

BREASIL is the King of the World, according to Irish legend, and the ruler of the fairy island HY BREASIL.

BRES was elected king of the TUATHA DÉ DANAAN, even though he was of mixed parentage, his mother being a Danaan and his father one of the FORMORIANS. However, he behaved badly towards his mother's people, heaping many insults upon their shoulders. Eventually, they rose up against him and ousted him from his position. He went off and joined the Formorians, fighting on their side against the Danaans, but lost a magical contest against Lugh and was forced to drink three hundred buckets of bad MILK, which killed him.

BRI LEITH ('The Hill of Leith') is the MOUND of MIDIR, King of the Fairies.

BRIDES on their wedding day are vulnerable to fairy attentions. Fairies may try to KIDNAP them and a girl who dies on her wedding night is liable to become a fairy.

BRIGHID, Brigit, Brigid or Bride ('Fiery Arrow') is one of the TUATHA DÉ DANAAN, and the daughter of the DAGDA. She was a goddess of FIRE, the patroness of poets, SMITHS, and healers. In Scottish folklore she ousts the hag of winter, the CAILLEACH BHEUR and ushers in the spring. She was Christianised as St Brigit.

BRITANNIA is the personification of the GENIUS LOCI or sovereign goddess of Great Britain. She is depicted as a female warrior, with trident shield and helmet.

BROCHS were ancient Scottish dwellings that resemble small hills or MOUNDS, composed of a round, stone house, covered with turf. Their remains are associated with the fairies, who are said to live in them.

BRODARICA VILA are Balkan WATER FAIRIES who come out on moonlit nights to bathe their children. They live in natural pools, streams and lakes.

BRODNICA SAMODIVA are Balkan WATER FAIRIES who live in a lake or brook. On moonlit nights, they bathe their children in the water. They drink from springs called 'wells of the fairies', and may be their guardian spirits.

BROKK ('Blacksmith') is a DWARF of Norse myth, an accomplished SMITH who, together with his brother Sindri, rose to Loki's challenge that the dwarfs could not equal certain magical items that he possessed. Despite the god's trickery he constructed the magical ring Draupnir, which dropped another eight like itself each night, and a magnificent hammer that would smash anything it was thrown at, and would always return to the hand of the thrower. It was called Mjollnir and was intended for Thor, the god of thunder.

BROLLACHAN is a type of Scottish HOUSE FAIRY with a ragged, hairy appearance, usually shapeless but sometimes with GOAT legs and hooves. Brollachans rarely speak but bleat like goats when startled. Others say that the brollachan is completely shapeless, having only eyes and a mouth, and can only take the shape of whatever it sits upon. It is only able to say two words: 'myself' and 'thyself'.

BROOM/ BROOMS or besoms are associated with fairies and WITCHES; both use brooms to fly. In many cases, however, it is used as a protection against evil spirits such as ALPE and PAINAJAINE. A broom has birch twigs for ritually sweeping and cleansing; birch is a tree of purification, dispelling negativity and associated with new beginnings. The twigs are bound to the pole with WILLOW, associated with the MOON goddess, ruler of water, the tides, the feminine, intuition and the unconscious mind. The shaft is made from ASH, associated with the sky god. Because the broom is both masculine and feminine, it is a symbol of fertility. In the old times women would ride broomsticks around the field, leaping as high as they could - the higher they leapt the higher the crops would grow.

BROONIE the fairy claimed that he was king of the TROWS. He was a helpful spirit, unlike the other trows, and people were glad to see him. He would guard the corn and cast protective spells on the crops on cold nights. The local people thought that he might feel a chill in the bad weather, and kindly made him a cloak. However, like any fairy given a gift of CLOTHES he disappeared, never to be seen again.

BROTHER MIKE was an English fairy captured in Suffolk. He longed to return to his own realm but was unable to escape, so pined away and died.

BROUNGER is a WATER FAIRY who lives in the sea off the east coast of Scotland and who heralds storms. He may have devolved from a thunder god. *See also* WEATHER FAIRIES.

BROWN DWARFS are German fairies who dress in brown, are very small and wear caps that make them invisible to anyone not wearing a similar cap. They are SHAPESHIFTERS.

BROWN MAN OF THE MOORS/MUIRS is a Scottish fairy, the master of the moors who punishes men for taking game. He has thick limbs, knobbly hands, curly RED HAIR and bare feet. He is always dressed in dull brown and carries a staff. Two men encountered him when they were hunting on the moors of Elsdon in 1744. The youngest man went down to the burn to drink and was startled to see a stout dwarf, dressed in clothes the colour of withered bracken, with red hair and glowing eyes. He berated the men for hunting animals, saying that for himself he only ate berries, nuts and apples. He invited the young man to go home with him to see for himself. Just then the older man called out and the Brown Man vanished. The older man told his companion that if

he had crossed the burn he might have been torn to pieces. The young man was shaken, and on the way home obstinately shot more game. However, the Brown Man had his revenge, since shortly afterwards the young man was taken ill and died within the year.

BROWN MEN live on Bodmin Moor in Cornwall and fiercely protect its animal life. They dress in the brown and autumnal colours of the moor on which they dwell, and have bright RED HAIR.

BROWNEY is a Cornish fairy who seems to belong to the same family as the non-Celtic BROWNIE, but how he travelled to Cornwall is unknown. He is the guardian of bees and is invoked when the bees begin to swarm. When this happens, the mistress should seize a metal pan and beat it calling "Browney! Browney!" and he will make the bees settle.

BROWNIES (s. **Brownie, Brounie, Broonie** or **Bruinidh**) are solitary HOUSE FAIRIES who become attached to particular houses or families and who do odd jobs about the house and farm, cleaning, tidying up or helping with the brewing. The only reward they ask is a bowl of cream or best milk, though the brownie of Bodesbeck Farm in Dumfries was offended when the farmer offered him even this for his hard work and went off in a huff declaring:

'Ca' Brownie ca',
A' the luck o' Bodesbeck
Awa' tae Leithan Ha.'

When a cock crows it is to let the brownie know it is time to go to bed. Some people think that brownies transform themselves into cocks during the day. The live in dark corners of the house, or in some cases nearby hollow trees or ruins.

A certain brownie on the Isle of Cara, off Scotland, disliked anything dirty and would put out soiled bedclothes at night. When visitors

were expected he would make sure the household was spick and span. In addition, he ground grain at night, helped in the threshing and the churning of milk. In return for his favours the dairymaids fed him warm MILK. The brownie was said to be stout and blooming. He had long flowing yellow hair and went about with a switch in his hand, with which he would slap anyone who made a mess. However, like most fairies he hated DOGS and would kill any left in the house at night.

Another brownie faithfully served a laird's daughter, becoming her friend and confidant. Whenever she wanted his company she would whisper into the chimney and he would appear. When the time of her marriage approached, he went unseen about the castle polishing the silver, dusting away the cobwebs and generally making things ready. The faithful brownie stayed with her through her marriage and even went out through the storm to fetch the midwife for her when no one else could get through.

Brownies are found in southern Scotland and the northern counties of England, occurring most thickly in the Borders. They are rarely seen, as they are very good at hiding and can make themselves disappear at will. They are small, shaggy haired and ugly, with flat faces, wrinkled skin, large eyes, pinhole nostrils and short brown curly hair, though their appearance varies from region to region. In Aberdeenshire it is said they have no separate fingers and toes, and in the Scottish lowlands they have nostril holes instead of a nose while some have huge noses but no mouths. They usually go naked, dress in rags or a brown hood and mantle; the easiest way to get rid of them is to offer them a gift of CLOTHES. The CAULD LAD OF HILTON haunted Hilton Castle in Northumberland until he was left a green cloak and hood, and went off singing. If Brownies are offended they can become malicious and turn into BOGGARTS.

There are various theories as to the origins of the brownie. Some think that the HOUSE FAIRY may be derived from the Roman household spirit the LAR FAMILIARIS, who is supposed to be an ancestral spirit. In the Shetland Isles, in the early eighteenth century, every family of substance had a brownie to which they made sacrifice. When the milk was churned a few drops were sprinkled in every corner of the house for him. When they brewed a few drops would be sprinkled into the hole in the 'brownies's stone'. There was also a special stack or corn called the 'brownie's stack', which was never fenced or roped like the others, but which no wind ever seemed to blow away.

Some think brownies are Teutonic in origin, since the term 'brownie' appears where the Teutons settled, spreading up into the lowlands of Scotland and into the Orkneys and Shetland. The brownie may get his name from his brown clothes and complexion. Brownies are often said to be the ghosts of DEAD servants, or be otherwise connected with the dead.

(The fact that Brownies do all the house and farm work for no more than their food was not lost on Lord Baden-Powell who named his packs of junior Girl Guides 'Brownies', as opposed to the more adventurous 'Wolf Packs' of boys - a pertinent comment on the sexual stereotyping of the era.)

BROWNIE CLOD haunted Fincastle Mill and no one dared go there at night. One evening, a girl was baking her wedding cake and ran out of meal and had to go up to the mill to grind some more. She made a fire and put on some water to boil. At midnight an ugly little brown man appeared and asked her who she was. She replied 'Me, myself'. As he edged closer she grew alarmed and splashed him with some boiling water. At this he grew angry and flew at her. In her fright she hastily poured the rest of the water over him, fatally injuring him. He limped home and when his mother

MAGGY MOULACH asked who had done this to him, he replied: 'Me, Myself'. However, Maggy heard the girl boasting about the whole incident and threw a three-legged stool at her, killing her on the spot.

BROWNIE OF ALTMOR threw about everything that was tidy, and tidied everything that was messy.

BROWNIE OF BALQUAM was also called 'the GHOST of Brandley Dhu'. He was once sent to fetch a midwife to his mistress. He took a special interest in the Goodwife of Furmenton, but her son eventually banished him.

BROWNIE OF GLENDEVON was offended by a gift of CLOTHES and went off in a temper declaring: 'Gie brounie coat, gie brounie sark, Ye'll get nae mair o'brounie's wark'.

BROWNIE OF JEDBURGH fetched a midwife to his human mistress and the laird desired to reward him. The servant had heard the brownie mutter 'Wae's me for a green sark!' the laird had the shirt made and laid it out for the brownie, who took it gleefully and was never seen again.

BRUDER RAUSCH ('Brother Rush') is a German HOUSE FAIRY with a sense of mischief - in particular he delights in getting people drunk. Later folklore described him as a DEMON who tempts those in religious orders from their vows.

BRUGH is a Gaelic term for the inside of a fairy MOUND where a group of fairies live. It is related to the word 'borough'. The Brugh na Boinne is a famous fairy mound near the river Boyne in Leinster, Ireland.

BUACHAILEEN ('Little Boys') are Scots and Irish fairies who appear as young men with pointed RED CAPS, though they can also SHAPESHIFT into animals if they choose. They are sometimes called 'The Herding Boys',

as they like to play tricks on shepherds and their animals. They keep herds of cattle themselves, and one who stole from the BEAN-TIGHE had his cattle cursed by her.

BUBAK is a Slavonic HOUSE FAIRY that makes a nuisance of itself by making banging and rattling noises.

BUCCA ('Spirit') is a Cornish term which refers to fairies and spirits of various kinds, including spirits of the wind or sea, fairies of the tin mines, spirits that cause or foretell shipwrecks, and even GHOSTS. The buccas were once taken very seriously and there are two kinds: the BUCCA GWIDDEN who is good and BUCCA DHU who is bad. Offerings were left for them: fishermen left a fish on the sands, a piece of bread was thrown over the left shoulder at lunchtime, and a few drops of beer spilled on the ground. The bucca was probably once a sea god, demoted to the status of a fairy. If a person is called 'a great bucca' it means 'a great fool'. The people of Penzance liked to torment the people of nearby Newlyn by calling them Buccas

BUCCA DHU ('Black Spirit) or **Bucca-Boo** is an evil Cornish fairy who may once have been a sea god. His status declined into that of a DEMON; as such he worked mischief in the tin mines and with the fishing fleets. The Bucca Dhu was the terror of children to whom he was held out as a kind of BOGEYMAN who would carry them off if they misbehaved. A bucca once stole a fisherman's net and the Paul choir chased him, praying all the time and the bucca fled over Paul Hill to Tolcarn where he turned the net into stone. The curious rock can still be seen. The name may have the same origin as the Welsh *bwcibo*, meaning 'DEVIL' or may be related to BWCA and the BUGABOO.

BUCCA GWIDDEN ('White Spirit') is a good Cornish WATER FAIRY who was probably originally a sea god. His

BUCKY

good offices were solicited by means of offering some bread from the first harvest, a fish from the catch or a small libation of ale.

BUCKY or **Buckie** is an evil fairy who inhabits the Lowlands of Scotland. He leaps up behind horse riders to garrotte them. In the English West Country the name Bucky is probably a familiar form of Bucca, a shadowy spirit who was perhaps once a god. When Devonshire children wanted to run through a dark passageway, they would offer up the invocation:

'Bucky, Bucky, Biddy Bene
Is the way now fair and clean?
Is the goose ygone to nest,
And the fox ygone to rest?
Shall I come away?'

BUFFARDELLO is a type of LINCHETTO, an Italian fairy who brings NIGHTMARES to sleepers.

BUG or **Bugge** (*pl.* **Bugges**) is an evil English fairy or DEMON which is never seen - only its terrifying presence is felt. The word first appeared in the fourteenth century and probably related to the Welsh BWG, a similar creature - in Welsh *bwgwth* means to menace or frighten. Wyclif used the word bug to describe a scarecrow, while Johnson described the bug as an amorphous spirit that presaged death or ill fortune. Thomas Moore spoke of *'such black bugges as men call devilles'*. Coverdale's 1535 translation of the bible substitutes 'bugges' for 'terror by night' and is consequently known as the *Bug Bible*. In the seventeenth century there was a saying *'to swear by no bugs'* meaning a genuine oath, while a conceited person was described as a bug. We are familiar with the word bug referring to beetles and grubs, a term that gained currency in sixteenth-century England, though in America it became a catch-all term for every type of insect. During the Second World War the term reverted to its original sense of a terror by night when it was applied to the doodlebug or flying bomb.

BUG A BOO or **Bugaboo** is a malicious English fairy who is held out as a threat to naughty children, whom it comes down the chimney to KIDNAP. The name may be derived from BUCCA DHU or the Welsh *bwcibo,* meaning devil. Though the term is virtually obsolete in England, it is still current in America in the sense of a threat or cause for concern. *See also* BOGEYMAN and BUG.

BUGBEAR is an English HOBGOBLIN in the shape of a bear who devours naughty children. The word is compounded from BUG and bear.

BUGGAN is a Cheshire BOGEY.

BUGGANE are ISLE OF MAN fairies who can alter their appearance, so their true shape is not known. Generally, they appear as black bulls or large rams and haunt old chapels to prevent their repair. One has continually pulled off the roof of St. Trinian's, near Greeba Mountain. A tailor once vowed to stay in the building long enough to make a pair of trousers, but fled at midnight when the buggane appeared. The monster was furious at not being able to catch the tailor, tore off its own head and threw it at him, but before the head could touch the man it turned to stone.

Bugganes also haunt water, particularly waterfalls, sometimes in humanoid form with huge heads and terrifying teeth and claws.

BUGGARS or **Buggers** are dangerous SHAPESHIFTING English GOBLINS. The word originates with the French *bougre,* a term of abuse applied to heretics. In English, it is a word usually applied to a sodomite.

BUGIBUS is an evil Old French GOBLIN. The term may be related to BUG or BULL BEGGAR.

BUGUL NOZ ('Night Shepherd') is a sad and lonely Breton fairy who is the last of his race. He is so ugly that he generally hides himself away and if he hears anyone approaching him, he will call out a warning, lest they be shocked, telling them that night is no time for lingering on the roads, but for being safely indoors. Sometimes Bretons see his tall and frightening figure outlined against the sky, as they wend their way home at twilight. He lives in the forest and takes care of sheep.

BUKURA E DHEUT ('Beauty of the Earth') is a powerful Albanian fairy who lives in an enchanted castle. She can be kind or malicious, as the mood takes her.

BULL BEGGAR, Bullbeggar or Bully-Beggar is nasty GOBLIN that dwells at Creech Hill in Somerset, England. It is tall and black and constantly howls with laughter or eerie shrieks. It once attacked a Bruton man who successfully fought it off all night with a HAZEL gad. It vanished with the cockcrow.

BU-MAN ('Cattle Man') is another name for a TROW. A protruding stone would be left in the floor of the byre so that milk offerings could be left for him.

BUNYIP is an Australian Aborigine fairy that inhabits the swamps. Bunyips look like small, plump humans, but are covered with mud. Their FEET point backwards. Some say they are frightening and malicious, while others say that they guide fishermen to good spots and protect them from dangerous swamp creatures.

BUSCHFRAUEN ('Bush Women') are small, shaggy German fairies. They are golden haired and have pendulous breasts and hollow backs. They live in hollow trees and guard the forests. They are offended if you peel bark from trees, bake caraway seeds into bread, or tell your dreams.

BUSCHGROSSMUTTER ('Bush Grandmother') is the Queen of the BUSCHFRAUEN.

BUTTERFLIES are the symbol of the SIDHE in Irish folklore. Fairies are often pictured as riding on the backs of butterflies. ANGELS and fairies were sometimes depicted with butterfly wings by medieval artists. In Celtic cultures, the butterfly is an emblem of the human soul, or perhaps a soul in actuality. The ancient Celts wore butterfly badges as a mark of respect for the ancestral spirits of the DEAD.

BUTTERY FAIRIES are English spirits who live in old abbeys and inns and steal any food not marked with a CROSS, especially butter, which they love. No one has ever seen one.

BWAGANOD are Welsh fairies who only appear for a few minutes at dusk, but they can choose any shape they like and delight in frightening humans.

BWYD ELLYLLON ('Fairy Food') is the food of the Welsh fairies, i.e. TOADSTOOLS.

BWBACH, Boobach or Bwbachod are Welsh relatives of both the BROWNIE and the BUG. They protect the house in which they live, but they are mischievous pranksters unless they are regularly fed. The bwbach has a double character as a HOUSE FAIRY and a terrifying phantom. Those GHOSTS who cannot rest because of the TREASURE they have buried may employ a bwbach to transport a human through the air to dig it up for them. When transporting humans thus, they will courteously ask how you would like to travel - above wind, mid wind, or below wind. If you choose above wind, the fairy will take you so high that you skim the clouds and are frightened to death. If you choose below wind you will be dragged through bramble and briar. If you ever find yourself in this situation, always choose mid-wind.

Bwbachs are small, stout and wear large RED hats, loincloths and fur cloaks. They hate teetotallers and people who stick their noses into other people's business. One bwbach developed a violent dislike to a Baptist preacher and took to pulling his stool away while he was praying, jangling his fire irons and frightening his maids. Finally the terrified preacher fled on his horse, but he had not escaped the bwbach's attentions as the grinning fairy was seen riding pillion.

BWCA are Welsh HOUSE FAIRIES who help out by churning butter, but only if the fireplace is swept clean and a bowl of cream is left by it at night. If all is not to their satisfaction they will not work but bang about, throw things and destroy clothes, pinch people and tell family secrets aloud. When they turn nasty they are very difficult to get rid of, and a CUNNING MAN will have to be called in to protect the household with holy water, IRON or ROWAN and RED THREAD.

One bwca worked hard, helping around a farm until a malicious maid gave him a bowl of urine instead of his usual basin of bread and milk. In disgust he moved to another farm where he worked willingly until another hardhearted girl began to mock him. Displeased, he moved to yet another farm where he became friendly with a manservant called Moses. When Moses was killed in battle the grief stricken bwca became malevolent and caused considerable damage until a local cunning man caught him by the nose and banished him to the shores of the Red Sea for fourteen generations.

BWCIOD is a solitary Welsh fairy only 30 cm tall (one foot), with purple eyes and a long, sharp nose. He can move incredibly fast. He loves to warm himself at human HEARTH fires and will turn nasty if anyone tries to get rid of him.

BUTTERFLIES

BWG is a malicious Welsh GOBLIN who goes around frightening people. This may be the origin of the better-known English word 'BUG'.

BWGANOD are Welsh BOGEYS.

BYSN is a Scandinavian fairy who lives in the forest. He is a SHAPESHIFTER and can appear as an animal or a tree, but usually looks like a little old man wearing a cap. He is often heard shouting through the forest and likes to trick any humans he comes across.

C'HORRIQUETS are a type of Breton KORRED.

CABBAGE-STALKS are used by some fairies as transport. They sit astride them and command them to fly with MAGIC words.

CABBYL USHTY or **Caval Ushteg** is a Manx fairy WATER HORSE, which resembles a real horse, apart from its back to front hooves. It sometimes entices people to ride on its back, but anyone who does so will be carried off into the water and drowned.

CACCAVECCHIA is a type of LINCHETTO, an Italian fairy who brings NIGHTMARES to sleepers.

CACCE-HALDE are Lapland WATER FAIRIES.

CAELIA is a Fairy Queen in British folklore, the lover of Tom a'Lincoln, ARTHUR's son, to whom she bore the Faerie Knight, in one old tale.

CAER is the Welsh term for a MOUND or barrow, sometimes called a FORT, equivalent to the Irish SIDHE. When *caer* appears in a name it usually refers to an otherworldly place, such as Caer Arianrhod, sometimes said to the Corona Borealis or a lost land sunk in Caernarfon Bay, a reef of stones that is covered at low tide. It is ruled by the Welsh weaver goddess ARIANRHOD ('Silver Wheel'). Caer Feddwidd or 'Fort of Carousal' is located in the OTHERWORLD, a paradise where the fountains run with wine, and no

illness or death is known. It is also known as Caer Rigor or Caer Sidi or Caer Siddi. Caer Wydyr, 'The Fort (or Isle) of Glass' is located in ANNWYN, which some associate with AVALON or Glastonbury.

CAER IBORMEITH was a SWAN MAIDEN who appeared to AENGUS OG in a dream. He visited Loch Bel Dracon one SAMHAIN eve and saw a flock of one hundred and fifty swans, each linked with a silver chain. Caer flew among them wearing a golden chain and coronet. Angus called to her and he also became a swan. They circled the lake three times, singing a magical song that put everyone in the vicinity to sleep for three days and nights.

CAIBE SITH is 'the fairy spade', a smooth slippery black stone shaped like the sole of a shoe. It can be put in water, which will then cure any sick people or cattle that drink it with fairy healing MAGIC, according to Scottish folklore.

CAIBELL is a Fairy King of Ireland who had a beautiful daughter. His friend Etar, the ruler of the neighbouring MOUND, also had a lovely daughter. Two human kings saw the fairy maidens and wanted to marry them, but the SIDHE kings objected. They appeared with their followers transformed into DEER to give battle to the presumptuous men. The contest took place at night so that the fairies did not possess an unfair advantage, and was so fierce that four hills were made from the antlers of the dead fairies. Sadly Caibell and both the human kings were killed.

CAILLAGE NY GROAGMAGH ('Old Woman of Gloominess') is a Manx HAG fairy who controls the weather. If IMBOLC (1st February) is fine she comes out, in the form of a giant bird, to gather firewood to warm her through the summer. If it is wet she stays in, and because she has no

firewood, has to make the rest of the year fine in her own interests. She is sometimes said to have fallen into the clefts of the rocks trying to step from the top of Barrule to her home at the top of Cronk yn Irree Lhaa.[15] *See also* CAILLEACH and WEATHER FAIRIES.

CAILLEACH ('Veiled One') is a HAG fairy probably derived from those Celtic goddesses who personified winter and who were transformed in the spring to lovely maidens. Several Cailleachs are found in Scotland and Ireland. Cailleach is also a name for the corn dolly, fashioned from the last harvested sheaf of grain. The corn dolly embodies the spirit of the grain, and it is ploughed into the first furrow the following spring. *See also* CAILLEACH BHEUR.

CAILLEACH BEARA, Beare or Bera ('Hag of Beare') is an Irish HAG fairy who lives in the Beare Peninsula and is associated with the harvest. She has two sisters, which seems to suggest she was originally part of a goddess triad. She lives in south-west Munster, believed to be the home of the DEAD, and here she dwelled for many years in perpetual youth, wearing out countless husbands who aged and died. She is also associated with mountains, and is said to be responsible for building several of them when stones fell from her apron.

CAILLEACH BEINNE BHRIC HORO ('The Carlin Wife of the Spotted Hill') is a large HAG, both broad and tall. She cares for a herd of red DEER (the Celtic totem animals for the feast of SAMHAIN). She will not allow them to descend to the beach, but feeds them on the watercresses that grow by the fountain high in the hills.

CAILLEACH BHEUR ('The Blue Hag') is a Scots Highland HAG fairy who lives on Ben Nevis. Stones that fell from her basket formed the Hebrides. Her face is blue with cold, her hair as white as frost and her cloak the colour of withered foliage, or some say blue and white. A carrion CROW rides on her left shoulder. She carries a HOLLY staff topped with the head of a carrion crow and if she touches anyone with it, they will die. At SAMHAIN (1st November) she strides across the land, beating down the vegetation with her staff and hardening the earth with frost. When her season has fully set in she brings the snow. As spring approaches her power begins to wane, until at BELTANE (1st May) she gives up her struggle, flinging her staff under a holly (or gorse) tree, and this is why no grass can grow there.[16] She then shrinks to a grey stone to wait until her season comes again. It is said that if anyone can find her staff they will have the power of destiny over the human race.

She is a folk survival of a winter crone goddess, called the daughter of Grianan, the winter sun . She is reborn each Samhain, the start of winter, and proceeds to blight the earth with snow and cold. She has been known to turn into a wild boar, an ancient symbol of approaching winter. (In Greek,Roman and Irish myth the wild boar kills the vegetation god.) She has two sons, one black and the other white. Each year one of them will steal her single eye and chase her north, before marrying the Summer Maid. According to another tale, she kept a lovely girl prisoner, but her son fell in love with the maiden. The two ran off together but the Cailleach launched bitter winds to keep them apart.

She is also the guardian of wells and streams. She guards a well near the summit of Ben Cruachan, which is inclined to overflow. She had to put a slab over it every sunset, and take it off every sunrise to prevent this. One evening she was so tired that she fell asleep and the water flowed down the hillside, drowning many people and beasts before forming Loch Awe. She protects DEER, PIGS, GOATS, wild COWS, and wolves.

CAILLEACH UISGE ('Water Hag') is a Scottish WATER FAIRY or HAG.

CAIRN MAIDEN is a Scottish fairy who revenged a human woman betrayed by her sister: Two sisters lived on the Isle of Mull, Lovely Margaret and Dark Ailsa. Margaret had a fairy sweetheart who visited her in secret; she was so happy that she told Ailsa and swore her to secrecy. But Ailsa betrayed her sister and soon everyone knew of the FAIRY LOVER. The offended fairy was seen no more.

Margaret grew distraught and spent all her time outdoors, wandering and pining for her lost lover. She laid a curse on Ailsa; that evil would come on her and her descendants. Ailsa thought nothing of it and got married; later giving birth to a son called Torquil. Margaret was heard prophesying that Torquil could climb and reap better than any other man.

This was true, when he grew to manhood Torquil had the strength of seven men, which proved his undoing. One year, when the corn was ripe, the fairy called the Cairn Maiden came out of her cairn and reaped the ripe corn every night with the strength of SEVEN men. Torquil took this as a challenge to himself. He waited one night and saw her setting to work. He took his sickle and tried to keep up with her. They harvested through the night until he came beside her, and grasping the last sheaf of corn in his hand, cut it. He turned to the maiden and thanked her, for he said want would be far from his door that winter. However, she replied that it was unlucky to cut the Corn Maiden early on a Monday morning and the young man fell dead at her feet.[17] (The Corn Maiden is another name for the corn dolly, made from the last sheaf of corn which contains the VEGETATION SPIRIT.)

CAIT SITH ('Fairy Cat') is a black CAT of the Scottish Highlands, with one white spot on its breast. It belongs to the fairies, but it may be that the cat is really a transformed WITCH.

CALCATRÁPOLE is a type of NIGHTMARE.

CALLICANTZAROI (CALLICANTZAROS), are Greek fairies who gather together around Mount Parnassos, riding chickens rather than horses. They are sometimes described as very small, slight and naked, with the FEET of horses and wearing RED CAPS or conversely, in other parts of Greece, as gigantic and hairy, with red eyes and large genitalia, relatives of CENTAURS or WILD MEN. At the winter solstice, they gather to celebrate the rebirth of the sun. They are all close to being blind, perhaps from staring at the sun. Sometimes other deformed fairies accompany them, such as the KOUTSODAIMONAS. When they are abroad it is necessary to take precautions against them, and farmers will carry brands of FIRE when they go out at night. Water containers must be protected against their mischief and it is wise to place some asparagus or hyssop about the house by way of preventing their entrance. If they get in, they are likely to urinate on the HEARTH or in the water butt. If there is dirty water around they will wash their genitals in it. Their favourite food is pork.

CALLIOPE or **CALLIOPEIA** ('Fair Voiced') is eldest of the nine MUSES, the patroness of epic poetry. She taught Achilles how to sing, and mediated the quarrel of Aphrodite and Persephone over Adonis. She is depicted with a writing tablet, wearing a golden crown.

CALLY BERRY is an Ulster HAG fairy who is constantly at war with the hero Finn Mac Cumhal and his followers. This probably signifies a seasonal battle between winter and summer (hag and bright hero), blight and growth. Her name is of similar origin to the CAILLEACH BHEUR ('Blue Hag') of the Scottish Highlands.

CAMENAE are the 'Foretellers' or freshwater NYMPHS of ancient Roman folklore. They once ruled the springs of Rome and their festival was on 13th October.

CANDELAS is a Sardinian WILL O' THE WISP, often seen just after sundown.

CANNERED NOZ is a Breton fairy and one of the many WASHERS AT THE FORD types: her appearance is an OMEN OF DEATH. Towards midnight, the Cannered Noz might be heard beating their linen in front of different washing places, always some way away from the village. They might ask passers-by to help them wring the sheets - if the person refuses, he will be wrung like a sheet himself. If you ever find yourself in this position, be careful to wring the sheet in the same direction as the washerwoman, for if you turn it in the opposite direction your arms will be wrung instead. The Cannered Noz are condemned to wash their winding sheets throughout the ages, unless they can find someone who will wring in the opposite direction, when they will be delivered.

CAOINEAG or **CAOIDHEAG** ('Keening Woman' or 'The Weeper') is a Scottish BANSHEE, one of the FUATH. She is rarely seen, but is heard wailing in the darkness by waterfalls, or wandering through the glens, or weeping on the banks of lochs and streams before a disaster overtakes a clan. One was heard keening every night by the Macdonald clan before the massacre of Glencoe.[18]

CAOINTEACH ('Wailer') is a type of CAOINEAG, or Scottish BANSHEE, who haunts the vicinity of Argyllshire and Skye. She appears as a small woman wearing a GREEN gown and a high crowned white cap. She has no nose and a single, monstrous front tooth. She screams to herald the deaths of members of the Macmillan, Matheson, Kelly, Shaw, Currie and MacFarlane clans. She used to also appear to the Mackay clan, until one member of the family felt sorry for her on a cold, wet night and put out a plaid shawl for her. Like any fairy given CLOTHES she disappeared, never to be seen again.

CAOINTEACH OF ISLAY is a BEAN-NIGHE, or Washer at the Ford fairy, and is very fierce. If anyone interrupts her washing she will strike at his legs with a wet sheet and he will lose the use of his limbs.

CAPELTHWAITE is a Northern English BLACK DOG.

CAPTIVES OF THE FAIRIES occur in many stories of people visiting FAIRYLAND and being held prisoner there for a number of years, usually SEVEN. Sometimes fairies KIDNAP human beings, especially pretty children, UNBAPTISED BABIES, young girls, and MIDWIVES, either to strengthen the fairy bloodline, aid them, or pay the TEIND they owe to hell.[19] Fairy kings often want to marry beautiful girls, and these are returned to the human realm after seven years, by which time they will have grown old and ugly - no doubt worn out by the demands of their fairy husbands- but having been taught the secrets of witchcraft to compensate them (see WITCH). In some cases, the fairies may leave a CHANGELING or STOCK OF WOOD in the place of the human. Other people have entered fairyland by accident, by stepping into a FAIRY RING, for example, or by eating FAIRY FOOD. Occasionally people have visited fairyland willingly, like THOMAS THE RHYMER.

CAPTURED FAIRIES occasionally feature in folk tales. SELKIE and ROANE brides may be had by the capture of their sealskins, a PERI bride by the capture of her CLOTHES, or a MERMAID bride may be won by the capture of her cap or belt. However, as soon as the fairies regain their property they will be off back to their own element.

Other captured fairies include the GREEN CHILDREN found wandering on an English hillside and the ASRAI, kidnapped by a fisherman, who died when she came into the sunlight. Indeed, fairies are never happy living in the human realm, and even those who have voluntarily married humans always long for FAIRYLAND and will return there in the end.

CARL HOOD is a hooded English fairy, of whom it is said "Old Carl Hood, who's aye for ill and never for good". He may be a derivative of Woden or Odin, the hooded god.[20] There are several hooded fairies, including possibly ROBIN HOOD. *See also* HOOD.

CASCORACH is a minstrel of the TUATHA DÉ DANAAN who lured St Patrick to sleep with his MUSIC.

CATs are something that fairies often transform themselves into, usually WHITE ones, but it is difficult to know whether a supernatural cat is really a fairy or its pet. In Ireland, ordinary cats are thought to be practically fairies themselves and on the ISLE OF MAN the cat is the only creature tolerated by fairies when they enter a house at night. Indeed, the tailless Manx cats were bred by fairies. The Celts believed that looking into a cat's eyes would enable you to see the fairies, or see into the OTHERWORLD.

Fairy cats come in a variety of forms. One wild breed, as large as dogs, are black with a white spot on their breasts, arched backs and erect bristles. In Scotland the *Cait Sith* ('fairy cats') have dark green eyes and very long ears, though many believe these are really WITCHES in disguise. Fairy cats still keep appearing in Britain; there are regular newspaper reports of unearthly cats, usually black. Sometimes they are the size of ordinary cats but are often much larger.

CATEZ is a Southern Slavonic woodland or field fairy which has a man's head, but the upper body, legs and feet of a GOAT. It haunts fields and waterfalls.

CATH PULUG ('Clawing Cat') is a monstrous fairy CAT which was slain by King ARTHUR or some say Sir Kay.

CAT

CAUCHEMAR is a French version of the NIGHTMARE which sits on the chest of a sleeper and rides him through his dreams.

CAULD LAD OF GILSLAND appears in a legend very similar to that of the CAULD LAD OF HILTON, but this cold lad is more GHOST-like than fairy.

CAULD LAD OF HILTON is a BROWNIE who haunted Hilton Castle in Northumberland until he was left a green cloak and HOOD, and went off singing. Brownies are always offended by gifts of CLOTHES and will disappear immediately.[21] His story is sometimes confused with that of a stable lad called Roger Skelton who was killed by his master in 1609 for falling asleep and not bringing his horse. His shivering GHOST haunts the castle, and anyone who sees it is affected with a creeping chill.

CAULDRON is a large cooking pot associated in folklore with fairies and WITCHES. Both are said to brew spells in cauldrons. Celtic stories contain a great number of MAGIC cauldrons, generally located in the UNDERWORLD. Some produce endless supplies of food, some restore life to the dead, while others confer the gift of wisdom. In ancient myth, the cauldron represented the womb of the Earth Goddess and her power to transform whatever is laid within it, for example transforming the seeds of autumn to the greenery of spring. Ceridwen had a cauldron that conferred inspiration and knowledge. LAKE MAIDENS kept another beneath a lake until Bran the Blessed retrieved it to restore to life men killed in battle. The TUATHA DÉ DANAAN were thought to have taken four gifts to Ireland - a spear, a sword, a cauldron and a stone, representing the four elements (fire, air, water and earth respectively) and the power of the ELEMENTAL kingdoms. In Christian times the symbol of the cauldron became translated into that of the Holy Grail.

CAVE FAIRIES is a term used by Lady Wilde to refer to the mound dwelling TUATHA DÉ DANAAN.

CAVES are associated with a great many fairies, including the Manx CUGHTACH, the French DRACS, DRAGONS, Scandinavian DWARFS, German DWERGERS, the Normandy FÉE, the GANDHARVAS of India, the KAKAMORA of the Solomon Isles, Hawaiian MENAHUNE, English PIXIES, BLACK ANNIS, Greek TRITONS, Shetland's WULVER and BLACK ERIC, the Spanish XANA, the German ZWERGE, the Indian AIRI, the Scottish BEITHIR, the BLUE MEN OF THE MINCH, OGRES, BOGEYMEN and numerous others.

Like burial mounds, caves are entrances to the UNDERWORLD, long associated with spirits. The ghosts of the DEAD are often said to dwell in an underworld kingdom, ruled there by the Lord of the Dead, himself often associated with fairies in the guise of such characters as GWYN AP NUDD, FINVARRA or ARAWN.

Caves were the first temples of our ancestors, who made animal paintings in them. These paintings were usually hidden and could have had no mundane purpose. They do not show all the species humans hunted and there is usually only one representative of any species. Perhaps our forebears realised that animals, as well as being a source of meat, also contain a spirit and this spirit might need appeasing after death.[22] Thus, ritual restitution was necessary. Blood and fat were mixed with RED ochre pigments and applied to cave walls deep within the earth to unite the spiritual and material planes. With the painting, the animal spirit was returned to the earth/cave womb of the Earth Goddess and its spirit could be reborn.

For the ancients, entrances into the earth like a cave, well or pothole was a literal opening into the body of Mother Earth's fecund womb. A number of sun gods (such as Zeus, Lugh and Mithras) are said to be born or reborn from a cave-womb at the winter solstice. Many burial mounds (as artificial earth wombs) are orientated so that the shaft of the sun at the winter solstice will strike a point in an underground chamber and generate the rebirth of the ancestral spirits entombed there.[23]

CEAIRD CHOMUINN ('Association Craft') can be bestowed by fairies on their favourites. If a SMITH, wight or other craftsman catches fairies working with his tools, he can compel them to confer on him the *ceaird chomuinn*, that is, assistance whenever he needs it. Almost any gift or skill can be passed on by the fairies, such as MUSIC, MAGIC, PROPHECY, or healing.

CEARB ('The Killing One') is an evil spirit of the Scottish Highlands.

CEASG is a Scottish MERMAID, also called *Maighdean na Tuinne* ('Maiden of the Wave'), with the upper body of a woman and the tail of a salmon. She will lure men into the sea in order to kill them, but if a man can catch her, she will have to grant him THREE wishes. She can be defeated by the capture of her SOUL, but this is located in a secret place.

CEFFYL is a Welsh WATER HORSE, an evil fairy that lives in streams or lakes.

CELLAR GHOSTS is a name is sometimes applied to HOUSE FAIRIES in Britain.

CENTAURS ('Those Who Round Up Bulls') have the upper bodies of men and the lower bodies of other beasts, usually horses (*hippocentaur*) but sometimes donkeys (*onocentaur*) or even fish (*ichthyocentaur*), as do many modern fairies who are half animal in appearance. In Greek myth Centaurs were the children of Ixion, a mortal man who tried to seduce the goddess Hera. Outraged at his impudence, Zeus formed a cloud in the shape of Hera and Ixion was deceived into mating with it. From this union the monster Centaurus was produced, who later mated with the horses on Mount Pelion who gave birth to centaurs. They are usually wild and unruly but one called Chiron was wise and skilled. He taught many of the Greek heroes including Herakles, and at his death was placed in the stars as the constellation Sagittarius.

It has been suggested that at some point in the early days of horse riding, a man mistook horse and rider for a single beast and this gave rise to a myth of centaurs. Alternatively, it may have been a term applied to the Scythians, who spent most of their time on horseback, rounding up their cattle, and who were reputed to have appalling manners and customs.

CÉOL-SIDHE ('Fairy Music') - according to Irish folklore the fairies charm people down to their realms with *Céol-Sidhe*, and no one who has heard it can resist its power and they are fated to belong to the fairies forever.

CEPHALONIA is the Fairy Queen of the Hidden Isle and mother of OBERON, a Fairy King.

_____

CERNUNNOS

CERNE ABBAS GIANT is one of Britain's many supernatural GIANTS and who is captured forever in this 55 m (180-feet) high chalk figure, which dominates a Dorset hillside. The locals maintain that he was a Danish giant who led an invasion of Britain. On reaching the hill he lay down to rest and the villagers cut off his head and left the outline of his figure on the hill as a warning to other invaders. The figure is over 2000 years old and has obvious fertility associations. Even today women sit on his large and obvious penis as a magical aid to conception.

CERNUNNOS ('Horned One') is an ancient pre-Celtic deity, perhaps the prototype of such horned fairies as PUCK. Like them, he is a nature spirit, the Lord of the Animals, both a hunter and protector of game. He is the god of life that arises from the earth, and also LORD OF THE DEAD and ruler of the UNDERWORLD. On the second century CE Gundestrup CAULDRON, he is depicted as stag horned, holding a torc and a SNAKE.

CERRIDWEN or CERIDWEN is a Welsh HAG or crone goddess associated with the PIG, the UNDERWORLD, and with fertility derived from the underworld, a prototype of many subsequent hag fairies. She brewed a magic potion in her CAULDRON that contained both knowledge and inspiration. This was intended for her ugly son Afagddu ('Utter Darkness') but was accidentally drunk by the little boy called Gwion who was set to stirring the cauldron. He spattered some liquid onto his thumb and when he sucked it to cool it, he was instantly privy to all the wisdom of the ages. When Cerridwen found out what had happened she pursued him in a variety of animal forms. He also SHAPESHIFTED into a variety of guises to evade her until eventually he turned into a grain of corn and she, in the shape of a black hen, ate him. He stayed in her womb for nine months before being reborn as the bard Taliesin ('Radiant Brow'). It has been argued that this story is the description of a shamanic initiation, or a metaphor for the changing seasons.

CHANGELINGS are fairy babies substituted for a kidnapped human one. Such stories occur all over Britain, Europe, Africa, India, the South Seas and the Americas. In Ireland a mother would place a pair of iron tongs over the cradle if she had to leave the baby unattended for a while. A wisp of straw would be lighted and a flaming sign of the cross made over the cradle before the child was lain in it.

Parents can soon tell that the baby in the crib is not their own but a fairy surrogate. A changeling may have a wizened or deformed appearance. It will probably be thin, weak or ailing and will cry continually. It may have a voracious appetite, be fond of dancing, be unnaturally precocious or make some unguarded remark as to its age. In Ireland all left-handed children are said to be changelings. Of course, these signs often meant that in the past any sick child was suspected of being a fairy child, and poor human babies were subjected to the terrible methods of detecting a changeling such as placing the suspect baby on a shovel and holding it over the fire saying:

'Burn, burn, burn
If of the devil burn;
But if of God and the saints
Be safe from harm'

or exposing the baby to the weather on a dunghill all day.[24] Others were given the poisonous leaves of the FOXGLOVE. When the changeling has been made to reveal its fairy nature it will disappear up the chimney, and the real baby will be found alive and well at the door, or back sleeping sweetly in its cradle.[25]

Fairies also steal away adults, especially pretty girls for wives or servants, and leave changelings in their place. A Cornish farmer called Mr. Noy came across one of these changelings on Selena Moor.[26] He said that he recognised family resemblances among the fairies, and some must have been recent changelings.

Belief in changelings was once very real and very frightening. As recently as 1895 a young woman called Bridget Cleary was burned to death in Ireland when her relatives thought she was a fairy changeling. When Bridget had failed to recover from an illness they had decided that she must be possessed by a malevolent fairy and tried to expel it with doses of URINE and herbs. When this failed her loving family resorted to the purification of FIRE.[27]

CHANNEL ISLES were once thought to be fairy islands, perhaps because of the many prehistoric graves, stone circles and monuments there. Locals believed that they had been built by *Les Petits Faîtiaux* (the fairies) to live in. The prehistoric sites themselves were sometimes called *pouquelaie* or 'fairy dwellings' (derived from POUQUE or PUCK).

English fairies once invaded Guernsey. A girl called Michelle de Garis fell in love with a beautiful, tiny man she found beneath a hedge. He was one of the Secret People of England (the Channel Islanders thought that England was FAIRYLAND) and they sailed away together, leaving as a gift for Michelle's parents a bulb which blossomed into the lovely Guernsey Lily. After a while more fairies arrived from England, all demanding brides like Michelle. The islanders refused to give up their women and tried to fight off the fairies, but lost the battle. The fairies married local women and this is why most islanders are short. The few tall people of the island are descended from the two human men who survived the battle. Native speakers refer to a small person as *aën p'tit faitot* meaning 'a little fairy'.

CHAO PHUM PHI ('Earth Spirit') are Thai spirits and are similar to HOUSE FAIRIES or household gods like the Roman PENATES.

CHERVAN is a Western European spirit that will act like a HOUSE FAIRY when well treated, but if annoyed will cause mischief.

CHERTOVKA or KHLEVIK is a female Russian DEMON or evil RUSALKA.

CHESS is played by the fairies of Scotland and Ireland, particularly the kings MIDAR and FINVARRA who are very fond of the game. Sometimes a fairy will challenge a human to a contest and ask for a human woman or other great prize if they win - which they usually do. In this manner Midar won Etain from her mortal husband. However, fairies do not always win, and the sidhe woman

BECUMA was banished back to fairyland when she lost a match.

CHEVAL BAYARD is a mischievous Normandy fairy who appears in the form of a HORSE but when humans get astride him he throws them into the bushes. He is the horse form of the LUTIN.

CHÈVRES DANSANTES ('Dancing Goats') are dancing French fairies which appear as the Northern Lights.

CHILDBIRTH is a dangerous time that leaves women vulnerable to the attention of fairies, both good and bad. Some evil fairies like the ELK will attack women or try to KIDNAP their new babies. Other kindly creatures, such as the Egyptian HATHORS, will protect birthing women. Should a woman die in childbirth she is liable to become a fairy herself. Such spirits include the Indian CHUREL, the Malayan LANGSUIR, the Aztec TZITSIMINE, and the Scottish BEAN-NIGHE.

CHILD STEALING is a very common phenomena of fairy lore and an astounding number and variety of fairies steal human children, including the Indian CHUREL, the Welsh BENDITH Y MAMAU, the Armenian ELK, the Greek GELLO, the German FRAU HOLLE, the Scandinavian HULDRE, the KORRIGANS of Brittany, the Spanish LAKE DEMONS, the Finnish SUKUSENDAL, the Irish SIDHE, the African ABIKU, the Brazilian ANHANGA, the Canadian APC'LNIC and the British BOGIE, among many, many others.

There are many theories as to why fairies steal human children. Some say they need to interbreed with humans to strengthen their bloodlines. Others that they like golden haired children because the fairy race tends to be dark and hairy. Yet again, others claim that fairies have to pay a TEIND to hell every seven years and use human children to do it with.[28] In Christian countries UNBAPTISED CHILDREN are considered to be particularly in danger. In Pagan cultures unnamed children are believed to be at risk from spirits. Children can be protected in a number of ways. A piece of IRON or steel may be placed beneath the cradle or hung above it. A PIN may be clipped in the child's clothing, a ROWAN branch hung over the cradle, a ring of FIRE placed around it, or the child can be wrapped in its father's shirt or trousers.

CHILDREN OF LIR were turned into swans by his jealous third wife Aoife, prophesying that until a King from Connacht in the north should marry a queen from Munster in the south, the children of Lir would be bound by the spell. It was nine hundred years before this happened, and the new king and queen of Connacht saw them return to human form. Alas, they were no longer lovely young SIDHE, but old and bent, and near death. A pious hermit baptised the old Pagans quickly, so that they were able to go to heaven.

CHIMBLEY CHARLIE is a HOB who haunts the Holman Inn near Blagdon in Somerset, England. He sits on the clavey (the beam above the fireplace), which is made from holly, or *holman* in the local dialect. A local farmer once scoffed at Charlie, and when he arrived for a meal at the inn Charlie had hidden all the silver and linen and the dinner had to be cancelled.

CHIMKE (a diminutive of 'Joachim') is a little German HOUSE FAIRY who helps around the house in return for a bowl of MILK each night.

CHIN-CHIN KOBAKAMA are Japanese HOUSE FAIRIES who pay particular attention to cleaning rugs and carpets. They appear as elderly men and women, but are very fit and active. They become nuisances if a home is not kept clean and tidy.

CHING are the Little People of China, only 23 cm (nine inches) tall. They live in the land of Hsiao-jen ko.

CHLEVIK is a Russian fairy who looks after the cattle sheds and the COWS in them, organising everything to his own satisfaction. If his rules are not adhered to he will become vicious and harm the cattle in his care.

CHOA PHUM PHI is a Thai HOUSE FAIRY.

CHOZYAIN or **Khlevik** also given as **Chozyainusko** ('Host') is a Russian HOUSE FAIRY, identical to the DOMOVOY.

CHRÜGELI is a CHANGELING of the Erdluitle.

CHURCH GRIM is an English fairy, known mainly in Yorkshire, who lives in a church bell tower.[29] It only leaves the church in dark, stormy weather, but delights in mischievously tolling the bell at midnight. During a funeral service it might appear to the clergyman, who can tell from its looks whether the deceased is saved or lost. The Church GRIM often takes the form of a BLACK DOG, and its appearance is an OMEN OF DEATH. There is a widespread belief that a spirit must guard a churchyard from the devil, and the church grim may be one of these spirits. *See also* KYRKOGRIM.

CHUREL, Chureyl or Dayan is an evil Indian VAMPIRE or WITCH, the GHOST of a woman who has died in CHILDBIRTH. She captures young men and sucks out their essence, until they are shrivelled and used up, or eats the hearts and livers of children. She has no mouth, and like many fairies, her FEET are on back to front. She cannot die until she has passed on her secret mantra to a successor.

CHURN-MILK PEG is a northern English fairy of the woodland in West Yorkshire, who appears as a DWARF woman in peasant clothing. She smokes a pipe. She loves nuts and will punish anyone who takes nuts from her tree with bloating and cramps. She hates lazy humans and will pinch them.[30]

CIN are SHAPESHIFTING Turkish fairies that are usually invisible but may appear as various animals, small humans, or even GIANTS. Sometimes they are friendly and will help humans; at other times they are malicious and are best avoided. It is best not to name them, but simply refer to them as *onlar* or 'they'. They are ruled by a king.

CINCIUT or CINICIUT is a form of NIGHTMARE.

CIPENAPERS (a contraction of 'kidnappers') is a Welsh term for the fairies and refers to their propensity to KIDNAP babies and young girls.[31] *See also* CHANGELINGS.

CITY OF JEWELS is the capital city of the DJINN, located in the country of Jinnistan. King Suleyman rules it.

CIUTHACH is evil Scottish fairy (possibly similar to an URISK), a CAVE dwelling GIANT or monster. He was originally a hero of the Picts.

CLIO is one of the nine MUSES, the patroness of history who introduced the Phoenician alphabet into Greece. She was the mother of Hyacinth. She is depicted with a scroll.

CLIONA, Clíodna or Cleena is an Irish fairy woman, the sister of AOIBHEALL and queen of the south Munster SIDHE. Some say that she is the daughter of the last Irish druid. She lives in an underground palace in Co. Cork. She is irresistible to men; some say that she is the most beautiful woman in the world. She appears accompanied by THREE magical birds, whose sweet song soothes the sick to sleep. They feed on the APPLE trees that grow in the OTHERWORLD. The O'Keefe clan claim that Cliona appears as their BANSHEE. She once lived in MANANNAN's country, but left there to live in Ireland with her mortal lover, Kevan. One day he went off to hunt in the woods and Cliona lay down beside the sea to sleep to the lullaby of FAIRY MUSIC, played by one of Manannan's minstrels. As she slept a wave caught her up and carried her back to the OTHERWORLD, leaving her lover desolate. The place is still called *Tonn Cliodhna* or 'Wave of Cliona' and lies at Glandore Bay in Co. Cork.

CLIONA

CLITON is one of the eight sisters of MORGAN LE FAY.

CLOAN NY MOYRN ('Children of Pride') is an ISLE OF MAN term for the fairies, referring to the notion that they were once angels, cast out of heaven for their rebellion against God.

CLOBHAIR-CEANN *See* CLURICAUN.

CLOTHES are a matter of some concern to the fairies. While some go naked and refuse to dress, others love smart garments, fine linen and costly lace. Solitary fairies like BROWNIES and HOUSE FAIRIES are often ragged in appearance, but they are offended by gifts of clothes and will promptly disappear forever if given a new suit, so if you have a helpful fairy don't be tempted to reward it in this fashion. Lewis Spence speculated that the fairy might have been expecting a human sacrifice, and would have been disappointed to discover no body inside the clothes. Or it may be the quality of the clothes that some fairies object to, chiding the giver for supplying a coarse hempen garment when a linen one was required. Headgear is also important. Diverse spirits favour RED CAPS and others GREEN caps, while LEPRECHAUNS prefer three-cornered hats.

You can make use of your own clothes to free yourself from fairy enchantments. If fairies are troubling you at night, place your shoes with the toes pointing outwards by the bed and throw your socks under it. If you are being PIXY-LED (tricked from your path by fairies) turn your clothes inside out and this will confuse the fairies long enough to allow you to make your escape. A GLOVE thrown into a FAIRY RING will enable a mortal trapped in it to make his or her escape.

While clothes hide the body, they often reveal a great deal more about the wearer than simple nakedness ever could. Their quality and cut communicate status and wealth, while the style may disclose the wearer's occupation, as in the case of a uniform. In days gone by this was more obvious than it is now. By his dress the yeoman farmer stood out from the nobleman, and the peasant from the artisan. In some cultures, it is still possible to tell whether a woman is married, widowed or single by her garments. During the Middle Ages the Sumptuary Laws operated in England and legislation defined even the type of fabric a class of person could wear - silks and velvets were strictly for aristocrats.

In folk tales, when a person changes their clothes they alter or lose their identity. The princess assumes rags to become a pauper and is only recognised by her relatives when she resumes her royal costume. Passing on clothes often means passing on the nature or status of their previous owner[32] and this may be why fairies object to being given human clothes. If a PERIs clothes are taken from her, she loses her fairy powers and must dwell as a human woman.

The ability to change shape or become invisible often depends on donning or removing some article of clothing, for example the SELKIES assume sealskins to swim in the sea and shed them when they come ashore. If these skins are hidden from them they cannot resume their seal shape or return to the water, and must abide as a human on land. Wearing animal skins takes on an extra dimension in shamanic practice, when wearing the skin of a creature indicates assuming some of its powers.

Many fairies are naked and prefer to stay that way, being completely unselfconscious about their undressed state. They don't share the human's prudery about nudity and implied sin that the bible claims descended on Adam and Eve when they were expelled from the Garden of Eden. It can be interpreted that fairies inhabit a more natural, innocent and freer realm of consciousness.

Many fairies wear pointed caps or hats, just as storybook WITCHES do. While some of this relates to MUSHROOM lore, pointed hats in stories are generally a code for powers of insight and intuition, but if the inner qualities fail to match up to the display it becomes the fool's cap.[33] The symbolism of the hat is as revealing as the symbolism of clothes. Types of hats define a viewpoint or bearing - the bishop's mitre, the judge's wig, the scholar's mortarboard, the businessman's bowler, or the workman's cloth cap. We still say of a person 'he is wearing his such-and-such hat today'.

CLOTHO ('Spinner') is one of the FATES who spins the thread of life. See SPINNING.

CLURICAUN, Cluricane, Clobhair-Ceann or Cluricaune is an Irish fairy from Munster who raids wine cellars and borrows sheep and dogs to ride them through the night. Cluricanes are almost unknown in the north of Ireland and it is not known whether cluricanes are a separate order of fairies or just LEPRECHAUNS on a spree. The cluricane is sometimes heard hammering and is said to be fond of making shoes, like the leprechaun, but in ancient tales these are of metal.[34]

He looks like a wrinkled little old man, dressed in antique style with a pea GREEN coat with large buttons and shoes with large metal buckles. His ensemble is topped off with a cocked hat in the French style. He makes shoes while whistling a tune, but if a human should catch a glimpse of him, he will vanish in an instant. He knows where hidden TREASURE lies, but if a man should leave a mark to guide him back to it, whether it be a bush with a broken branch, a ribbon tied to a thistle, a rock pile and so on, the cluricane will multiply the object so that the treasure is lost. He carries a small purse with a lucky shilling (*sprè na skillenagh*) in it. However many times he spends it, it always returns to his purse. He also carries a purse with a copper coin in it, and if anyone tries to rob him of the lucky shilling, this is the one they get. His favourite occupations are drinking whiskey and smoking tobacco. He is one of the few who know the true secret of making heather ale. People often dig up little clay pipes left by the cluricane, especially when they are ploughing in the vicinity of the fairy mounds.

One tale of a cluricane concerns Squire Justin Mac Carthy of Ballinacarthy, who was justly proud of the fact that he always served the finest food and the best wines. However, for some strange reason no butler in charge of the splendid wine cellar could be induced to stay in the job for any length of time. One day he returned from a hunting trip to find no wine available. The butler complained that he had been locked out of the cellar. Mac Carthy grew angry, and exclaimed that he might as well move if he had no control over his own house. Storming down to the wine cellar, he was astonished to be confronted by a tiny man sitting astride a pipe of port. His skin was wrinkled and his nose a boozy purple. 'I hear we are about to move house,' the cluricane said. 'Well, wherever you go, your cluricane Naggeneen will go with you.'

'In that case' replied Mac Carthy, philosophically, 'there's not much point in moving'. With that he seized a bottle of wine and went back to the feasting. For the rest of his long life, he had to fetch the wine himself. On his death, the cellar became depleted and some say the cluricane became so depressed by this he let himself go, though others say he turned cobbler and was seen at his work in the company of a foaming jug of ale.

CMOK (or probably **Tsmok**) is a Slavonic HOUSE FAIRY who appears in the form of a SNAKE.

CNOC is a little MOUND where fairies dwell. It is a Gaelic word meaning a knoll.

COBLYNAU, Koblernigh or **Coblyn** ('Knocker' or 'Sprite') are Welsh MINE FAIRIES, similar to the Cornish KNOCKERS. Though the coblynau are sometimes spotted working on seam faces, they do not actually mine anything, they are just pretending. William Evans saw a group of coblynau when crossing the mountains early one morning. They were busy working a fairy coal mine, some cutting coal, others loading it, but all was done in total silence.

Egbert Williams, his sister and two other girls also saw fifteen coblynau in a field at Bodfari. They were dressed in red and yellow with red spotted kerchiefs tied round their heads, and were capering madly in the manner of Morris dancers. They were the size of normal men, though they had the proportions of dwarfs. After a while, one of the coblynau broke away and ran at the watchers, who took fright and ran off while the copper-faced fairy leant on the stile, gazing after them fiercely.[35]

Others say that coblynau are only 45 cm (eighteen inches) tall, and very ugly, dressed in miners' clothes, with tiny picks, hammers and lamps. If miners speak disparagingly of them, they will throw stones at the culprits, but they will never really hurt anyone, and often guide miners to the best seams.

COBS are English HOBGOBLINS from Warwickshire and much feared. They were originally evil fairies who took the shape of HORSES (cob is another word for a saddle horse). From them came the now defunct HALLOWEEN custom of going out with a mock horse head covered in a sheet to frighten the timid.[36]

COCADRILLE is a curious forest fairy from central France who appears as a SNAKE with paws. Cocadrilles are deadly to cattle.

COCHION ('Red Ones') are little Welsh fairies. *See* Y GWLLIED COCHION.

COCKAIGNE or **Cockaygne** is a mythical OTHERWORLD or FAIRYLAND described in the thirteenth-century poem *The Land of Cockaygne*. It is a land of pleasure and ease, where the houses are made of cakes and the streets of pastry.

COCO, EL, is an Hispanic BOGEYMAN used to threaten babies who will not stop crying. It is said that he eats naughty children. He is black in appearance.

COHULLEN DRUITH are the feathered RED CAPS of the Irish MERROW sea fairies. If these are stolen, they cannot return to the sea. *See also* CLOTHES.

COINTEACH ('One Who Keens') is a Scottish BANSHEE.

CÓISTE-BODHAR ('Deaf Coach') is an immense black coach with a coffin on it, which sometimes manifests with a BANSHEE. It is pulled by headless horses and driven by a DULLOHAN. It rumbles up to a door and if the occupant answers it a basin of blood is thrown in his face.[37]

COLIN is a favourite name among Guernsey fairies and there are many stories of POUQUES called Colin. One old Guernsey MIDWIFE called

Lisabeau was called to a birth and found a lovely woman lying in bed with a sickly baby called Colin. She must have been bewitched for when she came to her senses she was back at home with the baby. She brought up the boy as her own. He remained very small but when he was fifteen he entered the service of the minister. A year later the vicar was returning home when he heard a voice saying 'Tell little Colin that the big Colin is dead.' The astonished minister did as he was bidden and was amazed when his servant said that he must depart immediately. That night he appeared before Lisabeau, seeming very upset. He asked her to bless him, as he had to go far away. With this, he vanished, never to be seen again.[38]

According to another tale Lé Sieur Dumont was returning home when he heard a little voice beside the path crying out 'Help me! Help me!' He was a kindly man and reached down, saying 'I am here. I will help you.' He felt a hand grab his own and could dimly see a small figure beside him. Lé Sieur Dumont continued home with the small waif still clutching his hand. However, when he stepped into the light of his kitchen he was horrified to discover that an ugly little fairy had him by the hand. The creature told him that his name was Lé p'tit Colin.

Despite his looks he proved to be very useful about the farm and was a caring nursemaid for the younger children. The family soon prospered with his help. On the other hand, all the neighbours hated the little fairy who was in turn rude and unpleasant towards them, causing them mischief whenever he could. Then one day Dumont heard a voice calling 'Tell Lé p'tit Colin that Lé Grànde Colin is dead.' The farmer did as he was bidden and on hearing the news the ugly little fairy sprang up with a grin and disappeared through the door, never to be seen again.

There is a menhir called the Fairies' Bat (*La Palaette ès Faies*), which serves to mark where two pouques played bat and ball. They were called Lé Grànde Colin and Lé p'tit Colin. Lé Grànde Colin was using the menhir as a bat. He hit the ball so hard that it disappeared from the field of play. When Lé p'tit Colin protested he grew angry and struck the bat into the ground and refused to play any more.

COLMAN GRAY or **Coleman Gray** is a little Cornish PISKIE who was adopted by humans. A miserable looking little piskie was found near a house, alone and incapable of making itself understood. Fearing the revenge of the fairies if they should fail to care for the creature, the family took it in and cared for it. The piskie soon recovered its health, and was so good-humoured that it soon became a family favourite. Then one day a voice was heard calling "Coleman Gray! Coleman Gray!" and the piskie sat up and exclaimed "Ah! My daddy has come!" and was off in an instant, never to be seen again.

COLT-PIXY is a guardian PIXY of apple orchards in Hampshire.

COLUINN GUN CHEANN ('The Headless Torso') is a Scottish BAUCHAN who was attached to the Macdonals of Morar, but would attack anyone else that crossed his path, and kill any man who passed by the river Morar after dark. He was eventually overcome by one of the MacLeods.

CONARAN is a Fairy King of the TUATHA DÉ DANAAN who sent his three HAG daughters to punish the Irish hero Finn Mac Cumhal for hunting his DEER. However, the THREE women were defeated and the king's MOUND burned.

CORANIEID are mysterious beings who made nuisances of themselves in Britain during the reign of the legendary King Lludd. They could overhear any conversation anywhere, and the money they passed out among the population was really only MUSHROOMS, infused by a magical GLAMOUR. They were killed when Lludd and his clever brother Lllefelys gave out crushed insects that were harmless to humans, but fatal to the Coranieid. The term Coranieid may be derived from the Breton KORRIGANED, though the *Trioedd Ynys Pyddein* states that the Coranieid came from Arabia.[39]

CORICS are a type of KORRED fairy of Brittany.

CORMORAN was a GIANT who built St Michael's Mount in Cornwall as a dwelling for himself and his wife. Jack the Giant-killer slew him, or some say King ARTHUR. He is the giant mentioned in the famous story of Jack and the Beanstalk.

CORNANDONET DÛ is one of country dwelling LUTINS of France.

CORPSE LIGHT is another name for the WILL O'THE WISP. It sometimes appears as an OMEN OF DEATH.

CORPSE-CANDLE is another name for the WILL O'THE WISP and sometimes appears as an OMEN OF DEATH.

CORRANDONNETS are a type of Breton KORRED.

CORRIQUETS are a type of Breton KORRED, who guard standing stones. They wear their hair tucked under broad brimmed hats, and are small and dark.

COTTINGLEY FAIRIES were the fairies supposedly photographed by two young cousins, Frances Griffiths and Elsie Wright, though both later admitted that the pictures were fakes. At the time the photographs fooled many people, including Sir Arthur Conan Doyle, the author of Sherlock Holmes.

COULIN ('Fairy Tunes') are the old ballads learned by human musicians from the MOUNDS of the SIDHE.

Carolan, the celebrated Irish bard, acquired his skills by sleeping out on a fairy hill at night when the fairy music came to him in his dreams and he played the air from memory.[40] He then had the power to make men laugh or cry. Many old Irish tunes are fairy songs such as *The Pretty Girl Milking the Cow* and *The Londonderry Air*. It is unwise to sing or whistle such tunes near a fairy hill, as the fairies don't like to hear their music on ordinary mortal lips.[41]

COURÉTES or **Carikenes** were introduced into Brittany by ancient Phoenician sailors. They intermarried with the local KORRED.

COURIL are little Breton fairies who haunt the old stone circles and standing stones. They have webbed feet and sightings of them have also been reported in Cornwall.

COVENTINA is a water NYMPH of northern Britain. Coins and brooches were thrown into her sacred spring at Carrawburgh on Hadrian's Wall.

COWS are a subject of great interest to fairies. European fairies frequently manifest as cows, usually WHITE in colour, while Egyptian fairies are associated with the cow-headed goddess HATHOR. Many fairies steal MILK from unattended cattle or attack them as they stand in the byre, only being deterred by special charms such as ROWAN and RED THREAD, or PRIMROSE bouquets.

Fairies keep herds of cattle themselves, customarily under a lake or beneath the sea where the animals graze on seaweed. Occasionally one of these *cro sith* or 'fairy cattle' appears on the shore as a gift for a human farmer. He is fortunate, as it will provide endless supplies of milk. There are several Scots legends of fairy cattle left as gifts, identified by their round ears. In Ireland a sacred white heifer would appear every MAY DAY to bring luck to a certain farmer. Sometimes though, the fairies send an enchanted cow into a mortal herd in order to steal cattle. If the farmer is not vigilant it will

lure his herd into a fairy MOUND and they will never be seen again. Sometimes when fairies steal away a cow the appearance of the cow is left but the substance is gone. The cow will pine away and die within a short time.

Otherworldly cattle are common in British and Irish folklore, recognised by their red or round ears. A herd of cattle descended from fairy cows have grazed the parkland around Chillingham Castle in Northumberland since the thirteenth century. They have the red ears and white coats of fairy cattle, and it is said that they will kill anyone who touches them. A white fairy calf haunts the countryside around Liphook in Hampshire.

According to an old belief if a man

CREIDDYLEDD

should give a cow to the poor, at his death the spirit of the animal will return to guide him to the OTHERWORLD. *See also* DUN COW.

CO-WALKER is a spirit double or *doppelganger* sometimes called a FETCH, Waff, or Reflex Man. It appears as the spitting image of some person; but when it appears it is an OMEN OF DEATH. The co-walker is possibly one of the fairies, sometimes seen at funerals by those with second sight. According to Kirk the Scottish and Irish will not eat meat at these gatherings, in case this brings them into contact with a fairy co-walker.

COWLUG-SPRITES are fairies of the Scottish/English Border counties who have cows' ears and haunt the villages of Bowden and Gateside on Cowlug Night.

COWRIE is a BROWNIE who haunted Goranberry Tower in the Scottish Borders.

COWSLIPS (*Primula veris*) are lovely spring flowers that are cherished and protected by the fairies. Cowslips unlock the doors to the fairy MOUNDS of the English West Country and access the TREASURE beneath them.

CRACKERBONES is an English GOBLIN from Somerset.

CRAMPS are a penalty for annoying the fairies.

CREDNE is of the TUATHA DÉ DANAAN, a worker in bronze who forges their weapons.

CREEPERS is an alternative name for TROWS.

CREIDDYLEDD is the fairy maiden for whose hand King GWYN AP NUDD and Gwythr, son of Greidawl, fight every MAY DAY. According to the story she married Gwythr but was abducted by Gwyn ap Nudd before the marriage could be consummated. King ARTHUR was appealed to and decreed that the two men should fight for her hand every May Day until Judgement Day. This is a seasonal battle between the powers of winter and summer for the hand of the Earth Goddess. It echoes similar tales of flower maidens or spring goddesses such as BLODEUWEDD and GUINEVERE.

CRIMBILS are the children of the Welsh fairies the BENDITH Y MAMAU. Sometimes the Bendith Y Mamau will steal a human child and leave a CHANGELING crimbil in its place.

CRIONS are French fairies who guard ancient standing stones. They are small, dark and shaggy. They like to force men to DANCE with them until they die of exhaustion. This is so hilarious to them they will laugh till daybreak.

CRODH MARA or **Crudh Mara** are hornless cattle that belong to the sea fairies, according to Scottish Highland folklore. The fairies sometimes give them to their favourites. *See also* COW.

CROM CRUAICH ('The Crooked One of the Hill') or **Crom Dubh** ('The Dark Crooked One') is sometimes cited as a fairy, though he was once an ancient agricultural god. His name associates him with the MOUNDS or the UNDERWORLD - just like the fairies, whose legends some think derive from such gods. Crom controlled the ripening of the crops and the fertility and MILK yield of COWS. To this end, offerings were made to him so that he should not blight the corn and spoil the milk. Into living memory, offerings were similarly made to the SIDHE for the same purpose, with milk and butter being placed on the fairy mounds. His festival was on 1st August, LUGHNASA, one of the great fairy festivals. In folk tales he appears as an archetypal Pagan converted to Christianity by St Patrick.

CRO-MAGNON MAN may be the source of fairies legends, according to some folklorists, who argue that stories of little people arose from distant race memories of this earlier breed of pre-Neolithic cave dwellers. Forty thousand years ago Cro-Magnon man started to move into a Europe that was still populated by Neanderthals, dark, hairy people with a very different appearance. The legend of the FORMORIANS could possibly describe such an encounter. (They were a swarthy race, described as monstrous and deformed, whom the TUATHA DÉ DANAAN drove out of Ireland.) Fairies are often depicted as shaggy or dark and hairy in appearance. Folk memories of Neanderthals may have given rise to legends of SATYRS, WOODWOSES and WILDMEN, and the RUSALKA in Eastern Europe.[42]

CROQUEMITAINE is an ugly French BOGEYMAN invoked to make naughty children behave: 'If you don't behave the Croquemitaine will get you'.

CROSS is one of the Christian symbols of which fairies are said to be afraid. Drawing a cross on cakes will stop fairies dancing on them. According to Irish folklore if a child is FAIRY STRUCK it will be cured if you give it a cup of water in the name of Christ and make the sign of the cross over it.

CROSSROADS are frequented by fairies and other spirits. The world over, crossroads are places of mystery, danger and magic. In Eastern Europe, they are the haunts of VAMPIRES, in Japan, evil spirits attack travellers there, and in India crossroads are ruled by Rudra, the god of evil powers. In England the evil OMEN of the BLACK DOG frequents crossroads, while in ancient Greece they were sacred to Hecate, the WITCH goddess of the UNDERWORLD. In many stories witches meet at crossroads: a trial record from seventeenth-century Sweden says that some witches danced there in order to summon up the DEVIL. It was the custom to bury suicides at crossroads with a stake through them, so that the GHOST could not rise and walk, or if it did it would be too confused to walk home, having four directions to choose from.

For the ancients any boundary, such as a doorway, was a magical a place between places, belonging to neither and therefore fraught with danger. This is why BRIDES are carried across the THRESHOLD. Imagine then how much more dangerous and magical is a crossroads, a boundary between four places.

CROW (*Corvus corone corone*) is a bird which often accompanies fairies, or may be one of their shapeshifting forms

Crows, RAVENS and other black carrion birds are interchangeable in many mythologies. The Greek for crow *corone* also yields *corax* or 'raven', while in Latin *corus* or 'raven' has the same root as *cornix* which means 'crow'.

Whether natural or supernatural, crows were considered to be OMENS, particularly of death; a crow in a churchyard is a portent of death. The crow is a carrion bird that feeds on corpses, known as birds of the scaffold, since they were often found perching and feeding on the old gibbets.

The crow was very much associated with WITCHES and witchcraft and was said to have the gift of PROPHECY, and therefore became an ingredient in many potions used in fortune telling.

The crow is a form taken by several ancient HAG goddesses and fairies, such as the Greek Coronis, the Irish BADB, and the MORRIGAN.

CROWD, THE, is a Manx term for the fairies.

CUACHAG is a Scottish Highland WATER FAIRY that haunts Glen Cuaich in Invernesshire. It is one of the FUATH and is highly dangerous.

CUCKOO is the *eun sith* or 'fairy bird' of TIR-NAN-OG. In the winter it disappears from the land and enters the fairy MOUNDS, not to be seen again in Britain and Ireland until the spring.

CUGHTACH is a Manx fairy that haunts CAVES. It is possibly one of the BUGGANES.

CULA is a French fairy, a SHAPESHIFTER so accomplished that it might appear as any one of a thousand different things, from a

boy to a flame, from a giant spider to a ball of wool. He is one of the LUTIN.

CULARDS are French WILL O'THE WISPS.

CÚLDUB is a mischievous fairy who, in ancient Irish legend, stole the food of the warrior band the Fianna and took it back to his MOUND. The hero Finn Mac Cumhal chased him but caught his thumb in the doorway of the mound. As he put his thumb into his mouth, he found he had knowledge of all things, past and present.

CUNNING MAN is the male equivalent to the village Wise Woman or FAIRY DOCTOR. Like the WITCH he may have acquired his knowledge of herbs, healing, potions and MAGIC from the fairies, or the knowledge may have been passed down from father to son. Certainly, the Cunning Man is able to cure those ills caused by fairy spells and ELF BOLTS. The most powerful Cunning Men were the seventh sons of seventh sons.

CURUPIRA, Curupuri, Caypór or **Cururipur** is a kind of forest HOBGOBLIN or WILD MAN of Brazil. He is ugly and deformed with RED skin, red eyes, back to front cloven FEET and long shaggy, RED HAIR. A

piercing cry of '*te wo yi*' sometimes resounds through the forests and this is attributed to him, though he is not generally considered very threatening. However, he does protect tortoises from hunters.

CUTTY SOAMS is a mischievous MINE FAIRY of the Scottish/English Border counties. He used to cut the ropes that pulled the coal trucks.

CWN ANNWN ('Hounds of ANNWN' or 'Hounds of Hell') are Welsh Hounds of the UNDERWORLD, red eared, white fairy dogs of the WILD HUNT. The Hunt is lead by ARAWN, or sometimes by GWYN AP NUDD who is both the King of the Fairies and the King of the Dead. It rides out on wild and stormy nights to pursue the souls of the newly dead. To hear it is an OMEN OF DEATH. The call of the dogs grows quieter the nearer they come, sounding 'like that of small beetles', but in the distance their cry is full of lamentation 'like that of a bloodhound'.[43] They are called *Cwn-wybir* ('Sky-dogs') since their eerie cries are heard from the air, and *Cwn bendith eu Mammau* ('Dogs of the Fairies').

CYCLOPS ('Round Eye') are one-eyed, man-eating GIANTS of classical Greek myth. The hero Odysseus escaped from one by blinding it. *See* FLY AGARIC.

CYHIRAETH is a Cornish BANSHEE who has long black teeth.

CYOERRAETH, Cyoeraeth, Kyhirraeth or **Cyhraeth** is a Welsh BANSHEE who can be either male or female. Cyoerraeth are sometimes heard but rarely seen, though they have long, black teeth, matted hair, withered arms and wings. They announce to the spouses of the dying that their husband or wife is about to pass away, or tap with their wings on the windows of a dying person, groaning loudly like sick people. They also herald shipwrecks by walking along the beach on stormy nights, carrying CORPSE-CANDLES, or warn of fatal disasters and epidemics with their groaning. On dark nights, they may be heard splashing in dangerous lakes and streams. Cyoerraeth was originally a Welsh goddess of the streams.

CYRENE is a water NYMPH of Greek myth, the daughter of the river god Peneus. She bore a son called Aristæus to the god Apollo. He is said to have invented bee keeping.

DA DERGA ('The Red Lord') is an OTHERWORLD character of Irish myth who owned a hostel that seems to have been an entrance into the UNDERWORLD of the DEAD. Conaire Mór, the King of Ireland, broke a number of taboos, which offended the fairies. Circumstances conspired to take him to the hostel of Da Derga, 'The RED Lord', where he met his death. A Red Lord also appeared in the tale of the GREEN KNIGHT, the alter ego of the Green Knight himself.

DACTYLS ('Fingers') are ancient Greek creatures, who seem to have been similar to EARTH FAIRIES or DWARFS. They were born from the fingerprints of the Titaness Rhea - five males from her right hand, five females from her left. They were SMITHS and magicians.

DÆMON or DAIMON is a Greek spirit, the representation or personification of a human personality. Though the word DEMON is derived from dæmon, it has a completely different meaning. Compare with GENIUS.

DAGDA ('Good God') is the chief god of the TUATHA DÉ DANAAN, later demoted to the status of a Fairy King. He owns a harp that can play itself and which calls forth the change of the seasons, a magical CAULDRON that supplies plentiful food and can restore the dead to life, and a club that can both kill and restore life. Every SAMHAIN he mates with the MORRIGAN.

The Dagda divided up the SIDHE or MOUNDS among the Tuatha dé Danaan, but forgot AENGHUS who was away at the time. When Aenghus returned he claimed the sidhe of Brugh na Boinne which the Dagda had assigned to himself. Naturally, the Dagda refused. Aenghus begged leave to be allowed to spend the night there and proceeded to do so, along with the next day. He then claimed that the mound was rightly his, since he had spent a day and a night there. The Dagda was forced to agree and had to move out.

DAHARI are the offspring of a DJINN named Sakhar.

DÁIN ('Dead') was a Scandinavian ELF who was very proficient with the runes (a method of divination).

DAIN, LÉ, is a Guernsey solitary fairy or GOBLIN with an evil reputation. The term is derived from an old Norman word for DEVIL.

DAIREANN is a fairy of the TUATHA DÉ DANAAN who offered herself as a bride to the Irish hero Finn Mac Cumhal. He refused her when she said that if they married he must stay with her for six months of every year. Angry at this rejection, she gave him drugged mead. For a time, he became mad, so much so that his war band tried to desert him thirteen times, and were only held back by the persuasion of Caoilte, his best friend.

DAKINI are fearsome female Hindu GOBLINS or VAMPIRES who suck blood from the newly dead, especially those who have been executed.

DAMA DAGENDA are jungle fairies of Papua New Guinea who attack travellers, inflicting sores and ulcers. For protection it is necessary to talk loudly or sing in a language they won't understand. While they are trying to work out what you are saying, you can make your escape.

DAMES BLANCHES ('White Ladies') or Demoiselles Blanches are the WHITE LADIES of Normandy who haunt ravines, fords, and bridges, preventing the passage of travellers unless they agree to DANCE. Should they refuse, they will be thrown into a ditch or tormented with evil spirits. The Dames Blanches are very beautiful, blond haired and clad in white, but betray their fairy origins with their snake-like tails or bird FEET. They cloak themselves in the white fog and wash their dresses every night in the streams.

DAMES VERTES ('Green Ladies') are fairies of eastern France who live in the forest, particularly in its CAVES or near waterfalls and springs, though they sometimes venture to its edges to play tricks on travellers. These range from the mischievous to the highly dangerous, such as dangling people over waterfalls by their hair. They like to lure young men to their doom, killing them with their extremes of passion and the violence of their lovemaking. They are very tall, beautiful, and dress in green, though they are usually invisible and the only sign of their passing is a ripple through the grass. They ride on the wind and breathe life into the ripening seeds of grain, visiting fields and orchards to bless them. Occasionally, they appear before fires and have even been known to work in human houses. When it rains, they may shelter behind trees or in the overhanging vines. They are VEGETATION SPIRITS. *See also* GREEN LADIES.

DAMNED SOULS are what some fairies are said to be, i.e. the damned souls of DEAD humans. Other fairies, such as the WILD HUNT, pursue the souls of the dead.

DANCE is an activity loved by fairies from all over the world, usually in forest glades under the moon. Such fairies include the Hindu APSARAS, the Normandy WHITE LADIES, the Dutch ALVEN, the Mexican JIMANIOS, the ancient Greek NYMPHS, the Danish ELLEFOLK, the Welsh ELLYLLDAN, the Algonquin ELVES OF LIGHT, the French FÉE, the Orkney TROWS, the Icelandic ILLES, the Hopi KACHINA, the Breton KORREDS, the Irish SIDHE, the Italian MASSARIOLI, the German NIX, the Tamil PEYMAKILIR, English ELVES and PIXIES, Scottish SELKIES, Norwegian THUSSARS, Icelandic VARDOGLS and the Slavonic VILA.

Fairies also dance on the village green and in fields and meadows, creating bright circles on the grass called FAIRY RINGS.

Humans may be drawn into a dance and some never escape, being forced to dance until they die of exhaustion. Others do get away, but they are never the same again. One young girl went to the well to fetch water when her foot slipped and she fell. When she got up she seemed to be in a strange place. About a blazing fire gathered a great crowd and they all looked at her. Then a beautiful youth asked her to dance but she complained that there was no music. He lifted his hand and instantly the sweetest music filled the air. The pair danced until the moon and stars set, and it seemed to her that she floated on air. The girl eventually returned home, but ever afterwards she heard the FAIRY MUSIC and pined away with longing.

DANDO AND HIS DOGS or Dandy Dogs is a Cornish version of the WILD HUNT, said to be led by the DEVIL himself or by Dando. The BLACK DOGs breathe fire and utter terrible cries. Dando was the name of a parson of St Germans who was given to all forms of disreputable behaviour and was passionately fond of hunting. One Sunday, he and his friends were out hunting over St. Earth way and were joined by a strange huntsman on a splendid fiery horse. At the close of the hunt, Dando called for a drink, but he had already emptied all the flasks and horns his servants had with them.

'Well, if you can't find any on earth, go to hell for it!', he cried. The stranger bowed and handed him a drinking horn. Dando drained it and declared it the best he had ever tasted. Then he fell to quarrelling with the stranger about whose bag the game belonged to and Dando declared he would go to hell rather than let the stranger have it.

'So you shall!', exclaimed the stranger, and seizing Dando, plunged with him and his dogs into the deepest pool, going down in a cloud of steam and fire. Dando and dogs are still heard early on Sunday mornings, pelting past in full cry.[44]

DANES is a Somerset name for the fairies. Fairy MOUNDS are also sometimes called 'Dane Forts', probably from DUN, since hill elves were known in Anglo-Saxon writings as *dunaelfen*. Dun also appears as a Scots term for a fairy hill. The name of the Dane Hills in Leicestershire - where BLACK ANNIS lives - probably has the same origin. It may be that *dane* derives from the Celtic goddess DANU, widely known as the mother of the fairies, or from the Scandinavian DÁIN, meaning 'dead' referring to a spirit or GHOST, or from DAIN, an old Norman term for a DEVIL.

DANU is a Celtic goddess, the mother of the TUATHA DÉ DANAAN, which literally translates as 'the People of the Goddess Danu'. She is the daughter of the DAGDA and is sometimes identified with Anu (Annis), and with AINE, the Irish moon goddess. She may have passed into fairy folklore as BLACK ANNIS, AINE, GENTLE ANNIE, and AYNIA.

Danu is probably Indo-European in origin and may be cognate with the Sanskrit water goddess Dánu ('The Flowing One').[45] Her name is found in the names of several rivers, including the Danube. She is paralleled in Welsh literature by Dôn, the mother of a race of warriors and may possibly be identified with the Greek Danaë, the foundress of the THREE cities of Rhodes. The cult of Danu probably reached Ireland with the Celts in the Iron Age. Originally a river goddess, she took on the attributes of a sovereign goddess of the land. She is often identified with Anu (from *anae* meaning 'wealth'), an earth goddess said to be the mother of the Irish gods. In turn Anu is sometimes identified with the MORRIGAN.

DAOINE BEAGA ('Little Folk') is a Scots Gaelic term for fairies in general.

DAOINE BEAGA RUADH ('Little Red Men') are the male fairies of Skye. They are called 'little RED men' as their clothes are dyed with lichen, while the fairy women are dressed in GREEN.

DAOINE COIRE ('Honest Folk') is a Scots Gaelic term for fairies in general.

DAOINE MARA ('Sea People') is a Scots Gaelic term for MERMAIDS and sea fairies. The males are hairy, bearded and have big mouths, flat noses, long arms and jaundiced looking skin.

DAOINE MATHA or DUINE MATHA ('Good People' or 'Peaceful People') is an Irish Gaelic term for fairies in general.

DAOINE SIDHE, Daoine Sith, Doane Shee ('People of the Hills') (s. Duine

waists. They wear GREEN and resent humans who wear this colour. They live in communities, each having its own abode called *shians* or *tomhans* - rock masses resembling turrets. The fairies are merry creatures, fond of MUSIC and DANCING. However, they are often mischievous or cruel to humans, who must deal with them carefully. Highlanders will not speak of them, especially on a FRIDAY. When the Daoine Sith take to their snow white HORSES and ride abroad, only the tinkling of the harnesses betrays their presence.

DAPHNE was a NYMPH in ancient Greek myth. She was transformed into a laurel tree to save her from the amorous advances of the god Apollo.

DARK MAN is a general term for fairies as many fairy beings are said to be dark complexioned. During the British WITCH trials, it was reported that witches kept company with 'the Dark Man', generally taken at the time to be synonymous with the DEVIL. *See also* FEAR DORCHA.

DARTMOOR HOUNDS is a Devonshire version of the WILD HUNT, a pack of ghostly dogs that fly through the night sky to pursue their quarry.

DATA JINN HITAM is the King of the BLACK JINN in Malayan folklore.

DAUGHTERS OF THE SUN are enigmatic fairy women who live on a mysterious island in the Okeefenokee Swamp in the southern USA. They have lovely faces, shimmering forms and musical voices. Travellers have occasionally encountered them, or their laughter has been heard echoing across the swamps.

DAUMLINGE ('Thumbling') is a little German fairy.

DAVY JONES is the spirit of the sea, according to the popular folklore of

---

DAOINE

Sith) is the form that the TUATHA DÉ DANAAN took when the Celtic Milesians invaded Ireland and drove them into the hollow hills. There, they dwindled in size and became the Daoine Sidhe, the small fairy folk. King FINVARRA, the high king of the Irish fairies, rules them in Connaught. He is fond of CHESS and no human has ever beaten him. His wife is OONAGH, the most beautiful woman in any realm, but he still likes womanising. In Munster there are THREE fairy queens, CLIODNA, AINE and AOIBHILL. The Daoine Sidhe like hurling (a traditional Irish ball game) and a contest was once

held between the fairies of Munster and Connaught. When Connaught were winning a fight broke out and the Munsters turned themselves into flying beetles and ate every green thing in sight, destroying the countryside until thousands of doves arose from the earth and ate them.

The Scots Highlanders called similar fairies the Daoine Sith. These fairies were once ANGELS but were cast out of heaven and are doomed to wander the earth until the Day of Judgement, when it is possible that God will pardon them. They are of supernatural beauty, small and perfect. The eyes of the women sparkle like diamonds and their dark brown hair falls in ringlets to their sailors. To 'go to Davy Jones' locker' is to be drowned or buried at sea.

DEAD Death occurs in the legends of just about every country in the world. These are usually tales of the wandering spirits of the dead, and in many places these have been incorporated into fairy folklore. (There was once a widespread belief that when a man slept or died his soul emerged from his mouth in the form of a tiny person.) Some fairies are expressly spoken of as ghosts, especially in Celtic countries where they are spirits neither good enough for heaven nor bad enough for hell, especially the souls of old druids and Pagans. In other parts of Europe, they are the ghosts of suicides, murder victims, unbaptised children or women who have died in childbirth. The WILL O'THE WISP is a dead child, DUNTERS are the victims of the Picts, BROWNIES and HOBGOBLINS are often the ghosts of dead servants.[46] The Irish said that if you had many friends among the departed you would have many friendly fairies, but that if you had many enemies among the dead there would be many fairies trying to do you harm.[47] Fairies are often ancestral spirits. In the original story of Cinderella, the fairy godmother was the spirit of her dead mother.

The fifteenth-century *Orfeo* talks of FAIRYLAND as the Land of the Dead.[48] The dead were seen in fairyland or among the fairy hoards, careering about with the UNSEELIE COURT of Scotland or feasting with GOBLINS in churchyards at HALLOWEEN. One young man was imprudent enough to go out on All Hallows Eve and encountered King FINVARRA and his Queen OONAGH. Their company was full of merriment and passed around much food and wine, but 'for all that they were the company of the dead'. He recognised a neighbour who had died many years before.

A Cornishman called Noy met his dead sweetheart among the fairy hoards.[49] One day he set out for an inn but when three days had passed and he hadn't returned home his servants went to look for him. He was discovered in a ruined barn and was amazed to discover that he had been missing for three days. He had got lost on the moor trying to take a short cut, but had discovered a farmhouse where they were holding a Harvest Home supper. Inside hundreds of richly dressed people were feasting, but they all looked rather small. He was staggered to recognise his former sweetheart, Grace Hutchens, dead four years. He knew then that the company inside the house were fairies. Grace warned him not to touch her, eat the FAIRY FOOD, or drink the cider, or he would be unable to leave. Mr Noy believed he knew a way to rescue them and took his hedging GLOVES from his pocket, turned them inside out and threw them among the fairies, who vanished, taking Grace with them.

Grant Allen proposed that fairies were folk memories of the NEOLITHIC dead, as fairies are associated with Neolithic burial mounds throughout Europe.[50] Some experts like Spence regarded a belief in fairies as stemming from the Neolithic Cult of the Dead.[51] The dead were buried, often in the foetal position, sometimes in elaborate cairns and mounds, to await a rebirth.

Entrances to FAIRYLAND are often said to be through burial MOUNDS and most British, Irish and Continental fairies are said to live in the hollow hills or beneath water in an underground country where the summer never ends. This is comparable with many ancient ideas of the afterlife. The Greeks believed that the souls of the good dwelt in Elysium, which means 'apple-land' or 'APPLE orchards'. It was a happy realm of perpetual day and the inhabitants could choose to be reborn on earth wherever they elected. The Celts believed that the afterlife was lived in a permanent summer, a land of the ever young: an apple orchard where the trees were always in fruit, such as AVALON ('Apple Land'). In fairyland the passage of time bears no relation to time in the real world as might be expected in a realm inhabited by souls after death.

People who are taken to fairyland are warned not eat the food there, or they will never be able to return to the human realms. This echoes ancient Egyptian mythology where the goddess Amenti was associated with the Land of the West, or underworld. She welcomed all deceased people to the Land of the Dead with bread and water. If they ate and drank, they could not return to the land of the living. In Celtic myth RED food was the food of the dead and was forbidden to mankind. The Moari fairies the PATU-PAIAREHE eat red fruits which are taboo to humans. The Greek goddess Persephone was bound to remain in the underworld after eating six seeds from a red pomegranate.

DECAIR is a fairy who appeared to the Fianna warrior band of ancient Ireland, leading a magical fairy HORSE. Thirteen warriors mounted the horse, whereupon it fled back under the sea to the OTHERWORLD taking the men with it.

DED MAROZ ('Grandfather Frost') is a Slavonic fairy with a long white beard, a RED coat and black boots. With his helper, the Snow Girl, he delivers ginger biscuits and presents on New Year's Day. He is the Russian FATHER CHRISTMAS. In Siberia he is called Father Ice.

DEDUSKA VODIANOI also given as **DYEDUSKA VODYANOY** or **Deduska Vodyanoy** ('Water Grandfather') is a Russian WATER FAIRY who drowns those who swim at midday or midnight. He lives in rivers, pools and lakes, especially those near water mills, though he likes to destroy mill wheels. He sometimes lures girls into his realms in order to marry them, and when they are about to give birth he

will fetch a human MIDWIFE to attend them. The midwife will be rewarded for her services with gold or silver. His daughters are the RUSALKI. Sometimes he will help fishermen by guiding fish into their nets.

He is a SHAPESHIFTER and often appears as bald and fat, with a long green beard, wearing green clothes and a hat made from REEDS, though he can appear as a handsome young man, and sometimes takes the form of a trout or salmon during the day. He hibernates during the winter and emerges in the spring to melt the ice. *See also* VODIANOI.

DED or **Dedek** is a Western Slavonic HOUSE FAIRY.

DEDUSKA ('Grandfather') or **Deduska Domovoy** ('Grandfather House Spirit') is a Russian HOUSE FAIRY who appears as an old man covered in hair, often in the likeness of a family patriarch. He wears a RED shirt, cloak and a red belt. Alternatively, he may manifest as a cow, a CAT, a DOG or a bear. In this case, the colour of the animal's pelt will match the hair of a family ancestor. However, most of the time the Deduska Domovoy is INVISIBLE.

He lives behind the oven or near the THRESHOLD of the house, in the cupboard, or in the stable, sometimes with his wife and children. He will protect the family, their home and their livestock from bad luck, keep the servants in order and do all kinds of chores about the place while everyone is sleeping. He is especially keen on SPINNING. To keep him happy he should be given something from each meal and white linen should be placed in his favourite room. The family that pleases its fairy will prosper in all things, but the family that fails to do him honour or uses bad language in

his presence will suffer his anger. He will revenge himself on the crops and cattle or leave the house altogether. The unprotected family will then fall ill and die.

In order to entice an alienated fairy home, the inhabitants must dress in their best clothes and go out in the evening and walk about their courtyard saying: 'Deduska Domovoy come and live with us and tend our flocks'. A cock is killed at midnight and its blood used to wash all the corners of the common room and courtyard.[52] Salted bread is wrapped in white cloth and put in the hall or courtyard while the family bows to the four quarters, praising the fairy and asking him to forgive them and return.

Each property has its own fairy and these fight with those of other households. The victors will settle in the homes of the defeated and cause trouble by throwing crockery about, making strange noises, injuring livestock and choking sleepers. To get rid of such a nuisance the human inhabitants will have to beat the hedges and walls of the house with rods, telling him to go home.

Without a Deduska Domovoy a house is unprotected so when a new home is built certain rituals must be performed to gain one. The first creature to cross the THRESHOLD is in some danger so a cat or cock is thrown inside. The head of a hen is buried in one corner of the main room, while some of the first bread broken in the house is buried in the right hand corner of the attic with an invocation to a fairy to come and protect the place and obey a new master. Since the Deduska Domovoy is sometimes thought to be an incarnation of an ancestral spirit, it is believed that there will be no happiness and prosperity in the house until the head of the family dies and becomes its protector.

When a family moves house, they will make every effort to take their house fairy with them. At the old house an old woman will clean the cinders from the HEARTH into a pan which she covers with a cloth. She then opens all the windows and invites the fairy to leave this house and go to the new one. She takes the cinders to the new house where the master and mistress wait with bread and salt at the gate. They bow low, take the pan into the house, and empty the cinders into the new grate. The pan is broken and buried in a corner of the room.

DEER and especially red deer (*Cervus elaphus*) are associated with fairies. Fairy women often assume the form of red deer. On the Isle of Mull deer are said to be the only cattle of fairies. During the winter they are protected by the CAILLEACH or HAG and her women, who herd and milk them. Tradition has it that no deer is ever found dead with age, and the shed horns are never found because the fairies hide them. Fairies

dislike deer hunters and throw ELF-BOLTS at them. When a slain deer is carried home at night the fairies press down on the bearer's back until he feels as though he is carrying a house. Should he stick an IRON or steel knife in the carcass it will frighten off the fairies and the body will become light again.

DEEVS are evil Persian fairies with their origins in the Zoroastrian religion. They are ruled by Arzshenk who lives in a palace in the mountains of Kâf, which surround the earth. These mountains are two thousand miles high and made of green chrysolite. One particularly malignant deev called Siltim haunted the forests, appearing in human form and doing injury to man. The deevs are constantly at war with the Peries (see PERI) who are good fairies, and when they capture one they hang it from the top of a tree in an IRON cage to torture it.

DEFORMITY/DEFORMITIES often betray a fairy origin. Though fairies appear in human form and can exert a GLAMOUR to make themselves seem as beautiful as they wish, there are always oddities. These include squint eyes, pointed ears, COW's tails, webbed FEET, feet back to front, or GOAT's hoofs. At one time, some DWARFS were regular visitors to a German village. They were delightful creatures, only a span high, but no one could ever see feet on them - they were always concealed. One day, ashes were spread out on the path and this revealed that their footprints were like those of goose feet. When the dwarfs discovered the trick they never visited again.[53]

Some fairy women have a frightful front tooth, or very long breasts. On the Isle of Mull, fairies only have one nostril. The Irish BANSHEE gives herself away by devouring a whole cow at a single meal.

Many believed that humans with disabilities or deformities were CHANGELINGS, or 'elvish-marked', stamped by the fairies as one of their own. The eighteenth-century critic

George Steevens wrote that the common people of Scotland 'have still an aversion to those who have any natural defect or redundancy, as thinking them marked out for mischief'.[54]

DELAK is a Latvian spirit who nurses new-born children.

DEMOGORGON is a mysterious being that lives in the Himalayas. Every fifth year the Italian fairies have to appear before him. In one story, King ARTHUR passed through the CAVE of the Demogorgon on his way to MORGAN LE FAY's palace.

His origins are obscure. He is certainly mentioned by medieval commentators on the classics and Conrad de Mare's *Repetorium* of 1273 called him the earliest deity of mythology. He is said to have resolved chaos into order.

DEMON is a term applied to any evil spirit or devil. Some particularly malicious fairies are described as demons, and according to Christian folklore, all fairies are demonic in origin (see DEVIL). The term is derived from the Greek DÆMON, which actually means the personification of a human personality or soul.

DEPARTURE OF THE FAIRIES. As farms, villages and towns appeared, the fairies retreated further and further into the wilder places, perhaps eventually disappearing altogether, going into the west with the setting sun. The last Fairy Rade was witnessed at the beginning of the nineteenth century by a herdboy and his sister at a hamlet near Glen

Eathie. A procession of dwarfish strangers rode by and the boy asked them who they were and where they were going. The leader replied 'Not of the race of Adam. The people of peace shall never more be seen in Scotland.'[55]

DERRICK is a Devonshire alternative term for a small, ill-natured PIXY, though they are also known in Hampshire where they are better tempered. There they dress in green and help lost travellers.

DEVANA is the name of a Western Slavonic forest fairy, a maiden huntress who roams the woodland with her bow and her dogs. The name is derived from DIANA, the Roman MOON goddess, whose name is found as a component of many fairy designations.

DEVAS is a term used by occultists to refer to nature spirits. The Theosophical Society, an occult group founded in the nineteenth century, believe that nature fairies or devas live in a hidden spiritual realm that co-exists with our own. Devas' bodies consist of the very finest of physical matter but they can manifest on the etheric level as animals, plants and people, reflecting the preconceptions of the observer. The energy flowing through them is often interpreted as hair and wings, though their normal state is a pulsating sphere of light with a bright nucleus. Their function is to give the material world its pattern and coherence; they hold the blueprint for material form.[56] Modern occultists refer to devas as 'The Middle Kingdom' or 'The Lordly Ones'. The term came into popular consciousness with the advent of the Findhorn Foundation in Scotland. Here Eileen and Peter Caddy set up a vegetable patch on very poor ground, growing huge vegetables and flowers aided by various nature spirits, fairies, elves and gnomes. Their associate Dorothy Maclean said that she was in touch with spirits called devas. She explained that these

materialised form, and supplied energy and guidelines to the GNOMES and fairies.[57] *See also* DEWAS.

DEVIL ('Little God') usually refers to the prime evil spirit of the Christian religion, though it may be applied to any evil spirit. In orthodox Christian doctrine, any spirit that is neither saint nor angel is demonic in origin, and fairies are included under this heading. According to Celtic folklore, those angels that were cast out of heaven for their pride became such fairies. Some fell to earth and dwelled there long before man, others fell into the sea and became water fairies. Others fell into hell where the devil

DIANA

commands them. They dwell under the earth and tempt humans into evil, teaching WITCHES how to make potions, spells, and enchantments.[58]

The term 'devil' actually means 'little god'. It is often the practice of a new religion to demonize the gods of the old, rival religion. Early Christians denounced the gods and spirits of the old Pagan religions as baneful and identified the old Pagan gods as devils. NYMPHS, DRYADS, SATYRS, and vegetation spirits dwindled into fairies and were condemned by the church as devils. King James I's *Daemonologie* equated fairies with devils in no uncertain terms and advised people who had them in their homes to get rid of them immediately. Writing in 1701, the Orkney vicar

Rev. John Brand said that fairies were evil spirits seen dancing and feasting in wild places. English Puritan writers of the sixteenth and seventeenth centuries lumped IMPS, devils and fairies together; they believed all fairies were devils.[59] Milton's *Paradise Lost* featured the old Pagan gods among the devils of hell.

DEVIL'S BIT SCABIOUS *Succisa pratensis* is a wild flower sacred to the fairies.

DEVIL'S DANDY DOGS are a Cornish pack of fire breathing BLACK DOGS, led by the DEVIL. They haunt the moors at night and will tear to pieces any man they find. Prayer may deter them. *See also* DANDO AND HIS DOGS.

DEWAS, **Devas** or **Diwas** are the spirits of trees and plants. In the early days of Buddhism there was some controversy as to whether trees had souls and it was decided they did not, but had certain resident spirits called dewas who spoke from within them. Among the Hindus dewas were gods, while the Persians viewed them as followers of the Evil One, Ahriman. *See also* DRYADS, DEVAS and TREE FAIRIES.

DI SMA ('The Little Ones') or **Di Smar Undar Jordi** ('The Little Ones Under the Earth') are small fairies from Gotland who wear grey or blue clothes and caps upon their heads. They dance on the grass creating FAIRY RINGS. If you want to be cured of an illness, lay a silver coin in the centre of the ring. Offerings of MILK, beer and flax seeds are also poured into the circle.

DIALEN is a type of WILDEN FRAULEIN (wild woman) from the Austrian/Swiss border. They have GOATS' feet.

DIANA is the Queen of the Fairies in Italian folklore. She is directly

related to the Roman maiden goddess of the MOON and hunt, armed with crescent moon bow and ARROWS, and the Graeco-Thracian ARTEMIS, a personification of virgin Nature. Roaming through the moonlit wilds, followed by her dancing nymph disciples, some say it is possible that the goddess Diana is the origin of the whole idea of a fairy queen and her attendants.

Late Roman sources and the inquisitors of the Middle Ages described her as the leader of the WITCHES.

DIIWICA

Leland argued that the ordinary people - especially the outcasts and the oppressed - clung on to the worship of Diana well into the Christian era, and that this developed into the doctrines of the Italian witches.[60] Diana was described as the protectress of the 'minions of the moon': thieves, harlots, witches and the ungodly.

One story that Leland recorded describes how the fairies, called the children of Diana, are born: Diana made all things, the stars in the firmament, and men and women, as well as GIANTS and DWARFS. One night a poor young man sat in a lonely place and was amazed to see thousands of shining white fairies, dancing in the moonlight. He exclaimed that he would love to be like them, free from care and the need for food. What on earth were they? They replied that they were moonbeams:

'We are children of the Moon,
We are born of shining light;
When the Moon shoots forth a ray,
Then it takes a fairy's form.'

The fairies told him that he was already one of them, since he was born when the moon, their mother Diana, was full. As such, he was favoured - if he should turn over the silver in his pocket once a month it would be doubled.

DID, Didko or **Diduch** is a Little Russian HOUSE FAIRY similar to, or identical with, a DOMOVIYR.

DIIWICA is a Lusitanian forest fairy and huntress, armed with a bow. Her name is derived from DIANA, the Roman goddess of hunt and moon.

DIMONIS-BOYETS are little Mallorcan fairies who are practical jokers, but friendly towards those humans they respect. A group of them once asked a miller's wife for some grain. She thought they had probably already stolen a good half bushel already, and replied: 'When you can wash this wool white, I will give you a sackful'. When the dimonis-boyets saw the wool they started crying; it was black and they knew they would never get it snowy white. The fairies left the island, but may return one day with a well-washed ball of wool to demand their reward.

DINNSHENCHAS are Irish fairies who protect cattle and serve the fairy AINE. They can SHAPESHIFT into any form. They avenge women harmed or raped by men.

DINNY MARA ('Sea Man') is a Manx MERMAN or sea fairy.

DIONES or **Dyonas** is the father of VIVIENNE, Lady of the Lake in Arthurian legend. His godmother was the MOON goddess DIANA.

DIREACH is a Scottish fairy of Glen Etive who has one hand sticking out of his chest, one leg sticking out of his haunch and one eye in the middle of his forehead. Direach may be an alternative term for the FACHAN.

DIREACH GHLINN EITIDH MHIC KALAIN ('Giant of the Moorland in Glen Eiti') is a one legged, one armed, one eyed fairy who was a woodcutter. Compare with FACHAN.

DIRNE-WEIBL ('Little Serving Maid') is a Bavarian fairy who appears dressed in RED carrying a basket of APPLES. She kindly gives these apples away to those she meets and after a short time, they turn into money. A Dirne-weibl is a sensitive fairy and often asks people to accompany her on her walks. If they refuse, she runs off into the wood, crying. In Germany, they are WOOD-WIVES who usually appear clad in white (as WHITE LADIES).

DÍSIR ('Goddesses') are supernatural females in Scandinavian myth who dispense fate in a similar fashion to FAIRY GODMOTHERS. They are associated with fertility and an autumn sacrifice was celebrated in their honour. They are also connected with the DEAD, and were sometimes referred to simply as 'dead women'. They appear in folklore as female ancestral spirits or HOUSE FAIRIES.

DIVE are female forest spirits or WILD WOMEN from the Italian Tyrol.

DIVA-TA ZENA is a Southern Slavonic WILD WOMAN who lives in the forests. She is covered with thick hair and is strong and feral. She throws her long breasts over her shoulders to nurse the children she carries on her back.

DIVJE DEVOJKE or **Dekle** are Slovenian forest fairies or WILD MEN. They live in the woods, but at harvest time come into the fields to help with the reaping. They will bind the corn into sheaves in return for food, which the farmers' wives leave out for them. They are generally kindly disposed towards humans, but will sometimes play tricks on solitary travellers. Since people have taken to using whips and goads they have largely disappeared and are now rarely seen.

DIVJI MOZ ('Wild Man') is a fierce Slovenian WILD MAN who lives in a deep forest CAVE and is very strong. Unless he is placated by offerings of food, he will cause serious harm, but to those who feed him he will act in a kindly manner and offer helpful advice.

DIVOUS ('Wild Brats') are CHANGELING babies substituted by the Bohemian wild women the DIVOZENKY.

DIVOZENKY ('Wild Women') are Bohemian WILD WOMEN. They are handsome creatures with large, square heads, thick, long black or RED HAIR, long fingers and hairy bodies. They live in underground burrows. They take grain from the fields and grind it to make their own bread. They also catch game and fish and eat roots such as liquorice. They make their clothes from SPINNING hemp. They know all the secrets of Nature and the properties of all the plants. They prepare various remedies and potions as well as salves to make themselves light and invisible. Divozenky are at their most powerful at MIDSUMMER.

They like to sing and DANCE, and storms are caused by their wild capering. Sometimes they will invite human men and women to join them in their merrymaking and these people will be well rewarded. They are generally on good terms with human beings and will sometimes visit villages in order to borrow utensils. If people treat them well, the wild women will repay them by cleaning their houses and looking after their children, or by harvesting the corn and tying-in sheaves. They may marry human men, in which case they make good wives and mothers, though they will vanish should anyone call them 'wild women' or affront them with a dirty grate or an unwashed kneading trough.

If anyone comes across a wild woman alone in the forest this can turn into a tricky situation. The fairy might spin him around until he become disorientated and loses his way. Wild women also waylay new mothers and substitute ugly, screeching CHANGELINGS called Divous ('Wild Brats') or Premien ('Changelings') for the human baby.

Wild Women hate the greedy and avaricious and will damage their corn, livestock and children.

DJABÉLK is a mischievous Polish fairy or IMP, fond of practical jokes. The term is now also used for a DEVIL.

DJADEK is a Silesian HOUSE FAIRY, the guardian of a home and family. Small statues were made of these creatures and placed in special niches near the doors in ancient times, and later on the mantelpiece above the oven. They are depicted as old men dressed in the local costume.

DJIN is the ELEMENTAL king of fire, in occult doctrine.

DJINN, Jin, Ginn, Jinn, Genie or **Jan** ('Spirit') (*m.* **Jinnee**, *f.* **jinniyeh**) are Arabian fairies mentioned in the Koran. A tradition from the Prophet says that the djinn were formed of 'smokeless fire', i.e. the fire of the wind Simoom, while others say they are the offspring of fire with fire in their veins instead of blood,

or alternatively they are composed of air. They were created 2000 years before Adam was made from earth, but will be annihilated at the Final Judgment. They were governed by a succession of forty (or seventy-two) monarchs named Suleyman, the last of whom, called Jan-ibn-Jan, built the Pyramids of Egypt. Prophets were sent from time to time to instruct and admonish them, but on their continued disobedience, an army of angels appeared, driving them from the earth to the regions of the islands, making many prisoners, and slaughtering many more. Among the prisoners was a young Jinnee named Azâzel (Azazeel, or El-Harith, afterwards called Iblees or Iblis from his despair), who grew up among the ANGELS, and became their chief. When Adam was created, God commanded the angels to worship him and they all obeyed except Iblees, who, for his disobedience, was tuned into a Sheytan or DEVIL, and he became the father of the Sheytans.

There are five varieties of djinn from the very powerful Marid, to the Afreet, the Sheytans (or Shaitan), and the Jinn to the least powerful order, the Jann (or Jan). When the Arabs poured water on the ground, let down a bucket into a well, or enter a bath, they would ask the permission of the djinn 'Permission' (*Destoor*) or, 'Permission, ye blessed!'.

Good djinn are very beautiful and the bad ones very ugly, though they are SHAPESHIFTERS and can appear as humans, monsters, CATS, ostriches, DOGS and SNAKES. The evil djinn cause sandstorms and waterspouts. When the *Zôba'ah*, a whirlwind that raises the sand in the form of a pillar of tremendous height, is seen sweeping over the desert, the Arabs, who believe it to be caused by the flight of an evil Jinnee, cry: 'Iron! Iron!'. All djinn hate IRON and can be bound with magic words and talismans to reveal the future. They can fly up to the heavens and listen to the words of angels. They have great powers of MAGIC. They are long lived, but can be destroyed by men, other djinn and shooting stars flung at them from heaven.

The djinn mate and have families like human beings. Their country is Jinnistan and its capital the City of Jewels, though they may take up abodes in wells, rivers, ruins, ovens and market places. While a human man may marry a female jinniyeh, a human female may not marry a male jinnee. The offspring of a human-djinn union has the attributes of both.

DJUDE is a small Southern Slavonic EARTH FAIRY.

DOAMNA ZÎNELOR ('Fairy Lady') is a lovely but cruel Romanian Fairy Queen who has some characteristics of an UNDERWORLD spirit or goddess, and is associated with spirits of the DEAD. She is called 'great lady', 'the queen of the mountains', 'lady of the shore' or 'the most beautiful woman'. She leads groups of SEVEN or NINE fairies that ride white horses and hunt deer with bows and ARROWS. She is possibly connected with DIANA.

DOAMNELE ('The Young Ladies') are Balkan fairies, referred to by this flattering term so as not to offend them, lest they retaliate by causing illness or loss.

DOBIE or Dobby is an English HOUSE FAIRY known mostly in the north, who, like others of his kind, is fond of helping humans. He joins workmen in their tasks. Unfortunately, he is so stupid that he is more of a hindrance than help. He is sometimes invoked to guard TREASURE, but anyone who can get one prefers an intelligent BROWNIE.

Conversely, in West Yorkshire, the Dobie is an evil fairy who garrotes unsuspecting horsemen. Dobies live in old barns or farmhouses, near old towers and bridges. The Dobie of Morthan Tower, Rokeby, is said to be the GHOST of the murdered wife of the Lord of Rokeby.

DÖCKÁLFAR are 'Dark Elves' (possibly identical to DWARFS), who live below ground and are generally evil.

DOGS hate fairies and chase them, but when they return all the hair is scraped off their bodies and they die soon after. However, fairies keep special hounds themselves. These *cu sith* ('fairy dogs') act as guides to the fairy realms and lead people into the UNDERWORLD. They are usually green or white with RED ears, though in Wales pure WHITE dogs are considered to be fairy dogs. In Eastern Europe fairy dogs have white rings around their necks and carry fairies around at night on their backs. The Irish hero Finn Mac Cumhal's dog Bran was of the fairy breed and was described as having yellow feet, black sides, a white belly, a green back, and red ears. Bran's venomous bite killed whatever it struck. The fairy dog makes its lair in the clefts of rocks and travels in a straight line. It barks only THREE times and by the time the third bark is heard the victim is overtaken, unless he has reached a place of safety.

Dogs are associated with death and the underworld. Even ordinary dogs are thought to be able to see GHOSTS and to be able to foretell disaster and the death of their owners - a dog howling at night is an OMEN OF DEATH. There are many tales of ghostly and phantom hounds, usually BLACK DOGS that haunt lonely places. Ghostly dogs haunt the northern and eastern coasts of Britain. This may be a folk memory of the Viking invaders who brought with them the stories of the Hounds of Odin. The mud flats of East Anglia are haunted by a phantom dog known as BLACK SHUCK or Old Shuck, a name derived from the Saxon word for the Devil, *succa*. He is variously described as having a single eye set in the centre of his head, or having glowing red eyes, or even as being headless, yet having glowing eyes suspended in front of him. A black dog is often associated with magic and witchcraft, demonic powers and death, and often appears as a warning of death.

Many legends of Britain and Europe tell of the WILD HUNT, a pack of ghostly dogs who fly through the night sky to pursue their quarry. The hunt was known to the Saxons as *Einherier* or *Herlathing*, the hunt is also called WISHT HOUNDS or DARTMOOR HOUNDS. The leadership of the hunt has been ascribed to HERNE THE HUNTER, King ARTHUR, the DEVIL, Charlemagne, GWYN AP NUDD, Odin and Woden. The prey is variously a white stag, a white boar, white-breasted maidens, or the souls of the damned. Some say the hounds are the souls of UNBAPTISED CHILDREN. One Cornish tale concerned a small black dog accidentally left behind by the hunt, which had to be looked after well and fed for a year before being claimed by the hunt or bad luck would follow. Perhaps one of the reasons dogs are associated with death and the underworld is because they are used to hunt down and kill prey.

Dogs have a long history as companions to humankind. There is evidence that in Palaeolithic times they shared humankind's homes and work, guarding houses, flocks and possessions. They have become the symbol of watchfulness and loyalty. As well as being mundane guardians, dogs were also guardian of the THRESHOLD, of Underworld TREASURE and the boundaries between the worlds. In Neolithic and Bronze Age burial sites ritually killed dogs have been found, buried to serve as spirit guardians.[61] Dogs feature in ritual sacrifice and early burial rituals; as recently as medieval times they were buried in doorways or the walls of buildings to protect the house.

Dog gall was made into a perfume and anointed onto walls to prevent evil spirits and witchcraft from entering a house. It was once a superstition that the first person to be buried in a churchyard would have to guard any subsequent buried souls, so it was the custom to sacrifice a dog to serve as a substitute - specifically a completely black one without a single white hair - and bury it in the foundation of the church. This is perhaps the origin of the English CHURCH GRIM and the Scandinavian KIRKOGRIM where a similar practice was current.

A dog spirit often seen conveyed the soul to the OTHERWORLD and hounds accompanied messenger gods and psychopomps such as Hermes and Mercury. In Greek myth Cerberus the THREE-headed dog guarded the entrance to the Underworld. The dog also was connected to the chthonic goddess Hecate. The Greek god of healing Asculapius is usually pictured with a dog companion. He bears in his hand a staff with two twining SNAKES symbolising resurrection from the UNDERWORLD. The jackal headed Egyptian god Anubis is usually pictured as accompanying Thoth, god of secret knowledge, and a dog accompanies the Phoenician hero Malkarth. It is a symbol of the Underworld, its guardian; it guards the secret knowledge of death and resurrection. The Welsh god of the Underworld had a pack of dogs with white bodies and red ears called the CWN ANNWN, or hellhounds. In Norse myth the dog Garm guarded the road to the Underworld. In some legends of the Underworld the entrance is through water and in folktales ghostly dogs lead travellers into pools and drown them. The Celtic sea god MANANNAN had such a pack. According to the *Mabinogion* two greyhounds were presented to Arawn, Lord of the Underworld. It is likely that the Celts ate dog meat as part of some underworld ritual.[62]

DOG OF BOULEY or Le Tchan de Bouole is a Jersey phantom hound or BLACK DOG, which appears on the Channel Island of Jersey when storms are brewing.

DOGIR are WATER FAIRIES who dwell in the River Nile, according to the northern Sudanese. They sometimes emerge to capture human women.

DOLA is a Polish spirit that embodies the fate of a human. It has its own ideas and preferences, and should a person go against their Dola's predilections then all will go awry. The fairy may appear as a person, a CAT or a mouse.

DOLYA is a Russian fairy that personifies a person's fate. She usually appears as an old woman, though she can manifest in a variety of forms. She lives behind the oven. A good Dolya will protect the person she is attached to from birth till death, taking care of his children, sending fish to his nets, bees to his hives, money to his purse and health to his body. An evil Dolya (sometimes called a Nedolya or Licho) thinks of nothing but herself, spending her time dressing up and making merry. A man with an evil Dolya will never prosper. Everything he tries will come to nothing. Furthermore, he cannot get rid of her, try as he might to lose her in the woods or drown her in the sea.

DOMOVIYR, Domovik, Domoviye, Domovoi or **Domovoy** ('House Spirit') is a generic Little Russian term for a fairy, though it usually refers to male HOUSE FAIRIES who, with their wives the domovikha or kikimora, look after a house and its residents. Beliefs concerning them echo those of the Russian DEDUSKA DOMOVOY. The creature is small and hairy from head to foot, even the palms of his hands. It wears RED shirts and blue girdles and lives behind the oven (see HEARTH), beneath the THRESHOLD, or in the stables or byre. When a family moves into a new house, they should put a slice of bread under the stove to attract a domovoi, since on him depends the prosperity of the household.

Once one is in residence, it will do various chores around the house as long as food is left out for it every night. If this is stopped the fairy will smash the pots and generally cause havoc. Domoviyr especially love to eat poultry and can get very cross if they feel they are not given their fair share. It is the custom to make an offering of a goose to the VODYANY every autumn, but if the domovoi realises one of his birds has been given to another fairy, he will be very angry. If a domovoi is heard murmuring all is well, but if he is heard groaning it portends misfortune. If he is heard weeping, this is an OMEN OF DEATH, and it is certainly unlucky to see one under any circumstances.

On 30th March they shed their skins and grow lighter ones for summer, and should not be approached during this difficult time. You should put some food out for them, but keep the cattle and chickens locked away. On 28th January, an offering of stewed grain must be made to the spirit, and to forget is a very serious mistake. You will have to call in a wizard to sacrifice a black hen, or the master of the house might go into the courtyard, face the moon, and summon the fairy, making him a gift of a red egg. If you move house, the oldest woman should take a coal from the old house to kindle a fire in the new home. when she arrives she should strike the doorposts and ask: 'Grandfather, are visitors welcome?', while the master and mistress welcome the fairy to the new dwelling and offer him bread and salt.

DOMOWIJE is the Polish equivalent of the Russian DOMOVIYR.

DÔN is the Welsh equivalent of the Irish DANU. She is the mother of the Welsh gods, later demoted to fairy status.

DONAS DE FUERA ('The Ladies from Outside') are Sicilian fairies. During the sixteenth and seventeenth centuries, the Spanish Inquisition accused WITCHES of trafficking with these fairies.

DONN or **DONN FIERNA** is a Fairy King in Irish folklore, Lord of the Fairy MOUND Knockfierna. On this hill are several dolmens known as GIANT's graves. In Co. Fermanagh, he is known as the ancestor of the Maguire clan, whom he helps in their battles. On stormy nights, he rides out on a white HORSE and people say: 'Donn is galloping in the clouds tonight'. He will fight local rival fairies, the winner carrying off the year's best potato crop.

Donn appears as a pseudo historical character, a leader of the Celts when they came to Ireland. His cult was once widely known in Ireland. Donn was the ancient Irish LORD OF THE DEAD. His name is derived from the Celtic *dhuosno* meaning the 'dark' or 'black one'. He lives on an island off the southwest coast of Ireland, called *Tech Duinn* 'the House of Donn', which is nothing more than a rock archway under which the sea flows.. The spirits of the DEAD were envisaged as following the course of the sun as it passed under the Arch of Donn's dwelling into the sea and thence to the UNDERWORLD. The dead gather at his house, *Tech Duinn,* before setting off to the ISLES OF THE BLEST.[63]

DOOINNEY-OIE is a Manx 'Night Man' who warns of approaching storms, sometimes by shouting, sometimes blowing a horn, or sometimes appearing in person, in the form of a misty man.

DOONIE is a Scottish fairy who appears in the form of a HORSE, or that of an old man or woman. It is generally helpful, even to the point of rescuing fallen climbers.

DÖPPELGANGER is an exact double that appears before and after that person's death.[64] Some think that every person has a döppelganger in FAIRYLAND. *See also* FETCH and CO-WALKER.

DOUBLE *See* CO-WALKER, DÖPPELGANGER or FETCH.

DRACAE or **Dracs** are French WATER FAIRIES who have a fabulous city under the River Seine, though many of them have emigrated across the English Channel and can be found haunting the lowland lochs and rivers of England and Scotland. Occasionally they can be found dwelling in damp CAVES. For fun they skim along the water on wooden plates.

Dracae like to mate with human men, and sometimes shed their natural purple globular state to appear as alluring women. Alternatively, one might manifest as a golden chalice rising from the water. If a man should reach out to seize the chalice, he will be grabbed and dragged down beneath the water.

Sometimes dracs abduct new human mothers to act as wet nurses for drac children, returning the women SEVEN years later unharmed, but so changed as to be virtually unrecognisable. Gervase of Tilbury (1211) was told by a woman that she had been taken underwater to nurse a drac child. While she was there, they had smeared her eye with grease from an eel pastry. When she returned to earth she happened to see the drac and went to greet him. He was amazed that she could see him and asked which eye she could see him with. She pointed out the eye that had been smeared with the eel grease. He poked it with his finger and put it out.[65] Similar tales are told across Europe.

DRAGONS appear all over the world. They are associated with the elements, the seasons, the weather, and various natural forces. In the Balkans, dragons are associated with WEATHER FAIRIES and demons of the storm. In Celtic myth, dragons are creatures of the OTHERWORLD. For the ancient Chinese the dragon represented the energy of the earth, stretching across countries in dragon lines. Some equate these with LEY LINES, since straight lines often link places with names relating to the dragon or worm, such as Dragon Hill, or with names dedicated to dragon slaying saints, such as St. George or St. Michael. These places are associated with fairies. Like fairies, dragons often guard a TREASURE in a deep CAVE.

DRAKES, Grak, Krat or Drachen are English, German and Scandinavian fire fairies who are said to smell like rotten eggs, and their presence is usually only betrayed by the stench, though they are sometimes glimpsed as a flaming ball. They only take on the character of fire when they fly, when they look like streaks of flame or fiery balls with long tails. Otherwise they look like small boys with RED CAPS and coats.

They are HOUSE FAIRIES who move into a house and keep the firewood dry and bring gifts of gold and grain to the master of the house. The bond is between the male head of the house and the male drake, and is a serious pact, often written in blood. (Originally the spirits of the drakes were kept imprisoned in carved mandrake roots.) The drake takes care of the house, barn and stables, making sure that the pantry and money chest are well stocked. They can travel the world in a split second, and bring their masters a present back from far away places. In return, the master keeps the drake fed and treated with respect. Should the drake be insulted the house will not be there long.

If you see a drake on its travels, take shelter, for they leave behind a poisonous sulphurous fug. If you quickly shout 'half and half' or throw a knife at the creature, then the drake may drop some of its booty in your lap. If two people together see a drake, they should cross their legs in silence, take the fourth wheel off the wagon and take shelter. The drake will then be compelled to leave them some of his haul. *See also* FIRE DRAKE.

DRAUGAR ('Walking Dead') are Scandinavian spirits that inhabit ancient burial MOUNDS and guard TREASURE. They are possibly synonymous with the HAUGBUI ('mound dwellers'). Sometimes said to be the ghosts of DEAD Pagans, they may injure both people and property. They still haunt Iceland to this very day, and the only way to defeat them is to decapitate them and cremate their bodies.

DROUG-SPERET is one of the country dwelling French LUTINS.

DRUGGAN HILL BOGGLE is a baneful BLACK DOG, which terrorised the district around Druggan Hill in Cumberland, north west England. He was associated with the GHOST of a murdered peddler, but as soon as the peddler's body was found and given a proper burial, the dog disappeared.

DRUS ('Tree') is a male DRYAD in Greek myth.

DRYADS (From the Greek *drus*, meaning 'tree') are NYMPHS of ancient Greek myth, who make their home in trees, usually OAKS, but unlike the HAMADRYADS who are one with their trees, they can leave their trees and DANCE in the forest. They are the companions of Artemis, the maiden goddess of the MOON and the hunt, or sometimes of Dionysus the god of wine. It is unlucky to see them or keep company with them.

DRYOPE was a NYMPH loved by the god Apollo. She was taught to sing and dance by the HAMADRYADS.

DUENDES (From *duen de casa*, meaning 'Lord of the House') are Spanish HOUSE FAIRIES. They appear as small, middle aged women with very long fingers, dressed in GREEN, grey or RED, or as old men wearing brimless, conical hats, dark hoods or RED CAPS. They live in isolated houses, towers and CAVES, though if they live with a human family, the fairies will move house when they do. They cannot be exorcised and, unlike most fairies, have no fear at all of priests or holy water. They come out at night, cleaning, repairing, or working as SMITHs. They are sometimes so house proud that they act like poltergeists to get rid of the human beings that make the place a mess. They will pinch sleepers, breathe down their necks, touch them with icy fingers, or pull off the bedclothes. They might move the furniture, throw stones at the windows, or ride humans through the night as NIGHTMAREs. Duendes also manifest in Belize where they appear as little old men, dressed in skins and wearing large

hats. These are sometimes known as Tata ('Grandpa') Duende.

DUERGAR or **Dvergar** are DWARFS of Scandinavian mythology, though similar beings occur in Saxon legend. They are also known as unpleasant fairies in Northern England who like to trick people in particularly nasty ways. For example, one lost traveller found a rough hut with a dying fire in it. Each side of the fire was a stone and a log. He sat down on one stone and made up the fire. After a short time a duergar entered and sat down without saying a word. When the fire burned down he broke a huge log in half and put it on the fire. When it burned down once more, he indicated that the traveller should do the same. The traveller suspected a trick and did nothing. When the sun came up the hut, fire and duergar disappeared and the traveller found that he was actually sitting on a crag with a sheer drop in front of it. If he had moved he would have fallen to his death.

The term duergar may be derived from the Icelandic *draugar*, which means 'GHOST' or 'walking DEAD'. The draugars are also called *haugbui* or 'MOUND dwellers', a common designation of fairies.

DUKHTARI SHAH PERIAN ('Daughter of the King of the Fairies') is the daughter of the King of the PERI. For a sight of her beauty men pine away, but should they behold her they will die.

DULCILE ('The Sweet Ones') are Romanian fairies referred to in flattering terms as 'sweet ones' so as not to upset them in case they damage the crops, or cause illness in cattle or children.

DULLOHAN or **Dallahan** are headless Irish fairy phantoms who drive the black coaches, which occasionally accompany BANSHEES. Sometimes they ride around on headless horses and wherever they stop someone will die. One dullahan used to stand on a Sligo street on dark nights in the form of a BLACK DOG and another, a headless

woman with a naked torso, used to mount the railings of St. James's Park at midnight. The ships on the Sligo quays were haunted by a dullahan who announced his presence with a sound like 'the flinging of all the tin porringers in the world' down into the hold.[66]

DUME is the ruler of the Mali fairies the WOKULO.

DUN is a rocky MOUND where fairies live in Scotland. *Dun* is also Anglo-Saxon for hill, as in *dunaelfen* or hill elves.

DUN COWS are quite a common phenomena and there are several Dun Cows in Scottish and English fairy folklore, such as the Dun Cow of McBrandy's Thicket, and the Dun Cow of Kirkham. They are fairy COWS who are either mischievous, or which give copious amounts of MILK. A DUN is a fairy hill.

DUNAELFEN is an Anglo-Saxon term for hill elves.

DUNNIE is a Northumberland BOGIE from north eastern England that takes the form of a HORSE that mischievously spills its riders in the mud.

DUNTERS are fairies of the England/Scotland border that haunt the old peel towers of the district. They make a noise like the beating of FLAX, or content themselves with moaning and whining all night. The sound is an OMEN OF DEATH. Some say they are the souls of the victims of the Picts, or possibly the GHOSTS of the ancient sacrificial victims whose blood was sprinkled on the foundation stones.[67]

DUSII are ancient Gallic spirits mentioned by St Augustine. They seem to have been wood spirits or HOUSE FAIRIES.

DUSKY ELVES is a third category added to those of LIGHT ELVES and DARK ELVES by Nancy Arrowsmith (*A Field Guide to the Little People*, 1977 p.13).

These she defines as the most numerous kind, tied to their environment, and most often seen by humans.

DVERG is a Swedish DWARF. According to Jacob Grimm, the word also means a spider, which like fairies, is famous for its SPINNING.

DVOROROI or **Dvorovoi** (*dvor*, meaning 'yard') is a Russian fairy guardian of yards. He often looks like the male head of the household and unless all is to his liking - including the colour of the farm animals - then he can turn very nasty. If this happens you will have to place a slice of bread, a piece of wool and some shiny gewgaw or other in the stables and say: "Master Dvorovoi, I offer you this gift so that you might look after the cattle". If this doesn't work, the head of the household will have to obtain the shroud of a corpse, weave it into a whip with THREE tails, dip it in wax and whip all the corners of the byre with it. The fairy should then behave.

DWARF (*pl.* **Dwarfs** or **Dwarves**) comes from the Old Norse word *dvergr*, in Old English *dweorg*, and in German *zwerg*. Some trace the origin of the word to the Sanskrit *dhvaras* meaning a ghost or phantom, or used as an adjective to signify 'deceitful'.

According to the Icelandic Eddas, when the gods created the world from the dismembered parts of the giant YMIR'S body, maggots fell from his decaying flesh and became the light elves and black elves, or SVARTALFAR, identified with the dwarfs.[68] The gods gave the dwarfs intelligence and great strength. Four strong dwarfs were set to hold up the Four Corners of the sky, while the rest went to live in the underground CAVES, out of the light. Early sources do not mention that dwarfs were short in stature, but emphasise that they were superb craftsmen and very wise. They possessed stones that gave them great strength, and others that made them invisible. The same sources also indicate that dwarfs were originally associated with the DEAD. They mine precious stones and metals, guard the earth and its riches, and are spirits of rocks and caverns, kin to the subterranean KNOCKERS and MINE FAIRIES that miners must appease.

The gods often needed the help of the wise dwarfs. In one Norse tale the trickster god Loki cut off the goddess Sif's lovely hair for a joke, but her husband Thor was so angry that Loki was forced to visit the clever dwarfs to find something to make amends. He met Ivaldi's two sons, gifted SMITHS. They worked fine gold threads that would take root and grow as hair would. In addition, they gave him an iron warship called Skidbladnir, which would fold up fine enough to fit in a pocket, and the spear Gungnir which nothing could turn from its mark.

The dwarfs were also called upon to help the gods in the matter of Fenris, the wolf son of Loki. This ferocious beast grew apace until the gods were afraid he would over run the world. They decided he must be bound, but no chain could hold him. Eventually they consulted the dwarfs, who fashioned a slender thread made with the footfall of a cat, the beards of women, the breath of a fish and other rare and impossible things. The gods tempted Fenris to try the strength of the rope, saying that since he had broken all the strong chains he had

been bound with, such a slender thread should prevent no challenge to him. However, Fenris suspected a trick and agreed to try the thread, but only if Tyr, the god of war, would put his hand in his mouth while he did so. The brave god agreed and the wolf was bound, but Tyr lost his hand.

In popular folklore, dwarfs live within the Scandinavian and German mountains. They move easily through the earth and are masters of all its minerals. They have short, squat bodies, grey skin and an aged look; they reach maturity at three and are grey at seven. Dwarfs don't like to show their FEET as they look like those of a goose or CROW, or point backwards. It is rumoured that there are no female dwarfs, but new dwarfs have to be fashioned from stone. Dwarfs cannot appear above the ground in daylight, since one ray of sun would turn them to stone. Some say they spend the day as TOADS. They occasionally steal human NEWBORN BABIES and leave their own children as CHANGELINGS. They can be quite helpful to humans, lending them china and utensils for weddings and baptisms. Though people used to have friendly relations with the dwarfs, most have migrated away from the mountains and are seen no more.

According to the people of Rügen in Germany, there are three kinds of dwarfs: White Dwarfs dress in WHITE, live beneath the hills in winter and frisk about the valleys on summer nights. By day, they can only come out in the form of a bird or butterfly. Brown Dwarfs dress in brown, are very small and wear caps that make them invisible to anyone not wearing a similar cap. They are shapeshifters. Black Dwarfs dress in black, are ugly and evil, but good at smith craft.

DWEORG is an Old English DWARF, or malignant DEMON, believed to be at the root of many evils. Anglo-Saxon leech-craft recommended the use of *dweorge dwostle*, or pennyroyal, to get rid of headaches caused by dwarfs.

DWERG is a Dutch DWARF, or in

Northern dialects, also a type of fairy. An underground echo is called *dwergmal* and is believed to be the fairies talking.

DWERGER are Gotho-German DWARFS who dwell underground or in CAVES.

DYBBUK (*pl.* Dybbukkim) is an unpleasant Hebrew spirit that has no material form of its own but must possess the bodies of human beings to perform acts of evil. Dybbukkim live in the shadowy abyss and feed off the energy of conflict.

DYONAS is the father of VIVIENNE, Lady of the Lake.

DZIANA is a Romanian forest fairy, patroness of hunting. Her name is composed from *zina* meaning 'fairy' and DIANA, the chaste Roman goddess of moon, wilderness and hunt.

DZIWITZA or Dziewona (*pl.* Dziwozony) is a Polish WILD WOMAN fond of hunting both day and night. She is tall, thin and pale. Her hair is long and tangled, while her breasts are so large and flabby that she has to throw them over her shoulders to prevent them getting in the way while she runs. Dziwozony roam the forests in groups accompanied by packs of DOGS and carry zylbas or javelins. They often appear to people who are in the forest at midday to frighten them, so it became a joke to say to people who were in the forest at noon: 'Aren't you afraid that the Dziwitza will come to you?' They are cruel and ruthless. Should they find a human in the forest they might tickle him to death. They sometimes force young men to become their lovers.[69]

DZIWJE ZONY ('Wild Women') appear at noon or dusk according to the Lusatian Serbs. They spend their time SPINNING hemp. If a human girl should spin or comb it for them, they will give her leaves that turn into gold.

EACHRAIS URLAIR ('Mischief of the Floor') is a female Scottish fairy who lives in palaces and provokes people, especially children, to mischief. She possesses a MAGIC wand, with which she turns people into animals.

EACH-UISGE ('Water Horse') is a race of Scottish fairy WATER HORSES that live in lochs and the sea. They sometimes trick people into riding them, carry them off into the water, and devour them, except for the livers. They may appear as human men in order to court women, but can be recognised by the fact they have water weed in their hair.

EAGER is a fairy of the River Trent in East Midlands of England. Bargees used to say that when the river was flooding, 'Eager was coming'. The name may be derived from the Gaelic for horse *each,* or possibly from Aegir, the Norse sea god.[70] The fairy may be a type of WATER HORSE.

EARTH FAIRY is a term applied to fairies who dwell under the earth in MOUNDS or CAVES, as opposed to those who dwell beneath lakes or wells, since most fairies are to be found below the surface of the earth. The term may also refer to nature fairies like DEVAS, VEGETATION SPIRITS, TREE FAIRIES, or earth ELEMENTALS like GNOMES.

EARTHLIGHTS is another term for WILL O'THE WISP type phenomena. One explanation for these strange lights is that they are electrical charges built up in areas of geological stress and slowly discharged as electrons

EGGSHELLS

into the air.[71] Earthlights have been witnessed in both Britain and Japan before earthquakes. The Celtic countries of Ireland, Scotland and Wales have a tradition of CORPSE CANDLES or fairy lanterns appearing as an OMEN OF DEATH.[72] Lights in pit tunnels have warned of impending disasters and haunt mines where catastrophes have claimed lives.

EARTHMAN is a term sometimes applied to a DWARF, particularly in Germany.

ECHO was a Greek NYMPH who fell in love with a youth called Narcissus, but he was only in love with his own image. He rejected her advances to gaze at himself in a pool, and eventually withered and became the flower that is named after him. She fled into lonely places and faded away, consumed by her love until she became no more than a voice. In many parts of the world the echo is thought to be a spirit. In Norway and Sweden, the echo is ascribed to dwarfs mocking human speakers.

EDDY O'ANNIS is one of the Orkney TROWS.

EGERIA is a Roman water NYMPH who lived in a grove and was consulted by King Numa Pompilius on political matters every evening. The Vestal Virgins went to her spring daily to collect water to purify the shrine of Vesta.

EGGSHELLS feature widely in fairy folklore. The method of discovering a CHANGELING by means of eggshells is used in many places around the world. Empty eggshells are arranged round the HEARTH and as the curious changeling gets up to examine them he will peer into each saying something like "This is but a windbag; I am so many hundred years old and I have never seen the like of this". An alternative method is to go through the motions of brewing water in halves of eggshells. The changeling will sit up and declare "I have seen the egg before the hen, I have seen the acorn before the oak, but I have never seen brewing in an eggshell before!" thus revealing its ancient age. It might even say "I'm fifteen hundred years in the world and I've never seen a brewery of eggshells before!"[73]

Eggshells are a favourite retreat of fairies. The judicious eater should break the shells to prevent fairies taking up lodging in them.

EINGSAUNG NAT is a Burmese HOUSE FAIRY.

EISENHÜTEL is a German HOUSE FAIRY of the RUMPELSTILTSKIN type, whose NAME has to be guessed.

EISIRT is the bard of the Irish fairy kingdom of Faylinn. He told his king, Iubdan, that there was a race of giants (humans) in Ulster and was clapped in irons for telling lies. Eventually he was released to prove the truth of his allegations, travelled to the court of King Fergus, and returned with Aeda, a dwarf who seemed huge to the fairies. Later the fairy king and queen visited the Ulster court, but were taken captive and only released when Eisirt led the SIDHE in plaguing the humans.

EKERKEN is a German HOUSE FAIRY who delights in disturbing human inhabitants by making strange noises, banging on the ceiling, creaking the doors, rattling the cutlery in the drawers and so on.

EKIMMU was an ancient Assyrian BANSHEE who wailed outside the door of a person about to die.

ELABY GATHON is a fairy invoked by nurses to watch over sleeping children, rather on the principle of setting a thief to catch a thief. She will prevent them from being kidnapped by fairies and substituted with changelings. Some think the word lullaby is a corruption of L'Elaby.

ELB or **ELBE** is a term for a female ELF derived from the old German tongue.

ELDER (*Sambucus nigra*) is a tree whose folklore varies from location to location. In some places, it is believed to be inhabited by a TREE FAIRY, in other places it gives protection against the fairies. Yet again, it may be a WITCH in disguise; the witch of the Rollright Stones turned into an elder tree. Certainly, the elder is inhabited by a spirit, and for this reason when it is cut, it bleeds real blood. In Lincolnshire, permission must be sought of the Old Lady or Old Girl: "Owd Gal, give me some of thy wood and Oi will give thee some of moine, when I graws inter a tree". If you cut the elder without permission, you risk losing your eyesight, your health, your cattle and your children. If you wound the tree, you must give it charms and offerings. If your child angers the tree, you must take the tree some wool and bread and say: "You elders and

eldresses, here I bring you something to spin and something to eat. Eat and spin and forget my child".

In Denmark, the elder tree was known to be under the protection of HULDA, and in England the Elder Mother or Elder Queen. She lived at its roots and was the mother of the ELVES. (According to Danish folklore, if you stand under an elder on MIDSUMMER Eve you will see the King of the Elves pass by.) It is safe to take a branch from the elder on January 6th without permission if you spit on the ground THREE times. This elder branch can then be used to draw a MAGIC circle in a lonely place for the purpose of demanding magic FERN seed, which will give you the strength of thirty men. Hulda will ensure that an unseen hand delivers a chalice, containing the seed.

ELDER MOTHER is the guardian of the ELDER tree in England, and her permission must be sought before picking any berries. She takes revenge on anyone who fells an elder by striking down his or her livestock with disease.

ELEMENTALS are spirits composed solely from one element. The theory that all things are composed of a combination of earth, air, fire and water was formulated by the Greek

scientist Empedocles (fifth century BCE). Aristotle and Plato accepted the idea and it persisted as accredited science until the seventeenth century. According to this philosophy, a perfect human would be a balanced combination of the four elements.

The ancients believed that a spirit inhabited every stream, hill, tree, and natural thing (*see* ANIMA). Following the theory of the four elements the Neoplatonists of the third century divided these spirits into four classes, each associated with one of the elements. However, it was the sixteenth-century alchemist, doctor and philosopher Paracelsus who gave them their familiar names.[74] He called the earth elementals pygmies or gnomi (singular gnomus) who could move through the earth as fish move through water. The derivation of the word is uncertain, but may relate to the Greek verb *gnosis* 'to know' or yet again to a word meaning 'of the earth'. He may have invented it. Though the term 'gnome' does not seem to pre-date Paracelsus (though the idea of earth spirits does), gnomes have captured the popular imagination as guardians of the earth. He called spirits of the air sylvestres or sylphs from the Greek *silphe* meaning 'BUTTERFLY' or 'moth'. They are described as almost transparent, very small and winged. Vulcans or salamanders (from the Greek meaning 'fireplace') were designated elemental spirits of the fire. They are usually portrayed as the newts of the same name. Nymphs or undines ('Wave') are regarded as representing water. In size and appearance, they resemble humans. In fact, they sometimes adopt human CLOTHES and marry mortal men. However, the man should be careful if goes near water as his fairy wife may be tempted to return to her natural element. Paracelsus said that if an undine female should desert her human husband then the man should not take another wife, since the marriage had not been dissolved. Through the marriage, the undine will gain a SOUL, and any children of the marriage will be human.

According to Paracelsus, while sylphs and undines are kindly disposed towards humans, salamanders cannot be approached or approach humans, and gnomes are usually malevolent. However, gnomes can be persuaded to become servants to a magician and: 'if you do your duty to him, he will do his duty to you'. He went on to say that elementals hate dogmatists, sceptics, drunkards, gluttons and the quarrelsome, while they love natural, child-like, innocent and sincere people: '...to him who binds or pledges himself to them they give knowledge and riches enough. They know our minds and thoughts also, so that they may be easily influenced to come to us'.

Paracelsus also declared that while humanity is made of THREE substances, the spiritual, the astral and visible or terrestrial and exists in all three, elementals live exclusively in only one of the elements. They occupy a position between men and pure spirits, though they have blood and bones, they eat, sleep and mate and produce offspring. They are not immortal but can succumb to disease. They live in dwellings that are made of special materials: 'as different from the substances we know as the web of a spider is different from our linen'. He said that elementals have no souls and are incapable of spiritual development.

Some occultists believe that fairies are elementals, spirit-beings made up of one element only - earth, air, fire or water. Sinistrari described beings of an intermediate nature between the angels and man, capable of independent thought and of choosing good or evil, composed of one of the four elements.[75] Ritual magicians, modern witches and Pagans call upon the spirits of the four elements. They maintain that they are beings who have developed along another line of evolution to humans. In the Cabala they are called the Shedim.

The word 'elemental' is occasionally used to describe nature fairies in general, or a kind of low-level spirit. One of the latter was seen by Lady Winifred Penoyer and two other women in Corsham churchyard in Wiltshire. It was described as an intently malevolent little man some 75 cm high (about two-and-a-half feet). Some magicians claim to create these spirits by magic.

ELF (*pl.* **Elves**) is a word that comes from the Teutonic languages: in Anglo-Saxon AELF, in Old Norse *âlfr,* and the Old High German is ALP. The term may originally have signified WHITE or shining spirits. It may be connected with the Latin *albus* and Sabine *alpus* meaning 'white' (the Alps are so called because they are covered in snow). Other cognate words are the Old English *ielfetu,* a swan, and the Greek *alphos* a disease characterised by white spots.[76] Originally, elves were ancestral spirits who brought fertility.

In Norse myth, there are two types-the light or white elves who are lovely and good, and the dark or black elves, who live below ground and are generally evil.[77]

Elves are particularly prevalent in Britain with many stories relating to them dating from as early as the eighth century. The term 'elf' or 'alf' occurs in personal names, such as Alfred. In England the word 'elf' is often interchangeable with the word 'fairy' but generally refers to trooping fairies, those who live in companies ruled by a king or queen and who dwell underground. They dress in GREEN or white. 'Elf' is sometimes applied to mischievous woodland spirits like PUCK and ROBIN GOODFELLOW or to small fairy boys. In Scotland, 'elves' are larger than fairies, being of human size.

In popular Scandinavian folklore, elves are said to live in certain groves and trees. They are fond of dancing in the moonlight, and the circles of brilliant green that sometimes appear in grass are attributed to them. They play mischievous tricks, steal things, and SHAPESHIFT into BUTTERFLIES, ALDER, aspen and WILLOW trees.

Danish female elves are beautiful from the front but hollow in the back. They play on stringed instruments and any young man hearing them falls in love. The male elf is said to have an aged appearance and to wear a low crowned hat. The Samoyeds of Siberia say that little elves haunt the woods and streams, and are ruled by a Great Spirit, the Forest Spirit and the River Spirit.

ELF BOLTS, Elf Arrows, Fairy Darts, Elf Shot or **Elf Stones** are arrowheads, called in Gaelic *saighead sith* (elf-arrows). They are manufactured by fairies and WITCHES for use in causing harm, shot at humans or livestock. Deaths have been attributed to them and it was once thought they could induce paralysis: the word 'stroke' for paralysis is derived from 'elf-stroke'.[78] In 1662 the Scottish witch Isobel Gowdie confessed to her dealings with fairies and testified: 'As for Elf-arrow-heidis, the Divell shapes them with his awin hand, and syne deliveris thame to Elf-boyes, who whyttis and dightis them with a sharp thing lyk a paking neidle.'

If a COW were suspected of being elf shot, then it would be necessary to send for a WISE WOMAN or CUNNING MAN who would examine the cow for hairless patches or lumps under the skin. She or he would then proceed to pierce the spot with a needle, and if the cow did not bleed the diagnosis was confirmed. Every wise woman or man had her or his own remedies, usually secret, but some of these might include firing guns over the cow, whispering in its ears or giving it drinks off silver platters.

Humans were also liable to elf shot, like the man sent lame for ploughing a TROW hill. Fairy darts were often aimed at the fingers, causing the joints to swell and go red and inflamed. Once two old women were seen passing a baby over hot coals then feeding it with a drink made from cinders in a cup of water to 'cure it of

fairy stroke'.[79] An eminent 'FAIRY DOCTOR' (a wise woman who specialised in curing fairy ills) made the cure of fairy darts her speciality and was sent for all round Ireland. She had no power unless she was asked to cure, and she took no reward until the dart was extracted and the cure effected. The treatment included a salve, the ingredients of which she kept secret.

In Scottish tradition, elves cannot throw the bolts themselves, but must compel some mortal whom they are carrying about to do so. If the victim is a friend, then the thrower can usually manage to miss, and the bolt will be found lying harmlessly beside the intended victim.

If you can find an elf bolt, it is a lucky charm and will guard against any further attacks by evil fairies. It can also cure wounds when rubbed on them. You should never give an elf bolt away, however, as this will be an invitation for the fairies to kidnap you. Elf bolts are often found in Ireland, Britain and Europe, particularly in the vicinity of fairy MOUNDS. They are the small flint arrowheads fashioned by Stone Age man.

ELF FIRE is an English name for the WILL O'THE WISP.

ELF LIGHT is another English name for the WILL O'THE WISP.

ELF LOCKS are the tangles in human hair or horses' manes caused by mischievous ELVES and fairies.

ELFAME or **Elfhame** ('Elf Home') is the Scottish name for FAIRYLAND.

ELFIN POX is the rash called *breac sith* ('elfin pox') in Scotland, which was thought to be due to the attentions of malicious fairies.

ELFOR are the Swedish equivalent of the Danish ELLEFOLK.

ELIMA (*pl.* **Bilima**) is a spirit of the Mongo-Nkundo people of the Congo, associated with fertility. It lives in trees, bogs, rivers and streams.

ELK are dwarfish creatures of Armenian folklore who steal the livers of living humans to feed themselves and their children. Once they have washed the liver and eaten it the human will die. They mainly attack women in CHILDBIRTH, sometimes stealing the child and leaving a CHANGELING behind. They can cause sterility and miscarriage. They can be stopped if a PIN is inserted into their clothes.

ELLEFOLK are Danish fairies who live on moorland, next to rivers, under the hills, or in marshes. They tend lovely gardens hidden in the moss at the edge of forests. Humans may glimpse their realm but once, then it will vanish never to be seen again. Ellefolk travel, by day or night, with equal ease through air, fire, wood, water or stone. They can pass though keyholes into human houses, riding on sunbeams.

The females are about 1.2 metres tall (some four feet), young and beautiful with long golden hair, but with drooping breasts, hollow backs and cows' tails. The males are shorter and look like old men wearing low crowned caps. Both sexes can see into the future and guard many ancient secrets. They are descended from Adam and his first wife LILITH.

The ellewomen like to seduce young human men by playing sweet music on stringed instruments and dancing beguilingly in the moonlight, weaving curious patterns with their steps. A few notes of the lovely music is enough to make a man lose his reason. If the men refuse to join the DANCE, the fairies will inflict sickness on them. If a man should glimpse a lovely ellemaid through the knot in a tree, he will forget his wife and children and follow her. If a woman should see an elleman sunbathing on the edge of the moors, she will be whisked away into the OTHERWORLD.

The ellemen are dangerous as their breath produces a pestilence. If cattle feed on hills where the ellefolk have spat or defecated, they too will be struck by illness. A farmer should take the precaution of asking the ellefolk's permission to let his cattle graze on their MOUNDS, and ensure that they do not mix with the large, blue fairy kine, which survive solely on dew. Ellefolk steal human food unless it is protected.

ELLEQUINDE is the Danish term for a female ELF.

ELLERWOMEN are lovely but hollow backed women of the HULDRE FOLK

ELLYLL (*pl.* **ELLYLLON**) are Welsh and Cornish fairies that closely resemble English ELVES. In Welsh *el*

means a 'fairy' or 'spirit' and they are one class of the PLANT ANNWN. They are tiny creatures, so small that they ride eggshells and wear mittens made of FOXGLOVE flowers. The ellyllon are ruled over by Queen MAB and dwell in hollows, dingles or inland lakes. They eat *ymenyn tylwyth teg* or 'fairy butter', a substance found in rock crevices in the shafts of lead mines, and *bwyd ellyllon,* 'fairy food', i.e. TOADSTOOLS.

Rowli Pugh encountered an ellyll. He lived on a farm in Glamorganshire and was widely known for his ill luck. Everything he did went wrong. Eventually, things got so bad that he decided to sell up and move to another country. As he sat musing over this, a little man appeared and asked him what the matter was. Rowli could only stare in surprise, but the ellyll said: 'There, never mind. I know all about you and your troubles. You are planning to go away, but now I have spoken to you, you will be able to stay. Only ask your wife to leave the candle burning when she goes to bed, and say no more about it." At this, the fairy disappeared.

The farmer did as he was asked. Every night his wife Catti set the candle out and swept the HEARTH before going to bed and every night the fairies would come and do her work – washing, mending, baking and brewing. The farmer took heart and now his crops were good, his cattle sleek and his pigs fat. So this went on until Catti decided to have a look at the fairies one night, and peeked through a crack in the door. There was a jolly company of ellyllon, working fast, but dancing and singing at the same time. Seeing them, Catti couldn't help laughing too, and at this the fairies took fright and disappeared like mist, never to be seen again. However, the farmer was now so well set up that he continued to prosper.[80]

ELLYLLDAN ('Fire Fairy') is a Welsh WILL O'THE WISP which can be seen dancing about on marshy ground, into which it may lead a hapless traveller.

Some say that the creature has died out, starved to death since farmers have drained the bogs.

Iolo the Bard described an encounter with an ellylldan during which he followed it down from a mountaintop into a marshy valley. It waited for him every time he stopped but each time dwindled away almost to a spark until he began moving again when it would glow and glide on. Eventually it shot away from him and joined a ring of its fellows, dancing around and around until the bard was lulled to sleep.[81]

ELM (*Ulmus sp.*) is also called 'elven' in England because the tree is considered to be the dwelling place of ELVES. According to legend, if an elm is cut down the one next to it will die of grief.

ELMO'S FIRE, ST. is a type of WILL O'THE WISP that appears at sea (thought by scientists to be caused by static electrical discharges during thunderstorms). It is accompanied by a crackling sound and is seen on ships' masts. When sailors see it they know that the worst of the storm is over and once asserted that the lights were the SOULS of the drowned. St Elmo is a corruption of St Erasmus, who died during a storm at sea in the fourth century. He told the sailors that he would come back from the dead and show himself to them if they were destined to be saved from the tempest. Sure enough, the light appeared at the masthead.

ELOKO (*pl.* BILOKO) is a vicious Congo fairy who sometimes appears as a GIANT with crocodile jaws and sometimes as a powerful DWARF. He wears only leaves and dwells in hollow trees.

ELVES OF LIGHT are Algonquin fairies from the Quebec area who dance in the forest. They are ruled by Queen Summer.

EMAIN ABLACH is a legendary FAIRY ISLAND usually identified with the real Isle of Arran or the ISLE OF MAN.

ENGUE is a type of NIGHTMARE fairy.

EPIMELIAN NYMPHS guard flocks of sheep in Italian folklore. According to an ancient tale, some shepherds saw them dancing at the Sacred Rocks of Messapia. The boastful shepherds claimed that they could DANCE better than the NYMPHS, and a contest began. It was soon apparent that the clumsy shepherds could not equal the light and graceful movements of the nymphs. The angry maids punished the men by transforming them into a grove of trees called the Place of the Nymphs and Youths. A voice of lamentation issued from the groves.

EQQO are Ethiopian fairies who dwell in wild places and who sometimes possess human beings to prophesy through them.

ERATO is one of the nine MUSES, the patroness of love poetry and mimicry. She is depicted with a lyre and a crown of roses.

ERDLUITLE (*f.* Erdbibberli) ('Earth Folk') are fairies found in Switzerland and Northern Italy. They live in the mountains, preferring the shelter of a CAVE, or a dwelling underground or beneath ancient standing stones. They have great power over nature and may cause floods, storms and avalanches. They bring fertility by dancing in the fields, and they protect all the farm animals as well as the wild mountain creatures. They milk the wild chamois and have the secret of making chamois cheese. They love to eat roots, peas, berries and pork. They are generally friendly towards humans, and may tell favoured farmers the best time to plant, or turn leaves into precious stones and gold. However, they do steal human children and leave CHANGELINGS called Chrügeli in their place.

In appearance, they are about 30 to 90 cm tall (between eighteen inches and three feet) with complexions the colour of new turned earth, dark hair that turns white as they age, and some have animal ears. Despite having duck-feet, these Swiss fairies sink if they try to swim. They are always hooded and wear smocks and long cloaks to hide their FEET.

ERDMÄNNCHEN ('Little Earth Men') are Swiss EARTH FAIRIES, a type of ERDUITLE. They are generally well disposed towards human beings, especially the poor (who called them big-eared dwarfs) and children, to whom they will give gifts of toys, sweets or money. Once one of the fairies pressed a piece of coal into the hand of a boy, who threw it away in disgust. However, when he found it the next day it had turned into a precious jewel.[82]

ERDWEIBCHEN or Herdweibchen ('Earthwives') are female ERLUITLE who influence all aspects of Nature, but may work in the farmhouse in the manner of a HOUSE FAIRY. They are excellent at SPINNING and are very lucky to have around. However, since Swiss farmers have gone over to mechanical methods of cultivation, the fairies are retreating into the wilder places, and the symbiotic relationship between man and fairy no longer exists.

ERINNYES are the ancient Greek Furies, spirits of vengeance, who track down murderers, particularly those who shed the blood of relatives. They have snakes for hair and bat-like wings. Their names are Alecto (Implacable), Tisiphone (Avenger), and Megaera (Disputatious). Like the fairies with whom they later came to be identified, they were addressed as 'The Kindly Ones' (*Eumenides*).

ÉRIU is a goddess of the TUATHA DÉ DANAAN later demoted to the status of a fairy queen. She gave her name to the land of Ireland, Erin.

ERL is the German term for an ELF.

ERLKONIG or Erlking ('Elf King') is an ELF who manifests in Germany and Denmark, wearing beautiful clothes and a golden crown. The Erlking

sometimes leads the WILD HUNT. His appearance is an OMEN OF DEATH. If he wears a pained look, the death will be painful. If he appears serene, the death will be peaceful.

Goethe wrote a famous poem about the Elf King, which Schubert set to music. It was based on an old legend: A father and son were riding on a single horse through a snowstorm. The boy became afraid and the father asked him what was wrong. The child replied that he could see the Elf King. The father soothingly replied that there was nothing there but the mist. But the Elf King beckoned to the boy, asking him to come and play with him. The boy cried out, but his father assured him it was only the rustling of the leaves. The boy eventually complained that the Elf King had wounded him. Finally, his father became alarmed and pressed hurriedly for home. When he reached the courtyard he bent down to wake his small son, but found him dead in his arms.

ERODIADE is a Queen of the Fairies, possibly synonymous with the WITCH goddess HERODIAS. The Italian carnival society of the Cavallino assembled under the banner of Erodiade. The society grew to prominence in the Middle Ages, appearing in processions, pantomimes and healing sessions, but may have had a very ancient, Pagan origin. It was exclusively male, they dressed in women's clothes and wore make up. They always gathered in odd numbers, such as SEVEN or NINE or eleven. The Catholic Church persecuted them as Pagans who worshipped the goddess DIANA.[83]

ERYTHRAEA ('The Red One') is a NYMPH, one of the HESPERIDES.

ESPRIT FOLLET ('Mischievous Fairy') is either a French HOUSE FAIRY, or a roguish spirit that lives beneath a dolmen.

ETAIN was the second wife of the fairy King MIDIR.[84]

ETAR was a Fairy King of Ireland. With his fellow fairy king CAIBELL he fought a battle against two human kings who wanted to steal their daughters.

EUMENIDES ('The Kindly Ones') is a flattering term for the dread goddesses the Erinnyes or Furies. The ancient Greeks called them 'The Kindly Ones' -just as people refer to the fairies - in an attempt to flatter them and deter their mischief.

EUR-CUNNERE NOE is a fairy of Brittany, similar to a BANSHEE. She appears as an OMEN OF DEATH.

EUTERPE ('Giver of Pleasure') is one of the nine MUSES, the patroness of MUSIC and flute playing in particular. She is depicted with a flute.

EYNHALLOW is Orkney's Holy Isle, which is said to vanish from time to time like a FAIRY ISLAND. It is the summer home of the FIN FOLK. It is located between the Orkney mainland and the Isle of Rousay and is often surrounded by mists and dangerous rip tides.

FACHAN is a Highland fairy of Glen Etive, Argyll, Scotland. He has one eye, one hand and one leg, one ear, one arm and one toe - in fact he only has one of everything, all lined up down the centre of his hairy, feathered body. He carries a spiked club with which he attacks any human who dares to approach his mountain realm. He hates all living creatures but especially birds, which he envies for their gift of flight. The fachan may be a distorted folk memory of the activities of Celtic seers who, when divining or casting spells, stood on one leg, with one eye closed and one arm extended. In other words, they stood not wholly in this world, had one eye closed, to look into the inner world, and had one arm acting in the OTHERWORLD. *See also* MUSHROOM and FLY AGARIC.

FADA is a generic term for a fairy in Provençal. These female fairies of France seduce young men. Should the lover of a fada become engaged to a mortal woman, then the fairy will ensure that he dies before he can consummate the relationship. The fadas used to be honoured on 31st December when houses would be cleaned and the doors and windows left open. A table would be laid with a white cloth, a cup, food, wine and a lighted candle. The fairy would enter bearing good luck in her right hand, and bad luck in her left. If she were pleased with the offering, she would reward the family.

FADAS are the Portuguese fairies, similar in character to the French FÉE.

FADET or **Farfadet** are tiny fairies who live in underground tunnels, according to the folklore of Poitou. They are black, covered in hair and are fond of crude jokes. One shocked three old ladies who were quietly spinning by the fire when he dropped his trousers, before disappearing up the chimney in a gale of laughter.

FADHAS are small, lovely Swiss fairies. They are generally friendly, and will always return what they have borrowed. If they break it, they will repair it for you. The inhabitants of one Swiss town could rely on a friendly fairy to prophesy what the following year would be like. In good years, the fairy would come down from the mountains, herding a flock of white goats, while in famine and plague years it would arrive with a flock of black goats.[85]

FAET FIADA ('The Look of an Animal') is the power of SHAPESHIFTING bestowed upon the TUATHA DÉ DANAAN by the god MANANNAN after the Milesian Celts invaded Ireland and forced them into hiding. It enables them to assume the appearance of animals in order to avoid detection.

FAËU BOULANGER, LE ('The Rolling Fire') is the WILL O'THE WISP in the folklore of the Channel Island of Guernsey. It manifests as a ball of rolling fire and a number of people have been astonished to find it rolling straight towards them. It is thought to be a spirit in pain, cursed to wander and vainly attempts to free itself from its suffering by suicide. It guards a hidden TREASURE. If you stick a knife in the ground with the blade uppermost it will try to fight it, and blood will be found on the blade the next day. If you need to avoid the Rolling Fire, turn your CLOTHES inside out and it will disappear.

People continue to see the Faëu Boulanger. Marie de Garis, in her book on the folklore of Guernsey, describes several instances, including one involving a man who was walking down La Rue de la Rocque at

FACHAN

Pleinmont. He saw a large oval shaped sphere of light floating a foot off the ground. It remained motionless as he regarded it, but when he took a step forward, it retreated slightly. They proceeded this way down the hill and the light vanished.[86]

FAFNIR is a Teutonic DWARF who murdered his father, the King of the Dwarfs, in order to steal his TREASURE. He refused to share it with anyone and turned into a miserly DRAGON, hugging his wealth to himself. Eventually the hero Sigurd killed him.

FÁIES is a type of French FÉE who is particularly tiny.

FAINEN is a Tyrolean WHITE LADY who can only be glimpsed by those born on a Sunday, or if she appears to kiss a child, or by those possessing a special amulet. She takes the form of a lovely girl with long golden hair, dressed in gauzy white.

FAIR FAMILY is a Welsh euphemism for fairies.

FAIR OF THE DEAD is an Irish name for the FAIRY MARKET.

FAIR FOLK is a Welsh euphemism for fairies.

FAIRY is an English word derived, by way of the French *fée*, from the Latin *fatare* meaning 'to enchant'. Variations on fairy include fayerye, fairye, fayre and faery.

The word *faërie* was originally the term for enchantment and only latterly came to refer to the race. It was more common to refer to a fay or fays. Side by side with the Latin derived term 'fairy' is the term PUCK, PHOOKA, POUKE or PIGHT. It has been argued that this is the Celtic designation, but this is unlikely since variations occur in Germanic, Scandinavian and Slavonic countries.

Some folklorists think that the whole concept of fairies originated in Italy with the Fatae or FATES and spread with the Roman Empire. These original Fates controlled the destinies of humankind, bestowing gifts upon newborn children - a concept recognisable in FAIRY GODMOTHERS - measuring their adult lives and finally ending them.

Fairies inhabit a realm which impinges on the human one, but which is rarely glimpsed. Fairies themselves are rarely seen, except under particular circumstances, at certain times, or by the use of certain herbs, potions or magic objects.

In the past it was considered unlucky to name the fairies, or even to use the word 'fairy' perhaps because to do so may have summoned them, or because using a name without its owner's permission was a threat or challenge. It was wise to call them 'the Good People', 'the Little People', 'The Gentry', 'the Mother's Blessing', 'Good Neighbours', 'Wee Folk' or 'the Hidden People', just as the ancient Greeks called the FURIES, the terrifying goddesses of vengeance, 'The Kindly Ones'. Talking about fairies was to invite disasters, the very least of which was the calamity of being struck by blindness.

FAIRY ANIMALS includes a number of creatures associated with the fairies in a variety of forms. In Celtic cultures, the BUTTERFLY is an emblem of both the human soul and the SIDHE. In Irish, British and European folklore fairies appear as cats and also keep pet cats. The tailless Manx cats from the ISLE OF MAN were bred by the fairies. The fairy King of the Cats dwells as an ordinary cat by day, living on the Isle of Man, and travels the country at night as a royal cat to avenge any slights given to him during the day.

Fairies are very interested in cows. WITCHES and fairies were often blamed for stealing MILK from cows, either by making milking motions from a distance, or by taking the form of a hare or hedgehog to suckle from the cow. Strange cows found on the seashore are called *cro sith* or 'fairy cows', because they are of no mortal breed but live under the water on seaweed. Otherworldly cattle are common in British folklore, recognised by their red or round ears, and are generous creatures that gave an unending supply of milk to their human owners.

The stag was one of the four sacred animals of the Celts. Red deer in particular are associated with fairies and in Mull, they are said to be their only cattle. Fairy women often assume the form of red deer. Fairies dislike deer hunters and throw ELF-BOLTS at them. During the winter, the stag herds are protected by the CAILLEACH.

Fairy dogs act as guides to the fairy realms and lead people into the UNDERWORLD. They are usually green or white with red ears, but Black Dogs appear in many areas of Britain as evil omens. Several legends of Britain tell of the Wild Hunt, a pack of ghostly dogs who fly through the night sky to pursue the souls of the damned.

A large number of fairies are associated with goats, either because they have goats' legs, or because they shapeshift into complete goats. English country people said that it was not possible to see a goat for twenty-four hours continually, as at some point he must go and visit either the fairies or his master the devil, to pay homage and have his beard combed.

Fairies love horses. When horses neigh at night, they are being ridden hard by fairies or witches. The TUATHA DÉ DANAAN kept magical fairy horses in the hollow hills. These were made of fire and flame and were as swift as the wind. There are also many stories of water horses called each sith, 'the unearthly horse' or 'fairy horse'.

According to Welsh folklore pigs originated in fairyland and the first seen by humans were a gift to Pryderi from the King of the UNDERWORLD. The sea god Manannan kept a magical herd of pigs in his underworld kingdom. There are tales of fairy pigs in the Isle of Man and at Andover in Hampshire, a spectral pig is seen on New Year's Eve.

The cuckoo is *eun sith* or 'fairy bird' of TIR-NAN-OG, coming from the words of the god/fairy ANGUS OG. It goes to the mysterious realm of the Land of the Dead in winter, entering the fairy mounds. In addition several other birds are associated with fairies, including the OWL, the CROW, the RAVEN, the wren, and the SWAN, while fairy WELL GUARDIANS appear in the form of FROGS, TOADS, and salmon.

FAIRY BANNER or *Bratach Sith* is a flag that belongs to the MacLeods of Skye. The faded brown silk flag is still kept in the drawing room of Dunvegan Castle. There are several legends telling how the flag came into the possession of the clan. Some say that a MacLeod married a fairy and she gave her husband the flag on the Fairy Bridge when she had to return to her own kin. Others say that a crusading MacLeod received it as a gift from a WATER FAIRY in the Holy Land, or won it from a she-devil. Yet again, the MacLeods trace their ancestry back to King Harald Hardrada. He was a Norseman who set out to conquer England in 1066 with a MAGIC talisman called Land-Ravager, a flag that guaranteed victory to its possessor. However, it does not seem to have worked for Harald, who was defeated by the English King Harold. Land-Ravager disappeared after the battle, but may have come into the possession of the MacLeods.

Legend says that when the fairy banner is unfurled in battle, victory always attends it, but it can only be used THREE times. The clan has used it twice, on both occasions against their enemies the MacDonalds, once at Glendale in 1490 and again at Waternish in 1520. Whenever the flag was taken into battle, whether it was unfurled or not, twelve champion swordsmen were chosen to defend it. During the Second World War, many young clansmen carried a photograph of the flag with them.

There are several conditions surrounding the use of the flag. At least a year and a day must elapse before each summoning of fairy help, and if a pregnant woman should see it, she will be taken in premature labour, while cows will cast their calves.

During the fifteenth century, the wife of the chieftain Iain Borb gave birth to a child. A fairy came to the castle, wrapped him in the flag and sang him a lullaby. When she left, the nurse remembered the words and melody, and since then, no nurse had been appointed to the MacLeod heir unless she knows the fairy song.

FAIRY BLESSINGS can be conferred on those mortals that the fairies take a liking to. They may protect their favourites from harm, give them great riches, beauty or magical powers. Fairies like simple, unpretentious, sincere folk and hate the nosy, boastful, quarrelsome and greedy. They detest people who give themselves airs and pretend to be what they are not. Fairies also love beauty and luxury and hate people who are mean and parsimonious.[87] They have a particular friendship with WITCHES, and in many cases, the witch receives his or her powers from the fairies in the first place.

In order to gain the friendship and blessing of the fairies you must take certain steps. Fairies appreciate being treated with consideration. It is wise to create a warm, tidy place by the HEARTH for them, leave the fire smouldering at night when you go to bed, put out water for them to wash in, and wine or MILK to drink or better still, a bowl of best cream. Leave the last apples on the tree for them and the last grain in the barrel, or the last few drops of milk in the pail. The first milk from the cow should always be spilt on the ground as an offering for them.

Remember that fairies don't like being spoken of by name, and don't like being called 'fairies'. It is as well to call them 'The Gentry' or some such flattery. They resent their MOUNDS, hills and trees being disturbed. Treat these places with caution and respect.

Fairies will always reward a good deed or kindness shown towards them. Take care to be kind to travellers, for they may be fairy princes in disguise. A fairy may appear in the guise of an old woman or poor man and ask you to share your food, take them to their destination, or even mend their broken wheelbarrow. If you pass the test the fairy may reveal hidden TREASURE, show you how to cast spells, reveal the power of herbs, save your life, or make someone love you. A sudden stroke of luck may fall upon you or your family. Fairies (WATER FAIRIES and MERMAIDS in particular) have the power to make human beings into great healers.

However, do not say 'thank you', as they will be offended. Do not offer them CLOTHES as a gift, or try to return more than is given or lent. Never mention what the fairies have done for you or speak of your relationship with the fairies, or they will turn against you.

FAIRY CHILDREN are produced when fairies mate, though very little is known about these offspring. Some say that fairy babies are seldom born and that each fairy man was proud to be thought a baby's father, for fairy men and women were not faithful to each other.[88] There are a great number of stories about fairies stealing human children and leaving fairy babies called CHANGELINGS in their place. It may be imagined that fairy parents are heartless and uncaring, but this is not the case. Some fairies have normal motherly instincts. Once when a human mother bent over the withered changeling she found in her child's cradle, the latch lifted and in came a fairy woman with her real child. 'It was the others who took it' she said. All she wanted was her own child back.[89]

Fairies also mate and have children with humans. Children of a human father and fairy mother grow up strong and powerful but with evil and dangerous natures.[90] They are often mystics, possess second sight and generally become famous in MUSIC and song, but they are passionate and vengeful. Their beautiful eyes and bold reckless temperament betrays their fairy blood. Many famous people are thought to have had one mortal and one otherworldly parent. These include Alexander the Great, the Queen of Sheba and MERLIN. Even Shakespeare was said to have been part fairy.

FAIRY DOCTORS specialised in curing those ills caused by fairy tricks and curses, such as the sickness caused by being struck by an ELF BOLT. Each fairy doctor would have his or her own remedies, which were usually kept secret. They might include the use of incantations, certain herbal salves and potions or spells involving IRON, silver or the BIBLE. One fairy doctor would tear pages from the bible and roll them into pellets to feed to the victim; another would make them drink water from a silver platter.

The secret knowledge of a fairy doctor would be passed from generation to generation. Some thought that the fairies themselves imparted the knowledge. The young girls that they stole away would be returned after SEVEN years, having grown old and ugly, but gifted with knowledge of herbs and spells.[91]

Though the term 'fairy doctor' is peculiar to Ireland, similar figures are found all over the world in the guise of WITCHES, WISE WOMEN, SHAMANS and CUNNING MEN.

FAIRY FESTIVALS coincide with the four fire festivals of the Celts and the solstices and equinoxes, universally celebrated by the ancient Pagans.

SAMHAIN marked the start of winter, and the ancient Celts celebrated it as a Festival of the DEAD. Good fairies such as the Irish Tuatha dé Danaan and the English Puck retire from sight until spring returns. Evil fairies, such as the Scottish Unseelie Court become very active, goblins are seen consorting with ghosts and evil omens such as Black Dogs and Washer at the Ford manifest. At YULE a wide variety of present giving fairies appear, such as the Icelandic Jola Sveinar, the Danish Julenisse, the Swedish Jultomte and, of course, Father Christmas. These are probably directly descended from Odin or Woden who rode out at Yule to reward good deeds and punish bad ones.

Good fairies are most active from BELTANE (May Day) to Samhain echoing the ancient return of the gods of summer and increase. One of the great fairy festivals is MIDSUMMER, the ancient celebration of the summer solstice. At this time they are said to have their greatest power and be at their most frolicsome. The fairies try to pass around the Baal fires in a whirlwind to extinguish them.

Herbs collected on the fairy days have great power for healing, divination and magic. They are gathered and taken home and dried on these days.

FAIRY FIRE is another name for the WILL O'THE WISP.

FAIRY FOOD is an odd idea as fairies do not eat much. Yet they drink in quintessences and ethereal essences, though they like spirituous liquors; and BROWNIES sometimes bake bread.[92]

Fairies are said to sip nectar from flowers and to love honey and MILK; any milk spilt by accident is regarded as a gift to the fairies. Some say they live on a diet of milk and saffron and eat neither flesh nor fish. Scottish fairies eat the root of the silverweed (*Potentilla anserina*), which is turned up by the plough in spring, the stalks of heather, barleymeal, and drink the milk of red DEER and GOATS.

Others say that fairy food consists of ordinary food from which they have taken the *toradh* (Gaelic 'the substance' or 'benefit') leaving only the semblance. According to Irish folklore any food left outside the house after sundown becomes the property of the fairies and is unfit for either human or animal consumption.

Those humans who eat fairy food are as hungry afterwards as before. Fairy food is not always what it seems as it is disguised by MAGIC. Sometimes if grace is said over the victuals, they turn out to be horse dung. A goblet of mead may reveal itself to be an acorn filled with brackish water or a seeming royal banquet nothing but faded autumn leaves. In Innisboffin (Ireland) it is said that if anyone is stupid enough to drink the fairy wine they will be dead before the year is out.

Mortals who return from the land of the fairy often pine away and die, though people rescued from FAIRYLAND rarely suffer the same kind of longing that affects those who willingly share the fairy feasts and dancing. People who are taken to fairyland are warned not to eat the food there, or they will never be able to return to the human realm. This echoes the idea, found in several mythologies, that the DEAD are welcomed to the UNDERWORLD with food, and once they have eaten this Food of the Dead, which is often RED in colour, they can never return to the living world. In ancient Egyptian mythology, the goddess Amenti was associated with the Land of the West, or underworld. She welcomed all deceased people to her land with bread and water. If they ate and drank, they could not return to the land of the living. The Greek goddess Persephone was bound to remain in the underworld after eating six seeds from a red pomegranate there. In Celtic folklore red food, such as ROWAN berries and FLY AGARIC mushrooms, was the food of the dead and was forbidden to mankind. The Moari fairies the PATU-PAIAREHE also eat red fruits which are taboo to humans.

FAIRY GODFATHERS or **Three Ursitory** appear three days after a child's birth to determine its destiny, according to Romany gypsy folklore.

FAIRY GODMOTHERS feature in many tales, appearing at the birth of a child to predict its future or bestow gifts upon it. Everyone knows the stories of Snow White and Cinderella. Fairies of this type include the FATA ('Fate'), the BÉFIND, HULDA, RODJENICE, SUDICE, DÍSIR, RÓZANICA, HATHORS, ROZANICE, URISNICI, NARÜCNICI, ROD, UDELNICY, SUDZENICI, ORISNICI, and SOJENICE, most of which dress in ˇWHITE and appear THREE days after the birth of a child to bless or curse it, according to the behaviour of its family. They will foretell its future, give advice and possibly favour the child with birthmarks. The house must be prepared for their arrival by being cleaned and thoroughly swept. The table must be laid with honey, bread and three white almonds. In parts of Greece water, coins and gifts are placed beside the food. The door should be left open and a light should be left burning. The house should be kept quiet. Once the fairy has appeared and the fate told, it cannot be changed.

These fairies also appear at marriages, and girls who want the help of the Fairy Godmothers make pilgrimages to CAVES, leaving offerings of cakes and honey. The fairies are then invited to the resulting weddings and honey glazed almonds are distributed to the guests in their honour. The fairies appear once more at death, to take the soul out of the world.

Possibly, these fairy godmothers are derived from folk memories of ancient weaver goddesses who spin, measure and cut short the lives of mortals such as the Greek Moerae or Fates, and the Scandinavian NORNS. *See also* SPINNING.

FAIRY GRIM is mentioned in *The Life of Robin Goodfellow* (1628). Grim is a common name of English fairies. Grim or Grimr was a title of the Scandinavian god Odin, meaning 'hooded' or 'masked' as the god was often known to go about in disguise among mortals. *See also* GRIM and HOOD.

FAIRY HART or **Fairy Hind** occurs in many stories to mark the beginning of a quest. The white hart often symbolises the pursuer's own soul, and the chase his quest for spiritual knowledge. A hart led King ARTHUR through a CAVE to MORGAN LE FAY'S palace, where he was shown the heavens and the earth. In another old tale from Somerset the Lord of Kilmersdon was distressed when a plague troubled his subjects. Riding homewards one MAY EVE he chanced to see the white fairy hart that dwelled in the forest among the other DEER. He followed it for a mile until it vanished. With it went all his care and dismay and he suddenly felt a great joy. In gratitude, he built the Lady Chapel at Kilmersdon Church.

FAIRY ISLANDS are enchanted lands inhabited by the fairy folk. They include AVALON, Emain Ablach, the Isles of the Blest, Lochlann, the Green Meadows of Enchantment, Ynis Gwydrin and HY BRASIL. Though humans have sometimes visited them, they are notoriously difficult to get to. Some are only seen in certain conditions, while some float and others are usually submerged. King ARTHUR, voyaging in his ship Prydwen, visited many such islands, as did the Irish saint Brendan. One thing is certain; if any IRON or steel is brought onto one of these islands it must stay put and cannot disappear or sink beneath the waves. A human visitor should remove nothing from a fairy island, as this will mortally offend the fairies.

FAIRY LAMB is a lucky fairy beast that occasionally appeared among flocks on the ISLE OF MAN. Its fleece was partially or completely RED. However, it had to be treated with caution. One lady saw a strange little lamb with a red saddle and a red bridle. She reached out to touch it but it sprang up and disappeared, which was as well, for if she had touched it she would have developed a paralysed or withered arm.[93]

FAIRY LANTERNS is another English term for the WILL O'THE WISP.

FAIRY LOVERS often seduce mortal men and women. The fairies can assume any form they like and may appear at village festivities as tall, dark, noble looking men to charm young girls, taking them as dancing partners. Afterwards the girl will move with a special fairy grace and then fade and die, and everyone knows that her soul has been carried away to TIR NAN OG where she will become the bride of a fairy king. If a man is tempted to kiss a young female fairy in the dance he is lost forever, and can never leave fairyland. *See also* FAIRY SWEETHEART.

FAIRY MARKETS are held all over Britain and Ireland, the most famous of which is at Pitminster in Somerset, in south west England.

Humans have occasionally visited these emporia. A man in the seventeenth century was riding by Blackdown in Somerset, England, when he saw a fairy market on the hillside. According to his description, the fairies were only slightly smaller that human beings, dressed in red, blue and green and wore high crowned hats. When he approached them, they disappeared. When he rode off, they became visible again.[94]

Ruth Tongue also recounted the tale of a man whose grandfather saw a fairy market in 1856.[95]

In Ireland the Fairy Market is called 'The Fair of the Dead' and is held on All Hallows Eve and it is sometimes the DEAD and sometimes the fairies that hold the market, though they are often confused as one and the same. The fair is crowded with fairies drinking red wine from little cups, eating and listening to the music of pipers and harpers.

FAIRY MARRIAGES are mentioned in many tales, and there are many anecdotes of humans who have married or become the lovers of fairies. These relationships always have conditions and taboos imposed on them, such as the fairy should never be struck or touched with IRON, or seen on a certain day. Should the fairy spouse leave for any reason, usually because of the breaking of a taboo, then the human partner will pine away and die. See MELUSINE, LADY RAGNALL, LLYN Y FAN FACH, PRESSINA, PENELOP, NIWAREKA, UNDINE and WILLOW.

One human who married a fairy was Kirwan of Castle Hackett, the great Connaught chief. A Fairy King asked his help against a hostile fairy tribe that had invaded his territories. This was granted and men and fairies together plunged into the lake and defeated the enemy. The Connaught men were rewarded with presents of gold and silver while Kirwan received a fairy bride. All of his female descendants were noted for their unearthly beauty.

FAIRY MISCHIEF was once said to be the cause of a number of diseases and disasters. Fairies used ELF BOLTS to cause harm, propelling them into humans or livestock. Deaths were attributed to them and it was thought they could induce paralysis; the origin of the word 'stroke' for paralysis is derived from 'elf-stroke'.

In addition, there are several other ills and mischief that were once attributed to fairy attentions: In Norway people fear the elf wind or *alvgest* which is the breath of elves and which covers the body of a person with blisters. Paralysis is often caused by the invisible presence of a FAIRY MARKET. Cramps are a punishment for annoying the fairies. Tuberculosis is caused by eating fairy food or by visiting a fairy hill at night. Fairies inflict impetigo and lice. Infantile paralysis indicates that the baby is a CHANGELING. Rheumatism, cramps and bruising are a punishment for annoying the fairies. If a child is left alone the fairies will appear and give its limbs a twist, causing childhood deformities. Fairies tangle human hair or horses' manes, causing elflocks. English fairies can steal your shadow, which will eventually cause you to fade away and die.

Some fairies are known to be thieves, but when they take something they take only its substance or spirit, so when a cow is elf-taken it appears to be struck down by some disease. It will lie down and refuse to get up. Though it will continue to eat, it will produce no milk. When it dies its flesh will turn out to be a stock of alder wood or some such rubbish. Fairies can also steal the spirit of the land itself. When this happens the fields appear to yield a crop but the ears of corn will not fill out, the harvest will be slender and the animal fodder without nourishment.

However, fairies can only take away what selfish humans deserve to lose. If you 'over look a child' (i.e. look on it with envy) then the fairies have it in their power. When people become miserly and refuse to share their possessions or do not value them, the fairies will take the goodness out of them. When a farmer grumbles about his crop, even if it is good, the fairies will take the substance out of it. When you mislay something and can't find it, no matter how hard you look, it is almost certain that the fairies have taken it.

FAIRY MUSIC is low and unbearably sweet, 'like that of the great PAN by the river'.[96] If you put your ear to a fairy MOUND, you may be able to hear the unearthly strains of lovely music, but be careful, you may be drawn into the earth and bound to live with the fairies forever.

Sometimes mortals are not drawn down into the earth, but one who has heard the fairy music will never be the same again. The spell remains on them, and they are haunted by the music until they die. They always have a dreamy look, for the fairy music is melancholy, a fatal charm for mortal ears. One man who heard the fairy music, when he fell asleep on a RATH, was haunted by the melody day and night until he grew mad and had no pleasure in life. He longed to be with the fairies again and hear them sing. He threw himself from a cliff into the lake near the fairy rath and so died.

Many young girls have been drawn away by the music and have danced all night with the fairies, though they are found fast asleep in bed in the morning. They remember all they have seen, and while they were with the fairies they learned the secrets of love potions, spells and charms.

It is dangerous for a young girl to sing when she is alone by a lake, for the fairies will draw her down to sing in the fairy palaces and she will be seen no more. Yet sometimes, when the moonlight is on the water and the waves break against the crystal columns of the fairy palace, you can hear her voice and know she is singing to the fairies.

However, some of the ancient poets and bards, like the famed Carolan, learned their craft by sleeping on fairy hills and mounds, allowing the magical music to enter their hearts and souls as they slept. Many old Irish tunes such as *The Pretty Girl Milking the Cow* and *The Londonderry Air* are fairy songs. It is unwise to sing or whistle such tunes near a fairy mound, as the fairies don't like to hear their music on mortal lips.

FAIRY OINTMENT is applied to the eyes of newborn fairy babies to enable them to see the invisible. In some cases, human MIDWIVES are called upon to perform this task. There are several instances of these women accidentally getting some of the ointment in their own eyes and afterwards being able to see the fairies coming and going. However, should the fairies discover this they will put out the woman's eyes with a rush or stick. Naturally, the ingredients of the ointment are secret, but probably include FOUR LEAFED CLOVER, WILD THYME and MUSHROOMS. One of the earliest tales, related in *Otia Imperialia* by Gervase of Tilbury (13th century CE), mentions eel fat.

FAIRY RADES occur in Scotland. During the Middle Ages, fairy aristocrats were thought to be human sized and very beautiful. They passed their time hunting, hawking, and feasting. Stories are told of the Fairy Rade (ride) when they rode in procession behind their king and queen, mounted on white horses hung with silver bells. One description comes from an old woman of Dumfriesshire in the early 1800s. 'A beam of light was dancing over them, more bonnie than moonshine. They were wee, wee folks with green scarves on. They rode on braw wee white nags with uncommonly long swooping tails and manes hung with whistles that the wind played on. This and their tongues when they sang was like the sound of a far away psalm'.[97]
The last Fairy Rade was witnessed at the beginning of the nineteenth

century by a herd boy and his sister at a hamlet near Glen Eathie. A procession of dwarfish strangers rode by and the boy asked them who they were and where they were going. The leader replied: 'Not of the race of Adam. The People of Peace shall never more be seen in Scotland'.[98]
The rades usually took place on HALLOWEEN when various spirits, GHOSTS and WITCHES are said to stir.

FAIRY RIDDEN is a frequent description of stolen beasts. Fairies and WITCHES like to steal HORSES at night and take them on wild rides across the countryside, returning them in the morning completely exhausted, with their manes in ELF-KNOTS. When the owner finds his worn out beast in the morning, he knows it has been 'fairy ridden'.

FAIRY RING is a place where fairies have been observed DANCING, making merry within a magical circle. This might be a prehistoric stone monument, a brighter green ring on the grass, or a circle of FAIRY RING MUSHROOMS. Shakespeare mentions fairy rings as 'orbs on the green' in Shakespeare's *A Midsummer Night's Dream*.
If humans join the fairies in their revels they become invisible to their companions outside the ring and may

find that it is impossible to leave, and be forced to dance until they collapse and die of exhaustion. Others may find that an evening spent in a fairy ring turns out to be many years in the human realm, and that when they return home their families and homes are no more. If someone sees an empty fairy ring and jumps into it, they will die young.

FAIRY RING MUSHROOMS (*Marasmius oreades*) are rings of mushrooms which appear on lawns and in meadows leaving a circular bare patch, or later in the year, a brighter patch of grass. They are said to be a favourite DANCING place of the fairies. It is now thought that some of these rings are very ancient indeed, some being as many as 600 years old.

FAIRY SWEETHEARTS are fairy women who sometimes become the lovers of human men. However, while some marry and make their mortal husbands happy, other fairy females exact a heavy price from their lovers, drawing away their life force. While she grows brighter and stronger, he wastes away and eventually dies. See FRAU WELT, LHIANNAN SHEE, NULIARKSAK and ORIANDE.

FAIRY TREES are the most usual place to find fairies is in the forest. They are closely connected to trees, either living in hollow trees or clearings, or manifesting as the spirits of the trees themselves. The particular trees associated with fairies varies in different parts of the world, but in most of western Europe they are the HAWTHORN, HAZEL, WILLOW, ELDER, HOLLY, BIRCH, OAK, ASH, ELM and ROWAN.
The ancient, primeval wildwood is dark and atmospheric, an untamed realm of Nature, untouched by man. It doesn't take much imagination to feel it to be the province of unearthly beings. It is deep in the forest that the hero meets the WHITE HART or the QUESTING BEAST, or encounters the lovely WHITE LADY by the fountain.

WITCHES like BABA YAGA dwell hidden in the forest, while in the clearings ELVES, fairies and PUCKS frolic. The frightening WOODWOSE and WILD MAN lurk in the undergrowth, outlaws such as ROBIN HOOD prowl, the WILD HUNT pursues its prey, and any minute supernatural ARROWS may fly through the trees. In Germany there are MOSS MAIDENS and WILD WOMEN and in Arabia the DJINN. In Greek and Roman forests, there are SATYRS, CENTAURS and CYCLOPS, PANS and DRYADS, HAMADRYADS and SILENI.

Much of the world's landmass was once covered in forest. Trees dominated the landscape, living inconceivable ages beyond the life of a single man. Deciduous trees were renewed each spring, while evergreens remained unchanging, even in the death-time of winter. Trees were widely venerated among early people and believed to embody the spirit of a god or goddess, or that of a vegetation or nature spirit. Trees were also oracles, the deity speaking through the whispering of the leaves. The tree itself was an *axis mundi*, the roots extending into the UNDERWORLD of the DEAD, tapping the ancestral wisdom there, and the branches extending into the realms of the sky gods, with the trunk connecting them to Middle Earth.

The ancient Chaldeans and Assyrians venerated the pomegranate and the cypress. The ancient Germans and Celts worshipped in oak groves. In Persian mythology, the cypress was the sacred symbol of the god Ahura Mazda. In India, Buddha was incarnated as a tree spirit forty three times before receiving enlightenment under a boab tree. In ancient Greece the goddess Artemis was associated with the cedar, the hazel and the willow, while the laurel was sacred to Apollo. Zeus/Jupiter was associated with the kingly oak. Several deities were imprisoned in trees, for example Attis and Osiris in the pine and Myrrha in the myrrh. At the festival of Dionysus

anyone with a tree in the garden adorned it to represent the god.[99]

At Christmas, we still honour the vegetation or evergreen tree fairy by decking the Christmas tree with lights and placing the fairy's winged image on the top. To this day in Britain and Ireland, some special trees, especially those near holy wells and springs, are hung with gifts or rags to solicit blessings or healing from their spirits.

FAIRY WATER is prepared by the fairies themselves, and enables a person to see fairies when they are present. It is similar in use and purpose to FAIRY OINTMENT.

FAIRY WIVEs are beautiful but troublesome. There are numerous anecdotes of human men who have married fairies. These are often LAKE MAIDENS who emerge from their underwater homes, dowered with COWS, to marry a human love. Such relationships always have conditions and taboos imposed on them, such as the fairy should never be struck or touched with IRON, or seen on a certain day. Should the fairy lover leave for any reason, usually because of the breaking of a taboo, then the human spouse will pine away and die.

Some marriages with fairies work out well. In the Orkneys Magnus O'Kierfea took a fairy bride in addition to his own mortal wife. On festival nights such as HALLOWEEN, Christmas and New Year's Eve he would be sure to set a place for her and the food would always be gone in the morning. With her aid he became a famous healer and they had three daughters.

FAIRYLAND or Fairy Land coexists with our own. There are tales of humans who have accidentally stumbled into it through entering a FAIRY RING, a FAIRY MOUND, walking through the mysterious MIST GATE or stepping onto a FAIRY ISLAND. In Wales there is a certain piece of turf, which if you step on it, will afford you a glimpse of fairyland,

though the turf can never be found twice by the same person.

In fairyland, the fairies spend their time feasting, dancing and making merry to the accompaniment of their skilled bards and musicians. Those humans who have visited fairyland, such as THOMAS THE RHYMER, join in with the revels and are honoured by their fairy hosts. However, visits to fairyland are fraught with danger. Time flows differently there, and humans who think they have passed a single year with the fairies may return to their homes to find them ruined by time, and their friends and relatives aged or long dead and buried. Any person who eats FAIRY FOOD will either be unable to leave fairyland, or will pine away with a longing to return to it.

Western concepts of fairyland seem to have derived from Celtic notions of the OTHERWORLD, the place of the gods and the DEAD which coexists with our own realm and which living humans sometimes gain access to. The Celtic Otherworld is a place of eternal feasting and drinking, music and dancing.

Some early writers located fairyland in the air. John Davies told Evans Wentz: 'They throng the air, and darken heaven, and rule this lower world. It is only twenty-one miles from this world to the first heaven'.[100]

FALLEN ANGELS who were cast out of heaven for their pride became fairies, according to Irish and Scottish folklore.[101] Some fell to earth and lived there long before man, as the first false gods of the earth. Others fell to the sea where they became MERMAIDS, SELKIES and other water spirits. Others were pure evil and fell to hell, where they are ruled by the DEVIL and tempt humankind with their GLAMOUR. They teach WITCHES how to make potions and cast spells. One fairy asked a man if she could be saved and he replied 'Yes, if she could say "our father who art in heaven" ' but she could only say 'our father who wert in heaven' indicating her allegiance was to Satan.

According to an Icelandic tale, those angels who neither supported nor opposed the devil when he was driven out of heaven were also cast out, but not to hell. They fell to the earth and were commanded to dwell in the rocks and mountains, becoming the ELVES and hidden people. They have no bodies but can appear in human form when they wish.[102]

It is said that a great Irish fairy chief asked St. Columb-Kille if there was any hope that they would one day be restored to heaven as angels. The saint replied that there was none, as God had fixed their doom. On Judgement Day, they would pass through death into total annihilation. At this the fairy chief fell into a great melancholy and sailed away from Ireland with all his court. They returned to their native Armenia to await the fateful day.

FAMILIARS are guardian spirits which accompany a person through life. One may manifest as a person or an animal. During the witch trials in Britain fairies were believed to be the familiars of WITCHES or it was thought that they worked together. James Walsh, a Dorset witch convicted in Exeter in 1566, admitted he learned how to bewitch people from fairies. Some fairies are said to be personal familiars such as the FYLGIAR, HALTIA, LEANAN SIDHE, OBERYCOM, LARS FAMILIARIS, PUCK-HAIRY, BAJANG and BAKRU. *See also* CO-WALKER.

FANE is an Ayrshire word for the fairies.

FANETTEN are French and German WATER FAIRIES of the Rhone Valley. They appear as lovely young women with golden hair, though there is always something wet and dripping about them.

FÄNGGEN or **FANGG** are female GIANTs who accompany the small and gentle FÄNKENMANNIKIN. They are bloodthirsty woodland spirits.
FÄNKENMANNIKIN is a small Swiss fairy, hairy and usually naked, though he will wear rough bark and furs when the weather is very cold. Fänkenmannikins are about 90 cm tall (around three feet) and have very acute hearing. They live in eastern Switzerland and the northern Tyrol, roaming the high meadows and taking great interest in mountain dairies. They live on chamois milk and can change leaves into gold. They can control all the winds except the hot, dry Föhn. When it blows, they hide in their CAVES. If you want to get rid of a Fänkenmannikin just give him a pair of shoes or suit of CLOTHES and he will disappear forever. Their female companions are GIANTs called FÄNGGEN.

FANTINE are kindly Swiss fairies of the Vaud valleys who bring good weather to farmers and who invented the device of putting bells on cattle to prevent them getting lost.

FAREFOLKIS is a Scottish name for the 'Fair Folk' or fairies. Some say this should really be Faring Folk derived from the Anglo-Saxon *faran*, 'to travel' because the fairies roam about at night and dance on the greensward.

FARFARELLI ('Little Butterflies') is Dante's name for the FOLLETTI, Italian fairies who, like BUTTERFLIES, are never still.

FARISEES is an English term in Somerset and Suffolk for the fairies. It is a contraction of the dialect double plural 'fairies-seez'. An alternative spelling is pharisees.

FARVANN is a fairy DOG of Scottish folklore. It bays THREE times when it is hunting, with a pause between each bay.

FATA (*pl.* **Fatae** or 'Fates') is a generic Italian term for a fairy or WHITE LADY; some are good and some are bad. They live in CAVES, rocks, springs and grottoes and are usually seen at noon, when they are at their most powerful. They are derived from the classical goddesses the FATES who determined the destiny of each human life. In Romance tradition, these multiplied and became a race of fairies. The Fatae appear soon after the birth of a child, as FAIRY GODMOTHERS, to bless or curse it, according to the behaviour of the family. They reward people who treat them well when they encounter them in the forest, and punish those who treat them ill. They are SHAPESHIFTERS and can appear in human or animal form. Every five years they have to travel to the Himalayas to appear at the temple of the DEMOGORGON. The Fatae sometimes appear as SNAKES.

FATA AQUILINA is one of the Italian FATA, a lovely NYMPH who dresses in WHITE.

FATA MORGANA is a famous Italian WATER FAIRY who can sometimes be glimpsed in the Straits of Messina. The phrase refers to a mirage that can sometimes be seen in the straits, an effect called in French *le château de Morgan le Fée*, since towers, houses and even whole towns are sometimes seen. *See also* MORGANA LE FAY.

FATA SIBIANA is one of the Italian FATA, a lovely nymph who is kind to her favourites, but cruel to those who offend her.

FATES are the trio in Greek myth, the THREE *Moerae*, who control human destiny. They are always clothed in WHITE. Their Greek name means 'phase' as in the phases of the MOON and they are in fact a manifestation of the triple moon goddess, the spinner and measurer of time (see SPINNING). The thread of life is spun on Clotho's spindle, measured by the rod of Lachesis and snipped by Atropos' shears. In stature, Atropos was the smallest of the three, but by far the most feared, relating as she does to the HAG of winter, the death goddess 'she who cannot be stayed'.

Prayers and pleas would not move them and even the gods could not alter the decrees of the Fates.

The Latin word *fatum* or fate referred to a pronouncement of destiny, a spoken sentence of doom fixed by the gods at birth. The word 'fairy' is probably derived from the Latin for fate *fata*, via the Old French *fée*. Shakespeare speaks of them as 'the Wyrde Systres' (*Macbeth*), a term derived from the Anglo Saxon *wyrd*, meaning fate, destiny, or the power that controls them. Wyrd Sisters is a term applied to the NORNS, another trio of fate goddesses. It is possible that The Fates were the original FAIRY GODMOTHERS; they were believed to assist at the birth of certain (if not all) humans. Long after the coming of Christianity, mothers would make ready for them when a baby was due, spreading out food and gifts to ensure their favour for the child. Just as the fairies were called 'good people' in supplication, the Fates were titled *Parcae*, or 'merciful'. Belief in them survived in parts of Greece well into the twentieth century.

FATHER CHRISTMAS or **Santa Claus** is a very special fairy that appears only once a year. Today he is usually portrayed in a RED and WHITE costume, though in the past this varied. The story that he wears red and white as the result of a Coca-Cola promotion is an urban myth and it is more likely that, like the RED CAPS of other fairies, his costume associates him with the FLY AGARIC mushroom. Like the northern shaman, he enters the house via the smoke hole or chimney, or perhaps, like other fairies and spirits, his method of entrance and egress is via the HEARTH.

It is usually claimed that he originated with St Nicholas, a fourth century bishop who saved three sisters from prostitution by leaving bags of gold in their stockings, which were hung up to dry. However, he has origins that are far more ancient. It is possible that he devolved from the

FATE

Scandinavian/Germanic god Odin or Woden, who rode the skies at YULE wearing a red, bloody, flayed animal skin, punishing the wicked and rewarding the good. It seems likely that he passed into English folklore, traceable in the character who appears as master of ceremonies in the mumming plays, and as the King of Christmas. Perhaps the figure may be older still, originating in the druidic midwinter festivities and the Roman Saturnalia. In European legends he rides a GOAT (Capricorn, the house in which the winter solstice falls) or a donkey, the latter a Saturnalian beast sacrificed with a holly club at the solstice.

In Britain, he is Father Christmas; in Germany and Austria Weihnachtman; and in southern Germany Kris Kringle. In France, he is Pere Noel, who dresses in red and arrives on a white horse to give out presents the night before Christmas. He is accompanied by Pere Fouettard ('Father Spanker') who punishes the naughty children. In Brazil he is called Papa Noel and children leave shoes out in the street to be filled with sweets and presents. In China, a similar character is called Dun Che Loa and children leave out stockings for him to fill. In Switzerland Samichlaus, dressed in a red robe, delivers presents to boys, while his wife Lucy, wearing a silk dress and cap, takes presents to girls. Some believe an angel, driving a sleigh drawn by reindeer, help out the couple. In Germany, he is also known as Pelze Nicol ('Furry Nicholas' from his fur costume), who is titled *Schrimmerlreiter* 'Rider of the White Horse' one of the titles of Odin. This character may be cognate with Belznickel who travels around at Christmas giving out both gifts and punishment, throwing sweets and presents in the air and smacking the naughty children as they bend over to retrieve them. He is also Aschen Klaus or 'Ash Nicholas' as he carries a sack full of ashes and a bunch of twigs. In some places, St Nicholas became merged with his helper KNECHT RUPRECHT to become Ru Klaus or 'rough Nicholas' from his shaggy appearance. St Nicholas is accompanied by various helpers such as Black Peter, Knecht Ruprecht and the Christkindl who hand out presents. He entered America with the Dutch Sinterklaas, Anglicised into Santa Claus.

FATHER FROST is the soul of winter in Russia, his icy embrace bringing death to helpless travellers. He leaps from tree to tree, snapping his fingers, causing them to be covered with frost. He is a SMITH, binding water and earth together with heavy chains. In one story he was impressed by the fact that, though his cold was nearly killing her, a girl was too polite to mention it. He spared her life. On New Year's Day he and his daughter drive their reindeer sleigh through Russia, rewarding good children with presents.

FATHER TIME is the spirit of the old year, portrayed as an old man clad in a long robe, carrying an hourglass and scythe. As the New Year strikes, he gives way to the New Year Child, who grows into a new Father Time as the year progresses. He may be associated with Saturn (or Greek Cronos 'time') whose festival was celebrated at the Winter Solstice.

FAULA or Fauna is the Roman spirit of the wildwood, the female counterpart of FAUNUS.

FAUN (*pl.* **Fauni**) is the gentler classical Roman equivalent of the SATYR. Fauns are mischievous woodland fairies with the heads and torsos of handsome young men, the legs of GOATS (or some say DEER) and small horns on their foreheads. They may be seen dancing with NYMPHS in woodland glades, playing a type of flute called a *shawn*. Fauns are the companions of the god of nature FAUNUS and are the guardians of the fields and forests. The Italian fairies the FOLETTI are said to be descended from fauns. Compare with PUCK, ROBIN GOODFELLOW, PAN, SATYRS.

FAUNAE or **Fatuae** are the female FAUNI. The mating of a male and female faun produces an INCUBUS.

FAUNI FICARII are bloodthirsty Sicilian fairies that frequent the neighbourhood of fig trees. The fig is unlucky because it is the tree on which Judas hanged himself and figs have never flowered since. Each leaf is said to harbour an evil fairy. It is imprudent for a man to rest beneath the shade of a fig tree, since a female fairy will appear with a knife in her hand asking him whether he will take the knife by the handle or the blade. If he says the blade she will kill him, if he says the handle, he will have luck in all he undertakes.

FAUNUS is a Roman nature spirit and patron of the fields and shepherds. He prophesies through the whispering of the wind in the trees. He is the leader of the FAUNI, and may be compared with the Greek PAN. Like many nature spirits he is half man, half GOAT in appearance. His female counterpart is called Fauna or Faula. Some say that there was originally a race of fauns who coalesced into one being called Faunus, others that the god came first and was multiplied into a race of fauns. Compare with PUCK, ROBIN GOODFELLOW, PAN and SATYRS.

FAY is an early word for FAIRY, derived from FATAE, the THREE Fates of the Romans. 'Fay' was originally the word for the being, while 'fairy' meant enchantment by a fay.

FAYETTES are French fairies who like to turn themselves into moles.

FAYLINN is a fairy realm in Irish folklore, ruled by King Iubdan and Queen Bebo.

FAYULES is another name for the French FÉE.

FEADH-REE is an Irish term for the fairies.

FEAR DEARG ('Red Man') is a Munster HOUSE FAIRY. He is around 75 cm tall (two-and-a-half feet), wears a RED CAP and a long, scarlet coat, has long grey hair and a wrinkled face. He is fond of playing pranks and likes to enter human homes to warm himself by the fire - it is unwise to refuse him.[103]

FEAR DORCHA ('Dark Man') summons mortals to the presence of the Fairy Queen. If the human should betray her secrets, the Dark Man will punish him by sending him blind or lame. In WITCH lore, the Dark Man is the protector of the

FAUNUS

coven who summons witches to the rite, or the term is sometimes used to denote the witches' god. During the witch trials, the Dark Man was said to be the DEVIL.

FÉAR GORTACH ('Hungry Grass') is enchanted fairy grass. If anyone should step on it they will immediately be consumed by a terrible, insatiable hunger which will be fatal unless they are lucky enough to have some food about them.

FEAR LIATH ('Grey Man') is an Irish fairy who appears surrounded by fog.

FEAR LIATH MOR ('Big Grey Man') or **The Grey Man of Macdui** is a large,

grey figure that haunts the Cairngorm Mountains. He is 3 metres tall (ten feet), has a dark complexion, and wears a black top hat. He skulks near a cairn to frighten climbers and walkers, sometimes chasing them for miles. He is more often sensed than seen, and those who have encountered him report ghostly footsteps, a sudden chill, and a high humming sound, a feeling of lethargy or despair, and even suicidal thoughts. The last reported sighting of the Grey Man was in 1950.

FEAR SIDHE or **Fir Sidhe** or **Far Shee** ('Man Fairy') is a generic term for male fairies in Irish Gaelic.

FEAR SIDHEAN ('Fairy Men') is a Scottish Highland term for fairy men.

FEAR-GORTA ('Man of Hunger') is an emaciated phantom who goes about Ireland during times of famine, begging alms and rewarding the giver.[104]

FEATHAG are Manx fairies that inhabit ELDER trees. They gather to mourn for their friends who have been cut down, and can be heard moaning and roaring in the wind. Once a fight broke out at their gathering in Balla Koig, and the next morning the townspeople found hundreds of fairy thumbs on the ground.

FÉE are fairies of France, the Alps and the Pyrenees. They are small and lovely but can turn themselves into trees, moss and stones, or simply become invisible. In the forest near Rennes they appear as magpies. Most of them are female, dress in WHITE linen and have long blond hair. Though they are young and beautiful, they always have some defect, like duck's FEET, a tail, or a hairy body. Others are HAGS with long teeth, with backs covered with seaweed and mussels. Local people believe that the fée are the oldest living creatures on the earth, born at the beginning of time. Some live in MOUNDS, dolmens and CAVES, while others inhabit the woods and forests caring for the plants and animals. Others erected dolmens on the plains, while those that live in the mountains control avalanches. Some fée travel on the wind or cloak themselves in fog. The storm fairies are dressed in the colours of the rainbow, and pass along following a lovely fairy who is mounted in a boat made from a nautilus and drawn by two sea crabs.

Sometimes they wash their clothes in springs and put them out to dry on Neolithic monuments. They are very proud of their white linen, and any disturbance of wash day chores will annoy them. At night they may borrow utensils or horses from a farmer, but will always return them unharmed by morning; any house they visit will be lucky thereafter.

The fée dance in FAIRY RINGS in the moonlight and should a human be foolish enough to try to join them he will be whirled about until he is exhausted, then flung up high into the air. Any man who loves a female fée may be killed by the ferocity of her lovemaking. If you lock stares with a fée, you are in danger of being drawn into an abyss. Queen ABUNDIA or Habundia rules them. It was widely rumoured that all the fée disappeared in the nineteenth century, but would return in the twentieth, when they would be more appreciated.

FÉE DES VERTIGES ('Fairies of the Mountain') are French fairies who appear as a flame, flitting about the mountains.

FEEORIN is a Lancashire collective noun for small GREEN fairies with RED CAPS and green skin. They like music and dancing and have sometimes helped humans.

FÉES DES HOULES ('Fairies of the Billows') are Brittany sea fairies who live in natural CAVES and grottoes. They are associated with the FIONS.

FEET may give away a fairy's identity. While many fairies can appear in human form in some cases this does not extend to their feet, which may be hoofed, webbed, clawed, backwards or even completely absent. Some fairies wear long smocks or dresses to try to cover this DEFORMITY.

A large number of fairies have cloven hoofs like those of GOATS. These include ROBIN GOODFELLOW, PUCK, NERIEDS, LESHIE, PANS, PILOSI, FAUNS, SATYRS, CATIZ, BAGINIS, BOABHAN SITH, CALLICANTZAROS, KORREDS and DIALEN. Others have bird feet, like the crow feet of the SLEIGH BEGGY, while the DAMES BLANCHE, DWARFS and ERDLUITLE have duck feet. Fairies of the nasty sort, including RASKAS, VETÀLA, CHUREL, CURUPIRA and the BUNYIP often

have backward-facing feet. KOBOLDS have feet for hands, while the PRANA DWARFS and the BAKEMONO have no feet at all.

According to Irish folklore, water in which human feet have been washed gives fairies the power of entry into a house. If fairies are trying to trick you or plague you, put your shoes on the wrong feet, and this will confuse them so that they leave you alone long enough to make your escape.

Feet are often important in myth. Feet are the parts of the body in touch with the earth and in ancient tradition the body receives energy from the earth this way. It was thought that the feet could show the nature of a person. Heroes such as Herakles and Achilles were identified by their feet.

FÉETAUDS are the male FÉE.

FEITHLINN was a fairy prophetess who appeared to the ancient Irish queen MEDB of Connaught on the eve of a battle. The lovely Feithlinn had skin as white as snow, her lips were as red as the rowanberry and her golden hair swept the ground. She wore a green robe clasped with a golden pin and a gold fillet upon her head. Seven gold braids for the dead were in her hand. Her voice was as sweet as the golden harp strings. She told the queen

that she was the prophetess of the RATH of Cruachan and foresaw bloodshed, power and defeat. The queen replied that her scouts had informed her that her army was both strong and well prepared. The fairy persisted 'I see bloodshed, I see victory!' The queen retorted that her enemies were afraid and she had nothing to fear from the Ultonians. The prophetess repeated that she saw bloodshed, conquest and death. The queen grew angry and exclaimed that the prophecy could not possibly apply to her. 'Be it thine and on thy own head' said the fairy and disappeared. Some time afterwards her own kinsman at Lough Rea murdered MEDB by the river Shannon to avenge the aid she had given the king of Ulster.[105]

FENNEL or **Finnen** is an Irish fairy who lives in a mound called Knock Fennel (Cnoc Finnine). Her name is derived from Finnen or Finnine from *fin* meaning 'WHITE'. She is the sister of AINE.

FER FE is a shapeshifting Irish fairy, also called the Lough Gur dwarf, and is the owner of the lough. He is the son of Eogobal of the Hill of Eogabail and foster son of MANANNAN. He is rumoured to be the brother of Aine and a druid of the TUATHA DÉ DANAAN. Well into the twentieth century local people took care to speak well of him.

FERIERS is a term for fairies in Suffolk in eastern England.

FERISH is a later Manx term for fairies, a corruption of the English word. *See also* FERRISH

FERISHERS is an eastern English Suffolk term for fairies.

FERLIES is an English North Country expression for the fairies.

FERN is a favourite plant of the fairies on the moors of Cornwall in south-west England. One woman sat on a fern and a fairy man instantly appeared and forced her to remain for a year and a day in FAIRYLAND to look after his son.

The date of January 6th is the time to appeal to the ELDER fairy, HULDA, for help in obtaining MAGIC fern seed, which will give you the strength of thirty men. Spit on the ground THREE times, cut a branch of elder, and use it to draw a magic circle in a lonely place. Hulda will see that an unseen hand delivers a chalice, containing the seed.

FERRIES is an Orkney term for fairies. These creatures are handsomer and gentler than the TROWS.

FERRISH or **FERRISHYN** are Manx fairies sometimes called Farm Fairies or Harvesters, since they like to lend a hand on the land, though they are more usually HOUSE FAIRIES. Unfortunately, they are not very bright. They generally go naked and are covered with patches of coarse, brown hair. Conversely, others say that they are a beautiful, secretive race. The name is probably derived from the Gaelic *fear sidhean* or 'fairy men'.

FETCH is a fairy double found in England and Scotland. It appears in the likeness of a person, and should anyone meet his or her fetch, it is an

OMEN OF DEATH. It is harmless to anyone but its double. A fetch is sometimes called a CO-WALKER, or in German tradition a DÖPPELGANGER.

FETCH CANDLE is another name for the WILL O'THE WISP, in this case an OMEN OF DEATH.

FETCH LIGHT is another name for the WILL O'THE WISP, in this case an OMEN OF DEATH.

FÊTE is a Breton term for fairies, derived from the Latin *fata* or FATES. The fathers, husbands and children of the fairies are thus called *Faito* or *Faitaud*.

FEUX FOLLETS ('Foolish Fires') are the WILL O'THE WISPs of Quebec, Canada. They look like blue flames and try to lure travellers into bogs.

FEY is a Scottish word that relates to the old English word *faege* meaning fated or doomed to die. If someone was described as fey, they were on the point of death. A person might be described as fey if he decided on a course of action that others believed would lead to his death. Later the word came to mean enchanted or struck by an ELF BOLT. Now the word is applied to one who can see into the OTHERWORLD of the fairies.

FIACHRA is the King of the Irish western SEA FAIRIES.

FIAMMETTA are Italian WILL O'THE WISPs who lead the DEAD into the OTHERWORLD.

FIERY DRAKE is a ball of flame that leads Peak District miners to the richest ores. *See also* DRAKES, FIREDRAKE.

FIN FOLK, **Fin-Folk** or **Finfolk** are amphibian SEA FAIRIES who appear in Scotland, especially the Orkneys, while in Wales and Cornwall similar creatures are called Sea Gardeners or the Lady's

Own. They look human and they live underwater, where they make fabulous gardens. The Orkney islanders regard them with dread, as they are known to be a race of dark sorcerers. They have always avoided contact with humans, perhaps because they have fins that are only partly disguised by clothes. Their legends may have been confused with the human race of Finns, also widely believed to be sorcerers. MERMAIDS are the daughters of fin-men and fin-wives, and should a mermaid seduce a human, she will lose her tail but not her beauty, unlike fin-wives who will grow old and raddled. The fin-folk dwell in the city of Finfolkaheem under the sea during the winter, while their summer home is Eynhallow, Orkney's holy isle, which is said to vanish from time to time.

Like the TROWS they occasionally KIDNAP humans, taking them down to their realms to become the spouses of one of the fin-folk. Once the fin-folk stole the wife of a man of Evie. He vowed to be revenged and performed a ritual at the Odin Stone at Stenness. After many adventures he set foot on Eynhallow, but the fin-folk escaped into the sea. The men prevented their return to the island by cutting crosses on the turf and circling the island with NINE rings of SALT.

FINFINELLA is a female GREMLIN who, during World War II, tickled RAF fighter pilots and bombardiers just as they lined up their sights.

FINFOLKAHEEM is the under-sea city where the FIN FOLK dwell.

FINVARRA or **Finnbearra**, also **Fionnbharra** or **Fionnbharr** or **Fin Bheara** ('White-topped'), is the King of the DAOINE SIDHE of the west or Connacht living in CNOC Meadha, and is called the Fairy King of Ulster.[106] He keeps friendly relations with the best families of Galway, especially the Kirwans of Castle Hacket, who always leave out a keg of Spanish wine for him at night. In return, the wine cellars at the castle are never empty. His fairy abode is beneath Knockma Hill, and his name may be an adjective applied to the hill. He sometimes abducts mortal women and takes them there.

Finvarra may once have been a god of the DEAD or UNDERWORLD, with some functions as a VEGETATION SPIRIT since he is deemed to have the power of bringing good harvests.

FINZ-WEIBL, or **Finzweiberl**, is a spotted Bavarian fairy WOOD WIFE or MOSS MAIDEN who wears a broad brimmed hat.

FIOLES are French WILL O'THE WISPs.

FION are tiny Breton fairies from the area near Ille-et-Vilaine. Their swords are the size of PINS. This may be another name for the LUTINS.

FIONNGUALA was a SWAN MAIDEN, one of the CHILDREN OF LIR.

FIR BOLG ('People of the Bogs') were the leaders of the fourth invasion of

FINVARRA

Ireland. They divided Ireland into the five provinces and ruled until the invasion of the TUATHA DÉ DANAAN. They subsequently dwindled into the first race of Irish fairies, sometimes described as monstrous GIANTS, but usually as little folk around 90 cm tall (about three feet), dressed in peasant clothing, favouring red checks and plaids. They are stouter and darker than the SIDHE, the second race of Irish fairies who descended from the Tuatha dé Danaan. Fir Bolg live in the old earthworks or RATHS, each ruled by its own monarch. They hate IRON, Christian symbols and holy water. They often have one human parent and are said to be mortal, though long lived. When one grows old his companions might swap him for a human being, popping him into the human's bed or cot as a CHANGELING, and kidnapping the human to serve them.

FIR CLIS or **Fir Chlis** ('Fallen Men') are Scottish fairies associated with the Northern Lights or Aurora Borealis, and are called the Nimble Men or Merry Dancers. They fight with the evil fairies the SLUAGH for the possession of a fairy lady. The red sky

beneath the northern lights is the 'pool of blood' from their battles. The blood falls to earth and solidifies into the *Fuil Siochaire* or bloodstones found in the Hebrides. Some say that the Fir Clis are FALLEN ANGELS.[107]

FIR DARRIG, Far Darrig, Fear Darrig or **Fir Dhearga** ('Red Man') is an unpleasant, ugly, fat Irish fairy with a rat-like appearance complete with long snout and tail, and dark, hairy skin. He wears raggedy old clothes and carries a shillelagh topped with a skull. These creatures live on the carrion found in the marshes near the coast and sometimes cause NIGHTMARES.

Conversely, according to W.B. Yeats, the Fir Darrig plays gruesome practical jokes, and appears as a man in a red coat and RED CAP.[108] According to Croker he is a little old man 75 cm tall, (two and a half feet), with a long red cloak and a red hat who likes to sit by the fire.

FIR DEA ('Men of the God' or 'Divine Men') is a Gaelic term for the TUATHA DÉ DANAAN.

FIRE can destroy all evil fairy MAGIC. In Ireland a threatened child, COW,

woman, house, or man was placed in a protective ring of fire. Burning embers were thrown into the water in which FEET had been washed to take away its power to admit fairies to the house at night. Candles or embers were carried around laying-in women (women in bed following childbirth) and around babies before they were christened to protect them from the attentions of fairy kidnappers. FAIRY DOCTORS would cure a FAIRY-STRUCK cow by passing a red-hot turf THREE times over and under its body. According to Lady Wilde, if fairies are seen coming through the door, burning embers should be thrown at them to scare them away. Such measures are unlikely to work against fairies which are part fire themselves, such as SALAMANDERS, the Arabian DJINN, WILL O'THE WISPS, or FIRE DRAKES.

FIRE DRAKES are DRAGON-like creatures with sinuous necks, bat wings, and massive jaws in Celtic and Germanic folklore. They cannot see well but have a good sense of smell. They are cunning and malicious, breathe fire from their mouths and guard TREASURE.

FIREPLACE FOLLETTI are Italian fairies who live in the HEARTH and fix young brides with their hypnotic stares, making them dissatisfied and dispirited. *See also* FOLLETTI.

FISHER KING in Arthurian lore is Amfortas, OTHERWORLD guardian or fairy guardian of the Holy Grail. He was wounded in the scrotum by a poisoned lance, and had to await the coming of the Grail Knight to restore him to health.

FLAX plants provide linen thread, one of the oldest known textiles. The spinning of flax is an important component of many fairy stories such as RUMPELSTILTSKIN. Flax was sacred to several spinning and weaving goddesses of the ancient world. SPINNING was anciently associated with women only, and was considered to be a magical act as the movements involved imitated the spinning of the cosmos and the procession of the zodiac through the heavens. Flax was placed as an offering on altars of the sun.

FLIBBERTIGIBBET is an English GOBLIN, mostly known in the Midlands and East Anglia, who likes to scare young girls in the dark. It used to be said that he 'mopped and mowed' between the ringing of the curfew bell and cockcrow.

FLORELLA is mentioned in an old magical manuscript as being one of the treasures of the earth, along with MAB and Tyton.[109]

FLOWER FAIRIES is a term occasionally used by occultists to refer to plant DEVAS. In the Balkans fairies are often born in flowers, or look after flowers and cause them to grow and fade. Rumanian and Balkan fairies each have their own plant emblem. Some southern Slavonic people believe that VILE are either born from plants, or from fairy mothers inseminated with dew.

Apart from this, flower fairies are largely a literary invention whereby each flower is assigned a fairy and is usually depicted clad in garments that resemble the flower. Cecily Mary Barker (1895-1973) illustrated a hugely popular series of Flower Fairy books.

FLY AGARIC (*Amanita muscaria*) is a red and white spotted mushroom closely associated with fairies. They are often depicted sitting on one, and the red caps many fairies wear may be a metaphor for the mushroom. Many fairies are characterised as red and shaggy - an apt description of the fly agaric.

Fly agaric is psychotropic and has a long history of use among European mystics and SHAMANS. In Finno-Ugric languages words denoting ecstasy and intoxication are traceable to root expressions meaning 'fly agaric'. The effects of the mushroom include auditory and visual hallucinations and spatial distortions. Subjects commonly report sensations of flying, or seeing little people or red-hatted mushrooms dancing. Fly agaric grows under BIRCH trees and the Siberian shaman's seven-stepped pole was made of birch. In other words, the shaman ingested the mushroom and flew up the *axis mundi* tree to the spirit realms, seeing the spirit of the agaric as a red-capped fairy.

The FATHER CHRISTMAS costume of white and red also suggests the mushroom. Siberian winter dwellings were excavated holes with a birch log roofs; the only entrance was through a smoke hole in the roof. Even the summer dwellings had smoke-hole exits for the spirit of the shaman to fly out of when he was in a trance. This might explain why Santa enters and exits through the chimney. Why does Santa bring gifts? The shaman is the middleman between humans and spirits and brings back knowledge from the spirit world. Ordinary individuals would write requests on pieces of paper and burn them, so their messages would be carried to the spirits on the smoke.

The Rig-Veda speaks of the mysterious soma; a plant that was considered a god, an aspect of Agni, the god of fire. The plant had no roots, leaves, blossoms or seeds but possessed of a single eye like the sun - the red cap of the fly agaric.[110] Spoken of as an eye, the cap of the fly agaric represents the opening of inner vision,

FOLLET

as well as the sun. A number of legends speak of one-eyed, one-legged creatures, and these may, in fact, be a code for psychotropic mushrooms. The FACHAN, a Highland fairy, has one eye, one hand, one leg, one ear, one arm and one toe all lined up down the centre of his body. He carries a spiked club with which he attacks any human who dares to approach his mountain realm. He hates all living creatures but especially birds, which he envies for their gift of flight. A number of writers have theorised that the fachan may be a folk memory of the Celtic shamans, who stood on one leg and closed one eye when casting spells. The usual explanation offered for this practice is so that one eye looks into the inner realms, and only standing on one leg symbolises not being wholly in one realm or another. However, it may be that the stance is in imitation of the mushroom that gives the shaman his power, the one-legged, one-eyed fly agaric. The fact that the fachan inhabits a mountainous region is significant, as that is where the fly agaric grows. His hatred of birds, which he envies for their flight, may be a distorted folk memory of the gift of flight the mushroom bestows.

There was also an Irish race of one-legged, one-eyed beings called FORMORIANS described as the oldest inhabitants of the land, a race of wizards who intermarried with the TUATHA DÉ DANAAN.[111] In Celtic folklore, all red food was taboo, including ROWAN berries and red nuts. Peter Lamborn Wilson has suggested that these may be masks for the mushroom in Irish myth, adding that the Celts were head-hunters, believing that all wisdom and power resided in the head. Perhaps these heads were not only human ones but also the heads of vision giving mushrooms.[112]

Mushrooms appear in Greek mythology in connection with the sun god Apollo. Carl Ruck speculated that the votive offerings sent to Apollo's shrine at Delos from Hyperborea (sometimes identified with Siberia and sometimes with Britain) were actually fly agaric mushrooms.[113] Along the route the offerings travelled lived a race called the Arimaspeans ('One-eyed'). The murder of the CYCLOPS ('Round-eye') occasioned Apollo's sojourn amongst the peoples of his northern homeland, Hyperborea. There was also a race of one-footed creatures called Shade-foots who, according to Aristophanes, were implicated in a profane celebration of the lesser Eleusinian mysteries. The Shade-foots were also known as Monocoli ('One-legs'). In Vedic Sanskrit soma is described as 'Not-born Single-foot'.

Fairy food, which is generally described as being red in colour, is prohibited for humans. Should they eat it, they can never return to the realm of men. This is comparable with the taboos placed on shamanic substances, forbidding them to ordinary men and women. Among the Selkup fly agaric was believed to be fatal to non-shamans. Among the Vogul consumption was limited to sacred occasions and it was abused on peril of death. The Indo-Europeans strictly limited the important ritual of soma to certain classes and the profane user risked death at the hands of the angry god. Amongst the Celts, red foods and mushrooms were taboo, designated as the food of the OTHERWORLD or the DEAD. As the mushroom aids the shaman to visit other realms in spirit flight, see spirits and contact the spirit or god within, Robert Graves argued that ambrosia, the food of the gods, was in reality hallucinogenic mushrooms.[114]

Descriptions of visits to fairyland might easily describe a drug-induced visionary experience - enhanced colours, unearthly music, spatial distortions, the loss of any sense of the passage of time, and food and drink tasting wonderful. However, when the traveller returns (or the vision ends) fairy gold turns to withered leaves or common rubbish.

FOAWR are Manx stone throwing GIANTS who like to ravish cattle. One caught a young fiddler called Chalse and carried him home for company, but the young man managed to escape up the chimney.[115]

FODDENSKKMAEND is a small Icelandic EARTH FAIRY.

FODLA is a Queen of the Irish TUATHA DÉ DANAAN, one of the THREE who met with the invading Milesian Celts. The others were Banba and ÉRIU.

FOG CAPS are hats the DWARFS wear to become invisible.

FOLATON or **Folatan** is a type of French HOUSE FAIRY or LUTIN.

FOLLET is an evil fairy of northern France who invades the homes of country folk and proceeds to pelt them with sticks and pots whenever they cross the THRESHOLD. They pester women who are SPINNING, rub cattle so hard they form scabs and make crude jokes. Neither water nor exorcism will get rid of them, though they are terrified of IRON and steel knives. They once lived under the old dolmens but moved into human habitations. If you are not driven into a rage by their antics, you will win their respect, and they may act as HOUSE FAIRIES, bringing you gifts, finishing off work, and taking care of domestic livestock. Though they are usually INVISIBLE, they may appear as little old men in the costume of a jester with parti-coloured coats covered with bells. Some with a more modern outlook wear RED coats and breeches and are armed with tiny swords. They have long hair, long beards and dark complexions. Sometimes they appear as GOATS, but have human voices.

FOLLETTI (s. **Folletto**) are Italian fairies who usually look and act like mischievous six-year-old children with their FEET on backwards, or are called 'little BUTTERFLIES' as they may appear in this form and are never still. The word folletti is used for the female of the species, as well as the plural of folletto, denoting the whole race. They appear under a variety of local names all over Italy. They are the offspring of FAUNS or SILVANS.

Folletti are generally well disposed towards humans, but can be mischievous and even downright malicious. They are particularly interested in sexual matters and may rape and torture women. Some cause madness, others cause NIGHTMAREs, while others contaminate pork. All types of folletti travel in whirlwinds, and are called 'Wind Knots' or 'Knots of Wind'. They are slight creatures who like to raise storms in order to ride on the wind and when swirls of dust are raised, this is the folletti at play. They cause the harsh storms that wreck crops, flood homes, and bring the snow. They are fond of blowing women's skirts up. Some types are exclusively WEATHER FAIRIES (see MACINGHE, MAZZAMARIEDDU, AMMAZZAMAREDDU, SUMASCAZZO, GRANDINILI, MAZZAMARELLE, BASADONE and ABRUZZO MAZZAMARELLE). They also play a game in which they ride on grasshoppers.

Wicked folletti are not easy to get rid of, and each Italian district has its own formula for exorcising them. In some areas only saints can banish them while in others brown haired girls can manage the job. If a member of your family has been driven mad by one you will have to gather one hundred and one eggs from a hundred and one different families and force the poor patient to eat thirty a day - after five days the folletto will be gone.[116]

FOOLISH FIRE is another name for the WILL O'THE WISP.

FOOTPRINTS can have a special importance in Ireland, especially at SAMHAIN. Then, if you throw dust from a footprint after a fairy host you can compel them to release any abducted humans. Some say that a footprint contains the life essence of its author and it is regularly used in magic (for example, in the USA black slaves took the earth from a beloved's footprint to make the loved one follow them, while a similar charm kept a spouse faithful).

FOREST SPRITES is a broad term for those fairies that live in forests and woodland, often inhabiting trees and caring for forest animals. There is a Swedish anecdote that concerns a forest sprite. A farmer called Jan Nilsson went off to make hay, accompanied by a serving girl. They both slept in the barn. One night the serving girl saw a strange woman enter the barn and lie down beside the farmer. She had lovely eyes, but the skin of her back was like tree bark. The next morning the girl asked Jan about his mysterious bed companion. He replied that he would be repaid for sleeping with the forest sprite and before long a huge bear came out of the woods and lay down beside the barn. Jan was able to shoot it without any trouble.

FORGET ME NOTS (*Myosotis sylvatica*) are little blue flowers guarded by fairies. Those searching for hidden TREASURE may carry them.

FORGETFUL PEOPLE or **Forgetful Folk** is a Scottish term for the fairies.

FORMORIANS or **Fomorians** (either from *Fomhoiré* meaning 'Sea Giants' or from *Fomhoisre* meaning 'Under-Spirits') are hideous monsters, formed from the leftover parts of various animals. They were the original inhabitants of Ireland. They fought every invading race, first the children of Partholan, who were destroyed by pestilence, then the people of Nemed, who had to pay the Formorians a tribute of two of their children and some cattle every November. Then came the FIRBOLGS who were driven out by the TUATHA DÉ DANAAN. Now the Formorians are forced to live in the sea, and can sometimes be seen coming ashore at night. Tory Island is their great stronghold. They each have a single leg, one hand, one eye in the centre of their foreheads, and three rows of sharp teeth. They represent the spirits of winter, death and disease. In Scotland, the Fomorians were a race of evil GIANTS. *See also* FLY AGARIC.

FORSO are Northern Australian spirits that must be placated with offerings or by human company if they are not to become vindictive.

FORTS are ancient earthworks associated with fairies. They are circular meadows surrounded by a MOUND, sometimes called a 'Dane Fort'.[117] It is said that when the ancient race moved out the fairies moved in. If a human should damage a fort, he or she will be punished with sickness.

FORTUNE is the name of an Italian SWAN MAIDEN. A human man fell in love with her and followed her to FAIRYLAND. They stayed there for two months and were very happy, but then the young man was seized with a desire to visit his mother. Fortune lent him a black fairy HORSE and accompanied him over the sea to his home. Everything seemed changed. They passed a great lord whose horse stumbled, and the young man was about to help when the fairy warned him 'Beware! That is the Devil!' and they rode on. However, he found that the land had changed and his mother was long dead and forgotten.

FOSSEGRIM are Norwegian WATER FAIRIES who live near waterfalls or beneath bridges. They have fine features, golden hair and the most beautiful singing voices. They dress in grey.

FOUCHI FATUI are Italian WILL O'THE WISPs that may be seen flickering over swamps or cemeteries and are sometimes said to be spirits of the DEAD. They are similar to, or identical with, the FIAMMETTA.

FOUL WEATHER is a Cornish fairy who appears in a tale similar to that of TOM TIT TOT. He performs work for a fee until his NAME is guessed.

FOULETOT or **FOULTA** is a French HOUSE FAIRY or LUTIN.

FOUNTAINS are frequently guarded by fairy women such as MELUSINE in enchanted forests. Such fairies live in underground grottoes during the day and inhabit the springs during the hours of daylight. However, they are at their loveliest at night when the moonlight turns them into pellucid creatures. Their voices are so pleasing that the night stops to listen to their songs. They have the power to transform the springs into healing waters. In fables of the Celtic OTHERWORLD, there is always a fountain, sometimes running with wine. To drink of this fountain bestows eternal youth. This may be identified with the Holy Grail and the UNDERWORLD magical CAULDRON of renewal.

FOUR LEAFED CLOVER (*Trifolium sp.*) is a common plant in Europe that allows you to see fairies and other spirits. A milkmaid accidentally picked a four-leaf clover with the grass she used to soften the weight of the pail on her head. When next she looked at her cow she saw dozens of fairies milking it.

An ointment of four-leaf clover will also open the Sight, as will carrying a charm made of seven grains of wheat and a four-leaf clover. According to Christian folklore the four-leafed clover represents the cross and enables its possessor to ward off WITCHES. Four-leafed clover will also dispel fairy MAGIC.

FOX FIRE is another English name for the WILL O'THE WISP.

FOXGLOVE (*Digitalis purpurea*) may be a corruption of 'folksglove', since fairies are said to wear the flowers as mittens. The Good Folk, like the flowers, inhabit woody dells, they conceal themselves under its green leaves and their caps blend in with the bell shaped flowers of the foxglove.[118] This has given rise to many of the plant's folk names— Fairy's Glove, Fairy's Cap, Fairy's Thimbles, Fairy Petticoats, Fairy

FRAU HOLDA

Weed, Little Folk's Gloves, Fairy Bell, Fairy Weed, and Goblin's Thimbles. In Gaelic the foxglove is called *Lusmore* or *miaran nan cailleacha sith* the 'Thimble of the Old Fairy Woman'. Growing foxgloves in your garden will attract fairies or if you want to keep fairies away, you should weed them out. Like other fairy flowers it is unlucky to pick them or take them indoors. In order to detect CHANGELINGS, the Irish used to give the juice of twelve foxgloves to the suspect baby. This would force a fairy to reveal its true nature (NOTE: this would be **deadly** poisonous).[119]

FRAIRIES is an eastern English name for fairies in the county of Suffolk.

FRAU ELLHORN is another name for the ELDER MOTHER.

FRAU GODEN is a leader of the WILD HUNT in German folklore. She had twenty-four daughters and they all loved hunting more than the thought of heaven. When they died Frau Goden became the Wild Huntress and four of her daughters pulled her carriage, while the rest became DOGS. If she comes to a CROSSROADS her carriage breaks.

FRAU HOLDA is a German HAG fairy who brings the snow in winter by shaking out her feather bed in the sky. When she washes her veil, rain falls. At YULE, she rides about in a wagon. She is the Mother of the ELVES and a patroness of WITCHES, appearing as a witch herself. Frau Holda is derived from the Germanic sky goddess Holda or Hulda, who was also a goddess of fertility, the HEARTH and SPINNING.

FRAU HOLLE is a Teutonic fairy who rides the wind and brings the snow by shaking the feathers from her quilt. She is cognate with FRAU HOLDA.

FRAU HOLUNDER is another name for the ELDER MOTHER.

FRAU SAELDE is similar to, or perhaps cognate with, FRAU HOLDA.

FRAU WACHHOLDER is a German juniper tree fairy that can be invoked to make thieves give up their booty. A branch of the juniper should be bent to the ground and held down with a stone while calling on the thief. The latter is then bound to present himself and give up his prize. The branch is then released and the stone replaced.

FRAU WELT is a German FAIRY SWEETHEART or SUCCUBUS, according to mediaeval clerics.

FRESHWATER MERMAIDS guard inland waters. When Aqualate Mere in Staffordshire was drained the men said that a MERMAID appeared and warned them she would destroy the two nearby towns if the lake were harmed. A mermaid also lives in the Black Mere near Leek and because of her animals won't drink the water. Two farmworkers of Child's Ercall in Shropshire saw a strange creature rising from a pond. They prepared to flee, but when the creature spoke, they realised it was a mermaid. She told them there was a TREASURE in the pond and they could have as much of it as they liked, if only they would come into the pond and take it. They waded into the water and the mermaid surfaced with a lump of gold as big as a man's head. One of the astonished labourers exclaimed that he had never had such luck in his life, but his remark offended the mermaid and she and the gold disappeared, never to be seen again.

FREY ('Lord') is associated with the VANIR or fertility spirits in Norse myth. He dwells in ÁLFHEIM, and rules the ELVES.

FRIAR RUSH appears as a HOBGOBLIN in English folklore. He is probably cognate with BRUDER RAUSCH.

FRIAR'S LANTERN is another name for the WILL O'THE WISP.

FRIDAY is the day, according to Irish lore, on which fairies have the most power since it is their Sabbath day. Knives should not be sharpened on a Friday, as this will make them angry. It is an unlucky day to start a new job, begin a journey, or hold a wedding, for the fairies are out to cause mischief and will spoil it if they can. It is on this day that they are most often up to their tricks with ELF-BOLTS, milk stealing and CHANGELING swapping. On Fridays, they are also wont to kidnap young girls as brides. A fairy story told on a Friday should be prefaced by the words: 'A blessing attend their departing and travelling! This day is Friday and they will not hear us'. This prevents Friday ill will coming on the narrator. According to the Gaels, Friday should not even be called by its proper name (*Di-haoine*) but referred to obliquely.

FRIDEAN are Scottish fairies who guard roads. Offerings of bread and milk should be made to them before setting out on a journey. They live under rocks.

FROCIN was a DWARF who betrayed King Mark's secret - that he had horse's ears - according to one of the

Arthurian tales. The indiscreet dwarf was beheaded.

FROGS feature in many folk and fairy tales. Sometimes a human being is turned into a frog for offending a fairy or WITCH. Other times, fairies themselves appear as frogs or TOADS.

The frog was a sacred creature for the Celts who associated it with healing. There is an ancient English healing spring at Acton Barnett, in Shropshire, where the guardian fairies of the well appear as frogs. The largest of the THREE is addressed as the Dark God.

FULL MOON

FROG STONES are yellowish stones that have the shape of a frog and are said to be lucky. They are fairy gifts reputedly found near large ponds and lakes.

FROHN are Swiss female forest fairies or WILD WOMEN who live in underground mountain CAVES.

FRUMOASELE ('The Nice Ones') are Eastern Balkan fairies referred to in flattering terms to avoid upsetting them.

FUATH are Irish or Scottish web-footed WATER FAIRIES. They have yellow manes and tails, large eyes but no noses. They are hairy all over, except for their faces. They have human bodies and dress in green. Sometimes they marry humans. Fuath is a collective term for a whole class of malignant fairies including DEMONS, SHELLYCOAT, the URISK and EACH UISGE.[120]

FUDDITU is a Sicilian fairy who loses his power if his RED CAP is stolen.

FUGLIETTI are Sardinian fairies, the souls of UNBAPTISED CHILDREN.

FUJETTU is a mischievous Calabrian fairy that causes trouble in those houses occupied by seven families.

FULL MOON nights are important to the fairies, and it is then that they are most often seen at their revels, dancing in the moonlight in forest clearings or in bright rings on the green. The MOON also has power over water and the tides of the sea, and its phases govern the activities of sea fairies, WATER FAIRIES and MERMAIDS.

FUMHNACH was first wife of MIDAR. She was so jealous of his second wife Edain that she turned her into a pool of water. The pool became a worm and the worm a fly. The perfume that the fly exuded was so lovely that Midar knew that it was Edain and was delighted to have found her. Enraged, Fumhnach caused a wind to blow the fly over a cliff, and poor Edain lay at the base of the cliff for seven years until AENGUS found her and restored her to Midar. Fumhnach again caused a wind to blow, and the fly was swatted into a goblet of wine, which was swallowed.

FUNERALS take place amongst the fairy folk too. The poet and artist William Blake witnessed a fairy funeral in his garden, with the corpse borne on a rose leaf. It was buried with ceremony and chants before the fairies disappeared.[121]

Observing a fairy funeral might prove to be an OMEN OF DEATH for the witness, as in the following story recorded by James Bowker: Two men were on their way home to Langton village in Lancashire one night when they heard the church bell ring a passing toll of twenty-six chimes. This startled the younger man, Robin, for he was just twenty-six years old and he wondered which of his contemporaries had died. The two continued on but as they reached the gate of the ancient abbey the gate opened and out came a dark figure, wearing a RED CAP. He was followed by a funeral procession. The two men peered into the face of the corpse and saw, to their astonishment, the likeness of young Robin. From that time the young man went into a decline and within a month he was dead.[122]

FUOCHI FATUI is an Italian WILL O'THE WISP, said to be a SOUL from Purgatory.

FURIES (The) were conceived from the blood that fell from the castrated genitals of Uranus, the Greek sky god, when it fell upon his wife Gaia, the earth. In appearance they were terrifying, with snakes for hair and hideous faces, grimacing and brandishing whips and burning torches. They barked like DOGS and delighted to scent human blood and suck it from wrongdoers, in VAMPIRE fashion. Their task was to avenge the murder of family members. Their Greek name is ERINNYES ('Furies') but they were also titled Maniai ('Raging Women'). However, it was unwise to call them by name, as to do so might summon them, so they were referred to as the Eumenides or 'Kindly Ones'. It is often the case that something frightening is given a flattering title, partly to avoid mentioning it by name and therefore summoning it, and partly to flatter. Such a practice can be seen in British and Irish fairy folklore where the fairies are referred to as 'The Gentry' or 'Fair Folk'. The Furies indeed became the Eumenides or Kindly Ones when the goddess Athene persuaded them to take on the role of guardian spirits of the city of Athens.

FUTTERMÄNNCHEN are helpful German fairies who feed farm animals and are a type of HOUSE FAIRY.

FUWCH GYFEILIORN was a fairy COW belonging to a band of fairies from the region of Llyn Barfog, a lake near Aberdovey in Wales. At dusk the fairies appear, clad all in GREEN, accompanied by their milk white hounds and milk WHITE cattle.

Once a farmer caught one of these cows and his fortune was made: it produced such butter, milk and cheese as was never seen. He called the cow Fuwch Gyfeiliorn and its fame spread. The farmer became rich beyond his dreams until one day he stupidly got it into his head that the fairy cow was getting old and he ought to fatten her for slaughter. The fatal day arrived and despite the pleading eyes of the cow the butcher raised his arm and struck her a dreadful blow. Suddenly there was an almighty shriek and the bludgeon went right through the head of the cow and felled NINE men standing close by. To everyone's astonishment a GREEN LADY arose from the lake and softly called to the cow. Together they disappeared back beneath the waters, never to be seen again.[123]

FYLGJA (pl. Fylgiar, Fylgia or Fylgjur, meaning 'Caul'), is a protective FAMILIAR spirit. According to Norwegian and Icelandic folklore a child born with a caul (fylgia) over its head will be accompanied through life by a fylgja. It follows its master closely, just one or two steps behind, and for this reason it is very impolite to shut a door behind a person too quickly. The fylgja may be heard knocking and banging around the house when visitors are about to arrive. The fairy may often be seen in its owner's dreams, usually in animal form and especially as a bear. A person may discover the appearance of his familiar by wrapping a knife in a napkin and reciting the names of all the animals he can think of. When he gets to the right one the knife will fall out of the napkin.[124] It only manifests during waking hours when the person is about to die, and its appearance gives an OMEN of the manner of death. A mutilated spirit means a painful death while a serene one indicates an easy death. These spirits occur in some of the early Icelandic sagas. In Iceland the familiar may also be called a Forynia or Hamingia, while in Norway it is also called a Folgie, Vardögl, Vardygr, Vardivil, Vardöiel or Ham.[125]

GABBYGAMMIES are strange gibbering fairies that once haunted Washer's Pit, a hollow that is now a bridleway close to a barrow between Fontmell Down and the village of Farnham in north Dorset, England. However, they now seem to have disappeared, since no one has seen them in many a year.

GABBLE RETCHETS *See* GABRIEL'S HOUNDS.

GABIJA is a Lithuanian fire spirit, mistress of the HEARTH fire, who was honoured by throwing salt on the fire and crying: 'Holy Gabija, be thou satisfied!'.

GABRIEL'S HOUNDS, **Gabriel Hounds**, **Gabriel Ratchets**, **Gabble Retchets** or **Ratchets** are a version of the WILD HUNT found in Northern England, primarily in Durham and Yorkshire. Their leader is Gabriel, who is cursed to lead the hounds until doomsday as punishment for hunting on the Sabbath day. The hounds fly through the air to chase the damned, baying all the while. Some say that they are the souls of UNBAPTISED CHILDREN. To hear them is an OMEN OF DEATH.

GAHE are spirits of the Chricahua and Mescalero Apaches that live underground. They were probably once fertility spirits.

GALGENMÄNNLEIN is a type of KOBOLD spirit inhabiting a carved mandrake root.

GALLEY BEGGAR is a jolly Somerset fairy who is occasionally spotted sliding downhill on a hurdle, from Over Stowey to Nether Stowey, with his head under his arm, laughing madly.[126]

GALLEY TROT is a BLACK DOG that haunts the headland north of Dunwich in Suffolk, England. He is also known in the North Country and some describe him as a white dog the size of a bullock that pursues anyone who flees from him.[127]

GALLITRAP is a FAIRY RING caused by PIXIES riding ponies in a circle. If you enter the ring you will be in their power.

GANCANAGH *See* GARCONER.

GANDHARVAS are shy little fairies who live under the hills and in the CAVES of India, where they play beautiful MUSIC.

GANDREID is the Norwegian WILD HUNT.

GANIEDA or **Gwendydd** is the twin sister of MERLIN.

GANS are Apache fairies who guard the mountains of south-western North America. They may be approached to drive away evil spirits and bring good fortune.

GARBH OGH set up her chair in the womb of the hills at the season of the heather bloom and then expired. She was giantess in Irish myth, though she may have once been a HAG goddess.

GARCONER, **Ganconer** or **Gancanagh** (*gean-canogh*, meaning 'Love Talker') is an Irish ELF who loves to seduce mortal women. He has bright black eyes and smokes a pipe. Any woman who yields to his sweet words and kisses is lost. She will pine away and die after he, inevitably, leaves.

GARGANTUA was a GIANT created by MERLIN to serve King ARTHUR. He carried a club that was 18 metres long (sixty feet) and helped Arthur to overcome Gog and Magog. *See also* GOGMAGOG.

GEANCANACH are the HOUSE FAIRIES of Northern Ireland, known in Meath and portions of Ulster. They like to warm themselves at the fireside and love to be offered drinks of MILK. They are small with slanting eyes and pointed ears. Though they have wings they do not fly but have been known to vanish and re-appear immediately in another spot, like a flickering light.

GEBHART ('Hard Luck'?) is a fairy of the RUMPELSTILTSKIN type, whose NAME has to be guessed.

GELLO are female VAMPIRE spirits, in Classical Greek myth, who attack children to drink their blood or kidnap them. Originally, there was only one Gello, a female DEMON who attacked children on the Isle of Lesbos.

GENIE *See* DJINN.

GENII CUCULLATI ('Hooded Spirits') appear in images of triads of hooded and cloaked DWARFS or GIANTS all over Celtic Europe during the Roman period. They may carry eggs or display phalluses. Many of the later hooded fairies, like Carl Hood, may have descended from them. *See also* GENIUS and HOOD.

GENITI GLINNE ('Damsels of the Glen') are ancient Irish Celtic or perhaps pre-Celtic NATURE FAIRIES later associated with the TUATHA DÉ DANAAN.

GENIUS, (*pl.* GENII) is a spirit which rules over a person, place or nation. Originally, the genius was a sort of male Roman HOUSE FAIRY who protected the household and the fertility of the family in it. In this he was helped by his female counterpart the Iuno or Juno. Its Greek equivalent was the DÆMON and Christian counterpart the guardian angel. Later the genius came to represent the personification of an individual's personality, or the spirit of a place or group of people such as a nation. These latter genii were depicted as SNAKES. The word *genius* is often used to denote the forest spirit, who exists in various forms worldwide. His voice is heard in the breeze or in the rustle of leaves. In some European countries, he is depicted carrying an uprooted pine tree.

GENIUS LOCI is the guardian spirit of a specific place. Many fairies are described as protecting individual localities such as certain groves, ancient sites and bridges. These fairies are often described as 'WHITE LADIES' and there are many of them throughout the world from the African SHAMANTIN

to the Irish BANSHEE. In Normandy, they are the fairies of ravines, fords, bridges, and other narrow places. A white lady appears in the Arthurian myths: GUINEVERE means 'white phantom', which indicates that she may have been of fairy origin, the guardian spirit of a place, maybe ALBION itself. Perhaps if Guinevere was the guardian spirit of Albion, MORGAN LE FAY was the *Mor Gwyn* ('white lady') of the Otherworld, AVALON, the magical island outside time and space where illness, old age and death are unknown.

GENTLE ANNIE or **Gentle Annis** is a HAG fairy of the Scottish lowlands who governs the storms. She causes the gales on the Firth of Cromarty from the south-west, where a gap in the hills allows the entry of squalls. She has a mild and innocent appearance and a polite manner, but she is evil and treacherous. A day may begin with fine weather, and the fishermen set out, then suddenly a storm brews up and the boats are in danger. Her name may be derived from ANU or DANU, a Celtic goddess. *See also* BLACK ANNIS, WEATHER FAIRIES and CAILLEACH.

GENTRY, THE is a flattering general term for fairies used in Ireland.

GERASI are Malayan GIANTS or OGRES who have tusks.

GHILLIE DHU or **Ghille Dubh** ('Dark Show') is a lone Scottish fairy of the Gairloch district. He is black-haired and clothed in GREEN leaves and moss. The Ghillie Dhu protects the trees from humans and may grab an unwary traveller and enslave him, though he has been known to return lost children to their homes.

Five lairds of the Mackenzies set out to shoot him, but luckily failed to find him.[128] *See also* BROWN MAN OF THE MOORS.

GHOSTS are spirits of the dead and sometimes synonymous with fairies,

particularly women who have died in CHILDBIRTH, unnamed or UNBAPTISED CHILDREN, suicides and murder victims. Such creatures include Spriggans, Sprites, Twyleth Teg, Will O'the Wisp, La Llorona, Redshanks, Peg O'Nell, Sea Witches, Shorthoggers of Whittinghame, Silkies, Soemangots, Achen, Bean-Nighe, Dunters, Duergar, Bergmoncks, Bucca, Brownies, Churel and the Dogs or cursed leader of the Wild Hunt.

GHOULS or **Ghul** (*f.* **Ghulla**) are a variety of fairy or DJINN, in Arabic folklore, the offspring of Ibis (Satan). They can adopt many forms, including those of lovely women, but always have asses' hooves instead of FEET. They live in the desert and attack travellers. If the unfortunate victim fails to kill the ghoul with the first punch, he is doomed, as any subsequent blows will only give it more strength. Children are threatened into good behaviour with mention of the ghoul as a type of BOGEYMAN. In European folklore, the ghoul has become a creature that dwells in churchyards and feasts on the flesh of the dead. The term is sometimes synonymous with GOBLIN.

GIANE are Sardinian fairies who live in caves. They are 1.5 metres tall (around five feet), have long hair, steel fingernails, and long breasts which they throw over their shoulders. They wear furs and pointed hats made of animal skins. They spend their time SPINNING and embroidering, and usually carry small spinning wheels in their pockets. They can make white veils that can cover whole valleys (the mist). They are accomplished weavers and a piece of their cloth is very lucky. Their lovely songs can enchant humans and draw them to the fairy CAVES, where they will be pounced on. The giane will suck their blood, like VAMPIRES. They also eat humans, giving birth THREE days later to new gianes, born with a taste for raw meat. These children are carried in baskets on their backs. Giane are also expert diviners, and foresee the future by gazing into their spinning wheels. Some say that nowadays the giane have become smaller and dress in peasant clothes, the women covering their heads with kerchiefs. Male and females live together in caves, eating meat and herbs. They weave and sing songs of enchantment.

GIANTS are sometimes synonymous with fairies and it has proved to be impossible to write about fairies without mentioning giants. Sometimes fairies appear as giants or are said to have been giant in stature until humans drove them underground. Giants are found all around the world, from the Scandinavian YMIR, the first man and creator of the human race, to the Irish FORMORIANS, the Greek TITANS, the Norse JÖTUN, Goliath in the bible, and the Greek CYCLOPS.

Giants are always said to have lived in the far past, perhaps in primordial times before the creation of gods and men. In many cultures, they fought with the gods and the chief god created the earth and heavens from the body of a slain giant. They seem to be personifications of the primeval forces of the nature such as frost, volcanoes and earthquakes and so on, as opposed to the forces of the sky such as thunder or rain which belong to the gods. Giants are often said to dwell underground or have close links with the earth, just like fairies.

Many places are said to have been inhabited by races of giants. Early Danish historians accounted for the huge rocks near burial MOUNDS, cairns, and other structures by stating that giants must once have peopled Denmark. The British Isles were said to have been inhabited by a race of giants until the last two, Gog and Magog (or some say one called GOGMAGOG) were defeated by Brutus. Legends say that giants built the megalithic monuments such as Stonehenge. Many more giants appear in folk tales, including Amerant, who was killed by Guy of Warwick, Ascapart, slain by Bevis of Hampton, Bell from Leicestershire, the Cornish giant Bolster who fell in love with St Agnes, the giant of St Michael's Mount who was killed by King Arthur, Leon Gawr who founded the city of Chester, and Wade who was buried in North Yorkshire, near Whitby.

GIDOLIN is a DWARF that appears in early Arthurian legend, keeping the flasks of HAG's blood warm on the hearth of hell. The knight Culhwch had to fetch the flasks as part of his quest to marry Olwen.

GILTINE ('Sting' or 'Harm') is a Lithuanian spirit who brings death. She dresses in white and appears at the house of the doomed person and then strangles or suffocates them.

GIMLÉ ('Fire Proof') is the home of the Light Elves, the LIOSÁLFAR, in Norse myth. It is a shining hall situated in the third heaven.

GIMP is of the Orkney TROWS.

GIOGA is the Queen of the SEA TROWS.

GIRLE GUAIRLE is an Irish fairy who, like TOM TIT TOT and RUMPELSTILTSKIN, agreed to spin FLAX for a mortal woman, on condition that she should remember the fairy's NAME. The woman was bewitched and forgot it. She was very frightened of the consequences but she accidentally overheard some fairies singing of Girle Guairle. Thus she was able to greet the fairy with her true name. The angry fairy disappeared in a huff. See also SPINNING.

GITULIUS is a Western Slavonic BROWNIE or KOBOLD.

GLAISEIN or Glashan ('Grey Headed Man') are Manx HOUSE FAIRIES who are physically very strong. Sometimes they journey from farm to farm, threshing corn and helping out at the sheep folds, though more often they skulk on the hillsides, watching the farmers. Recently they have taken to magnetising stones on the edges of roads to pull cars off the highway. Both male and female glashans go naked, and the males sometimes abduct mortal women for wives or rape lone women they come across. They often take the shape of grey foals or yearling lambs.

GLAISTIG (from the Gaelic glas, meaning 'grey' and stig, meaning 'small, creeping object') is a Scots fairy, a small, GREEN dressed woman with yellow hair right down to her feet, though her face is grey and wan. Alternatively, in Skye she is said to be tall, thin and dressed in WHITE. Some say that she is half GOAT under her clothes.

The glaistig is actually a human woman under fairy enchantments and to whom fairy powers have been given. She is stronger than other fairies and one yell of hers, heralding times of joy or sorrow, wakes the echoes of distant hills. She is always alone, unless she happens to be accompanied by one of her own children.

The glaistig mournfully haunts castles, houses and cattle folds, and confines herself to servants' work. She might be seen herding her COWS up to their pastures in the evening, or sunning herself on a distant rock, or coming to the fold at dusk for her allowance of MILK. One glaistig was said to live on Iona in a hole in the rocks and the people poured milk into a hollow stone for her. She is particularly interested in the dairy, and resents it when people are not grateful for her services.

A glaistig is sometimes useful, and sometimes mischievous and troublesome. People are generally afraid of meeting her as she might harm them, should she be in the mood to. Some say that she drowns people or sucks their blood like a VAMPIRE. A vicious glaistig met a weaver going home with a bundle of cloth at a stream. She caught hold of him and pummelled him all night in the water, saying he was better for being washed.

At Lochaber in Inverness a blacksmith once captured a glaistig and refused to release her until she gave him a herd of cattle. As soon as she had produced the cattle, the SMITH demanded a house that no fairy or evil spirit could enter. The glaistig called upon every fairy in the district and the house was built in a single night. The smith then gave the glaistig leave to go, and she put out her hand in farewell, but the ungrateful man seared it with a red-hot IRON. The poor fairy fled to the Hill of Finisgeig where she bled to death. To this day, the vegetation there is stained RED.

Glaistigs are known to be kind to those of weak intellect, and sometimes take such unfortunates under their wing. Like other fairies, they detest DOGS and will avoid a house with such a pet, or make their displeasure known in some manner. Another way to keep them out of the house is to place a shoemaker's awl at the door.

GLAISTIG UAINE is a Scottish female HOUSE FAIRY or GREEN LADY who watches over old houses and castles.

GLAMOUR or **Glaymore** is a Scottish word, introduced into English literature by way of Sir Walter Scott, and is a type of fairy MAGIC which can make one thing seem to be another; as Scott wrote:

'...had much of a glamour might
Could make a ladye seem a knight;
A nutshell seem a guilded barge,
a sheeling seem a palace large,
And youth seem age, and age seem youth:
All was delusion, nought was truth'.[129]

For example, a fairy can make a rude CAVE seem to be a palace, or a nutshell full of brackish water seem to be a golden goblet full of the finest wine. Fairies can also enhance their own appearance by means of glamour, making themselves appear more beautiful, and their clothes more rich and costly.

The only way to see through fairy glamour is to have the eyes touched with FAIRY WATER or a FAIRY OINTMENT, or perhaps with a FOUR LEAFED CLOVER.

GLAS GHAIBHNEACH ('The Grey Cow with White Loins') was a fairy COW that belonged to an Irish master SMITH. She gave inexhaustible supplies of MILK, which fed everyone around. However, she objected to having her generosity abused and when a woman milked her to have extra to sell she took herself off across the sea to Scotland.

GLASHTIN or **GLASTYN** are Manx WATER HORSES; they look like ordinary horses except their hooves are back to front, or some say they are WATER BULLs, half horse and half bull. They can SHAPESHIFT and appear in human form, when they are very attractive to human females. A special ARROW is needed to overcome a glashtin called a *baodhag* ('fury of the quiver').

GLASS CASTLE is the OTHERWORLD palace of the MOON goddess or fairy ARIANRHOD in Welsh folklore.

GLASS MOUNTAIN is the Polish OTHERWORLD.

GLITEN is one of the sisters of MORGAN LE FAY who dwell with her in AVALON, according to Welsh folklore.

GLITONEA is one of the sisters of MORGAN LE FAY.

GLORIANA is the Queen of the Fairies of England, according to Edmund Spenser (1552-99) in his unfinished poem *The Faerie Queene*. However, she is probably a purely literary creation and the poem an allegory of the struggle between good and evil, in which Gloriana represents Queen Elizabeth I and Duessa, Mary Queen of Scots, while fairyland stands for England.[130]

GLOVES when tossed into a fairy ring will disperse the revellers. In one Cornish tale a farmer called Noy threw his glove down at a fairy gathering and house, orchard and all the company disappeared.[131] It is possible that the throwing down of a glove was a challenge to the fairies. Gloves feature widely in custom and folklore, often as a symbol of authority or intent. For example, putting on your gloves is a sign that you are leaving . If you forget to take your gloves when you leave a house and have to go back for them you must sit down before putting on the gloves, or you will never return to that place again. During the Middle Ages, a glove was thrown down as a challenge to honour; to pick it up was to accept the challenge. In later ages, to be struck with a glove meant a challenge to a duel.

GLOWER is a fairy strongman.

GLUCKSMÄNNCHEN ('Lucky Mannikin') is a type of KOBOLD which inhabits a carved figurine.

GNOME or **Gnomus** (*pl.* **Gnomes** or **Gnomi**) is an ELEMENTAL fairy of the earth, according to the sixteenth-century alchemist Paracelsus (1493-1541).[132] He referred to them as PYGMIES or gnomi (singular gnomus) who could move through the earth as fish move through water. The derivation of the word is uncertain, but may relate to the Greek verb *gnosis* 'to know' or yet again to *ge-nomos,* which means 'earth-dweller'. The word is most familiar to us in connection with the gnomon, the pointer on a sundial, the 'knower of time'.[133] Gnomes do not seem to pre-date Paracelsus (though the idea of EARTH FAIRIES does) but gnomes have captured the popular imagination as guardians of the earth - particularly the suburban garden - depicted as jolly faced little men wearing RED CAPS. In this role they are said to live for a thousand years and reach maturity at the age of a hundred.

GOATS are associated with fairies, especially in connection with fertility or corn. Goats were sacred to various Celtic deities and to fairies like Bucca and Puck. Some fairies shapeshift into goats, while others have goat's hooves, horns or legs. These include Fauns, Brollachans, Catez, Robin Goodfellow, Sileni, many VEGETATION SPIRITS, Bockmann, Dialen, Glaistig, Goat Heads, Gryphons, Haferbock, Goatman, Gwyllion, Hibla-Bashi, Kirin, Ki-Lin, Nereids, Silvani, Silvanus, Urisk, Kornböcke, Leshie, Purzinigele, Phooka, Pilosi and Puck. Russian woodland fairies are said to appear as part human but have the ears, horns and legs of goats

Fairies have a particular love of goats. They visit goats to comb their beards every FRIDAY (or perhaps Wednesday), their Sabbath day. English country folk said that it was not possible to see a goat for twenty-four hours continuously as, at some point, he must go and visit either the fairies or the DEVIL to have his beard combed.

For the ancient Greeks and Romans, the goat represented virility: goats are fertile and reputedly lusty. PAN, the Greek god of the wild, was the son of Amalthea ('goat'). Both he and his SATYRS had the legs, horns and beards of goats.

GOAT HEADS are evil Irish fairies associated with LEPRECHAUNS and FORMORIANS.

GOATMAN is a creature that appears in America in the folklore of Virginia. It has the upper parts of a human, and the lower parts of a GOAT. In this respect it resembles NATURE FAIRIES and spirits.

GOB, Ghob or Ghom is the king of the earth ELEMENTALS, in occult lore.

GOBAN is an Irish SMITH who frequently plays a major part in fairy tales. He is the Celtic equivalent of WAYLAND SMITH and is derived from the Irish smith god Gobniu who forged weapons for the TUATHA DÉ DANAAN.

GOBELINE or Gobelins are French BOGEYS. The word often occurs from the fifteenth to the seventeenth centuries, but first appeared in an eleventh-century account by Oderic Vitalis who wrote of a demon called Gobelinus. The name may relate to the Italian *gobbo,* meaning a hunchback, a description often applied to fairies.

GOBELIN are German HOBGOBLINS.

GOBELINUS is a certain GOBLIN who haunted the vicinity of Evreux in France in the eleventh century.

GOBLIN ('Spirit') is sometimes a generic term for the uglier and more unpleasant fairies such as BOGGARTS, BOGIES, GHOULS and BOGLES, or just mischievous HOUSE FAIRIES. However, it may also refer to the groups of fairies that live underground, especially in churchyards, or in the clefts of rocks or among the roots of ancient trees. Then again, some claim that the race of goblins originally emerged from a cleft in the Spanish Pyrenees and proceeded to spread all over Europe. They are mostly seen on HALLOWEEN, when they consort with ghosts and tempt humans to eat

FAIRY FOOD. Goblins sometimes appear as little deformed humans or animals. A smile from a goblin can turn milk sour or curdle the blood.

The origin of the term 'goblin' is not known for certain. It may be derived from the Greek *kobaloi* meaning 'evil spirits'. The Latin form was *cobalus,* developing into the French *gobelin* and the English goblin and perhaps the Welsh *coblyn* meaning 'KNOCKER', 'fiend' or 'sprite'.

GOBLIN OF GLEN MOR is a Scottish GOBLIN, said to be some 75 cm tall (two-and-a-half feet) and very aggressive. He lives at Glen Gloy.

GOBLIN-GROOM is an English HOBGOBLIN 30-60 cm tall (between one and two feet), with dark skin.

GOFANNON is the blacksmith of the Welsh fairies, the Tylwyth Teg, actually an ancient Brythonic SMITH god.

GOGMAGOG was the leader of a ferocious group of British giants, the original inhabitants of Britain, according to the twelfth-century historian Geoffrey of Monmouth. Brutus, the grandson of Aeneas of Troy, landed in Britain with his followers and was attacked by the giants under the leadership of Gogmagog. The Trojans captured Gogmagog and forced him to wrestle with their champion Corineus, who hurled him over the cliffs to his death. Two statues at the Guildhall in London commemorated the pair. The original statues were destroyed in the Great Fire of London in 1666, and were replaced by two new figures that were erroneously titled Gog and Magog, the last of the British giants.

GOLDEMAR is a German HOUSE FAIRY who dwelt in the home of Neveling von Hardenburg. He is said to have been kindly treated but would not tolerate anyone threatening his dignity.

GOBLIN

When one man tried to trip him up, he killed and roasted him before taking off, never to be seen again.

GOMMES are French MINE FAIRIES.

GOOD NEIGHBOURS or Good Neighbours from the Sunset Land is a flattering term for fairies in both Scotland and Ireland.

GOOD PEOPLE is an English and Irish expression for fairies in general, though similar expressions are found throughout the world, as in the African YUMBOES and the Malayan BEDIADARI.

GOOSEBERRY WIFE is a fairy from the Isle of Wight who takes the form of a big, hairy caterpillar to look after green gooseberries.

GORGONS are MERMAIDS, in modern Greek folklore, half women and half fish. According to one tale their mother is the sea and their father Alexander the Great. They will swim up to a ship and ask if he is still alive. If the sailors say "no" the mermaid will cause a storm, if they say "yes" she will strum her lyre and make the sea calm.

In Classical Greek myth there were THREE gorgons: Medusa, Sthenno and Euryale. They had snake locks instead of hair, and their glance was so awful that it turned any onlooker to stone.

GORSKA or Gorska Diva is a mountain fairy of Bulgaria.

GORSKA MAKVA is a HAG fairy of Bulgaria who prowls through villages at night to torment children. Placing an IRON knife beside the cradle, or an axe beneath it may protect a child.

GOSSAMER is something that fairies are often said to be clad in, or they have gossamer wings. They spin the light, wispy gossamer that is often in evidence in the autumn, caught on bushes or drifting on the air. Gossamer is a fine film of cobwebs and the term may be derived from the middle English *gos somer* meaning 'goose summer' referring to Martinmas in early November when gossamer is seen and when goose is traditionally eaten, a custom dating from very ancient times.

GOTWERGI is a male ERDLUITLE.

GRAC'HED COZ are Breton HAG fairies.

GRAK *See* DRAKES.

GRAMPUS is a dolphin-like fairy creature that lives in the sea. However, a certain land-bound one dwelt in a yew tree by Highclere Church in Hampshire, England and chased the villagers until it was banished to the Red Sea.

GRAND COLIN is a Channel Islands' fairy from Guernsey. *See also* COLIN and LE GRAND COLIN.

GRANDINILI are FOLLETTI from Friuli, in Italy, called 'little hail people' who bring the hail but are driven away by the sound of church bells.

GRANT occur in several types, each of which adopts an English village. A grant appears as a small, strange HORSE, walking erect. He warns when there is trouble approaching by walking through the village at sunset, setting the dogs to barking and the horses to whinnying. During World War II, several villages claimed that their grant had warned them of approaching air raids. However, Gervase of Tilbury (1211) described the grant as a DEMON, and said that its appearance was an OMEN OF DEATH.

GRASS is used by some fairies as a form of transport. They sit astride blades of grass and command them to fly by use of MAGIC words.

GRAVEYARD MOULD or soil from a churchyard is considered to be a useful counter charm against the spells of fairies and WITCHES.

GREEN is very much associated with fairies. They are often described as wearing green clothes, coats, and caps. Some even have green skin. In Ireland, green is so much the fairy colour that it is unlucky for humans to wear it. In Scotland any woman dressed in green is sure to be a fairy. The fairies most associated with green are the NATURE SPIRITS, woodland fairies, and those solitary fairies dwelling in the wild. Green of course, is the colour of growing things. After the cold, death-time of winter the spring returns with a flurry of fresh green growth. It is therefore a symbol of regeneration, the spirit of vegetation, hope, beauty, harmony, and eternal life. As a natural colour, it is peaceful and soothing.

Ancient religion was chiefly concerned with agriculture and fertility, entreating the gods and nature spirits to provide the corn. In Britain, this spirit of vegetation is still portrayed on MAY DAY by the GREEN MAN, Jack in the Bush, or Jack in the Green, in the guise of a mummer clad in green leaves and fresh boughs. He also occurs on numerous inn signs and church carvings. May Day is also connected with ROBIN HOOD, and in England it was once called 'Robin Hood's Day'. He was the outlaw of the greenwood who dressed in Lincoln green, and may have been a spirit of the forest himself. In Germany, the May King is concealed in a frame and covered with BIRCH boughs and flowers.

In parts of Russia and the Balkans, the Green Man is called Green George, who masquerades as a tree. He was ducked in a pond to make sure enough rain would fall in the summer. Green is also connected with water as the bringer of life. In Mohammedan lore, the Green Man is Khidr who drank from the fountain of life and turned green. He now lives alone, travelling the world and protecting sailors.

Evergreens like HOLLY and ivy preserve the green vegetation spirit though the winter. The druids kept some evergreens as a home for the nature fairies in winter.

Green is also described as the colour

of envy. This may be because it is a colour of the gods and spirits. Whatever the origin of the belief, the correspondence of green and envy has passed into folk custom. In Scotland, it was the custom that if a girl married before her older sisters she should give them a present of green stockings, while in England an older sister should dance at her younger sister's wedding wearing green stockings.

GREEN CHILDREN have turned up in several English villages, unable to speak English and with strange, GREEN tinged skin. Their finders concluded that they were fairy children who had wandered away from their homes and were unable to find their way back.

One such incident occurred in Suffolk, when a boy and a girl with green tinged skin were found at the mouth of a pit. Their speech was unintelligible. They were taken to the house of Sir Richard de Calne at Wikes. They wept and seemed to be hungry, but would not touch the food put before them. Eventually they were induced to eat some beans, but would touch nothing else.

The boy was always languid and depressed and shortly died, but the girl gained in health and began to eat other food and gradually lost her green colour. She was baptised and lived for many years in the service of Sir Richard, but was rather loose and wanton in her conduct. She said that all the inhabitants of her own country were green. They had come from St Martin's Land where the sun never shone. She and the boy had been following their flocks when they heard the sound of sweet bells. They wandered into a cavern and found the mouth where they were struck senseless by the light of the sun and lay for a long time. They were terrified by the noise when people arrived and wanted to flee, but could not find their way back to the cavern and were caught.[134]

GREEN GIANT *See* GRONJETTE

GREEN JEAN haunts West Wemyss Castle in Scotland. She is a GREEN LADY.

GREEN KNIGHT is a fairy GREEN MAN. He appears in one of the Arthurian tales that explores the concept of the seasonal battle between representatives of summer and winter. As ARTHUR and his court were celebrating YULE, a Green Knight appeared and issued a challenge to the company: was anyone brave enough to take the axe he carried and chop off his head, a compliment he would return in a year's time? Sir Gawain leaped up, seized the axe and cut off the knight's head. To everyone's amazement, the Green Knight merely picked up his head and bid Gawain to meet him in a year's time at the Green Chapel.

A year passed and Gawain rode off to meet the Green Knight. Eventually he came to a castle and its Lord, a RED headed man, invited the knight to remain with his wife and himself until the time should come to keep the appointment. Each day Gawain hunted with the Red Lord, but each night the Lord's wife came to his room to try to seduce him. Being an honourable knight Gawain refused, but on the last night the lady came to him with a MAGIC green garter, which would protect its wearer from any kind of weapon. She said she would exchange it for a kiss. Seeing a chance to save his life for no more than a kiss, Gawain agreed.

The next day, he set off to the Green Chapel, a CAVE in the woodlands. The Green Knight stepped out and Gawain meekly kneeled before him and bowed his head. The Knight raised the axe high and brought it down, but just stopped short of the neck of Gawain, who couldn't help flinching.

Ashamed of his cowardice he apologised and bade the knight strike again. Once again the axe came down and stopped short, but Gawain held himself steady. Raising the axe once more the Knight struck, merely nicking Gawain's neck.

Gawain looked up and instead of the Green Knight, there stood his host, the Red Lord. The Lord praised his courage in meeting the challenge and said that the two blows that didn't touch him were in reward for his constancy in refusing the seductions of the Lady of the castle.

The third blow, which cut him, was for giving in to temptation and kissing the lady.

GREEN LADY/GREEN LADIES is a term for DRYADS. In England, fairies dwelling in OAK, ELM, APPLE, WILLOW, HOLLY and yew trees.

Permission had to be sought from the fairy before cutting down the tree. PRIMROSES were planted beneath the trees as an offering to the Green Lady to solicit her blessings. One Derbyshire farmer was certain that he owed his prosperity to the fact that every MIDSUMMER EVE he climbed the hill behind his house and laid primroses at the foot of the three trees that stood there, hailing them as his 'Green Ladies'. As he lay dying, he entreated his three sons not to forget the custom. The two elder sons thought it superstitious nonsense, but the younger one obeyed his father's wishes, and each Midsummer climbed the hill to pay homage to the TREE FAIRIES. This annoyed his eldest brother, who took out his spite by chopping down one of the trees. He died within the year. The second brother blamed the trees, and cut down another. He died within a few months. The youngest continued to honour the remaining Green Lady, who rewarded him with a long and prosperous life.

In Scotland, the term Green Lady (*Glaistig Uaine*) has a somewhat different meaning. There any woman dressed in GREEN must be a fairy, as the colour is unlucky for humans. The *bean chaol a chot uaine 's na gruaige buidhe*, or 'slender woman of the green kirtle and of the yellow hair', can change white mill water into red wine, and weave the threads of spiders into tartan plaid. She turns the stalk of the fairy reed into a pipe, the music of which can soothe the most troubled spirit, or rouse them into merriment. She might entice human men to stay with her in her fairy bower, but when they leave, though only a day has passed in fairyland, many years have passed in the world. Some Green Ladies act as HOUSE FAIRIES.

There are a large number of Green Ladies that seem to be somewhere between a fairy and a GHOST. For example, Ballindalloch Castle is haunted by a Green Lady. When her lover jilted the lady of Newton Castle

GREEN MAN

at Blairgowrie, a WITCH advised her to wear the green fairy CLOTHES. To win them she had to sit all night on the Corbie's Stane (RAVEN's Stone). The experiment failed and she died. At midnight on HALLOWEEN, her gravestone turns THREE times and she walks as a Green Lady. West Wemyss castle is haunted by a Green Lady called Green Jean.

GREEN LADY OF CAERPHILLY is a lonely fairy that haunts a ruined castle and sometimes appears as ivy.

GREEN LADY OF HELLASAY is a Scottish fairy that will only show herself to a MacLeod.

GREEN LADY OF LLYN BARFOG is the fairy who appeared at the lake of Llyn Barfog, which is near Aberdovey in Wales. At dusk fairies appear, clad all in GREEN, accompanied by their milk white hounds and milk white cattle. Once a farmer caught one of these cattle but misused it. A GREEN LADY arose from the lake and took the cow back below the waters, never to be seen again.[135]

GREEN LADY OF SKIPNESS is a GRUAGACH who helped out the inhabitants of Skipness Castle near Loch Fyne by defending them against danger and bewitching their enemies. She would warn the family when a death was imminent, sometimes appearing as a bunch of trailing ivy.

GREEN MAN/GREEN MEN is the vegetation spirit of the wildwood depicted in church carvings and pub signs all over Britain in the form of a severed head with branches and leaves emerging from the mouth. At one time, most of Britain was covered with forest and there are many legends of the forest fairies called WOOD WOSES, fairy WILDFOLK, green men or WILD MEN. Those who saw them described them as GREEN people, powerful fairies who could sometimes be appealed to for help and had to be placated if they were angered, as their ELF BOLTS or flint arrows were deadly. These green spirits represent the raw, untamed, primal force of nature. The green clad wildmen passed into folklore as fairies, often given the name of HOB, Robin, ROBIN GOODFELLOW or ROBIN HOOD.

GREENCOATIES is a Lincolnshire fenland term for fairies in general, believed locally to dress in GREEN.

GREENIES is a Lancashire term for fairies in Northern England.

GREENSLEEVES is the name of a fairy wizard in a Scottish tale.[136]

GREMLIN/GREMLINS are modern English fairies who cause problems with machinery by blocking pipes, loosening screws and generally tinkering about. The Royal Air Force first discovered them during World War II. There are many tales as to how this came about, but the commonest one ascribes the discovery to the comical character and accident-prone Pilot Officer Prune, who

described the gremlin effect on aircraft. Gremlins are 15-50 cm high (6 to 20 inches), green, blue or grey in colour with horns or big ears. The term may be derived from the Old English word *gremian* meaning 'to vex' though Pilot Officer Prune claimed it was arrived at by amalgamating 'Grimm's fairy Tales' with 'Fremlin's Elephant Ales.'

GRENDEL is a legendary creature who appears in the famous eighth-century Old English poem *Beowulf*. He was man-shaped, had the strength of thirty men and lived in a watery lair with his mother. He regularly raided the hall of the Danish king until killed by the hero Beowulf. He was possibly a TROLL, OGRE or a GIANT, though some think he may have been a DRAUGAR. *See also* BLACK SHUCK.

GREY MAN OF MACDUI *See* FEAR LIATH MOR.

GREY NEIGHBOURS is a Shetland term for the TROWS.

GRIAN is the Fairy Queen of north-east Leinster in Ireland. She lives in the MOUND called Cnoc Greine. She fled with the hero Diarmaid - all over Ireland there are cromlechs and cairns called 'the bed of Diarmaid and Grian'. She was once a sun goddess.

GRIGS are tiny British fairies about the size of a grasshopper. They dress in

GREEN and wear RED CAPS, which some say are made of flowers. They are always happy and jolly, hence the expression 'as merry as a grig'. In 1936, two workers were crossing Stanmore Common in Middlesex when they saw grigs playing in the bracken. Two of them pulled on their red caps and disappeared, but the third was in such a panic that he pulled his cap too hard and fell into it like a sack. One of the men saw it and reached out to pick it up, exclaiming that it was a fine red hat. The other warned him to leave it alone, but the first pulled it onto his head. The grig in the hat began to pull his hair and beat him about the head and the man dragged off the cap exclaiming that there was the mother and father of all hornets inside it. The grig shot out of it as it lay on the ground and cried: 'You was told to leave it lay'. All the bracken rang with the laughter of the grigs and the men ran like hell.[137]

GRIM is an English GOBLIN that 'do like a skritch OWL cry at sicke men's windows' and 'When candles burne both blue and dim,/Old folks will say, 'Here's fairy Grim'.[138] This fairy title was once much more common, as evidenced by the number of English place names such as Grim's Dyke, Grimley ('grove of the goblin') etc. There is a Fairy Grim in *The Life of Robin Goodfellow* (1628). Grim or Grimr was a title of the Norse god Odin, meaning 'hooded') or 'masked' as the god was often known to go about in disguise among mortals. *See also* CHURCH GRIM and HOOD.

GRIG

GRIM REAPER is a name given to Death, probably from the same root as 'GRIM', meaning 'hooded' as he is usually depicted as a hooded skeleton.

GRINDYLOW is a malignant Yorkshire WATER FAIRY.

GROAC'H LANASCOL ('Fairy of Lanascol') is a Breton fairy who appears in the guise of a HAG, bent and twisted with her hands leaning on a crutch with which she stirs the golden leaves in the autumn. Then (probably in the spring) she appears as a lovely maiden, wonderfully adorned and accompanied by strange, silent, little black men. If she stops before a tree, the tree will bend down as if to receive her commands. If she looks into a pool, it trembles to its very depths.

GROAC'H VOR is a Breton MERMAID or sea woman.

GROGAN is an Ulster HOUSE FAIRY closely related to the GRUAGACH.

GROGOCH is an Irish HOUSE FAIRY, probably cognate with the Ulster GROGAN and the Scottish GRUAGACH. It is known throughout Antrim, Rathlin Island and Donegal. Though it is usually invisible, it may occasionally be glimpsed in the guise of a small, naked old man, covered in RED HAIR. A grogoch feels neither heat nor cold and lives in a CAVE or hollow, or the large leaning stones that appear about the countryside which are known as 'Grogochs' Houses'. A grogoch will occasionally help out about the house or farm in return for a jug of cream, but if offended will cause trouble and a priest will have to be called in to get rid of it.

GROMER SOMER JOURE ('Lord of the Summer's Day') is an OTHERWORLD being of Arthurian legend.

He demanded that Arthur should discover what women most desire. The answer was revealed by LADY RAGNELL, the HAG bride of Sir Gawain.

GRONJETTE is a green giant who haunts the Grünewald ('Greenwood') on the Isle of Möen. He is a spectral hunter who hunts on horseback carrying his head. His prey are the WOOD-WIVES and he was once spotted carrying a dead one across his saddle saying 'SEVEN years have I chased her, now in Falster I have slain her'.[139] *See* WILD HUNT.

GROVES of trees and the mysterious forests they stand in are frequented by fairies. Sacred trees have played a part in the folklore of most countries and were worshipped as spirits and deities. *See also* TREE FAIRIES.

GROVE DAMSELS or **Grove Folk** are Swedish ELVES who live in groves and protect the trees.

GRUAGACH ('Long Haired One') is a castle haunting type of GLAISTIG, in Scotland. It may be either male or female, and attaches itself to grand houses and castles, though it is the building it is attached to, not the family. If the house is demolished it will disappear, never to be seen again. The gruagach appears or cries out whenever joy or sorrow is coming to the family. It goes around tidying up at night, sweeping the floor, and re-arranging the furniture. When it is heard doing so you can be sure that visitors are about to arrive. It is a temperamental creature, sometimes it will finish the washing, or at other times, despite the noise of work, things may be found in disorder or tradesmen's tools ruined. To prevent a gruagach messing about with the SPINNING wheel the band must be taken off at night. When servants annoy it the 'Long Haired One' will punish them by knocking over water pitchers, unmaking the beds, putting dust in the meat, or slapping people on the side of the head.

Milkmaids were always careful to propitiate them by pouring MILK on certain stones for their consumption, otherwise the gruagach would allow the cow to trample the corn, or if further offerings were neglected, cause the death of the cow. In the Highlands, the stone, which the milk is poured into, is called *Leac na Gruagaich* or 'flag-stone of the Gruagach'. One Scottish minister reported that 'the fairy queen who watches over cows is called Gruagach in the islands and she is often seen'. People used to say they were the spirits of ancient druids, living on milk left for them by those whose priests they had once been. On Skye, there were altars to gruagachs where offerings were left.

In Ireland, the term is applied to a variety of fairy beings such as OGRES, GOBLINS, GIANTS and even human magicians, druids and heroes.

Gruagach means 'long haired one' or possibly, 'hairy one' and they may once have been NATURE SPIRITS, gods or WILD MEN. *See also* HAIR.

GRYLA are Faeroe Island mountain fairies, described as having shaggy pelts like sheep. They are said to be very dangerous and are best avoided.

GRYPHONS are Welsh fairies who have the heads of HORSES and the bodies of GOATS. They can speak in the human tongue. They blight any crops left in the fields after HALLOWEEN.

GÜBICH is a demon-fairy who roams the forests of Harz and frightens people. He is held out as a sort of BOGEYMAN to children.

GUERRIONETS is a type of KORRED who wears broad brimmed hats.

GUGWES or **Djenu** are creatures known to the Micmac Indians of Canada. They are giants and have the faces of bears. Some say they are ape-like.

GUILLYN VEGGEY ('Little Boys') is a Manx term for the fairies.

GUINEVERE ('White Phantom') is Arthur's legendary queen who may have been of fairy origin: her name suggests that she was a WHITE LADY, the guardian spirit of a place, perhaps Albion itself. She always dressed in GREEN, the fairy colour, was captured by ARTHUR and married at BELTANE, the traditional time of marriage for NATURE FAIRIES and gods, though an unlucky month for humans. She may be a later form of the Welsh goddess BLODEUWEDD (Guendoloena in the *Vita Merlini*) who began life as a maiden composed of flowers and finished as an OWL (perhaps the 'white phantom'), as befits a seasonal goddess of life and death.

GUINGAMEUR is the king of AVALON in some stories, and the lover of MORGAN LE FAY.

GULL is an ELF, an associate of ROBIN GOODFELLOW.[140]

GUMNUT BABIES are Australian fairies that live in the town of Gumnut in the Bush. They love music and dancing and are attended by insects. Their names are Bib, Bub, Snugglepot, Cuddlepie, Ragged Blossom, Narnywo, Nittersing and Chucklebud.

GUNNA is a Scottish Highland fairy who lives alone - some say he has been banished from fairyland. He wears fox skins. Sometimes he helps humans to look after cattle.

GURIUZ are north Italian fairies that bring good weather to farmers. They are a type of ERDLUITLE. *See also* WEATHER FAIRIES.

GURT DOG is a Somerset BLACK DOG.

GUTER JOHANN ('Good John') is a German HOUSE FAIRY.

GWARCHELLS are small Welsh fairies, gentle and kindly unless they are shown disrespect. They live underground and generally avoid sunlight.

GWARTHEG Y LLYN ('Kine of the Lake') are magical milk-white COWS owned by a band of fairies that haunt Llyn Barfog, a lake near Aberdovey, Wales.

GWARWYN-A-THROT was a friendly BWCA who helped out on a farm in

Monmouthshire. She helped a maidservant who was descended from the fairy BENDITH Y MAMAU. Gwarwyn-a-Throt did all her work for her - SPINNING, washing, ironing, and teasing the wool. All he required in payment was a bowl of milk or a sweet loaf. No one ever saw the fairy, including the girl. One night, out of sheer mischief, she substituted a bowl of urine for his usual bowl of milk. The next morning the bwca grabbed the girl by the neck and beat her black and blue.

The fairy was not heard of for two years until he was discovered working at another farm in the neighbourhood, called Hafod y Ynys. There he worked for a pleasant girl who fed him with bread and milk. He refused to show himself to her, and her curiosity grew until she could stand it no longer. She tricked him one day by telling him that she was going out. Sneaking back, she heard him working away at the spinning wheel singing:

'How she would laugh if she knew
That my name is Gwarwyn-a-Throt'.
The maid called out to him that she now knew his name.

'What is it then?', he asked. 'Gwarwyn-a-Throt, she replied. At this, he left the spinning wheel moved to a nearby farm where he became friendly with a servant called Moses. But Moses went off to fight against Richard Crookback and was killed at Bosworth Field. Gwarwyn-a-Throt became very wicked and troublesome. Eventually, a CUNNING MAN was able to lay him and banished him to the Red Sea.[141]

GWAZIG-GAN is a type of KORRED.

GWENDYDD is the twin sister of MERLIN.

GWENHIDW ('White Enchanter') is the Queen of the Welsh fairies the TYLWYTH TEG, according to some. She is possibly a form of GUINEVERE.

GWERDDONAU LLION ('The Green Meadows of Enchantment') are occasionally glimpsed by sailors. They are fairy islands beneath the waves between England and Wales, somewhere in the Bristol Channel between Somerset and Pembrokeshire. The islands are rarely visible, and are only seen by accident. During the nineteenth century some sailors landed on the islands and joined the fairies in their revels, but when they sailed away and looked back, the islands had vanished. In the fifth century, the British King Gavran made a voyage in search of these islands, but whether he ever found them is not known, since he was never seen again. He may be there still, feasting with the fairies.

Fairies from the islands are reputed to have once regularly visited the markets of Milford Haven and Laugharne, silently making their purchases and always leaving the right money. The people of Milford Haven had a special ability to see the fairy islands and knew that the fairies went to and fro via a subterranean tunnel under the sea. Some claimed that the island fairies were really certain druids who could not enter heaven because they were Pagans, but who were not wicked enough to enter hell.

GWRACH Y RHIBYN ('Hag of the Dribble') is a Welsh BANSHEE who appears at CROSSROADS, stream banks, or on the sides of mountains. She is a withered HAG with black teeth, tangled hair and bat-like wings. If you encounter the hag and she shrieks: 'My husband! My husband!' your husband will die. If she shrieks: 'My child! My child!', then your child will die and so forth. Sometimes she enters into the body of the person she intends to warn and will be carried along until a stream or crossroads is reached, when she will begin to shriek. She is called the Hag of the Dribble because the stones she dribbled from her apron formed the mountains. See also WASHER AT THE FORD, BANSHEE, CYHIREATH and CYOERRAETH.

GWRAGEDD ANNWN ('Wives of the UNDERWORLD') are fairy maidens who dwell beneath the lakes in the Black Mountains of Wales. They are exquisitely beautiful and sometimes come ashore to marry mortal husbands, bringing herds of fairy COWS as dowries. They must never be touched with IRON or struck, or they will return to the lake taking their cattle with them. People have reported seeing the towers and hearing the bells of their underwater lands. One legend says that the Gwragedd Annwn were once human women, who were turned into fairies by St Patrick when he returned for a visit to Wales. They berated him for abandoning his native land for Ireland, and insulted him in no uncertain terms. Several old Welsh families claim descent from the Gwragedd Annwn. See also LADY OF THE LAKE and MORGAN LE FAY.

GWYDION is the King of the fairies of North Wales or perhaps the TYLWYTH TEG, though some say that GWYN AP NUDD holds that position. His name is derived from the Welsh father-god.

GWYLLGI, HOUND OF DARKNESS is a phantom Black Dog that haunts Pant-y-Madog in Pembrokeshire. It has blazing red eyes and baleful breath; it runs from the castle to the town.

GWYLLION ('Hag Fairy') are the mountain fairies of Wales, usually frightful HAGS who lead wanderers astray. A Gwyllion called the 'Old Woman of the Mountain' haunts Llanhyddel. She looks like a poor old woman wearing a four-cornered hat, ash coloured clothes, and with a pot upon her head. She leaps up before the unwary traveller crying: 'Wwb!' or 'Wow up!' and anyone who sees her or hears her cry will be sure to be lost.

The gwyllion roam the hills caring for herds of GOATS, combing the goats' beards every Wednesday, the Welsh fairies' sabbath. They can take the form of goats themselves.[142]

The gwyllion dislike mortals

intensely and often lead them into swamps or just stare at them with a malicious expression. They once had the power of flight, but somehow lost it. They fear storms and will sometimes seek out mountain huts for shelter. They also fear IRON or steel knives, and if you can corner one with a knife it must grant you a wish, but then the whole tribe of the gwyllion will hate you forever, and you will never be able to travel safely in the mountains again. Evan Thomas once found himself surrounded by gwyllion while travelling in the mountains, heard the sound of a bugle and the noise of invisible hunters riding by. Directly he drew out his knife, the fairies vanished.[143]

On stormy nights the gwyllion often sought shelter at the homes of people in Aberystruth, where they were made welcome, the inhabitants taking care to bring them clean water and that no knife or cutting tool should come near them.

These creatures are often referred to in Welsh poetry and the term often seems to mean a ghost or DEAD soul, allowed to return to the earth in a visible form.

GWYN AP NUDD is the Welsh King of the UNDERWORLD who leads the WILD HUNT and rules the TYLWYTH TEG. The entrance to his kingdom is through the Welsh lakes, or beneath Glastonbury Tor in England. He once summoned St. Collen (or Tollen) to meet him on the Tor. The saint had objected to Gwyn ap Nudd being called both the king of fairies and the king of ANNWN, the underworld. At first the saint was reluctant but eventually went armed with a flask of holy water. On top of the hill, he saw a fair castle and troops of minstrels, comely youths and graceful, pretty maids. King Gwyn ap Nudd, seated on a golden throne, greeted him courteously and bade him share in the feast. The saint refused to eat the FAIRY FOOD and dowsed Gwyn ap Nudd with holy water, which caused him to disappear.

Gwyn ap Nudd is often mentioned in Welsh poetry. He is named as the son of Nudd, the Lord of the DEAD. Each MAY DAY he fights Gwythyr for the hand of the maiden CRIEDDYLED and this contest will carry on until doomsday - a description of the seasonal battle between the powers of blight and the powers of growth. Gwyn ap Nudd also appears in the Arthurian tales, which assert that it was ARTHUR himself who made Gwyn both the ruler of the DEAD and the king of Annwn. Gwyn ap Nudd is particularly associated with the Vale of Neath (Nudd is pronounced 'neath') and is traditionally depicted with an OWL.

GYL BURNT TAYLE is an old English name for the WILL O'THE WISP.

GYRE-CARLIN is a HAG fairy of Scotland who rides the storm and can confer skills in SPINNING. She is often accompanied by a small child, which she takes home and bathes before bedtime. Some describe her as the Fairy Queen of Fife. She is sometimes called Nicnevin, and it is under this guise that she rides the storm. This name may be derived from the Gaelic *nic neamhan* meaning 'Daughter of Heaven'. It seems likely that she was once a seasonal crone goddess.

GYTRASH or **Guytrash** are evil northern English fairies that appear at night as large HORSES, donkeys or shaggy BLACK DOGS with webbed feet, lurking silently by the side of the road to waylay travellers. A gytrash has drooping saucer-shaped eyes and walks with a splashing sound – the '*trash-trash-trash*' sound of old fashioned boots.[144] Occasionally, a friendly gytrash will help a lost person and show them the way home.

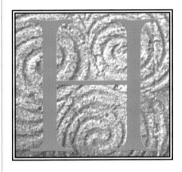

HAAF-FISH is an Orkney term for the SELKIE.

HABETROT is a lowland Scots fairy and the patroness of SPINNING. A shirt woven by her is efficacious against any ill. She appears in a story that has elements of similarity with the tales of TOM TIT TOT and RUMPELSTILTSKIN.

There once was a lazy young girl who hated spinning and avoided it whenever she could until her mother shut her up with her spinning wheel and five skeins of FLAX, saying that she wouldn't let her out until she had spun them. The girl picked up her spindle but soon made her fingers and lips sore with her bungled attempts. Bursting into tears she climbed through the bedroom window and fled into the fields. Near the stream she found a self HOLED STONE, through which, as everyone knows, one can see fairies. Peering through the cleft the girl was amazed to see into a fairy MOUND where a strange little woman sat spinning, pulling out the thread with a huge, long lip. She was none other than the fairy Habetrot. It was soon arranged that the fairy would spin her thread.

The mother was delighted with the smooth thread, and ran back and forth boasting how her daughter had spun so well. A passing laird thought what a good wife the girl would make, and married her, bragging of all the spinning she would do after the wedding. He presented his bride with a new spinning wheel and plenty of fresh flax.

The unhappy girl went down to the holed stone and called on Habetrot. The kindly fairy considered the problem and advised the girl to bring her husband to visit the fairy spinners. The couple was shown into the mound and the laird was horrified at the deformed backs and lips of the women.

'Yes, we were all bonnie once, until we took up the spinning', Habetrot said, 'Yon girl will soon be the same after pulling out the thread with her sweet red lips and bending her lovely young back over the wheel!' The laird was horrified at the prospect of his lovely young bride losing her looks. He took his wife home and forbade her to do any spinning, passing it all on to the fairies instead. So all worked out well in the end.

HABUNDIA *See* ABUNDIA.

HACKELBRAND is the leader of the WILD HUNT in Germany. Legend makes him the GHOST of a hunter called Hans von Hacklenberg who died in 1521 and who did not want to go to heaven but wanted to continue hunting. It is possible that Hacklenberg was originally an epithet applied to the German chief god Woden.

HADA or HADAS is a Spanish generic term for a fairy, similar in character to the French FÉE or FADA.

HADES is a type of FÉE, as well as being a Greek god of the UNDERWORLD.

HAFERBOCK ('Oat GOAT') is a corn spirit in German folklore.

HAG OF BEARE *See* CAILLEACH BEARA.

HAG OF THE DRIBBLE *See* GWRACH Y RHIBYN.

HAG STONE *See* HOLED STONE.

HAGS appear in many folk and fairy tales, ugly withered old women, sometimes human and sometimes fairies or WITCHES. They often bring sickness, death or winter, devour humans or cook them in their CAULDRONS. In English literature of the Renaissance period the words 'hag' and 'fairy' were synonymous.

These tales are folk memories of the crone goddesses of death and winter since they are most often abroad between BELTANE and SAMHAIN. At the beginning of summer they either disappear from sight or turn into lovely young maidens.

The hag goddess was also the sagacious old woman. For example, The Hag of Scone chose the ancient Scottish kings, and it is her spirit that resides in the Coronation Stone of Scone, now returned to Scotland after being part of the coronation throne in Westminster Abbey in London for many centuries. (*See also* Badbh, Befana, Black Annis, Gentle Annie, Caillage Ny Groagmagh, Cailleach, Cailleach Beara, Cailleach Bheur, Cailleach Uisge, Gyre-Carlin, Gwrach Y Rhibyn, Gorska Makva, Gwyllion, Frau Holda, Garbh Ogh, Holda, Járnvidja, Madgy Figgy, Korrigan, Kriksy, Kulshedra, Muireacrtach, Miru, Vargamor, Lady Ragnall, Loathly Lady, Nicnevin, Nocnitsa, Old Hag, Peg O'Nell, Peg Prowler, Plaksy, Snow Queen, Washer at the Ford, Whuppity Stoorie, Túnridur, Woman of the Mist, Yama-Uba, Yuki Onna and Baba Yaga.)

HAG RIDDEN horses are those which have been stolen by WITCHES and

fairies. They ride them through the night and bring them back at dawn, exhausted or 'hagridden'.

HAG RIDERS are the riders of the WILD HUNT in some Norse myths, female *túnridur* or 'HAG Riders'.

HAG-KNOTS are tangles in HORSES manes. WITCHES and fairies make them to use as stirrups when they steal horses at night to hag-ride them (i.e. ride them wildly over hill and dale, bringing them back exhausted).

HAIR of fairies differs form that of humans. Indeed, there is something very strange about it and many fairies have hair that is preternaturally long and beautiful. Water fairies in particular may be seen seductively combing such lovely hair. Sometimes a fairy may be recognised because the hair is green, like the Vodianoi, or composed of seaweed, like Tangie, or watercress like the Kelpie, moss like the Leshie or even SNAKES, as in the case of Yama-Uba. Sometimes the hair is always wet and refuses to dry as with the Morgans and the Rusalka.

RED HAIR often betrays an otherworldly origin and a variety of spirits such as the Pech and the Morrigan have red hair. Witches too are discovered by their red hair. Many fairies go naked, and these are often covered in red hair.

A huge number of fairies are described as very hairy, or partly or completely covered in hair, like an animal. Usually these are nature fairies, protecting forests and wild places, though they are sometimes the protectors of the home. The word 'hairy' even forms part of the name of several fairies like Hairy Meg, Puck-Hairy, Red Hairy Men, and the native name of the famous Bigfoot, Sasquatch means 'Hairy Man'. Wild Men and Wood Woses are commonly described as hairy, shaggy figures.

Sometimes the state of the hair

indicates that the fairy is a creature that lives outside of normal human conventions. The hair may be unkempt and tangled. Otherwise, in contrast to the hair of human women in some societies, fairy hair is worn long, uncovered or unbound. This is true of the mermaids who shamelessly display their hair, the gorgeous hair of the Sidhe, and the flowing wet hair of the Rusalka.

Perhaps in all of these instances the state of the hair is an indicator of the wild and free character of the fairy who lives close to nature and is not restricted by the conventions that bind human societies. The ancients saw the hair as a seat of the life-force and for men cutting the hair symbolised loosing power and potency, as in the

HAMADRYADS

case of Samson. Cutting hair also symbolises death, the ultimate loss of potency, as in the death of the setting sun as it loses its last rays.[145] Hair may be cut as a sign of mourning, or as a symbol of an initiation as when the tribal shaman has all of his hair cut off, or a monk when he shaves off part of his hair in a religious tonsure. Dishevelled hair is a sign of mourning or of hopelessness, or the matted hair of a type of ascetic.

For women long, loose hair symbolises freedom, youth, virginity and magical power. Cutting the hair is related to losing virginity - ancient Greek girls offered up their shorn hair

in temples after this rite of passage. In some cultures, girls tie up their hair when they reach womanhood, or married women cover it, symbolising a loss of freedom. It was believed that the cutting of a woman's hair deprived her of the power to work magic and cast spells.[146] The Vily have very long fair hair and should they lose a single strand they will die. *See also* CRO-MAGNON MAN.

HAIRY JACK is a BLACK DOG that haunts a barn in Lincolnshire.

HÄKELMÄNNER are German WATER FAIRIES who appear wearing RED CAPS and carrying harps. They are SHAPESHIFTERS and may turn into horses, bulls or fishes.

HALF-HANNIKIN is a little Somerset HOUSE FAIRY who cleans up at night.

HALLOWEEN or **All Hallows Eve**, falls on 31st October. Traditionally, it is the time when WITCHES, fairies, GHOSTS and all sorts of spirits are released from the UNDERWORLD and freely roam abroad for the night. On this night, fairy MOUNDS open and reveal the inhabitants inside. It was once the custom to take precautions to protect individuals and property from the attentions of evil or mischievous spirits at Halloween. These included protecting the house with HOLLY.

Halloween is derived from the ancient Celtic festival of SAMHAIN, which marked the start of winter. On this night, the Celts believed that the veils that separate the human realm from the OTHERWORLD are thin, and spirits may pass freely through. After this time the spirits of winter, blight and death walk the land until spring.

HALLUCINATIONS can be brought on by mental disturbance or the use of alcohol or psychoactive drugs. Some claim that the sight of fairies is purely an hallucination. Certainly, SHAMANS in many cultures have used narcotics to help them attain a state of consciousness in which they can interact with spirits. FLY AGARIC is commonly mentioned in conjunction with fairies, spirits and shamans. However, this is only one of a number of psychoactive drugs used by shamans that generate sensations of flying, visions and perceptual enhancement.

Kevin Callahan documented the experience of Ojibwa Indians who saw little people for about thirty minutes during hallucinations induced by Atropine plants from the Deadly Nightshade family.[147]

Even alcohol withdrawal has been known to induce fancies of little people.[148]

HALTIA are Finnish fairy FAMILIARS; some take the role of an individual's GENIUS, developing THREE days after his or her birth, others protect the house or bath house like a type of HOUSE FAIRY.

HAMADRYADS are the NYMPHS of particular trees in Greek myths. They are female to the waist and their lower parts form the trunk and roots of the tree. Their trees grow only in secluded spots where they are unlikely to be encountered. When their tree dies so does the nymph, and if the tree is cut down a cry of anguish can be heard escaping it.

An ancient story is told of a man called Rhoekos who saw an OAK ready to fall to the ground and ordered his slaves to prop it up. The nymph who had been about to die asked him what reward he would like. He said he would like to become her lover and she agreed, on condition that he should avoid the company of every other woman, and a bee would be her messenger to him. One day the bee appeared as he was playing draughts and interrupted his concentration. He made a rough reply to it, which so angered the nymph that she sent him blind.

HAMINGJA, **Hamingia** or **Ham** ('Luck') is the spirit of a person's or a family's luck in Norse myth, often personified as a stately woman. In one of the Icelandic sagas a man dreams that a lovely woman is travelling towards him from a certain direction, and interprets this as his grandfather having died and his hamingja now coming to live with him.[149] *See also* GENIUS, DÆMON, DÖPPELGANGER, FYLGJA.

HANTU HUTAN are forest fairies of the Malay Peninsula that are generally considered to be malevolent. No one dare enter the forest alone, and the fairies are entreated with prayers not to injure travellers.

HAPTALAÖN, LÉ ('Snatchheel') is a Guernsey fairy who lies in the long grass of orchards to catch those children who are trying to scrump unripe apples. If he ever catches one he will grab it by the leg and carry it off to his home and it will never be seen again.[150]

HÅRDMANDLE/HÅRDMANDLENE is a male ERDLUITLE. These fairies return stray animals to their owners and make cheese from their own chamois herds. This cheese has magical properties. If you are given some, it will grow back to full size each time you bite it, but if you fail to eat it all, it will vanish forever.

HARES are often associated with fairies and WITCHES. The hare is connected with lusty fertility and with madness, especially during the mating season

HARE

when they may be seen boxing or leaping in the air, allegedly resembling a coven of dancing witches. Like many animals sacred to the older religions, the Mediaeval Christians changed the hare into an animal of ill omen, saying that witches and fairies shapeshift into hare forms to suck cows dry. There are many stories of wounds inflicted on hares being found the next day on women.

Hares were sacred to the ancient Celts who associated them with MOON and hunting deities. Killing and eating the hare was taboo, but this restriction was lifted at BELTANE, when a ritual hunt and consumption was made. Folk survivals of this observance still persist. Until the end of the 18th century a hare hunt took place in the Dane Hills, near Leicester led by the mayor and corporation. This hare was associated with Black Annis, a fearful HAG fairy said to live in a CAVE in the hills known as Black Annis's Bower, which she had gouged out of the hillside with her own claws.

In Europe, the hare is also associated with the corn spirit. Hares hide in cornfields until the last reaping, the last sheaf is often called 'the hare', and its cutting called 'killing the hare', 'cutting the hare' or 'cutting the hare's tail off'.

HARLEQUIN is a character originating in the Italian Commedia del l'Arte and later very popular on the English stage. His origins are in the character of HELLEKIN or Harlekin, a leader of the WILD HUNT.

HARP is the musical instrument beloved by Celtic fairies, who excel in its playing. The MUSIC of the fairy harp is often used to lure humans into FAIRYLAND.

HATHOR is the Egyptian term for fairies, derived from Hathor, the ancient COW-headed goddess of love, beauty and childbirth. When a child is born, SEVEN Hathors appear as FAIRY GODMOTHERS to plan its life.

HAUGBAI is a Norse 'BARROW-WIGHT'.

HAUGBONDE is the old Norse guardian spirit of a farm.

HAUGBUI ('Barrow Spirit') See HOGBOY, BARROW-WIGHT and DRAUGARS.

HAUSBÖCKE ('House Goats') are German HOUSE FAIRIES that have something of the GOAT about them, like their field-dwelling cousins the KORNBÖCKE, or 'Corn Goats'.

HAUSMÄNNER ('House Men') are German HOUSE FAIRIES. They are sometimes helpful, and sometimes mischievous, but always demand a reward for their labours.

HAUS-SCHMIEDLEIN ('Little House Smith') is a Bohemian KNOCKER who predicts the death of a miner by knocking THREE times. Lesser misfortunes are signalled by the sound of him digging or pounding.

HAVFINE are Norwegian MERMAIDS and are temperamental creatures. It is a bad OMEN to see one.

HAVFREUI are MERMAIDS of Gotland, described as female TROLLS who live in the sea, sometimes helpful to fishermen and sailors, other times playing evil tricks on them. The havfreui keep COWS that they bring out to graze on the night of YULE. One man decided to capture one of these fairy beasts, and when the water woman appeared with her animals, he threw his IRON axe so that it hit the

cow without hurting it, but from then on, the cow was under his power. Next spring he was out hunting seals on the ice when the ice cracked and he was stranded on a floating block. The water woman appeared and said that she would save him as long as he gave her back her cow. He refused and almost froze to death before he was rescued.

HAVFRUE are Scandinavian female WATER FAIRIES or sea-maids that appear when a thin mist hangs over the sea. They may be seen sitting on the surface of the water combing their long golden hair with golden combs, or driving their snow white COWS to feed on the strand. To see them portends disaster.

HAVMAND or HAVEMAND are Danish male WATER FAIRIES or MERMEN. They have black beards, fish tails and green hair.

HAWTHORN (Crataegus monogyna) is a tree very much associated with fairies; they meet beneath its shade. It is said that when the OAK, ASH and thorn grow close together it is a favourite haunt of the fey folk and those solitary hawthorns growing on hills or near wells are boundary markers to the world of the fairies. Until recent times an Irish peasant would sooner die than cut down a hawthorn because of its sacredness to fairies, believing they generally stood in the middle of a fairy ring. Any human who sleeps beneath one, especially on MAY EVE, is in danger of being taken away by fairies. In some parts of Brittany and Ireland it was considered dangerous to pluck a leaf from old and solitary trees especially those growing in unfrequented spots and on moorland. Fairies are very protective of hawthorns, and a blooming tree should never be trimmed as it angers them, and always the tree should be trimmed east to west.

HAZEL (Corylus avellana) is another tree with many fairy connections. A fifteenth century spell for summoning fairies

involved burying hazel wands under a fairy hill. Hazel was called *bile ratha* in Ireland, meaning tree of the RATH (a fairy dwelling). Boiling jam was stirred with a hazel or ROWAN stick to prevent the fairies from stealing it. In Ireland hazel is associated with wisdom, and in England with fertility and divination.

Hazel is the commonest wood used to make a forked divining rod used for divining water and buried treasures. The divining rod was connected with ELVES and PIXIES who have all the treasures of the earth in their keeping. Hazel was traditionally cut at MIDSUMMER, one of the great fairy festivals.

There is an ancient Celtic story, which tells that Sinend, daughter of Lodan son of Lir, often visited a well in FAIRYLAND. There stood the hazels of wisdom and inspiration that in the same hour bore fruit, blossom and foliage which fell upon the well in the same shower. On one occasion the waters broke forth in anger and overwhelmed her, washing her up on the shore of the river Shannon where she died giving the river its name. This is a cautionary tale, a warning that the gifts of wisdom and inspiration may not be attained without a degree of risk.

HAZEL THICKET FAIRIES live in English hazel thickets and punish anyone unwise enough to pick the unripe nuts with bloating and cramp.

HEALING and the power to heal are assocted with fairies, particularly WATER FAIRIES. Their help is solicited with offerings of PINS and coins thrown into wells, streams, and lakes. To this day in Britain and Ireland, some special trees, especially those near holy wells and springs, are hung with gifts or rags to solicit blessings or healing from their spirits. Early Scandinavians seeking healing would redden the outside of a fairy MOUND with the blood of a sacrificed bull, then offer the meat as a meal to the ELVES.[151] Fairies can bestow the gift of healing on their favourites. SHAMANS and WITCHES receive their powers from spirits or fairies. The famous witch Biddy Early (d. 1873) used a blue bottle, which they gave her, for healing and prophecy. Fairy objects such as the fairy spade (a smooth slippery black stone) are useful for healing. They can be put in water, which will then cure any sick people or cattle that drink it. A UNICORN's horn is a restorative able to cure many diseases, act as an antidote to poison and even to raise the dead.

HEARTH is the place in a house most associated with domestic spirits. They often try to gain access to a house in order to warm themselves by it and are much angered if they are kept out. They like to DANCE on the hearth and often enter by flying down the chimney or exit by flying up it. A discovered CHANGELING will make its escape up the chimney. Some fairy homes lie beneath human hearths, and the hearthstones are their doors. Sometimes the fairies living there will reach up and steal cakes baking on the hearth.

The hearth was once the central focus of the home, providing warmth and food. It was the place of the fire, which meant the difference between freezing and surviving, eating and starving. As such it was sacred and the focus of many customs. The fire had to be kept burning, and was only put out at certain times of year, to be re-lit from a sacred flame. Because the smoke rose to the sky, it was a message rising to the spirits or gods, while below the hearthstone lay the UNDERWORLD. Therefore the hearth was also a domestic *axis mundi* via which the gods or spirits could enter the home and a shaman's spirit could travel out. This is possibly why FATHER CHRISTMAS enters the house via the chimney. HOUSE FAIRIES may originate in the ancient belief in household gods or spirits that protected the home, like the Roman LARES. The hearth was their means of entrance and egress, their shrine and altar flame.

HEATHER (*Calluna vulgaris*) is the moorland and heathland plant upon which fairies are said to feed. An Irish myth tells of the death of the giantess Garbh Ogh (probably a HAG goddess) who set up her chair in the womb of the hills at the season of the heather bloom and then expired.

HEATHER PIXIES live in the north of England and in Scotland. They spend their time SPINNING. They are diminutive creatures with translucent wings.

HEDLEY KOW is a BOGGLE that haunted the village of Hedley on the Hill in Northumberland, and who liked to play mischievous tricks. He would turn himself into a truss of straw on the path of old women gathering kindling. If they took it up to carry it away it would become so heavy that they would be forced to lay it down. The straw would get up and shuffle away with a laugh and a shout. One of his most outstanding disguises was that of two girls who led two men into a bog before disappearing. The kow would also imitate the voices of the lovers of female farm servants, give all the cream to cats, unravel knitting, or put the SPINNING wheel out of order. The kow has not been reported since the middle of the nineteenth century, so he may have died or simply moved away.

HEERWISCHE is a German WILL O'THE WISP.

HEIMCHEN are German fairies that follow in the train of BERCHTE.

HEINZEMANNCHEN or HEINZELMÄNNCHEN is a small EARTH FAIRY or DWARF in German folklore. These fairies are small and dress in GREEN or RED with RED CAPS. They have RED HAIR and beards, and some of them are blind. They may SHAPESHIFT into CATS, children, bats, SNAKES or roosters. Heinzemannchen act like HOUSE FAIRIES; working at night for people they like or owe favours to. They will do most of the work about house and farm if they are fed once at week and on holidays, but will leave if they are slighted by being laughed at, given CLOTHES, rushed or not fed. They curse those who have upset them and this is not a thing to be taken lightly. They will also leave if the house burns down and a wagon wheel is left in front of it.

HEINZLIN ('Little Heinz') is one of the tribe of German HOUSE FAIRIES, the HEINZEMANNCHEN.

HEIZEMÄNN is a HOUSE FAIRY found in the Cologne region.

HEJKADLO is a Bohemian fairy that calls out to distract travellers from their path.

HELIKE is the willow NYMPH in ancient Greek myth.

HELLEKIN or **Harlekin** is a leader of the WILD HUNT; a priest called Wachin saw him in the vicinity of St Aubin in Anjou in 1901.[152] He was accompanied by a troop of noble ladies, churchmen and men, all in black on black horses carrying black banners. Wachin recognised many of them as people he had known who were DEAD. Hellekin devolved into the character of Harlequin on the Italian and English stage.

HEMÄNNER ('Hey-Man') is a variety of Rumanian fairy that tries to distract travellers from their path by calling out to them.

HENKIES or **Henkie Knowes** is an alternative name for TROWS, or according to K.M.Briggs Orkney and Shetland TROOPING FAIRIES who limped as they danced.[153] They live in hills called 'henkie knowes'.

HERLA is an ancient king of Britain who was visited by a small man, riding a GOAT. He had goat's feet himself and was very hairy. This creature invited King Herla into a fairy MOUND to attend a feast. When he left the king of the UNDERWORLD gave him a small DOG, with the injunction that he must not dismount from his horse until the dog did. Herla left with his followers, warning them not to touch the earth until the little dog led the way, but one of his men was so overjoyed to be back in the human realm that he disobeyed, and was instantly turned to dust. As the king and his followers journeyed through the countryside it soon became apparent that they had been inside the fairy mound for many centuries, not a few nights, and they were no more than ancient history in the minds of those now living. The little dog never leaped down from the horse, so Herla and his men are forced to wander the length and breadth of Britain still.[154] *See also* OISIN.

HERMAN is a GIANT who lived on one side of Burrafiord in the Shetland Isles. On the other side lived the giant Saxie. The two quarrelled at every possible opportunity. One day, Saxie refused to lend Herman his CAULDRON to boil an ox and they began to throw rocks at each other. Saxie's rock dropped into the water and is now called Saxie's Baa, while Herman's embedded itself in the cliffs and is now called Herman's Hellyac.

HERNE THE HUNTER may once have been an ancient British stag god equivalent to the Gaulish Cernunnos. His name may be derived from the call of the stag that sounds like 'Heeern'. Herne the Hunter is said to still haunt Windsor Great Park and to walk round Herne's OAK at midnight every winter. He rides out with the WILD HUNT at the midwinter solstice (*see* YULE). He is described as a mighty, bearded figure with a huge pair of stags horns on his head. He wears chains, carries a hunting horn, and rides out on a black HORSE with a pack of ferocious hunting hounds. Some traditions make him the father of ROBIN HOOD. *See also* BLACK DOGS and DEER.

HERODIAS is a Channel Island fairy known as the Queen of the Witches. She causes sudden gusts of winds by shaking her petticoats. Herodias is the name of a Gaulish mediaeval WITCH goddess,[155] possibly from the same root as the Etruscan Aradia, the goddess of the witches and daughter of DIANA in the Italian witch cult.[156]

Like Diana she was cited in the mediaeval witch charges, the tenth century *Canon Episcopi* stating she was worshipped by witches, a claim repeated in the *Malleus Mallificarum*. She is mentioned in the bible as playing a part in the execution of John the Baptist, though this may be a much later insertion.

She appears in a fifteenth-century tale as the wife of Sir Orfeo. She fell asleep beneath a 'fair YMPE tree' one MAY afternoon, and dreamt of the King of the Fairies who told her that if she should return to the same tree on the morrow, then she should go with him to FAIRYLAND, the Land of the DEAD. And though Sir Orfeo surrounded the tree with a thousand well-armed knights, she was still KIDNAPPED by the fairies. Orfeo went off to live like a WILD MAN in the forest, sleeping on the ground, eating nuts and berries and growing hairy and shaggy. One day he saw the fairies and their king passing and recognised his wife among the throng. He was able to win her back.

HERR JOHANNES See RÜBEZAHL.

HESPERA ('Evening Light') is one of the HESPERIDES.

HESPERIDES are the THREE guardian NYMPHS of the tree which bore the golden APPLES of immortality in Greek myth. The tree lies on an island in the far west, where the sun sets. They are Aegle, which means 'brightness', Erythraea 'the red one' and Hespera 'evening light.' Their names refer to the sunset when the sky is the colour of ripening apples.

HERNE

HETHER-BLETHER is one of two magical FAIRY ISLANDS situated near Orkney (the other is HILDALAND). It rises from the sea on certain days and is a home of the FIN FOLK.

HEY-HEY MEN or HEY-MAN are found from southern Germany through to the Balkans. Though they are rarely seen, their voices are frequently heard calling 'Hey! Hey!' If you are silly enough to follow them you will lose your way. If you laugh at them, they will kill you. These fairies are SHAPESHIFTERS but usually appear as small men wearing large brimmed hats to hide their faces. They wear RED cloaks and carry whips. *See also* HEMÄNNER.

HIBLA-BASHI is a type of VAMPIRE in Iranian folklore. In appearance, it is half man and half GOAT, like a SATYR.

HIDDEN ISLE is a fairy island is ruled over by Queen Cephalonia, the mother of OBERON.

HIDDEN PEOPLE is an English term for fairies in general.

HILDALAND is one of two magical FAIRY ISLANDS situated near Orkney (the other is Hether-Blether). It rises from the sea on certain days and is the summer home of the FIN FOLK. The name may be derived from the word *hildring*, which means 'mirage' or from HULDRE-land. If a person should happen to see the island, they should keep a piece of IRON in their hand while they row towards it, and this will stop it disappearing.

HILL FOLK is a Scottish term for the fairies.

HILL JOHNNY is one of the Orkney TROWS.

HILLE BINGELS is the wife of the house fairy HINZELMAN.

HILLMEN See HOGMAN.

HILL-TROWS is another term for the land TROWS of the Orkney islands.

HINKY PUNK is a WILL O'THE WISP in Devon and Somerset:
One leg and a light,
and lead you into bogs'.[157]

HINZELMANN or Heinzelmann is one of the tribe of German HOUSE FAIRIES the HEINZEMANNCHENS. This blond fairy wore a RED CAP and lived with his wife Hille Bingels in Lüneburg Castle during the sixteenth century. He had his own room and was allowed to eat with his master at high table. However, things had not always been so amicable. At first, the master tried to get rid of him, even calling a priest to exorcise him - all to no avail. The master gave in and departed for Hanover, but failed to see the little white feather that went with him. This proved to be the house fairy and the poor man realised he would have to make the best of it. The two returned and lived happily in the castle with Hinzelmann performing many useful services for his master in return for his crumbs and sweet MILK.

HIPCHE appears in a German tale. A merchant fell in love with a poor girl and asked her to marry him. She knew that he would expect a big dowry and sold herself to a fairy for a pile of gold. She agreed that if she had not discovered its NAME within a year. He should carry her off. By the end of the year she still had not guessed, when a shepherd came to her and related how he had seen several odd creatures dancing around a fire. One was singing that the mistress did not know that his name was Hipche. Thus, the lady was able to tell the fairy its name and save herself. Compare with RUMPELSTILTSKIN and TOM TIT TOT.

HIPPOCENTAUR is a type of CENTAUR, half-man and half-horse.

HOB or HOBB is a Midland and northern English designation for a fairy, sometimes a type of HOUSE FAIRY. These shaggy creatures often guard roads and lonely places, and can be either helpful of malicious as they choose. J.R.R.Tolkien, famed author of *The Hobbit* and *Lord of the Rings,* a West Midlands man, probably derived the name of his fictional Hobbits from hobs. Certainly, the Shire, the hobbit homeland was based on the rolling countryside of the English Midlands.

There is a small cave called Hob Hole, near Runswick Bay in North Yorkshire, which was home to a hob. Local people thought he had the power to cure whooping cough, and ailing children were taken up to the cave by their parents who recited:
'Hob-hole Hob!
My bairn's gotten t'kink cough.
Tak't off! Tak't off!'
Hob was undoubtedly once a woodland god. In Old England the populace would adjourn to the woodland on MAY DAY to indulge in sexual license which encourages the fertility of the land by sympathetic magic. Any child of these 'greenwood marriages' was entitled 'Hobson' (Hob's son) or Robinson (Robin's son). Hob may be a familiar variation of Robin. It used to be a term applied to the country bumpkin. There was a phrase 'to play the hob' meaning to work mischief. The Puritans later termed Hob a DEMON.

HOB HURST is a HOB who haunts lonely woods in Derbyshire, England. There is a Bronze Age barrow near Chatsworth House in Derbyshire, which is called Hob Hurst's House. At Deepdale in Derbyshire is Thirst House, which is a CAVE beneath Topley Pike, said to be the home of a hob. The name is an abbreviation of Hob o'the Hurst's House, 'hurst' meaning a wooded place. A farmer is once said to have encountered the hob, and to have put it in his bag. It cried out so piteously, that he let it go and it ran off to seek the sanctuary of its cave.

HOB-AND-HIS-LANTHORN is a WILL O'THE WISP of the Midlands.

HOBBIN is a Warwickshire alternative term for a HOB.

HOBBLEDY'S LANTERN is a Warwickshire WILL O'THE WISP.

HOBBY LANTER is an East Anglian and Wiltshire WILL O'THE WISP.

HOBERDY'S LANTERN is a Warwickshire WILL O'THE WISP.

HOB-GOB is an alternative name for the English HOBGOBLIN.

HOBGOBLINET is an uncommon variation on the English HOBGOBLIN- or perhaps just a smaller hobgoblin.

HOBGOBLINS ('Hearth Spirits') are found throughout England and the Scottish lowlands. They are hairy, good-natured (but sensitive) HOUSE FAIRIES who turn into nasty BOGGARTS if they are slighted. Rather than domestic houses they are associated with farms, particularly dairies. They love the warmth of fire and move into human homes to be near one. Once in residence, they may get up to all sorts of mischievous tricks. One Herefordshire hobgoblin would steal all the household keys if he was upset. The family would have to beg for their return by placing a cake on the stove, sitting in a circle round the fire quietly with their eyes closed until the hobgoblin had eaten all he wanted. He would then throw the keys against the wall and the family could go about its business.[158]

In appearance, hobgoblins are about 30-60 cm tall (between one and two feet), have dark skin and either go naked or wear ragged clothes. The Puritans used the word 'hobgoblin' – a compound of hob and goblin - to refer to satanic forces, and these fairy creatures gained an evil reputation. Bunyan described them as dark and mean featured. It is rumoured that they guard TREASURE.

HOBMEN is an English North Country name for HOUSE FAIRIES.

HOBTHRUSH or **Hob Thrush** is a Yorkshire fairy. The terms HOB and hobthrush are used interchangeably, though it is possible that hob once referred to a domestic fairy, while hobthrush meant an open-air one. In Derbyshire, the term is generally given as HOBTHRUST. They are friendly spirits attached to particular localities.[159] Perhaps they were once GENII LOCI.

HOBTHRUST or **HOB THRUST** is a HOUSE FAIRY or HOB who lived in a barrow in Derbyshire, England, called Hob Hurst's House. He is said to have been particularly friendly and helpful towards a certain cobbler. Another of the same name lived at a cave in Mulgrave Woods in Yorkshire.

A Hobthrust lived at Starfit Hall at Reeth in Yorkshire, but was driven away when a reward of CLOTHES was left out for him:

Ha! A cap and a hood!
Hob'll never do mair good![160]

See also HOB HURST.

HOBYAHS were wicked Scottish and English GOBLINS, also found in New England, who were in the habit of kidnapping humans and making them slave in their mines, digging for gold. When they were no more use, the hobyahs would eat them. Eventually the hobyahs met their just deserts when a BLACK DOG ate them all.

HÖDEKEN ('Little Hat') was a KOBOLD who lived in the palace of the Bishop of Hildeshein. He was generally kind and obliging, helping out the bishop and warning him of forthcoming events. However, he fell under suspicion when a scullion, who had regularly abused the fairy and thrown dirty water over him, was found strangled, chopped into pieces and cooked. The bishop was forced to exorcise his little friend.

HOLED STONE (Men an Tol, Cornwall, England)

HODEKIN is an English forest ELF or an alternative title for ROBIN HOOD.

HODGEPOCHER or **HODGPOKER** is an obscure sixteenth-century term for an English HOUSE FAIRY or HOBGOBLIN.

HOGBOY or **Hogboon** or **Hug Boy** are Orkney fairies who are less malevolent than the other resident fairies, the TROWS. They are shadowy in appearance and live in the MOUNDS, and protect domestic animals from trows and sometimes mend farm implements. In repayment, ale and MILK is poured onto the mounds. If anyone tries to disturb the mounds, however, a hogboy will appear as a small grey man in tattered clothes and set upon the intruder. Every mound has one, even the Maes Howe, a barrow in Orkney. The term 'Hogboy' is derived from the Norse *haugbui* ('mound dweller') or BARROW-WIGHT, or *haugbonde*, the Old Norse guardian spirit of farms. The Norwegians believed that after death a person's spirit continued to live near his home, especially the founding ancestor, usually buried beneath a large mound called a *haugr*.

HÖGFOLK are handsome Scandinavian fairies who live in the hills. They are midway between the nature of humans and ELVES.

HOGMEN or **Hillmen** are the most feared of the Manx fairies. At HOLLANTIDE they move their abode, and one should not venture out then. They use well-trodden paths running in straight lines between the fairy MOUNDS. *See also* LEY LINES)

HOIHOIMANN is a German version of the HEY-HEY MAN who tries to distract travellers from their path by calling out to them.

HOLDA, FRAU (also **Holle, Hollen, Hoide, Holda, Holde, Hulda, Huldra, Huldu, Hulla, Hulle, Frau Holle,** or Dame Venus) is a beautiful fairy of German folklore who brings the snow by shaking out the feathers from her bed in the sky. Between Christmas Day and Twelfth Night, she rides around in a wagon. Her realm is reached through the bottom of a well and she is associated with water and lakes. Though she is generally benign, and particularly interested in SPINNING, she gets annoyed by ill kept houses.

Holda was originally a goddess of the hearth and spinning, demoted to a fairy BOGEY WOMAN in Christian times. As a sky goddess, she rode about on the winds in a HAG form accompanied by WITCHES. As a hag fairy she rides in a type of WILD HUNT accompanied by the spirits of UNBAPTISED CHILDREN, sometimes gathering up humans into the train, after which they are forced to remain in her realm until Judgement Day. German Jews once performed the *Holle Kneish* to protect newborn children from her. After a child is born a group of children surround the crib and invoke Holda to name the child.

HOLED STONES, Hag Stones or Limmell Stones are naturally holed stones with a magical reputation. Fairies can be seen through them, especially those rocks worn through by water, like the one at St Nectan's Glen in Cornwall. Small holed stones are used as amulets for protection, fertility, and HEALING.[161]

Single holed stones or necklaces of such stones were hung up as charms in houses, cow byres and stables to protect them from the attentions of malicious fairies and WITCHES. These talismans could still be found on English farms as late as the 1950s.[162] They safeguarded against horses being stolen and HAG RIDDEN. Farmers often tied the stable keys to HAG stones to make a dual charm of holed stone and IRON. A holed stone also protects from fairy spells and the evil eye, perhaps because the stone resembles an eye. One under the pillow protects from NIGHTMARES.

Holed stones, small or large, are believed to have great restorative power. In Cornwall small decorated stones called ADDER stones, adder's beads or snake stones were once in demand as magical charms for both fertility and healing. They were sometimes steeped in water or ale, which was used to transfer the healing energy.[163] Several megaliths are holed, such as the Men an Tol in Cornwall. People still crawl through the stone to solicit healing. The act of emerging from the stone symbolises rebirth from the womb of Mother Earth, healed and whole, while the disease returns to the UNDERWORLD.

The Men an Tol holed stone is flanked by two upright dolmens and together the THREE stones represent male and female powers. Many marriages and betrothals were solemnised at such stones with the couple holding hands through the stone to plight their troth. Small holed stones were carried as fertility charms.

For the ancients any holes in the earth, such as CAVES and wells, were regarded as entrances into the womb of the Earth Goddess. Holed stones were symbols of the Goddess and the power of her womb, and were regarded as powerful talismans. Holed stones have been found in Stone Age dwellings. They were used as spindle whorls, a function that continued for millennia. In ancient times, SPINNING was a magical act, the province of women under the auspices of the spinning and weaving goddess. This goddess, identified as ARIANRHOD in Wales and Isis in Egypt, but having many names worldwide, is seen reflected in the many spinning fairies, such as HABETROT. Interestingly, the heroine of the story first sees Habetrot, patroness of spinning, through a holed stone.

HOLLANTIDE (Gaelic *Laa Houney*), is the Manx name for the day on which winter begins. It is cognate with SAMHAIN and was originally celebrated on 11th November - Old Samhain before calendar changes. On this day the Hillmen or HOGMEN move their abode. The MOUNDS open and the fairies can be seen feasting inside.

HOLLOW HILLS fairies are often said to live beneath the ancient burial MOUNDS or in CAVES, the Hollow Hills of folklore, where they feast and dance. Sometimes at night, these hills are said to sparkle with light and if you press an ear to the hill, you will hear their revels.

HOLLY (*Ilex sp.*) is an evergreen that represents continuing life through the winter, though it is thorny and difficult. The druids brought some indoors as a home for the nature fairies during the winter. The GREEN KNIGHT in the story of Gawain was a Holly Knight, carrying a holly club, their contest being the bi-annual fight of the Oak King and the Holly King, Summer and Winter, for the hand of the goddess CREIDDYLAD.

Holly protects against the spells of WITCHES and fairies. Collars and whips of holly wood protect horses from their attentions and the wood is used for doors and windowsills for the same reason. No witch or fairy can cross a THRESHOLD made from holly wood, and a holly hedge keeps them off the property. At HALLOWEEN holly was strewn before the house and hung over the doors to prevent fairies and WITCHES entering. Holly is associated with HAG fairies and Crone Goddesses such as The Blue Hag, or CAILLEACH BHEUR, who brought winter to the Scottish Highlands. On the eve of BELTANE, she gave up the struggle and flung her staff under a holly tree. Holly was sacred to the Morrigu, or MORRIGAN, the Irish goddess of death.

HOLZRÜHRLEIN BONNEFÜHRLEIN is a German DWARF who fell in love with a human girl and wanted to marry her. A cowherd and a shepherd lived in a forest and were firm friends. The cowherd had a daughter and the

shepherd a son. The two children were inseparable from birth and when they grew up, they agreed to marry. Then an ugly dwarf appeared and asked for the girl's hand, bringing many valuable presents. Though the girl's mother had no intention of accepting the dwarf as her son in law, she continued to accept all the gifts. Then one day she could stand the repulsive dwarf no more and announced that no matter how many offerings he should bring he would never marry her daughter! At this he grew angry and declared that they had accepted his largess and he would return at noon the following day to claim the girl unless they could guess his NAME by then. Now it chanced that the shepherd's son was herding his flocks near a CAVE when he heard the dwarf gleefully singing that he would soon have the maiden because her family would never guess that his name was Holzrührlein Bonneführlein. Thus, the cowherd's wife was able to tell the dwarf his name and marry her daughter to her true sweetheart, the shepherd's son. Compare with TOM TIT TOT and RUMPELSTILTSKIN.

HOMESPRITE is an alternative English term for a HOUSE FAIRY, a spirit that performs domestic tasks around the house while its inhabitants are sleeping in return for food and a warm place by the HEARTH.

HOMMES CORNUS are fairies of Gascony, a type of KORRED. They guard the standing stones there. They are all males, so how they reproduce is not known. They wear their hair loose, are small, dark and shaggy.

HONGATAR are Scandinavian TREE FAIRIES.

HOOD are important in fairy lore. There are several hooded fairies, including Carl Hood, ROBIN HOOD, GRIM and the Romano-Celtic Genii Cucullati ('Hooded Spirits'). Images of triads of hooded and cloaked

DWARFS or GIANTS appear all over Celtic Europe during the Roman period carrying eggs or displaying phalluses, obviously marking them as fertility spirits. So, why do fertility spirits have hoods? An obvious association is the 'hood' of the phallus, the foreskin. This is further compounded by the fact that 'Robin' (as in Robin Hood) was once a nickname for the phallus.

According to Robert Graves hood or *hod* also means a 'log', especially the YULE log, perhaps referring us back to tree spirits (*see* TREE FAIRIES) and renewal at the winter solstice. There is plenty of hood symbolism around at Yule. FATHER CHRISTMAS goes about in his RED hood, delivering gifts. Odin, called *Grimr* or 'hooded' rode the skies, dressed in his bloody animal skins, rewarding the good and punishing the bad. On Old Christmas Day (January 6th) the Haxley Hood Game takes place, ostensibly to celebrate the return of a red hood to Lady Mowbray in the fourteenth century. It is presided over by the Lord Boggan with a wand of thirteen willow withies and the hood itself (now a coil of rope bound in leather) is fought over by the two sides. It seems clear that in the latter case we have another instance of our recurrent theme of the seasonal battle between summer and winter here and its ritual re-enactment. The thirteen willow wands probably represent the thirteen lunar months of the year.

Another explanation might be that the hood conceals the identity of the supernatural being so that it might go amongst mankind undetected. Odin was called GRIM or Grimr meaning 'hooded' or 'disguised' as the god was often known to go among mortals in this aspect. For humans wearing a hood, mask or disguise may have a sacred or ritual purpose, relinquishing the old identity with the old CLOTHES. Disguising or 'guising' is still a feature of the Yuletide celebrations, with participants wearing fancy dress.

HOOKIES is a Lincolnshire term for the fairies.

HOOTER is a name given to three different fairies. Firstly there is one who tries to lure people into bogs and swamps by calling out to them. The second is the WHOOPER, a Cornish swan spirit. The third is a type of BLACK DOG.

HOPFENHÜTEL ('Hop Cap') is a German HOUSE FAIRY who wears a RED CAP. He protects the home and helps in the brewing of beer.

HORSES are of great interest to the fairies. They take great delight in horsemanship and are excellent riders. They sometimes entice young human men to ride out with them, and will dash along like the wind. Afterwards, those young men are the most fearless riders in the country and people know that they have hunted with the fairies. When horses neigh at night, they are being ridden hard by fairies or WITCHES.

The horses of the TUATHA DÉ DANAAN are stabled in the Hollow Hills. They are made of fire and flame and are as swift as the wind. They are shod with silver and have golden bridles. A cavalcade of SIDHE knights has SEVEN score steeds, each with a star-like jewel on its forehead, and seven score horsemen, all king's sons, clad in GREEN mantles fringed with gold, wearing golden helmets and carrying golden spears.[164] These fairy horses live for one hundred years. However, it is possible that they have died out completely, as there is a legend that the last of them was owned by a lord of Connaught, and was sold at his death. Refusing to be mounted by its base born buyer, it threw him to the ground and bolted, never to be seen again.

Some fairies occasionally turn themselves into horses, including Lazy Lawrence, Lutin, Phooka, Puck, Robin Goodfellow, Adh Sidhe, Boggart, Boobrie, Brags and Gytrash.

Other fairies appear exclusively in horse form, such as Knops, Linchetti, Painajainen, Pickatree-Brag, Tatterfoal, Cheval Bayard, Cobs, Dunnie and the Grant. Some of these are known to bring NIGHTMARES. There are many stories of fairy WATER HORSES that live beneath lakes or under the sea. These include the Kelpie, Muirdris, Näkh, Neagle, Neugle, Nickur, Noggles, Nuckalavee, Shopiltees, Tangie, Wihwin, Aughisky, Cabbyl Ushty, Each-Uisge and the Glashtin. *See also* SHAMAN.

HORSESHOES when hung over the house or stable door, will keep evil fairies and other spirits out; it is usual to hang the horseshoe points up to keep the luck in, though in Dorset it is traditional to hang it the other way. *See also* IRON.

HOST, THE *See* UNSEELIE COURT.

HOSPODÁRÍCEK is a Southern Slavonic HOUSE FAIRY who appears as, or is symbolised by a SNAKE. He is also called Hospodárícek or Hospodar or Domovnícek (see DOMOVOY). He lives behind the oven and if anyone should harm him they will be struck with misfortune, as will his whole household and family. If the fairy dies so will the master of the house. If he is well treated he will bring the home luck and prosperity and becomes very attached to the family, especially the children whom he will watch over when they are alone. He will warn the family of any impending danger. Sometimes two snakes live in the house, male and female.

HOTEI or **Hoteiosto** is the Japanese equivalent of FATHER CHRISTMAS. He looks like an old monk and gives gifts to good children. He has eyes in the back of his head in order to spot naughty children.

HOTOTS are WATER FAIRIES of Armenia folklore. They lure humans, horses and cows into swamps and rivers to drown them. They always appear covered in mud and slime.

HOUGGÄ-MA are Swiss WATER FAIRIES, similar in character to the Russian VODIANOI.

HOUPOUX are French fairies that try to lure people into bogs by calling out to them.

HOUSE FAIRY/FAIRIES is a general term for those fairies that dwell in human homes, guard them, and occasionally undertake domestic tasks in return for a small reward, such as a bowl of cream or a warm place by the HEARTH. Such spirits are found throughout the world, from the Hawaiian Menahune to the Scottish Brownie, from the Spanish Duende to the German Hausmänner, from the Russian Igosha to the Finnish Kodin-Haltia, and from the North American Shvod to the Cambodian Àràk. There are numerous other examples listed in this book .

House fairies were once a common feature of English domestic life. In the twelfth century, a spirit called Malekin caused a commotion in the Suffolk home of Sir Osborn de Bradwell by discoursing learnedly in Latin on scriptural subjects. A Danish Kobold became clerk to an archbishop.[165]

House fairies often have a mischievous side and like to play tricks on the human inhabitants of a dwelling. Such pranks might include rattling the fire irons, smashing crockery, hiding objects, or just making a mess. House fairies are notoriously hard to please, capricious and easily offended. Some house fairies object to the presence of a cat or a dog, and most of them will disappear for good if given a suit of CLOTHES.

The belief in house spirits is very ancient. In Persia and China it was always the custom to make offerings to the house spirit before entering a

dwelling, while a similar custom in northern Europe involved taking bread and salt when visiting a home. In modern Indonesia, elaborate ceremonies are performed to protect people entering a new home and to propitiate the spirits within it. In many parts of the world, blood sacrifices were made to the spirit of the place whenever foundations were laid for a building. Animals or even human victims were buried alive under the cornerstones to provide protective spirits - it is still thought lucky to live in a corner house. Animal and human skulls were embedded in the walls to placate the household deities. In Bolivia, llama foetuses are sometimes still buried under the foundations of a house.

In ancient Rome, the house fairy or spirit was called the LAR FAMILIARIS ('household lar'). It was given monthly offerings of garlands on the hearth as well as daily offerings at mealtimes. The lar protected the house and its wealth and was invoked on family occasions. Though some Victorian writers claimed that the concept of household spirits may have spread with the Roman empire, there is enough evidence to prove that a belief in such spirits evolved independently in places as far apart as China, Western Europe and South America. In later ages, this creed dwindled to a superstition about naughty fairies and today is reduced to belief in good or bad atmosphere in a house.

HOWE is an Orkney term for a fairy MOUND.

HOWLAA is a Manx fairy that howls before storms.

HSIEN is a Chinese term for an immortal spirit. The character for *hsien* implies a person that lives on a mountain.[166] The term is usually applied to humans who gain immortality, though it may be applied to fairy-type spirits.

HU HSIEN are malicious Chinese Fox Spirits who are also powerful SHAPESHIFTERS.

HUACAS are ancient Incan NATURE FAIRIES that looked after the fields and the harvest.

HÜAMANN is a German HEY-HEY MAN who tries to seduce travellers from their path by calling out to them.

HUCKEPOTEN or Huckpoten is a German WILL O' THE WISP.

HULDA is described as Queen of the Dwarfs, in one Nordic saga. See HOLDA.

HULDEFOLK or Hulde are Faroe Island fairies of the MOUND FOLK type.

HULDRA or Huldre ('Hidden Folk') (*f.* Hulder; *m.* Huldre-kall) are Scandinavian ELVES and fairies. According to Icelandic folklore, Eve was washing her children in the river when God appeared suddenly and frightened her. She hid those children not already washed, and when God asked if all her children were present, she replied 'yes'. God told her that those hidden would be hidden from man forever, and they became the Huldre Folk. (The Grimm brothers relate a variation on this tale in which Eve only shows God the beautiful children and hides the ugly ones. He tells the lovely children they will be kings and princes and seeing this generosity Eve brings out the ugly, dirty children, and God tells then they are destined to be peasants, servants and scullions.)

The girls are very beautiful in front, but have hollow backs and COW's tails. They appear as WHITE robed forest NYMPHS who sometimes like to lure young men into the mountains to become their lovers, but the men are always marred in some way afterwards, anything from being unable to grow a beard to going mad. The huldre may be heard singing a beautiful melody called the *huldrlaat*. They can cause deformities in people by licking them with their tongues.

There is a tale of a huldre minister who debated with a parson. He told him that in the bible it said that in the beginning, God created a man and a woman, but in the second chapter, it stated that a woman was created out of Adam's rib. The first woman was Adam's equal in every way, but God said it wasn't good for man and woman to be equal, so he sent her and her offspring away, and put them in the hills to live. They are without sin, but stay in the hills except when they want to be seen. The children of Eve, on the other hand (mankind) have sin, which is why God gave them the New Testament, while the Huldre-folk only need the Old. The parson had to agree, and never went back to his pulpit again.

Two viceroys rule over each tribe of huldre, and every two years they sail to Norway to report to their ruler. They will take away UNBAPTISED children and replace them with *umskiptinger* or CHANGELINGS. On the night of the New Year, they move their dwellings, and if you can encounter one at this time, it can be forced to foretell your future.

The name may be derived from the goddess Hulda. *See also* HOLDA.

HULDRE-FOLK is the Norwegian term for fairies. See also HULDRA.

HULDUFOLK is the Icelandic term for the fairies. *See also* HULDRA.

HULTE is a male Swedish woodland fairy or WILD MAN.

HUMBLEKNOWE BRAG is a BRAG that appeared near Sedgefield near the River Tees in north east England to avenge two beggars turned away on an icy night by a cruel man, the woman cursing him as she went. One night the master was away from home when the mistress of the house was tormented by terrible noises, and the sound of something galloping around and around the house. Smoke billowed from the grate and suddenly the lights went out. The next morning the master was brought home by two farm labourers, having been thrown from his suddenly startled horse. He had lain senseless in the freezing night and would have perished but for the two men who helped him.[167]

HUNKY PUNKY is a Cornish WILL O' THE WISP.

HUNTIN is a West African DRUS of the silk-cotton tree. The particular trees in which he dwells are surrounded by a girdle of palm leaves and thus marked out for protection against injury. If the tree needs to be felled the fairy must be propitiated with offerings of fowls and palm oil.

HUSBUK ('House Goat') is a Scandinavian HOUSE FAIRY, which has something of the GOAT about him. He lives in human houses and is a fertility spirit.

HÜTCHENS are Scandinavian KOBOLDs or HOUSE FAIRIES who wear RED felt hats.

HUTZELMANN (from *hüten*, meaning 'to watch over') is a German HOUSE FAIRY.

HY-BREASAIL is a fairy island that only appears above the waves every SEVEN years. The sea god MANANNAN condemned it to its fate, but allows it to surface periodically so that the inhabitants can catch a breath of air. If fire or IRON is brought onto the island, it will remain in sight, as it once did when a red-hot ARROW was fired into it. Many have tried to find Hy Breasail. Maps have even existed, which usually depict it as round, divided in the centre by a river, leading to comparisons with Atlantis.

HYTER SPRITES are East Anglian SHAPESHIFTING fairies. They appear as various birds, including green-eyed sand martins and carrion birds. Usually, they try to avoid humans, but have been known to band together to mob individuals to scare them or admonish irresponsible parents who neglect their children. In this same vein, they sometimes return lost children.

HYTER SPRITES

ICHTHYOCENTAUR is a type of CENTAUR that is half-man and half-fish.

IELES ('They') or **DINSELE** ('They Themselves') are strange VAMPIRE fairies who come from Romania and look like large CATS that walk on two legs. They lie at CROSSROADS awaiting human victims to suck their blood, but they cannot go into the middle of the crossroads. If a human steps into their circle they will steal a piece of his leg bone and replace it with a wooden wheel spoke. However, if the man returns to the same place one year later, they will restore the bone.

Sometimes they are seen with a plough and are connected with fertility, dancing in the garden on the green grass, or feasting in the cornfields. Sometimes they appear in carts and are able to travel the whole world in a single night, sailing over the NINE seas and through the nine countries.

Once a year they revisit the spot they visited the year before, dancing in the same ring they danced in the previous year. They may force humans to join them in their DANCE, and a piper who does so will become a master of his instrument, or they may enchant a musician, carrying him away with the power of their music while he is sleeping. In return for the gift of song, he will have to give them part of his body, usually his little finger.

If you want to please the fairy, leave an offering near his spring consisting of WHITE foods such as MILK, eggs, cheese, or a white hen, laid upon a clean, white cloth. This should be offered to all passers by. If someone is ill, a similar offering should be made at his house by nine women, walking nine times round the house and casting a spell nine times over the sick person. The colour of the sacrificial foods suggests an offering to the DEAD.

IGNUS FATUUS ('Foolish Fire') is a Latin term for a WILL O'THE WISP.

IGOSHA is a Russian HOUSE FAIRY, the spirit of an UNBAPTISED CHILD. Igoshi have no hands or legs and love to play nasty pranks on householders. They can be kept friendly with gifts of spoons, mittens or bread.

IHK'AL are fairies of the Mexican Tzeltal Indians. They are hairy and have taken to the modern device of rocket backpacks to enable them to fly.

ILEANA COZÎNZEANA ('Ileana the Fairy') is a Romanian fairy who brings the dawn, waking up during the night to usher in the next day. She is said to have eyes like the sun, and was probably originally a goddess of the dawn. She keeps a herd of COWS.

ILLES are Icelandic TROLLS who can only emerge from their underground lairs after sunset. They are naked, hairy and dark, though they can SHAPESHIFT into beautiful women that make men fall in love with them. The men will then pine away and die. If they touch a person he will become sick and they also sometimes suffocate people. They are skilled musicians and love to DANCE in the moonlight.

IMBOLC or **Oimelc** is an old Celtic festival that marks the first stirrings of spring, celebrated on February 2nd. It was Christianised as Candlemas. On this day the HAG or CAILLEACH fights her rival the maiden goddess, in the shape of BRIGHID. This is sometimes symbolised by a DRAGON fighting a lamb, as this festival marks the time of first lambing and MILK.

IMD ('Ogress') is a TROLL-WIFE in Norse mythology.

IMP or **YMPE** is a small DEMON or wicked fairy. The name is derived from the Old English *impe* meaning 'young shoot' implying that the imp is a 'chip off the old block' of his father the DEVIL. In Anglo-Saxon there was a verb *impian*, related to the Latin *impotare* meaning 'to put upon' or 'implant'. It describes the technique of grafting, known to both Greeks and Romans. Gardeners called this imping, and the new buds are called imps. In Langland's *Piers Plowman* we find the following:

'I was sum-tyme a frere
And the conventes Gardyner for to
    graffe ympes;
On limitoures and listre lesynges I
    ymped'.

The term also applies to the male scion of a noble house (with scion also meaning graft or shoot) as in the epitaph carved in the Beaumont chapel at Warwick:

'Here resteth the body of the noble Impe Robert of Dudley, sonne of Robert Erle of Leycester'.

The term began to be applied to petty fiends and spirits, with such phrases as 'imp of hell'. There was a proverb: 'No marvel if the imps follow when the devil goes before'.[168] Dr. Johnson defined the word as 'a subaltern devil'.

IMPET is a type of IMP, presumably one even smaller than usual.

INCANTRICES is an alternative term for the FATAE.

INCUBUS (*pl.* INCUBI) (from the Latin *cuba,* 'to lie' and *in* 'upon') is a masculine spirit who sexually assaults women in their sleep. Should the woman become pregnant from the encounter she will give birth to a wizard. The magician MERLIN's father was said to have been an incubus. A peony flower in the bedroom will keep away this evil spirit. In Latin *incubo* refers to a 'NIGHTMARE' and is connected with the word *incubare* meaning 'to lie on' (the female *succubus* means 'to lie beneath'). Some say that incubi, and their female counterparts the succubi, are FALLEN ANGELS, though in Italian folklore incubi are the results of mating between male and female FAUNS. Possibly, they were originally herd spirits who gave animals bad dreams.[169]

Modern theorists suggest that incubus experiences may result from the medical condition of sleep paralysis, during which the mechanism that keeps the body inactive during sleep fails to switch off for a short while after awakening. *See also* MART and ALP.

INDRA or **Inder** was the supreme god of the Hindu triad, replaced in the Middle Ages by Brahma-Vishnu-Shiva. Like many supplanted gods he was ridiculed by his successors and demoted to the status of King of the Fairies. He is known to be lecherous. He lives in Koh Qaf, land of the fairies.

INDRIK is a horned Russian spirit, the Lord of the Animals. He lives on a sacred mountain where no other foot may tread. When he moves the earth trembles. He is sometimes kind to human beings and once rescued some people from a drought.

INSULA POMORUM ('Isle of Apples') is an alternative name for AVALON given by Geoffrey of Monmouth in the *Vita Merlini.*

INVISIBILTY is a gift of the fairies. Most fairies can become visible or invisible to human eyes at will, or be visible to one person while being invisible to another. To see fairies that don't choose to be seen, a human will need to employ certain herbs or magical potions, or be in the right place at the right time (*See* SEEING FAIRIES).

Fairy kingdoms are also invisible since they exist in another dimension to that of humankind, though they sometimes appear for a brief instant to mortal eyes. In some cases, this happens on certain days of the year - as in the case of several FAIRY ISLANDS - and in other cases if you access the appropriate trigger in the vicinity, e.g. treading on the right blade of grass or stepping through an unseen doorway in a stone circle. Certain herbs such as PRIMROSE will open fairy MOUNDS.

IRODIA, IRODIADA or **IRODITA** are Romanian fairy names derived from HERODIAS.

IRON is a metal that terrifies fairies. Show them any kind of iron and they will vanish immediately. To protect yourself, your family and your property from the unwanted attentions of evil or mischievous fairies, keep a knife or a nail in your pocket and under your pillow at night. A horseshoe hung over the door will keep fairies and other spirits out of the house.

However, unlike other fairies DWARFS are SMITHS and can work in iron with complete impunity.

The tradition that iron gives protection from fairies may have sprung from some dim memory of the Celtic invasions. The Celts were armed with iron, while the aboriginal races they defeated had weapons of bronze or stone.

IRRBLOSS is a Swedish WILL O' THE WISP.

IRRLICHTER ('Crazy Light') is a German WILL O'THE WISP.

IRUDICA is a Dalmatian fairy that rides the black storm clouds and brings bad weather to the Balkan coast. She is accompanied by hail and lightening. Her name is derived from HERODIAS.

ISKIOS is a Greek spirit that manifests at CROSSROADS during the time of the new moon. It is a figure that develops from the soul of a DEAD man and appears in animal form, perhaps a DOG or a GOAT.

ISKRZYCKI ('Spark') is a Polish HOUSE FAIRY who lives inside the stove. He mumbles and grumbles but will protect the house and its inhabitants, as long as he is fed and treated properly.

There was a certain house in Poland where all the children died in a mysterious fashion. No one wanted to live there and for many years it stood empty until a poor man and his family, attracted by the cheap rent, moved in. As they arrived, the man opened the door and called out: 'Good day to whoever lives here'. The iskrzycki, pleased to be given proper respect, replied, 'Good day and you are welcome, just so long as you clean the stove every day and don't let the children mess with it'. The man politely thanked the fairy and from then on, the house was peaceful. However, the family were still very poor, and one night the children complained that they were hungry. Suddenly, there was a strange noise, and turning round, they found their friendly iskrzycki dragging a huge crock of gold out of the stove. 'You've taken good care of me,' he said, 'and in return here is a present for you!'[170]

ISLE OF ARRAN is situated off the west coast of Scotland in the Firth of Clyde, is sometimes identified with the fairy island of EMHAIN ABHLACH, once the home of the Celtic sea god MANANNAN.

ISLE OF MAN is a very real island in the Irish Sea, but it was once a fairy domain, and there are many fairies still living there, though they are rare since the coming of the railways, as they object to the IRON of the rails.

The island is steeped in fairy folklore and the inhabitants say that if you put your ear to the Dalby Mountain you can hear the fairies or *Sheean-ny-Feaynid* ('sound of the infinite'). No islander would cross the Ballona Bridge (Fairy Bridge) without offering his or her greetings to the little folk beneath.

The island is named after the Celtic sea god MANANNAN and was created when the GIANT Fin Mac Cumhal scooped out a chunk of Irish land and thrust it into the sea. The hole that was left became Lough Neagh. The dense mists that often envelop the island are said to be the result of a MERMAID's curse: she punished the whole island when a youth rejected her advances.

There are two types of Manx fairies, the first are good, gay and beautiful, the second sullen and vindictive, living apart from men and other fairies in clouds, on mountains, or in seashore CAVES.[171] Manx fairies vary in size from that of human children to smaller, deformed beings. Most dress in GREEN, wear RED CAPS, have large ears, and are about 180cm tall (two to three feet). At night, Manx fairies steal HORSES and go hunting, accompanied by multi-coloured fairy DOGS. They are easily offended, as a drunken farmer discovered when he swore at a group of them. The next day his horse and all his cattle died, and forty days later he was dead too. Some types of fairies are peculiar to the Isle of Man including the Fynoderee, Buggane, Cughtach, Dinny Mara, Dooinney-Oie, Foawr, Glaisein, Howlaa, Cabbyl-Ushty, Ferrishyn, Hillmen, Ben Varrey, Arkan Sonney, Tighe Fairies, Tarroo-Ushtey, Sleigh Beggy, Lhiannan Shee, Moddey Dhoo, Sea Sprites and the Caillage Ny Groagmagh.

Islanders learned to protect themselves from the attentions of fairies with such magical charms as iron, SALT and the BIBLE. On 11th May, *Oie Voaldyn* (Old May Eve), or on MAY EVE, the islanders would gather *Cuirn* or rowan without the aid of a knife, and make crosses of the sprigs to put over the door to keep the fairies out. On this day the fairies were particularly active, as were WITCHES, and to propitiate them greenery and primroses were strewn on the THRESHOLD. *Bollan-feaill-Eoin* or ST. JOHN'S WORT was placed in the byres and folds. Fires were lit on the hills to frighten away the fairies, and on this day, it was unlucky to give away FIRE.

ISLES OF THE BLEST, or **The Fortunate Islands**, are Irish fairy or OTHERWORLD islands, only seen in the mist along the RED path of light from the setting sun, as viewed from the western coast of Ireland. The ancient Greek Pythagoreans also wrote about the Isles of the Blest. They believed that at death the soul passed through the air, then the waters above the air, finally landing on the Isles of the Blest, situated on the MOON.

ITCHETIK (*pl.* Itchetiki) are WATER FAIRIES in Russian folklore. They are the souls of babies drowned by their mothers. They like to live in whirlpools, or by water mills. To see an itchetik or to hear one slapping the water is a very bad OMEN. Itchetiki look like small, shaggy men.

IUBDAN is the king of the fairy realm of Faylinn, in Irish folklore.

IVALDI is a DWARF of Norse myth.

JACK FROST is the English fairy who brings frosts in winter, painting windowpanes with elaborate icy patterns. He nips noses, fingers and toes in his icy grip. Similar fairies appear elsewhere, such as the Russian FATHER FROST.

ISLE OF MAN

JACK IN THE GREEN is an English folk character who was impersonated in processions by a boy dressed in leafy greenery. He may be identical with the NATURE SPIRIT depicted in churches as the GREEN MAN, a forest creature that guards the greenwood.

JACK O'KENT is an English GIANT who joined efforts with the DEVIL to dam the weir at Orcop Hill in Herefordshire to make a fishpond. They accidentally dropped their stones on Garway Hill, where they are now known as the White Rocks.

JACK O'LEGS is a fabled GIANT of Weston in Hertfordshire, England, who was an accomplished archer, and like ROBIN HOOD, he robbed the rich to feed the poor. Eventually he was ambushed by the rich bakers of nearby Baldock, who tied him up and put out his eyes with a red-hot poker. They then told him that he could fire one last ARROW. Where it fell should mark his burial place. He rallied himself to shoot, and the arrow fell three miles away in Weston churchyard, where his grave can still be seen.

JACK O'THE BOWL is a Swiss HOUSE FAIRY who does small household tasks in return for the bowl of cream which is placed on the cowshed roof for him every night.

JACK O'THE BRIGHT LIGHT is a name for the WILL O'THE WISP.

JACK O'THE SHADOWS is death.

JACK ROBINSON is a name for Puck.

JACK-A-LANTERN, Jack O'Lantern or **Jacky Lantern** is an English bog or marsh fairy, similar to a WILL O'THE WISP, who likes to trick humans. Until the fenland swamps of East Anglia were drained at the beginning of the twentieth century, Jack-a-Lanterns commonly haunted the marshes at night. Their glowing flames bewitched travellers and led them to their deaths in deep bogs.

Shakespeare used the expression 'played the jack with us' in *The Tempest*. Whistling is said to attract them and to escape their clutches, you should lie face down on the path until they go away. One later tale accounts for the origin of Jack-a-Lantern. Long ago there was a farmer called Jack who was so clever that he once tricked the DEVIL into climbing a tree from which he could not escape. Old Nick pleaded with Jack to let him down and Jack, thinking he was being very sharp, replied that he would, on condition that the devil would never allow him into hell. The devil had to agree. Eventually, when Jack died he went straight down to hell, but according to his promise, the devil could not let him in. Jack went off to heaven, but he had been so wicked in his life that he was not allowed in there either. In despair, Jack hollowed out a turnip and made a lantern out of it, and now wanders everywhere with his lamp trying to find somewhere to stay.

The name Jack-a-Lantern is now given to the hollowed out pumpkins or turnips that are used as lanterns at HALLOWEEN.

JACK-IN-IRONS is a Yorkshire GIANT who haunts lonely roads, clattering his chains.

JACK-MUH-LANTERN is a JACK-A-LANTERN type fairy that made an appearance on the southern seaboard of the USA. It was a terrifying creature 1.5 metres tall (about five feet), with goggle eyes, a large mouth and a body covered in long hair. It went bounding through the air like a giant grasshopper. It compelled any man who saw it to follow it into the swamp, where he would be drowned.

JACKY MY LANTHORN is a Somerset name for a WILL O'THE WISP.

JALPARI is a Punjabi WATER FAIRY who likes to seduce human males. If they refuse her she will kill them. Sacrifices of animals or flowers are made at the sides of rivers to placate her.

JANN or **JAN** is the least powerful order of the Arabic fairies, the DJINN.

JÁRNVIDJA ('Iron Hag') is a TROLL-WIFE who is associated with the mysterious IRON Wood (Járnvid). In this wood a giantess gives birth to a race of wolf sons, one of which will devour the sun at the end of the world (Ragnarök), and spatter the sky and all the heavens with blood.

JASHTESMÉ are Albanian NYMPHS.

JEAN DE LA BOLIETA is a mischievous western European mountain fairy who will act as a HOUSE FAIRY if treated well, but will cause havoc if he is slighted.

JEANIE OF BIGGERSDALE is a Yorkshire spirit that haunts the Mulgrave Woods and who is highly dangerous, being intent on murder.[172]

JENDZYNA is a Polish spirit, synonymous with the Western Slavonic JEZE and the Russian BABA YAGA. She is an evil, ugly creature that steals children and harms adults. She appears in fairy tales as Jaga-baba, Jezibaba or Jendzibaba.[173] She is a forest spirit, leader of a host of fairies, probably once a HAG aspect of an ancient goddess.

JENNY BURNT TAIL is a Cornish WILL O' THE WISP.

JENNY GREENTEETH is a WATER FAIRY of the River Ribble in Lancashire. She haunts the stepping stones near Brungerley and every SEVEN years claims a victim by grabbing a hapless traveller and pulling them beneath the water to drown. Children are warned not to go near the water, or Jenny Greenteeth will get them.

She is sometimes associated with the green plants growing in the water, or alternatively the green scum that floats on top of it indicates her presence.

JENNY WI' T' LANTERN is a North Yorkshire WILL O'THE WISP.

JETINS are Gallic fairies, a type of KORRED, who guard standing stones. They have loose hair, and are small, dark and shaggy.

JEZERKINJA are Baltic WATER FAIRIES that live in streams, brooks, lakes and springs. They are possibly their guardian spirits.

JEZE, Jezenky or **Jezinky** ('Lamias') are unpleasant ancient Western Slavonic spirits that have the faces of women, bodies of PIGS and legs of horses. They live in CAVES and KIDNAP children, feeding them on dainty morsels. They lull people to sleep and put out their eyes.

JIMANINOS ('Little Children') are winged fairies of Mexico and Central America. They look like small children. (Some say they are the souls of dead children.) Playing tricks, they dance among people at the festival of the DEAD, El Dia de Muerte (2nd November).

JIMMY SQUAREFOOT is a Manx fairy that sometimes looks like a PIG, and sometimes like a porcine man. A stone throwing GIANT rides him.

JINN *See* DJINN.

JIN TANAH are Malayan EARTH FAIRIES that have power over the forest and its inhabitants.

JOAN IN THE WAD is an English WILL O'THE WISP from Somerset.

JOAN THE WAD is an English WILL O'THE WISP from Cornwall.

JOHN BARLEYCORN is a legendary figure, renowned in folk ballad and song, and is the British spirit or personification of barley. He was once a vegetation god, planted in the spring, growing to manhood and cut down with the harvest.

The term 'John Barleycorn' is sometimes used to refer to alcohol in general.

JOHN TUCKER is an English HOUSE FAIRY from Devon.

JOLA SVEINAR is a small Icelandic fairy that delivers Christmas gifts.

JOLEREI ('Yuletide Host') is the Nordic WILD HUNT that rides out at YULE, led by the old god Odin, to claim the souls of the DEAD. It is death for a Christian to see it.

JÖTUN (*pl.* **Jötnar**) is the Norse term for GIANTS, related to the verb *eta*, 'to eat'.[174]

JÖTUNHEIM ('Giant-home') is the home of the Norse GIANTS, located in the far north.

JOULUPUKKI ('Yule Buck') is a Finnish fairy who delivers presents at Christmas. It takes the form of a GOAT, or man in a goat skin and horns. At first, it did not give presents but demanded offerings, though today he is a more benevolent creature.

JÜDEL is a German field spirit or KORNBÖCKE which has something of the GOAT about it. Though perhaps originally a fertility spirit, he is an unpleasant character who kidnaps and slaughters human children.

JUDI (*s.* **JUDA**) are Southern Slavonic or Macedonian WATER FAIRIES which are similar to VILE. A juda has a SNAKE-like body and long hair. She lives in rivers and lakes. Judi are sometimes seen sitting on the riverbanks combing their hair, or dancing in the meadows. If a man enters the water the fairy will unloose her hair, coil him in it, and drown him. If a person joins her DANCE he or she will also be destroyed. Judi bring hail and storms to damage crops.

JULBUK ('YULE-Buck') or **Jolabukkar** is an Icelandic horned fairy, dressed in furs and part GOAT. It lives in the woods in summer, the fields in autumn and, gradually inching closer to human habitation as the year progresses, he visits human houses at Christmas, or rather, YULE. If he is well fed, he will leave without causing any harm, but if not he will spill the beer in the cellar and make the stored grain rot. He was originally a VEGETATION SPIRIT.

JULENISSE ('YULE Nisse') (*pl.* JULNISSEN) is a Norwegian or Danish NISSE who delivers Christmas gifts. He looks like a little old man in RED clothes and a RED CAP. Julnissen live in dark corners or under the stairs and creep out at night to eat the porridge that children are careful to leave out for them. They were probably originally HEARTH spirits or household gods.

JULTOMTE ('YULE Tomte') (*pl.* JULTOMTEII) is a Swedish TOMTE who delivers gifts on Christmas Eve, and should be rewarded with a special seasonal rice pudding if he is to behave well during the coming year. In times past he gave a secret knock at the door and delivered little gifts called *julklapper.* He is the King of the Fairies.

JUNO or **Iuno** is the female form of the GENIUS. The name is derived from the Roman goddess Juno, Queen of Heaven, patroness of marriage and protectress of women.

JUNONES are ancient Roman spirits that protect women, but were originally souls of the DEAD.

JURUTA or **Jurute** is a Polish or Lithuanian sea fairy or MERMAID who lived in an amber palace under the waves. She fell in love with a human sailor, but the thunder became jealous and caused a storm that sent the sailor to the seabed and caused the amber palace to shatter. Whenever there is a storm over the Baltic, you can hear the cries of the sailor and pieces of amber drift to the shore. Juruta was originally a sea goddess, beloved of the thunder god Perun.

KABOUTER MANNIKIN or **Kaboutermannikins** relates to wooden mannikins fashioned from fairy trees (or mandrake roots) in such a way as to imprison the TREE SPIRIT within the image. These were kept in locked boxes, which only the creature's master was allowed to open, or the spirit would escape and wreak its revenge. To teach children not to open mannikin boxes, toy boxes were made housing scary puppets that jumped out when the lid was raised - the Jack in the Box. If a man wanted to sell his mannikin, then it must be for less than he paid for it.

Kaboutermannikins are also known as fairies who live near river banks and harbours and who enter houses on moonless nights to help with the work in the manner of HOUSE FAIRIES. They live in mills, caves and in the roof beams of old houses and castles. They are known in northern Germany, the Netherlands and Belgium.

KACHINAS are a variety of supernatural beings of the Hopi and Pueblo Indians of the south western part of North America. They represent the powers of nature and may be ancestral spirits or the souls of good people. There are a variety of kachina including the Cloud Beings, Corn Maidens, Star Spirits, Dawn Spirits and Lightning Spirits. The Hopi believe that many of the human DEAD join the Cloud People.

The kachinas have instructed the Hopi and Pueblo Indians in many skills. They visit from midwinter to midsummer, then return to the OTHERWORLD for six months. The spirits keep themselves to themselves, unless they are specifically summoned by humans, when they cannot refuse to attend. Their help is sought on various occasions such as seasonal celebrations, house building, harvesting, hunting, kiva building, road making, rain making, or soliciting better crops, more babies and healthier animals. They are invoked by Kachina Dancers, who wear masks that represent the spirits. These dancers imitate the kachina and are sometimes possessed by them.[175]

KAHUI-A-TIPUA are Maori fairies from New Zealand who have faces like DOGS. They may belong to the MAERO.

KAKAMORA or **Kakagora** are tiny Pacific Ocean fairies from the Solomon Isles who have long, sharp nails. They live in CAVES or trees, and are ruled over by a king and queen. Though they are generally unthreatening, they are strong enough to kill and devour a human being if the fancy takes them. However, they are afraid of the colour WHITE, and any white article will deter them.

KAKUA KAMBUZI is a central African fairy who protects the incense trees.

KALAU are evil Siberian fairies that bring sickness and death to humans, sometimes as a punishment for a crime, sometimes just for evil's sake.

KALFATER is a German fairy that may be found on board ships.

KALKADOON are Australian aboriginal spirits that live in the Dreamtime. They are GIANTS in stature.

KALLIKANTZARI or **Karakondzuli** are Macedonian fairies that appear between Christmas and the Epiphany, during the twelve days of chaos, coming up from the UNDERWORLD to try to cut down the World Tree that supports the Earth. They take the form of CENTAURS or DOGS, wolves, or hideous hairy men with animal legs, appearing at human settlements to trash the furniture, urinate on the floors, ravish the women and KIDNAP the children. They eat only raw dog meat and snails. At the end of the Twelve Days people have to drive them back to hell with noisy ceremonies and processions. If you are born during the Twelve Days of Christmas you risk turning into a Kallikantzari, or they might be the souls of DEAD foreigners. They are possibly a folk memory of Dionysian revellers. *See also* CALLICANTZAROS.

KÅLLRÅDEN are Swedish WATER FAIRIES that appear as lovely women who make their home on the riverbanks or in underwater dwellings. They come to the surface to comb their hair.

KALO ('Beautiful') in Greek folklore is the Queen of the Mountains, who leads her fellow NYMPHS through the hills.

KAMI are the NATURE FAIRIES of the Japanese Shinto religion. They are aided by ELEMENTAL beings that live beneath the sea.

KAPPA are strange Japanese WATER FAIRIES which have webbed and clawed hands, trunk-like noses, GREEN skin, round eyes and tortoiseshells on their backs. On the tops of their heads are small depressions filled with water, the source of their power. Their heads must always be wet and they cannot survive out of water for very long. They travel around on cucumbers. Despite their ludicrous appearance, they are highly dangerous, lurking at the edge of water to lure in humans and animals to eat. To escape, you should trick the kappa into spilling the water from its head, or toss it a cucumber, which it loves even more than human flesh. Sometimes kappas can be helpful, and teach human beings medical skills like bone setting.

KARAWATONIGA are Melanesian fairies of a human-like appearance, with luxurious HAIR. They inhabit the seashore and are generally kindly disposed.

KARLÁ are Lithuanian fairies; small, gentle and kindly, unless they are crossed or ill treated.

KÄSERMÄNNER ('Cheese Men') are German fairies living in the mountain huts where cheese is made. Though they are sometimes classified as WICHTLN they are more like GIANTS.

KARLIKI are Russian DWARFS of the UNDERWORLD. They are said to have fallen from heaven with the DEVIL.

KARZELEK is one of the Polish MINE FAIRIES, who lives in the tunnels and guards underground TREASURES of gems, gold and crystals. He will help miners and lead them to good seams, but if insulted will cause cave-ins, rock showers or throw the culprits into deep chasms. He does not like whistling, swearing or bare heads. Karzeleks look like small miners, nearly a metre tall (about three feet), complete with picks and shovels, or like naked children or even just flickers of light.

KASHA are Japanese GHOULS that feed off any human bodies left unguarded.

KATAJATAR are Scandinavian TREE FAIRIES.

KATZENVEIT is a DEMON fairy who haunts the German forests of Fichtelgebirge and frightens people. He is held out as a sort of BOGEYMAN to children.

KAUKAS are Lithuanian HOUSE FAIRIES.

KAUKIS are small Russian fairies.

KEGRIM is an English GHOUL or GOBLIN of the south west. One haunts the churchyard of Launceston in Cornwall. The term is possibly a contraction of CHURCHGRIM.

KELPIES (s. KELPIE) are Scottish WATER FAIRIES who appear as grey horses that encourage people to ride them. Once a person is astride, the Kelpie will run off into the water, drown its passenger and devour him, leaving only the entrails on the shore.

They are known to eat animals, humans and other fairies that venture too close to their lairs. To see a kelpie is an OMEN OF DEATH or great misfortune.

If you want to catch one and make it work for you, have the sign of the CROSS made on a bridle and slip it over the kelpie's head; it will then serve you and do your bidding.

Kelpies sometimes appear as men to seduce young women, but their HAIR always looks like seaweed or watercress. A handsome young man courted one young girl, but when she discovered the seaweed and shells in his hair she realized he was a kelpie. He instantly turned into a horse to chase her in order to kill and eat her and would have done so if she had not been saved by a fairy bull.[176] One kelpie also appeared as an old woman and was put to bed by a bevy of girls. During the night, he sucked the blood of all but one, who escaped over running water. In this respect, the Kelpie is a VAMPIRE.

A kelpie lives at Loch Coruisk on the Isle of Skye of the west coast, while another in the north east, at Corgarff in Aberdeen, tricked a man who was trying to cross the swollen River Don. The beast offered to take him across, but halfway, it submerged itself, dragging the man with him. However, the man managed to escape and the kelpie threw a boulder after him, which can still be seen and is known as 'The Kelpie's Stone'.

KENNA is the daughter of OBERON.[177]

KEPETZ are small and gentle European fairies.

KERIONS are a type of KORRED.

KESHALYI ('Spindle') are the good fairies of Romany gypsy folklore. They are associated with SPINNING and MAGIC. They are very long lived, but this is not without problems for the female Keshalyi as at the age of 999 they are handed over to the demon LOÇOLICO, the result of a divorce

KELPIE

settlement between the Fairy Queen and the King of the Demons. The Keshalyi are ruled by Queen Ana.

KEYHOLES represent chinks in the armour of the house, apertures through which spirits may enter and which must therefore be rendered secure. If the IRON key is left in the lock, all is safe – evil fairies and NIGHTMARES cannot enter. The Irish believed that it was important to stop up the keyhole during CHILDBIRTH in order to prevent fairies stealing the baby.

KHITKA is a Russian fairy, an aspect of the RUSALKA, who abducts human beings.

KIDNAP/KIDNAPPING seems to be a common activity of fairies of all nationalities. They steal human adults and children, though they only take the young and fair, and never bother with old people. The Welsh sometimes call the whole fairy race *cipenapers*, a contraction of 'kidnappers'.[178] People most in danger of being snatched include laying in women, UNBAPTISED BABIES, blond children, pretty girls, those sleeping beneath HAWTHORN bushes and anyone wandering near fairy MOUNDS at night.

Male fairies sometimes marry human girls, or make them into maidservants. Later, when they have lost their youth and beauty, they may be released. SEVEN years is the usual period of captivity. The idea that spirits kidnap living humans, particularly babies, has been known from ancient times. These demons are often rumoured to be the spirits of human women who were either barren or who died in childbirth. *See also* CHANGELINGS, CHILD STEALING and WITCHES.

KIELKRÖPFE ('Keel Crop', i.e. a bottomless pit or hollow legged) are South German CHANGELINGS with huge appetites, bad tempers, and who are subject to fits of howling and screaming. They have wrinkled skin and over-large heads with ugly features but bright eyes. To get rid of one, you must trick it into revealing its advanced age.

KIKIMORA, or Shishimora, is a female DOMOVIYR or Russian HOUSE FAIRY. Kikimora are tiny creatures who live behind the oven or in the cellar. If a home is well looked after they will help out, doing small domestic tasks. They love SPINNING and will tear and ruin the work of women who rise from their spinning wheels without first making the sign of the cross. When they are upset they make strange noises and tickle the children awake at night. To appease an upset kikimora wash all your pots and pans in FERN tea. They are usually invisible but sometimes appear to those about to die. They look like normal women, but wear their hair loose as opposed to Slavonic women who normally have their heads covered. If you look carefully, you will see that they also have chickens' FEET.

KILAKAI or Kilyakai are Papua New Guinea forest fairies that steal babies and corrupt them with demon energies. They also steal livestock and cause sicknesses like malaria with tiny poisoned ELF BOLTS. They look like small, wizened tribesmen.

KI-LIN ('Male-Female') is the Chinese version of the UNICORN. It has one horn, but is a GOAT-like creature, rather than a HORSE. The legend originates in Tibet, where the beast is depicted in the ancient temples. The circle containing the body of the Lama was drawn with a ki-lin horn. From Tibet, the legend was introduced into China. The creature is so gentle it will not even step on a blade of grass for fear of damaging it. The backward sweeping horn is tipped with flesh, indicating that it is not for violent purposes. The name 'Male-Female' indicates that it is a symbol of the harmony of opposites, like the yin-yang symbol - a male horn on a female body. The creature appears to signal the birth of a very holy person, or to herald the reign of a great ruler. One appeared at the birth and death of Confucius. *See also* KIRIN.

KILLCROPS are the children of PIXIES, which they substitute for human babies. The word is possibly related to *kielkröpfe* the German term for CHANGELINGS.

KILLMOULIS is an ugly Scottish BROWNIE who has no mouth but eats by stuffing food into his huge nose. He kindly does work around mills, but often proves more of a hindrance than help as he is so fond of pranks, like blowing ashes over shelled oats. He makes his home by the HEARTH or the oven, and wails if sickness or misfortune threatens the miller's family. He has been known to fetch the midwife for his master's wife.[179]

KING FROST is a Russian fairy with power over the weather. *See* DED MAROZ.

KING OF THE AUXCRINIER is a MERMAN of the Channel Isles, whose appearance heralds a storm.

KING OF THE CATS is often referred to in Celtic folklore. He dwells as an ordinary CAT by day and travels the country at night as a royal fairy cat to avenge any slights given to him during the day.

A young Scottish man had dealings with the King of the Cats. He had been walking home across the mountains when a mist descended and he could not find his way. A strange light had appeared and he had followed it until it came to rest beside a large OAK tree. As he looked into its hollow trunk, it seemed that he gazed into a church where a funeral was taking place. Later, as he related his adventures to his friends, the cat that sat on the hearth seemed to be paying great attention. When the young man recounted that the coffin and torches had been borne by cats, and that a sceptre and crown lay on the coffin the cat sat up and exclaimed: 'By Jove! Old Peter's dead and I'm the King of the Cats'. He rushed up the chimney and was seen no more.

KING SIL or Zel is a fairy king said to sit, wearing golden armour, on his horse inside the famous prehistoric mound called Silbury Hill, near the equally magical village of Avebury in Wiltshire in southern England.

KINKACH MARTINKO is a GOBLIN that appears in a Slavonic tale about a lazy girl called Helen who span her hemp into gold thread on condition that she guessed his NAME.[180]

KIRATA are Indian forest fairies. The females are golden NYMPHS while the males have the upper bodies of tigers and the lower halves of men.

KIRIN is a similar creature to the UNICORN. It appears in Japan as a GOAT-like beast with cloven hooves, a single horn and a beard. It is a gentle fairy that brings good luck - and its image and name are applied to an interanationally sold Japanese beer!

KIRKEGRIM ('Church Grims') are Danish fairies found in churches, living in dark places in the nave. They appear as a 'grave sow' and punish sinners. *See also* CHURCH GRIMS and KYRKOGRIM.

KIRKONWÄKI ('Church Folk') are Finnish fairies who live beneath the altars in churches. When a female is experiencing a difficult labour, should a Christian woman lay her hand on the altar all will be well, and the fairies will reward the woman with gold. In appearance the kirkonwaki are small and misshapen.

KIRNIS is a Lithuanian fairy who is the guardian of the cherry tree. *See also* TREE FAIRIES.

KIT IN THE CANDLESTICK is a southern English WILL O'THE WISP from Hampshire.

KITTY CANDLESTICK is another English WILL O'THE WISP from Wiltshire.

KITTY WI' THE WISP is a northern English WILL O'THE WISP from Northumberland.

KIT-WITH-THE-CANSTICK is yet another name for a WILL O'THE WISP.[181]

KLAAS VAAK is the Dutch equivalent of the SANDMAN, a fairy who brings sleep to children.

KLABAUTERMANNEKEN are Dutch fairies who inhabit the figureheads of ships to guide and protect the vessel. Presumably they are the TREE SPIRITS who originally inhabited the wood.

KLAGE-WEIB ('Wailing Woman') is a German OMEN OF DEATH, like the Irish BANSHEE. On stormy nights when the MOON shines faintly, she stalks, seeking out those about to die. She is of gigantic stature, with a death-like aspect. Her eyes are black and hollow and she is wrapped in grave clothes. She stretches her arm over the house of the one to die, lamenting, and crying into the darkness. One of the inmates of the house will die within the month.[182]

KLAKADOON are Australian Aborigine GIANTS who live in the Dreamtime.

KLAUBAUF ('Thief') is a German fairy, one of the KORNBÖCKE, who has a long beard, horns, long fingers and a long nose. He carries a sack and dresses in shaggy furs. He lives in the woods in the summer, and the cornfields in the autumn. He is a scary character who gnashes his teeth and roars loudly when he is angry. He steals and murders human children when he can catch them.

KLAUBAUTERMANN or **Kluterman** ('A Ship's Kobold'), is a German fairy found on boats and ships. These fairies wear red jackets and RED CAPS and love to smoke a pipe.

KLEINMANNEKEN ('Little Man') is a small Swiss EARTH FAIRY.

KLIPPES or **KLIPPIES** are Lowland Scots TROOPING FAIRIES with brown faces.[183]

KLOPFERLE ('Knocking Elf') is a noisy German HOUSE FAIRY.

KLIPPOTH is a Hebraic term used for DEMONS or their realm, and for ELEMENTALS.

KLUDDE is a Belgian WATER FAIRY who hides in the half-light of dawn and sunset to attack travellers. The kludde appears as a horrible BLACK DOG covered in chains that rattle and give a warning of its presence. However, it is a SHAPESHIFTER and can appear as a black CAT, a black bird or a giant SNAKE.

KLWAKWE is a man-eating GIANT that appears among the Penobscot native Americans of Maine.

KNECHT RUPRECHT ('Servant Rupert') or **RÜPPEL** is a German HAUSBÖCKE who appears at Christmas, in a procession with two other figures, usually with the infant Jesus. While the Christ child gives out gifts, Knecht Ruprecht threatens punishments for bad behaviour. He has a long beard, dresses in shaggy clothes and furs, and carries a staff called the *Klapperboch*, which is dressed in GOAT skin and topped with a wooden goat's head with clacking jaws. He carries a sack of ashes.

KNIRFIKER ('Little Fucker') is a fairy of the RUMPELSTILTSKIN type, whose NAME has to be guessed.

KNOCKERS or **Knackers** are fairies that live in the tin mines of Devon and Cornwall in south west England. When the mines were in operation they sometimes guided miners to good seams by tapping or 'knocking'. Their favours had to be rewarded with food, traditionally a bit of pasty or tallow. However, they were not always well disposed towards the

KNOCKERS

the Jews who had crucified Christ and were punished by working out their penance below the earth. Despite this they sing carols on Christmas Day, Easter and All Saints' Day. Compare with COBLYNAU and KOBOLD.

KNOCKFIERNA is a large hill on the Limerick Plain in Ireland and there are many fairy related tales about the *poul-duve* or 'black hole' of Knockfierna. Here, it is said, is an entrance to a fairy castle.

KNOCKY-BOH is an English BOGGART who knocks and rattles behind the walls and wainscoting of houses, waking sleepers and frightening children.

KNOPS are HOBGOBLINS from the West Midlands of England who are much feared in Warwickshire. They were originally demon HORSES and may be the origin of the 2nd November (All Souls Day) custom of using a mock horse head covered in a sheet in order to frighten the timid.

KNOWE is word which refers to the outside, visible part of a fairy MOUND.

KNURREMURRE ('Rumble-Grumble') is a cross-grained old TROLL who lived in Denmark. He once thought that his wife was having an affair with a young troll and vowed to kill his wife's lover, who decided that he should lie low for a while. Accordingly, the young troll turned himself into a tortoise-shell tomcat and leaving the troll hill behind, journeyed to the nearby town of Lyng. He established himself in the house of an honest man called Plat where he was treated well, given plenty of milk and a warm place by the fire. So he dwelled contentedly. Then one day he was licking his plate when old Plat came home and told the CAT that he had been passing the troll hill when a voice issued forth, instructing him to inform his cat that Knurremurre was dead. The cat sprang up on his hind legs and made off back

miners and sometimes pulled faces at them or performed grotesque dances. Whistling offended them, as did swearing, and brought ill luck or a harmless shower of stones.

The knockers at the closed Chaw ('Raven') Gulley on Dartmoor are particularly vicious. A RAVEN (which some say is the original one from the ark) warns them when anyone tries to enter 'The Roman Mine' to look for the TREASURE which is buried there. The knockers will kill anyone who lowers himself into the shaft by cutting the rope. The body is found laid out on the surface the next day because the knockers cannot devour Christians.

Knockers have been described as small, ugly and thin limbed, with hook noses and mouths like slits, which stretch from ear to ear. Some said that knockers were the spirits of to the troll hill, no doubt to make up lost time with the widow.[184]

KOBLERNIGH is a Welsh MINE FAIRY. *See* COBLYNAU.

KOBOLD, Kobolde or **Kobalt** is a spirit found in Germany, Denmark, Sweden, Austria and Switzerland as both a HOUSE FAIRY and MINE FAIRY. The first record of the term occurred in the thirteenth century in Latin as *coboldus* which refers to a mountain spirit.

Kobolds appear to have been wooden figures depicted with their mouths open, probably laughing and there was an expression 'to laugh like a kobold'. Possibly they were carvings meant to embody the spirit of the tree or plant (usually boxwood or mandrake root) from which they were cut, or kobolds may once have been household gods, and the wooden figures images of them; certainly, the spirits of the fairies were contained within the image. This spirit might manifest in the likeness of the figurine, or as a CAT, a child, or a worm. Kobold figurines have various names around Germany such as Galgenmännlein, Oaraunle, Glucksmännchen, Allerünken and Alraune. It is possible to catch a kobold spirit by going into the woods at MIDSUMMER and finding a bird on an anthill. This will be the kobold in disguise. You will then have to talk to the bird and when you have lulled him into a false sense of security, catch him and put him in a bag to carry him home. Treat him well and he will do work around the house.

Kobolds are usually described as mine fairies, living underground in subterranean passages. In 1635, Heywood commented that they were found around the places where ore was dug, and known to the Greeks and Germans as *Cobali*. Sixteenth-century miners often came across ore which not only failed to yield silver or copper, but when heated gave off poisonous fumes. They attributed this ore to the agency of evil fairies that stole the silver. The useless ore was named after the demons and called cobalt. This name found its way into English and was at first associated with the ore, described as being impregnated with arsenic, copper and silver which: 'being sublimed, the flores are of a blue colour these the German mineralists call *zaffir* (sapphire)'.[185] This produces the deep cobalt-blue pigment known throughout the ancient world. When the Swiss Chemist Brandt isolated the metal in 1742, he named it cobalt, after the ore.

One possible origin of the word of kobold is the Greek *kaballoi* meaning 'horse-riders', associating them with primeval creator spirits like the TITANS, or *kabalos* meaning a 'rogue'.

As mine fairies, they take pleasure in frustrating miners' work. If they are neglected or insulted, they become malignant. However, they will sometimes take a particular miner under their wing and direct him to rich seams, and in former times if a man was seen to find more seams or possess more skills than his fellows, it was said that he was under the protection of the kobolds.

Sometimes kobolds move into German and Swiss dwellings as HOUSE FAIRIES. They begin by strewing sawdust on the floor and dropping dung into the MILK. If the shavings are left where they are and the milk is drunk, then the kobold will know that he is welcome, and make himself at home. Once lodged, the kobold will not move for any reason, even if the house burns down, though some kobolds will follow a favourite family to a new home. Nevertheless, they will make nuisances of themselves unless they are well treated and fed regularly. They particularly like to hide objects and push people over, though a happy kobold may sing lullabies to the children. Some say that the word kobold is derived from *kobwalt* or household god.

Kobolds are usually depicted as very ugly beings, around 60 cm tall (about two feet), with dark green or dark grey skin, with hairy tails and feet instead of hands. They wear conical hats, pointed shoes and dress in RED or GREEN.

KODIN-HALTIA is a Finnish HOUSE FAIRY.

KODUHALDJAS is an Estonian HOUSE FAIRY for whom food and drink are left out.

KOH QAF is the land of the fairies in Hindu folklore. It is ruled over by King INDRA.

KOPUWAI ('Water Stomach') was a man-eating OGRE of Moari myth. It had a dog's head and hunted his prey with a pack of two-headed DOGS. He was known to drink vast quantities of water. The Maoris eventually trapped him in his CAVE and smoked him out of a hole in the roof. When he tried to make his escape, they battered him to death.

KORANDON is a type of KORRED.

KORK is one of the Orkney TROWS.

KORNBÖCKE ('Corn-Goat') is a German fairy who guards the grain and causes it to ripen, riding on the breezes which ripple the cornfields. Like other GOAT spirits, he is associated with corn and fertility. When the grain is harvested he retreats into the last sheaf, and when it is cut he dies or, if it is left, he hibernates within it until spring. He is sometimes found in amongst the stalks in the guise of a cornflower or appears as an ill-tempered goat, though he can appear as a bird, CAT, wolf or insect. He was originally a vegetation god.

KORNIKANED is a type of KORRED. These fairies carry small horns attached to their belts.

KORN-KATER is a fairy that protects the grain fields.

KORRED or Korrs are fairies that have large heads, red eyes, dark skin, hairy bodies, spiky hair, cloven feet, sharp noses, spindly arms and legs and cat's claws. The males have rough, cracked voices, and always carry leather purses containing hair and a pair of scissors. The females are rarely seen, as they tend to stay at home. Korreds are usually found in Brittany, though they are also known in Gascony and the Pyranees. Considering the close ties between Cornwall and Brittany, the Cornish SPRIGGANS may well be related.

They guard the dolmens, the TREASURES stored beneath them, and the stone circles of Brittany. Some say that they erected the megaliths, being strong enough to carry the huge stones on their backs, and that they now live beneath them. Some may also live in caves, under heaths or under sea cliffs; wherever they live, it is always under sea level.[186] Their special day is WEDNESDAY, and their great feast day the first Wednesday in May, which they celebrate with feasting and dancing. They love to dance and the vigour of their movements leaves a circle burnt in the grass. Should a human male be drawn into their DANCE, he will be whirled around until he drops dead of exhaustion, while any girl who joins the ring will bear a child nine months later resembling some man of the village that she has never slept with.

Though they jealously guard the old stones, the korred will deal fairly with humans. If you leave a scythe, knife, or other tool overnight by the stones, together with a small payment, you will find it sharp in the morning. You might even leave your pigs in their care if, when the pig is slaughtered, you invite the korred to the smoking and give him a piece of fat.

KORRIGAN, Corrigan (pl. Korriganed, Corriganed or Corrikét) are female fairies known in Brittany and Cornwall, guarding the springs and fountains situated near standing stones. A woman may catch sight of a bathing korrigan with impunity; but if a man should chance to see a naked fairy, he must marry her within three days, or lose his life. They appear as beautiful blond maidens by night and fearsome red-eyed HAGs by day, though they are SHAPESHIFTERS and can also appear as spiders, SNAKES and eels. They like pretty children, whom they will kidnap and substitute fairy CHANGELINGS for them. They whistle to call others to assembly and mushrooms grow where they dance. They can travel from one end of the world to the other in the blink of an eye.

By night a korrigan haunts the forest of Broceliande as a lovely maiden and may be encountered by streams and fountains. She seduces men by using her MAGIC wand to create a GLAMOUR that makes the woods seem to be a sumptuous palace, but at the first light of dawn everything is revealed in its true state and she is transformed into a hideous hag. One of her victims was the knight Sir Roland, who at dawn saw the repulsive crone who ran shrieking into the forest, while the knight fell to his knees to give thanks to God for his deliverance.

Men who fall in love with a korrigan's comely night-time form will often pine away and die of love for her. It is also said that if a man loves both the beautiful and ugly korrigan, she will be able to remain lovely forever.

They are the granddaughters of NINE holy druidesses of ancient Gaul. Each Spring, they drink the secret of poetry and wisdom from a crystal goblet. Any man who interrupts their ritual will die. They remain Pagans and are enraged by the sight of a priest's cassock and the name of the Virgin Mary. Thomas Keightley speculated that the legends of the Korrigans of Brittany might have derived from a college of priestesses that dwelled on an island in the Seine, described by Pomponius Mela as human sorceresses.[187] See also LADY RAGNALL.

KORRIKS are a type of KORRED that guard standing stones. Some say that they are the descendents of CARIKINES, fairies introduced into Brittany by Phoenician sailors.

KORRS are a variety of KORRED who guard standing stones.

KOURICANS are Breton fairies living beneath the ancient dolmens.

KOURILS are a type of KORRED.

KOUTSODAIMONAS ('Lame Demon') is a hideous fairy that accompanies the CALLICANTZAROI or the NEREIDES during the Twelve Days of Christmas in Greece, though he is also known as far afield as Malta. He is small with a large head, lolling tongue, a hump on his chest and huge genitals, which he takes no trouble to hide. He follows the processions of Callicantzaroi, cursing and swearing. When the cock crows on the 5th January he is the last of the company to disappear, hanging on in the hope of making some final act of mischief. He is a serious threat, and once blinded a princess. If he gets into a house he will rape young girls and push his horns into the bellies of pregnant women. To keep him away hang a sieve and a BROOM by the door, suspend some pork bones in the chimney and burn incense at night throughout the Twelve Days of Christmas. If you have no incense burn old shoes - he really hates the smell!

KOW ('Spirit') is an old word used to refer to fairies in the north of England. See HEDLEY KOW.

KRAKEN is a Scandinavian sea creature big enough to swallow a whole boat. It is round, flat and submerges itself to create a whirlpool. The Vikings had many tales of Krakens, and one entered Scalloway Bay in Shetland in the nineteenth century.

KRAMPAS ('Cramper') is an Austrian fairy that looks like a DEMON, with staring eyes and a long, lolling tongue. He spends the winter searching for naughty children to punish.

KRASNOLUDI or **Krasnoludki** ('Red People') are Polish fairies similar to the LUDKI.

KRATTI is a Finnish spirit who guards property.

KRAVYAD is a Hindu GHOUL that consumes the flesh of the dead. It is named after the flames of the funeral pyre.

KRIKTSY ('Shrieks') are Russian NIGHTMAREs or Night-Hags. In Eastern European folklore, this HAG fairy prowls through villages at night to torment children. The villagers protect their babies by placing an IRON knife beside the cradle, or an axe beneath it.

KRISS KRINGLE or **Kris Kringle** (German 'Christ Child' from *Christkindl*) is synonymous with FATHER CHRISTMAS in southern Germany, and brings gifts at Christmas. However, in earlier German and Austrian folklore the Christ Child himself brought the presents to good children.

KROSNYATA is a small and kindly European fairy, of the QUIET FOLK variety.

KRSNIK, **Kresnik** or **Karsnik** ('Red Person') is a Slavonic good fairy or family GENIUS which guards the household and battles against the other resident spirit, the evil VLKODLAK.

KRUZIMUGELI is an Austrian DWARF who plotted to steal away a queen from the royal palace: A king wanted to get married, but only to a girl with black hair and eyes. A number of candidates presented themselves, but none had both attributes. Meanwhile, deep in the forest a charcoal burner's daughter heard of the

KRUZIMUGELI

king's quest and decided to offer herself, since she had the blackest eyes and ebony hair. On her way to the palace she met a dwarf who asked her what she would give him if she became queen. She replied she had nothing to give him. He smiled and told her that she would become queen, but he would visit her in THREE years time and she must remember that his NAME was Kruzimugeli or she would belong to him.

It all passed as the dwarf predicted and after three years of royal wedded bliss he was due to appear. The queen tried in vain to remember his name and grew sadder and sadder as the day of his appointment grew nearer. Then one day the royal forester reported to her that he had observed a strange sight in the woods. A little man had been dancing around a fire singing "It is as well that the queen does not know that my name is Kruzimugeli".

When the dwarf appeared she was able to tell him his name and he disappeared in high dudgeon. *See also* RUMPELSTILTSKIN.

KUBERA is the ruler of the fairy YAKSHAS. He lives on a mountain high in the Himalayas and guards mounds of TREASURE. He appears as a pot-bellied DWARF carrying a moneybag or a pomegranate.

KUGARVAD is the European KING OF THE CATS.

KULAKS are Burmese DRYADS to whom prayers must be offered before cutting down a tree.

KUL-JUNGK is an evil fish spirit of the Inuit (Eskimo) people. It lives in deep water and has a human shape. In past times, when the ice broke in spring, images of fish made from BIRCH were taken to the fishing place and left as offerings to the spirit.

KULSHEDRA is a creature of Albanian folklore. Every year, each St George's Day (23rd April), a DRAGON-like creature called a Bolla awakes. After twelve years, it transforms itself into a huge HAG called Kulshedra with pendulous breasts and a hairy body.

KUNAL TROW, or **Kurnal Trow**, is a particular species of TROW that dwells on the Shetland Island of Uist. There are no females. The males are therefore forced to marry human women, but giving birth to kunal trow offspring kills the unfortunate wife. After this, a human wetnurse has to be KIDNAPPED to look after the child. When the child reaches maturity, the father kunal trow dies.

KUNDRIE or **Cundrie** is the fairy Grail Maiden of Arthurian legend, a guardian of the Holy Grail.[188] She also has a HAG or LOATHLY LADY aspect, which indicates she is a goddess of sovereignty.

KUSHTAKA is a fairy of the Tlingits (Native Alaskans). These fairies usually appear as small men, though they may also manifest as land otters. They steal human babies and if they keep them long enough these become fairies too. The Kushtaka are generally malicious and malevolent and the tribal SHAMAN has his work cut out keeping them under control, though on occasions the Kushtaka may take it into their heads to be helpful.

KUWALDEN is a race of fairy beings encountered by a Roman called Publius Octavus in the year 470. He was living at Lugdunum (which is now Leiden in the Netherlands), when he met a tiny man wearing a RED CAP, a blue shirt and green trousers. He had a white beard and said he came from a race called Kuwalden, of whom there were only a few in the world. He drank MILK and cured sick animals about the villa.[189]

KYRKOGRIM ('Church Grim') are Swedish fairies who live in churches, usually under the altar.

They have been known to punish the impious, but usually they do not take any interest in the goings on in the church, except for foretelling the deaths of the parishioners. A kyrogrim appears in the form of a lamb. Perhaps this is because, in the early days of Christianity in Sweden, a lamb was buried beneath the altar and some say that they derive from souls from this animal sacrifice. *See also* CHURCH GRIM.

LA DORMETTE is a female French fairy who brings sleep to children, like the English SANDMAN.

LA LLORONA ('Weeping Woman') is an Hispanic BOGEY WOMAN who is said to be the GHOST of a woman who slew her children after being betrayed by a man. She haunts watersides and preys on men who drink or commit adultery.

LA PLATA DWARFS are DWARFS who were spotted in Argentina in the 1980s, having emerged from a well in the grounds of an abandoned house. They were GREEN and with wrinkled skin, like old men.

LABYRINTHS often appear in myth and folk tale. The hero of a story may be guided to the centre of the labyrinth by a mysterious woman, who leads him with a thread, as in the story of Theseus and Ariadne in the labyrinth of the Minotaur. The SPIRAL labyrinth is often inscribed on Stone Age tombs and MOUNDS. It spirals inwards along one path, and outwards again along another. It symbolises the soul's journey into the UNDERWORLD, the Land of the DEAD or FAIRYLAND, and then outwards again to rebirth. The anti-clockwise spiral represents the death journey, moving down towards death and the underworld, and then the spiral unfolds into a sunwise journey of rebirth.

LACHESIS ('Measurer') is one of the three FATES.

LADY OF DEATH is another term for the Irish or Scottish BANSHEE, an OMEN OF DEATH.

LADY OF THE LAKE is a beautiful fairy that appears in one of the Arthurian tales. She snatched the baby Lancelot from his real mother and disappeared with him into the depths of a lake where she tenderly brought him up in her underwater kingdom, preparing him for greatness. She also supplied ARTHUR with his magical sword Excaliber, a gift from the land of the fairy, whose sheath safeguarded its owner from harm. Some call her VIVIENNE, in the *Morte D'Arthur* Thomas Malory called her NIMUE and she has also been called NINIANE. She may have been one of the GWRAGEDD ANNWN, the Welsh fairy maidens who dwell beneath lakes in UNDERWORLD kingdoms.

LADY RAGNALL is a KORRIGAN type fairy who married Sir Gawain: King ARTHUR was once captured by an evil knight who only freed him when he agreed to return within a year with the answer to the riddle: 'What is it that women most desire?' Arthur sought far and wide for the answer, questioning everyone he met. Some said a good husband, some said nice clothes, while others said jewels or children. He knew that none of these answers was the true one, and began to despair. Eventually, as the year drew to a close, he came upon a hideous old fairy HAG who agreed to tell him the answer. However, she had one condition: that a handsome young knight of the court should marry her. Arthur regretfully entreated his knights for one who would submit himself to such an unappealing match. The brave knight Gawain stepped forward and pledged his hand in a most courtly and chivalrous manner to the frightful crone, Lady Ragnall. She smiled and told Arthur the answer to his riddle: 'Sovereignty'.

The marriage of the ill-matched couple was celebrated and the pair was duly escorted to the bridal chamber. Gawain gazed at the down-turned bed and steeled himself to honour his commitment, but as he turned to his loathly bride, she was instantly transformed into a lovely young maiden. She informed him that she was under a spell, but now that he had married her, she was able to appear as a beautiful maiden either at night in their bed, or at the court during the day. He could choose which it should be. The knight considered that she would be embarrassed to appear so ugly before the splendid court and told her that

LABYRINTH

the choice should be hers. When he thus proved unselfish, granting the thing that women most desire into the bargain, she revealed that this enabled her to break the spell entirely and become beautiful all the time.

This is the story told by the Wife of Bath in Chaucer's *Canterbury Tales*, though its original is ancient. The fairy is a goddess of sovereignty whom the sacred king must symbolically marry in order to rule. In the winter, she has the face of a hag of blight, in the spring a comely maiden.

LAILOKEN ('Twin') is a naked, hairy Welsh WILD MAN who made several prophecies. He was encountered by St Kentigern of Scotland and said he was being punished for his sins by living apart from men. He lived at the court of Rhydderch Hael and revealed to King Meldred that the queen was an adulteress. He shares some similarities with MERLIN who also had to live as a wild man for a time, as a punishment for starting a war.

LADY OF THE LAKE

LAKANICA is a Polish meadow NYMPH.

LAKE DEMONS are Spanish WATER FAIRIES who live in a lake on Convagnum in Catalonia. They kidnap human adults and unwanted children to act as beasts of burden, keeping them for SEVEN years before returning them to mortal realms.

LAKE MAIDENS *See* GWRAGEDD ANNWN.

LAMAS are spirits of ancient Chaldea who took an interest in the welfare of humans. They appeared as female hybrid creatures with wings.

LAMIA (*pl.* LAMIÆ) are fairies who appear as beautiful women or SNAKES, or perhaps a combination of the two. The original Lamia was a lover of the god Zeus and bore him two children, but the god's jealous wife Hera stole the children. In revenge, Lamia vowed to steal any human children that she came across and her bitterness caused her to turn into a flesh-devouring monster. The term *lamia* generally came to mean a seductive supernatural female, such as a SUCCUBUS, VAMPIRE or LEANNAN SIDHE who sucks the life force from a human partner, and to be used as a poetical allegory for beautiful harlots who destroy their lovers. Sometimes, WITCHES are referred to as lamiæ. The creatures were a type of noon demon (like the Balkan POLUDNICA), as noon is seen as a time for ghosts in the Mediterranean.

One early Greek tale relates how a young man called Lycius fell in love with an exquisite woman and married her. At the wedding feast, she trembled under the gaze of a philosopher who had guessed what she was. She hissed, turned into a serpent and disappeared. Lycius died of a broken heart.

LAMIA OF THE SEA is a Greek sea fairy, the queen of the SIRENS, who

dances on the waves and causes waterspouts and whirlwinds. She sings beautifully. One Greek shepherd boy drove his flocks right to the edge of the sea, despite his mother's warnings. He took out his pipe and began to play. Instantly the lamia appeared and challenged him to a contest to see who could play and dance the longest. The boy, being a foolish lad, accepted the challenge. He played and danced without stopping for three days and nights before he collapsed from

LAMMAS

exhaustion. The lamia was as fresh as she was at the beginning. She took his sheep and left him lying on the sand, near to death.

LAMIÑAK or **Lamignak** are fastidious Pyrenean Basque fairies who live in underground grottoes near water, CAVES, woods and mountains. They guard fountains and springs. When their hair is well brushed they bathe in the water, singing. To see them is counted as lucky. Sometimes they will give advice to humans, but it is usually misunderstood, since they say the opposite to what they mean. If they say the sun is shining, it will rain. If they say it is warm, it may well snow!

LAMMAS ('Loaf Mass') is an Anglican Christian festival, celebrating the start of the harvest at the beginning of August. Celtic fairies celebrate it, since it coincides with the ancient Celtic festival of LUGHNASA.

LAND OF YOUTH is the Irish fairyland, called *Thierna na oge* or TÍR NAN OG. It lies beneath the water and above the earth. The sun always shines, trees are always in blossom and there are lush fields and woodlands. Magnificent palaces house the happy fairies. Here old age and death are unknown, so it is called the Land of Youth. Sometimes humans have entered it by accident, by stepping over a hidden boundary at a magical time, or some humans have been taken there by fairies.

LAND UNDER THE WAVES (in Gaelic *Tirfo Thuinn*) is a Celtic FAIRYLAND.

LANDÁLFAR ('Land Elves') are Icelandic protective ELVES or spirits. It was once believed that if they were driven from the land, then Iceland would be open to invasion.

LANDVÆTTIR ('Land Wights') are Icelandic protective spirits or NATURE FAIRIES that live within the stones, streams, trees, rivers and features of the landscape. There was a legal requirement that Icelandic long ships had to remove their dragon head carvings when approaching home to prevent them frightening away the Landvættir. They can appear large or small, as animals, DRAGONS or GIANTS. A multitude of Landvættir in various forms chased away a scout of King Harald's invasion fleet.

LANGSUIR or **Langsuyar** is an evil Malayan VAMPIRE fairy, the spirit of a woman who has died in CHILDBIRTH. She has long, sharp nails, green robes, and floor length long black HAIR that hides the hole in the back of the neck where the langsuir sucks the blood of children. If her hair and nails are cut off she will become harmless and can even marry a human man and bear children. To prevent a DEAD woman rising as a Langsuir place glass beads in her mouth, needles in her hands and eggs under her armpits.

LANTERN MEN is an alternative English name for WILL O'THE WISPs.

LAR (*pl.* LARES) are protective spirits of ancient Rome. The best known is the LAR FAMILIARIS ('household Lar'), which protected the home like a HOUSE FAIRY. Though there was a single Lar to each house, Lares were usually depicted in pairs. According to Ovid a small DOG was often portrayed with a Lar, as both stood for watchfulness. He said that both guarded the house, both were faithful to their masters, and Lares were as wakeful as dogs. Like dogs they protected the family but were antagonistic to strangers. He added that CROSSROADS were dear to the Lares and dogs alike.[190] The Lares

Praestites were the protectors of the Roman people, the Lares Grundules protected the thirty civil divisions, the LARES COMPITALES guarded boundaries and the Lares Vicinales various neighbourhoods. The Lares Semitales were venerated for their protection of paths and the Lares Viales for their protection of highways. The title 'Lar' was also applied to some gods such as SILVANUS, god of the forest.

The annual feast of the Lares was the Compitalia, celebrated soon after the winter solstice (*see* YULE), when merrymaking accompanied the performance of theatrical farces. Some other elements of the festivals gave rise to later Christmas customs. The Compitalia called for the use of artificial light, and the Lares traditional sacrificial victim was the PIG, traditional Christmas fare for centuries. Slaves and freedmen especially venerated the Lares, as it was one of the few state cults to which people of all stations were admitted.

LAR FAMILIARIS ('The Household Lar') is the oldest manifestation of the LAR, or Roman HOUSE FAIRY. It protects the house and its wealth, and sometimes even gives warning OMENS to the householder. Each family had its own lar to which it would make offerings and libations of MILK. In return, it would ensure the prosperity of the family and sometimes punished those who offended against them.

This household Lar was given monthly offerings of garlands on the HEARTH, as well as daily observances of food and wine at mealtimes. It was always invoked on family occasions. Each householder's GENIUS was propitiated along with the Lar Familiaris. Lares were ancestral spirits, usually the spirit of the founding ancestor of the family.

Most probably, their worship dates from the time that relatives were interred beneath the floor of a family dwelling. The Lar's shrine was usually the HEARTH, the heart of the home. Though each house had only one Lar (which came to symbolise the home itself), they were usually depicted in pairs.

Some folklorists argue that the whole concept of house fairies originated with the Lares (or the similar PENATES) and spread with the Roman Empire.

LARES AUGUSTI were protective spirits of Augustus Caesar, who converted the cult of the LARES VICINALES into the worship of Lares Augusti, Lares of 'Increase' associated with the worship of his GENIUS (his personal creative force).

LARES COMPITALES guard boundaries (a *compita* is a boundary marker). At important intersections marble altars stood, with temples housing statues of two lares accompanied by a GENIUS LOCUS. At small intersections there might be an altar of stuccoed brick against a wall, on which would be a painting of two lares, dressed as Greeks with goblets, together with a toga clad genius, holding a sacrificial saucer and cornucopia. Many boundaries run along a path or road and the lares compitales were worshipped at both rural and urban CROSSROADS. Sometimes they were the chief deities of a hamlet. At the junction of two roads two lares would be worshipped.

LARES GRUNDULES ('Grunting Lares') are named after the traditional sacrifice of a PIG to the LARES. They are thirty in number and protected the thirty civil divisions of ancient Rome.

LARES PRAESTITES protected the citizens of ancient Rome.

LARES SEMITALES ('Path Lares') were venerated for their protection of paths (*semitae*) in ancient Rome.

LARES VIALES ('Highway Lares') protected highways (*viae*).

LARES VICINALES ('Neighbourhood Lares') were worshipped in a public cult of LARES vicinales. Freedmen mayors and slave attendants supervised their regular worship in each district.

LARVA is a little spirit mentioned by Monachus Sangallens in the ninth century. It appears to be a HOUSE FAIRY who enters a house and plays with the SMITH's tools and it can be heard working, though not seen. It takes human form and presents the master of the house with a pitcher of wine that is never empty.

LASA are ancient Etruscan spirits of fields and meadows who are identical in many ways with later European fairies. They were also associated with the UNDERWORLD. The Roman LARES may have evolved from them.[191]

LÁTAWICI is a Polish fairy. If a child should die without being baptised, he will wander about the earth for SEVEN years, begging to be baptised. Should he not be granted this boon he will be turned into a Látawici. *See* UNBAPTISED CHILDREN.

LAURIN is the DWARF king who appeared in the *Heldenbuch* ('Hero Book') and an old German poem, in which Dietrich of Bern and his warriors broke into Laurin's garden and laid waste to it. The dwarf appeared magnificently arrayed with helmet, banner and shield to defend his property. His MAGIC ring and girdle endowed him with the strength of twenty-four men, and his mantle rendered him INVISIBLE at will. On the advice of Hidlebrand Dietrich struck off the dwarf's fingers, broke the girdle, pulled off the mantle, and so was able to vanquish him. The dwarf then pretended to forgive his attackers and invited them all to a banquet deep in the mountains. Once there, they were in his power and he was able to take them all prisoner. However, Laurin's queen had no

reason to love her husband since he had KIDNAPPED her, and she took her revenge by freeing all the captives. Another great battle ensued with Laurin backed by a hoard of dwarfs. Once again, the humans were victorious and Lauren's hill was plundered of its TREASURES. The dwarf was forced to earn his living by becoming a buffoon.

LAÚRU is a lascivious southern Italian fairy of Puglia and is one of the FOLLETTI. He is handsome with twinkling eyes, black curly hair, soft velvet clothes and a sugar loaf hat. He tries to seduce mortal women. If the woman refuses, he will visit her with NIGHTMARES until she gives in, though these can be prevented by the useful measure of hanging bull or ram horns above the door. If he likes you, he may reveal the whereabouts of hidden TREASURE, or the sequence of winning lottery numbers.

LAZY LAWRENCE is an English fairy from Somerset and Hampshire who is associated with HORSES and sometimes takes the form of a pony himself. He guards orchards and gives cramps to APPLE scrumpers.

LE BARBOUE ('The Bearded One') is a Channel Island BOGEYMAN used by mothers to frighten naughty children.

LE CRIARD is one of the country dwelling LUTINS of France.

LE FAEU BÉLENGIER is a Channel Island WILL O'THE WISP and is a spirit condemned to wander in pain while seeking deliverance from its suffering.

LÉ GRAND COLIN is a Guernsey fairy who stuck his bat into the ground in a fit of pique when his young son objected to him hitting the shuttlecock out of sight. It is now a menhir called La Longue Rocque, also known as The Fairy's Battledore.

LE GRAND VENEUR is a WILD HUNTSMAN who haunts the forest of Fontainebleau when the wind blows through the trees.

LE PETIT HOMME ROUGE ('The Little Red Man') is a Normandy HOUSE FAIRY.

LE RUDGE-PULA is a type of NIGHTMARE fairy who enters and escapes through a keyhole or other hole in the bedroom.

LEANAN SIDHE, Leanhaun Shee (Irish), Leannán Sí (Irish), Leannan Sith (Scots) or Lhiannan Shee (Manx) means something like 'fairy love', 'fairy sweetheart', 'fairy mistress' or 'fairy FAMILIAR' and might apply to a being of either sex. These Scots, Manx and Irish fairies seek the love of mortals and if the mortal refuses, then the fairy must become their slave. However, if the mortal consents, they are bound to the fairy and cannot escape, except by finding another to take their place.

As a lover, the leanan sidhe is very passionate, but their human partner pays the price of the relationship with a short life. The embrace of the fairy draws life and breath from them while the fairy becomes bright and strong, this is particularly true in the case of the Isle of Man LHIANNAN SHEE who is more like a VAMPIRE who sucks the life from her lover.

A leanan sidhe is also a muse who gives inspiration to her poet or musician lover. She sometimes takes the form of a woman to inspire men in battle with her songs. Those she favours have brilliant careers, but die young.[192]

A member of the Scottish clan MacLeod, called The Forester of the Fairy Corrie, who served with the Earl of Argyll's troops in 1644, had a *leannan sith* who followed him everywhere in the shape of a white FAIRY HIND. Its presence irritated the earl and he ordered the forester to kill

it. MacLeod told the earl that he would obey; though it meant his own death. As the shot hit the fairy, it gave a shriek and disappeared, while the forester fell down dead.

A leanan sidhe inspired the poetess Eodain and it was she who helped Eugene, the King of Munster, to gain victory over his foes. After this he gave himself up to a life of luxury and went to SPAIN for NINE years where he married the king's daughter. Then he returned to Ireland with a band of Spanish followers to find his kingdom ruined, with drunkards and wastrels feasting in his halls. The nation blamed the king for neglecting his duties and would not listen to him or help him. So he sent for Eodain to give him counsel. She told him to govern like a true hero, as it is by strength and justice that kings should rule. Heartened by her words he overthrew his enemies and brought peace back to the land.

LEIMONIADES ('Mead Nymphs') were the NYMPHS who frequented meadows in Greek mythology.

LEPRECHAUN, Leprechan, Leprochaune, Luchorpan, Lubrican, Lubberkin, Luricane, Lurican, Lurikeen, Lurigadaune, Leprehaun, Lepracaun or Leipreachán is an Irish lone fairy cobbler who makes all the shoes for the fairy gentry. Leprechaun or Leprochaune is the Leinster name for them, though they are called CLURICANE in Co. Cork, Luricane or Lurican in Kerry, Lurikeen in Kildare, Lurigadaune in Tipperary and Loghery-man in Ulster.[193]

These names may be colloquial derivations of *Luach'rman* meaning 'DWARF', *lughchorpán* meaning 'little body' or the term may be derived from *luachair* meaning 'a rush' i.e. a man the height of a rush or a being that dwells in boggy places, as many fairies are said to.[194] Yet again, the leprechaun may be *Leith Brogan* meaning 'Artisan of the Brogue' or 'One Shoe Maker' as they are only ever seen working on

one shoe, never a pair.[195] It is also possible that the leprechaun may be derived from LUGH-CHROMAIN, a diminished form of the god Lugh.[196] On a different track the Grimm brothers thought the word leprechaun derived from *prèachán* or *prìachan* meaning 'raven'.[197] This too might relate back to Lugh who had the raven as his totem bird.

Leprechauns are small, withered and dressed in a homely fashion, green jerkins, waistcoats with silver buttons, leather aprons, blue stockings and silver-buckled shoes. They often have cocked or three-cornered hats and they have been known to turn upside down and spin like tops on them. They love whiskey and tobacco, smoking small pipes. They live under the roots of trees and in deserted castles.

To get the leprechaun's legendary pot of gold away from him, you must see him before he sees you. One leprechaun showed one farmer the single RAGWORT in a field under which there was gold. The man marked it with a red ribbon while he went to get a shovel. When he came back there was a red ribbon on every ragwort.[198]

LES ÉCLAIREUX, or just ÉCLAIREUX, are French WILL O' THE WISPS.

LES PETITS FAÎTIAUX are Channel Island fairies that live in the old burial MOUNDS and hills and are sometimes heard tinkling silver bells. They come out on moonlit nights to DANCE with WITCHES.

LESHIE, Leshiye, Lieschi, Lesiy, Lesovik (s. Leshy, Leshi or Leszi) ('Wood Spirit') are Russian fairies, the offspring of human women and DEMONS. They are always present in clumps of trees, particularly BIRCH trees, and where the FLY AGARIC mushroom grows. If you are walking through the forest and hear the murmur and rustle of leaves, this is the

LESHY

leshiye talking about you. Once in the forest, you are in their power.

Leshiye are often described as GREEN with tangled hair and bark-like skin, or blue with green hair and eyes. Some say that they have only one, lashless eye or the horns and feet of a GOAT, like PAN or PUCK. Leshiye are SHAPESHIFTERS who may appear as tall as trees or as small as mice - when they are wandering the forest they are big but when they appear on the plains they do not exceed the height of a blade of grass. They can also assume the shape of OWLS, wolves, bears, hares, old men clad in shaggy furs or may even take the shape of someone you know in order to lead you astray.

Usually there is only one Leshy in a wood, though there may be several in which case they are ruled by a czar. A

Leshy may live alone in the forest or in a CAVE, or with his wife and children, called the lisunki, and several other fairies. Some live in deserted forest huts, and will get very annoyed if a human tries to rest there. They may be heard moving through the forests with a rustle of wind (winds always blow about the Leshiye), laughing, or whistling or making noises like animals. If you hear an echo in the forest, it is a Leshy. If you see a whirlwind, this is a leshy dancing with his bride. Hurricanes are leshiye fighting.

Leshiye are the guardians of the forest, owning its birds and animals, especially bears. The year 1843 was renowned throughout Russia as the year of the Great Squirrel Migration when thousands of squirrels left the forests of Vyatka. Naturally, this was ascribed to the actions of a leshy.[199]

Leshy have strict rules about what people can and cannot do in their domain - humans are not allowed to whistle or shout there. Leshiye also hate thieves, and should one enter the forest they will torment him. If a herdsman enters the forest, he will have to pay for use of the grazing by offering the leshy food and MILK.

Leshiye are fond of tricking travellers; brushing away footprints so that they cannot retrace their steps or making every tree and landmark look the same. They may remove signposts and boundary markers. They have been known to go as far with their pranks as tickling travellers to death. They also lure lovely young women into the forest and rape them. When kidnapped humans return from the clutches of the fairies, they are often mute or even

LEPRECHAUN

covered in moss. They will never again be normal and will have a vague manner and act in strange ways. Leshiye also KIDNAP human children and substitute stupid, ugly CHANGELINGS with voracious appetites. Even if the child should be returned, it will grow up into a useless vagabond.

For protection, wear your shoes on the wrong feet, or your CLOTHES back to front. If you suddenly fall ill in the forest, this may be because of a Leshy trick. Wrap up a slice of salted bread in linen or take some suet, sweets or blini and leave this on a tree stump as an offering. When shepherds have to enter the forest, they will placate the Leshy by making an offering in the shape of a COW. In a similar fashion, a huntsman will leave a piece of salted bread on the stump of a tree and the first kill he makes.

You can invoke a leshy by the following method: cut down some birch saplings and arrange them in a circle with their points to the centre. You should then enter the circle, ascend one of the stumps and face the east. Bend down and look through your legs saying: 'Uncle Leshy ascend thou, not as a grey wolf, not as an ardent fire, but as resembling myself.' The leaves then tremble and the fairy appears in human form, agreeing to give service in return for your soul.

Leshiye are only active from spring to autumn. They disappear in the winter, and hibernate in the UNDERWORLD, to return with the spring.

LESIDHE is a solitary Irish fairy who is a forest guardian and who looks like foliage until he moves. He may imitate birdcalls and sometimes lead travellers astray.

LESNI MUZOVE are Western Slavonic forest fairies, a type of LESHY, covered in shaggy green hair. They hibernate during the winter and sleep in abandoned forest huts.

LESNI PANY is a female forest fairy of Western Slavonic, wife of the LESNI MUZOVE.

LESOVIKHA ('Wood Spirit') is a female LESHIE who appears as a WHITE LADY as tall as a tree, or as a young girl or an ugly HAG with pendulous breasts.

LEY LINES are the mysterious straight paths joining geographical points of significance. Although the theory of ley lines is usually dated to Alfred Watkins (1921), straight lines known as fairy paths or ghost roads were spoken of for several centuries previously. A correspondent of Evans Wentz (1911) spoke of fairy paths as lines of energy that circulate the earth's magnetism. While the straight alignments between ancient sites were only noted by scholars in the eighteenth century, tales of these straight fairy paths were current among the peasantry since who knows when.

Straight lines seem to be associated with the sacred or the supernatural, perhaps because straight lines do not occur in nature - while nature is full of curves and bends, the straight is otherworldly, associated with gods, spirits, fairies and ghosts. In many places, it is believed that spirits travel in straight lines. In Ireland fairies pass from one mound to another on straight paths between the raths, and humans will be punished for interfering with them. In China, bad spirits travel on straight paths, so straight paths are unlucky for humans.

It is widely believed that the dead must travel by the shortest route and in a straight line. This gives us the basis for a fashionable theory about ley lines- that they were death roads or corpse ways for the dead to travel to the burial ground. In Holland, mediaeval funeral routes called *doodwegen* ('deathroads') or *spokenwegen* ('ghostroads') are still detectable, converging on cemeteries. Similar paths called corpse ways, coffin paths and church roads are found in Britain. This death road theory may be connected with the idea of shamanic flight paths, since the SHAMAN in trance is thought to be undergoing a type of death in order to visit the world of spirits.

LHIANNAN SHEE or **Lliannan-She** ('Fairy Sweetheart') is a Manx version of the Irish LEANAN SIDHE. She lives in the wells and springs of islands where she waits to encounter young men. If one speaks to her, she will follow him always, being only visible to him. The lovers of the Lhiannan Shee have short lives, since she drains not only the vitality of her lovers, but sometimes their blood too, just like a VAMPIRE.

L'HOMME VELU is a French fairy, one of the country dwelling LUTINS.

LI'L FELLAS is a Manx term for fairies, a contraction of 'little fellows'.

LIBAN was a young Irish woman, drowned in a flood in the year 90, who then developed a salmon's tail, and became a MERMAID. She swam about the sea for 500 years with her DOG, who was transformed into an otter. Eventually, St. Comgall helped her get to heaven.

LICHO is a Russian fairy who personifies an evil destiny. *See* DOLYA.

LICKE is a female fairy associate of ROBIN GOODFELLOW, a HOUSE FAIRY or cook.[200]

LIDERC or **LIDERCZ** is a Hungarian HOUSE FAIRY that appears as a hermaphrodite chicken. It can travel equally well through fire and air, and will carry out any task set for it, such as finding TREASURE, but it never rests, and so can become very wearisome for its owner. The only way to get rid of one is to keep setting it impossible tasks until it dies of rage. A magician may gain a Liderc by growing one in the first egg laid by a black hen, which he must carry under his armpit until it hatches.

LITTLE PEOPLE

LIEKKOS is a Finnish WILL O'THE WISP. It is an OMEN OF DEATH or misfortune for all that see it. Some say that Liekkos were once children who were kidnapped by a WITCH during a midwinter candlelight procession. They can only return to earth by replacing one of their number with a human child.

LIGHT ELVES *See* LIOSÁLFAR.

LILE is a fairy woman from the Isle of AVALON who appeared at the court of King ARTHUR bearing a sword in a magical scabbard. The knights were asked to draw it forth, but only Balin was able to do so. Afterwards the fairy asked him to return it, but he refused, wishing to keep the sword. At this, she prophesied that with it he would kill his best friend and bring about his own destruction.

LILE HOB ('Little Hob') is a HOB that haunts the roads at Blea Moor in North Yorkshire, England, and hops onto passing wagons.

LILITH was the first wife of Adam, whom he put aside for Eve. She is often said to be the mother of DEMONS or fairies, and to be a SUCCUBUS, LAMIA, or VAMPIRE. God formed her from mud and earth and married her to Adam. However, she was not happy, and objected to taking the subservient position during the act of lovemaking - she wanted to be on top. When Adam tried to force her to lie beneath him, she flew away. THREE angels found her beside the Red Sea where she was happily copulating with demons, giving birth to a brood of children called *lilin* or *liliot* at the rate of a hundred a day.

According to Jewish folk tradition, Lilith preys on NEWBORN BABIES. Girls were vulnerable up until they were twenty days old and boys until they were eight years old. Protective measures have to be taken against her, including the drawing of magic circles. She is also a succubus who attacks men through their dreams, sucking their blood like a vampire.

The legend of Lilith suggests an alternative creation myth embedded in the biblical book of Genesis. She is probably a pragmatic demonization of an earlier goddess.

LILITH

LIMMIADES are the NYMPHS who frequent lakes and pools, in classical Greek myth. In popular folklore they are thought to be human SOULS condemned to walk the earth in punishment for some ill deed. Sometimes they appear as WILL O'THE WISPs.

LINCHETTI (s. Linchetto) are Tuscan fairies who bring NIGHTMARES. They creep through the keyholes and press down on sleepers' chests, making it hard for them to breathe; this can kill babies, the old and the frail. To discourage a linchetto, hang a strand of curly hair over the bed and the fairy will spend all its time trying to straighten it, and forget to make a nuisance of itself. Alternatively, scatter FLAX seeds over the bedroom floor and it will spend all night trying to pick them up. Linchetti are fastidious creatures who hate mess and will not linger in an untidy house. To make one so disgusted that it will leave and never come back, eat some bread and cheese while sitting on the chamber pot. They appear as horses, or one type just has long ears, though he is usually invisible. He lives in the barn, rather than the house, and torments horses he doesn't like, tangling their manes. Those he favours, however, he will feed until they are sleek and glossy.

LINCOLN IMP is a tiny IMP, about 30cm tall (one foot), who is said to have caused havoc in Lincoln Cathedral in England - until an angel turned him to stone and placed him on a pillar in the cathedral's Angel Choir, where he can still be seen.

LIOSÁLFAR, Ljósálfar or Light Elves were created from the maggots that fell from the deacying body of the giant Ymir, in Norse myth, along with the Dark Elves or DÖCKÁLFAR. They dwell in the air, in ALFHEIM (or GIMLÉ) situated in the third heaven. They are ruled by the god Freyr and are happy and benign. They are 'fairer to look upon than the sun', according to the 13th century Icelandic writer Snorri Sturluson.[201] Their women were the most beautiful ever seen and the Old English word ælfsciene ('elf shining') denoted great beauty.[202]

While the light of the sun kills the dark elves, there is a connection between the sun and the light elves. They are described as 'whiter than the sun'. The sun goddess Sol was titled Alfrodull ('Elf Beam') or Glory of Elves.[203]

In contrast, the Döckálfar were blacker than pitch and lived underground. People made sacrifices to the elves at barrows and MOUNDS. These consisted of offerings of MILK and honey, while images of the elves were carved on doorposts for luck. It may be that WHITE LADIES are a later form of the Liosálfar. The name yields alve and thus possibly the Danish ELLEFOLK.

LIPSIPSIP are the DWARFS of the New Hebrides in the Pacific. They live in trees and rocks and are inclined to eat humans who offend them.

LISS are ancient Irish earthworks or forts associated with fairies. According to folklore when the ancient race moved out the fairies moved in. Earthworks are sacred to the Fair Folk. No tree on them should be cut down, nor should anything be built on them. If a man should be rash enough to attempt either sacrilege the fairies will blast his eyes or give him a crooked mouth.[204]

LISUNKA ('Fox', or perhaps 'Sly Spirit') is a female LESHIE or forest fairy of Russia.

LISUNKI are the children of the LESHIE, the Russian forest fairies. They are sometimes substituted for human children in the manner of CHANGELINGS.

LIT ('Hue') is a DWARF of Norse mythology. He was accidentally kicked onto the funeral pyre of Baldur by the god Thor.

LITTLE DARLINGS is a general euphemism for fairies.

LITTLE FOLK is another general term for fairies.

LITTLE MAN is a description often applied to male fairies. Often the colloquial name of the fairy in many languages means simply 'little man', such as the KLEINMANNEKEN.

LITTLE PEOPLE is another general term that refers to the fairies.

LITTLE RED MEN are American fairies in Tennessee, living in the woods near the Mississippi River. They are the size of ten-year-old children and wear cast-off human clothes.

Many other fairies are similarly described. A whole tribe of little RED men lives in Glen Odder near Tara in Ireland. A group of little red men live in Uganda and the names of many fairies simply mean 'red men' such as the FEAR DEARG, NAIN ROUGE and DOINE BEAGA RUADH.

LITTLE SPIRITS are tiny fairies of the native American Sioux. They are only about 4 cm (an inch-and-a-half), and guard their territory near the Whitestone River by firing ELF BOLTS at any trespassing humans.

LITTLE WASHER BY THE FORD is another title of the WASHER AT THE FORD.[205]

LLYN Y FAN FACH, LADY OF appears in a Welsh fairy legend. A young man was grazing his cattle on the banks of Llyn y Fan Fach when he saw a lovely fairy maiden sitting on the shore, combing her HAIR. He thought that he had never seen a woman as beautiful, and tried to entice her to come to him by offering her gifts of bread. She smiled and shook her head, but this only made him more determined.

Eventually, after many attempts, he persuaded the fairy to marry him. She warned him that if he should strike her more than twice, she would vanish forever. As her dowry, her father bestowed upon the couple many fairy sheep, GOATS and COWS, which all emerged from the lake at the call of the fairy woman.

They married, and for many years lived happily on a small farm near Myddfai, having three lovely sons. One day, the couple were preparing to go to a christening, and the man asked his fairy wife to get the pony, while he collected something from the house. Returning, he found her still standing in the same spot. Fearing they would be late, he tapped his wife on the shoulder and told her to hurry. She turned to him with a sad expression, for he had struck her once.

A few months later they went to a wedding, and the fairy burst into tears. Embarrassed, the man struck her on the shoulder and bade her be quiet. She turned to him and said: 'I am weeping because their troubles are just beginning, and so are ours, for you have struck the second blow.' This frightened the farmer, and he took care not to strike his wife again in all the years that passed - until one day they attended a funeral, and his wife burst out laughing. Enraged, he tapped her on the shoulder and asked what was the matter . She replied: 'When people die, their troubles are over, and so is our marriage, for you have struck the third blow.'

With that, she disappeared into the lake, taking all her fairy animals with her. The farmer never saw her again, but she returned occasionally to instruct her sons in the art of herbs and medicine. They became the famous physicians of Myddfai.

LLYR is the Welsh King of the UNDERWORLD and the sea, the equivalent to the Godelic MANANNAN.

LOA are a group of Voodoo spirits or gods who usually personify natural forces like fresh water springs or protect certain places such as CROSSROADS. They are often interested in human activities and their worshippers seek their help. Compare with NYMPHS, LARES.

LOATHLY LADY is a British term for a type of ugly HAG fairy, who was once perhaps the goddess of the sovereignty of the land, whom the sacred king would have had to marry. In the stories, the Loathly Lady has to be won over or married, as in the tale of LADY RAGNALL. Some Loathly Ladies become transformed into lovely maidens when they are married, as the hag goddess of winter is transformed into the maiden goddess of spring. In Arthurian stories, she is associated with the Holy Grail and tests the fitness of the candidates.

LOB is an evil Welsh GOBLIN that appears as a dark cloud and feeds off the energies arsising from conflict and arguments.

LOB-LIE-BY-THE-FIRE is another term for LOBS.

LOBS are English HOUSE FAIRIES. They are very large and strong with long, thin tails. They will help out around the farm for a warm spot by the fire and a bowl of MILK. The name seems to be derived from the Indo-European root word *lobh* meaning to cheat or be cunning.

LOCHLANN or **Sorcha** is an underwater fairy kingdom off the west coast of Scotland.

LOÇOLICO are the UNDERWORLD fairy DEMONS of Romany folklore. When they reach the age of 999 the lovely females of the fairy tribe the KESHALYI are forced to marry male Loçolico.

LÖFVISKA are Danish TREE FAIRIES.

LOG OF WOOD can be a substitute for a mortal. According to Irish fairy folklore, the glance of a fairy can exert a death like trance. This enables the real body of the person affected to be carried off to FAIRYLAND, while a log of wood or fairy CHANGELING is substituted, clothed with the shadow of the stolen form. It is possible for a FAIRY DOCTOR to bring the victim back from fairyland, but they will always have a far-away spirit look.[206]

LOHJUNGFRAU is a German MOSS MAIDEN.

LOIREAG is a female WATER FAIRY of the Hebrides, small and sad looking. She is a patroness of weaving and SPINNING, presiding over the warping, weaving and washing of the web. She will punish any women who neglect the traditional ceremonies of these occasions. The Loireag loves MUSIC, but dislikes harsh singing voices and weavers singing out of tune.[207]

LOLOK are small spirits that appear in the folklore of the Minahadsa of Indonesia.

LORD OF THE DEAD is one of the roles which several fairy kings serve alongside that of Lord of the UNDERWORLD. Such kings include ARAWN, GWYN AP NUDD, BARINTHUS and FINVARRA. In each case. they are derived from ancient gods of the DEAD, and their names often means 'WHITE'. *See also* CAVES, FAIRYLAND and GHOSTS.

LORDLY ONES is a flattering term for fairies in general.

LORELEY, **Lore Lay** or **Lorelei**, is a lovely German WATER FAIRY. These fairies are the SIRENS of the Rhine who play their harps and sing sweetly to lure sailors onto the rocks. Those who see them go mad or blind.

In one tale, Lorelei was the name of a human girl, so lovely that men could not resist her. The outraged citizens of the town began to mutter that she must be a WITCH, or possessed. The bishop was forced to put her on trial. She told him that though every man who looked into her eyes fell in love with her, this was not her wish. She had only loved one man who had left her and gone far away; she wished to die.

However, the bishop could not bring himself to proclaim a death sentence, and ordered that she should enter a convent and dedicate herself to God. Arrangements were duly made and three knights summoned to accompany her to the nunnery. As they travelled along a high path overlooking the River Rhine, their charge asked them to grant her one last glimpse of the river. As they glanced down she happened to notice a boat far below them and cried out that the boatman was her long lost lover. With this, she leapt from the precipice into the water.[208]

LOSKUTUKHA ('Ragged Spirit') is a Russian fairy, an aspect of the RUSALKA. She tickles people, but this is not really a laughing matter as she tickles them to death.

LOST ISLAND is the FAIRYLAND home of PRESSINA, mother of MELUSINE.

LOUMEROTTES are French WILL O'THE WISPS.

LOVERS, THE is a generic euphemism for fairies.

LUBBER FIEND are LOBS, according to Milton:

'…how the drudging Goblin set
To ern his Cream-bowle duly set
Then lies him down the Lubber Fiend,
And strecth'd all out the Chimney's length,
Basks at the fire his hairy Strength.'

LUBBERKIN is an Elizabethan diminutive of Lob (*see* LOBS), referring to a PUCK like spirit.[209]

LUCHORPÁIN is a sea dwelling LEPRECHAUN. Luchorpáins can take humans beneath the waves in perfect safety by putting herbs into their ears or putting a magic cloak over their heads.

LUCIA ('Light') is a GOBLIN that leads the WILD HUNT in Swedish tales. She is an old Pagan goddess also transformed into the Christian saint St. Lucia, whose festival is celebrated on 13th December. The festival is called 'Little YULE' and it is the start of the Yule festivities which celebrate the reborn sun. The house must be cleaned in preparation, all the SPINNING and weaving finished, and candles lit. The youngest daughter of the house is called the Lucia Bride and represents the maiden goddess who overcomes winter. She wears a crown of candles and presents her family with cakes baked in the shape of sun wheels. She is accompanied by the Star Boys, dressed as TROLLS and DEMONS who represent the chaos of winter, which will be overcome by the re-rebirth of the light.

LUCHTENMANNEKENS ('Men of the Air'?') are Dutch WILL O'THE WISPs, the SOULS of boundary mark movers.

LUDKI ('Little People') (*s.* **Ludek**) are DWARFS of Slavonic folklore. They love singing and MUSIC, playing instruments that resemble cymbals. They live in family groups

and hold large feasts to celebrate weddings and other grand occasions. However, the various Ludki families are rivals and often wage terrible wars against each other.

In contrast, they generally behave in a kindly manner towards humans, attaching themselves to particular households in a fashion similar to that of the HOUSE FAIRY. In return for gifts of millet they will do favours for the human family. If the Ludki borrow pots, churns or farm equipment they will offer good recompense to those who lend them willingly, but if people grudge them their due they will punish the offenders in a cruel fashion.

The Lusatian Serbs believed that the Ludki were the first inhabitants of the land but they were Pagans and could not stand the sound of church BELLS, so fled the country and are rarely seen now. It was the Ludki who taught humans how to build houses. They are experts in many types of crafts, especially that of the SMITH.

They are small with large heads and bulging eyes. They wear bright clothes and RED CAPS. They speak their own strange language and once they have said one thing will then proceed to state the opposite. They live in the mountains, in forests, underground or in human houses. Their own dwellings resemble baker's ovens, but are furnished in the usual way.[210]

In some ways, the Ludki are unlike other fairies; they are mortal and grow their own crops. They sow their own corn and make their own coarse brown bread, though they also eat wild berries and roots. In times of need they will steal human turnips, beans and grain. When a ludek dies his fairy relatives burn the body and put the ashes into pots which are buried in the earth. At the funeral, all the other Ludki will weep into small jars which are also buried when they are filled. In such a way, the Serbs explained the ancient funeral urns and lachrymatories found in graves.[211]

LUGH-CHROMAIN ('Little Stooping Lugh') is an Irish fairy, possibly the origin of the LEPRECHAUN. The name is derived from that of the god Lugh, patron of the arts and crafts. When the old gods, the TUATHA DÉ DANAAN, were driven underground by the Celts, he diminished in people's minds and became 'little stooping Lugh', a fairy craftsman.[212]

LUGHNASA ('Games of Lugh') is one of the great fairy festivals. It coincides with the start of the grain harvest. Several fairies become active at this time, such as the German KORNBOCKE who causes grain to ripen, and the Russian POLEVIK who kicks awake sleepy harvesters. In Britain and Ireland fairies hold processions or move house at Lughnasa, and sometimes a line of lights can be seen moving from one hill to another.

Lughnasa, also given as Lughnasadh, was an ancient Celtic festival marking the start of the harvest at the beginning of August. It is named after the Irish god Lugh ('Shining One'), a deity cognate with the Welsh Lleu and the Gaulish Lugus, who is sometimes compared to the Roman Mercury.[213] He was a king of the TUATHA DÉ DANAAN and introduced the festival to commemorate his foster mother Tailtu (a daughter of the FIRBOLG king), an agricultural deity who expired after clearing a forest. The festival took the form of funeral games, similar to the original Olympics. Possibly the games celebrated the funeral of Lugh himself. Lugh once fought a battle with Balor, the Dark One, and originally the battle may have been an annual one between summer and winter, the forces of light and the forces of dark with the dark gaining ascendency. The last Lughnasa games were held in 1169.

Lughnasa is still celebrated by the Anglican Church as Lammas ('Loaf Mass'). The name of the ancient festival survives in modern Irish as *Lúnasa* (August), Manx as *Luanistyn* (August) and in Scottish Gaelic as *Lúnasad*, the Lammas festival. In Welsh, the festival is called *Calan Awst* (the first of August).

LUGOVNIK or **Lugovik** ('Meadow Spirit') is a male Russian meadow NYMPH.

LUIDEAG ('The Rag') or **Luideac** is a monster fairy that haunts Lochan Nan Dubh Bhreac on the Isle of Skye. She has a squat appearance and an evil, murderous nature.[214] She kills any men she catches.

LULL is a female fairy associate of Robin Goodfellow.[215]

LUMB BOGGART is a BOGGART who laid siege to a house in Bradwell in Derbyshire, after the bones of a woman were found under a staircase in the village in 1760. The haunting became noisier and nastier with time, until an exorcist was called in. He commanded the boggart to assume the form of a small fish and go to live at Lumb Mouth, the source of the local beck. Once a year, on Christmas Eve, it takes the form of an ouzel and flies round the village.

LUOT-CHOZJIK

LUNANTISHEE or **Lunantishess** or **Lunantisidhe** ('Moon Fairies') are Irish fairies that guard BLACKTHORN bushes and will not allow a stick to be cut on November 11th or on May 11th (Old SAMHAIN and Old BELTANE) or ill luck will follow. They appear as wizened, bald old men with pointed ears, long teeth and have long arms and fingers. They dance in the moonlight and dislike humans.

LUNDJUNGFRUR is a female Swedish wood TROLL that lives in trees near houses, but is invisible to humans.

LUNETE is the fairy cousin of NIMUE, the Lady of the Lake, from whom she learned MAGIC.

LUOT-CHOZJIK is a female fairy of Lapland who protects the reindeer as they graze untended in their summer pastures.

LUPEUX are French fairies that try to lure people into bogs by calling to them.

LURIDAN was a BROWNIE that inhabited the Isle of Pomona for seven years.[216]

LUSMORE ('The Great Herb') and refers to the FOXGLOVE, which is often mentioned as a fairy plant.[217]

In one Irish tale, Lusmore was a hunchback who wore a sprig of foxglove in his hat. He was driven from his home because of his DEFORMITY. One night he heard the FAIRY MUSIC, endlessly chanting 'Monday, Tuesday', but never getting any further. He became so annoyed that he shouted: 'Wednesday'; and the fairies were so pleased with this they swept him into their dances and when he awoke the next morning his hump was gone. Hearing this, another hunchback determined to have his own hump removed by the fairies. Accordingly he stationed himself at the MOUND and heard the fairies sing, but without waiting for the right place he exclaimed: 'Wednesday, Thursday!' The fairies were so angry at having the rhythm disrupted, they gave him Lusmore's hump on top of his own.[218] The same tale is told all over Europe with minor variations.

LUTIN or **Bon Garçon** ('Good Boy') are mischievous fairies, found in France (especially Normandy and Brittany) and some Swiss Cantons.

They can SHAPESHIFT into animals, small RED-clothed monks, boys, wolf-headed men and inanimate objects like flying spindles, gusts of wind, and travelling flames. They can appear or become invisible at will. They live near stagnant water, in CAVES, and appear on moors, dunes and near standing stones. The country lutins are sometimes called Lutins Noirs or Araignée Lutins. They love pretty girls and good wine. The name may be derived, by way of *netun* (the old name for lutins) from NEPTUNE.

Sometimes, they act like HOUSE FAIRIES (though some say they will only stay for one year), helping the servants, blowing up the fire in the HEARTH, supervising the cooking, and quieting the crying baby. Lutins also help out in the stables and byres.

If they are slighted, however, they become spiteful, upsetting cooking pots, tangling knitting and SPINNING, knotting horses' manes, drying the milk in cows, and stripping the backs of sheep.

One woman always sprinkled her trivet with water to cool it, before setting it back on the hearth - just in case the lutin should burn himself by sitting on it. If lutins start behaving like poltergeists in your house, sprinkle the floor with FLAX, which will get rid of them.

Lutins sometimes lurk around at CROSSROADS to attack travellers. Occasionally one will appear in the guise of a HORSE, but when a person mounts it the lutin will gallop off and finally throw the unfortunate rider into a ditch.

They might also rip the horns of COWS, block roads and throw travellers into ditches or off cliffs. They disguise seashells as pieces of gold and laugh themselves silly when humans try to collect them. On the other hand, they have been known to warn humans of impending disaster, and to take a friendly interest in children and HORSES, often pampering their favourite horse in the stable. Sometimes they rescue shipwrecked sailors and guard fishermen's nets.

LUTINS NOIRS ('Black Lutins') are a country dwelling variety of LUTIN.

LUTKI or **Lútky** are Hungarian DWARFS who love music and singing. They live on mountains or in mines. They usually like humans, though the sound of church BELLS drove them from the world, and they are rarely seen these days.

LY ERG is a fairy who dresses as a soldier. His red stained hands betray his bloody nature.

LYGTE MEN are a Swedish type of WILL O'THE WISPs, the SOULS of men who surreptitiously move boundary-markers.

LYKTGUBBE or **Lyktgubhe** is a Scandinavian WILL O'THE WISP.

LYONESSE is a legendary lost land believed to lie off the coast of Cornwall, between England and Britany - and the site of ARTHUR's court after his death. St Michael's Mount is said to be the part of Lyonesse that still lies above the surface.

LYSGUBBAR is a Swedish field fairy who protects the crops and causes them to grow.

MAANVÄKI are Finnish MOUND FOLK. Ancient and skilful, they are busy from dusk till dawn.

MAB ('Baby') is queen of the Welsh fairies, the ELLYLLON. In sixteenth- and seventeenth-century literature, she was described as the midwife of the fairies, 'quean' meaning muse or midwife from the Saxon *quen* 'woman', though perhaps it was not babies she midwifed, but MAGIC and dreams. She is also said to steal human children and leave CHANGELINGS in their place. She is supposed to tangle horses' manes at night.

It may be that she was better known in England than Wales, and was certainly familiar to Midlanders. Shakespeare, a Warwickshire lad himself, described her as a midwife of dreams in *Romeo and Juliet* but replaced her with TITANIA in *A Midsummer Night's Dream*. Herrick and Ben Jonson wrote of her as Queen of the Fairies, while Drayton had her as the wife of OBERON in *Nymphidia* (1627). She may be an incarnation of the legendary Irish queen or goddess MEBD or Maeve, though this link is tentative.

MAB-LED is a Warwickshire term for being PIXY-LED, or led astray by fairies.

MABUZ is the son of the LADY OF THE LAKE, according to Arthurian lore. He may be derived from the Celtic god Mabon ('Son'), the son of the Great Goddess Modron, whose cult was widespread in Britain. He is possibly the British equivalent of ANGUS OG, 'The Young' god.

MAC GRENÉ ('Son of the Sun') is a king of the TUATHA DÉ DANAAN. His wife was called Eriu.

MACHA ('Battle') is said to be a fairy that riots and rejoices among the slain, in the form of a hoodie CROW.[219] She is the daughter of the Fairy King MIDAR. Macha was originally an Irish goddess of fertility. She was also a warrior and built the fortress of Ehmain Macha, the ancient capital of Ulster. While she was pregnant, she was forced to run a foot race against the horses of Conchobar. As a result of this, she died giving birth to twins. She became the patroness of games and HORSES, cognate with the Welsh Rhiannon and the Gaulish Epona. After her death, she became part of the MORRIGAN trinity, with BABD and NEMAIN. As Macha the RED, she was a battle goddess to whom the heads of the slain were dedicated on the Pole of Macha.

MACIC are Southern Slavonic fairies of two varieties, the land macic and the sea macic. The land fairy helps out on farms, while the sea fairy keeps his own counsel under the waves, though he is fond of sweet cakes.

MACIEW are Russian HOUSE FAIRIES who are well behaved if treated fairly and fed each day, but they will play tricks if they are slighted.

MACINGHE is one of the FOLLETTI, and is a dangerous Sicilian wind fairy who violates human women.

MADGY FIGGY is an English supernatural HAG or WITCH from Cornwall.

MAERO were the first inhabitants of New Zealand, according to the later arrivals, the Maoris. They are hairy beings with long nails, which they use to spear fish.

MAEROERO-REPUWAI is a variety of Maero. They are tall with good-looking females.

MAG MELL is a Celtic OTHERWORLD underwater kingdom called the Plains of the Sea, where gods and heroes live. Here the fairies move as they would on land, herding flocks of fish, and walking through forests of seaweed.

MAGAE is an alternative term for the FATAE.

MAGGY MOULACH, Meg Moulach, Hairy Meg or **Hairy Mag** - in Gaelic *Maug vuluchd* - is a Highland BROWNIE who had a stupid son called BROWNIE-CLOD. After slaying the girl who killed him, Maggy found a new home at the farmhouse of Achnarrow in Banffshire and worked so hard that the farmer dismissed all the other servants. At this, she went on strike and the farmer was forced to hire them all back again. She was attached to the Grant family and used to stand behind the laird when he was playing CHESS to show him what moves to make.[220]

MAGIC is something which all fairies are capable of, in some form or other. Most are expert SHAPESHIFTERS and can manifest as a variety of animals such as BLACK DOGS, white CATS, COWS, DEER and birds, or even fire, moss, plants and trees. A similar type of magic is the GLAMOUR, which makes something appear to be what it is not. Usually, glamour is used to make a person or place seem more attractive than it is; for example, a cave may seem to be a magnificent palace or rags to be glorious robes.

Most fairies can also become invisible or visible at will and seem to appear and disappear in the blink of an eye. This magic is also used to disguise their kingdoms, which can only be located at certain times and in certain conditions, or by the aid or special herbs and potions.

Many fairies are fond of MUSIC, and possess great skill as fiddlers, pipers, harpists and singers. Fairy music is very seductive to human ears, and a person may be enchanted into a FAIRY RING or a fairy MOUND by a lovely tune, and then be incapable of leaving for many years. When eventually they do they will pine for the music, waste away and die. WATER FAIRIES such as MERMAIDS seduce sailors and fishermen with their SIREN songs, luring them beneath the waves where they drown them.

Many fairies possess magical objects, such as rings or girdles, that confer the power of invisibility; or magic wands to cast a number of spells; or cauldrons which can supply endless amounts of food or even revive the dead.

In Norse mythology, dwarfs are skilled craftsmen and SMITHS who can make magical objects. They made fine gold threads, which took root and grew to replace the shorn hair of the goddess Sif, an iron warship called Skidbladnir, which would fold up fine enough to fit in a pocket, and the spear Gungnir which nothing could turn from its mark. Other dwarfish wonders include the golden boar Gullinbursti, endowed with magical life, the magical ring Draupnir, which dropped another eight like itself each night, and a magnificent hammer that would smash anything it was thrown at, and would always return to the hand of the thrower. It was called Mjollnir and was intended for Thor, the god of thunder.

MAGLORE is a French FAIRY GODMOTHER, one of the BONNES DAMES.

MAGUT is a male, well-groomed Italian fairy who dresses in RED and has a loud, booming laugh. He sometimes helps out on the farm, but does not like to get dirty. He may give TREASURE, such as gold, to women he likes.

MAHJAS KUNGS are Latvian TREE FAIRIES who live in groves behind human houses.

MAHR were ancestral spirits of the ancient Slavs and Germans. They appeared in the form of moths to disturb the sleep of humans and drink their blood. A race of giant VAMPIRE Mahr moths lived in the Carpathian Mountains, and could only be killed by returning the wandering SOUL to its owner and running a stake through its heart, or exposing its lair to daylight.

MAHRT is a German fairy who sits on the chest of a sleeper to cause NIGHTMARES. The sleeper is said to be mahrt-ridden. One farm worker was mahrt-ridden so often that he

MANANNAN

asked the companion who shared his room to stop up the keyhole and knotholes, so they could capture the wicked fairy. The next time that his friend saw that the man was having bad dreams, thrashing and moaning in his sleep, he leapt up and stopped up the knothole with some straw. Next morning, they found a lovely girl crouching in the corner. Each claimed her for his own and they fell to arguing. Finally it was agreed that the nightmare sufferer should marry her. Though the couple seemed happy, the woman often asked her husband to show her the knothole where she entered the room. At first he declined, but when she said she would like to visit her mother one last time he showed her. No sooner had he done so than she flew out of it and was never seen again.

MAIDENLAND is another name for the realm beneath the lakes, where the LAKE MAIDENS raised Sir Lancelot, in Arthurian legend.

MAIGHDEAN MARA ('Sea Maiden') is one of the Scottish MERMAIDs.

MAIGHDEAN NA TUINNE ('Maiden Beneath the Waves') is one of the Scottish MERMAIDs. *See* CEASG.

MAJAHALDJAS is an Estonian HOUSE FAIRY who is rewarded for his helpful domestic activities with food and drink.

MAL-DE-MER ('Evil of the Sea') are sea fairies who live off the coasts of Brittany and Cornwall. They project lights onto rocks, which fool ships into thinking they have reached harbour. The ships are then wrecked and the fairies can possess the souls of the drowned sailors. The term *mal de mer* is used in modern French to denote seasickness.

MALEKIN was found in eastern England, at Dagworth Castle in Suffolk. The thirteenth-century chronicler Ralph of Coggeshall (1207) related that Malekin claimed to be a human CHANGELING stolen from her mother in a cornfield, but she had adopted the fairy nature and was INVISIBLE except when she chose to show herself, when she looked like a child wearing a WHITE tunic. She ate the food left out for her and spoke to the chaplain in Latin and the peasants in a broad Suffolk accent. She said that she had been in captivity to the fairies for SEVEN years but would soon regain her freedom and recover her human form.

MALIENITZA is a small and gentle European fairy of the QUIET FOLK variety.

MALINGEE is a fearful Australian Aboriginal night fairy. He avoids humans if he can but if he is provoked he will attack them with his stone knife. It is best to get out of his way, though his knocking knees and burning eyes give fair warning of his approach.

MALLEBRON is the servant of OBERON, in French folklore. He often travelled to the Holy Land with knights on Crusade, and saved many of them from death.

MAMAGWASEWUG are Canadian forest fairies. They are small and mischievous, seemingly similar to their European cousins like PUCK and ROBIN GOODFELLOW.

MAMALIC is a Southern Slavonic fairy that lives in the ceilings of houses and helps out on farms. If he doesn't get what he wants he will cause trouble.

MAMUCCA is a little Italian fairy who dresses as a monk and takes pleasure in hiding household objects, watching the fun while people search for them. When he does this, people say 'the mamucca is having a whirl'. Eventually, he will appear with a big grin on his face and return the missing item.

MANANNAN is the chief fairy of the Isle of Man, after whom the island is named. He was once a Celtic sea god. He takes the form of a THREE-legged wheel that is the Manx symbol. He is a master of deep MAGIC. When the TUATHA DÉ DANAAN were defeated by the invading Celts and forced to flee into the MOUNDS of Ireland, he gave them three gifts to help them survive: the first was the *faet fiada*, the power of shapeshifting; the second was a herd of magical PIGS which regenerated after being eaten; and the third was the elixir of eternal youth. He is an older deity than the Danaans, and is called Manannan Mac Lir or Manannan, Son of the Sea. He corresponds to the Welsh god Manawyddan.

MANDEGLOIRE is a spirit that lives in mandrake roots in French folklore. He can reveal hidden TREASURE.

MANII are ELEMENTAL spirits of the west and water, in Italian occult lore.

MANITOU are fairies, but also the spirit that is contained within manifest Nature. According to the Algonquin tribes of Native Americans, everything contains spirit or manitou. People have guardian manitous, which may manifest in dreams in the forms of animals. Sometimes manitous are described as fairies that live in tribes and have small horns or antlers on their heads. They play tricks on humans and possess strong magical powers. *See also* PUCK.

MANNEGISHI are a race of little people known to the Native American Cree people. They have big heads and eyes, thin bodies and no noses. Like similar European fairies, the Mannegishi are fond of playing tricks.

MANNIKIN ('Little Man') is a German term for ELVES.

MANO is the name for a small EARTH FAIRY in Hungary, the Balkans and Western Slavonic regions.

MARA or **Mera** is a Norse GOBLIN who attacks sleepers, robbing them of their powers of speech and motion.

The term has passed into English in the word 'NIGHTMARE', i.e. a NIGHT MARA, a female DEMON of the night who attacks sleeping men, sits on their chests and causes them to have bad dreams.

MÄRA-HALDDO is a Lapland SEA FAIRY.

MARANTULE is a type of NIGHTMARE that enters a bedroom through the keyhole and sits on the chest of the sleeper.

MARA-WARRA is an Irish MERMAID or MERROW with a splendid under water palace lavishly decorated with gold and jewels.

MARATEGA is an Italian fairy who sometimes appears as part of a triad with Rododesa and BEFANA to spin the destinies of humankind. Together they are FATES or FAIRY GODMOTHERS. In appearance, Maratega is ancient, brittle looking, and can stretch herself to great heights.

MARCRA SHEE ('Fairy Cavalcade') is a Gaelic term for the fairies or TUATHA DÉ DANAAN.

MARGOT or MARGOT-LA-FÉE is one of the Normandy FÉE, also called *Ma Commère Margot* ('My grandmother Margot') and even *Bonne Femme Margot* ('Good Woman Margot').

MARID is a powerful order of DJINN.

MARIE MORGANS *See* MORGENS.

MÂRISHÂ is the daughter of a NYMPH in a Buddhist legend. The imprisoned sages in the centre of the ocean threw up fire and storm against the tree that threatened to cover all the earth. The god Soma interposed and dreamed of re-populating the earth by mating with Mârishâ, the daughter of a nymph.

MARKOPOLEN is a Prussian TREE FAIRY that lives in the roots of a tree, under the supervision of the PUSCHKAIT.

MARMAELER are the children of the Scandinavian sea women the MEERWEIBER.

MÅRT ('Torturer'?) is a German fairy that sits on the chest of a sleeper to cause him or her NIGHTMAREs. The male is a mår and the female a måre. The pressure of the spirit will deprive the sleeper of speech and movement. It creeps up on a sleeper with a noise like a gnawing mouse or slinking cat. It can be captured with an inherited GLOVE, or by stopping up all the entrances to the room, including keyholes.

MARTI SEARA ('Tuesday Evening') is a Rumanian fairy who controls SPINNING.

MARTINES or **Martes** are Breton fairies that appear as huge women with a large quantity of brown HAIR, fiery eyes and huge breasts with which they try to suckle any passers-by they can catch.

MARUI is a type of NIGHTMARE who enters through the keyhole and sits on the chest of a sleeper.

MARY KINNEY is an Irish mermaid who was loved by a fisherman. He stole her cap so that she could not return to the sea, so she married him and bore him two children. One day when the children were playing they found the cap and showed it to their mother. She seized it and returned to the water.

MARY PLAYER is an English MERMAID who can sink a ship by circling it THREE times.

MARZANNA is a Polish spirit who appears dressed in otherworldly WHITE. She is the personification of winter, a HAG of death. Every spring an effigy of Marzanna, together with her BROOM, was 'drowned' to symbolise the end of winter and return of spring.

MASKIMS were SEVEN evil fairies of ancient Chaldea against whom an incense of white cedar was an infallible protection.

MASSARIOLI, **Mazapegul** or **Massariol** ('Little Farmer') are north-eastern Italian male HOUSE FAIRIES and are known as the 'jolly little farmers' who help out in farm houses, look after livestock and braid horses' manes every FRIDAY. They like to lure young women to the mountains to dance with them, but always leave them unharmed. These fairies dress well, invariably in RED, and look like elderly men with large red hats. They laugh like horses and are kindly creatures.

MASTER OTTER is a supernatural Irish beast that represents all otters. An inch of his skin will protect a man from being wounded, a horse from injury, or a ship from wreck. He appeared once at Dhu Hill (Black Hill) accompanied by a hundred ordinary otters.

MASTER PISCA is a mischievous PWCA who haunts an old Welsh farm at Trwyn in Monmouthshire.

MAUTHE DOOG is a local name for the Manx MODDEY DHOO, a BLACK DOG.

MAVJE or NAVJE ('Dead') are Slovenian WATER FAIRIES cognate with the Russian MAVKY.

MAVKY or MAJIKY ('Dead') are the SOULS of children either drowned by

their mothers or drowned UNBAPTISED CHILDREN. They look like beautiful babies or young girls with curly hair. They run about naked or clad only in a WHITE shirt. When the MOON is bright, they sit in the branches of trees to entice young humans towards them by laughing and giggling. Should a person fall into their clutches they will be tickled to death or drowned in deep water.

In summer, they are found swimming in the rivers and lakes. They may also live in the woods or on the steppes where they are sometimes heard crying pitifully that their mothers allowed them to die unbaptised. If you happen to hear one weeping in this way you should say "I baptise thee in the name of the Father, The Son and the Holy Spirit" and this will set them free. If after SEVEN years no one has performed this service for them they become WATER FAIRIES.

MAWKIN is an English ghost or FETCH.

MAY DAY is celebrated on the first day of the month of May and marks the start of summer in many countries of the Northern Hemisphere. The ancient Celts called it BELTANE, beginning the celebration on May Eve. A number of fairies become active around this time, particularly those associated with vegetation, the spring and summer, and forests spirits such as PUCK and ROBIN GOODFELLOW. In England, May Day was called ROBIN HOOD's Day and was celebrated with Morris dancing, circling the maypole, and gathering HAWTHORN blossoms from the greenwood. Fairies are particularly active on this day and sometimes may be glimpsed about their business. Anyone sleeping beneath a hawthorn on May Day is liable to be kidnapped by fairies.

MARY PLAYER

MAZAPEGOLO is an Italian fairy from the region of Forlì, being a type of LINCHETTO, who brings NIGHTMARES to sleepers. To get rid of him you must induce a brown haired girl to eat some bread and cheese while sitting on a chamberpot and threatening to shit on his face. Understandably, he will leave in disgust and never come back.

MAZIKEEN, Mazikin, Shideem or Shehireem are winged fairies of Jewish folklore. They can SHAPESHIFT, foretell the future, perform MAGIC and make themselves INVISIBLE. They were created when spirits lay with both Adam and Eve after the couple was banished from the Garden of Eden. Mazikeen have been known to marry human women, and there is a tale of a holy man summoned by a mazikeen to circumcise a baby born to his human wife. The girl cautioned the man not to eat the FAIRY FOOD, or he would be unable to return to the human world. *See also* MIDWIFE.

MAZOE is one of the sisters of MORGAN LE FAY who dwells with her in AVALON.

MAZZAMARELLE are FOLLETTI known in the Calabria, Lazio and Abruzzo areas of Italy, where they appear as little boys with silk hats and castenets, who ride the whirlwind. They get into houses where they knock and rattle about.

MAZZARUOLO was an Italian fairy written of by Florio in 1598 as a type of HOUSE FAIRY, a sprite, or 'LAR in the chimney'.[221]

MEDB, Maeve or Medhbha ('Intoxication') is a SUCCUBUS or fairy, in Irish folklore, perhaps cognate with the Welsh Queen MAB - though this link is tenuous. In earlier legend, she was Medb, the Queen of Connacht, who brought

MEDB

about the downfall of the hero Cuchulainn by trickery. When she went to battle she rode in an open car, accompanied by four chariots, one before, one behind, and one each side so that her crown and royal robes should not be defiled by dust. She was originally a goddess, ostensibly a goddess of war and destruction, though perhaps in actuality a sovereign goddess, a personification of the land. In one story she appears in HAG form as a WELL GUARDIAN, to Niall. She grants him a drink and when he agrees to mate with her she changes into a young girl and awards him the kingship of Ireland.

MEERFRAUEN ('Merwomen') (*s.* Meerfrau) are female German sea or WATER FAIRIES.

MEERJUNGFERN ('Mermaid') are German MERMAIDS

MEERMANN is a German MERMAN.

MEERMINNEN are Dutch MERMAIDS or sea women.

MEERWEIBER is a sea-fairy or MERMAID of Scandinavia.

MEISTER HÄMMERLINGE (Master Hammerlings') are German MINE FAIRIES.

MEKUMWASUCK are little people of the Passamaquody Native American people of the modern-day Canadian/US border. They are about 60 cm tall (about two feet) and somewhat ugly. They live in the forests and their faces are covered with HAIR. If one looks directly at you, you will be struck with a disease.

MELALO was the child of a union between the Queen of the Fairies, ANA, and the King of the Demons, in Romany gypsy folklore. He looks like a two-headed bird and causes insanity among humans.

MELCH DICK or **Melsh Dick** is an English North Country fairy who appears as a DWARF man in peasant clothing. He loves nuts and will punish anyone who takes nuts from his tree with bloating and cramps. He hates lazy humans and will pinch them.

MELIADES, **Meliads** or **Melian Nymphs** were the Flock NYMPHS of ancient Greece who protected sheep.

MELIOR was the sister of MELUSINE.

MELISSAI ('Bees') were often the mothers or nurses of heroes and infant gods, including the infant Zeus, who fed on sacred honey. His nursing nymphs retained the title *Melissai* or 'bees'.

MELPOMENE ('Songstress') is one of the nine MUSES, the patroness of tragic drama, with a lovely singing voice. She is depicted with the mask of tragedy, boots and a crown of cypress.

MELUSINA, **Melusine** or **Merlusine** is a WATER FAIRY; some say the daughter of a Scottish king and a fairy mother, cursed to become a

SNAKE every Saturday from the waist down. The royal houses of Luxembourg, Rohan and Sassenaye all claim descent from Melusine. The counts of Lusignan cliam her name signifies *Mère des Lusignans* ('mother of the Lusignans').

In a French version of the tale, Elinas, King of Albania, married the fairy Pressina with the taboo that he should not witness her laying-in. She bore him the triplets Melusina, Melior, and Palatina, but the king, forgetting the taboo, rushed in to see them, and the fairy and her daughters disappeared.

They went to the mysterious Lost Island, where the girls grew up. When they were fifteen, Melusina determined to be revenged on her father and set out for Albania with her two sisters. By magic, they imprisoned him and all his wealth inside a high mountain. Pressina was outraged by this unfilial act and cursed Melusina to become a snake every Saturday until she should marry a man who would agree never to see her on that day. Melusina wandered the world and eventually arrived in the forest of Colombiers in Poitou, where all the fairies welcomed her and made her their queen.

It chanced that Count Raymond was travelling in the forest and arrived at the Fountain of Thirst, also called The Fountain of the FAYS. There he saw THREE comely fairy women disporting themselves, the loveliest of which was Melusina. Naturally, they fell in love and were married, with the condition that Raymond should not see her on a Saturday. Their marriage was happy, despite the fact that their children were all horribly deformed. However, it was not to last. The Count wondered why he could not see his wife on a Saturday and began to suspect that she had a lover. Concealing himself in her chamber he saw the horrible truth. Before his eyes she transformed into a writhing

serpent, grey, white and blue. Still, he loved Melusina and knew that if he ever revealed that he was aware of her secret she would have to leave him.

It then came about that one of their sons, the vile Geoffrey, burned his brother and a hundred monks to death as they sheltered in an abbey. As Melusina went to comfort her husband he cried out: 'Go, thou foul snake, contaminator of my race!' Thus, the entire evil destiny that had lain in abeyance came to pass. Melusina told her husband that she must leave him and spend her time in pain and misery until Doomsday. She added that when one of her race was about to die at Lusignan she would appear, and when the castle was about to gain a new lord she would appear hovering in the air, or in the Fountain of Thirst.[222]

In the Luxembourg version of the legend she married Count Siegfried, the founder of the country. In this case she asked to be alone on the first WEDNESDAY of the month, when she would retire to the caverns beneath the city. Inevitably, Siegfried spied on her and discovered that she became a MERMAID with a fish tail. She jumped out of the window into the River Alzette and he never saw her again. (All over Europe there are similar stories of men who accidentally discover their wives to be mermaids.)

In Germany, Melusina is not only a water fairy but a woodland and mountain fairy as well. The German version of the story concerns a young man who lived at Stollenberg Palace. He was out hunting by the Stollenberg Mountain when he heard the voice of a woman asking him to redeem her by kissing her three times. She told him that her name was Melusina and that if he complied with her request she would be his bride. He saw that she had an angelic face, golden hair and blue eyes but her hands had no fingers and instead of feet a snake's tail peeked from

beneath her skirts. Nonetheless, she was enchanting and he kissed her THREE times. Expressing her delight, the maiden disappeared.

The next morning he went off to find her again. This time, she not only had a snake's tail but also a snake's body, a DRAGON's tail and wings. But her face was so exquisite and her mouth so seductive that he again gave her three kisses. She smiled joyfully and disappeared.

That night. he could not sleep with thinking of the extraordinary Melusina and as soon as it was light he set off to find her once more, following the sound of her sweet singing voice. But what now? Instead of the beloved face he expected she now had the head of a TOAD, lifted up waiting to be kissed. He could not bring himself to kiss her the requisite three times. In revulsion, he fled, leaving behind the fairy's cries of anguish and disappointment.

He left the district for good and married a normal girl. As they celebrated the wedding feast a crack opened in the ceiling and a drop of moisture fell into a dish of food. Anyone who ate from this dish fell down dead. Then a snake's tail emerged from the ceiling and the wedding party broke up in chaos.

Violent cries were known in France as *cris de Melusine* from the scream Melusine gave as her husband betrayed her. In Germany, during a storm, they say: 'Melusina is crying for her children'; and on Christmas Eve, they brush the crumbs from the table, so that Melusina might also have something to eat.

Like many Pagan deities and fairies, she has acquired the title Saint Melusina. According to Gerald Gardener Melusine was one of the names given to the WITCHES' Goddess. Her name may derive from the Breton *melus* meaning melodious.

MEN OF PEACE is a Scottish term for the fairies.

MENA is an Italian spirit of love and marriage.

MENAHUNE, Menehune or **Menihuni** are Hawaiian fairies that live in the forests and emerge at night to play tricks on people or sometimes to punish or reward those they take an interest in. They are of uncertain temperament, one day being playful, the next malicious and dangerous. They are credited with any unexplained event. The islanders avoid them unless certain special favours are needed from them.

In olden times, some of the females intermarried with humans, but did not know how to make a fire or cook food, because they only ate raw vegetables themselves. Those descended from human-menehune parents are able to call on the services of their fairy kin. Menahune are expert builders and craftsmen and may act like HOUSE FAIRIES to do such things as preparing wedding feasts while the humans sleep.

They are tiny beings, about 15 to 60 cm tall (6 inches to two feet), with long black HAIR to their knees - which covers their nakedness - and pointed ears. They are fond of dancing and singing. They also like to dive from high cliffs into the sea at night, so if you hear a splash it may be a menehune, though they are rarely seen. They have tiny bows and shoot little ARROWS to pierce the hearts of angry people and make them feel love instead. They are afraid of OWLS and when they play too many mischievous pranks the owl god of Paupueo summons the owls to drive them back into the forest.

When the first Polynesians arrived on the island of Hawaii they found that the menehune were already there, living in the CAVES but having already built dams, fishponds and temples. They are said to have hidden TREASURE.

MENTERS is a northern English term for fairies in Yorkshire.

MEREWIPER are German WATER FAIRIES or WATER MAIDS encountered in the River Danube. They were mentioned in the thirteenth-century *Nibelungenlied*.

MERLIN or **Myrddin** the magician was half-fairy. Or, according to the Christian version, he was fathered by an INCUBUS, but saved from evil by being baptised. As a child he demonstrated his magical powers and saved himself from being a human sacrifice by telling King Vortigern that his fortified tower kept collapsing because two DRAGONS, one RED and one WHITE, fought beneath the foundations. Merlin arranged the conception of ARTHUR by magically disguising Uther Pendragon as King Gorlois, so that he could seduce Gorlois' wife Igraine. Merlin took the resulting child and arranged for him to be fostered by Sir Ector. Later, Merlin acted as adviser to the young King Arthur and is also said to have built Stonehenge.

There are various tales as to his eventual fate. Some say he fell in love with NIMUE and taught her magical secrets, which she used to imprison him in a HAWTHORN tree. Others say he went mad and lived as a WILD

MAN in the woods. There are even theories that he may originally have been a god, perhaps an aspect of Mabon or Cernunnos.

In contrast, some propose an historical origin for him as there are records of a sixth-century bard called Myrddin who became insane after the Battle of Ardderyd (allegedly in the year 574) and lived in the woods.[223]

MERMAIDS are legendary creatures who have the upper bodies of lovely women and the tails of fish, though the Scots say that under the fish scales are normal human legs. They may occasionally be seen sunning themselves on rocks as they gaze into mirrors while combing their long hair. Like the SIRENS, they have sweet voices and sing to lure human lovers into the depths of the waves, or to summon storms that wreck ships.

The early church took a dim view of mermaids, saying that they were DEMONS who tempted the righteous. In Irish legend, St Patrick banished old Pagan women from the earth by turning them into mermaids. The mermaid of Iona was offered redemption if she relinquished her sea home, but this she was unable to do and her tears became the grey-green pebbles of the island's shore.

Like other fairies, mermaids are said to have no souls but they can gain one by marrying a human. They make good wives and caring mothers and for this reason many men have sought them. The Clan McVeagh in Sutherland, in the north-east of Scotland, claim descent from a union between a mermaid and a fisherman. To capture a mermaid it is first necessary to secure her MAGIC cap, her belt or comb and hide it. If she finds it she will return to the sea, which is her greatest desire. In a Scottish tale Johnny Croy got round this by contracting a SEVEN-year marriage with a mermaid and agreed to leave with her at the end of the arrangement. They duly sailed away to sea after the seven years, together with six of their children, having to leave the seventh because Johnny's mother had taken the precaution of branding it with a cross.

Mermaids also have the power to grant gifts. One day, Lutey of Cury was beachcombing near the Lizard, in Cornwall, when he found a mermaid stranded in a rock pool. She asked him to return her to the sea and he agreed. In gratitude, she granted him THREE wishes and he chose the power of breaking WITCHES' spells, the power to force FAMILIARS to do good for others and that these powers should be passed on to his descendants. She also rewarded his kindness with two other gifts: that his family should never want and the power to call her whenever he wanted by aid of her magic comb. He then carried her down gently to the sea and true to her nature she tried to bewitch him into entering the water with her, but his dog barked and broke the spell: he remembered his wife and children at home. She slid away, saying that she loved him and would return in nine years. She was true to her word and the family became famous healers. After NINE years Lutey was fishing with his son and the mermaid rose

MERMAIDS

from the sea. Lutey told his son it was time to keep his promise and sank beneath the waves with the mermaid, seeming quite happy.[224]

Belief in mermaids was still widespread in coastal areas of Britain in the nineteenth century. As recently as 1947, an eighty-year-old fisherman from the Isle of Muck in the Inner Hebrides claimed he had seen a mermaid near the shore, combing her hair.

The word 'mermaid' may derive from the French for sea, *mer,* or be a corruption of meremaid or merrymaid. It is possible that the concept of mermaids derives from ancient beliefs of fish tailed goddesses such as Atargatis, the Semitic moon and love goddess, known in Greece as Derketo, and from later forms of such deities like Aphrodite who was 'foam born' in the sea. Aphrodite (the Roman Venus) is the goddess of love, fertility, and fair sailing, often accompanied by her sacred dolphins, TRITONS and TRITONIDS. Like mermaids, she is depicted with a mirror and comb, the Greek names of which signify the female vulva. In early astrology her mirror represented the planet Venus. Like the goddesses, mermaids are connected with love and the moon. In Tudor England, 'mermaid' was a term for a prostitute, with Anne Boleyn being characterised as a mermaid.

MERMEN have been spotted over the years and, in contrast with their women folk, are said to be ugly with a wild appearance, GREEN hair, snub noses and large mouths, sometimes with green or fish teeth. Gervase of Tilbury (1211) said there were many mermen about the coasts of Britain. In Scotland and Scandinavia, they may appear as horses, while in the Mediterranean they are half-man and half-fish. They are generally antagonistic, causing storms and tidal waves, and it was once the task of any ship's captain to placate the mermen, making appropriate offerings. The bodies of the dead were given into their care, but they might also steal the

souls of the drowned, imprisoning them in their underwater homes. In 1723, Denmark instigated a Royal Commission to disprove the existence of mermaids but to their surprise they encountered a merman near the Faeroe Isles with deep set eyes and a black beard.

MERPEOPLE ('Sea People') is another English term for MERMAIDS and MERMEN.

MERROW, Moruadh or **Murrughach** (Gaelic from *muir* 'sea' and *oig* 'maid') are Irish mer-people, human above the waist and fish below. The males have green teeth and hair, pig eyes and red noses, but are jovial and friendly. The females are beautiful and gentle but have webbed fingers. They wear feathered RED CAPS, *cohullen druith,* and if these are stolen, they cannot return to the sea. In this regard the caps are similar to the seal skins of the SELKIES. Female merrows have been known to fall in love with the fishermen they come across and a woman of Bantry was said to be the child of such a marriage; she was covered all over in fish scales. Fishermen are afraid of merrows, because to see them means a storm is coming. Both male and female merrows sometimes come ashore in the form of small, hornless COWS.[225]

MERRY DANCERS may be an English translation of the Gaelic *Na Fir Clis* according to some[226] (though I take it to mean 'the fallen men') and refers to the Northern Lights, thought to be dancing fairies.

MERRYMAIDS are Cornish MERMAIDS.

MERWIFE is another English term for a MERMAID.

MERWOMEN is an alternative English term for MERMAIDS.

MESITCH is the patron of both hunting and the woods. He can be sometimes

seen riding a boar with golden bristles through the forests. He was probably once a god of the Circassians.

METSHÄNHALTIA is a Finnish fairy or HALTIA who rules the forests. He dresses in lichens and usually appears as an old man with a grey beard. If he wishes, he can stretch himself to peer over the treetops.

METSHELDIJAS is an Estonian fairy who rules the forests. He dresses in lichens and usually appears as an old man with a grey beard. If he wishes, he can stretch himself to peer over the treetops.

METSIK is an Estonian forest fairy who is inclined to injure COWS if he is not placated in an elaborate ceremony during which an image of him is made.

METTEN are North European FATES or FAIRY GODMOTHERS.

MEYLANDT is the FAIRYLAND of German folklore.

MHOWAH or **MHAOAH** is a forest GIANT of the nomadic Bhîl tribe who provides them with wood, bread and the water of life.

MICKLETON HOOTER is an English spirit from Warwickshire, who makes a booming noise and is sometimes identified with the DUN COW.

MICOL is the Fairy Queen mentioned in the British Museum manuscript Sloane 1727.

MIDAR, Midhir or **Midir** was also once an Irish god associated with rebirth, but is best known as the Fairy King of the TUATHA DÉ DANAAN who fell in love with the mortal Queen Edain, the wife of the King of Munster. Disguising himself as a wandering bard, Midar went to their court and challenged the king to a game of CHESS, the winner to name the reward. Midar easily won and demanded the queen as his prize, saying he would return to claim her in one year. As the day approached the King of Munster set guards around the palace and ordered them to kill any stranger who approached. At midnight, the king looked up to see a stranger in the middle of the hall, carrying a golden HARP. Midar sang and played such enchanting FAIRY MUSIC that the court was struck silent and found themselves unable to move as he spirited Edain away.

The King of Munster then realised that his strange visitor was a fairy and sent messages to all the rulers of Erin that they should destroy the forests where the SIDHE were known to dwell. Still his bride was not returned. He then ordered that the stables of the sidhe should be blocked up so that their HORSES would starve, but the magic horses rushed out like whirlwinds. The kings forgot about the search for Edain in the rush to take hold of the fairy beasts with their silver hoofs and golden bridles.

In despair, the King of Munster sent for his druid, threatening to put him to death unless he could discover where the queen was hidden. The druid searched all over Ireland and after carving four oghams on four wands of HAZEL it was revealed to him that deep in a hill in the very centre of Ireland the queen was hidden away in the palace of Midar, chief of the fairies.

The King gathered a great army and dug down into the hill. Eventually he reached the gate of the fairy palace. Midar sent up fifty beautiful fairy women to distract the warriors, all so like Edain in form that the king could not tell whether his wife was there or not. But when Edain saw her beloved husband, the enchantment fell from her and she embraced him. Happily he carried her back to Tara.

MIDDLE KINGDOM is a term used by occultists to refer to nature spirits, fairies and DEVAS.

MIDDLE WORLD MEN are the Manx fairies, according to Sir Walter Scott, since they inhabit a world somewhere between heaven and earth, and because they are souls neither good enough for heaven nor evil enough for hell. (This should not be confused with Tolkein's Middle Earth, by which he means the world inhabited by humans.)

MIDNIGHT is one of the times when fairies are most likely to be seen, probably because it is a 'THRESHOLD time' between one day and the next and belonging to neither one. For the Celts, all thresholds were magical, whether it was times between times or places between places.

MIDSUMMER (and especially Midsummer Eve) is one of the most mystical times of the year when all sorts of MAGIC and enchantments are in the air. WITCHES, spirits and fairies are abroad. In Ireland it is one of the great fairy festivals and they move amongst human kind, frolicking around the midsummer bonfires and playing all sorts of tricks ranging from innocent pranks to inflicting death. It is at this time that they most often steal away human women to become their brides.[227] Fairies particularly associated with Midsummer include the AMADAN-NA-BRIONA, PILWIZ and TROW.

It may be necessary to take precautions against the attentions of malicious fairies. According to Irish folklore they try to pass around the Baal fires in a whirlwind in order to extinguish them, but may be kept off by throwing FIRE at them. Humans can protect themselves from fairies by leaping through the fire and their COWS by driving them through the embers, passing glowing coals THREE times over and three times under the body of each animal. Needless to say, these measures had to be taken with some caution if human and bovine burns were not to ensue.

Midsummer is one of the most ancient of festivals, derived from Pagan celebrations of the summer solstice, but Christianised as St John's Day. Pagans celebrated it as the day marking the peak of the sun god's power, the longest day before his decline and 'death' at the winter solstice. Midsummer Day is now celebrated on June 24th, while the solstice usually falls on or about 21st June in the Northern Hemisphere.

MIDWIVES are often summoned to attend fairy births. It usually turns out that the woman in labour is the mortal wife of a fairy man who needs a human midwife to help her give birth. The story generally involves some fairy ointment which the midwife accidentally rubs on her eye that enables her to see fairies. She later greets a fairy and he asks her which eye she sees him with. When she answers, he puts it out. Similar stories are found all over Europe.

There is a Swedish tale of a midwife summoned to the birth of a TROLL. One evening, a farmer and his wife were sitting at the door when a small, dark complexioned man appeared, dressed in old grey clothes. He asked the farmer's wife to accompany him to help his wife, who was in labour. The couple was sure that the man was a troll but thought the fairies might curse them if they refused to help. So the woman took some linen and accompanied the troll. The good wife was gone a long time, but returned unharmed. She told her husband that she had been conveyed to a chamber as if by the wind. The birth was normal and afterwards the troll had offered her some FAIRY FOOD, which she refused. She was then returned by the wind. The next day the pair found a pile of silver on the shelf, the gift of the trolls.

The serving maid Eilian of Garth Dorwen ran off with the TYLWYTH TEG (the Welsh 'Fair Folk'). Nine months later her old mistress, the midwife of Llandwrog, was summoned to a birth. She was taken to a large cave in which there was a magnificent room, with a woman on a fine bed. After the birth the husband asked the midwife to anoint the baby's eyes with magic ointment. As she did so her own eye began to itch and she rubbed it, accidentally getting some of the salve into it. Instantly she saw that the cave was really small and poor and that the wife was on a bundle of rushes and withered ferns. She recognised Eilian, her old servant. Some weeks later she encountered the fairy husband in the market place at Caernarfon, and asked him how he was getting on. He inquired which of her eyes had she seen Eilian with. When she told him, he put it out with a bulrush.

The story is paralleled in a German tale. A midwife was taken to a hidden chamber and attended the birth of an ELF. The fairies kept her with them for a few days, but she noticed that each time they went out they rubbed their eyes with a salve that they kept in a glass jar by the door. She smeared a little on her right eye. Eventually, the woman was allowed home and given as her reward the sweepings behind the door. She arrived home and her husband was overjoyed to see her again. Then she emptied her apron onto the table and the sweepings had turned into a big pile of gold.

Some time later, she attended a market in Frankenberg and saw a number of elves in the crowd, playing tricks and stealing from the stalls. They were invisible to everyone else. She called out to them and they inquired which eye she could see them with. When she told them her right, she instantly went blind in that eye, and never saw through it again.

MIESIAC or **Mesiats** is the Russian spirit of the MOON who marries the sun at the beginning of summer. He abandons her at the beginning of winter and returns to her in the spring. She has powers of healing.

MIKAMWES is a forest fairy of many native North American tribes. He frolics in the moonlit glades and seems to resemble the mischievous PUCK in temperament.

MILK is a favourite food of fairies. Some fairies keep herds of magical COWS that give unlimited supplies of milk. Others steal milk from mortal COWS. One milkmaid accidentally picked up a four leafed clover which enabled her to see the little people. She was amazed to witness dozens of them milking her cow. In Ireland, after milking the cow, a thumb was dipped into the pail and a cross drawn on the flank of the beast to protect it. Any spilt milk belongs to the fairies. The first few drops were always dripped onto the ground in Ireland and Cornwall. It is possible that the latter belief stems from the ancient practice of pouring libations on the ground as an offering to spirits. In some areas, milk was poured into stone hollows as an offering to the fairies. A good Irish housewife would always leave out a dish of milk or cream for the fairies and never completely drain the churn or milk pail, as the dregs were the prerogative of the little people. One fairy mother was overheard to say that she would knock over the milk pail so that her child could drink its fill.

HOUSE FAIRIES and BROWNIES generally undertake their work asking only a dish of milk or cream as a reward. After churning the milk for butter, some must be left for the fair folk, but during the operation, a live coal was placed under the churn to protect it from the attentions of the little people, who might either steal the butter or prevent it setting.

In ancient times, milk was sacred, a symbol of feminine care and sustenance, and associated with many goddesses personified as nurturing mothers. The stars were thought to be drops of milk from the breasts of a goddess and this is how the Milky Way got its name. The Celts called it 'The

Track of the White Cow'. Milk was also sacred to moon goddesses because of its WHITE colour, the MOON sometimes being seen as a milk pitcher that filled and emptied each month with its waxing and waning.

MIMIS are fairies of the Australian Aborigines that live in rock crevices. They are thin and long limbed and generally eat yams and roots, though they may devour an unwary traveller. Strong winds can blow them away or break off their brittle arms and legs.

MINE FAIRIES are the masters of all that lies under the earth: all the metals and minerals of the mines belong to them. When miners venture into these fairy realms, they encounter spirits who may either aid or hinder them. Mine fairies may lead favoured miners to rich seams or punish those who swear or whistle with showers of stones, cave-ins, or simply wrenching the miner's head off his shoulders. They are often dressed as miners themselves, with leather aprons, miniature picks, lamps and hammers. They are usually about 45 to 60 cm tall (between 18 inches to two feet). It was once the custom for miners to leave offerings for them in the form of food. In Istria they were given gifts of CLOTHING twice as year and they were very upset if forgotten.

They are known throughout Europe, but especially in Wales, Scotland, Cornwall, Germany, Yugoslavia, Rumania and Austria. Mine fairies include the German Mine Monk who wears a blue jacket and a hood, which gives him his clerical nickname. The Romany fairies the Pcuvus guard the treasures of the earth while the Welsh Tylwyth Teg y Mwn guide miners to rich seams. The South German Wichtlein warns of miners' deaths by tapping three times; and their presence in a mine indicates rich seams. In Scotland similar fairies are called Black Dwarfs and in Wales Coblynau are sometimes spotted working on seam faces, though they do not actually mine anything, they are just pretending. Some mine fairies are mischievous like Cutty Soams. The Polish Karzelek, if insulted, will cause cave-ins, rock showers or throw the culprits into deep chasms. Knockers are fairies that live in the tin mines of Devon and Cornwall, who guided miners to good seams by tapping or 'knocking'. The German Kobold take pleasure in frustrating miners' work.

MINE MONK is a German MINE FAIRY or KOBOLD who dresses in antiquated miner's garb, including a green miner's hat, a blue jacket and a hood, which gives him his clerical nickname. *See also* RÜBEZAHL.

MIRI are Albanian FAIRY GODMOTHERS or FATES.

MIST GATE is the wreath of eerie mist often surrounding fairy MOUNDS, FAIRY RINGS, stone circles and other magical places. Should you find a gap in the mist, you will be able to pass through into the OTHERWORLD. This is more likely at the magical 'time between times' of BELTANE or SAMHAIN, MIDSUMMER, dusk, dawn, or MIDNIGHT.

MITTWINTERFRAU ('Lady of Midwinter') is a Croatian HAG fairy who leads a procession of DEAD souls between Christmas and Twelfth Night. Her followers either reward or punish people, according to their deserts. She controls SPINNING and is connected with rites to ensure a good flax crop.

MNÁ SIDHE, **Mná Sídh** or **Mná Sige** ('Women of the Sidhe') is an Irish collective term for female fairies, but which once referred to goddesses.

MOB, THE is a Manx term for the fairies.

MODDEY DHOO ('Black Dog') was an Isle of Man BLACK DOG that roamed Peel Castle. Every night it warmed itself before the guardroom fire, and at first the soldiers were afraid, but eventually they got used to it. Then one night, during the reign of the English King Charles II, a drunken soldier boasted that he would patrol the castle alone, and dared the dog to accompany him on his rounds - he would find out whether it was a real animal or a demon. The ghastly dog arose from his place by the fire and followed the man. Fearful cries and screams issued from the corridor, but not a man dared venture from the room. The foolish soldier returned white and gibbering. He died three days later, never speaking of what he had seen. The black dog has not been seen since, but some say it still haunts the castle, unseen.[228]

MOESTRE YAN is a house LUTIN recorded in the eighteenth century.

MOINE TROMPEUR is a French fairy, or LUTIN, of the countryside.

MOIRA ('Fate') is a single being, an early Greek goddess of fate, who may have been the origin of the Three FATES.

MOKUSA or **Mokosh** is the Polish personification of fate and patroness of women's occupations such as SPINNING and weaving. Women would leave strands of fleece by the oven or HEARTH as offerings to her. She was originally a goddess, often titled 'Moist Mother Earth', and was Christianised as St. Paravaskeva.

MOLLYNDROAT ('Servant of the Druid') is a Manx fairy who agreed to spin thread for a woman. Like the tale of RUMPELSTILTSKIN, GIRLE GUAIRLE and TOM TIT TOT, she had to guess his name to prevent him harming her. *See also* SPINNING and NAME.

MONACHICCHIO is an Italian fairy from Calabria who dresses like a monk with a RED hood twice the size of his tiny body. He guards underground TREASURE: if you steal his hood, he will have to tell you where it is.

MOMMET is an English night spirit, though the term is also used to refer to a scarecrow.

MOMUR is the FAIRYLAND ruled by OBERON in French romance.[229]

MONACHETTO is an Italian fairy associated with CAVES, tunnels and anywhere under the earth, something like a GNOME.

MONACIELLO ('Little Monk') is an Italian fairy of Naples who guards hidden TREASURE and is known to pinch people and steal their clothes. Though he can turn himself into a CAT, he generally appears as a drunken monk or cardinal, though his eyes are red and sparkle like fire. If anyone manages to steal his RED CAP, then they can demand treasure for its return.

MONOCOLI ('One-leg') are creatures who, according to Aristophanes, were a race of one-footed creatures, also called Shade-foots who were implicated in a profane celebration of the lesser Eleusinian mysteries. The term is probably a code for a sacred MUSHROOM.

MONOLOKE is a type of KOBOLD that inhabits a figurine of white wax and which wears a blue shirt, a black velvet waistcoat and who goes barefoot.

MOOINJER VEGGEY ('Little People') is a Manx term for fairies.

MOON, THE is connected with fairies, who are more likely to be abroad in the eerie moonlight than the bright glare of the sun. It is then that they are seen dancing and feasting in forest glades, stalking through the streets of villages and towns, or perhaps hard at work in houses and

The moon itself is said to have magical power: as the moon waxes it sends out growth energy to the earth that affects all things as they grow, causing them to increase or decrease in size. It is most often associated with the feminine, women's menstrual cycles and the waxing and waning of the womb.

The moon is associated with many ancient goddesses who are said to be the moon or to represent its powers. These include Arianrhod, Isis, Hathor, Astarte, Artemis, Diana, and Ishtar. In some cases these goddesses are said to be the progenitors of the fairy race, or in other cases fairies have accumulated some of the lore of the goddesses, such as the Irish Aine. The name of the Roman moon goddess Diana is found as a component of many fairy designations. In Romania, she became Dziana, among the Slavs she was Diiwica (Lusatia), Devana (Western Slavonics) and Dziewona among the Poles. Diana's Greek counterpart is Artemis, the maiden goddess of the moon and the hunt, Apollo's sister. Her bow is the crescent of the moon and her ARROWS the shafts of moonbeams. Her companions are the Dryads.

The moon, or the moon goddess, rules moisture and the tides. Dew forms at its richest on moonlit nights. It is possible that the concept of mermaids derives from ancient beliefs of fish-tailed goddesses such as Atargatis, the Semitic moon and love goddess, and from later forms of such deities like Aphrodite who was 'foam born' in the sea. Mermaids are connected in folklore with love and the moon, like the goddesses.

The word fairy itself is probably derived from the Latin *fata* ('fate'), based on the Three Fates of the Greeks. Some say that these figures are the origins of fairy belief. They always appear clad in white and are an incarnation of the triple moon goddess. Their Greek name means 'phase' and the moon goddess is the spinner and measurer of TIME. An amazing number of fairies are

MOON

barns. Some fairies, such as Dwarfs and Trolls, can only venture forth at night as sunlight will kill them or turn them to stone. Others, like the Corrigans and Gwyllion, change form in moonlight, shapeshifting from ugly HAGS or goats into beautiful maidens. Some fairies travel on moonbeams.

The phases of the moon affect fairies and their powers. The energies of evil fairies grow with the darkness and they are more potent at a crescent or dark moon. The Russian Vodianoi become young and voracious at the new moon, but age with the old moon. At certain phases of the moon, the Scottish Highland fairies may be seen inside their MOUNDS, feasting and drinking, since their habitation is raised on pillars for a short time. If a horse should be tethered at Wayland's Smithy under a full moon, the owner returning in the morning will find it newly shod.

While all that happens under the light of the sun is apparent, what happens during the night, under the mysterious light of the moon, is hidden. In occult lore the moon rules growth and the secret forces of nature.

associated with SPINNING, such as Frau Holda.

MILK, which appears in numerous tales as the fairy food of choice, is also sacred to moon goddesses because of its white colour, the moon sometimes being seen as a milk pitcher that fills and empties each month with its waxing and waning. The Egyptian moon goddess Hathor, the milk giving mother, is depicted as cow headed.

The moon is strange and enigmatic; itself often regarded as a FAIRYLAND or a realm of the DEAD, inhabited by spirits. While the sun is constant in the sky each day, the moon waxes and wanes each month, and for THREE nights disappears completely. It is noticeable that there is an increase in crime, drunkenness, accidents and excitability during the days of the full moon. The word 'lunatic' is derived from *luna,* the Latin for moon. Small wonder that it is associated with magic, fairies and spirits. WITCHES also work by the light of the moon and commune with fairy spirits under its light. The Roman moon goddess Diana is their patron.

MOOSWEIBCHEN ('Mosswives') are German fairies who steal children and replace them with CHANGELINGS called Wechselbälge. They are sometimes chased by the WILDE MÄNNER.

MORA are Polish ancestral spirits, VAMPIREs which appeared in the form of moths to disturb the sleep of humans and drink their blood. Some say the Mora is the wandering soul of a living man or woman, which leaves the body when its host is asleep. Sometimes this happens when two souls inhabit one body, or perhaps a person may be born as a Mora. In this case, he is recognisable by the fact that his bushy eyebrows meet in the middle. The Mora assumes a variety of shapes, perhaps a white shadow, a leather bag, a CAT, a white mouse, a white HORSE and so on. In this shape, it enters human dwellings at night to try to suffocate the inhabitants.

Perhaps it will send them to sleep and then induce horrible nightmares before choking them and sucking their blood. It is particularly fond of attacking children, though it will also prey on domestic animals.

In Russia, Mora is another term for a HOUSE FAIRY or KIKIMORA. *See also* MAHR.

MORAG is a monstrous WATER FAIRY that haunts Loch Morar, the deepest loch in Scotland.

MORAVA are Southern Slavonic ancestral spirits, VAMPIREs which appeared in the form of moths to disturb the sleep of humans and drink their blood. *See also* MAHR and MORA.

MORGAN is a Welsh lake spirit.[230] Morgans appear in Breton folklore as sea dwelling spirits, male and female. *See also* MORGENS.

MORGAN LE FAY ('Morgan the Fairy'), **Morgana Le Fay** or **Morgen** has many legends. There are several Morgans, and they may or may not have had a common origin. In one version, Morgan le Fay is the 'haughty fairy' of Continental legends, in yet another she appears in the Arthurian tales where her role and character varies considerably according to

different authors, though she is generally said to be the half-sister of ARTHUR. Mythological clues point to the fact that she may be derived from an ancient goddess.

According to the courtly romances, she was a playful virgin, dark, slim and straight limbed, warm and sensual. Malory made her the wife of Urien and the mother of Yvain, a rather tempestuous, malefic woman who tried to murder both her husband and King Arthur, and who had a number of lovers.[231] MERLIN is said to have taught her magic, as he did VIVIENNE, and their stories are sometimes confused; they may once have been the same character.

Yet again, she is said to be the ruler of AVALON, the magical island outside time and space where illness, old age and death are unknown. The island is covered in APPLE orchards and inhabited by nine sisters of which Morgan is the most beautiful and most powerful. She has knowledge of SHAPESHIFTING and can turn herself into any animal or bird, and knows the properties of all plants for healing and MAGIC. As Arthur lay dying after the battle of Camlann, Morgan appeared with a ship of women and carried Arthur to the Isle of Avalon. In this guise, she is Morgen, a goddess of the druids, perhaps related to Modron or Matrona, the Welsh divine mother goddess; the author of Sir Gawain and the Green Knight called her 'Morgan the goddess.' She has aspects of maiden, mother and crone.

Morgan is certainly related to the LADY OF THE LAKE and to the fairy rulers of enchanted islands. Her name may be derived from the Welsh *môr* 'sea' and *gân* 'a birth' i.e. 'born of the sea'. To some authors her name also suggests the battle goddess of the TUATHA DÉ DANAAN Morrigan or MORRIGU ('Queen of Nightmares') who also appeared in the form of a RAVEN. Morrigan is a triple goddess incorporating the

MOROZØKO

aspects BABD ('Raven'), Nemain ('Frenzy') and Macha. Babd is used in Gaelic tradition as a generic name for a bad fairy.

Again, the name may arise from the Welsh *Mor Gwyn* meaning WHITE LADY. This would make her a spirit of place, possibly a sovereign goddess of the land who had the power to confer kingship.

MORGENS, Morgans, Mari-Morgans, Marie Morgans, Sea Morgans or **Morganezed** are Breton WATER FAIRIES that lure sailors down to their underwater palaces of crystal and gold. Some authors think that they may be related to MORGAN LE FAY. The Mari-morgan (sea morgan) called DAHUT was responsible for the destruction of the city of Ys. The Morgen is eternally young, eternally seductive. By days she sleeps in her underwater grotto, by night she rises to the rocks. Droplets of water become precious jewels at her touch, as white as her dazzling body. Sitting in the moonlight she combs her hair with a golden comb, singing a song whose charm is irresistible. Any sailor who hears it will be drawn to his destruction, for as soon as she touches him, the man will die. The frustrated morgen is left clutching nothing but a corpse, and her passionate nature remains unfulfilled. The soul of the man has lost its chance of heaven, the Pagan touch of the Morgen condemning his ghost to eternal wandering through the sea, open-eyed and knowing no comfort.

Morgans are also known in England. Ruth Tongue was told a story of a sea morgan in Cornwall in 1916.[232] A fisherman came down in the owl-light into St Audries Bay. He had heard singing down there and was curious; though he tried to be quiet, he scared off all the morgans who fled into the sea. However, in their hurry they had left behind a baby-morgan chuckling under the cliff waterfall. Now the fisherman had had a baby daughter who had died and he and his wife

were still broken hearted. So he took the baby home and laid it in the empty cradle. His wife was overjoyed and took to the baby at once, though she could never get its HAIR dry, even in the sun. All went well for a while, and the girl grew up as girls will, except that she spent a great deal of her time paddling in the pond and stream. Then one day a nosy neighbour exclaimed that the girl should dry her hair like a good Christian and that paddling in the pond was unchristian and she should go and swim in the sea. Then she heard a strange song coming from the distant sea. 'Whatever is that?' she asked. 'That's my song,' replied the girl. 'Someone wants me. There will be a storm tonight.'

The nosy neighbour declared that the girl was a WITCH and ran to rouse all the Doniford and Staple men to chase her away. The girl ran from them, laughing because they couldn't catch her. She ran down to the sea and out onto the rocks. A great wave swept her into the water and she was never seen again.

MORGUE is a French FAIRY GODMOTHER, one of the BONNES DAMES

MORONOE is one of the sisters of MORGAN LE FAY who dwells with her in AVALON.

MOROZKO is a Russian fairy who brings the ice and causes the frost fractures in trees. There is a tale of a maiden lost in the forest who heard a cracking and saw Morozko leaping from fir to fir, snapping his fingers.

MORRIGAN, Mór Ríagan/Mór-Ríoghain ('Great Queen'), **Morrigu** ('Queen of NIGHTMARES') or **Mor-Ríoghain** ('Phantom Queen'), is the RED-HAIRED battle goddess of the TUATHA DÉ DANAAN, a triple goddess incorporating the aspects BABD ('Raven'), Nemain ('Frenzy') and Macha ('Battle'). The Morrigan gives warning of

coming battles, urges on her chosen side, and finally takes the form of a crow or RAVEN to feed upon the dead on battlefields. The heads of those killed in battle were dedicated to her. In this role, she is the protectress of the land.

There is some confusion as to the true meaning of her name, since in Irish an accent on a single letter can alter the meaning of a word, and the old manuscripts are either unclear or vary. She may be the Great Queen or the Phantom Queen, or the Queen of Nightmares. At any rate, in addition to her function as a battle goddess it seems clear that she also has functions as a goddess of agriculture and irrigation (she mates with the Dagda and urinates on the land).

It is possible that she was the original of the death herald the BANSHEE. Those warriors who heard the SIREN songs of the Morrigan were destined to die in battle, while those who did not might have wit enough to live. Thus, her song is an OMEN OF DEATH, like the wail of the banshee. She is said to choose the loveliest maidens to become Banshees.

Some students of mythology think that she may also be the original template of MORGAN LE FAY, though the link is tentative and there are more convincing candidates.

MORTRIDEN ('Mare Ridden') is a German term for a NIGHTMARE believed to be caused by an ELF or ALP sitting on the chest of a sleeper.

MOSS MAIDENS are German fairies who spin the moss for the forests. They live in communities, are grey and covered in moss to blend in with the trees. Their faces are old and withered. They are ruled by the Bush Grandmother, an ancient creature with white hair and mossy feet. Be careful when you walk through the forests, as they are angered at any damage done to saplings. They will be revenged on humans who peel bark from trees, tell their dreams, or bake caraway seeds in bread. They help humans they like and have healing powers, knowing all the properties of the forest herbs including the little blue flowers called *ache-no-more* which helps women in childbirth. They help the crops to grow and turn the leaves brown and gold in the autumn. They raise their children in moss cradles strung high in the treetops. Such fairies are known throughout Central Europe.

MOSS MANNIKINS are the male equivalents of MOSS MAIDENS. They are rarely seen and live only in virgin forests. They are also called Forest Fathers.

MOSWYFJES are Flemish MOSS MAIDENS.

MOTHAN or trailing pearlwort (*Sagina procumbens*) is a plant that protects its possessor from fire and the attacks of fairy women. If fairies are stealing your MILK, lace it with, or feed the cows, on the plant, and it will render them powerless.

MOTHER OF THE TREES is a Thai DRYAD. One of them inhabits every tree.

MOTHER'S BLESSING is a flattering general term for fairies in Ireland and Wales.

MOUND/MOUNDS are associated with fairies and are credited with having magical properties. From Scandinavian to Celtic and Slavonic folklore, earth mounds are described as occasionally glowing or giving off a strange light. They are also the home of GHOSTS, who live there in company with the ancestors. At certain phases of the MOON the Scottish Highland fairies may be seen inside their mounds, feasting and drinking, since their habitations are raised on pillars for a short time. They are also the home of GHOSTS, who live there in company with the ancestors.

Burial mounds, dating from the NEOLITHIC period onwards, are found throughout Europe. There are upwards of 40,000 in Britain alone. They vary in size from a few feet across to about 90 metres in diameter (over 300 feet). Some contained TREASURE and other grave goods, while others seem never to have had any occupants and their function is still obscure. Tumuli or earth heaps, found on hills and inside earthworks may have had a defensive purpose, while the several types of barrows contain chambers that may have been used for burials.

It seems likely that some mounds had a ritual purpose. They were not sealed, but the interred bones were brought out to witness special events, allowing the tribe to commune with the ancestral DEAD. Other barrows were designed so that at certain times of year shafts of sunlight would strike the inner chamber. This is possibly a symbolic fertilisation of the earth womb, also allowing the souls of the dead to attain rebirth or travel to the OTHERWORLD.

These barrows were probably also used for magical initiations with the candidate going into the burial chamber, symbolically dying and entering the ground. He or she would lie in the earth womb while experiencing visions of the OTHERWORLD, and then emerge through the narrow passage, which represents the birth canal, being 'reborn' into the daylight. It seems that their connection with ancestral spirits, magic and the Otherworld is preserved in fairy folklore.

MOUND FOLK is a name applied to a great many fairies, who are often said to live in mounds, but Scandinavian fairies in particular are referred to as mound folk, berg folk or hillmen. These include Trolls, Thusser, Maanväki, Huldre, Hulde, Pysslinger-Folk and Skogsrå. They are usually tall, thin creatures that live inside the hollow hills with their wives, children and animals. They are nocturnal - in fact daylight turns them to stone or ages them drastically, so they must be inside before the cock crows THREE

times. While humans sleep, the mound folk are busy with their cattle and horses, or with baking, brewing, sewing, dancing and making music so sweet and poignant that the trees and stones must move in time to it. Should a human hear the fairy tunes he will be forced to go on dancing until he dies of exhaustion, unless someone can creep up behind the fiddler and cut the strings of his violin. The male mound folk are expert SMITHS and produce beautiful jewellery, useful pots and formidable weapons. Every full moon the Icelandic mounds are raised up on RED pillars and it is possible to look inside. On New Year's Eve, the mounds rise up and the folk move house.

MOURIE is a WATER FAIRY that inhabits Loch Maree in Scotland. Offerings of coins and rags used to be left for him on an island in the loch. It seems likely that he was once an ancient Scottish god of lochs and lakes whose feast day was 25th August. This may have been a first fruits LUGHNASA ceremony (held later as the harvest ripens later so far north). Well into the seventeenth century, people sacrificed bulls, adorned wells, monuments, and stones, and poured milk upon hills as oblations. He was connected with the island of St. Ruffus, commonly called Ellan Moury. The name of the island may be a corruption of *Eilean a Mhor Righ'* meaning 'Island of the Great King', perhaps a sacred king who stood for the god and ruled on the island.[233] The local people used to speak of 'the god Mourie' well into the seventeenth century, much to the disgust of the church.[234]

MPFUNDLWA is a DWARF in Tsonga (Africa) folklore. He is mischievous and likes to play tricks.

MU are forest fairies of Papua New Guinea and are only 60 cm high (about two feet). Generally, they are benevolent and will help lost children.

MUCALINDA is the King of the Hindu WATER FAIRIES the NAGAS

MUGWORT (*Artemesia vulgaris*) is a magical herb sacred to MERMAIDS and to Artemis, Greek goddess of the MOON.

MUIRDRIS is a hideous WATER HORSE that inhabits Loch Rury in Ireland. When Fergus Mac Leda came face to face with the horse he was so frightening that his face was permanently disfigured.

MUIREARTACH, Muileartach or Muilearteach ('One of the Seas') is a Scottish HAG fairy who appears as a bald crone with sharp teeth, only one large eye, and a bluish-grey complexion, or as a sea SNAKE. She causes storms off the Scottish coast. She was once a crone goddess whose husband was a sea god. She stole a cup from the Fianna warriors, but was eventually defeated by Finn Mac Cumhal (the Irish hero), who tore her to shreds. She may be synonymous with the CAILLEACH BHEUR.[235]

MUMA PADURA is a Romanian forest fairy that goes into the forest to help children who have strayed there and become lost.

MUMIAI are Indian fairies who punish people of the lower castes for stealing or having dirty habits. They drive them out of the villages by trampling their gardens, breaking their crockery and tossing out their belongings.

MUMPOKER is an English BOGEYMAN who may be found on the Isle of Wight.

MUNYA is a central European fairy who is a daughter of the VILA. She is the lightening and plays in the clouds with her two brothers, who are thunder.

MURDHUACHAS are Irish WATER FAIRIES that have the torsos and heads of seals or walruses. They sometimes sing unearthly songs that lure ships onto the rocks of Ireland's Atlantic coast, or occasionally they decide to be useful and help sailors find their way home in the fog.

MURRAUE is a fairy that presses on the chest of a sleeper to cause them NIGHTMAREs and temporary paralysis. It is known in the German region of Wendische-Buchholz. When one has manifested in a room, the fear it causes will not abate until the sun comes up. When it rains, be careful not to stand underneath a pine twig that has deformed into a tangled nest, as if water drops on you from it, a murraue will visit you in the night. A human agent can send it; and a person whose eyebrows meet in the middle is called a murraue. Those born on a Sunday may become one. In a family of SEVEN same sex siblings, one will be a nightmare but will know nothing about it.

MURYANS or Meryons (from the Cornish *murrain,* meaning 'ant') are tiny Cornish fairies. Some believe that fairies end their days as ants since every SHAPESHIFTING operation reduces them in size. Those who take the forms of animals grow smaller and smaller with every change until they are lost in the earth, as ants.[236]

Some say they are the spirits of DEAD druids. In Cornwall, it is thought to be very unlucky to kill ants, as they might be the final forms of tiny fairies. If you place a piece of tin in a bank of ants at the waxing of the MOON it will be turned to silver.[237]

MUSAIL is the Russian king of the forest fairies, associated with the ROWAN tree.

MUSES are NYMPHS or goddesses of inspiration, in ancient Greek myth. They were invoked with WILLOW wands and were the companions of Apollo. Their provinces were as follows: Clio (memory and poetry, or history as we call it today), Euterpe (flute playing), Thaleia (comedy), Melpomene (tragedy), Terpsichore (dancing and lyric poetry), Erato (love poetry), Polyhymnia (mime), Urania (astronomy) and Calliope (epic poetry).

MUSHROOMS are connected with fairies. The magical rings where they dance are circles of mushrooms. English OAKMEN offer food to passing mortals that turn out to be poisonous fungi disguised by magic. The Swedish PARA can be made to appear by taking a certain mushroom, frying it in tar, salt and sulphur and beating it with a rod. Fairies are commonly depicted sitting on top of the red and white spotted mushroom, FLY AGARIC (*Amanita muscaria*), and they commonly also wear RED CAPS, probably a code for the mushroom.

MUSIC *See* FAIRY MUSIC.

MÜTZCHEN ('Little Cap') is a German HOUSE FAIRY, one of the HEINZMANNCHEN.

MUZAYYARA are Egyptian fairies. They are beautiful, with hair down to their knees, but they have IRON breasts with FIRE glowing at the nipples. They try to seduce human men.

NAAKI are Finnish WATER FAIRIES.

NACHTMÄNNLE ('Night Man') is a type of NIGHTMARE.

NACHTMART ('Night Torturer) is a type of NIGHTMARE. *See* MÅRT.

NÄCKEN or **Naecken** are Swedish male WATER FAIRIES who lure people to them by playing fiddles. If you want to improve your own playing, hang your fiddle under a bridge that spans a Näcken-haunted stream for THREE consecutive Thursday nights. The Näcken will play it on each of these occasions, and after the third night, two fiddles will be found. If you pick your own fiddle, you will be a great and famous musician, but if you should choose the Näcken's he will claim your soul.

NAGA-IOKA is the UNDERWORLD fairy kingdom of the NAGAS.

NAGAS are Indian NYMPHS of earth and water. They protect wells, streams, waterfalls, lakes and rivers. They can appear as beautiful maidens, humans with SNAKE tails or as full serpents. Their enemy is Garuda, the king of the birds. Similar antagonism between the serpent power of earth and water and the bird power of sun and air is found in many mythologies.

Nagas can become invisible and have magical powers. They lived on earth until Brahma relegated them to the UNDERWORLD, where they established the kingdom of Patala-Ioka or Naga-Ioka. There they dwell in jewelled gold palaces, spending their time dancing, feasting and drinking. Their king is Mucalinda, who sheltered the Buddha for a week after his enlightenment. Several royal families of India claim descent from Nagas.

NÄGENDÜMER is one of those SPINNING fairies whose NAME has to be guessed. Once upon a time a girl had to spin a certain amount of FLAX everyday, but she could never finish her task. Then one day a little man appeared saying that he would do her spinning for her if she could guess his name. She tried in vain to guess, but to each name she tried, he shook his head. He left her, turned himself into a bird, and flew back and forth singing that it was a good job that she didn't know his name was Nägendümer. A passing shepherd chanced to hear and related the strange story to the girl, so that when the man appeared she was able to tell him his true name. The fairy was angry but kept his promise.

NAGGENEEN is a CLURICAUN who served Justin McCarthy.

NAGUMWASUCK are North American fairies of the Passamaquoddy people. They are known to be small (only about 90 cm or some three feet tall) and ugly, though they are rarely seen as they usually hide. They occasionally help humans, especially hunters. They may sing when there is a death in the tribe, or dance at weddings. Some say that they have now left the earth, paddling away in a stone canoe because people stopped believing in them.

NAIADS or **Naiades** are the water NYMPHS of running water, rivers and springs, fountains and streams in Greek myth.

NAIN ('Dwarf') is a type of small Breton EARTH FAIRY or DWARF with a hideous, black, hairy body, a voice like a very old man, and sparkling black eyes. Nains like to play tricks on mortals who fall into their power. They are often thought of as evil spirits condemned to live on earth for a time.

NAIN ROUGE ('Red Dwarf') is a BROWNIE of Normandy who looks after local fishermen. He is an expert SHAPESHIFTER, and sometimes is mischievous. Two fishermen were once surprised when a young boy who was accompanying them suddenly turned into the Nain Rouge and threw one of the fishermen into the sea. The fairy beame annoyed that he could not touch the other, since the man had crossed himself with holy water that morning and thereby spoiled the dwarf's fun.

In the USA, the Nain Rouge is an evil fairy and some paint a cross on their doors to prevent it entering the house.

NAJADE are Slavonic WATER FAIRIES.

NÄKH or **Näkinein** are refractory Estonian WATER FAIRIES who sometimes appear in human form, or sometimes one will take the form of a WATER HORSE. They are expert SHAPESHIFTERS and can appear in a variety of other forms. It is thought that the true form of the females is something like a MERMAID, with a human head and torso and a fish tail. Both the males and females lure humans into the water with their sweet singing, where they will drown them. Any sight of a Näkh is an OMEN OF DEATH by drowning.

NAKK are Estonian WATER FAIRIES. The male has a lovely singing voice, and uses it to lure humans into his giant mouth in order to eat them. The females are lovely with long HAIR, which they comb with golden combs. They sometimes have fish tails like MERMAIDS.

NAME There is an ancient belief that by naming something you invoke it. Therefore, according to the old folklore, fairies are only referred to obliquely as 'the good folk', or 'mother's blessing' or some such flattering term to avoid inadvertently summoning them up to cause mischief.

In earlier times, and in tribal societies, the naming of a thing or person was a great responsibility. The true name of something encapsulates its essential nature. Even today, in many societies, religions and cultures, a child is named in a solemn ceremony; and there is often an accompanying belief that the name chosen will affect the child, in some way shaping its character. Often, a child is not felt to be a person at all - or to have its own individual identity - until it is formally named. Un-named or unbaptised children were considered to be at risk of being kidnapped by fairies and jealous spirits.

In some primitive societies, the naming does not take place until some time after birth, but the child is called by something that is not the *real* name, which is not disclosed. In Europe, the name was often kept hidden until the christening, even from the mother. This stems back to the old belief that people, animals, places, gods and spirits have real names that are concealed. If a person can discover the real name then they will have the being in their power, and the real name can be used to work magic against its owner. Magicians use words of power, which include the names of gods and spirits, tapping into the essence and energy of the being when the name is intoned correctly. This belief is exemplified in many fairy tales, when the secret name of a fairy is discovered and it loses its power. Examples include Gebhart, Girle Guairle, Hipche, Holzrührlein Bonneführlein, Kruzimugeli, Mollyndroat, Eisenhütel, Kinkach Martinko, Knirfiker and Rumpelstiltskin. Once the fairy's name is guessed, it has no more power.

Often a person takes a new name with a change of status, for example a boy will assume a new name when he comes to manhood, a woman when she marries, a priest when he is ordained, and a WITCH or magician when initiated. Some fairies (see Puddlefoot for example) will disappear in a huff when given a name, which presumably changes their status. An old Mesopotamian demon called Kubu, the ghost of a stillborn child, could never get any older as he had never been properly named.

NANNY BUTTONCROP is a northern English fairy from Yorkshire who makes sure children are tucked up warm in bed.

NAPOEÆ are the dale NYMPHS who frequent the valleys in Greek myth.

NARBROOI is a spirit of Papaua New Guinea who draws out the SOULS of those he loves and carries them away to the mist enshrouded treetops. When a person falls ill, a friend should go to the trees to endeavour to recover the soul. Attracting the attention of the fairy, one should then light a cigar. Then, as the smoke curls up, the spirit will appear in it as a young and elegant man, who will say whether he has the soul or not. He can be persuaded to give up the soul in return for an offering. The soul is then carried back to the sufferer in a straw bag, which is emptied over him. Sometimes Narbrooi reneges and takes the soul back again, and the victim dies.

NARUCNICI (*narok* meaning 'destiny') are Southern Slavonic FAIRY GODMOTHERS who decide the destiny of a newborn child. They wear WHITE dresses.

NASNAS is an evil fairy in Islamic lore who takes the form of an old man

He waits by the side of a river and asks travellers to carry him across on their backs. However, once he is on board he will not let go and rides them until they die of exhaustion. *See also* OLD MAN OF THE SEA and NIGHTMARE.

NATROU-MONSIEUR is a French HOUSE FAIRY or LUTIN.

NATS are the nature fairies of Burma. There are four different kinds of tree Nats: The Akakasoh dwell in the topmost branches; the Shekkasoh in the trunk; the Boomasoh in the roots and the wood fairies Hmin range through the forests and violently shake those they meet, causing malaria. The victim must be placed beneath the tree beneath which he last rested, from where the ague spirit descended to him, and ceremonies must be performed to exorcise the spirit.

Prominent among the Nats is the Thirty-Seven, the spirits of warriors and heroes. They have power over weather, crops, health, and animals and must be propitiated with food and flowers.

The most important Nat is Tha Gya Min who is associated with the beginning of the Burmese year. He is depicted standing in a lotus supported by three elephants.

NATURE FAIRIES/SPIRITS represent trees, specific localities, streams, wells, vegetation or the weather and other natural forces. *See* VEGETATION SPIRITS, OLD GODS, TREE FAIRIES and WEATHER FAIRIES.

NAV, Navi or **Navjaci** ('Dead') are Southern Slavonic fairies, the spirits of UNBAPTISED CHILDREN, usually invisible creatures though they may take the shape of birds. As they wander around, pitifully weeping and searching for their own mothers, they attack women in childbed. If a kind person says the baptismal words over them, they will be set free.

NAVJE ('Dead') are Slovenian fairies, the souls of UNBAPTISED CHILDREN. They fly about in the form of big black birds, pleading to be baptised and allowed to go to heaven. If a person should baptise them and set them free, he will win their eternal gratitude. However, if he should mock them or whistle at them he will arouse their anger.

NAVKY ('Dead') are WATER FAIRIES of Finland who appear as RAVENS or crows or as pale children who cling to the branches of riverside trees and wail piteously. In this guise, they try to lure people into the water by pretending to be drowning. Sacrifices were once made to the navky or their permission asked before crossing a stream or swimming in a lake.

NAW are evil Slavonic fairies or DEMONS who are the spirits of the DEAD, especially those who died prematurely or under tragic circumstances.

NEAGLE, **Noggle**, **Nuggle** or **Nyaggle** is a Shetland WATER HORSE.

NECK is a Scandinavian WATER FAIRY who sits on the surface of a river or lake, playing a HARP. He is good looking with golden hair and a RED CAP, though his nature is not pleasant, as he demands a human sacrifice every year. However, he sometimes takes pity on lonely youths spurned by their lovers by disciplining the cruel girls. He is afraid of IRON and steel and these can be used to render him harmless if you want to go into the water. Take a needle and repeat the following charm:

'Neck, Neck, needle thief
You are in the water, but I am on the land
Neck, Neck, needle thief
You are on the land but I am in the water!'

NECKER are Dutch MERMEN. They are small and sad, spending most of their time sighing.

NEGROES OF THE WATER are WATER FAIRIES of South America, known especially in Argentina, Brazil and Paraguay, who attack boats. They have webbed hands and feet.

NEKRSTENCI are Croatian fairies, the SOULS of the unbaptised DEAD, or those who committed suicide.

NEJKY ('Dead') are WATER FAIRIES of Little Russia, the souls of DEAD children. *See* MAVKY.

NELLY LONGARMS is a nasty WATER FAIRY of north-west England who pulls children into ponds to drown them.

NEMAIN ('Frenzy'), **Neman**, **Neamhan** or **Nemainn** is one of the THREE aspects of the MORRIGAN, she is the 'counfounder of enemies' and causes members of the same band to fight each other in mistake for the enemy.[238] She appears in the shape of a CROW.

NENNIR is a WATER HORSE.

NEOLITHIC is the archaeological terminology for the New Stone Age. Some authors have claimed that legends of fairies arise when one culture takes over another and drives out the original inhabitants. Professor Margaret Murray contended that legends of fairies were folk memories of the Neolithic peoples who continued to populate Europe into the Bronze Age.[239] Mediaeval English literature described fairies as being small in stature (of the size of twelve-year-old children) and the average height of a Neolithic man was approximately 1.5 metres (around five feet). Like Neolithic man, fairies were said to have no knowledge of agriculture, but to keep small herds of cattle and subsist on what they could gather or hunt. The tradition that iron gives protection from fairies may have sprung from some dim memory of the Celtic invasions. The Celts were armed with IRON, while the race they defeated had weapons of bronze or stone. Those stone arrowheads called ELF-BOLTS (the darts reputedly used by fairies and witches to do harm) are actually Stone Age flints. In all areas where pre-Celtic Neolithic monuments, cairns and stone circles exist, they are associated with fairies such as the KORREDS of Brittany and

the SPRIGGANS of Cornwall, who are said to guard them.

However, current research suggests that the so-called Celtic invasions within Europe may never have taken place on the scale that was previously thought: they may have been cultural offensives rather than physical ones. Moreover, since fairies are known world wide, this theory of an aboriginal Neolithic race driven to retreat from civilisation and dwell in secret does not stand up to close examination.

NEPHILIM appear in Genesis. The ANGELS of God took wives among the daughters of men, and the result of these unions was the Nephilim, or 'Fallen Ones'. In Greek, this was rendered *gigantes* or 'earth born', often confused with GIANTS in the various myths about them. These gigantes corrupted humans; so God was determined to purge the earth of both evil species and sent the Flood, sparing only Noah and his family.

NEPTUNES are small French fairies described by Gervase of Tilbury (1211), which he said the British called PORTUNES. The name is obviously derived from the Roman god of the sea, Neptune, and they are mischievous WATER FAIRIES. Neptunes sometimes grab the bridles of night travellers and lead them into ponds. It is said that if you can capture one, it must grant you a wish. Gervase described them as only about 1.5 cm tall (half an inch), and said that they roasted frogs for their suppers.

NEREID/NEREIDES ('Honeyed Ones') are the sea NYMPHS of Greek mythology, the fifty daughters of Doris and the sea god Nereus. One of them was Thetis, mother of Achilles. Pliny described them as being rough and scaled all over, though they were usually portrayed as young women with shell head-dresses riding hippocamps (a cross between a horse and a dolphin). Each rules over a

NEREIDES

particular body of water. They have beautiful singing voices, which they use to entertain their father, and are known to protect sea travellers. The Phoceans of ancient Greece claimed descent from the nereid PSAMATHE who turned herself into a seal in a vain attempt to escape from the advances of Aeacus. (The ancient Greeks believed that a seal's body conceals a woman.) They are related to the Russian RUSALKA and have special days during March, August and MAY DAY.

In modern Greece, the term is applied to all kinds of female fairies. Some are beautiful while others are ugly. Some have GOATS' or asses' feet and GREEN hair. They are long lived but not immortal for 'a crow lives twice as long as a man, a tortoise twice as long as a crow, and a nereid twice as long as a tortoise.'[240] If offended, they strike people with blindness, dumbness, epilepsy or mutilate them. If a man sees them they will strike him blind, send him mad, or drown him. They are envious of human mothers and kill their babies with fever, though a kindly Nereid may bless a child. A black cross should be laid on the THRESHOLD and food left for the fairy to prevent harm. Some Nereids marry human men, but inevitably leave their husbands and children to return to their own world. If a man can capture the fairy's WHITE shawl he can force her to marry him, but as soon as she regains the shawl she will be off, back to the mountains or sea, leaving her husband and children without a second thought. Many modern Greeks claim descent from Nereides.

The fairies cause whirlwinds which are greeted with the charm:

'Milk and honey in your path'.

The fairies may harm you if you leave home at noon or midnight. If a human is harmed by one of these creatures, he or she should wait a week, a month or a year and then go back to the place the incident occurred and leave a gift of honey for the fairy, then leave without looking back.

NERUSNICA is a Serbo-Croatian fairy akin to a FAIRY GODMOTHER or FATE. Her favour can be won with the correct offerings.

NEOLITHIC STONE CIRCLE

NESRECA is a fairy that personifies an evil fate. *See* SRÉCA.

NESSIE is a famous monster of Loch Ness and is only one of many fairy SNAKES, monsters, WATER HORSES or WATER BULLS said to inhabit the lochs and waterways of Scotland. The first recorded sighting of Nessie was by St Columba fourteen centuries ago. He told one of his monks to swim across the loch to fetch a boat. When the poor man was half way across, the monster appeared and was about to attack the swimmer when the saint commanded it to go back and leave the man alone. The monster had no power to resist the saint, and disappeared beneath the water. From that day to this, Nessie has never harmed any one. She is described as having two humps, flippers, a sinuous neck and small head. *See also* WATER FAIRIES, KELPIES, NEUGLE and WATER HORSES.

NETUN is an old name for LUTINS, derived from NEPTUNE.

NEUGLE lives in Njugals Water in the Shetland Isles. He is a WATER HORSE akin to a KELPIE. Anyone foolish enough to mount the horse will be carried beneath the water never to be seen again.

NEVYN is a lovely Welsh MERMAID who once married a human man called Ivan Morgan. They had a son called Nevydd who died of shame when he found out that his mother was a mermaid. His body was taken to the shore to be buried, but when a wave touched the coffin he sprang out fit and well and sailed off in a fairy ship.

NEWBORN BABIES are at risk of being kidnapped by fairies until they have been named. See UNBAPTISED BABIES and NAME.

NHANGS are evil MERMAIDS that lure unfortunate human men to their deaths beneath the sea, in Armenian folklore.

NIÄGRUISAR are HOUSE FAIRIES who live in the Faeroe Islands. They are small, wear RED CAPS, and live in high trees near houses. They bring luck unless their trees are felled.

NIAMH is the daughter of the king of TIR NAN OG, the Irish land of the fairy. She took the hero OISIN there, where he remained for THREE hundred years, though it seemed to him that he had only been there a week.

NICHOLAS PIPE is a MERMAN who was described by Walter Map, a contemporary of Geoffrey of Monmouth.[241]

NICKEL or Nickelmänner is a German term for a GOBLIN or mischievous WATER FAIRY, and may be the origin of the use of the expression 'Old Nick', meaning the DEVIL, or perhaps while Old Nick was the devil, the nickels were his little IMPS. One Nickel dwelled in the cloudy lake on the Isle of Rügen. Many years ago some men tried to fish there but when they looked round for their boat they spied it in the treetops. One cried out: 'who the devil put that there?', and was astounded by the reply from an invisible source: 'It wasn't the devil but me and my brother Nickel!'.[242]

Nickel is also a mischievous MINE FAIRY, inhabiting the copper mines of Germany. When the miners dug up useless copper-coloured ore from which no copper could be obtained, they called it *Kupfernickel* or 'copper nickel', naming it after the fairy. We still call this metal nickel.

NICK-NOCKER is a noisy German HOUSE FAIRY.

NICKUR, Nykur or Ninnir is an Icelandic WATER FAIRY that looks like a grey or black horse with its hoofs on backwards, though it can SHAPESHIFT into other forms. It lives in rivers, lakes and the sea. In winter, when the ice cracks with a loud booming noise, men say that the nickur is neighing. Male and female nickurs mate in the water, though a nickur stallion may come ashore to mate with an earthly mare. All horses descended from a nickur lie down when they pass through water that comes up to their bellies.[243] The nickur will appear on land near fords that are difficult to cross, to try to tempt a human rider onto his back. Like other fairy WATER HORSES, once a human rider is astride he will run off into the sea. A nickur cannot bear to hear the word 'DEVIL', its own name (Nickur or Ninnir) or anything that sounds like it. If it does it will immediately return to the water where it lives.

NICNEVIN is a Scottish HAG fairy who rides the storm:
'Nicnivin with hit nymphs is in nomber anew'.[244]
She is also said to ride out with the WILD HUNT, after the sun sets. She will take those without protection. *See also* GYRE-CARLIN.

NICOLAI CHUDOVORITS is a Russian fairy who travels through the air on his reindeer drawn sleigh to deliver gifts to human houses on the Feast of the Epiphany (6th January), before disappearing up the chimney with the smoke.

NIDAVALLIR is the dwelling places of the DWARFS, in Norse myth.

NIGHT-HAG is an evil fairy who wanders about at night and attacks sleeping people, causing them nightmares. Such creatures include the NIGHTMARE, the MARA, and the Russian KRIKSY.

NIGHT FOLK is a general British term for fairies, since they are usually active at night.

NIGHT HUNTSMAN is an alternative term for the WILD HUNTSMAN in Germany. A Night Huntsman haunts the Wyrth Forest and on St. Bartholomew's night (August 24th), he frequents Buller Mountain. There are several tales of men who have encountered the hunt and have been shocked to have dismembered human legs thrown at them.

NIGHT MARA is a Norse GOBLIN that attacks sleepers, robbing them of their powers of speech and motion. The term has passed into English in the word 'NIGHTMARE' i.e. a night MARA, a female DEMON of the night who attacks sleeping men, sits on their chests and gives them bad dreams.

NIGHTMARE was originally an evil Norse fairy who attacked sleepers, robbing them of their powers of speech and motion, giving them bad dreams. She was the MARA, a female DEMON of the night. She perches on a Mare's Nest, a term which has come to signify a great discover that turns out to be moonshine. *See also* NIGHT MARA.

NIGHT STEALERS is another name for the Orkney TROWS.

NIGHT WASHERS are Breton fairies who may be seen washing the linen of the dead on the banks of rivers. They may call on humans to help them, and will drown anyone who refuses. *See also* WASHER AT THE FORD.

NIKKISEN are Manx WATER FAIRIES who may be seen on the nights of the full MOON, when they lead the souls of the drowned in a procession.

NIKSA or **Necksa** is the king of the water ELEMENTALS in occult doctrine. The name is derived from NICKUR or NIXIE.

NIMBLE MEN is another name for the Fir Clis, the Scottish sky fairies associated with the Northern Lights or WILL O'THE WISPS.

NIGHTMARE

NIMUE was the LADY OF THE LAKE according to Thomas Malory in his classic *Le Morte D'Arthur*. She was the daughter of Diones and the goddaughter of the goddess Diana. MERLIN saw her dancing in the forest and fell in love with her. Diana officiated at their marriage, after which the Lady of the Lake kept Merlin prisoner in an enchanted castle, or possibly a CAVE or MOUND. This may echo the idea of the initiate or poet spending time in the glass or spiral castle in order to gain knowledge of the goddess's secrets of life and death. She may be one of the Welsh GWRAGEDD ANNWN, fairy maidens who dwell beneath the lakes in the Black Mountains of Wales, or may be identified with the Irish goddess NIAMH or the Welsh goddess Rhiannon.

NINE is a very magical number. There are nine SIRENS and nine MUSES, nine sisters of MORGAN LE FAY, nine daughters of RÂN, nine waves of the sea, and nine SUDICKY appear to determine the fate of a child. BLODEUWEDD was created from nine types of flowers and a SKRZAT and a SETEK hatches after nine days. SIRENA has nine eyes. In tales people disappear for nine nights, nine months, nine years, or nine hundred years. Spells are performed over nine successive nights or involve doing things in nines, such as making nine rings of salt. A CAT has nine lives.

A human baby gestates for nine months, and this is one reason for the number's mystical reputation. It is also three times three, or the number of the triple goddess or holy trinity tripled. It is the last number of the single number scale before the number one repeats on a higher level as ten. For all of these reasons, it is regarded as the number of completion and initiation.

NINGYO is a Japanese WATER FAIRY. It has a human head and a fish body. It cries pearls instead of tears. Eating a Ningyo confers eternal youth and beauty.

NINIANE is one of the names given to the LADY OF THE LAKE in Arthurian legend. *See also* NIMUE and VIVIENNE.

NION NELOU is a country dwelling type of LUTIN or French fairy.

NIS or **Nisse** is a Scandinavian solitary HOUSE FAIRY. In appearance, the nis is very small. Around the year 1200, a statue was found in a fisherman's cottage, just less than 15 cm (six inches) high, with an inscription which stated 'Nisse, actual height'. A nisse has the face of an old man, wears grey clothes and a pointed RED CAP, unless it is Michaelmas Day, when he wears a round one. He loves music and dancing in the moonlight.

One year, there was a drought in Jutland and two nis of neighbouring farms tried to help out their respective homes by stealing grain from each other's stores. For a while, they did not realise what was happening and couldn't work out why the grain stores got no bigger when they kept putting more grain in the barn until one day they met in the lane, each on the way home with his booty. They started to fight and the winner made off with both sacks of grain. The loser went back to his farm, knowing that the other would be along at midnight to steal again. He woke up the farm hand, who was astonished to see him, and asked his help. The brownie told the labourer that the enemy nis would soon appear in the form of a flaming twelve-spoked wheel, while he himself would appear as an eight-spoked wheel. The farm hand must break his rival's spokes to defeat him. As predicted, the twelve-spoked wheel appeared and the man beat out its spokes. Afterwards the farm prospered.

NISSEN GOD DRENG ('Good Lad') is a Scandinavian version of ROBIN GOODFELLOW.

NISKEN are German HOUSE FAIRIES that will look after the house and barn if well fed, or if slighted they will play tricks. They are small, strong, and appear like old men with wizened faces and bright eyes, wearing peasant clothes with RED stockings and GREEN jackets. They live in dark corners of the house, or in the stable or barn.

NIWAREKA is the daughter of the king of the fair-haired Polynesian fairies the TUREHU. She married a mortal prince called Motaora.

NIX/NIXEN ('Nothing') are German fresh WATER FAIRIES. They are rarely seen as they will dive beneath the surface as soon as a human comes near them, leaving only a ripple on the water. They wear RED CAPS. The Grimm brothers recorded a tale of a nix that attended the annual July dance at Laibach in 1547.[245] The whole community gathered in the market place next to the fountain, which was shaded by a lovely linden tree. After everyone had feasted, they got up to dance. Suddenly, a handsome young man appeared and asked if he could join in the revelries. When people shook his hand, they found it to be cold and clammy, though it appeared normal. After a while, he led a flighty young girl called Ursule Schaferin to the dance floor and they whirled wildly around, faster and faster, moving away from the dance floor and towards the river. When they reached the river, the youth leapt in, carrying the girl with him. She was never seen again, though fishermen reported further appearances by the nix.

Sometimes, the strange singing of a nix is heard drifting across water, but the sound of it drives humans mad. A nix may steal a human baby and leave a wizened green CHANGELING in its place. They have been known to mate with young human women and occasionally human midwives have been called in to attend the births of such unions. Their children are called URCHINS.

Nixen can be friendly towards humans, perhaps warning them of drownings or teaching them to fiddle in the elfin manner. However, should the fairy teach a man the *Elf King's Tune* he is doomed to play forever unless he can play it backwards, note for note, or unless someone cuts the fiddle strings from behind.

NIXIE is a female German WATER FAIRY. Nixies love to seduce young human men and sometimes visit village dances disguised as beautiful girls, or appear in the water as lovely women with long, golden hair and blue eyes. They will try to seduce handsome young men into the water. If the men succumb, they will never be seen again. Nixies are malignant, trapping sailors' souls in lobster pots to prevent them reaching heaven.

NJUZU is a southern African WATER FAIRY of Zimbabwe who sometimes appears as a human-headed fish, or at other times as a lovely woman who lures young men to their deaths. Children were once sacrificed to the Njuzu, but many of these fairies have now disappeared from the vicinity of human habitations, as they cannot stand all the noise that people make.

NOCNITSA or **Nochnitsa** ('Night Spirit') is a HAG fairy who prowls through villages at night to torment children in Eastern European folklore. Placing an IRON knife beside the cradle, or an axe beneath it protects a child.

NOGGLE is a western European fairy who appear as small a grey HORSE. Noggles live individually along the edges of streams and waterways. When humans build near their streams or dam the watercourses it annoys them immensely and they have been known to block up water wheels and chase people away.

NOKKE are Swedish WATER FAIRIES that can be heard singing at sunrise and sunset. They are very shy and you will never see one.

NORDRI ('North') is one of the four DWARFS who hold up the sky, which is formed from the skull of the giant YMIR. The others are Sudri ('South'), Austri ('East') and Vestri ('West').

NORGGEN, Norg, Nork, Nörke, Nörkele, Nörglein or **Lörggen**, are male fairies, said to be among the oldest in existence. They are found throughout the Tyrol and northern Italy as far north as the German

border. They are 60 to 90 cm tall (two to three feet), with blazing red eyes and glossy beards. They dress in old-fashioned coats covered in moss or in green breeches and coats and three-cornered hats. Though they are forest fairies, they also appear inside mines and human houses, usually between the first quarter and full MOON.

They can be friendly towards humans, advising them when to plant the crops and so on, though they will steal anything they can get their hands on, including MILK, geese, cows and clothes. They are usually avoided as they are so bad tempered. They are also WEATHER FAIRIES, and if annoyed can ruin the harvest, or breathe on the roads to cover them with ice. They mate with the WILD WOMEN. For the story of a Nörglein, see PURZINIGELE.

NORNS are the Three FATES of Norse legend. They are Urd, Verdani and Skuld (Past, Present and Future). They sit beneath the world tree Yggdrasil and determine the fates of humankind. However, the Scandinavians also believed that there was also a race of lesser norns who visited every child at birth to shape its life in a similar fashion to a FAIRY GODMOTHER. Some of these norns were descended from the gods, others from ELVES, and others from DWARFS. Good norns are responsible for good lives, and bad norns for miserable lives.

NORTHERN LIGHTS are said to be the elves dancing at night.

NUADA is a king of the TUATHA DÉ DANAAN who lost his hand in a battle. The physician-druid Dianecht made him a hand of silver and he was ever afterwards known as Nuada of the Silver Hand, *Nuad Airgeat lamh*.

NUALA is Queen of the Munster SIDHE and FINVARRA's consort.[246]

NUCKELAVEE is a Scottish sea fairy and one of the FUATH. He appears on land riding on a monstrous horse - or perhaps the horse and rider are one. His head is like a man's, but some ten times larger and his mouth projects like a pig's. He has no hair and even no skin.[247]

Others describe the nuckelavee as a huge WATER HORSE with flippers and blazing eyes. It has long arms, a huge head, and no skin, black blood flowing in yellow veins, red muscles and white sinews. It smells like a pile of rotting eggs and fish. If you see one it is as well to remember that it cannot cross running fresh water and dislikes rain; it never visits the land while it is raining.

The nuckelavee's evil breath can wilt the crops as they stand in the field, blighting them with mildew. He can sicken the livestock, cause epidemics among humans, and is responsible for droughts.[248]

According to the Orkney islanders, if it were not for the SEA MITHER keeping him a prisoner in the summer and his fear of fresh rainwater in the winter, he would have overrun the land.

NULIARKSAK is an Inuit spirit of the Arctic lands, a kind of SUCCUBUS or female FAIRY SWEETHEART. She sometimes marries a human man and may bear his children, but they will be INVISIBLE. The male equivalent is called a Uiirsak.

NUNNEHI ('Moon Eyed People') is a Cherokee term for fairy-like spirits.

NURSES According to Irish folklore, young women who are often carried off by fairies to be wet nurses to their offspring. Such a nurse is allowed to return to her own child after sunset. However, sometimes she will return shrouded in black like one of the DEAD, hissing like a SNAKE. When she enters the house her husband must throw water over her in the name of God and she will be restored to her own shape. The husband must ask no questions but give her food in silence. If she falls asleep on the third night he can tie a RED THREAD across the door, which will prevent the fairies taking her again.

NY GUILLYN BEGGY ('The Little Boys') is an ISLE OF MAN term for the fairies.

NY MOOINJER VEGGY (' The Little Kindred') is an ISLE OF MAN term for the fairies.

NYKER is a WATER FAIRY who lives in a deep pool called Nikkesen's, on the Ballacoan stream on the Isle of Man. The fairy or fairies who live there will entice humans into the vicinity and drag them into the water, never to be seen again.

NYKUS is a Polish WATER FAIRY, similar to the NICKUR. It lives in ponds, lakes or rivers and may tempt humans into the water in order to drown them. He looks like a human but on land he is powerless and may be captured and forced to perform domestic tasks.

NYMPH(S) ('Young Girl', 'Bride' or 'Nurse') is a term applied to female nature spirits and fairies, often regarded as minor goddesses. It derives from one of the oldest traditions of ancient Greece where nymphs were believed to inhabit and guard rivers (potamid), running water and streams (naiads), lakes, meadows, mountains (orestiads or oreads), oak trees (dryads and hamadryads), ash trees (meliads) and the sea (nereids or oceanides). They are all beautiful in appearance, personifications of youth, charm and femininity.

Traditionally, the MOON goddess Artemis is accompanied by nymphs, hunting in the wild places of the earth. Nymphs were often the mothers or nurses of heroes and infant gods, including the infant Zeus, who fed on sacred honey. His nursing nymphs retained the title *Melissai* or 'bees'.

NYMPH

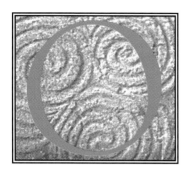

O'DONOGHUE is an Irish fairy who lives beneath the Lake of Killarney. He rises every MAY DAY morning with his train, garlanded with spring flowers, to the sounds of beautiful music. It is said that he once ruled the surrounding lands, but one day he walked out onto the surface of the lake and sank beneath it, where he now rules his new underwater kingdom.

OAF is a fairy child, a CHANGELING left in place of a stolen human baby. It grows up misshapen or a half-wit. The word is derived from AELF or 'elf'.

OAK (*Quercus robur*) is a tree that has numerous associations with fairies. The majority of fairies are to be found in woods and forests, particularly oak groves. ELVES and fairies are often said to dwell within the hollow trunks of oaks. In southern England, a New Forest rhyme advises:'Turn your cloaks for fairy folks are in old oaks' - for to turn your cloak inside out protects you from being distracted from your path by fairies.

The German forest fairies, the WOOD-WIVES, frequent the old sacred forests and oak groves. SALVANELLI, the weather fairies of southern Italy, live in hollow oak trees. In England, unfriendly dwarfish creatures called OAKMEN live in the saplings which grow from felled oaks. In Greek myth, DRYADS and HAMADRYADS are the spirits of the tree itself.

The concept of tree spirits is very ancient and very widespread. Romans believed that men, NYMPHS and FAUNS had a common origin, all springing from the oak. Buddhists believe that trees have a spirit called a DEVA. GREEN LADIES is a British term for dryads dwelling in oak, ELM, APPLE, WILLOW, HOLLY and yew trees. Permission had to be sought from the fairy before chopping down the tree and PRIMROSES planted beneath the trees as an offering to the fairy.

The oak is associated with the light half of the year, midsummer and the sun. In Celtic Pagan belief, the spirit of the Oak King fought a bi-yearly battle with the Holly King for the hand of the Earth Goddess. This is exemplified in the story of the GREEN KNIGHT.

OAKMEN or **Oak Men** are the most widespread tree fairies in England; sometimes they are merged with OAK trees, like HAMADRYADS, and sometimes they appear as forest DWARFS who offer tempting food to passing mortals, which will turn out to be poisonous fungi, disguised by fairy GLAMOUR. They inhabit copses where saplings have grown from felled oaks. If BLUEBELLS are growing in a copse, it invariably indicates the presence of oak men; and mortals should be warned to avoid the area. Oak men become extremely angry and dangerous if their tree is cut down. They also guard all the forest animals and punish those who harm them, such as foxhunters. The rain that gathers in their oak hollows has powerful magical healing qualities.

OANNES are fish-headed sea spirits of the ancient Chaldeans, derived from the Sumero-Semitic god Ea-Oannes, Lord of the Deeps, who was served by a priesthood in fish-head head-dresses, the origin of modern bishops' mitre head-dresses. The Oannes rose from the sea to teach humankind the sciences and arts, and returned each night to the sea.

OARAUNLE is a type of KOBOLD which inhabits a figure carved from a mandrake root.

OATMEAL sprinkled on CLOTHES or carried in the pocket protects against malicious fairies. In Mull mothers used to fill the pockets of boys travelling at night with oatmeal.

OBERON appears in many stories - mainly from the Middle Ages - in which his origins and character vary enormously. He first appeared in the mediaeval French romance *Huan de Bordeaux*[249] as Alberon, a DWARF king, either the brother of MORGAN LE FAY or her son by Julius Caesar. In this aspect, he is said to be the king of AVALON and one tale explains that when ARTHUR was mortally wounded he was taken to Oberon's kingdom and became his heir. Others say that his mother was Cephalonia, Queen of the Hidden Isle and at his christening, her ladies in waiting bestowed many gifts upon him, though an evil fairy cursed him with short stature. In another story he was the father of ROBIN GOODFELLOW by a mortal girl.

Spenser named him as the father of the fairy queen Gloriana and Shakespeare immortalised him as the king of the fairies in *A Midsummer Night's Dream*. In contrast to Shakespeare's beautiful king, Oberon is usually described as an ugly dwarf, only about a metre (or three feet) high. Some trace his origins back to the dwarf ALBERICH, who was the jester at the court of Dietrich of Bern. Others say he was a hideous dwarf called Tronc whom the fays turned into a handsome fairy and gave a kingdom.

He is wont to meet wayfarers in the forest and tries to get them to speak to him. If they do, they are lost forever, but if they remain silent, Oberon will cause it to rain and hail and a great black river to appear. However, this is an illusion and can easily be waded through.

OBERYCOM is a FAMILIAR spirit in early renaissance folklore, possibly the original of OBERON.[250]

OBOROTNI ('Changed One') is a Russian fairy CHANGELING.

OBLAKINJE VILE are Baltic WEATHER FAIRIES. If the sun shines when it is raining, it means that they are combing their HAIR.

OCEANIDES are the NYMPHS of the oceans, daughters of the god Ocean, in ancient Greek myth. A chorus of Oceanides appears in Aeschylus's *Prometheus Bound*.

ODMIENCE ('Changed One') is a Polish fairy CHANGELING.

OGRE (f. Ogress) is a term occasionally used to signify any monstrous, evil being, but more specifically it applies to a class of large, deformed and ugly fairies. They are usually hairy, fearless and stupid. Their favourite food is human men. An ogre may be male or female, though the females are sometimes called 'ogresses'. Ogres appear to have originated in France, and the term first appeared in Perrault's *Fairy Tales* (1697). This ogre may have been a development of the earlier ORCO found in Ariosto's *Orlando Furioso* (1516) and the ancient ORC, perhaps derived from the Roman god of the UNDERWORLD, Orcus ('Pig'). Creatures called 'orcneas' are mentioned in the Anglo-Saxon poem *Beowulf*. Ogre type figures appear in the folklore of Native Americans, Indias, Japanese, Scandinavians and the Basques. In Norse mythology ogres make the storms and hit the earth with their IRON clubs, causing earthquakes. They are larger and fatter than men, but shorter than giants. Their dense skin can be anything from white to ebony; they have round ears, and prominent lower canines. They can see in very dim light and like to live in CAVES.

OHDOWS are North American fairies that are small and live underground. They use their powers to stop GIANTS and DEMONS emerging from under the earth to cause earthquakes and other disasters.

OISIN or **Ossian** was the son of Finn Mac Cumhal (chief of the Fenian warriors of Ireland) and Sadb, a DEER-woman. He was hunting one day when NIAMH of the Golden Hair, daughter of the god MANANNAN, approached him. She had chosen him for her lover and together they journeyed to the fairyland TIR NAN OG. After THREE hundred years he expressed a wish to see his home and she lent him a fairy HORSE, with the caution not to let his feet touch the earth. He was dismayed to see that all had changed, and St Patrick had converted Ireland to Christianity. Even the men seemed feebler. He saw three men trying to move a rock and as he lent down to give them a hand his saddle girth suddenly snapped and he fell to the earth. The horse vanished and he instantly became ancient and blind. St Patrick found him and tried to convert him to Christianity, but Oisin could not see the point of an afterlife where there was no feasting, hunting or loving beautiful women and preferred to stay a Pagan.

OISIP is a Russian WATER FAIRY who appeared as a SNAKE and took a mortal wife.

OITEAG SLUAIGH ('People's Puff of Wind') occur in Highland folklore: when the fairies leave home in companies they travel on eddies of wind, known in Gaelic as *oiteag sluaigh*. People on night journeys have been lifted up and carried off by these supernatural winds, and have spent the night madly careering through the skies. On being dropped to earth they usually return to the house they last left, too stupefied to recognise the house or its inhabitants. Other returned travellers may find themselves on a distant hill, or in some inaccessible place they could never have reached on their own. Even in daylight, some have been carried from one island to another, in great terror lest they fall into the sea. By throwing one's left shoe at the *oiteag sluaigh*, or an IRON knife, or soil from a molehill, or one's bonnet, the fairies are made to stop what they are doing and return whatever or whoever they are taking away.

OLD BLOODY BONES is the Cornish version of RAWHEAD AND BLOODY BONES.

OLD GIRL is the English spirit of the ELDER tree.

OLD GODS may be the origins of many fairies, perhaps even of the vast majority, are traceable to the old gods and nature spirits of Paganism. When Christianity spread across Europe, the old gods were either designated Christian saints (the goddess Brighid, for example, became St Brigit) or entirely demonized. However, they were remembered among the ordinary people as spirits that were occasionally seen and still had to be honoured lest they should be angered. It may be that the old gods eventually passed into folk memory as spirits or fairies.

This theory is most clearly illustrated by the legend of the TUATHA DÉ DANAAN ('People of the Goddess Danu'), a race of gods who dwelled in Ireland. They were tall and fair and had many talents. When they were eventually conquered by the Celts they dwindled in size and retreated to the hollow hills becoming the DAOINE SIDHE or 'People of the Hills'. In many places until quite recent times offerings of MILK were poured onto MOUNDS or the standing stones these old gods were said to have built. Some of the baking and the harvest had to be left for the 'fairies' and various precautions taken so as not to offend them.

A large number of named fairies are directly traceable to specific old gods. Leicestershire's BLACK ANNIS was once the goddess Anu, the SHONEYS are descended from the Norse sea goddess Sjofn, the Rumanian fairy ILEANA was once a goddess of the dawn, AINE was a goddess of the Tuatha dé Danaan, Gwydion, who rules the TYLWYTH TEG, was once a Celtic god. There are literally thousands of examples.

Even the word 'fairy' is derived from the Greek goddesses the FATES (from the Latin *fata* via the Old French *fée*). They are an aspect of the triple MOON goddess, the spinner and measurer of time. The thread of life is spun on Clotho's spindle, measured by the rod of Lachesis and snipped by Atropos' shears. Atropos relates to the HAG of winter, the waning or dark moon death goddess, reflected in hag and CAILLEACH fairies.

Like goddesses of fate, a number of fairies are associated with SPINNING and flax, including FAIRY GODMOTHERS, who appear to bless or curse a child at birth. These weaver goddesses were once considered the most powerful, spinning the thread of life and weaving the fabric of the cosmos. The Weaver Goddess appears in many mythologies in various forms. The Three Fates are paralleled in Norse myth by the THREE Norns, Urd, Verdani and Skuld. Arianrhod is the Welsh weaver goddess. Her name means 'Silver Wheel', the spinning wheel of the moon and the stars. She is mistress of Caer Arianrhod, situated in the Corona Borealis, a Celtic OTHERWORLD or FAIRYLAND. It is the Spiral Castle to which the soul journeys at death.

The Egyptian Isis was the patroness of weaving but she also wove MAGIC and could heal, as all fairies and WITCHES are said to be able to do. The Egyptian goddess Meith was a magician and her symbol was a weaver's shuttle. She was titled 'The Opener of the Ways' and conducted souls to the underworld. This idea of following a linen thread into or out of the UNDERWORLD is echoed in other cultures. Ariadne led Theseus out of the underworld MAZE of the Minotaur by means of a thread, while the witch goddess Hecate lead the corn goddess Demeter into the underworld with a thread to find her daughter Persephone (Spring). The underworld is reputed to

be where the fairies live, and many of them, like LEPRECHAUNS and DRAGONS, guard TREASURE.

It can be no coincidence that the festivals most associated with fairies are the four fire festivals of the Celts (SAMHAIN, LUGHNASA, IMBOLC and BELTANE) and the solstices and equinoxes universally celebrated by Pagans (OSTARA, MIDSUMMER, YULE and the autumn equinox). Seasonal winter/death goddesses may be discerned in various hag fairies like the CAILLEACH BEINNE BHIC HORO who cares for red deer (the Celtic totem animal for Samhain), the CAILLEACH BLEUR who beats down vegetation and FRAU HOLDA who brings the snow. At Yule, particularly in Scandinavian and Germanic countries, a wide variety of present giving fairies appear. The Icelandic Jola Sveinar, the Danish Julenisse, the Swedish Jultomte and of course FATHER CHRISTMAS deliver gifts. These are probably directly descended from Odin or Woden who rode out at Yule to reward good deeds and punish bad ones.

The various HOUSE FAIRIES around the world, such as the Spanish ANCHO, the Polynesian ATUA, the Russian BAGAN, the Irish BEAN-TIGHE, the Scots BODACHAN SABHAILL, the Welsh BWBACH and BWCA, the Japanese CHIN-CHIN KOBAKAMA and the Chinese CHOA PHUM PHI, are similar in character to the Roman LARS FAMILIARIS, household gods that guarded each family.

OLD HAG is the fairy who causes NIGHTMARES in Newfoundland.

OLD LADY OF THE ELDER TREE is a Lincolnshire name for the ELDER MOTHER.

OLD LUK OIE ('Old Close Your Eyes') is a Danish fairy who brings sleep, like the SANDMAN. He wears a silk jacket that changes colour with the light, and carries two magic umbrellas. He blows fairy dust into the eyes of children to make them sleep. If he opens the

umbrella with pictures painted on it, the child will have lovely dreams. If he opens the plain umbrella, the child will have dreamless sleep.

OLD MAN CROOK is a helpful Devonshire fairy who lives in the vicinity of the town of Bideford in south west England

OLD MAN OF THE SEA is an evil DJINN who persuades men to take him on his back to cross a stream or reach some fruit, and then will not dismount. Such a figure occurs in many folk tales often in the form of a HAG.

The title 'Old Man of the Sea' also refers to the Greek sea god Proteus, who is the most masterful SHAPESHIFTER of all. He is able to assume any form he desires and if a human can catch him he will be forced to keep one shape until he is let go, and answer any question his captor desires, as to the past, the present or the future. Most WATER FAIRIES are said to be shapeshifters, perhaps referring to the fluid and changeable nature of water itself, which is only given shape by the vessel that holds it.

OLD MAN WILLOW is an English fairy of the WILLOW tree, often thought to reach out and snatch at passers by in lonely places. An old Somerset rhyme runs:

Ellum do grieve, Oak he do hate,
Willows do walk,if Yew travels late.

OLD ONES is a generic term for fairies.

OLD PEOPLE is a Cornish term for fairies.

OLD SHOCK or **Old Shuck** *See* BLACK SHUCK.

OLLAVITINUS is Prince of the SEA TROWS.

OLLPHIAST is a monstrous sea spirit found in Co. Meath, Ireland.

OLYROUN is a fairy king, the father of TRYAMOUR.

OMANG are small fairy creatures of the Batangs.

OMENS can be drawn from the appearance of some fairies, usually of ill fortune. These include the SKRIKER, AKUMA, BAJANG, ITCHETIK and KELPIE.

Through the ages people have believed that the future casts its shadow before it, and that omens occur as a warning of a fate to be avoided. However, since the aforementioned fairies are all evil in nature, it is doubtful whether they are performing a friendly service, but rather bring the evil with them. The unexpected appearance of a fairy is rarely a good omen. Fairies like to carry out their good deeds in secret, unseen at night or in an invisible form.

OMEN OF DEATH Some fairies appear to herald the death of an individual. These include the TCHI-CO, WASHER AT THE FORD, WILD HUNT, ACHERI, BADBH, BANSHEE, COISTE-BODHAR, MORRIGAN, BLACK DOG, BLACK SHUCK, BODACH GLAS, BODCA-AN-DUN, BOGGART, CORPSE CANDLES, FETCH, FYLGJA, GABRIEL'S HOUNDS, KELPIE, KLAGE-WEIB, LIEKKOS, NÄKH, AOIBHILL, CANNERED NOZ and the CYOERRAETH.

While some of these beings are evil, and bring the bad fortune with them, others are motivated by a friendly feeling towards an individual or family. See also OMEN.

ONE WITH THE WHITE HAND is a pale fairy that flits out from the BIRCH copses to seek out young men travelling alone the moors of Somerset in south west England. Taunton schoolboys used to have a tale of the spirit that rose out of a coppice of BIRCH and OAK at twilight to drift after rash travellers so swiftly they could not elude her. She was as pale as a corpse, and her long, thin white hand was like a blasted branch. If she brushed a man with her hand he would go mad, if she touched his breast he would die, and the mark of the white hand would be found over his heart. It is said that a brave man with a handful of SALT laid her.[251]

ONLAR ('They') are Turkish fairies that appear as male or female, dwarfs, GIANTS or animals. They usually live among the garbage of rubbish tips in the city.

ONNERBÄNKISSEN is a small and gentle European fairy of the QUIET FOLK type.

ONOCENTAUR is a CENTAUR, half-man and half-donkey.

OONAGH, Donagh or Una is the Queen of the DAOINE SIDHE in Co. Tipperary, wife of King FINVARRA. Her golden hair sweeps the ground and she is robed in silver GOSSAMER, glittering as if with diamonds, but they are dewdrops that sparkle all over it. She is more beautiful than any woman of the earth.[252] She lives in Knockshegouna 'the fairy MOUND of Oonagh' east of Lough Derg, which is the most sacred lake in Ireland, situated in a lonely spot in Co. Donegal in the province of Ulster. It is still sacred to Irish Catholics and associated with the Purgatory of St Patrick and with the transportation of human souls to purgatory. In the middle of the lake, Giraldus Cambrensis (*Topography of Ireland* 1186) described an island divided, occupied in one part by good spirits and the other by evil ones. On the latter part were NINE pits, and anyone spending the night in one of them would be seized upon by malignant spirits. St Patrick spent the night there and was granted a trip to both heaven and hell.

OOSER is another name for the WOODWOSE and occurs in the folklore of the English county of Dorset.

ORA is the Albanian version of the FAIRY GODMOTHERS or FATES.

ORANG BUNYI ('The Voice Folk') are Malayan fairies that none may see, but which all may hear. Their voices sound human and they can be heard calling to each other in the forests. Anyone who answers their calls of distress will lose his way and not be able to retrace his steps. He is then led further and further on until the Voice Folk become visible to him and his doom is to become one of them.

ORC is a huge sea monster with big teeth, according to the Roman writer Pliny. It likes to eat human men and women. Tolkien used the name for the creatures that formed the evil army in *Lord of the Rings*.

ORCHI (s. ORCO) are Italian GIANTS that live in the clouds and come down to feed on animals, humans and other fairies. Their descendants are the smaller ORCULLI. They have beards and smell like rotting corpses. A single touch from them can make a cow sick. They fear CATS. The Orco was a gigantic horror, mentioned in Ariosto's *Orlando Furioso* (1516) who had no eyes, but bones sticking out where his eyes should have been. He ate men but not women. He may be the original of the OGRE.

ORCULLI are capricious Italian fairies who live in caves in the area of Friuli in northern Italy. They often appear as bearded males, though they are shapeshifters and can appear in any form they like. However, an orcullo can be recognised by its awful smell.

OREAD, Orends or Oriades are mountain NYMPHS of Greek mythology.

ORIANDE or Orianda is a particular FAIRY SWEETHEART of French and Italian romance.

OSENJA is a malevolent southern Slavonic spirit that evolves from the evil soul of a DEAD person. It may appear during the Twelve Days of Christmas or at the dark moon.

ORISNICI ('Establishing') are Southern Slavonic FAIRY GODMOTHERS who decide the fate of a newborn child. When a child is born, a supper is provided for them and all the relations are also invited to partake.

OSKOREI is the Norwegian WILD HUNT, the host of the unforgiven DEAD who appear at the site of a murder and sometimes take the killer with them. The Oskorei also appears in the guise of a hunter and hounds riding out at YULE.

OSTARA (21st March) is a busy festival for Scandinavian fairies. It is then that they are at their most active. If they are denied their rightful portion of the festival feast, you will have to give them twice as much at MIDSUMMER or you will be troubled until the next Ostara.

At the spring equinox, as the weather starts to brighten and the earth blossoms, a number of fairies start to become busy.

The DOMOVIYR (Russian cellar fairies) shed their skins and grow lighter ones for the summer. The Russian river fairies, the RUSALKI, appear bathing in lakes and sitting on the shore combing their hair in the moonlight.

OTHAN is a Gaelic word for a green elevation in wet ground where fairies live.

OTHERWORLD is a term often used to refer to FAIRYLAND. In Celtic myth, the Otherworld is the realm of the gods, spirits and the DEAD. It exists parallel to the known world, intertwined with it, as symbolised by the two strands of Celtic knotwork. It can be accessed on special days or at special times, such as MIDNIGHT, dawn, and dusk, SAMHAIN, and BELTANE or MIDSUMMER; in certain places such as FAIRY RINGS, MOUNDS and stone circles or sometimes by accident through a MIST GATE or by stepping on a STRAY SOD.

The SOULS of the especially blessed are also called there after death. It is a land where the trees are always in fruit and blossom, where illness and old age are unknown, and where there is continual music, feasting and dancing. The Irish call it Tir Nan Og, the Land of Youth, while the Welsh call it Annwn. It is also called AVALON, Tír Fó Thuinn, Tír Tairngiri, Útgard, Booyan, Cockaigne, Caer Arianrhod, Elysium and Fairyland.

The Otherworld came to be the realm of the fairies or the SIDHE, sometimes the same as the UNDERWORLD, but sometimes not.

OUPH is an Elizabethan English variant on the word ELF and Shakespeare wrote of: 'urchins, ouphs and fairies, green and white'.

OVINNIK (*ovin* meaning 'threshing barn') are Russian fairies that live in barns and care for livestock, or they are HOUSE FAIRIES who look after a potter's drying kiln, appearing as a black CAT with burning eyes. An ovinnik will be angered and burn down the kiln if it is fired on a feast day, or if he is not honoured for his help by the sacrifice of a cock. He will burn down the threshing shed - with the farmer's children in it if he can manage it - if he is not given the last sheaf or offerings of blini.

OWD LAD is an English term for a TREE FAIRY, usually an OAK spirit.

OWLS are associated with fairies such as GWYN AP NUDD, the Lord of Death, HAGS and the WILD HUNTSMAN. Like most night-flying birds, the owl is a bad omen in many parts of the world, a herald of death. The owl was associated with Adam's first wife, LILLITH. She fell from grace to become one of the four wives of Satan. From this association with Lillith the name of the screech owl or tawny owl, *Strix aluco*, came to mean a VAMPIRE.

The owl may have been associated with the Greek SIRENS, winged sisters who sang to lure sailors to their deaths. There were THREE of them (or possibly NINE in earlier myths) and had titles like 'Persuader', 'Bright Face', 'Bewticher', 'Virgin Face', 'Shrill Voice', and 'The Whitened One', which might be descriptions of owls.

In the northern hemisphere, many owl species are very vocal in November (the death time of the year) and then fall silent until February. As such, they are the servants of the crone goddess, and in Scotland the owl is known as *Cailleach* which means 'HAG' and is the *Cailleach Oidhche* ('the Hag of the Night') and *Cailleach Oidhche Gheal* ('Hag of the Night Moon') and is linked to the CAILLEACH BHEUR, the blue faced hag of winter and death. It is also the death bird, 'the Bird of the Corpse'. One tale says that the owl is the servant of one of the ten UNDERWORLD kings. In most of Europe, owls were associated with WITCHES, who were thought to be able to turn themselves into them. The SKOGSRÅ appear as owls.

PA HSIEN are the Eight Immortals of Chinese myth, often translated as The Eight Fairies or Eight GENII by English-speaking Chinese. They are eight male and female spirits, some of which were once mortal humans. They live on an OTHERWORLD island paradise.[253]

PACH is an associate of ROBIN GOODFELLOW.[254]

PADFOOT is a fairy BLACK DOG that haunts the north of England. He has fiery eyes and drags a chain behind him. His name comes from the padding sound of his feet. Occasionally he appears as a white dog. His appearance is an OMEN OF DEATH or ill fortune.

PAINAJAINEN are Alpine fairies who appear as small, white HORSES that ride through the mountains. They bring NIGHTMARES to children, which can be prevented by placing a piece of IRON or a broom beneath the child's pillow.

PAJANVAKI are Finnish fairies, the guardians of metals or perhaps the ELEMENTAL spirits of the metals.

PALA is an ELEMENTAL spirit of the North and the Earth in Italian occult belief. *See* PALOS.

PALATINA is one of the sisters of MELUSINA.

PALOS is the ELEMENTAL spirit of the North, who influences creativity and intellect, in Italian occult belief.

PAMARINDO is an evil Italian fairy, one of the FOLLETTI. He is lazy and cruel. He steals animals from farmers and eats nothing but their meat. When he whistles the animals are compelled to follow him and he will lead them on a wild run, faster and faster, until he comes to the edge of a cliff, where he will roll into a ball and bounce off. The animals follow him over and are dashed to pieces on the rocks below. He is easily spotted since he is grotesquely fat, taking up the entire width of the road. He dresses in RED and both his hat and shoes are made of copper. He inhabits the region around Gemona in northern Italy.

PAN is the most powerful nature spirit of all, the Greek god of the wild, son of the god Hermes by a NYMPH of Arcadia. The ancient writer Servius described him as being:

'Formed in the likeness of nature with horns to resemble the rays of the sun and the horns of the moon; his face is ruddy in the imitation of ether; he wears a spotted fawn skin resembling the stars in the sky; his lower limbs are hairy because of the trees and wild beasts; he has the feet of a GOAT to resemble the stability of the earth; his pipe has seven reeds in accordance with the harmony of heaven; his pastoral staff bears a crook

in reference to the year which curves back on itself, and finally, he is the god of all Nature'.

He roams the mountains, pursuing game in the valleys, playing his pipe in the groves and travellers in the woods often hear his music. His call is said to give rise to 'panic', an overwhelming fear in all that hear it.

There are a variety of nature and woodland fairies similar in appearance to Pan, e.g. ROBIN GOODFELLOW, PUCK, SATYRS and FAUNS.

PANDAFECHE is a type of NIGHTMARE that sits on the chest of a sleeper and rides him through the night.

PANS or **PANES** are a race of male nature fairies with GOAT attributes. They may be the precursors of PAN.

PANTEGANE are Italian fairies, cognate with the AGUANE and mates of the PANTEGANI. They protect the lower slopes of the Alps and their meadows.

PANTEGANI are Italian Alpine fairies, cognate with the SALVANI and mates of the PANTEGANE, they protect the lower slopes of the Alps and their trees.

PARA is a Finnish KOBOLD or HOUSE FAIRY who can be persuaded to become the servant of a human. He steals MILK from other people's cows, carrying and coagulating it in his stomach so that it can be disgorged into the churn of his human mistress. It is said that she can make him appear by taking a certain MUSHROOM, frying it in tar, salt and sulphur, and beating it with a rod. The Para will quickly appear and entreat her to spare him. If a Para should become a nuisance, he is very difficult to get rid of. Some churches kept exorcists specifically to deal with Paras.

PARALDA is the king of the air ELEMENTALS in occult and Italian doctrine.

PARANA DWARFS are creatures that have been seen in recent times in Parana (Argentina). They have small horns, no feet, can fly and disappear in clouds of black smoke.[255]

PARIBANOU is a fairy mentioned in the Arabian Nights who appeared to Prince Ahmed and presented him with a magic tent which would fold up small enough to be carried in a pocket, but expand large enough to shelter an army.

PARTHOLAN or **Partholon** is the Celtic Lord of the UNDERWORLD, who came to Ireland from the west, the place of the setting sun, or FAIRYLAND. He fought the FORMORIANS for rulership of the land. The Celts considered that they were descended from him.

PARZAE are Northern European FAIRY GODMOTHERS or FATES.

PATHS BETWEEN THE MOUNDS are straight paths which fairies use to process between their homes. It is unlucky to build on the paths between the mounds. One of the Irish seers, interviewed by Evans Wentz in 1911, reported that these fairy paths were magnetic arteries through which the earth's magnetism circulated: an early LEY LINE theorist.

PATRE, LE ('The Father') is a French HOUSE FAIRY or LUTIN, who is well behaved when well treated, but will play mischievous tricks when slighted.

PATU-PAIAREHE are Moari fairies that dwell in bushes and the fairy flax that grows in the forks of New Zealand's forest trees. They are not visible to humans but their songs are sometimes heard. They eat RED fruits, which are taboo to humans unless the fairies are first propitiated, as red fruit belongs exclusively to the fairies. The Patu-paiarehe play tricks on people who enter the forests, calling out and leading them astray. *See also* FAIRY FOOD.

PAVARÓ is an Italian fairy with a DOG's head, long arms and IRON teeth and nails. He protects bean fields by slashing the legs of anyone who damages the crops. His arms are so long that he can reap several acres at once.

PAYSHTHA or **Pastha** or **Piast-Bestia** is an Irish water DRAGON who guards hidden TREASURE.

PCUVUS or **Pchuvushi** are Romany EARTH FAIRIES or MINE FAIRIES. According to gypsies, clumps of nettles mark the places where subterranean passages lead to their realms. Here they guard the TREASURES of the earth including precious metals and gems.

PEALLAIDH ('The Shaggy One') is a Scottish URISK from Perthshire.

PEARLIN JEAN is a HAG fairy or WITCH spirit who stalks the length and breadth of Scotland at HALLOWEEN, haunting town and countryside alike. She has the eyes of a CAT.

PECH, Pecht or **Picts** are fairies of Lowland Scotland that live underground. They have long arms, RED HAIR and use their enormous feet as umbrellas. It is said that they are responsible for building Edinburgh Castle.

PAYSHTHA

PECHMANDERLN are German fairies, perhaps a subspecies of WICHTLN, who glue sleepy children's eyes together with pitch.

PEEDIE FOLK are Orkney fairies who live in the burial mounds and maybe synonymous with the TROWS.

PEERIE FOOL or **Peerifool** ('Little Fool') is a little fairy who appeared in an Orkney tale: There was once a widowed queen of the Orkney Isles who had three daughters. They lived in a small cottage with a single cow and a kale patch. They found that their kale was being stolen. The eldest princess offered to keep watch all night to see what happened. In the middle of the night a huge GIANT came and started cutting the kale stalks. When she asked him why he was stealing the vegetables, he took her by the arm and leg, threw her into his basket on top of the kale leaves, and went off with her too.

When they reached the giant's home he told her that each day he would go out and she would have to milk his cow and put it to graze on the hills, then she should take the wool, wash and tease it and spin it to make cloth. The next morning he went off and she put on the porridge to make herself breakfast, when all of a sudden a number of *peerie* ('little') yellow-haired folk appeared and asked her for some food. She refused them, saying there was none to spare. This was a big mistake, for the fairies cursed her and she was unable to card the wool or spin it. When the giant came home and found none of the work done he skinned her down her back and over her feet and hung her from the rafters, among the hens. Exactly the same fate befell the second sister.

The third night, the youngest princess set out to watch the kale patch. She saw the giant come and asked him why he was stealing her mother's vegetables. He picked her up and took her home, like the other two sisters. The next morning he gave her the same tasks that he had given the other two. So, she milked the cow and put it out to graze, then put on the pot, and began to make porridge for herself. When it was ready the PEERIE TROWS came about and asked her for some. She told them to fit themselves out with cutlery and crockery and they were welcome. So, some got heather twigs, others got broken dishes and one thing and another, and had their share of the porridge. After they were finished, one trow asked her if she had any work to do. She replied that she had some fleeces to tease, spin and weave. He told her that the fairies would take it away and make it into cloth for her, on condition that when they returned she should guess his NAME. The princess thought that this would not be difficult and agreed to the deal.

That night an old woman knocked on the cottage door and related to the princess a strange tale. She had found a high MOUND and heard singing coming from inside it, saying,

'Tease, teasers, tease,
Card, carders, card,
Spin, spinners, spin,
For Peerie Fool is my name'

She put her eye to a crack and saw that inside a great many fairies were working away, carding and SPINNING.

The next day the fairy came back to the princess with all the wool made into cloth, and demanded she should tell him his name. She guessed several names and at each he jumped up and down with glee, crying 'No'. Just when he thought he had won she said 'Your name is Peerie Fool'. The trow threw down the wool, and ran off, very angry.

The princess found her sisters hanging in the rafters. She restored their skin and tricked the giant into taking them all home to the queen. They emptied a cauldron full of boiling water over him, and that was the end of the giant.[256]

PEERIE TROWS ('Little Trows') These Shetland TROWS are so small that they live under toadstools. See also PEERIE FOOL.

PEERIFOOL See PEERIE FOOL.

PEESTERALEETI One of the Orkney TROWS.

PEG O'NELL is a water HAG of the River Ribble in Lancashire, England. She demands the sacrifice of a life every SEVEN years and will be satisfied with a small animal or bird, though if this is not offered she will take a human life.

The River Ribble was sacred to Minerva during the Roman occupation and an unknown water goddess before that, and Peg O'Nell is likely to be a folk memory of this goddess. However, some say that Peg is the GHOST of a servant from Wadden Hall, drowned as a WITCH. See also WATER FAIRIES.

PEG PROWLER or **Peg Powler** is a water HAG of the River Tees in north eastern England. She is GREEN with long hair and sharp teeth. If people wade in the water she pulls on their ankles and drags them down to drown. *See also* WATER FAIRIES.

PEG WI'TH' LANTERN or **Peg-A-Lantern** is an English WILL O'THE WISP who waves her lantern on dark nights on Lantern Pike in Derbyshire.

PEGGY WI' T' LANTHORN is another northern English WILL O'THE WISP form Yorkshire. She has been known to lead humans to safety after they have been misled by evil BOGGARTS on the moors.

PEHTRA BABA is a Balkan HAG fairy who appears between Christmas and the Epiphany leading a procession of DEAD souls. She controls SPINNING.

PELLINGS is a half-fairy Welsh tribe, living near Mount Snowdon. They are the descendants of PENELOP.

PELZE NICOL ('Furry Nicholas') is the German FATHER CHRISTMAS.

PENATES are house spirits of ancient Rome which seem to have been similar to HOUSE FAIRIES, in that they dwelt with particular families to help and protect them. Images of the Penates were made of wax or ivory and had special shrines in the house. They were worshipped along with the domestic goddess Vesta and were responsible for the house's food supply and the success of the harvest. A fire was kept burning in their honour and they were given SALT and the first portion of each meal.

They were once gods of the storeroom, but were later demoted to fairy status. They were connected with the LARES; the spirits of the DEAD or ancestors, and the terms are sometimes interchangeable. The *Penates Publici* were the protectors of the Roman state and were worshipped in a state cult.

PENELOP or **Penelope** is a fairy who appears in a Welsh tale. Near to the Snowdonian village of Beddgelert is a place that the locals call the 'Land of the Fairies'. It was once commonplace to hear the lovely music of the fairies there, and see their dancing and mirthful sports. A youth lived in the vicinity. He was brave and determined, and spent many evenings watching the fairies. One evening he spied them on the shore of Llyn y Dywarchen and his eyes were drawn to one of the fairy ladies. Her skin was like alabaster, her voice as lovely as the nightingale's and as unruffled as a zephyr in a flower garden on a summer's noon, her feet moved as lightly in the dance as the rays of the sun on the lake. He instantly fell passionately in love with her. So powerful was the youth's desire that he ran headlong into the throng. He seized the fairy maiden in his arms and bore her into his house. He bolted the door with IRON so that the pursuing fairies could not enter.

Now the youth began to plead his cause to the exquisite lady. With soft words, he wooed her. At first she would not hear of it, but in due time, seeing that he would not allow her to return to her people, she seemed to relent. She said that she would not marry him, but would become his servant if he could guess her NAME. He agreed, but guessing all the names he could think of got him no nearer his goal. All were wrong.

Then one night he was returning from the market at Caernarfon when he saw a number of fairies ahead of him, near the path. He thought that they might be planning to rescue their sister and decided to creep up close to them and endeavour to overhear what they were saying. As he did, he found that they were indeed speaking of the abducted fairy. One of them cried out pitifully: 'Oh Penelop, Penelop! Why didst thou run away with a mortal?'

The youth returned home and called out: 'Penelop, come here!' The fairy lady came to him in astonishment and asked who had betrayed her name. He said nothing and she began to weep and bewail her fate. However, she was true to her word and began work in earnest, cleaning, washing, SPINNING, weaving and keeping the farm better than any housewife in the district. The holding began to prosper and the young man pestered her to

marry him. Finally, she agreed with the condition that if he should ever touch her with IRON, she would return to the Fair Folk.

So they were married and for several years lived quite happily together. She bore him two children who were as lovely as fairies themselves. Then one day the couple went out to catch a filly in the field. Together they drove it into the corner and the youth attempted to throw the bridle over it. But alas, his wife chanced to move into the way and the iron bit caught her cheek. She vanished immediately and was never seen again.[257]

It is interesting to encounter a Welsh fairy, connected with spinning, called Penelope. She no doubt gets her name from the wife of the Greek hero Odysseus, who span and wove to discourage suitors while her husband was away. According to Robert Graves, *penelope* means 'with a web over her face'.[258]

PENELOPE OF THE LOWLANDS was a Fairy Queen who, for twenty years, guided Goodwin Walton (through the medium Mary Parish). She told the alchemist that the Fairy Queen would one day marry him and endow him with riches. Unfortunately, other fairy ambassadors always turned up when he was about to go and meet her where she lived on the heath at west Hounslow (near what is now London's Heathrow airport) where the entrance to FAIRYLAND was supposedly located, with its marble palaces and horses the size of dogs.

PENETTE is a type of French HOUSE FAIRY or LUTIN.

PEOPLE OF PEACE is an Irish euphemism for the fairies.

PEOPLE OF THE HILLS is an Irish euphemism for fairies.

PERCHTA or **Frau Percht** is a Germanic/Slavonic fairy, a form of BERCHTE, who carries the souls of

DEAD and yet-to-be-born children around with her, as she tends the plants. She brings the storms and leads the WILD HUNT, accompanied by the souls of humans who have died an unnatural death. She was originally a fertility spirit, a bride of the sun. Her festival was celebrated in Austria well into the twentieth century in Salzburg, when the people wore masks; pretty ones representing spring and summer, ugly ones representing autumn and winter.

PERE NOEL is the French name for FATHER CHRISTMAS, a special once a year fairy visitor.

PERI or **FEROUERS** are the Persian good fairies, formed from FIRE, who are constantly at war with the DEEVS, the evil fairies. The lovely Peries feed on perfume, which repels the ugly Deevs as a happy side effect. They lived on the earth before humans. Originally the Peris were not so benign, and were the servants of the Lord of Evil, Ahriman. They were responsible for bad weather, poor harvests, comets and eclipses of the sun. In Islamic folklore, they became transformed into lovely maidens who guide human souls to paradise. Some claim that *peri* is the origin of the word 'fairy', imported into Western Europe with the Crusaders.

One story relates how a merchant's son dressed himself as a wandering dervish and travelled far from home. At sunset, as he rested at a pool, four doves descended and at once were transformed into lovely Peries. They disrobed and started to bathe. The man quickly gathered up their garments and hid them in a hollow tree. The peries looked in vain for their clothes and begged the young man to restore their garments. He consented on condition that one should become his wife. This was agreed and he took his new wife home, carefully concealing from her

the fairy clothing without which she could not escape. After ten years he again had to travel and left the fairy in the charge of an old woman, to whom he revealed his secret. While he was away the Peri cajoled the old woman into letting her put on the fairy CLOTHES for an instant, so that she might momentarily regain her native beauty. No sooner had she put them on than she vanished.

PERI BACALARI ('Fairy Chimneys') are natural rock formations in Turkey which are said to be the home of the fairies.

PERI-BANOU is a fairy or PERI who gave Prince Ahmed a magical APPLE which cured any disease.

PERIWINKLES (*Vinca major*) are wild flowers that attract fairies.

PERRY DANCERS is a name for the Northern Lights, thought to be fairies, in the eastern English county of Suffolk.

PERSÉVAY is a French HOUSE FAIRY who will be very helpful unless upset, when it will cause havoc.

P'TITES GENS ('Little People') is the Guernsey term for fairies. The Little People were very kindly disposed towards humans and mainly lived at the north end of this Channel Island. However, as time passed and they saw that humankind was becoming more evil they decided to forget human wickedness by drinking the water of a magic fountain, which caused oblivion. They all trouped off to the fountain and drank, but alas, it had no power to work on fairies, only humans. With the pain of their memories as vivid as ever they gathered together inside an ancient cromlech and hanged themselves with blades of grass. The trilithon was called *lé gibet des fairies* ('the fairies' gibbet') and near it was *la fontaine des faïes* ('the fairies' fountain'). Sadly these monuments no longer exist as the landowner broke up the stones

for building work and converted the fountain to a well.[259]

PETIT JEANNOT or **Jeannot** is a French HOUSE FAIRY or LUTIN.

PETITCRIEU was a fairy DOG given to the Arthurian hero Tristan by Duke Gilan. It came from AVALON and was a tiny, wondrously coloured beast with a tinkling bell around its neck.

PEY is a Tamil VAMPIRE fairy from Sri Lanka that drinks the blood of fallen and wounded warriors.

PEYMAKILIR is a female Tamil GHOUL who dances madly as she devours corpses.

PHARISEES is a strange English term for fairies in Suffolk, probably derived from the dialect double plural 'fairieses'. An alternative spelling is Farisees. The word is also known in Sussex, Hereford, Warwick and Worcestershire.

PHI is a Thai fairy that ranges through the forests and violently shakes those he meets, causing an ague. The victim must be placed beneath the tree he last rested under, from where the malaria spirit descended to him, and ceremonies must be performed to exorcise the spirit.

Phi were nature fairies who inhabited trees, streams, open spaces, mountains, valleys and so on, in the manner of NYMPHS.

PHI NANG MAI are Thai DRYADS. Even though these are part of the pre-Buddhist mythology, the sacred trees around temples are known as *Phi nang mai* 'female tree spirit'.

PHILYRA is the NYMPH of the linden tree in ancient Greek myth.

PHOOKA, Phouka, Pooka or **Púca** is an Irish goblin who can appear as a GOAT, a HORSE, a DOG, a bull or an eagle. He is always black with blazing eyes and usually has something of the

goat about him. His name may be derived from *poc*, which means 'he-goat'.[260] The term pooka appears in Middle English and stands for the devil. He may take the form of a shaggy colt with chains, a goat, ass, dog, eagle, bull and even, like the Kilkenny Phooka, a fleece of wool that rolls around the fields near the Dun of Coch-na-Phuca, making a buzzing noise to frighten the cattle. The term phooka is often used to refer to the DEVIL and 'playing the phooka' means playing the devil[261] i.e. being wicked.

The Irish call HALLOWEEN 'Phooka Night'. After this time the Phooka blights any crops remaining in the fields and makes the BLACKBERRIES unfit to eat,[262] a service performed by the devil in France.

The Brothers Grimm thought that the Phooka was comparable with the German MAHR in that it sits among the REEDS and ALDER bushes and leaps onto the back of a passing traveller and rides them until they are exhausted. The Phooka delights especially in haunting the dreams of drunkards. Phookas are horse dealers, and one might appear as a swarthy man mounted on a good horse, or might visit a racecourse in an invisible form.

In horse form, the Phooka offers rides to weary travellers, then takes off at a mad pace, before dumping them in a ditch and galloping away laughing. When he is not bruising and battering travellers with wild rides, the Phooka can be friendly and if he is well treated he will help farmers and millers. One day Phadrig fell asleep in an old mill, and when he woke he was astounded to witness six little fairies and an old man in tattered clothing who directed them to mill the corn. He felt sorry for the old Phooka in his tattered clothes, so one day he bought a fine silk suit and laid it out on the floor of the mill. The delighted Phooka put it on and declared that he was now a fine gentleman and would grind the corn no more.[263] *See also* PUCK.

PHOOKA NIGHT is an Irish name for HALLOWEEN. *See also* PHOOKA.

PHOOKA SPIT is an Irish term for a snail. *See also* PHOOKA.

PHYNNODDEREE, Fenoderee or **Fenodyree** ('Hairy man of the Wild Woods') are hairy, long-armed powerful Manx HOUSE FAIRIES who are more than willing to help farmers they like, though they are not very bright and one was once tricked into trying to fetch water in a sieve.

A Fenoderee once volunteered to bring in a shepherd's flock, but was gone for what seemed to the shepherd to be a very long time. Eventually, the phynnodderee turned up, tired and breathless, complaining that the little brown sheep had given him more trouble than all the rest. The shepherd checked his flock and was astonished to find a hare, rounded up with the sheep.

One farmer of Ballochrink was so grateful to a Fenoderee that he laid out a suit of CLOTHES for him as a gift, but the fairy was so offended by these that he lifted up each item in turn and described the ills that each would bring with it. Then he went off to be alone at Glen Rushen.

PICKATREE-BRAG or **Picktree Brag** is a fairy that assumes the form of a pony or small HORSE to prowl around the vicinity of Chester and Durham. Should anyone try to ride him, he will tip him or her into a pond and go off in a high good humour.

PIGS are a matter of great interest to fairies and a number of fairy pigs also appear in various locales. There are tales of fairy pigs in the ISLE OF MAN. At Andover in Hampshire, a fairy pig is seen on New Year's Eve. Pigs are allied to gods and goddesses of the UNDERWORLD, which may account for their association with fairies, also associated with the DEAD and underworld realms. In Celtic legend, pigs are mystical creatures, originating with the spirits in the OTHERWORLD. Their flesh was associated with feasts of the dead and was otherwise taboo. In Celtic myth, swineherds were honoured as magicians and prophets.

PIGHT is another term for PUCK.

PIGMY or **Pygmy** have been proposed as a folk memory of a forgotten race of human beings, which originated the concept of fairies. One whimsical hypothesis[264] suggested that fairies were a tribe of African or Mongolian pygmies that migrated into Europe.[265] Certainly, fairies are often described as being small, and there are many legends of pigmies around the world. The ancient Egyptian pharaoh Assa spoke of seeing a pigmy brought from the land of Punt (Somaliland). Homer mentioned an annual warfare between pigmies and cranes, probably the origin of the Greek PITIKOS, miniature fairies who every year are threatened by migrating cranes and have to take arms to drive off the birds from their tiny cattle.

PIGWIGEON, Pillywiggin or **Pilliwiggin** is an English term for a very small fairy. In popular folklore, they are tiny, delicate creatures who live amongst wild flowers.

PILOSI are nature fairies or WILD MEN of ancient Gaul. They look like hairy men with the legs and feet of GOATS. A HORSESHOE nailed to the HEARTH will encourage them to the fireside. They were mentioned by Isidorus at the beginning of the seventh century.

PILWIZ or **Bockschitt** is a German fairy who takes pleasure in causing ELFLOCKS in human hair or beards. It lives in the mountains, where it fires ELF-BOLTS at trespassers. The pilwiz has dark skin, likes to wear linen and three-cornered hats. He comes out at night with a sickle tied to his left foot to raid cornfields. To stop this, a farmer must either catch the pilwiz in the act, which will cause it to die for a year, or throw corn cut by the pilwiz into a newly dug grave. Both these operations are highly dangerous. The first act should be carried out at noon on St. John's Day (MIDSUMMER's Day), but if the pilwiz should see the farmer first, the man will die. For the second remedy, the farmer should take care not to let any of his sweat fall into the grave, or as the ears of corn rot he will sicken and die. A much easier option is to take some stubble from the pillaged field and hang it up in smoke, which will cause the troublesome fairy to waste away. The farmer might also throw an IRON knife with three crosses cut in it at the fairy, crying: 'Take that, Bilbze!'

PIN is the usual offering to the fairies or guardian spirits of a wishing well. Pins are generally considered to be lucky and you must be sure to pick it up if you see one on the ground. Pins will even protect you from the attentions of some evil fairies. An old rhyme runs:

'Find a pin, pick it up
And all day long you'll have good luck'

PINCH is an ELF associated with ROBIN GOODFELLOW.[266]

PINKET is WILL O' THE WISP from Worcseter in the English Midlands. They are said to be the spirits of UNBAPTISED CHILDREN.

PISACA is a Hindu GOBLIN or GHOUL that lives on human corpses but which is sometimes seen in water upon which the sun is shining.

PISGIES are the small, white moths that flit about in the evening, in Cornwall, south west England. They are thought to be the souls of DEAD children. *See also* PIXIES and BUTTERFLIES.

PISHASAS are evil fairies which are much dreaded in India. When women move about the forests, they must propitiate the Pishasas with offerins laid in crevices, sacred stones and hollow trees.

PISHOGUE is an Irish fairy spell, the equivalent of the Scottish GLAMOUR, which makes one thing seem to be another. The term can also mean a tall story.[267]

PISKIES (s. pisky or Pisky) are Cornish PIXIES. They are described as dapper little old men with bright eyes and white waistcoats, green stockings and highly polished shoes that gleam with diamond dew. Some say that they ride around on snails. Belief in them was once absolute, and every cottage had a 'pisky pow' placed on the roof's ridge tiles to give the fairies a dancing place. They live in the prehistoric structures scattered across the Cornish countryside, which are sometimes called 'Piskies' Halls' or Piskies' Craws' (a craw being a shed). They were often called 'the mite' or little ones. When a ring of MUSHROOMS appeared in a field in the morning, the old folks would point to them and exclaim that the fairies had been dancing there.

In the town of Penzance, people believed in two kinds of piskies, one dwelling on land, the other on the seastrand, and this was sometimes identified with the BUCCA. Those humans favoured by the piskies (usually WITCHES) were given a green ointment with which to annoint their eyes. This would make them invisible and in this condition, they could join in the fairy revels. After HALLOWEEN you cannot eat the blackberries, since the fairies have gone over them, making them unfit.

A legend tells of a boy from St Allen, near the small cathedral city of Truro, who went into a copse to pick wild flowers. He disappeared for THREE days, but was later found sleeping in the very copse where he had vanished. The boy told his family that he had followed a beautiful bird song into the woods, then night fell, the stars were shining, and he realised that each star

was a piskie. They had led him into a CAVE with marvellous crystal pillars that were studded with jewels of every colour. He had been fed on the purest honey and the piskies had sung him to sleep. When he woke up he was back in the copse.

Many Cornish folk believe that pixies are the SOULS of the prehistoric dwellers of Britain, and they are getting smaller and smaller until they will eventually vanish completely.

PITIKOS are miniature fairies of the Greek Islands that are only 30 cm high (about one foot). Every year they are threatened by migrating cranes and have to take arms to drive off the birds from their tiny COWS. Homer mentioned an annual warfare between pigmies and cranes.

PITZLN is a German HOUSE FAIRY.

PIXIE, Pisgies, Pixys, Piskies, or **Pigseys** (s. **Pixie** or **Pixy**) are little GREEN fairies found in the English West Country. Dartmoor in particular is alive with them and many places there are named after them including Pixie's Holt, Pixie's Cave and Pixie's Parlour. They like to dance in the shadow of standing stones and caper at stream edges, and the bells they wear are often heard tinkling across the moors or sounding deep within their fairy MOUNDS. They steal the wild ponies at night and wildly ride them across the heath, twisting and knotting their manes. Some say that they can turn themselves into hedgehogs if they choose. In Devon, pixies are said to be the souls of DEAD children.

One of the pixies' favourite games is to lead travellers astray, and this is called being pixy-led. One Devonshire farmer could not find his way out of his own fields until he remembered to turn his coat inside out, whereupon the pixies flew away into the trees, where they sat and laughed.

A woman, accompanied by two children, crossed the northern borders of Dartmoor. When she got home one

of the children was missing. All the neighbours set out with lanterns and eventually found him sitting beneath a large OAK tree, known to be the haunt of pixies. He said that he had been led away by two large bundles of rags that had stayed with him until the lights of the lanterns appeared, when they vanished.[268]

Though usually mischievous, pixies can be as helpful as HOUSE FAIRIES. Some Dartmoor pixies threshed the wheat a farmer left in his barn, and every morning he found a fresh pile of grain. In return he left them bread and cheese. One day all the wheat was harvested and all the grain threshed, but he still heard the sound of flails at night and the next morning there was yet more grain. He didn't question where it was coming from and continued to leave bread and cheese until his grain stores were filled to bursting.

The name pixie may relate to a Scandinavian word PYSKE, denoting a small fairy.

PIXY-LED is a term for being led astray by fairies. In the English Midlands, the equivalent is Mab-led. Should you find that you are lost in familiar territory it may be the fault of mischievous fairies. To find your path again, turn your CLOTHES inside out and this will confuse them long enough to allow you to escape.

PLAKSY is a HAG fairy who prowls through villages at night to torment children in Eastern European folklore. A child is best protected by placing an IRON knife beside the cradle, or an axe beneath it.

PLANINKINJA VILA is a Balkan mountain fairy, living on high peaks or in CAVES.

PLANT ANNWN ('Underworld Family') are the Welsh fairies that dwell in the UNDERWORLD realms beneath water. Arawn (once a Celtic god of the underworld) rules them.

They come out to hunt and possess much wealth in the form of COWS.[269] In Celtic stories the entrances to the OTHERWORLD is often through water. *See also* WATER FAIRIES.

PLANT RHYS DWFEN ('Family of Rhys Dwfen') are beautiful, small and, unusually amongst their kind, honest Welsh fairies. They are ruled over by the mysterious Rhys Dwfen. The land where they live is INVISIBLE because of a certain herb that grows on it. The Plant Rhys Dwfen amuse themselves by going to local auctions where they love to outbid all the other buyers. They are possibly half-human.

PLENTYN-NEWID ('Changeling') is a Welsh fairy baby left in place of a human one.

PLUTO is the Roman god of the UNDERWORLD and the DEAD, demoted to a king of the fairies by mediaeval writers.[270]

POBEL VEAN ('Small People') are the small and gentle fairies of Cornwall in south west England that pass their time in feasting and dancing. The female fairies are pale and fair, and wear crinolines and pointed hats. They are adorned with fine lace and jewels. The males are dark skinned and dress as hunters or soldiers or wear pale blue coats and green breeches. They wear tricorn hats decorated with lace and silver bells. Both males and females have large, brown eyes, and never seem to be older than twenty-five or thirty. They are believed to be the living souls of old Pagans who, having refused Christianity, are doomed to remain alive, decreasing in size until they vanish completely. You can see the Pobel Vean if you place a four-leaf clover on your head.

PODOVNA are Balkan WATER FAIRIES that live in springs, streams and lakes. They come ashore on moonlit nights.

POGANICA is a Dalmatian WEATHER FAIRY that rides the racing storm clouds, bringing hail and rain to damage crops.

POKEY-HOKEY is an eastern English BOGEYMAN.[271]

POLEDNICA ('Midday Spirit') is a Bohemian fairy that appears as a WHITE LADY or as a HAG who wanders about the fields at midday or haunts human houses. When sudden winds gust, she is amongst them and her touch causes sudden death. Occasionally, she will appear as a young girl carrying a whip. Should she cross the path of a young man and strike him with the whip he will die at an early age. If women who have recently given birth are foolish enough to go out at midday, they are at risk of being ambushed by the Polednica. Should a child be left unattended in the fields at harvest time it may be KIDNAPPED by her. Naughty children are threatened with the words: 'if you don't behave, the Polednica will carry you off!'

POLEDNICE is a female western Slavonic fairy who carries off women in childbed and keeps them for a year.

POLEVIK or **Polevoy** (*pole*, meaning 'field') are fairies of the Russian cornfields that grow with the grain and after the harvest shrink to the size of the stubble. A polevik will retreat before the harvesters and hide in the last few stalks or corn. When these are cut he gets into the hands of the reapers and is taken to the barn with the final sheaf.

If people wander into the fields at the wrong time, they disturb the fairies who will cause them to cut themselves with the sickle, though if you say the paternoster backwards for thirty minutes you will be safe. The bark of a certain tree will cure any wound inflicted by the fairy. A polevik often kicks awake harvesters who have fallen asleep on the job.

After late September, they claim any grain that has not been harvested. Sometimes farmers in Poland pour them libations and leave grain in the fields for them. It is said that cornflowers attract the polevik and that they like to spin FLAX. The males dress in white but have GREEN hair and dark skin, while the females are clad in WHITE and have dark complexions and hair, appearing at noon carrying sickles. They are most often seen at noonday or dusk and it is unwise to sleep in the fields at these times. The Polevik rides about the fields on horseback and will trample down the sleepers or inflict illness on them. He strangles drunkards who trample the grain. The polevik was probably once a vegetation god or corn spirit, now demoted to the status of a fairy.

POLEWIKI ('Field Spirit') are Polish field fairies equivalent to the Russian POLEVIK. *Pole* means 'field', hence the name of the country 'Poland'. He appears as a DWARF with grass for hair and eyes of different colours, wearing a completely black, or a completely WHITE outfit. He appears at noon or sunset and will harm anyone that he finds asleep or drunk during the harvest period. If you have thus angered a Polewiki and have been struck by disease, then you must place two eggs and an old rooster in a ditch when no one is looking.

POLONG are evil sea fairies of the Pacific who fought some of the traditional Maori heroes of New Zealand.

POLTERSPRITES are German shapeshifting HOUSE FAIRIES who delight in going poltering i.e. making a dreadful noise about the house. Though today people tend to think of poltergeists ('knocking spirits') as ghosts they are probably synonymous with these noisy fairies, who have cousins all round the world, like the knocker, kobold etc. They scamper over the ceiling while you are trying to sleep, rattle the pots and pans while you are eating your dinner, bang the wainscoting, make the doors creak and throw stones at the roof while you are sitting quietly. They prophesy a death in the family by making an even greater racket. They may appear as squirrels, CATS or little old men dressed in grey or GREEN, or become invisible by putting on their *tarnkappen* or RED CAPS.

POLUDNICA ('Midday Spirit' or 'Lady Midday' from *poluden*, meaning 'noon') is a Moravian spirit who looks like an old woman or HAG in a WHITE dress. She has matted hair, slanting eyes and an unpleasant face. Instead of feet she has HORSE's hooves. She carries a scythe.

The Eastern Slavonic peoples believe that the Poludnica appears as a lovely young girl dressed in white. She walks about the fields and twists the necks of those she finds working there at midday, causing them severe pain. She lures young children into the corn in order to steal them away. The Siberians see her as an old woman or HAG with thick, curly hair who is nearly naked and lives in clumps of nettles or reeds. She KIDNAPS naughty children.

In some regions, noon is a traditional time for ghosts and spirits. Lady Midday is also the whirlwind that often manifests in spinning dust clouds during the heat of noon in the summer. In tales, she appears when the day is hottest and weakens people or drives them mad, perhaps sunstroke personified, illustrating the dangers of working in the midday heat.

POLUDNICA, Potudniówka or Przypotudica (Midday Spirit') is a dangerous Polish fairy who looks like a tall woman dressed in a long WHITE robe, carrying a sharp sickle. In the summer she stays in the woods or fields and chases humans who venture there, asking them riddles or difficult questions. If they cannot answer, she

will punish them with various illnesses or bad luck. When she leaves her usual haunts to hunt women and children SEVEN huge BLACK DOGS accompany her. During stormy weather, she may suddenly appear in cottages. The Poles attribute a variety of natural phenomena to her.

POLUNOCNICA ('Female Thing of Midnight') is a Slavonic female DEMON who torments children in the middle of the night.

POLUVIRICA ('Half Believer') is a Slavonic forest fairy who appears naked, with pendulous breasts, a long face and three braids of hair down her back. She usually carries a child. The Poluvirica is the spirit of a dead Pagan.

POLYHYMNIA or POLYMNIA ('Many Hymned') is one of the nine MUSES, the patroness of sacred poetry who inspired many of the great poets, as well as mime, agriculture, geometry and meditation. She is usually depicted looking reflective or veiled.

POPPELE is a noisy German HOUSE FAIRY.

PORESKORO is the child of ANA, Queen of the Fairies, and the King of the LOÇOLICO or DEMONS in Romany folklore. He has four dogs' heads, four cats' heads, and a tail like a snake with a forked tongue. He causes all the worst diseases seen amongst humankind, such as plague and cholera.

PORTUNES or Portuni are Britain's oldest recorded fairies, described by the historian Gervase of Tilbury (1211). He reported that:

'It is their nature to embrace the simple life of comfortable farmers, and when, on account of their domestic work, they are sitting up at night, when the doors are shut, they warm themselves at a fire, and take little frogs out of their bosom, roast them on the coals, and eat them'.[272]

Portunes have the features of old men with wrinkled cheeks, and they are of a very small stature, according to Gervase *dimidium pollicis* or half a thumb tall, though some say he may have meant *pedis* making it half a foot tall, or six inches (15 cm).[273] They wear coats made of tiny patches of cloth. They live in deserted farmhouses. Though they have the power to serve and not to injure, they are fond of practical jokes. They sometimes grab the bridles of night travellers and lead them into ponds, then go off laughing heartily. In other respects they act as HOUSE FAIRIES carrying goods into the house and finishing farm chores faster than any human could. These tasks they would carry out in return for a bowl of MILK or dish of cream. It is said that if you can capture one, it must grant you a wish.

POTAMIDS are NYMPHS that inhabit and guard rivers in Greek myth.

POULPIKANS are old Breton fairies that live in dank places such as swamps and bogs. They are hairy, small and dark. They are possibly a type of KORRED.

POUQUES are the solitary fairies of Guernsey in the Channel Islands, perhaps the equivalent of the English PUCK. The term pouque was synonymous with DEVIL and they were cited as such during the WITCH trials. Many confessed to seeing a pouque, a little man wheeling around a barrow load of parsnips.

Unlike the handsome English fairies that are reputed to dwell on Guernsey, the pouques are stunted, ugly, with shaggy hair and long, powerful arms. They dress in tattered clothes. They may be mischievous or downright bad tempered but will occasionally act like HOUSE FAIRIES and help out around the house or farm, especially at harvest time. If a maid puts out some unfinished knitting and a bowl of cream, she may find the bowl empty and the knitting finished in the morning. However, like other such helpers, they are offended by gifts of CLOTHES and will disappear forever if given any. Pouques dislike lazy people and instead of helping them will punish them with kicks and punches. Pouques will always reward a good turn done to them. The islanders think of them as Pagans as they are frightened away by Christian symbols and any talk of religion.

Pouques possess a magical GLAMOUR that can make objects appear to be other than they are, such as making a CAVE seem to be a splendid hall filled with gold. There are several tales of MIDWIVES being taken to a magnificent chamber to attend a fairy birth, when she accidentally gets FAIRY OINTMENT in her eye, she sees that the chamber is only a cave. When the pouques find that she has the magical sight, they put out her eye.

The fairy women spin FLAX grown in field above their MOUNDS. The flattened holed discs sometimes dug up are called *les rouels des faitots* or 'the fairies' SPINNING wheels'. They are thought to be lucky charms.[274]

POVODUJI is a WATER FAIRY from the Italian-Southern Slavonic border, similar to the Russian VODIANOI.

POWRIES haunt the peel towers and ruined fortresses of the Scottish Borders. They make a sound that resembles the beating of FLAX. When this sound grows particularly loud, it heralds death or disaster. They are related to or possibly identical with the DUNTERS.

POZEMNE VILA are Balkan mountain fairies who live on high peaks, hilltops, or sometimes valleys and CAVEs.

PRÃY are evil fairies of Cambodia that inhabit trees and lay in wait to attack travellers by throwing ELF BOLTS at them, injuring or

sometimes killing them. Some say that they are the spirits of women who have died in childbirth, or the spirits of UNBORN CHILDREN.

PREMIEN ('Changelings') are CHANGELING babies substituted by the Bohemian wild women the DIVOZENKY.

PREINSCHEUHEN is a Bavarian fairy who lives in the oat and millet fields to protect the grain.

PRESSINA is the fairy mother of MELUSINA.

PRIMROSE (*Primula vulgaris*) is a fairy flower. It can make the INVISIBLE appear visible, and to eat primroses is

PROTEUS See *THE OLD MAN OF THE SEA*

a sure way to see fairies. If you touch a fairy rock with the correct number of primroses (probably thirteen) in a posy, it will open to FAIRYLAND and fairy gifts; but the wrong number opens the door to doom.

In one story, a young girl touched a fairy rock accidentally with a bunch of primroses and the fairies came out, gave her many prsents and showed her the way home. An old miser heard the tale and tried to repeat the experiment. However, he had the incorrect number of primroses in his bouquet, and was never seen again. Like other yellow flowers, primroses are associated with the DEVIL. If a nosegay has thirteen primroses, it must be negated by the addition of violets, or it is unlucky to take it into a house or church.

In Ireland, primroses are scattered on the THRESHOLD in order to

prevent fairies from entering a house. In south west England, in Somerset, thirteen primroses were laid under a baby's cradle as protection against it being stolen by fairies. In central England, in Buckinghamshire, primrose balls were hung over the house and cowshed door on MAY EVE to protect them from malicious fairy attentions.

PRIPOLDNICA or **Prezpoldnica** ('Midday Spirit') is a fairy of the Lusatian Serbs who looks like a young woman or HAG, dressed in white and carrying a sickle. She guards the growing corn from thieves and punishes anyone who treads the ears down.

She will leave the woods where she lives at midday to appear to people working in the fields. These unfortunates will have to talk to her about a single subject - without hesitation or deviation, presumably - for one hour. If they fail they will fall ill or even forfeit their heads. She might also ask difficult questions about the cultivation of hemp or FLAX and again, those who cannot answer correctly will be punished. Her favourite victims are young children or women who have recently given birth.

PROMETHEUS was the progenitor of the first ELF, a male fairy that married a FAY or female fairy from the Gardens of Adonis, and from them the nation of fairies descended.[275]

PROPHECY is a gift possed by all fairies. Yet, whilst able to see the future, they do not often choose to share it with humans. Nevertheless, they are able to confer the gift of prophecy on their favourites such as Biddy Early and other WITCHES.

The word prophecy is derived from the Greek and means 'speaking before'. However, the original meaning was slightly different, and the job of a prophet was to allow a god or spirit to speak though him or her, as the

priestesses at Delphi acted as the oracles of Apollo. A prophet was a SHAMAN, communicating with spirits and bringing back their messages to the wider community.

PROSERPINA is the Roman goddess of the UNDERWORLD and the DEAD, demoted by mediaeval writers to a queen of the fairies.

PROTECTION FROM FAIRIES is an important requirment. According to Irish, British and European folklore, unless careful precautions are taken, evil fairies may gain entrance to your property by a variety of methods, where they will delight in causing untold damage. They can gain admission into homes by means of the last of the baking, called the *fallaid bannock,* unless a hole is put into it, a piece broken off, or a red hot coal placed on top of it. They can also enter by means of the water in which men's FEET have been washed. Unless the fire has been properly raked and banked up to keep it alive for the night, the fairies will come down the chimney.

There are several effective methods which can be employed to protect against the attentions of fairies:
- If fairies are troubling you or if you are being pixie-led on a journey, turn your CLOTHES inside out and this will confuse them long enough to allow you to make your escape.
- If a friend has been dragged into a fairy ring, toss one of your GLOVES inside and the revellers will disperse.
- To keep fairies out of your bedroom scatter FLAX on the floor.
- Fairies will not enter a house with ivy growing on the walls.
- Fairies are terrified of IRON and they will vanish immediately on being shown any form of the metal. Keep a knife or a nail in your pocket and under your pillow at night. In Russia a scythe was hung over the house door at night. A horseshoe hung over the door will keep fairies out.
- Fairies are afraid of Christian

symbols such as bibles and crucifixes; drawing a cross on cakes will stop fairies dancing on them.
- There are a number of old Pagan symbols which will keep out fairies, such as a HOLED STONE, or a PIG's head or pentacle drawn on the door.
- A ROWAN cross tied with RED THREAD will offer protection when hung in a high place in the house or byre.
- The besom or BROOM can be placed beside the HEARTH to prevent fairies coming down the chimney.
- A Witch Bottle (a glass bottle containing sharp objects such as nails and PINS, ASHES, SALT and rowan wood) can be buried before the doorstep.
- Bells scare away fairies. The bells on Morris Men's costumes offer them protection from fairies and other spirits.
- Fairies don't like to catch sight of themselves in mirrors, so a mirror facing any point where they might enter a house, such as opposite a door or window, will deter them.
- FIRE is the great preventative against fairy magic - a ring of fire will protect a child, a cow, a woman, a house or a man (BEWARE! This is obviously as equally dangerous to the person being protected).
- If oatmeal is sprinkled on clothes or carried in the pocket no fairy will approach. To prevent fairies taking the baking, a final bannock is made with a hole through it.
- Stale urine can be sprinkled over cattle, doorposts and the walls of houses on the last evening of every quarter of the year to keep off the fairies.
- Trailing Pearlwort (known in Gaelic as mothan or moan) protects its possessor from fire and the attacks of fairy women.
- ST. JOHN'S WORT prevents the fairies carrying off people while they sleep.
- When children were pining away and were fairy-struck, the juice of twelve leaves of FOXGLOVE were

given (please note that this is deadly poisonous).

- On the last night of the year fairies are kept out by the holly decorations. The last handful of reaped corn should be made into a harvest maiden or corn dolly and hung up in the house to keep them out till the next harvest.
- Parents should adorn their children with daisy chains to protect children on May Eve.
- A mulberry tree in your garden will keep away fairies. At the dangerous times of Midsummer and Midwinter you should dance around it counter-clockwise - possibly the origin of the rhyme 'Here we go Round the Mulberry Bush'.
- Ground ivy is a magic charm against the unwanted attentions of fairies.

PSAMATHE is one of the NEREID.

PSCIPOLNITSA is the Wend (German Slav) version of the POLUDNICA. She appears carrying shears, a symbol of death.

PSEZPOLNICA is a southern Slavonic field spirit equivalent to the POLUDNICA.

PSOTNIK or Psotnica are Slavonic ELVES or mischievous fairies.

PUCA are English fairies that inhabit wells, barrows and pits. The word is an Old English form of PUCK.

PUCK, Poake or Pouke is a mischievous English fairy of the woods who likes to play tricks on humans and can make them dance with his sweet piping. He is sometimes described as the jester of the fairy court and appears in this role in Shakespeare's *A Midsummer Night's Dream*. In mediaeval times he was characterised as a DEMON but later became associated with the good but mischievous ROBIN GOODFELLOW, Jack Robinson and even ROBIN HOOD.

Puck can SHAPESHIFT into a HORSE, which will trick people into riding it. He may act like a helpful HOUSE FAIRY if he feels like it, or mislead travellers as a WILL O'THE WISP. In parts of Worcestershire peasants claimed to be 'Poake led' into ditches and bogs by the mysterious fairy before it disappeared with a loud laugh. In the Midlands this was called being 'pouk-ledden' and is the same as being PIXY-LED.

He is sometimes described as having the head of a youth and the body of a GOAT. Like the god PAN he has a lusty nature, small horns on his head, and carries musical pipes. It may be that he is the fairy remnant of the ancient horned gods or nature spirits, since there originally seem to have been a race of pucks. He is never seen between HALLOWEEN and the vernal equinox and is usually accompanied by a variety of animals. Other descriptions have him as rough and hairy or as an innocent child, but he is a shapeshifter and can appear as a horse, eagle, or a donkey.

He is related to the Welsh PWCA and the Irish PHOOKA, the Norwegian PUKJE, the Danish PUGE, the Swedish PUKE, the old

Norse PUKI, the Latvian PUKIS, the German PUKS and the Baltic PUK. The derivations of these names are usually given as meaning a DEMON or malignant spirit and in *Piers Plowman*, Langland called Hell 'Pouk's Pinfold'. Pouk was used in mediaeval times as a nickname for the devil.

PUCK-HAIRY is a creature that appears in seventeenth-century accounts as a HOBGOBLIN or witches FAMILIAR.

PUDDLEFOOT is a BROWNIE who haunted Altmor Burn in Perthshire. He could be heard splashing and paddling in the burn, and then he would go on wet feet to the nearby farm. If everything were left untidy he would tidy it, but if everything were left neat he would mess it up. It was counted unlucky to meet him on the road at night. Then one night, a man was returning, drunk, from the market and heard the brownie splashing about in the water and cried out convivially, 'Well, Puddlefoot, how is it with you?' The brownie was horrified. 'Oh, no!' he cried, 'They've given me a name! They call me Puddlefoot!' and disappeared, never to be seen again. It seems that giving a brownie a NAME is as effective as giving him a suit of CLOTHES.

PUG is a small DEVIL or PUCK.

PUGE is a mischievous Danish fairy analogous with PUCK.

PUK is a Baltic HOUSE FAIRY that sometimes appears as a small DRAGON. They are known to retrieve stolen treasure and restore it to the master of their chosen household. They are probably related to PUCK and PHOOKA.

PUKE is the Swedish form of PUCK.

PUKI is the Old Norse form of PUCK.

PUKIS is the Latvian and Lithuanian form of PUCK.

PUKJE is a Norwegian fairy analogous with PUCK.

PUKMIS are the wild spirits of the woods, the souls of men who have nearly drowned, in the folklore of the Nootka tribe of Native Americans.

PUKS is the Low German form of PUCK.

PULCH is a wood fairy who dwells in the Kammerforst, punishing those who steal wood or damage forest trees.

PULTER KLAES is a noisy German HOUSE FAIRY, synonymous with a POLTERSPRITE or KNOCKER.

PULTER-CLAAS is the Dutch version of PULTER KLAES. The name seems to mean something like Nick-Knocker, since Claas is short for Nicolaus.

PUMPHUT is a German HOUSE FAIRY who will work hard for food once a week and on holidays. He will do most of the farm work as well as the housework, clean out the stables and byres and chastise lazy servants. He can foretell the future and is loyal to his chosen human family, unless slighted, when they will leave. He wears a RED CAP.

PUNDACCIÚ is a Sardinian fairy who dresses like a monk with seven RED hoods. If one of these is stolen, he will die.

PURZINIGELE ('Tumbling Goat'?) is one of the many fairies whose NAME must be guessed.

Long ago a rich and mighty count was hunting in a forest when a NÖRGLEIN suddenly appeared before him. The little man said that the count had trespassed on his territory and must pay a penalty. He demanded the count's death or his beloved wife in payment. The count apologised for infringement and offered anything in his power except his dear wife. Eventually the dwarf seemed to relent a little and said that if the count's wife could guess his name within THREE attempts in one month's time she should be free. Otherwise, he would seize her and make her his own wife.

With a heavy heart the count returned home and told his wife all that had happened. She became pale and wept. The previously happy castle and its environs became a sad place. The weeks went by and the time came for the dwarf to make his first call. The countess guessed: 'Fir, Pine, Spruce', since she thought a forest spirit might have the name of a tree, but none of these was his name. He returned the next day and she guessed again: 'Oat, Buckwheat, Maize'; but none of these was right. The dwarf disappeared with a grin, promising to return the next day arrayed for his wedding.

The countess was close to despair, knowing that unless she correctly guessed his name at the next attempt she would belong to the repulsive dwarf. She wandered in the woods, hoping for some inspiration and all at once came upon a lonely cottage. From within the cottage a voice issued, singing gleefully: 'It is good that the countess does not know that Purzinigele is my name!'

The next morning the dwarf turned up bright and early dressed in his finest doublet of red and gold. 'Well?' he asked. 'Pur,' hazarded the countess.'Wrong!' he answered.'Goat', she tried again.

The dwarf blushed and hesitated, since the word 'GOAT' (*ziege*) was indeed part of his name. He hurriedly said 'No, not right, guess again and be quick!'

'Purzinigele!' exclaimed the countess, triumphantly. The dwarf stamped his foot and disappeared in high dudgeon.[276] *See also* TOM TIT TOT and RUMPELSTILTSKIN.

PUSCHKAIT is a grumpy Prussian TREE FAIRY.

PUTZEN or **Butzen** ('Cleaner') is a German HOUSE FAIRY, possibly a subspecies of WICHTLN, but sometimes thought of as a ghost or REVENANT.

PUU-HALIJAD is a male Estonian fairy that lives in groves of trees behind houses.

PWCA or **Pwcca** are Welsh HOUSE FAIRIES, possibly related to the English PUCK, who can be helpful or unpleasant as they chose. It used to be the custom to leave food out for them.

One pwca tried to lure a man over a cliff one night by leading him on with a lantern, and indeed, the name pwca is sometimes applied to the ELLYLLDAN or Welsh WILL O'THE WISP. There are many tales of peasants returning home when they see a dusky figure before them, holding a lantern or candle over its head. After following it for several miles, the peasant finds himself on the brink of a precipice, with a raging river below him. The pwca jumps across the chasm, laughs and disappears.

A number of them are said to dwell in Cwm Pwca (Pwca's Valley) in Breconshire, and some claim that this was the original location of Shakespeare's *Midsummer Night's Dream*, and that Shakespeare was informed of the traditions of the Welsh fairies by his friend Richard Price.[277]

PYSKE is a Scandinavian term for a small fairy. *See also* PISKEYS, PIXIE.

PYSSLINGER-FOLK are Swedish fairies or MOUND FOLK, and expert shoemakers.

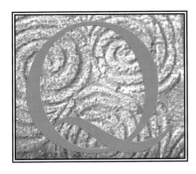

QUAELDRYTTERINDE is a NIGHTMARE fairy.

QUATERNICA leads a band of lost souls that appear in midwinter according to Balkan folklore. She is possibly cognate with the Slovene MITTWINTERFRAU and PERCHTA or HOLDA as leader of the WILD HUNT.

QUEEN OF THE SHORE is a modern Greek sea NYMPH who sings to lure men into the water in order to drown them, like an ancient SIREN.

QUEEN PICEL is the Queen of the LEPRECHAUNS of Blarney in Co. Cork, who rides a dragonfly.

QUEEN SUMMER rules the Native American fairies the ELVES OF LIGHT. Her presence causes winter to melt away and awakes the hibernating elves.

QUERXE are small and gentle fairies of the Harz Mountains region of eastern Germany.

QUERCIOLA is an Italian fairy who favours lovers and sweethearts.

QUETRONAMUN is a small fairy of the Araucanian Indians of Chile and Argentina. It has only one foot, possibly a code for a sacred MUSHROOM. Compare with SHADE FOOTS and FACHAN.

QUIET FOLK or 'Still Folk' is a common term for fairies found throughout Germany, Denmark, Holland, Poland, England and Russia. Such fairies generally live underground and avoid the sunlight, are small in stature, gentle and peaceful. They are master craftsmen, can brew beer, make bread, are excellent at SPINNING and skilful BLACKSMITHS. However, if they are wronged or slighted in any way, they will cause disruption, illness and madness.

RAGWORT (*Senecio jacobaea*) is a fairy plant. Fairies sometimes bury their TREASURES beneath ragwort stalks and these weeds are used as HORSES by fairies when they want to fly. The magic words to make them work are: 'Horse and Hattock!'. In saying this, the fairies are echoing the confession of the Scottish WITCH Isobel Gowdie (1662) who claimed witches flew by putting wild straws and corn stalks between their legs crying: 'Horse and hattock in the devil's name'. One Cornish man rode a ragwort to FAIRYLAND and back again. The association of ragwort, horses, witches and mischievous fairies may come from the fact that ragwort causes fatal poisoning in horses.

RAINBOWS are often associated with fairies. The LEPRECHAUN's pot of gold is found at the end of the rainbow, and the entrance to the OTHERWORLD may be via a Rainbow Bridge.

The ancient Norse folk believed that the rainbow bridge Bifrost accessed Asgard, the home of the gods. In Germanic countries the tradition still lingers that the rainbow is used by the souls of the dead to pass into heaven. Some Polynesian tribes say that a rainbow is a ladder to heaven. Archer gods, such as the Hindu Indra and the Finnish Ukko, used the rainbow as a bow to shoot thunder ARROWS. The Greek goddess of the rainbow was Iris, the emissary of the gods. In some cultures, the rainbow is associated with divine messages of forgiveness or blessing.

Conversely, in some parts of the world a rainbow is considered to be a bad omen or the manifestation of a DEMON. The Karens of Burma suppose that the rainbow is an evil spirit that devours human souls, while the Zulus of southern Africa consider that it is a supernatural SNAKE that descends to earth to drink from waterholes. Should any man be bathing in the pool he may be seized and eaten.

RAKSA or RAKSHASA are Hindu GOBLINS or GHOULS who haunt the cemeteries and like to eat human flesh or steal the MILK from COWS. Their power grows with the darkness, especially at the new moon, but they disappear with the first rays of the rising sun. Raksas can SHAPESHIFT but in their natural form they have red eyes and are betrayed by some DEFORMITY, like two mouths, tusks, bull's heads, bloated bellies or backward facing FEET and hands. Sometimes, the females appear as beautiful women in order to seduce holy men, afterwards devouring them. As soon as a female raksa conceives, she gives birth to a fully-grown raksa. The Raksas are ruled by a ten-headed king called RAVANA.

RÂN is the queen of MERMAIDS and WATER FAIRIES. She was originally a Norse goddess, the wife of Aegir, the sea god. She is very beautiful, can see the future and loves MUSIC. The souls of those drowned at sea go to live in her realms. It was in her honour that sailors wore a piece of gold in the form of an earring. When bad weather threatened the ship, they would throw it in the waves to placate her. Her daughters are the NINE Waves of the Sea.

RARASH is a Slavonic HOUSE FAIRY that lives in the HEARTH and appears as a hen, or as a small boy with claws. It will steal from neighbouring farms to bring gifts to its chosen family.

RAROG ('Whirlwind') is a Russian DWARF who turns himself into a whirlwind. To defeat him it is necessary to throw an IRON knife into the whirlwind. He also appears as a falcon or a dog.

RAROHENGA is the FAIRYLAND of the Polynesian fairies the TUREHU.

RATH is an ancient earthwork or fort, a circular meadow surrounded by a MOUND with overgrown furze bushes, sometimes called a 'Dane's Fort'. It is associated with fairies. It is said that when the ancient race moved out, the fairies moved in. They are sacred to the fairies, and if humans damage them, they will be punished with sickness. No mortal is allowed to cut down a tree on a rath or carry away a stone from one. According to Lady Wilde, the fairies would punish him by blasting his eyes or giving him a crooked mouth.

RAVANA is the ten-headed, twenty-armed king of the demon RAKSAS. He ruled the kingdom of Lanka until he was defeated by the Hindu god Rama, who stormed his castle in retaliation for the demon-kind having kidnapped Sita, Rama's wife. Ravana was imprisoned in a mountain for a thousand years, but can only be killed by a mortal.

RAVEN (*Corvus corax*) is considered to be a mysterious bird, associated with spirits, gods and fairies, though in early stories the raven is interchangeable with other members of the crow family. Ravens are carrion birds and were once a common sight, feeding on the corpses of the slain after a battle. This made them symbols of death and war; associated battle deities such as MACHA ('Raven'),

MORRIGAN, BABD and Nemain who could all take raven form. The Morrigan would become a raven on the battlefield and foretell the outcome of the conflict to the Dagda. Some say that her later Arthurian counterpart was MORGAN LE FAY who also appeared as a raven. In many places in Britain, ARTHUR is thought to have become a raven after death, and countrymen tip their hats to ravens in consequence. To kill one was a crime, and insulted Arthur.

Ravens are guardians of the UNDERWORLD fairy treasure. A fierce raven is said to guard the gold in the Chaw ('Raven') Gully mine in Cornwall. A stone obtained from raven's nests is called 'the raven stone' or 'stone of victory' and it helps to discover fairy TREASURE and aid in PROPHECY,

RAVIYOYLA DJINS are southern Slavonic fairies who have the appearance of lovely women. They know all the secrets of healing with herbs and can even bring the dead back to life.

RED is a colour that occurs in connection with fairies in a variety of ways. Some fairies are simply called 'red men' (Red Fairies, Red Hairy Men, Fear Dearg, Nain Rouge, Doine Beaga Ruadh), while others are described as having RED HAIR, as dressing in red, or as wearing RED CAPS.

It is tempting to dismiss this colour connection as having wholly to do with the FLY AGARIC mushroom; fairies are often depicted sitting on the red and white spotted cap of this fungus, and the red caps many wear may simply be a metaphor for the mushroom. Fly agaric is hallucinogenic and has a long history of use among European witches and SHAMANS as an aid in contacting spirits.

However, red is deeply linked with the supernatural. It is the colour of witchcraft; in fairy tales WITCHES often wear red cloaks, have red hair or

wear red caps. According to W. B. Yeats, Irish witches put little red caps on their heads before flying off to the sabbats. In England, the Sussex witch Granny Smith was nicknamed Old Mother Redcap.

Red is also associated with death in the Celtic world. Red food is described as the food of the DEAD, and is taboo for humans (see FAIRY FOOD). At death blood stops and congeals, so the red of flowing blood is a symbol of health, life, vitality, and strength.[278] During early burials corpses were painted with red ochre to endow them with renewed life. In Mesolithic Ireland, red ochre was applied to tools to give them magical potency. At the Hostel of Dá Derga ('the Red'), a doomed king saw THREE red haired riders, accoutred with red equipment, riding on three red horses.[279] Red horsemen convey the dead to the house of DONN, the god of the dead.

As the colour of spilt blood, red is a symbol of warning, danger, murder, cruelty, war, destruction, and Mars, the planet of war. The red-haired MORRIGAN is the Irish goddess of battle and death; red flags are employed by socialist revolutionaries; red meant a call to arms for the ancient Romans; the French revolutionaries wore red caps; and we still say 'caught red handed' when a person is discovered in the act of committing a felony.

There is a further connection between red and death. When the sun sets, it often turns red and is enveloped in red clouds. For the ancients, the sun was a god who died each night and sank into the UNDERWORLD to dwell with the dead. The red clouds are the flowing red hair of the death goddess who receives him each night and gives birth to him each morning as the birth-bloodied goddess of dawn. Such a goddess appears in triple aspect as the HESPERIDES, guardian NYMPHS of an APPLE island in the far west. They are named Aegle, which means 'brightness', Erythraea 'the red one', and Hespera 'evening light.'

Additionally, red is the colour of completion and harvest. In Roman times, red-haired puppies were sacrificed to influence the ripening of the corn, while in Egypt red-haired men were buried alive as a sacrifice to the god of the dead, Osiris.

In some cultures, red represents influence and authority. In China, the highest officials wore red buttons as a sign of their rank. Roman Catholic cardinals wear red hats and kings often dressed in red. Red carpets are still unrolled for VIPs. It is a powerful colour, emblematic of FIRE, and as such is protective, effective against psychic attack. Red coral has been worn since Roman times against the evil eye, while RED THREAD protects against evil witches and fairies. This protective ability extends to red plants, such as ROWAN.

RED CAMPION (*Silene vulgaris*) is a wild flower sacred to the fairies.

RED CAP or **Red Comb** is one of the bloodthirsty Scottish fairies. *See* REDCAPS.

RED CAPS are worn by many fairies, including Barabo, Buachaileen, Bwbachs, Clircaun, Dunter, Feeorin, Fudditu, Grigs, Hutchers, Kinkach Martinko, Kuwalden, Spriggans, Trolls, Niãriusar, Nisse and Nixie. The red caps may be a symbol for the FLY AGARIC mushroom, which has a red cap with white spots. Fly agaric is psychotropic and has a long history of use among European mystics and shamans. The effects of the mushroom include auditory and visual hallucinations and spatial distortions. Subjects commonly report sensations of flying, or seeing little people or red-hatted mushrooms dancing. *See also* RED.

RED ETIN ('Red Giant') was a particularly nasty THREE-headed OGRE who dwelt near Preston in the Scottish Borders. Once upon a time, there were two poor widows who were neighbours. One had two sons, and the other only one. The eldest son of the first widow decided to go off to seek his fortune. As a parting gift, he gave his brother his favourite knife, saying that as long as it remained bright and clean, they would know that he was well, but should it become rusted, he would have met with misfortune.

After a few days travel the boy came upon a shepherd who told him that the sheep he was guarding belonged to Red Etin, a fearsome ogre who had not yet met the man who could defeat him. The lad continued on his way, and as night fell came to a castle where he decided to seek shelter. The old woman that let him in made a space for him by the kitchen fire and told him to be careful, as the castle belonged to Red Etin.

Suddenly, the door flew open and the ogre himself marched in, all three of his noses sniffing for human blood. Seeing the boy he roared: 'Be he live or be he dead, his heart tonight shall kitchen my bread!' Seizing the youth in his massive hands, each head asked the youth a different question: Was Scotland or Ireland the first to be inhabited by men? Was man made for woman, or vice versa? What was made first, man or beast? The boy could only shake his head in bewilderment. At this the ogre struck him, and the unfortunate youth was turned to a pillar of stone.

Far away, his brother saw that the blade of the knife had turned rusty, and knew that some misadventure had befallen the lad. Bidding farewell to his mother and neighbours, he shouldered his pack and set off to discover what had become of his brother. Though the two widows waited anxiously, no word came, and they concluded that the second son had also been overcome by some misfortune.

The remaining boy saw that it fell to him to discover what had happened to his two friends, and despite his mother's entreaties took the same road as the other two. He travelled for several days, and soon his small supply of food was exhausted. As he sat down to eat his last bannock, a poor old woman approached and looked hungrily at the small loaf. Feeling sorry for her, the lad broke it in two and gave her half. In gratitude, the old woman, who was really a fairy, whispered to him the answers to three strange riddles and went on her way. Next the youth met the shepherd, who informed him that the sheep he guarded belonged to Red Etin the ogre and added, 'now I fear his destiny is at hand.'

When the boy reached the castle, he was shown into the kitchen and was just seating himself before the fire when the door flew open and the fearsome three-headed ogre marched in, all three of his noses sniffing for human blood. 'Be he live or be he dead, his heart tonight shall kitchen my bread!', he cried and seized the boy. Each of Red Etin's gruesome heads asked the youth a different question: Was Scotland or Ireland the first to be inhabited by men? Was man made for woman, or vice versa? What was made first, man or beast?

In reply, the boy whispered the answers the old fairy woman had given him. The ogre realised that he had met his match and fell back with a cry. The boy seized the wood axe and with one blow, cut off all the ogre's heads. No sooner was this accomplished, than the two other boys were released from their spell. The three happily returned home to their joyful mothers.

The remains of Etin's castle can still be seen in the Scottish Borders, near Preston in Berwickshire. And the answers to the three questions? Only the boy and the fairy know.[280]

RED HAIR is considered to be very unlucky. It is associated with the supernatural and with death. In Ireland, people with red hair were considered so unlucky that many houses would not grant them admission. The Celtic death and battle goddess MORRIGAN has red hair, and so do many fairies and legendary witches. In some cases, it is the red hair that betrays a character's fairy or supernatural origin. The ancient Egyptians associated red hair with evil gods like Set and numerous eastern and African DEMONS have red hair. There is often an instinctive, irrational aversion to red hair in some minds; Judas is said to have had red hair, and Indian Brahmins were forbidden to marry girls with red hair. *See also* RED.

RED HAIRY MEN are diminutive fairies of West Africa found on the Ivory Coast.

RED-HEADED MAN or **Red Haired Man** is an ambiguous figure. Although RED HAIR is usually regarded as being unlucky, in several fairy tales a red-headed fairy man is the one who acts as a benevolent *deus ex machina*.[281] He may warn people not to eat FAIRY FOOD, break fairy spells or free humans imprisoned in fairyland.

RED THREAD is used as a protective measure against fairies and WITCHES in both Britain and Ireland. The thread is bound around a cross of ROWAN wood and hung above the door or cattle byre:
 'Rowan tree and red thread
 Leave the witches all in dread'
 Red thread across the door will prevent fairies entering a property and a necklace of red thread is worn by a child as a protection from the Indian spirit the ACHERI.

REDCAPS, Red Caps, Red Combs or **Bloody Caps** are vicious Lowland Scottish fairies that haunt the peel-towers (fortified towers or farmhouses) of the Borders and abandoned castles where violence has been done. They climb the towers to attack travellers and try to re-dye their caps in the blood of their victims.

When the blood dries the colour disappears, and the Redcap will look for a new victim. If you hold a cross or cross-handled sword before one he will disappear, leaving only a talon-like fingernail behind. In appearance, a Red Cap is a short (1. 2 metres or about four feet), stocky old man with long, grey hair with a RED CAP, wearing heavy boots and carrying a staff. He has sharp talons for fingernails, red eyes and long protruding teeth. Redcaps may foretell disasters by making a noise that sounds like the beating of FLAX. *See also* DUNTERS, POWRIES.

REDSHANKS are fairies of Dolbury Camp, Somerset. They are said to smoke little pipes and be the ghosts of Danes killed in this area of south western England.

REED (*Phragmites communis*) is called in Gaelic *cuigeal nam ban sithe* 'the Distaff of the Fairy Woman'. Because of its thick root, the Celts identified the reed with a submerged DRYAD. Pipes were originally made from reeds and in Celtic legend, the fairies invented the bagpipe.
 In Greek myth, the god PAN fell in love with a water nymph called SYRINX and pursued her until she reached the river Ladon, where she cried out to her sister nymphs to enable her to cross it. Pan reached out to grasp her, but instead found his arms filled with reeds. Hearing the breeze as it passed through the reeds make a low musical sound, he plucked seven of them and made a pipe, which he named Syrinx. The pipe had SEVEN reeds in accordance with the harmony of heaven, which was said to contain seven sounds.

REFLEX MAN is another British term for a DOUBLE or FETCH.

REGIN ('Powerful One') was a particular DWARF in Norse myth. He was cunning, sly and skilled in magic. He became the foster father of Sigurd,

forged a powerful sword for him, and taught him all the noble skills. He encouraged the young man to kill the DRAGON Fafnir, which had stolen his TREASURE. However, he afterwards plotted to murder Sigurd, but because the hero had licked the blood from the dragon's heart he understood the language of birds and was forewarned by them.

REMORA is a sea spirit that sucks at the keel of a ship and enchants away the sexual potency of men and women, like an INCUBUS or VAMPIRE.

REVENANTS are human spirits returned from the DEAD to make mischief among the living. Several fairies are revenants, the commonest form being women who have died in CHILDBIRTH or UNBAPTISED CHILDREN.

RHAGANA is a Slavonic TREE FAIRY.

RHEUMATISM is inflicted on those who have offended the fairies.

RHIANNON is the daughter of the Welsh King of the UNDERWORLD. She married Pwyll and gave birth to a son called Pryderi. However, evil spirits snatched him from his cradle and smeared the blankets with DOG blood, making it appear that Rhiannon had killed her baby. She was punished by having to carry all the visitors to the palace on her back, like a HORSE. She was eventually vindicated by the return of her child. The Birds of Rhiannon, a flock of blackbirds, herald otherworldly happiness. She is entitled Rigantia, meaning 'Great Queen'.

RHOEA is the NYMPH of the pomegranate, in ancient Greek myth.

RHYS DWFEN is the ruler of the Welsh fairies the PLANT RHYS DWFEN.

RIBHUS are NATURE FAIRIES, the sons of INDRA in Hindu folklore. They

RHIANNON

look after streams, crops and various crafts. The name is from the Sanskrit *ribhu,* meaning shining or shiny.

RITTMEIJE ('Forced Ride') is a female fairy who presses on the chest of a sleeper to cause NIGHTMARES, known on the German island of Baltrum.

ROANE ('Seal') is an Irish or Scottish island race of fairy seal people, similar to the SELKIES. They are gentle, shy and retiring, desiring only to be left in peace. The females sometimes swim ashore and cast off their sealskins to dance in the moonlight as human maidens. If a fisherman can steal a roane's skin, he can force her to become his wife for as long as he can keep the seal skin hidden. As soon as she finds it she will don it and return to the sea.

ROBGOBLIN is an uncommon variation of 'HOBGOBLIN'.

ROBIN GOODFELLOW is a mischievous English fairy who loves to play tricks on mortals, perhaps rushing between their feet as a HARE, transforming himself into a HORSE and carrying them away, or appearing as a WALKING FIRE. He sometimes leads people astray in a manner similar to being PIXY LED or appears as a WILL O'THE WISP; a term for being lost is 'Robin Goodfellow has been with you tonight'. People so bewitched would only find their way when they turned their caps or cloaks. He seems to have possessed the ability to be in several places at once. However, he can also be kind and helpful and only expects a bowl of cream as a reward. He is sometimes said to be the son of OBERON and a mortal woman.

Faith in Robin Goodfellow amongst the ordinary people was once absolute, though Reginald Scot wrote in 1584 that belief in him was less strong than it had been. However, he was to become a popular figure in ballads and mummers plays for many years afterwards, appearing wearing calfskin and carrying a BROOM or flail, with ruddy hands and face. He is a solitary being, a fairy of the HOBGOBLIN or HOB type. He has the head of a handsome youth and the body of a GOAT. Like the god PAN he has a lusty nature, small horns on his head, and carries musical pipes. It may be that he is the fairy remnant of an ancient horned god. He is never seen between HALLOWEEN and the vernal equinox and is usually accompanied by a variety of animals.

Some later tales make him synonymous with PUCK, including Shakespeare's *A Midsummer Night's Dream,* though he is generally more benevolent. He may be synonymous with ROBIN HOOD as a fairy spirit or god of the forest. However, the puritans called him a DEVIL and condemned him along with all the other fairies. The term 'goodfellow' was applied to a rogue, a petty thief or a glutton.

ROBIN HOOD is one of the great legendary heroes of England, but his origins are perhaps less than human. In Britain, some of the ancient NATURE SPIRITS and gods passed into folklore as woodland fairies, often given the name of HOB, Robin or ROBIN GOODFELLOW and this may be the real origin of the legends of Robin Hood. Consider his name, his GREEN clothing, his forest home, and his deadly ARROWS. Perhaps he was the nature god of the ordinary people who could seek him in the forest.[282]

A depiction of Robin and his men at the fourteenth-century chapter house at Southwell Minster in Nottinghamshire shows them as twelve green men merging with various sacred plants such as HAWTHORN, and ivy.[283] In some traditional WITCH covens, the Lord is addressed as Robin and the Lady as Marian. *See also* HOOD.

ROBIN ROUNDCAP or **Robin Round Cap** is an English HOBGOBLIN of the ROBIN GOODFELLOW or PUCK variety who appears around Haliwell in Yorkshire.

ROCK CANDY MOUNTAIN is the magical FAIRYLAND or OTHERWORLD spoken of by American hobos, or tramps, many of whom hope one day to find it. It is popularly known from the song made famous by the American singer Burl Ives. In the Rock Candy Mountain, the streams run with cold beer, food can be picked up off the ground, the snow on mountain tops is ice cream, while cigarettes and dollar bills grow on trees.

ROD is a male Slavonic spirit who represents ancestral SOULS. He is partner to the RÓZANICA, a type of FAIRY GODMOTHER who appears at the birth of a child. The pair were once Slavonic gods.

RODJENICE or **Rojanice** ('To Give Birth') are Croatian FAIRY GODMOTHERS who dispense fate at the birth of a child. They are very beautiful with pale faces. They wear WHITE clothes, cover their heads with a white veil and wear gold and silver jewellery. In their hands, they

hold burning candles. When a child is born people place offerings near the stones of the CAVES where the fairies live.

RODODSA or **Rododesa** is an Italian fairy who sometimes appears as part of a triad with BEFANA and Maratega to spin the destinies of humankind, a version of the three FATES or FAIRY GODMOTHERS. She can change her fingers into sweets, which she breaks off and gives to children.

ROGGENMÖHME ('Aunt in the Rye') is a fairy who protects the grain. Any children who venture into the corn fields are suckled at her poisonous black breasts. Her companion is the PILWIZ.

ROJENICE are the Southern Slavonic FAIRY GODMOTHERS or FATES who appear as three WHITE ladies. One midwife observed them leaning over a new born child. The first said that the boy would become a great priest, the second said, no, he would die as a soldier, while the third exclaimed that he wouldn't grow to be a man at all, but would be burned to death by lightening on his eighteenth birthday.

The worried midwife communicated what she had heard to the child's mother, a wealthy woman who declared that no expense would be spared in saving her son from his fate. She caused a great fortress to be built around him, with NINE successive walls, each inside the other. As the day of his birthday dawned a storm raged. A bolt of lightening struck the fortress and causes a fire to rage through it. The boy was unable to escape in time, through the nine locked gates in the nine encircling walls, so his death was caused by a bolt of lighting on his eighteenth birthday, as the fairy foretold.

RÖPENKERL is a German HEY-HEY MAN who tries to seduce travellers from their path by calling out to them.

ROSEMARY (*Rosemarinus officinalis*) is a herb that attracts fairy folk, though it is a protection against evil spirits.

ROWAN (*Sorbus aucuparia*), or Mountain Ash, is a tree that draws its name from the old Norse word 'runa' meaning 'a charm'. The rowan is associated with protection, particularly from WITCHES and fairies. In the Scottish Highlands, a rowan tree would be planted outside the house to prevent evil from entering. A branch of rowan would be tied over a cradle to prevent the fairies stealing a girl-child.[284] For a protective charm rowan was be gathered at BELTANE (May Day) and bound together with RED THREAD to form an equal-armed cross. Or, according to a Scottish charm:

'Rowan, amber and red threid
Puts witches to their speed'

Country folklore also advises that boiling jam should be stirred with a rowan stick in order to prevent the fairies from stealing it.

In Druidic belief, the rowan was associated with prophecy and divination, whilst an Irish legend tells how a rowan was guarded by a FORMORIAN and bore berries that conferred immortality.

RÓZANICA are Polish FAIRY GODMOTHERS who are present at the birth of a child as arbiters of its fate; celebrations to welcome the birth of a child were called *róziny*. The male equivalents of these spirits are called Rod and these represent ancestral spirits. It was believed in ancient times that all souls were re-incarnations of ancestors and that no new souls were ever created. *See also* ROZANICE.

ROZANICE ('Mother') is a Slavonic FAIRY GODMOTHER who determines the fate of a child at its birth. The name is derived from *roditi* meaning 'to give birth' and Rozanice was an ancient Russian deity. Along with her

male partner Rod, she was offered bread, cheese and honey. The Western Slavonic people believe that they appear as WHITE LADIES or HAGS. In either case, they are very tall, pale and almost transparent, though their eyes sparkle with life. The Rozanice may bewitch the unwary, whilst in other traditions, these goddesses of fate may be clad in sparkling robes, while their hair is sprinkled with jewels. Again, they may appear dressed very simply, with just a garland of flowers about their heads to ornament them. Whoever sees one of these fairies will be stupefied with horror and be unable to move.

RÜBEZAHL ('Account Keeper') or **Herr Johannes** is a Bohemian fairy, sometimes described as a MINE FAIRY of the KNOCKER type, the ruler of the wind who can summon either snow or sunshine. He lives in the wooded slopes of the Reisengebirge Mountains ('Giant Mountains'). He dislikes humans and deals roughly with those who cross his path. He may variously appear as a hunter, a charcoal burner or a herb gatherer, but his true form is a ragged, brawny ELF. He is known as the Master of the Mountains and can make people's ears and noses grow long, turn fruit into dung and gold, cause horns to appear on people's heads and make straw turn into horses.

In Germany, Rübezahl watches over children who get lost in the woods, protecting them from danger. During the year he busies himself making presents until at Christmas he travels with St Nicholas to deliver them to good children.

RUDICA is a Dalmatian weather fairy who rides the storm, bringing hail and lightening to this part of the Balkans. Her name is derived from HERODIAS.

RUMPELSTILTSKIN is a DWARF who appears in a tale collected by the brothers Grimm: [285] A miller foolishly boasted to the king that his daughter was so clever that she could spin straw into gold. The avaricious king immediately locked the girl into a room with a SPINNING wheel and a pile of straw, warning her that if she failed to produce the gold promised by her father she should be put to death. As the girl cried out in despair - for her father's claim was nothing more than an idle boast - a dwarf appeared and offered to perform the task in return for her necklace. She agreed and he span the straw into threads of the finest gold.

The king was both amazed and delighted. He locked the girl into a larger room with more straw, again with the injunction that should she fail to spin the gold she would be put to death. Again the dwarf appeared and span the gold in return for the girl's ring.

Inevitably, the king showed the maiden into a yet larger room, filled with yet more straw. This time he informed her that should she fail to turn the straw into gold she would die, but should she succeed he would make her his wife. The dwarf appeared, but the girl was out of jewellery, and instead he exacted a promise that when she became queen her first child should be given to him.

The king married the maiden and a year later their first child was born. Even before the christening, the dwarf appeared, demanding his fee - the royal princeling. The queen began to weep and the dwarf seemed to relent, saying that if she could guess his NAME within THREE days, she should keep the baby.

Though she guessed many names and servants were sent out to discover more, none proved to be the name of the dwarf. On the last night, she began to despair until a messenger informed her he had overheard a little man singing a rhyme about his name being Rumpelstiltskin. When the dwarf returned the queen was able to tell him his name: 'Rumpelstiltskin'. The thwarted mannikin, in his fury, stamped his foot so deep into the ground that he tore himself in half pulling it out.

His name is sometimes humorously translated as 'Wrinkled Foreskin', though sadly this is probably not authentic. Similar legends of fairy spinners with names that have to be guessed appear in the folklore of England, Scotland, Russia, France, Iceland and Austria. In Germany, the term *Rumpelgeist* is used to denote a poltergeist.

RUSALI are Romanian WEATHER FAIRIES, related to the Russian RUSALKA. They are malevolent and bring storms and hail. They appear in the Rusalia Week just before Whitsuntide as stooping, ugly old women. At night they wail so that people think the wind is blowing. They sometimes sing like girls and sometimes like the DEAD, and are often thought to be the souls of women who died as brides or committed suicide.

RUSALKY or **RUSALKI** (*rus* meaning stream) (s. **RUSALKA**) are Russian WATER FAIRIES or wood NYMPHS. They are the spirits of UNBAPTISED CHILDREN, unwed mothers, or DEAD human women not given proper funeral rites or who were murdered near water. (In the latter case, their fates can be undone by revenging their deaths, or in some cases, their families may appease them by giving them gifts of pancakes, red eggs, or alcohol.) They appear as young girls about seven years of age, or more usually as lovely, pale, lithe young women with gorgeous breasts and flashing eyes. They have long green or blond hair, worn loose. This hair is always moist and if it should ever dry out then the fairy will die. When they choose to cover their alluring bodies Rusalki dress in GREEN leaves or unbelted WHITE shirts. They have pleasing voices and musical laughs. They live in forests,

meadows and fields, or in lakes and streams. Large groups of Rusalki dwell in streams, under rapids or in the depths of rivers. On clear summer nights, they come to the surface and frolic about in the water, splashing and playing joyously.

They first appear on Holy Thursday. In the sixth week after Easter, they move into the trees. Their special time is at Whitsuntide, when they are most active, bathing in lakes and rivers or sitting on the shore combing their hair in the moonlight asking women for dresses and girls for a skirt. At that season women hang strips of cloth torn from their dresses on the branches of birch trees to propitiate them.[286] The Rusalki wash these and spread them out to dry. They weave cloth and wash it in the

stream, leaving it on the bank to dry. Should a human step on one of these, he will become weak or lame. Girls perform a circle dance and swear promises of loyalty and friendship. Young men and women place bread, cheese and butter on the riverbanks while others weave garlands and cast them into the waters.

In the seventh week after Easter, the water nymphs gather feathers and straw to make underwater nests. During this time humans are forbidden to sew, spin or do any field work. At Whitsuntide, people stay indoors at night and do not bathe in the streams and rivers, clap their hands or do any field work that might offend the nymphs. Only WITCHES dare swim in the water with the Rusalki. At the end of the spring festival called the *Rusal'naia nedelia* ('mermaid week'), when people celebrated the new vegetation with dance and song, an effigy of a Rusalka is taken out of the village back towards the forest or stream. It is blessed and thrown back in the water, or broken up and the parts buried in the fields. Young girls offer them garlands to solicit their help in gaining rich husbands.

In late spring, Rusalki play about the fields, woods and meadows, clapping their hands and frolicking. Their laughing voices may be heard echoing about the forests. They are fond of music and dance in the moonlight, making fairy rings on the grass. However, travellers should beware. A man caught up in their games is likely to be tickled to death. They are fond of SPINNING and hang their yarn to dry in the trees.

They are associated with fertility: they walk the land at MIDSUMMER and where they step, blue flowers grow. The Rusalki run about the meadows and when they move through the grain, this causes it to grow. They dance among the corn decked with poppies and cornflowers until June 29th. The grain can sometimes be seen waving and their

movements cause this.

The Rusalki have power over the wind and rain. They live in water during the autumn and winter, but return to the land in spring and summer - perhaps to bring it much needed moisture. If they comb their hair, it causes a flood. As 'sky women' they couple with the thunder spirits to bring summer storms. When the first snow falls, they hibernate in their winter nests until the spring.

These lovely nymphs can be very dangerous. The Rusalki sing SIREN songs to lure men to their deaths by drowning or tickling. No man is able to resist the smiles of the Rusalki, but should he approach one he will be pulled beneath the waters and drowned, unless he should have the luck to be wearing an amulet of wormwood. They entangle fishermen's nets, create floods by breaking dykes and cause storms, hail and heavy rains. Precautions may have to be taken against these evils using various charms, IRON pokers, garlic, or the sign of the CROSS.

It is likely that the various rites associated with the Rusalka are remnants of ancient goddess worship. Indeed, her Ukrainian name *Bohynia* means 'goddess'. Her behaviour and appearance contrasts with that expected of human women in a Christian society she is free spirited, chooses her lovers where she will and wears her hair lose and uncovered.[287] In a patriarchal society, such feminine freedom is considered dangerous and when a Rusalka lays hands on a man, he loses his life - a warning against promiscuity.

RUSH is a plant that Irish fairies sometimes use as horses, straddling them and saying the magic words 'Borram! Borram! Borram!' in order to make them fly. Some fairies, such as the LEPRECHAUNS, are described as being only the height of rush.

RYM ('Roaring') is a TROLL-WIFE in Norse myth.

SA-BDAG are Tibetan NATURE FAIRIES who look after particular mountains, villages or fields.

ST. JOHN'S WORT (*Hypericum perforatum*) is a plant sacred to the fairies on the Isle of Man. If you step upon it, the fairies will lead you astray on your journey. Elsewhere, the herb is used to cure illnesses caused by ELF-BOLTS and fairy spells, such as stitch, cramps and itches or to break fairy enchantments. Indeed, it is currently very fashionable as a natural alternative to synthetic anti-depressant drugs.

ST. MARTIN'S LAND is the name of the subterranean FAIRYLAND described by the GREEN CHILDREN found in the tale of Ralph of Coggeshall. It is lit only by the twilight, and there is no heat or cold there.

SAKHAR is a DJINN who built the fabulous brazen city of Baladu Nuhasir in Africa.

SALAMANDERS are ELEMENTAL fairies of the fire, according to the alchemist Paracelsus (1493-1541). They are usually portrayed as the newts of the same name.

SALBANELLI (*s.* Salbanello) are the fairy children of a SALVANELLO and a WITCH in Italian fairy folklore.

SALEERANDEES are Welsh fairies, scaled beings that resemble lizards walking on two legs. They are cold blooded and seek out human fires. Though their appearance is frightening, they are not harmful. The name may be a corruption of 'SALAMANDER'.

SALGFRÄULEIN is a female Tyrolean fairy who dresses in WHITE and sits beneath a larch tree, singing.

SALT repels evil fairies and other spirits. It is possible to prevent a child being stolen by fairies by tying up a little packet of salt in its dress. A pinch of salt was placed in a baby's crib to protect it from evil. Salt prevents the corruption and decay of food and has become a powerful symbol of defence against malfeasance.

SALVANELLI (*s.* Salvanello) or Salvanel are fairies of Italy and the Alps. They are small, have curly RED HAIR, brown skin, wear RED and live in hollow OAK trees, CAVES, and woodland. They like to raise storms so that they can ride on the wind. They are merry fellows who love to play tricks, misleading travellers and leaving them stranded on high mountain ledges, stealing MILK, tangling the manes of horses and riding them all night so that they are exhausted in the morning. They also like children and will KIDNAP them, particularly little girls - they have been known to return little boys in disappointment. These children will be treated kindly and raised in a woodland cave. A Salvanello is the child of a SALVANO (a male forest spirit) and an AGUANA (a female stream NYMPH). They mate with WITCHES to produce the SALBANELLI.

SALVANI (*s.* Salvano) is the northern Italian name for the SILVANI. A Salvano is the protector of the forest, of human size but very hairy with something of the GOAT about him. The salvani mate with the AGUANE to produce SALVANELLI.

SAMANACH ('The SAMHAIN One') is a male Scottish fairy who kidnaps children at HALLOWEEN. This fairy is shapeless and coarse, and lives in seashore caves.

SAMCA or Samtsa is a malevolent Russian fairy, created from the DEAD soul of an evil man. It appears during the dark times of the year, especially the Twelve Days of Christmas, and during the dark moon.

SAMHAIN is an ancient Celtic festival, known in modern times as HALLOWEEN, celebrated at the beginning of November. The hours of light have diminished; the days are short. The powers of growth and light are in decline and the powers of darkness and cold begin to gain dominion.

Similar festivals are celebrated around the world marking the start of winter and the ascendance of the powers of blight, decay and death. The ancient Celts celebrated it as the New Year festival. It may seem a strange time to begin the marking of a new year, but for the Celts, in all calculations of time, night preceded day, and the dark days of winter preceded the light of summer.[288]

Any boundary was important magically. These times and places were dangerous, one might enter the OTHERWORLD through them accidentally, or the Otherworld might pass through into our own. The time when one season passed to another was particularly tricky, especially the two hinges of the year, BELTANE (May Day, the start of summer) and Samhain, when the Otherworld came very close. Samhain is the pivotal point of the year itself, when one year passes to the next, and the doors between the worlds stand open.

At Samhain, the cattle were brought down from the summer pastures to the safer lowland winter ones. Any beast that could not be kept through the winter would be slaughtered. This is one of the reasons Samhain was called 'The Festival of the DEAD'. Some of the animals would have been ritually sacrificed to propitiate the powers of winter (like Irish offerings at Samhain to the FORMORIANS, Gods of Blight), and to feed the spirits of the dead that came to visit the Samhain feast.

After Samhain, ghosts, spirits and evil fairies walk the land. Good fairies such as the Irish TUATHA DÉ DANAAN and the English PUCK retire from sight until spring returns. Wicked fairies, such as the Scottish UNSEELIE COURT, become very active from now until Easter along with CAILLEACHs and HAG fairies, probably once crone goddesses of winter who ruled over the season. Evil omens such as BLACK DOGS and the BEAN-NIGHE or WASHER AT THE FORD also appear. Fairy MOUNDS open at Samhain and you might get a glimpse inside. At HOLLANTIDE (11th November, old Samhain) the HILLMEN or Hogmen, the most feared of the Manx fairies, move their abode, and one should not venture out then.

After Samhain, all the crops left unharvested belong to the fairies. In Ireland, Halloween is called PHOOKA Night and after this time he renders all the crops unfit to eat and spoils all the BLACKBERRIES. Welsh gryphons blight any crops left in the field after Halloween and the LUNATISHEE will not allow BLACKTHORN to be cut on November 11th (Old Samhain before calendar changes).

SAMODIVA are winged Southern Slavonic WEATHER FAIRIES, the equivalent of the Croatian Vily. To capture one, simply steal her CLOTHES when she removes them to bathe. The term entered the Romanian language as a euphemism for the DEAD.

SAMOGORSKA is a southern Slavonic mountain fairy who inhabits the high peaks, hilltops or sometimes the valleys.

SAMOVILA *See* SAMOVILY.

SAMOVILY or **SAMOVILA** is the southern Slavonic equivalent of the Russian RUSALKI. She is a WATER FAIRY who sings sweetly to lure young men to their deaths in her dripping arms. She is the spirit of a bride who died on her wedding night, or some say she is the spirit of an UNBAPTISED BABY.

SAND YAN Y TAD is the Breton WILL O'THE WISP. At its finger ends are five lights, which spin round like a wheel.

SANDMAN is a kindly European fairy who brings sleep and pleasant dreams to children by sprinkling their eyes with magical sand. He is also found in North America.

SANKCHINNIS are Indian female DRYADS that inhabit trees and can sometimes be seen standing at the foot of their trees at midnight. A Brahmin's wife was once attacked by one who shut her up in the trunk of the tree.

SANTA CLAUS is the American FATHER CHRISTMAS, an Anglicised form of the Dutch Sante Klaas.

SANTE KLAAS is the Dutch FATHER CHRISTMAS.

SÂNTOADERI are Romanian fairies who appear as horses or centaurs, or perhaps a human who has something of the horse about him, such as horse shoes or a tail. They appear in groups of SEVEN, NINE or twelve, visiting villages and rattling chains and beating drums. They appear during Lent with the DEAD. If people venture out of their houses at night, these creatures will ride them like beasts or trample them underfoot. They break into houses to dance on human bodies or bring illness with them. However, they only punish those who break their taboos by SPINNING and weaving during the duration of their visit to earth. They carry away human souls.

Their patron is St Theodore and women perform rites three weeks after Easter on Todorusale Day. The ceremonies are devoted to the fairies to ensure healing and fertility. On this day, the Sântoaderi dance with the IELE. They (or St Theodore) bring in the summer.[289] In Romanian folklore, St Theodore, with twelve horses, six black and six white - the six months of winter and six of summer - chases the sun, which at the beginning of spring deviates and moves northwards. The six white horses defeat the six black ones (the six light months of summer versus the six dark months of winter).

SARNA BURHI ('Woman of the Grove') is a Bengal DRYAD who dwells in a sacred grove called Sarna.

SASABONSUM are forest fairies of the West African coast that dwell in silk-cotton trees. If the earth around one of these trees is RED, it identifies it as the abode of a Sasabonsum. He attacks and devours unwary travellers at night and the red is said to be the blood wiped off him as he goes to his UNDERWORLD home after a night's carnage. No one goes near such trees at night. In appearance, he is enormous and red in colour, with straight hair. The Sasabonsum is a friend of WITCHES and can give the power of becoming witches to those who desire it. His wife is SHAMANTIN ('Tall Ghost').

SASQUATCH ('Hairy Man') or **BIGFOOT** has been seen many times in the forest regions of North America, the first recorded sighting being in 1811. It is described as being between some 2-3 metres tall (between seven and eleven feet), covered in thick fur or hair, with long arms, and a flat nose. Several expeditions have set out to find Bigfoot, but all have failed and those photographs and films that exist purporting to depict the creature are contentious. Some people think Bigfoots belong to a natural but unknown species, while others believe them to be spirits. Descriptions of their appearance tallies with that of a large number of (mainly) forest fairies around the world, including the Schrat, Trolls, Urisk, Ved, Wood Wose,

Boggarts, Brollachan, Callicantzaros, Fuath, Gruagach, Hobgoblin, Illes, Korreds, Maero, Ogres, Phynnodderee and Pilosi.

SATIA ('Satisfaction') is mentioned in documents of the Middle Ages as a Fairy Queen or Italian WITCH goddess (along with ABUNDIA) with a following of female dancers.

SATYRS are the companions of the Greek gods Dionysus and PAN. They are NATURE SPIRITS of the fields and woods. They are covered with bristly hair, have GOAT legs and feet and small horns on their foreheads, extremely large genitals, flat noses and pointed ears. Stories associate them with sexual license and they appear incessantly chasing various NYMPHS. They came to represent debauchery.

SAUVAGEONS ('Wild Ones') are female Breton fairies, incredibly old members of the FÉE race.

SCAZZAMURIEDDU is a small Italian fairy from Lecce who wears a RED CAP and guards hidden TREASURE,

which he may occasionally reveal to favoured humans. He lives in human dwellings as a HOUSE FAIRY but he likes to seduce human women. He loves children and knows which numbers will win the lottery.

SCHACHT-ZWERGEN ('Shaft Dwarfs') are Austrian MINE FAIRIES.

SCHLORCHERL is a Romanian fairy that tries to lure people into swamps by calling out to them.

SCHNEERFRÄULEIN ('Snow Maiden') is a German WILD WOMAN who dresses in white and wears crystal jewellery. These fairies live in larch and beech forests.

SCHRAT, SCRAT or SCHRATT is a large, hairy forest fairy of German folklore. He has a great aversion to bad mannered guests.

SCHRÄTLEIN is a variety of German fairy, perhaps a smaller version of the SCHRAT.

SCHRÄTTELI is a type of NIGHTMARE in German folklore.

SCHRECKSELE ('Soul Shocker'?) is a type of NIGHTMARE.

SCHRETEL (probably cognate with SCHRAT) was first mentioned in a thirteenth-century poem which related how the King of Norway journeyed to see the King Of Denmark in order to make him a present of a bear. On the journey, he stopped at the house of a Dane to ask for shelter for the night. The man welcomed him, but warned him that the house was plagued by a fairy. Though he had never seen it, he had heard it banging about and throwing the furniture around. Moreover, it was likely to kill anyone who stayed there overnight.

Neveretheless, the King decided to rest there, and he and the bear made themselves comfortable by the fire, both falling asleep in the warmth.

Suddenly, the schretel appeared, 'three spans high' and wearing a RED CAP. He sat by the fire and roasted himself a piece of meat before looking curiously at the bear. He had never seen such a creature before and wondered what it was. Then, true to his custom, he whacked the bear across the head with the meat spit. This bear leapt up and a fight broke out between beast and fairy until, at last, the vanquished fairy fled.

The next morning, the Dane returned, surprised to see the Norseman and his bear still alive. The king and his bear went on his way, while the puzzled Dane hitched up his plough and went out to work his fields. He was amazed when the bedraggled and torn Schretel appeared before him, angrily demanding whether he still possessed his great cat. Thinking quickly, the man replied: 'Yes, and today she gave birth to five fine kittens'. At this, the Schretel took fright and declared he would never enter the house again.

SCHRIMMERLREITER ('Rider of the White Horse') is a German term for FATHER CHRISTMAS. His name is far older, being one of the titles of Wodin, who rode the skies at YULE, rewarding the good and punishing the bad.

SCHWARZBRAUNEN MÄDELEIN ('Black-Brown Maiden') was known to the miners of Europe. The German miners sang a song:
To the black-brown Maiden in the night,
To her they are bound'
Western Slavonic miners would pray to the lady before starting work, leaving offerings of water, tea and eggs for her. She has been Christianised into St Barbara, patroness of miners, gunners and others in danger of sudden death.

SCRAT is often the name for the devil or a demon, but also a German fairy. See SCHRAT.

SCRATTEL is small hairy forest spirit of Germany.

SEA FAIRIES poulate the world's oceans very widely. In the watery depths, dwell MERMAIDS, NYMPHS, ELEMENTALS and MERMEN, as well as monsters like the KRAKEN and the OLD MAN OF THE SEA. These spirits control the weather and the water, raise storms, and have the power to cause shipwreck, drowning and death. The appearance of one of them is usually an OMEN of disaster.

In ancient times, it was the practice to placate the spirits of the sea with a sacrifice before setting out on a voyage. The ancient Romans would offer a bull, while in other places criminals were thrown over cliffs. The Vikings ran the keels of their longships over prisoners to coat them with blood. Even today, we break a bottle of champagne over a new hull. If the sea spirits were denied their tributes, they would take another by sinking the ship and taking the souls of the sailors to dwell with them in their fabulous underwater cities. For this reason, sailors have always taken many precautions so as not to offend the spirits. They often had tattoos of nymphs, TRITONS and mermaids, and would avoid saying the word 'PIG' or swearing while on board. If this taboo were broken, they would have to stick an IRON knife in the mast to avert the ill fortune.

Like the sea itself, many sea fairies are personified as lovely and seductive, but treacherous. The best known of these is the mermaid. It is possible that the legend of the mermaid has its origins in the goddesses who rose from the sea, like Venus/Aphrodite, or the fish tailed Atargatis and Derceto. The sea is associated with the Great Mother Goddess whose names include Maia, Mary, Mara, Marian, Maria and Miriam; all names derived from a root word for sea. Sea goddesses are usually also goddesses of love and the MOON, drawing the tides, rivers, dew and flow of human life. Ancient mariners would have a tattoo of a star to honour the goddess Venus as they steered by her star. She was also the prototype of the ship figureheads.

SEA MAIDS is another term for MERMAIDS.

SEA MITHER ('Sea Mother') appears in the folklore of the Isles of Orkney. She represents the powers of summer and life, is the mother of all that lives in the sea and brings seasonal calm to the island waters. Her enemy is Teran, the spirit of winter, who stirs up the waves and winter gales. Every spring, at the equinox, the Sea Mither begins to battle with Teran to bring in the summer. At the end of the fight, which may go on for weeks, he is bound and imprisoned at the bottom of the sea. Then, the Mither will bring warmth and growth back to the sea and the islands until the autumn, when the Teran escapes and they fight once again at the autumn equinox. This time, Teran is victorious and the Sea Mither is banished. During the winter, he will wreak havoc on both sea and land, whipping up storms, bringing ice and cold, and drowning the fishermen. Lying at the bottom of the ocean, the Sea Mither hears their cries and waits for spring, when she will rule once more.

SEA SPRITES are coastal fairies of the ISLE OF MAN and are the guardians of the sea. They sail in broken seashells and occasionally help humans.

SEA TROWS are a particular species of TROWS that dwell in the sea, having been banished there long ago by the land trows. Sea trows live at the bottom of the sea and sometimes surface disguised as seals. In their natural state, they look like misshapen, wizened monkeys with heads that slope to a sharp angle at the top. They have round, flat feet and webbed fingers and toes. Their hair looks like seaweed, and so the sea trows are often called TANGIE ('seaweed'). They are known to be stupid but not evil, though they like to play tricks on humans, stealing bait and fish from anglers' lines. They are most often spotted on the strand uncovered by the tides and rarely venture very far inland, as they are slow and clumsy out of water. *See also* SELKIES and ROANE.

SEA WITCHES are prominent in British folklore, variously described as evil fairies, spirits, GHOSTS or living humans who have sold their SOULS to the devil to become WITCHES. They can control the weather, and lurk along the coastline of Britain to attack ships and wreck them on the rocks. Sir Francis Drake is said to have solicited the help of the Sea Witches in order to defeat the Spanish Armada in 1588. They raised a storm that wrecked many of the ships.

SEBILLE was an incarnation of the LADY OF THE LAKE who had an affair with Alexander the Great and became an ancestor of ARTHUR in this manner.[290]

SECOND SIGHT is afforded to few people. According to Scottish folklore, only those with such clairvoyant powers may see the fairies. Possessing second sight often indicates fairy blood somewhere among the ancestors.

SECRET FOLK is a euphemism for the fairies.

SECRET PEOPLE is a term for the fairies of England.

SEEFRÄULINE is a German LAKE MAIDEN who wears a shimmering WHITE dress. She has blond hair and blue eyes and knows all the healing herbs of the forest.

SEEHIRT is a mischievous Western Slavonic fairy.

SEEING FAIRIES is not the gift of everyone. According to the old folklore, people born in the morning cannot see fairies or the spirit world, but those born at night can see both fairies and the ghosts of the dead. People who have fairy blood themselves can also see fairies. Young girls, just prior to puberty, are more likely to be able to see fairies. A person whose eyes have been touched with FAIRY WATER or the application of a FAIRY OINTMENT can see fairies when they are present. Certain herbs, such as THYME, PRIMROSE and FOUR LEAFED CLOVER can aid in seeing fairies. An old recipe to make a potion to enable you to see fairies ran thus:

Take a pint of Sallet oil and put it in a glass, first washing it with rose water. Then put thereto the budds of hollyhocke, of marygolde, of young hazle and the topps of wild thyme. Take the grasse of a fairy throne Then all these put into the glasse… dissolve three dayes in the sunne, and keep it for thy use.' [291]

If you see the fairy before it sees you, all is well. But according to Manx folklore, if the fairy sees you first, it is dangerous.

You are more likely to see fairies at one of their great festivals: BELTANE, SAMHAIN, MIDSUMMER and YULE; or on a FRIDAY. On any day, the most likely times are those of dawn and dusk, noon and midnight.

SEELIE COURT

SEELIE COURT ('Blessed Court') are aristocratic Scottish TROOPING FAIRIES who live together in hierarchic courts and take part in FAIRY RADES (rides), riding out in processions, which are sometimes witnessed by humans. They are often compassionate towards humans and always repay a human kindness. These are the good fairies of Scottish folklore, as opposed to the bad fairies of the UNSEELIE COURT ('Unblessed Court').

SEEMÄNNLEIN

SEEMÄNNLEIN is a German WATER FAIRY who appears as a young man wearing a RED CAP. He has curly golden hair, green teeth and carries a golden harp, though he can change into a fish-man or bull.

SELIGEN FRAULEIN ('Venerable Woman') is a type of Tyrolean WILD WOMAN or forest spirit. Some say that there are very few of them left as they have been hunted to near extinction by the WILDE MÄNNER, who seek to destroy them. They can only be saved by sheltering on a tree stump on which THREE crosses have been cut, and they will reward woodcutters who are kind enough to mark trees this way. They protect the trees and animals (especially chamois and deer) from hunters. They MILK chamois in underground milking parlours. They are fertility spirits who make the hay and flax grow faster, and who help in harvesting, milking and herding, SPINNING and weaving. They are experts at healing with herbs, and sometimes rescue lost travellers. Farmers say that since they have been driven out, the land is less fertile. They will flee if a man should touch their HAIR, or swear in their presence, if they are struck or called by their real NAMEs, or if they are given gifts of CLOTHES. They love bells and dancing. According to the writer and researcher Nigel Pennick,

selig is a term applied by the German Catholic Church to a person one step below sainthood, and this implies that these fairies are, or were once, honoured creatures.

SELKIE (pl. Selkies, Silkies or Selchi ('Seals') are Orkney and Shetland fairies that take the form of seals in the sea, but when they come ashore they shed their seal skins and assume human form. Some say they are bewitched humans who can come ashore on MIDSUMMER Eve, cast off their seal skins, and resume their true shape. Others say that they are fairies and can only take a human shape at certain times, perhaps only every Johnsmas Eve (Midsummer Eve), though others say that it is every ninth night.

Once ashore and in human form, the selkie-folk will dance on the seashore and if they are disturbed they will grab their skins and run back to the sea. If a man can steal and hide the shed skin he can force a selkie maid to marry him, though if she ever finds her skin she will put it on and be off back to the sea. The man will pine away and die of a broken heart. Though the female selkies sometimes marry humans, they can never settle: their dual nature means that they are not truly happy either in the sea or on the land.

Descendants of such unions have webbed fingers and toes or a horny substance on their palms and soles. The Mac Codrum clan from North Uist in the Hebrides claim descent from selkies; they are known as *Sliochd nan Ron,* the Offspring of Seals. A distant ancestor stole the skin of a seal maiden as she danced and kept it hidden for many years, during which time she bore him many children.

The male selkies also come ashore to make love to human women, to whom they appear very seductive. Island men who do not keep their wives satisfied risk their wives taking selkie lovers. If a human woman wants to attract a male selkie for a lover, she should go to the sea and drop SEVEN tears in it at high tide. Generally, the

male selkies have no love for humans, causing storms and overturning the boats of seal hunters and fishermen.

According to folkore of the Orkneys, selkies are FALLEN ANGELS, thrown out of heaven and into the sea after offending God. Others say that they are the souls of drowned humans, allowed once a year to resume a human shape. Tales of seal people are found all over Shetland, Orkney, the Hebrides and Faeroe Islands. Seals are a common sight in these parts and the name of Orkney is derived from the Norse *Orkneyjar* meaning 'Seal Islands'.

SERVÁN ('Servant') or **Sarvén** are mysterious fairies, found in Switzerland and northern Italy, who have never been seen by human eyes. Their existence is only detected by the footprints they leave behind after they have worked their nocturnal mischief. They steal keys, scissors, needles, pens and spectacles, laughing themselves silly as people try to find them. They also delight in pulling the covers off the bed, knotting cows' tails and covering MILK churns in moss. However, if they are well treated and given a bowl of cream each night, they act as HOUSE FAIRIES, living next to the stove, and helping out with the housework.

SETEK or **Sotek** is a Bohemian fairy who looks like a small boy with claws in place of nails. He is a kind of HOUSE FAIRY or protective spirit that protects the flocks and byre. It is very lucky to possess a setek and will result in wealth, good harvests and health. In the winter he lives in the oven to keep himself warm, while in the summer he may stay in the sheep shed, though he may burrow into the flour barrel, the peas or live in a wild pear tree.[292]

To breed a setek, carry an egg for NINE days in your armpit. The hatched fairy can go for nine years without eating or drinking, but after that will return to the place of his birth to cause trouble.

In Slovenian folklore, the setek was a good sprit who haunts the places where SALT is kept, or lives in the cattle sheds. A portion of all the meals cooked must be laid out for him or he will cause the fire to go out, the pans to crack, or the cows to yield blood instead of milk. He is only the size of a thumb so he can hide in all sorts of nooks and crannies to cause mischief for those who offend him.

SETLANO is an Italian fire elemental.

SETTIANO are ELEMENTALS of the South and of Fire, in Italian occult lore. They have influence over the subconscious.

SEVEN is a number that appears frequently in fairy stories. It is the usual number of years for a human to be AWAY, a captive, in fairyland. A stolen CHANGELING can be free after seven years and young girls are returned after seven years, transformed into WITCHES. According to Lady Wilde, the fairies meet at the Siodh-Dune every seven years to lament and mourn at having been cast out of heaven. She adds that every seven years the fairies have to pay a *teind* (tithe) to hell.[293] Every seventh year on May Eve, fairies fight for the rights to the harvest, for the best ears of grain belong to them.[294]

Some fairies appear in groups of seven, such as the Seven Whistlers, the Egyptian Hathors, and the ancient Maskims. Fairies eat food called 'seventh bread' (*See* SILVERWEED). When the nymph Syrinx was transformed into reeds, Pan used seven of them to create a pipe in accordance with the harmony of heaven, which has seven sounds. Jenny Greenteeth demands a sacrifice every seven years and the island of Hy-Breasail appears above the surface of the waves once every seven years. A person born into a family of seven same sex siblings is liable to become a MURRAUE, while the seventh son of a seventh son can become a Cunning Man with power over fairy spells. A shaman's birch pole has seven steps to ascend into the OTHERWORLD.

The number seven has a mystical aspect too. The ancients knew only seven planets; and we still talk of the seven days of the week, the seven deadly sins, seven colours of the rainbow, and the Seven Wonders of the World. In the bible, God is said to have created the world in seven days; and in the Book of Revelations there are seven stars, seven angels, seven trumpets, seven seals and seven vials of wrath. Similarly, life cycles are said to run in seven-year periods; for example, just think of the phrase 'the seven year itch'.

The reputation of the number seven as magical relates to its link with the moon. In ancient times all reckoning was based on the moon cycle of twenty-eight days. The moon has four phases which are divided into periods of seven days each. Occultists were quick to observe that if you add all the numbers from one to seven the total comes to twenty-eight, reinforcing the power of the number. According to the principles of numerology it is the number of completeness, inner rhythms, virginity, and reflection.

SEVEN WHISTLERS are Lancashire wild geese, a manifestation of the WILD HUNT in north-west England. They are an OMEN OF DEATH.

SHADE FOOTS were a race of one-footed creatures who, according to

Aristophanes, were implicated in a profane celebration of the lesser Eleusinian mysteries. The Shade foots were also known as Monocoli ('One-leg'), possibly a code for a sacred mushroom. *See also* FACHAN.

SHADOWS are considered to be more substantial in fairy lore than merely the physical manifestation of light and shade. English fairies can steal your shadow, which will eventually cause you to fade away and die. However, if you can manage to steal a fairy's shadow he or she must grant you a wish.

SHAG is a North of England BLACK DOG. To touch it means certain death.

SHAGFOAL or **Tatterfoal** is an English fairy from Lincolnshire, similar to a BRASH or the HEDLEY KOW.[295]

SHAIBAR is a male Arabian fairy who is very small, though his beard is some nine metres long (30 feet) and he has two humps, one in front and one behind. His sister is PERI-BANOU.

SHAITANS, **Sheitans** or **Sheytân** are evil DJINNS, the children of the DEVIL. They are extremely ugly and live in the shadows, feeding on excrement. They can SHAPESHIFT but are always recognisable by their cloven hoofs. They bring evil and disease to humans and try to tempt them to wickedness. In pre-Islamic times, the Shaitans were very different. A Shaitan was a type of MUSE or GENIUS inspiring poets and prophets.

SHAMAN is a gifted person able to communicate with the spirit world. Fairies are said to dwell in MOUNDS, caves or underground in general and a common shamanic experience is the visit to the UNDERWORLD. Shamans and WITCHES are said to receive their powers from spirits or fairies who can confer gifts of healing, magic and prophecy.

In nearly all cultures, shamans work with local spirits and animal totems,

SHAMAN

which are also creatures of spirit. In Europe, these often appear as fairy animals to signal the beginning of a spiritual quest. Fairies are said to ride HORSES, or turn into them to trick the unwary into mounting them and then taking off on a wild ride. Gods and shamans tether their horses to the World Tree, the *axis mundi* via which journeys to all realms is possible. The horse spirit carries the shaman into other worlds.

A shaman's drum is often referred to as his 'horse', since the drumbeat is a vehicle that enables him to travel to other realms. The Irish horse

Aonbharr carried the hero Conan to the OTHERWORLD. THOMAS THE RHYMER was taken to the realm of the fairy by the milk white steed of the elf queen, and TAM LIN escaped from the fairy realm on a stolen white horse.

In Greek myth, the horse of Otherworld journeying was Pegasos - better known in its later Latin form of Pegasus - who was the horse of Apollo, the Muses and the inspiration of poetry. On Helicon, there was a spring called Hippocrene ('the horse well') which was horse-shoe shaped and was said to have been made when Pegasus ('of the springs of water') stamped there; poets drank its waters for inspiration. If a poet said; 'I am mounting my Pegasus', he meant that he was inspired to write poetry. Poetry and bardship was a serious business, not mere rhyme making, it meant being touched by the gods and being given divine inspiration from the other realms. Many famous poets and musicians are said to have learned their craft in the Otherworld or the realm of the fairy.

The ancient Celts, among others, had a taboo on eating RED food, which was believed to belong to the fairies or to the ghosts of the DEAD. Its use was confined to shamans and to feasts of the dead. This recalls the taboo nature of FAIRY FOOD, which humans are forbidden to eat or they will not be able to leave Fairyland.

SHAMANTIN ('Tall Ghost') is an African DRYAD and the wife of the evil forest fairy, SASABONSUM. She is white and very tall, a description of the silk-cotton tree. She is kinder than her husband is and if she comes across a traveller she will teach him the ways of the forest, which herbs a can be eaten and which will cure disease, the language of the animals and where they go to drink. *See also* WHITE LADIES.

SHAPESHIFTER/SHAPESHIFTING is a power possesed by most fairies. They can alter their original forms in order to appear as lovelier than they are, or as various animals such as COWS, DEER, eagles, HORSES, BLACK DOGS and CATS, though these may be the original forms for all we know. They can also manifest as moss, trees, herbs, columns of fire, stones and balls of light. The Cornish believe that each shapeshifting operation makes fairies diminish in size until they become ants. The god MANANNAN gave the TUATHA DÉ DANAAN the power of shapeshifting so that they would be able to remain hidden from the occupying Celts.

SHEAGH SIDHE or Slooa-Shee ('Fairy Host') is a Gaelic term for fairies or TUATHA DÉ DANAAN.

SHEFRO (also given in Gaelic as *sia bhrugh, sithbhrog, sithbhrogh, siohbhrogh* or *sioghbhrugh*) is a general Gaelic term for the TROOPING FAIRIES who live in communities, though the shefro itself is more correctly the fairy dwelling.[296] A Shefro wears a FOXGLOVE flower for a cap.

SHEHIREEM or SHIDEEM are Hebraic fairies. *See* MAZIKEEN.

SHELLYCOATS are Scottish WATER FAIRIES that haunt shallow woodland pools. They are covered with shell-like scales of red or purple and have the general appearances of fishes with large mouths and eyes. They can take off their shell coats if they wish, but this renders them weak and powerless. Shellycoats are able to fly, and the rattling of their coats may warn you when they are approaching. They like to play pranks on travellers looking for water to refresh them.

Two men encountered one near the banks of the Ettrick river. When they heard a mournful voice calling: 'Lost! Lost!'. They thought it was the voice of a drowning person and quickly tried to find him. They followed the sound all the way to the source of the river, through the long night. The voice then descended the opposite side of the mountain and the two men realised that they had been tricked, and angrily gave up the pursuit. They heard the Shellycoat laughing loudly.[297]

SHEOGUES, Sheoques, Shoges, Sigh Oges or Sidheog ('Young Spirits' or 'Little Spirits') are Irish fairies who live in thorn bushes or RATHS. Their FAIRY MUSIC sometimes leads humans away from safe paths into bogs or into the fairy MOUND, though occasionally it has inspired great bards and poets like the famous Carolan, who learned his tunes from sleeping on a fairy rath. Sheogues are usually well disposed towards human beings, though they sometimes kidnap children and leave CHANGELINGS in their place, which will die after one year.

SHIANS are the dwelling places of the Scots highland fairies the Daoine Sith.

SHINSEEN are Chinese fairies who haunt forests and mountains. They sometimes appear as old men with long beards or as young maidens wandering in the forest in the moonlight. They are generally benevolent.

SHISIMORA is an alternative name for KIKIMORA, a Russian female HOUSE FAIRY that may act like a NIGHTMARE.

SHOCK is a malicious SHAPESHIFTING English fairy that can appear as a DOG, a COW, or a man with a donkey's head.

SHONEY, Shony or Spony is a type of KELPIE that haunts the Isle of Lewis in the Outer Hebrides. Usually thought of as male, Shoney was once a sea god, or perhaps goddess, as his name may relate to the Norse *Sjofn*, a sea goddess. The inhabitants of the nearby Isle of Lewis made an offering of a cup of ale to the Shoney well into the nineteenth century. In the weeks before HALLOWEEN, pocketfuls of malt were brought into the church of St Mulray, then combined and brewed into ale. A man would wade into the sea with a cup of this ale, and (in Gaelic) offer the Shoney the ale in return for good catches and seaweed to enrich the soil: "Shoney, I give you this cup of ale hoping that you will be so kind as to give us plenty of sea-ware for enriching our ground the ensuing year".[298] Some say that there are several Shoneys, and they are bad tempered, stupid and squat, with pointed ears and sharp teeth.

SHOOPILTEES or Shopiltees are little WATER HORSES or ponies that play about the Shetland and Orkney Islands, though they have not been seen in more than a hundred years, so they may have died out. They are similar to the KELPIE in character and live off the blood of the drowned.

SHORTHOGGERS, OF WHITTINGHAME are Scottish fairies, similar to SPUNKIES, and are said to be the ghosts of UNBAPTISED CHILDREN.

SHUCK MONKEY or Shug Monkey is a BLACK DOG that haunts eastern England in the area of Balsham and Wratting in Cambridgeshire. It is unusual for an English fairy in that it has the face of a monkey.

SHVOD is a HOUSE FAIRY of North American folklore. He is usually helpful, but parents sometimes refer to him as a kind of BOGEYMAN as a threat to coerce children unto good behaviour.

SIA BHRUGH, Sioghbhrugh or Siohbhrogh is a Gaelic general term for TROOPING FAIRIES who live in communities.[299]

SIB is a female fairy associate of ROBIN GOODFELLOW.[300]

SIBILLE are Abruzzo fairies, the WHITE LADIES who haunt the Italian linden trees and sacred groves guarding TREASURE.

SIDHE, Shee, Sí or Sith is the name for the fairies in Irish and Scottish Gaelic.

In the various manuscripts of the old folklorists the word is also given as sia, sigh, sighe, sigheann, siebhra, sirchaire and siogidh. The word sidhe actually means a burial MOUND, hill or earth barrow. In myth, when the Milesian Celts invaded Ireland, the resident TUATHA DÉ DANAAN were forced to retreat into the barrows, each leader being awarded a particular mound by the DAGDA. The term sidhe came to refer to the OLD GODS themselves and eventually to fairies, other spirits and anything supernatural, including WITCHES. From this we have compound words and phrases such as leannan sidhe meaning a fairy familiar, siogh-dhraoidheachd meaning enchantment by fairies or spirits, sigh ga'oithe or siahean-ga'oithe meaning a whirlwind, so called because the fairies are said to raise it, and the mysterious twilight is called sia, because that is the time fairies are most active.[301] A blast or blight, again believed to be caused by fairies, is called sidhe, sidheadh or sigh. In Scotland the term sith is applied to whatever is unearthly, for example breac sith or 'elfin pox' refers to hives or spots that appear suddenly on the skin.

The sidhe, generally speaking, are very tall and thin, and eternally young and beautiful in appearance. They are usually dressed in WHITE, have sweet voices and long flowing HAIR. They spend their time caring for their animals and living a quiet life unless they are disturbed. They can curse humans with illness, madness and death for breaking fairy taboos or trespassing on fairy property. They kidnap human children and replace them with CHANGELINGS, and steal away pretty girls to become fairy brides. It is wise to leave them offerings of food, water, milk, tobacco or whiskey. Spilt milk is regarded as an offering to the fairy folk with the cry 'there's someone the better for it'. They move house at BELTANE and SAMHAIN.

SIDHE DRAOI are Celtic DRYADS or TREE FAIRIES.

SIFRA is the dwelling pace of the SIDHE It is a fairy palace, situated in the heart of a MOUND or barrow. Its walls are made of silver and the pavements of gold, while the banqueting hall is lit by the glimmer of diamonds. Anyone digging into the fairy mound to steal the gold will be warned by strange voices, sounds, and storms and should take heed, or disaster and even death will follow.

SIGGER is the GIANT who gave his name to Sigger Hill in Orkney. He loved fishing and put a rock in the sea to fish from, but decided he needed a stepping stone as well. He found a suitable rock, and was struggling down to the sea with it when his wife saw him and cried out: 'Oh Siggie! Many an evil stane has laid on dy back!' This so startled Sigger that he stumbled and the boulder fell on top of him. He lies imprisoned beneath it still.

SIGH-OGE means 'young fairy' and if a man should kiss a sigh-oge he will fall in love with her and be lost forever - since he will pine away with longing and have no interest in the life around him.

SI'LA are DJINN who cannot change their shape but are very dangerous and evil.

SILENI are creatures of classical Greek myth, originating in Albania. They are similar to SATYRS. In appearance, they have horses' ears and sometimes the legs of HORSES or GOATS too.

SILENTLY MOVING PEOPLE is a Scottish term for the fairies.

SILI FFRIT is the name of a little Welsh Fairy.[302]

SILI-GO-DWT is the name of a little Welsh Fairy.[303]

SILKIES are small and dainty English North Country fairies dressed in

white or grey silk, who haunt Denton Hall in Northumberland. A silkie acted as a HOUSE FAIRY for the Hoyle family, doing housework such as cleaning out the hearth, laying the fires and laying bunches of flowers on the staircase. However, she took a dislike to the new tenant who moved in after World War II and began to act like a poltergeist - so much so that he had to move out. Briggs describes silkies (for some say there are more than one) as being 'between ghosts and brownies'.[304]

SILVANI ('Wooded') are Italian wood fairies, half man and half GOAT with long claw-like nails, dressed in the skins of a bear, wolf or wild bull. They are always hungry. They are larger than the FAUNS, but in any case are rarely seen. They are named after the Roman nature god Silvanus (sometimes identified with PAN and FAUNUS). Hesiod described the silvani as a 'useless and crafty tribe', though they guarded herds, houses and land boundaries in Roman times. In popular folklore they sometimes appear as winged NYMPHS, dressed in animal skins or RED costumes, indeed, they are attracted to anything red. They protect wildlife and the trees of the forests and mate with the AGUANE.

SILVANE ('Wood Women') are the female version of the Silvani, with whom they mate to produce the FOLLETTI.

SILVANUS is a Roman nature god sometimes identified with PAN and FAUNUS. *See also* SILVAN.

SILVERWEED (*Potentilla anserina*) is a favourite food of the fairies. One of its old names was 'seventh bread'.

SINIPIIAT or **Blue Maidens** are Finnish fairies who look after the flowers.

SÎNZIENE are female Balkan fairies who appear once at year at the MIDSUMMER solstice.

SINTERKLAAS is a Dutch name for FATHER CHRISTMAS or Santa Claus.

SIODH-DUNE ('Mount of Peace') are ancient burial MOUNDS and a favourite retreat of the Irish fairies. According to Lady Wilde the fairies meet there every seven years to lament and mourn at having been cast out of heaven.[305]

SIRENA is a MERMAID of the island of Guam. She was once an ordinary girl, who loved to swim. One day her mother sent her on an errand, but Sirena forgot, and spent the afternoon playing in the river. Her angry mother exclaimed that since she loved swimming so much she should become a fish. To avert the curse her godmother quickly said: 'Leave the part of her that belongs to me!' Meanwhile, Sirena, swimming in the river, became aware of a strange sensation, and discovered that from the waist down she was a fish. She swam out into the Pacific Ocean and is sometimes seen by sailors. She can only be caught with a net of human hair.

To the Pech Indians of Honduras in Central America, Sirena is the nine-eyed mother of all the fish, or perhaps a WATER FAIRY. Sirena lives in every river. Her permission must be sought before taking any fish. Offerings were left for her on the riverbanks.

SIRENS ('Entangled') are Greek sea NYMPHS who lure men to their deaths with songs of enchantment. They inhabit an island called Anthemoessa ('Flowery') near Scylla and Charybdis and surround themselves with the bleached bones of their victims. The CENTAURS died when they heard them, as they were so enchanted they forgot to eat. Odysseus is one of the few men to have heard them and lived. When his ship passed the Sirens' isle he ordered his men to stop up their ears with wax, while he had himself lashed to the mast so that he could listen without dashing himself overboard.

The sirens once entered a singing contest with the MUSES and lost, whereupon the muses plucked out all of the sirens' feathers and made crowns from them. However, in the original stories, the sirens were bird women, psychopomps sent to collect the souls of men but in later tales they were depicted as MERMAIDS. The number of them has also varied. Homer mentioned two, naming only one, Himeropa ('Arousing Face'). Others wrote of THREE, Thelchtereia ('Enchantress'), Agaope ('Glorious Face'), and Peisinoe ('Seductress'). They later appear as Parthenope ('Virgin'), Ligeia ('Bright Voiced'), and Leucosia ('White Goddess').

The term 'Siren Song' is used poetically to refer to any seductive music or endearments that lure people from their chosen paths. Most FAIRY MUSIC has this effect.

SITH are the Scots equivalent of the Irish SIDHE, usually called the People of Peace. As well as an Irish Celtic influence, there are Scandinavian

SIDHE

touches to these creatures, though they speak the old Gaelic among themselves. Smaller than the Sidhe aristocrats, the SEELIE COURT are just over one metre tall (three to four feet), with RED or blond hair. They live in Elfhame and process through the countryside in processions known as 'fairy rades' (rides). The UNSEELIE COURT or evil fairies are often dark and ugly and it is necessary to take precautions against them in the form of protective horseshoes of IRON, or rowan and red thread.

SITHBHEIRE is the Gaelic term for a CHANGELING.

SITHEIN is a Scots Gaelic term given to any place the fairies take up residence.

SIZE does matter in the fairy world. Most people think of fairies as delicate, miniature, butterfly-winged creatures, but very few fairies actually look like this. According to the old accounts, they are of human size or larger; and some are even described as GIANTS.

Some believe that as time passed they shrank in size to become very small. In a Cornish story of the fairies of the Gump, they were so tiny that a man could cover a whole fairy feast with his hat. Many British fairies are described as being the size of young children. Writing in 1705 John Beaumont described as follows an experience with fairies:'…the two that constantly attended myself appeared both in Women's Habit, they being of a Brown complexion, and about Three Foot in Stature; they had both black, loose Network Gowns, tyed with a black Sash about their Middles, and within the Network appear'd a Gown of Golden Colour, with somewhat of a Light striking thro' it…they had white Linen Caps on, with Lace on them, about three Fingers breadth.'[306]

SJANKA or SENKA ('Shadow') is an evil Southern Slavonic spirit created from the DEAD soul of a human who has either committed suicide or died an unnatural death. It brings the storms and hail.

SJENOVIK or SJEN ('Shadow') is a spirit of the Slavonic Montenegrins, a type of GENIUS who presides over a house, a lake, a mountain or a forest. It may appear in human form, as a cat, a dog, some other domestic animal, or more likely a SNAKE.[307]

SKAANE was a TROLL who could be controlled once his NAME was guessed.

SKEKLAR is a Shetland TROLL who has fifteen tails and carries fifteen children on each tail.

SKILLYWIDDEN was a fairy captured at Treridge, Cornwall in south-west England, and taken into a human household.[308] However, he managed to return to his own people eventually.

SKOGSJUNGFRU is a female Swedish woodland fairy or WOOD WIFE.

SKOGSRÅ are Swedish wood spirits which may be regional versions of MOUND FOLK, THUSSERS or TROLLS. They are present whenever a violent whirlwind appears and the trees are shaken to breaking point. The rapacious female skogsnufra are violent in their lovemaking with several seventeenth-century death certificates citing the cause of death as: 'involvement with a skogsnufra'.

These creatures appear as small, young and beautifully dressed women, but have claws instead of nails, long breasts and flowing hair. Look carefully, as they have hollow backs and cow tails. Their sweet voices entice men into the woods, and once a man answers, he is in their power. If he refuses, he is no better off, since the fairy will cast an invisible net over him from which he can only be freed by the sound of church bells. Once the fairy has made love with a man, he can never be free of her. When she is absent, he pines away and if she leaves him, he will die. Any children born of the union will be monstrous creatures that might be swapped for human babies, or will be ugly humans with fairy powers.

Be warned, if you hear a voice in the woods asking you questions, never answer 'yes' but only 'he'. If they lead you astray turn your coat inside out or say the paternoster backwards. Carry garlic and leave a few coins on a tree stump at the entrance to the forest. If hunters meet the skogsnufra, they must offer her part of their catch, since all the creatures of the forest are hers. The skogsrå are forest spirits who cannot move far from their trees. They punish people who offend them. The female sometimes appears as an OWL, but is afraid of thunder, wolves and the WILD HUNT. She can be wounded by one of her own hairs fired from a shotgun. The males are called skovmann and are very dangerous shapeshifters who can grow and shrink. They look like little old men wearing wide brimmed hats, but with cow tails, or sometimes appear as horned owls. They ride the storms and whirlwinds.

SKOGSRÅT is a male Swedish woodland fairy or WILD MAN.

SKOODEM HUMPI is one of the Orkney Islands TROWS.

SKOUGMAN is a male Swedish wood fairy or WILD MAN.

SKRAT or Skratec is a Slovenian spirit who lives in the mountains and forests, hiding in the dark caves there, or perching in beech trees. He is made very angry when people shout in his vicinity. At night, he visits villages, especially the SMITH's forge where he will hammer away until dawn. He can appear in many shapes such as an old man or woman, a boy, a CAT, a DOG or a goose, though he is naturally covered with hair.

His services may be obtained for the price of an egg from a black hen, plus your own self, spouse and children.

This pact must be signed in your own blood. In return, the skrat will bring you whatever you wish, placing things on your windowsill, or flying down your chimney in the shape of a fiery BROOM to bring you money. (The flaming broom or staff is an attribute of a Slavonic god of death called Flins or Velyn. He was called der Abgott Flins meaning 'false god' or Pagan god, in sixteenth-century German writings.[309]) In addition to everything else you have promised him, you must leave him a bowl of millet gruel on the windowsill whenever he visits.

SKRATA or Skriatek is a Slovak HOUSE FAIRY who appears in the form of a drenched chicken.

SKRATTI ('Giant') is an Icelandic term for a GOBLIN or monster. The devil's nickname 'Scratch' is probably derived from a cognate old Scandinavian word.

SKREE is a Scottish spirit, possibly a type of BANSHEE, who has red eyes and black, leathery wings. The night before the Battle of Culloden (1746), it was seen shrieking over the opposing English and Scottish armies.

SKRIKER is a North of England OMEN of doom in Yorkshire and Lancashire. It usually appears as a BLACK DOG with saucer eyes and large feet. It wanders around the woods in an invisible form, screaming horribly. It is probably the same being as the TRASH.

SKRÍTEK ('Hobgoblin') is a Slavonic HOUSE FAIRY who lives in the stable or behind the oven. He will do work about the house, especially SPINNING and tending the flocks. The family set out a portion of their meals for him, especially on Thursday or at Christmas, when THREE bits from every dinner are assigned to him. If he is not given his due, like other house fairies he turns nasty and storms about the house, breaking pots, damaging livestock and injuring people. If a family is going to be absent from the house for a while, an image of the Skrítek is placed on the HEARTH to guard the home while they are away. This image depicts him as a small boy with his arms crossed, wearing a crown. The name may be derived from the German SCHRAT.

SKRZAT, Skrzatek or Skrzot is a Polish HOUSE FAIRY who appears in the form of a bird, often a wet chicken dragging its wings and tail behind it, emitting small sparks. Carrying a strangely shaped egg beneath your armpit for NINE days may breed one. It lives in the hayloft and steals the corn. In bad weather, it will move into human dwellings - lucky for the inhabitants, as it will bring them good fortune and wealth.

SKULD is one of the three NORNS, Scandinavian spirits of FATE.

SKY WOMEN are an aspect of the Russian WATER FAIRIES the RUSALKA. In this guise, they couple with the thunder spirits to bring the summer storms.

SLÄTT is a TROLL that can be controlled once his NAME is guessed.

SLEAGH MAITH ('Good People') is an Irish term for the fairies.

SLEIGH BEGGY, Sleih Beggey, Yn Sleigh Veggy ('The Little Fellas' or 'Little Folk') or Mooinjer Veggey are the original inhabitants of the ISLE OF MAN, and are always spoken of in flattering terms by the islanders. They live underground near ancient circles, CAVES, riverbanks or beneath water. They are small and naked with CROW's feet and their footprints are sometimes seen in the ashes strewn in the hearth at HALLOWEEN (a form of divination). They own tiny horses, but are very attracted by the larger Irish and English racehorses and will steal them if they can. A horse found lathered in its stable may have been ridden by the Beggy. They are rarely seen by humans, and will only travel along their own straight paths. They are deterred from entering a house by the presence of ASHES and SALT, silver and all yellow flowers except broom.

SLOOA-SHEE ('Fairy Host') is an Irish Gaelic term for the fairies or TUATHA DÉ DANAAN.

SLUAG ('Host' or 'Fairy Host') are malevolent Scottish Highland fairies, the Hosts of the Unforgiven Dead, damned souls of DEAD humans forced to haunt the scene of their sins forever. They fly about in black clouds like starlings, up and down the face of the earth, haunting the scenes of their sins. They draw humans up into their wild flights and rarely let them go again. They are associated with the UNSEELIE COURT. Sometimes they are seen as sky ELEMENTALS, which may be closer to their original role as spirits of storms and winter weather.

SLUAGH are the Irish host of damned SOULS, equivalent to the Scottish SLUAG, who fly in from the west and try to take the souls of the dying with them. If all west facing windows in the sick room are kept closed, this will thwart them.

SMALL PEOPLE is a generic term for fairies in general, though it is particularly applied to the small and gentle fairies of Cornwall, the POBEL VEAN ('Small People').

SMALL RED MEN are little East African fairies found in Uganda.

SMITHS and IRON play a part in protecting people and animals against malignant fairies, evil spirits, witchcraft, and the evil eye. IRON bracelets or iron objects placed beneath their cribs or pillows protect children.

Blacksmiths are the possessors of magical power themselves. While ordinary humans hang lucky horseshoes with the points upright, so that the power does not leak out, smiths hang them point down to pour the power on to their anvils. In the past, the smith was one of the most important members of the community. He made its tools and weapons, working with iron, a metal that changed the face of the ancient world. Iron falls from the sky in the form of meteorites, a gift of the sky god, or must be extracted from deep in the UNDERWORLD belly of Mother Earth. The metal itself was mysterious, magnetic and stronger than any other. Its smelting and forging processes were akin to magical rituals.

The Celts grouped smiths with Druids as having the power of casting spells and curses.

In myth, there is a connection between trades that use fire and magic.[310] The magical reputation of the smith persisted in Europe into the nineteenth century and is still extant in India and Africa. In Britain, it was believed that smiths were blood charmers (healers) and could foretell the future. They possessed the secret of the Horseman's Word, which when whispered into the ear of the wildest horse would calm it. Even the water the smith used to cool metal had magical properties. People swore oaths by his anvil; and in some places he had the authority to marry couples, as at the famous Gretna Green in Scotland.

Supernatural smiths dwell underground in the Land of the Dead. There are tales of people being rejuvenated in the smith's fire or re-forged by a supernatural smith. In Indian, African and Christian cultures the smith is associated with spirits of fire, underworld deities, and enemies of the sky gods. Many ancient gods are said to have been smiths, such as the Egyptian Ptah, the Greek Hephaestus, the Roman Vulcan, the Irish Lugh and the warrior god Goibniu. Smith gods often forge the thunderbolts for the thunder gods.

Though most fairies are afraid of iron, some fairies are smiths, including DACTYLS and KORREDS. In Russia FATHER FROST is a smith, binding water and earth together with heavy chains. In Scandinavian myth DWARFS are the supernatural smiths, dwelling deep in the earth and possessing all the secrets of magical metallurgy, forging Odin's spear and Thor's hammer. Northern European fairy smiths include ALBERICH and REGIN, while in England there is WAYLAND SMITH, variously described as a dwarf, ELF or GIANT. If a horse is left overnight by his MOUND it will be found newly shod in the morning.

SMOK is a Slavonic HOUSE FAIRY that appears in the form of a SNAKE.

SNAKE is a form in which guardian spirits and WATER FAIRIES often appear, particularly the protectors of wells, springs and rivers. In the west of Wales, a well in Pembrokeshire contains a golden torc guarded by a fairy-serpent, which bites the hand of anyone who tries to steal it. The Maiden's Well in Aberdeenshire, Scotland, is reputed to contain a winged serpent. The Creek Native Americans believe a horned serpent will sometimes appear at a certain well. Arabs believe that DJINNS, in the form of DRAGON or serpent spirits, live in wells.

A snake's movements are sinuous and wave-like, like the course of a river or stream. It was once believed that all water contained a spirit-serpent. In Celtic folklore, snakes and wells are associated with healing. Because the snake sheds its skin each year and appears renewed, it was believed to be immortal.

The snake was regarded as a powerful guardian spirit and was encouraged in temples and homes - snakes were often kept as pets. There are many tales of serpents guarding underground TREASURE under a lake, in a CAVE, or on an island in the far west of the ocean. The snake is a link with the UNDERWORLD from its habit of living in the earth. Snakes are often found in graveyards and were once thought to be communicating with the DEAD, or to be the spirits of the dead themselves.

In myth, the snake (or DRAGON, for the two are often synonymous) is sometimes seen as ruling the winter half of the year and the underworld. It is defeated yearly or nightly by the god of the summer or the sun. The sun god Apollo slew the python at Delphi with his sun ray ARROWS, while St. George killed the dragon. The sun 'dies' nightly, and passes through the Underworld realm of the serpent or dragon. In Greek myth, Ge, the earth goddess, gives the Tree of Immortality as a wedding gift to Hera. It is located in the HESPIRIDES, an island in the far west, and guarded by the daughters of night and the serpent Ladon. The APPLES of the tree represent the sun, which sets or dies nightly in the west and journeys through the underworld, lair of the serpent or dragon, to be reborn each dawn in the east.

SNEGUROTCHKA or **Snow Maiden** is the daughter of Frost and spring in Russian folklore. The heat of the sun melts her when she discovers human emotions and falls in love.

SNOW QUEEN is a beautiful but cruel Danish fairy that brings the winter snows. She lives in a white winter palace and has no children of her own. To be loved by her means death. She may be the later form of a winter HAG goddess.

SOD OF TURF can be more than just earth and grass. According to the folklore of many lands the fairies may steal a human child and leave an ugly CHANGELING in its place. In previous times, Irish parents might place the suspected changeling in a ring of fire to see if it would turn into a sod of turf.

SOEMANGOTS are Indonesian spirits, thought to be the GHOSTS of the DEAD on the island of Sumatra. If a man loses his way in the forest it is because they are casting spells on him. He must split a rattan and creep through the opening, throwing the fairy off the track.

SÖETROLDE are Scandinavian WATER FAIRIES who appear as young men wearing RED CAPS.

SŒURETTES ('Little Sisters') are Breton fairies who act like ancient Greek maenads, rampaging over the hillsides and preying on men.

SOLTRAITS are a type of French HOUSE FAIRY or LUTIN.

SOJENICE ('Givers of Fate') are the Slovenian FAIRY GODMOTHERS who decide the destiny of a new born child. On the night after the birth, a table is set out in the room where the mother lies. On it are placed wax candles, wine, bread and SALT as offerings to the fairies to solicit a happy fate.

SOMODIVES are southern Slavonic forest fairies not to be trifled with. A song relates how the young shepherd Stoïan was warned by his mother not to lead his flock through the forest of the samodives, nor to play his flute when crossing the forest because at the first note a samodive would come and wrestle with him. The shepherd disobeyed, leading his flock into the forest and playing his flute. A young man with ruffled hair appeared to challenge him. They wrestled for THREE days, then the samodive invoked his sisters The Tempests, who carried the shepherd over the trees, beat him, tore him to pieces and destroyed his flock.[311]

SOTRET is a type of French HOUSE FAIRY or LUTIN that delights in making a noise, rattling pots and pans and banging about.

SOULS may be restriced only to mortals, for some authorities state that fairies do not possess souls. According to Irish folklore, this makes them jealous of the human race. Some fairies, like UNDINE, try to marry a human to gain a soul. Paracelsus declared that while man is made of THREE substances, the spiritual, the astral, and the visible or terrestrial and exists in all three, elementals live exclusively in only one of the elements. They have no souls and are incapable of spiritual development.

Conversely, other tales speak of fairies as being the souls of human DEAD, especially UNBAPTISED CHILDREN, women who have died in CHILDBIRTH, suicides, the victims of murder, or the damned. HOUSE FAIRIES (such as the Cauld Lad of Hilton) are often said to be the ghosts of dead servants. Other stories describe fairies as the souls of Pagans who existed before Christianity or Druids who refused to convert: souls neither good enough for heaven nor evil enough for hell, but expelled to the middle world.

There are some fairies who try to capture human souls. MERMAIDS like to snare the souls of sailors, while the WILD HUNT, in its various incarnations, chases the souls of the damned.

SOWLTH or Soullh are luminous, shapeless fairies of light in Ireland.

SPAIN is sometimes equated with FAIRYLAND or the Land of the DEAD in Irish tales.

SPEIR-BHEAN is a lovely woman who appears in a vision of the OTHERWORLD and leads the dreamer into a closer experience of fairyland.

SPINNING is an ancient human activity that has also long associated with a large numbers of fairies. Either they spin themselves or maliciously destroy the spinning of humans. Such fairies include Berchte, Frau Holle, Giane, Girle Guairle, Gruagach, Gwarwyn-A-Throt, Gyre-Carlin, Habetrot, Heather Pixies, Hedley Kow, Holda, Keshalyi, Loireag, Mollyndroat, Terrytop, Tom Tit Tot, Tsirk-Tsirk and of course Rumpelstiltskin. Fairies can be seen through the holed stones that are used as spindle whorls. They are said to have taught the skill of spinning to humans.

Some of these fairies are traceable to ancient spinning and weaving goddesses, who spin the thread of the cosmos and weave the web of fate, such as the Scandinavian NORNS and the Greek FATES. In many tales, it was a goddess who gave the gift of FLAX to humankind and taught the arts of spinning and weaving. According to

German myth, it was the Goddess HULDA, or Holda. Like goddesses of fate, FAIRY GODMOTHERS appear in a triad to bless or curse a child at birth: one who spins, one who weaves and one who cuts the thread of life.

The Egyptian Isis is the patroness of weaving but she also weaves MAGIC and can heal, as all fairies and WITCHES are said to be able to do. Like fairies, spinner/weaver goddesses are associated with the UNDERWORLD and the DEAD. The Egyptian weaver goddess Meith conducted souls to the underworld. Ariadne led Theseus out of the underworld MAZE of the Minotaur by means of a thread, while the witch goddess Hecate led the corn goddess Demeter into the underworld with a thread to find her daughter Persephone

STONEHENGE

(Spring). A number of Celtic gods were depicted with wheels and wheel decorated altars and tombstones.

Several fairies are said to destroy any spinning left on the wheel at YULE or Christmas. This has its origin in the fact that many sun gods and goddesses span the cosmos or the sunbeams in the hours before dawn. At Yule ('Wheel'), the midwinter solstice, when the sun stands still, all forms of spinning and weaving were forbidden. The Lapps forbade the turning of any kind of wheel, including cartwheels and churns.

SPIRALS are marked on many ancient tombs, coins, floors and CAVE walls. It represents the journey through the LABYRINTH that the soul travels into death and the UNDERWORLD and outward to rebirth. The spiral maze is the one created by the SPINNING and weaving goddess, which encompasses

the cosmos itself. In Welsh legend, the weaver is Arianrhod, mistress of Caer Arianrhod, the Spiral Castle of death, initiation and rebirth. Out of her own body she spins the thread of being, and weaves it to form matter: the cosmos itself. The arms of the Milky Way extend in a spiral. She is lady of FATE who spins the thread of destiny and weaves the web that joins all life together. Her spinning wheel is the wheel of the stars, her threads the threads of life, death and rebirth. Her castle reflects the spiralling thread. The ancients saw it as the Corona Borealis at the North Star, where souls regenerated. The spiral shape, which is the basis of the spider's web, is an ancient and almost universal symbol of regeneration and rebirth.

SPOORNE is a little fairy mentioned by Reginald Scot in the *Discoverie Of Witchcraft* 1584.[312]

SPÓR is a Slavonic fertility spirit. Families would invoke such spirits to bring blessings on corn and cattle.

SPOTLOGGIN is a fairy who haunts a ditch near Evesham in the county of Worcestershire, England.

SPRIGGANS (from the Cornish *sperysyan,* meaning 'spirit') are evil south westrn English fairies from Cornwall, reputed to be the ghosts of GIANTS or humans. They guard hidden TREASURE buried beneath pre-historic stones. One night a man tried to dig up the treasure buried under Trencrom Hill. As he neared the gold all about him went dark, thunder crashed and lightening streaked the sky. By its light, he saw a large number of spriggans swarming out of the rocks. At first they were small but they swelled in size until they were as big as GIANTS. He managed to escape, but without his treasure. He was so shaken by his experience that he took to his bed and never worked again.[313]

Spriggans are destructive, causing whirlwinds to blight crops and stealing from human houses. A troop of spriggans used to meet at the cottage of an old woman to divide up their booty. They left a coin for the old woman each time, but she wanted more. One night, she turned her shift inside out, a sure remedy against fairies, and they were forced to flee. She seized all the treasure, but suffered agonies each time she wore her shift.[314]

Spriggans are small, wizened and ugly with oversized heads, but they can inflate themselves when they want to be intimidating. A band of smugglers brought some booty ashore near Long Rock in Cornwall. Three of them went to make arrangements while the other three rested. Tom Warren of Paul heard music and went to tell the intruders to go away. He saw tiny people dancing and playing music dressed in green with RED CAPS. Tom was amused and shouted a rude greeting to them, but the dancers sprang up, armed with bows and ARROWS, spears and slings and seemed to be getting bigger and bigger. Tom ran back to his mates and they were forced to put out to sea under a hail of stones that burned like coals. No spriggans will touch SALT water but the men were forced to stay put until cockcrow.

Spriggans find it highly amusing to kidnap human babies and replace them with ugly spriggan CHANGELINGS.

SPRITE (From the Latin *spiritus,* meaning 'a spirit' in the sense of a soul or ghost) is used as a general term for fairies or a reference to the elusive spirit fairies of more ethereal realms. In popular folklore, sprites change the colours of the leaves in autumn.

SPUNKIES are short and unpleasant Scottish fairies, with very long arms. They steal children and leave ugly CHANGELINGS in their place.

In Somerset, in south-west England, they appear like WILL O'THE WISPS, carrying candles and leading travellers astray at night. On MIDSUMMER's Eve, they go to the churchyard to meet the newly DEAD. Some say that the spunkies themselves are the SOULS of UNBAPTISED CHILDREN, condemned to wander until doomsday.

SRECA is a southern Slavonic fairy that personifies the fate of a human being like the Russian DOLYA. A good Sreca appears as a lovely girl SPINNING golden thread. She will bestow health and riches on the person she is attached to. A bad fate, sometimes called a Nesreca, will bring nothing but misfortune. In this case she appears as an old woman with bloodshot eyes who spends all her time sleeping and takes no care of her owner's affairs, though she also spins. She may be driven away unlike the Russian Dolya.

STAFIA ('Shadow') is the Romanian spirit guardian, or GENIUS, of a person, family, or village. It is possibly the soul of a DEAD ancestor. It appears as a SNAKE, dragon or some other creature, perhaps a RAVEN or bull.

STAR FOLK are lovely spirits of the Algonquin Native American people. These beings live among the stars but sometimes descend to marry humans; but they can also cast spells on people to make them fall ill.

STAR SPIRITS are beings that inhabit star shaped talismans used by Thai farmers to protect their crops.

STENDEL is a variety of NIGHTMARE that sits on the chest of a sleeper and rides him through his dreams.

STICHIO ('Shadow') is a Macedonian spirit guardian of a person, family, or village, and is possibly the soul of a DEAD ancestor. *See also* GENIUS.

STILL FOLK is a Scottish term for the fairies.

STONEHENGE is the famous megalithic site but also the haunt of fairies.

STOCK OF WOOD is what Celtic fairies may leave behind when they steal human babies or adults. Shaped in the likeness of the person, this stock appears to be alive for a short while, but soon ceases to function and the relatives then realise their loss.

STOICHEION/STOICHEIOI ('Shadow') is a Greek guardian spirit of a person, family or village, possibly the soul of an ancestor, occasionally thought of as a HOUSE FAIRY. It appears as a SNAKE that curls up in the warm ashes of the HEARTH.

STOPAN is a southern Slavonic HOUSE FAIRY.

STRAKH ('Fear') is a Bohemian fairy who bursts out of the forest to clutch men by the throat and squeeze out cries of terror.

STRANGERS is a regional English term for fairies in Lincolnshire.

STRASHILA is a noisy Eastern European HOUSE FAIRY.

STRASZYDLO is a Slavonic HOUSE FAIRY who is a nuisance, making noises in the night, rattling pots and pans and thumping the walls.

STRATTELI ('Nightmare') is an Italian wood fairy. *See* STRUDELI.

STRAW can be another form of fairy transport. Its blades are used by some fairies and WITCHES, who twist them into horse shapes then sit astride them, using magic words to command them to fly. Some fairies transform themselves into straw, or can spin it into gold.

STRAY SOD is an enchanted piece of turf that should be avoided. If you step on this piece of grass, you will lose your way, even if you are in your own back yard. This echoes the ancient Irish belief in the Sod of Death (*fód bháis*), whereby everyone has such a sod allotted to them, and will die as soon as their destiny takes them to the spot.

STRENTU are gigantic Hindu creatures covered in scales. They like to eat humans.

STRIBÓG is a Slavonic wind fairy.

STROKE is an illness caused by a clot or haemorrhage in the brain and often results in the paralysis of one side of the body. It used to be thought that it was caused by being struck by an ELF BOLT, aimed by a fairy or WITCH.

STROKE LAD is a member of the Irish SIDHE who comes at the end of every fairy procession. Presumably he causes strokes.

STRÖMKARL is a Norwegian WATER FAIRY who wears a RED CAP, red stockings and a red cape. He plays a harp or a fiddle and sings beautifully in order to seduce young girls.

STRUDELI is an Italian woodland fairy who, in partnership with STRATTELI, attacks fruit trees. A Twelfth Night ceremony is undertaken to frighten them both away. The boys of the village walk in procession making noises with horns and cowbells.

SUCCUBUS (*pl.* **Succubi**) (from the Latin *cubare* meaning 'to lie', and *sub* meaning 'beaneath') is a female spirit who sexually assaults men in their sleep in order to conceive a DEMON child. A BLUEBELL in the bedroom will keep her away. She is the female counterpart of an INCUBUS and both are related to the various NIGHTMARE fairies.

SUD ('Judgement') *pl.* **Sudy** are the Russian spirits of FATE or judgement.

SUDICE ('Givers of Fate') are Slovenian FAIRY GODMOTHERS who bestow fortune on a newborn child.

SUDÍCKY are Bohemian FAIRY GODMOTHERS who decide the destiny of a newborn child. When a woman has given birth they send her into a deep sleep and place the baby on a table while they ponder its fate. Usually THREE fairies will appear, the oldest being the most powerful. Like the Greek FATES one spins, another measures, while the third cuts the thread of life. On other occasions one, four, five, SEVEN or NINE fairies may come, led by a queen.

The Bohemians believe that the fairies may be persuaded to grant a favourable destiny by being bribed with presents and offerings. When a woman goes into labour a table is made ready for them, covered with a white cloth and laid with bread, SALT, butter, cheese and beer. When the child is christened food is left on the table at the feast for the spirits.

SUDRI ('South') is one of the four DWARFS who hold up the sky, which is formed from the skull of the giant YMIR, in Icelandic myth. The others are Nordri ('North'), Austri ('East'), and Vestri ('West').

SUDZENICI are Southern Slavonic FAIRY GODMOTHERS who decide the destiny of a newborn child.

SUJENICE or **Sudjenice** are Croatian FAIRY GODMOTHERS who decide the destiny of a newborn child.

SUKUSENDAL is a Finnish fairy, which can be either male or female, that sexually assaults sleepers, like an INCUBUS or SUCCUBUS. It also steals human children and leaves CHANGELINGS in their place. Like other fairies it is deterred by placing an IRON knife or nail under the bedclothes.

SULEYMAN is the king of the DJINN.

SUMASCAZZO is an Italian FOLLETTO who causes dust whirls and eddies in Sardinia, and his appearance is a bad OMEN.

SUMMERLAND is the British OTHERWORLD paradise, where the souls of the DEAD feast and rest before rebirth. It is sometimes said to overlay the physical realm of the south west of Britain, and one of its entrances is through Glastonbury Tor.

SUMSKE DEKLE ('Woodland Maidens') are Croatian woodland fairy maidens, covered in hair. They have never been heard to speak; though their wild shrieks are sometimes noticed echoing around the forests. When humans leave food out for them they will return the favour by cleaning their houses.

SVARTÁLFAHEIM ('Black Elves' Home') is an UNDERWORLD realm, the home of the black or dark elves called SVARTALFAR or DOCKALFAR.

SVARTÁLFAR or Swartalfar ('Black Elves') are the Norse ELVES or 'black spirits', possibly synonymous with DWARFS. They live in an UNDERWORLD kingdom away from the sunlight, which would turn them to stone. They are as black as pitch in appearance.

SWAN is the bird form in which fairies or enchanted humans sometimes appear. They can be recognised by the golden chains around their necks.

SWAN MAIDENS appear in Norse, Greek, Celtic, Indian, Malayasian and Thai stories, from *The Arabian Nights* to the Welsh *Mabinogion*. The motif of a fairy maid who first appears as an animal such as a seal (SELKIE), WHITE HIND or swan is a common one. She may challenge the hero or lend him magical aid. Sometimes swan maidens appear as guides to the DEAD, taking them to the Far Northern OTHERWORLD, through the swan-veils. The VALKYRIES were such swan maidens who could discard swan plumage to become human. Any man who could steal the plumage could command them. Some swan maidens are human women changed into immortal fairy swans, recognisable by the golden chains around their necks.

SWAN VEILS in misty layers, according to Norse folklore, are said to cover the entrance to the far northern OTHERWORLD.

SWAN MAIDEN

SWARTH (Swarthy or Black?) is a Scottish Borders term for a FETCH, possibly derived from swartalfar or SVARTALFAR, meaning 'Black Elves'.

SWETYLKO is a western Slavonic WILL O'THE WISP.

SYLPH is an air ELEMENTAL according to the alchemist Paracelsus. The word is derived from the Greek

silphe meaning 'BUTTERFLY' or 'moth'. Sylphs live in the mountain peaks and sometimes their voices are heard on the wind, though they are rarely seen. Sylphs are described as almost transparent, very small and winged or alternatively tall with long feathered wings, large, hawk-like eyes and angular faces.

SYLVANS are Greek woodland fairies, beautiful but dangerous. They lure travellers to their deaths in the forests.

SYLVESTER is a spirit of the woods, according to the alchemist Paracelsus.

SYLVESTRES are the spirits of the air also called sylphs, which Paracelsus named from the Greek *silphe,* meaning 'BUTTERFLY' or 'moth'. They are described as almost transparent, very small and winged. *See* ELEMENTALS.

SYRENKA is a Polish MERMAID who lived in the River Vistula River in Warsaw. One day, three peasants decided to curry favour with the prince by catching her and presenting her as a gift. They stopped their ears with wax so as not to be enchanted by her singing, and netted her as she sat on a rock, combing her hair. After

SYLVANS

SZÉPASSZONY ('Beautiful Woman') is a Hungarian fairy, a lovely WHITE clad woman with long hair. She walks on top of the world so that she can see what is happening everywhere. Individual fairies protect particular villages and protect them from demons bringing illnesses. The szépasszony dances in storms and hail showers, appears and disappears at will, and is at her most powerful at noon.

She may travel in company with others of her kind, singing and dancing in the air from midnight till cock-crow. She likes to seduce young men and appears in the moonlight, bathing in streams or combing her golden hair. She casts evil spells on humans and a sickly child may be said to have been 'suckled by the Fair Lady'.

One method of her casting a spell is via the water that drips from the eaves to form a puddle. Anyone who steps into this puddle will fall under her power. You must not disturb her when she is dining at the crossroads, as you will become ill. She performs much of her magic at the CROSSROADS, washing her legs then cooking beans in the water, before pouring it onto the centre of the roads; if a person then steps on the spot he will get an abscess. If you step on the plant called szépasszony grass (or 'wrong grass'), you will lose your way. However, the szépasszony grass gathered in a fairy place has curative properties, as does the herb called szépasszony milkbread. It is not good to lie on the ground before St George's Day (23rd April) as the fairy might carry you away. If you sleep outdoors on Whitsun night, she will steal your bones.

The szépasszony is sometimes thought of as a human or supernatural WITCH and during the witch trials it was reported that human witches consorted with the szépasszony, dancing with them and joining their feasting.

keeping her in a barn overnight, they set off to see the prince, leaving her in the care of a young shepherd. She begged him for her freedom, and very moved by her pleas, he agreed. She plunged into the river and swam away, but promised that if the city were ever in difficulty she would arm it with sword and shield. For this reason, she appears on Warsaw's coat of arms.

SYRINX was a water NYMPH beloved by PAN, who pursued her until she reached the river Ladon, where she appealed to her sister nymphs for help. They turned her into a bed of REEDS and when Pan reached out to grasp her, he found his arms full of reeds instead. He heard the wind rushing through the reeds, making a pleasant musical sound; this inspired him to pluck SEVEN of them to make his famous pipes.

TALONHALTIJA is a Finnish fairy that protects the home, rather like a HOUSE FAIRY. It is sometimes said to be an ancestral spirit.

TAM LIN is the eponymous hero of a Scottish folk ballad. A maiden called Janet went into Carterhaugh Wood in the Scottish Border country. She wished to pick wild roses near a certain well that lay in a clearing there. No sooner had she plucked a single blossom than a tall, handsome ELF appeared before her. The pair dallied together all that afternoon and fell in love. The elf told her that he was really not a fairy at all, but a human knight under enchantment, held in bondage to the Fairy Queen. His name was Tam Lin, and he was the grandson of the Earl of Roxburgh. Janet determined to rescue him; an endeavour that her lover explained was possible, but full of danger.

The following SAMHAIN Eve Janet proceeded to the CROSSROADS and hid behind a thorn bush, to await the passing of the FAIRY RADE. Eventually, to the sweet sound of the music of lutes and pipes, a procession came into view led by the lovely Queen riding a black HORSE, and followed by pale fairy lords and ladies. Among them was Tam Lin on a white horse, recognisable by the fact that he was wearing only one GLOVE. As instructed, Janet sprang out from her hiding place and pulled him from his saddle.

By malignant fairy GLAMOUR, Tam Lin was transformed into a SALAMANDER lizard, and Janet nearly lost her grip. Then the lizard became a huge, coiling SNAKE. Janet was

terrified, but hung on. The serpent became a bear, but she held it fast. The bear became a SWAN, which flapped against her breast. At last, its struggling stopped and Janet found that she held only an IRON bar. This was the end, she knew, and cast the bar into the well. There it steamed and a moment later a naked man stepped from the well, her lover Tam Lin become human again.

The Fairy Queen blazed with anger. She turned her gaze on Tam Lin, amazed that a mortal could have bested her. She cried that had she known that a woman could have won him, she would have torn his heart from him and given him one of stone. At this she wheeled away, all her band following, and disappeared into the trees.

There are many recorded sung versions of this song on record.

TAMARA is a Cornish water NYMPH who was changed into the River Tamar by her father, an UNDERWORLD figure, when she refused to choose between the sons of two Dartmoor GIANTS who sought her hand in marriage.

TAN NOS is a French WILL O'THE WISP.

TANGIE or **TANGYE** (Derived from the Danish for 'seaweed') is an evil WATER HORSE that haunts Shetland. It has long shaggy hair and is covered in seaweed. Tangie can also appear as an old man. Some say that there is a race of mischievous Tangies who tempt people to ride on their backs and duck them under the water. *See also* BLACK ERIC.

TANGOTANGO is a Maori fairy of New Zealand who fell in love with a young god called Tawhaki. She stayed with him until she became pregnant, when she left him to give birth to her daughter alone.

TANKERABOGUS or **Tantarabobus** is a BOGEYMAN, known in the south west of England, especially in Devon

and Somerset. He goes after naughty children in order to punish them. The word is sometimes used for the DEVIL. It is possible that it gave rise to the American word *bogus*, once treated as slang but now part of the English language, a noun that describes anything counterfeit. It was first used by a reporter in 1827 in Ohio, but a Dr Willard of Chicago commented that when he was a child it was common practice to refer to anything ill-looking or dubious as tantarabogus.[315]

TAPAIRU ('Fairest of the Fair') are water NYMPHS of the Pacific islands, the four daughters of the female DEMON Miru, an ugly HAG who lives in the UNDERWORLD. The daughters are very beautiful and rise to the upperworld at sunset and comb their tresses in the moonlight or join human dancers in their revels. They live in the pool that leads to AVAIKI, the UNDERWORLD, and seduce men into their mother's realm where she will ply them with drink, then roast and eat them.

TAPIO is a Finnish fairy, once a powerful god, to whom all the wild beasts of the forests belong. He reigns his forest kingdom along with his beautiful wife. Any hunter has to appeal to them before he kills any forest beast. They also protect domestic COWS and those people who stray into the forest.

TARANS ('Fire'?) are Scottish fairies, spirits of UNBAPTISED CHILDREN condemned to wander about the woods until Doomsday, bewailing their fate.[316] Meeting one is very dangerous, and possibly even fatal, but dousing them with holy water and speaking the words of the baptismal rite can save these sad souls. In the Scottish Lowlands and in south west England in Somerset, they are called SPUNKIES.

TAROGOLO is a spirit who seduces humans and then destroys their genitalia, according to the Papau New Guinea folklore of the Lakalai people of the island of New Britain.

TARROO-USHTEY is a fearsome WATER BULL that lives in the seas surrounding the ISLE OF MAN, though similar animals are found all around Britain. It sometimes leaves the sea to feed and mate with domestic COWS. One farmer had to abandon his farm when the Tarroo-Ushtey took against him.

TARTARO is a one-eyed GIANT in Basque folklore, similar to a CYCLOPS.

TATTERFOAL is an English GOBLIN who appears in Lincolnshire in the form of a HORSE.

TATTERMAN is a German BUGBEAR or scarecrow.

TAWA-O-HOI is an evil MAERO who lives under Mount Tarawera in New Zealand. The Maori say that he likes to eat humans.

TCHI-CO is a saucer-eyed BLACK DOG that haunts the St Peter Port area of the Channel Island of Guernsey, clanking its chains. Its howls are a sure omen of death for those who hear them.

TEIGUE OF THE LEE is one of the Irish HOUSE FAIRIES.

TEIND or **Kain** is a form of giving the Devil his due! According to Scottish folklore, the fairies have to pay a tribute to the DEVIL every SEVEN years in the form of a human. This tithe is called a *teind or kain*. It is said that this is why they kidnap us.

TEINE SITH ('Fire Fairy') is the Scots Gaelic fairy light or WILL O'THE WISP of the Hebrides.

TENGU are Japanese nature spirits, part of the Shinto religion. They are SHAPESHIFTERs who can appear as any animal, but usually manifest as RED-clad, winged fairies carrying feathered fans. They are born from eggs. They have great magical powers, which they will not share with humans.

TENNIN are lovely fairy maidens of Buddhist lore. They wear feathery robes and live in the OTHERWORLD. They are sometimes encountered on the highest summit of the mountains.

TEPEGOZ is a one-eyed GIANT in Turkish folklore, similar to a CYCLOPS.

TEPENTIREN is a fairy of the RUMPELSTILTSKIN type, whose NAME has to be guessed.

TERAN is a spirit of the Orkney Islands who brings the winter and its attendant storms. (For his story, see SEA MITHER.)

TERDELASCHOYE is a name given to MORGAN LE FAY in Wolfram von Eschenbach's *Parsifal* (1200).

TERPSICHORE ('Whirler') is one of the nine MUSES, the patroness of dancing and mother of the SIRENS. She is usually depicted plucking a lyre.

TERRE DE LA JOIE ('Land of Joy') is the Land of MORGAN LE FAY in French romance.

TERRYTOP is an English GOBLIN from Cornwall who consorted with the famous St. Leven WITCHES. Squire Lovel of Trove rode to Churchtown to hire help for the cider making. As he was passing through the village he heard a tremendous din at Janey Chygwin's cottage door and was dumbfounded to see her beating her stepdaughter Duffy about the head, calling her a lazy slut. The girl protested that her SPINNING and knitting were the best in the parish. The squire immediately resolved to take Duffy with him, since he was in need of a girl to spin his wool and knit him fine stockings.

When they reached Trove, the squire's half-blind housekeeper (one eye had been put out by a wizard) showed Duffy up to the attic where the knitting and spinning was done. However, the truth was that Duffy really was an idle slut who could neither knit nor spin. The garret was piled with fleeces of wool and she looked miserably at them for some time before wailing: 'Curse the spinning and knitting! The devil may spin and knit for all I care'. No sooner had she spoken, than a quaint little man appeared and offered to do the work for her, telling her she should be a lady of leisure. However, if at the end of THREE years she could not guess his NAME, she would have to go with him. Duffy wasted no time in consenting to the compact.

All the spinning and knitting was done beautifully by the little man. Duffy only had to look under the black lamb's fleece to find lovely yarns and stockings. The squire and his housekeeper heaped praise upon the indolent girl, while she did nothing but sleep and go to dances at the nearby mill. However, Old Bet the miller's wife was a WITCH and realised that Duffy's work was done by a GOBLIN.

Things went on for nearly three years. All the chests and coffers of the manor house soon became filled with fine thread and hose. The squire was unwilling to lose such a useful and willing girl to another man and decided to marry Duffy himself. While he spent his days hunting and drinking she kept the goblin busy producing underclothing, stockings, bed linen and embroidery.

The three years promised by the goblin were coming to an end and Duffy began to get worried. She decided to consult Old Bet and was advised her to fetch a jug of her strongest ale from the cellar. Taking this and her *crowd* (a sieve covered in sheepskin) the witch threw her red

cloak over her shoulders and set off into the night.

Meanwhile, Duffy waited up for her husband as Bet had instructed. He came in at midnight drunk and rambling, describing a weird encounter. He told her that as night fell he went down to Lamorna Bottoms where his dogs put up a HARE. He chased it at a wild pace until it ran down the fougou hole.[317] The dogs went in after it and the squire after them, OWLS, and bats flying about his head. He went on a mile or more, though the tunnel was not meant to be so long. As they came to a broad pool of water the dogs ran back, howling and afraid. Undeterred, the squire pressed on and turning a corner, saw a glimmering fire where there were St. Leven witches in scores. Some were riding on RAGWORT stems, others on BROOMS, some were floating on three-legged stools and some, who had been milking the good COWS in Wales, had come astride enormous leeks. There was Bet with her *crowd* in one hand and the jug of ale in the other. Suddenly a little man appeared, dressed in black. Bet struck her *crowd* like a drum and kept up a vigorous beat. The goblin danced around all the women, but every time he went by Bet he took a good swig of the ale. It wasn't long before he was blind drunk and began to sing: 'Duffy, my lady, you'll never know…what? That my name is Terrytop, Terrytop..Top!'

The watching squire had laughed at all the fun, but as soon as the throng was aware of his presence, the lights went out and they all disappeared. Hearing this story Duffy began to chuckle. The next day the goblin appeared. 'Well', he asked 'are you ready to accompany me? Have you guessed my name?'

'Perhaps your name is Lucifer?' mused Duffy. The goblin scoffed and bid her guess again.'Could it be Beelzebub?' The goblin conceded that he might be a distant cousin.

'Well, in that case your name must be Terrytop! Deny it if you dare.'

'A gentleman never denies his name,' replied the goblin, and disappeared in a puff of fire and smoke. All of his knitting and spinning immediately fell into ashes along with him, just as the squire was wading through a brook on the moors. He blamed his subsequent cold on Old Bet getting her revenge for him chasing her while she was in the form of a hare.[318]

TEUFEL ('Devil') is a German term for a GOBLIN.

TEUZ are Breton fairies who live in bogs or swamps. They are small, dark and shaggy.

THABET are evil Burmese fairies, ugly monsters with long tongues. They dislike humans and attack them when they get the chance.

THAGYA MIN is the most important NAT or Burmese nature fairy. He is associated with the beginning of the Burmese year. He is depicted standing in a lotus supported by three elephants.

THALEIA or **Thalia** ('Flourishing') is one of the nine MUSES, the patroness of comedy and whimsical poetry. She is depicted with the mask of comedy, an ivy crown and a shepherd's crook.

THIEVES and fairies can often be synonymous. Many fairies are known to be thieves, but when they take something they take only its substance or spirit, so when a cow is elf-taken it appears to be struck down by some disease. It will lie down and refuse to get up. Though it will continue to eat, it will produce no milk. When it dies its flesh will turn out to be a stock of alder wood or some such rubbish. Fairies can also steal the spirit of the land itself. When this happens the fields appear to yield a crop but the ears of corn will not fill out, the harvest will be slender and the animal fodder without nourishment.

Fairies can only take away what selfish humans deserve to lose. If you 'over look a child' (i.e. look on it with envy) then the fairies have it in their power. When people become miserly and refuse to share their possessions or do not value them the fairies will take the goodness out of them. When a farmer grumbles about his crop, even if it is good, the fairies will take the substance out of it. When you mislay something and can't find it, no matter how hard you look, it is almost certain that the fairies have taken it.

THEMSELVES is an ISLE OF MAN term for the fairies. They are sometimes said to be the SOULS of those that died in Noah's Flood.

THETIS is a NEREID, or sea NYMPH, of Greek mythology. She was the mother of Achilles.

THÉVADAS are spirits of pre-Buddhist Thai mythology that inhabit the stars and planets and all the spaces in between. The places of the earth are inhabited by spirits called PHI.

THEY is an ISLE OF MAN term for the fairies echoed in many parts of the word such as the Turkish Onlar ('They') and the Romanian Ieles ('They').

THEY THAT'S IN IT is another ISLE OF MAN term for the fairies.

THIRTY SEVEN, THE are prominent among the Burmese nature fairies the NATS. They are the spirits of warriors and heroes. They have power over weather, crops, health and animals, and must be propitiated with food and flowers.

THITIS is of the sisters of MORGAN LE FAY who dwells with her in AVALON.

THIVISHES ('Thieves'?) seem to exist in large numbers throughout Ireland; though whether they are GHOSTS or fairies it is hard to determine.

THOMAS BOUDIC is a particular house LUTIN of French fairy folklore.

THOMAS THE RHYMER was a mortal who spent time in FAIRYLAND. He had been playing his lute beneath a HAWTHORN in the woods when a beautiful fairy riding a horse emerged from the trees to listen. Eventually, she dismounted and he tried to kiss her. She warned him that such an act would bind him to her for SEVEN years, but he did not hesitate. They journeyed together through the night to a bright meadow in which there were two paths, one to perdition and one to righteousness, but the fairy queen explained that for lovers and poets there was another path, a twisting third way that led to fairyland. While in the fairy UNDERWORLD he was shown another hawthorn tree, which also bore magical APPLES. The Queen of Elfland warned him that it bore all the plagues of hell, and also conveyed the gift of PROPHECY.

After seven years, Thomas returned home but his songs were sweeter and more poignant than ever before. He was also able to foretell the future, as in fairyland he had eaten an APPLE whose flesh had the power of truth, a parting gift from the fairy queen.

On his seventy-eighth birthday, he was holding his annual party when he was told that two white DEER, a male and a female, were heading through the village to his house. He knew this to be a summons to fairyland and followed them back there, where he still sings and plays.

In fact, there was an historical Thomas the Rhymer; a poet and prophet of the Scottish Borders called Thomas Rymour of Erceldoune (c. 1220-c.1297) who was said to have predicted the death of Pope Alexander III and the Battle of Bannockburn.

THREE is a number that appears regularly in fairy tales: three fairy godmothers, three blind mice, three bears, three little pigs, three wishes, three guesses, three kisses, three gifts and third time lucky. Magical spells are often performed in threes: spit on the ground three times before cutting ELDER; pass a hot coal three times round a cow to purify it; knock three times to open a fairy MOUND. Mary Player swims three times around a ship to sink it, and the magical swans flew three times around a lake to put everyone in the vicinity to sleep. Mine Fairies knock three times and the Otherworld DOG barks three times as a warning of impending disaster. Cerberus, the Greek canine guardian of the UNDERWORLD had three heads, as do some ogres like Red Etin. Then we have the three FATES and the three NORNS, three SIRENS, three GORGONS, three HESPERIDES, three aspects of the MORRIGAN, and the three faces of BRIGHID.

Three is regarded as the number of completion. One stands alone; two creates opposites while three reconciles them, for example as in the trinity of male, female and child. Time has three phases, past, present and future. Creation has a beginning, middle and an end. Space has three dimensions, length, breadth and thickness. Gods and goddesses often appear in trinities like the holy family of Isis, Osiris and Horus; the three aspects of the Moon Goddess, maiden, mother and crone; and the Christian trinity of God the Father, Son and Holy Spirit.

THRESHOLDS can be significant, even hazardous, locations. A number of fairies live beneath thresholds, including the FOLLETTI. The threshold is a dangerous place, neither inside nor outside, but a boundary between the two - a place between places. When a person crosses a threshold, they move from one state to another and are in danger from the spirits that dwell *between*. For this reason a bride - in a threshold stage of life - is carried across the threshold into her new house. Sometimes, the first thing to cross the threshold of a new house is in so much danger that a cock or some other animal is thrown in by way of a sacrifice. In Ireland, PRIMROSES were scattered on the threshold because fairies are unable to pass them. In England, thresholds were made of HOLLY wood, since no witch or fairy could pass over these. Other charms included sprinkling the doorposts with blood and hanging sacred objects on them. In parts of Britain, protective patterns ('step patterns') were drawn on the doorstep in salt, chalk, or actually reproduced in mosaic. These took the form of knotwork and 'tangled thread' patterns.[319]

In many cases, it was thought unlucky to tread on the threshold itself, and people were always careful to step over it. It was often believed to be the dwelling place of certain gods and spirits, such as the Indian Lakshmi and the Roman Lima and Limentius. Frazer recorded that the followers of the Philistine god Dagon took care not to tread on the threshold of his temple.[320] To avoid offending these deities, corpses and pregnant or menstruating women had to leave by the back door.

For the Celts boundaries of any kind were dangerous and gave access to the OTHERWORLD. These included such in between things as a CROSSROADS, the shore between sea and land, MIDNIGHT (the time between one day and the next) and SAMHAIN, the time between one year and the next). The place where the sun sets is another kind of threshold, giving access to the UNDERWORLD.

THRUMMY CAP is a north-eastern English cellar HOUSE FAIRY in Northumberland, who has the appearance of an old man. He wears a cap of weavers' thrums.

THRUMPIN is an attendant spirit, in the English/Scottish Border counties, which accompanies every human with the power of taking his or her life.[321] *See also* FETCH, GENIUS and DÆMON.

THUMBLING is an English term for a small fairy.

THUNDER-ARROWS is a name given in Germany to belemnite fossils. Also known as thunderbolts or ELF-BOLTS, it was once believed that they were cast down from heaven with the lightening. They are lucky charms and protect the house and dairy from lightning and the attentions of evil spirits.

THURSDAY is a bad day for Scottish fairies. They cannot be abroad on Thursdays, because it is St. Columba's Day:

'God be between me and every fairy,
Every ill wish and every druidry;
To-day is Thursday on sea and land,
I trust in the King that they do not hear *me*'

Thursday is named after the Norse thunder god Thor, traditionally an enemy of DWARFS and ELVES.

THUSSERS (Giant'?) are Norwegian fairies who live in communities beneath MOUNDS near the fjords. At night, the mounds open and the thussers emerge to dance and play fiddles in the moonlight. Should a human approach they will hurry away and hide. They are expert metal workers.

THYME (*Thymus vulgaris*) is one of the herbs sacred to fairies. At midnight on MIDSUMMER's night, the King of the Fairies dances with his followers on wild thyme beds. In Shakespeare's *A Midsummer Night's Dream* OBERON tells PUCK:

'I know a bank where the wild thyme blows
Where oxlips and the nodding violet grow'

It is an ingredient of many magical potions, dating from around 1600, which allow those who take them to see fairies. One simple charm is to make a brew of wild thyme tops gathered near the side of a fairy hill plus grass from a fairy throne. Like other fairy flowers, wild thyme is unlucky if brought indoors.

TIB is a female fairy associated with ROBIN GOODFELLOW[322] and is an attendant of Queen MAB. Tib was well known in the English Midlands and there is a Tib's Hall in Birmingham.

TIDDY MUN ('Little Man') or **Yarthkin** ('Earth-kin') is a WATER FAIRY of the East Anglian Fens, a region of eastern England that largely lay under water until drains and ditches were dug. Tiddy Mun could control the mists, call up disease from the marshes, and control the water. He is appealed to, in order to calm the waters but can be dangerous when angered. He lives in the green water holes and comes out in the evenings when the mists rise into the darkling (twilight). He limps along like an old man with long white hair and a long white beard, all matted and tangled, wearing a long grey gown that hides him in the mist or dusk. He whistles like the wind and laughs like a peewit. He was thought to be better natured than most of the local fairies and sometimes helped people. When the floodwaters rose to the cottage door a family would go out and call: 'Tiddy Mun wi'out a name; tha watters thruff!' When they heard a noise like a peewit they knew that Tiddy Mun had heard them, and would go home.

When the fenlands were drained, the Tiddy Mun became so angry that he brought pestilence on children and cattle until he was pacified with lustrations and prayers.[323] Tiddy Muns are also called YARTHKINS.

TIDDY ONES ('Little Ones') are English fairies of East Anglia who can be helpful to humans, but will injure children and cattle if they are offended. TIDDY MUN was appealed to to withdraw the floodwaters of the fens.

TIDY PEOPLE is another name for the YARTHKINS.

TIGERNMAS or **TIERNMAS** ('Lord of Death') is an ancient mythical king of Ireland who seems to have associations with the UNDERWORLD and the craft of the SMITH, which he introduced to Ireland, along with mining and the WEAVING of tartans.

TIGHE FAIRIES are Isle of Man HOUSE FAIRIES that go out and about at night in pairs to do household tasks for humans. However, they will not enter a house where a CAT lives.

TIME in the realm of the fairy passes differently from time in the human realm. Those humans who have visited fairyland believe that they have been absent from their homes for a single night; whereas, in reality, they have been many years in fairyland. All they knew is long passed away and their friends and relatives are long dead (see OISIN).

Alternatively, a person may think that he has spent many years in fairyland, but has been absent from the mundane world for only a few minutes. This occurred in the case of the Welsh shepherd from Pembrokeshire who joined a dance in a FAIRY RING and found himself in the Otherworld. He lived happily for several years among the fairies, feasting and drinking with them in their lovely palaces. However, he was warned that he must not drink from a magical fountain that stood in the centre of the gardens. Inevitably, he eventually broke the taboo and plunged into the water. He instantly found himself back on the hillside, with his flock of sheep, having been absent for only a few moments of ordinary time.[324]

TIPUA are SHAPESHIFTING Moari GOBLINS from New Zealand.

TÍR FÓ THUINN ('Land Beneath the Wave') is an Irish FAIRY ISLAND.

TIR INNA MBAN or **Tir Na Mban** ('Land of Women') is an Irish fairy island. In one Celtic legend, the sea god MANANNAN summoned the hero Bran and his followers to the FAIRYLAND Tir inna mBan, the Isle of Women, which was supported on four bronze pillars and solely inhabited by women. There they were entertained royally, but after a year, they decided they would like to see Ireland once again. As they left, the women made them promise not to set foot on land.

Eventually, their ship sighted Ireland and the adventurers shouted news of their exploits ashore. The incredulous inhabitants replied that Bran and his ship were only an ancient legend. At this, one of the sailors was so disturbed that he determined to wade ashore and find out what was going on, but as soon as his feet touched the land, he crumbled to dust. The crew realised that they could never return home after being in the realms of the fairy, and sailed away, never to be seen again. *See also* OISIN, THOMAS THE RHYMER.

TIR NAN OG or **Tir-na-Oge** is 'The Land of Youth' of Irish legend. When the TUATHA DÉ DANAAN fled from the physical realm of Ireland they went to the OTHERWORLD paradise of Tir Nan Og where they live feasting, hunting, lovemaking and playing music. It is always spring here, and there is no ageing, illness or death or even work as there is always fruit on the trees. They can indulge in their love of fighting with impunity, as anyone killed will rise again the next day.

TÍR TAIRNGIRI ('Land of Promise') is an OTHERWORLD kingdom ruled by the Irish sea god MANANNAN or perhaps the fairy king MIDAR.

TISIPHONE ('Avenger') is one of the ERINNYES, the ancient Greek Furies, spirits of vengeance.

TITANIA is a famous fairy whose name derives from a title of the goddess DIANA.[325] In mediaeval folklore, Titania is rarely mentioned, but she was immortalised by Shakespeare's in *A Midsummer Night's Dream* as the Queen of the Fairies. She rules a fairy court situated near Stratford upon Avon (Shakespeare's birth place), with her husband OBERON.

TITANS ('Lords') were the race of GIANTS that ruled the SEVEN planets in ancient Greek myth, a male and female Titan to each. Later the Olympian god Zeus devoured them. According to one school of thought, the Titan Prometheus is the progenitor of the fairy species, while the Titaness Rhea gave birth to the Dactyls who were DWARFS or earth fairies.

According to Hesiod, the Titans are confined in the dank, dark UNDERWORLD. The entrance to their domain is in the western Mediterranean: 'where day and night draw near and greet each other as they pass on the great threshold of bronze', i.e. the place of the setting sun.[326]

TITTELI TURE is a fairy of the RUMPELSTILTSKIN type, whose NAME has to be guessed.

TOADS (*Bufo bufo*) were often the FAMILIARS or the SHAPESHIFTING forms of evil fairies and WITCHES. Mediaeval alchemists thought the toad represented the primal elements of nature and its dark and damp environment gives it lunar and UNDERWORLD associations.

Two girls once saw a massive fat toad that turned out to be a fairy. One joked that if it ever had a baby she would be its godmother, the other quipped she would cook for the christening. A few days later an old woman knocked at their door and invited them to the baptism of the toad's child, reminding them of their promise. They were taken to an isolated location where all sorts of strange looking guests had gathered to attend the ceremony. The service proceeded and the girls filled their parts. When they departed, they were astonished to have their aprons filled with coal from the hearth. They hurried home, scattering most of the coal as they went. However, when they arrived at their door and crossed the THRESHOLD, every bit of coal that remained had turned to gold.

TOAD STONES are fossils, once believed to come from the foreheads of TOADS, which are a protection against fairies and WITCHES. They prevent MILK being bewitched.

TOADSTOOLS, fungi and MUSHROOMS, with their unearthly shapes and rapid growth, are often associated with fairies. This is evidenced by some of their English names, which include Yellow Fairy Club, Slender Elf Cap, Dune Pixie-Hood and Dryad's Saddle. *See also* FAIRY RING MUSHROOMS, FLY AGARIC.

TOD LOWRIE is an English fairy from East Anglia, a peculiar, primeval spirit that has to be pacified or it will bring blight.

TODMĀDCHEN ('Death Maiden') is a German term for an IMP.

TODORCI or **Todorovici** are southern Slavonic fairies who appear in the form of HORSES during the spring. Sacrifices were offered to them to ensure fertility.

TOGGELI is a Southern European fairy who is a type of NIGHTMARE.

TOICE BHREAN ('The Lazy One') is an Irish WATER FAIRY, the guardian of Lough Gur, a lake in Co. Limerick in Ireland. Because she neglected to watch over the well that she was appointed to oversee, it flooded and created the lake. Every SEVEN years a mortal drowns in the lake, taken by the BEAN-FIONN.

TOKOLOSHE, Tikoloshe (Xhosa) or **Tokkelossie** (Afrikaans) is an evil South African fairy that is covered with black hair, though he has human hands and feet. He has the power to become INVISIBLE. He lives beside streams and likes to frighten humans by throwing stones into the water or making small beasts squeak as he strangles them. He sometimes helps burglars.

TOLCARNE TROLL is a Cornish fairy who lives at the Newlyn Tolcarne. He is said to date back to the time when the Phoenicians sailed to Cornwall. He looks like a pleasant little old man, dressed in a tight fitting leather jerkin, with a HOOD over his head. He lives within the rock. He can become invisible at will. He often sailed away with the Phoenician traders who came for the tin, visiting Tyre and assisting at the building of Solomon's temple. You can call up the fairy by holding in your hand THREE dried leaves (OAK, ASH and HAWTHORN) and pronouncing a charm, the words of which are a closely guarded secret and have to be passed from man to woman, to man, and so on.

TOLMAN or **Tulman** is a Scots word for a small green knoll or hummock where fairies live.

TOM DOCKIN is a fairy from the north of England, who has IRON teeth, and eats children.[327]

TOM POKER is an East Anglian BOGEYMAN who lives in dark closets.

TOM THUMB was originally a fairy in English folklore,[328] though later just a very small man in a seventeenth-century tale.[329] According to legend, MERLIN prophesied that a woman would bear a son no longer than her husband's thumb. This happened and the boy grew to manhood in four minutes. His godmother was the Queen of the Fairies, and she bestowed on him several magical gifts, including a ring of invisibility, a cap of knowledge, and SEVEN league boots. He attended the court of King ARTHUR.

TOM TIT or **Tom Tit Tot** is an alternative name for an English HOBGOBLIN. There is a famous tale of a Suffolk hobgoblin called Tom Tit Tot who spins FLAX for a girl who must become his wife unless she can guess his NAME.

TOMALIN is a fairy knight and relative of OBERON.[330]

TOMHANS or **Shians** are rock masses resembling turrets. By day they just look like part of the rock, by night they are sometimes splendidly illuminated by fairy light.

TOMTEVÄTTE are Norwegian HOUSE FAIRIES that look after the house and farm animals, but who will become malevolent if they are not respected and fed every day.

TOM-TIT is a Lincolnshire name for an English HOBGOBLIN.

TOMTRÅ (s. **TOMTE**) (from *tomtgubbe,* meaning 'old man of the house') are Swedish HOUSE FAIRIES who take pride in a well kept home, but will torment lazy housekeepers until they mend their ways. Unless everything is kept clean and tidy they will leave, and this is a shame as a happy tomte ensures a prosperous family. The tomte must be rewarded with a cosy fire and food; some say he should be fed at ten in the evening, and again at four in the morning. He should not be tormented with excessive noise, like the sound of wood chopping in the yard. If annoyed he will play tricks like pinching children, waking sleepers and letting the cows out. He will take every THURSDAY off as his day of rest, when he should be given extra food and butter in his porridge. Because this is his day off, he will be very annoyed at anyone caught SPINNING. At Christmas, he should be given a little piece of grey cloth, some tobacco and a shovel full of clay. The tomtrå always wear brown clothes and GREEN caps. They are

accomplished fiddlers and like to dance in the moonlight. As they care for the farm animals, they occasionally feel entitled to steal hay and MILK.

TONTTI or **TONTUU** is a Finnish HOUSE FAIRY who will look after the house and stock if well treated and fed regularly, but who will play tricks or leave if he is mistreated.

TOOTH FAIRY leaves a silver coin under the pillow in exchange for a child's shed milk tooth.

TOPIELEC ('Drowner') is a Polish WATER FAIRY, similar to the Russian VODIANOI.

TRAPANI FRATUZZO is a little Sicilian fairy who dresses like a monk, but wears an enormous roof tile on his shoulders to hide himself. He wears a RED hood and guards underground TREASURE. Catch his hood and he must tell you where it is. Steal his hood and he will move heaven and earth to get it back, since he cannot live without it. Don't give it back until you have the treasure above ground, or you will never see daylight again.

TRAS is a Bohemian fairy who bursts out of the forest to attack humans.

TRASGU is a HOUSE FAIRY of northwest Spain who attaches himself to a particular family, and will follow them when they move houses. He is small and dresses in RED.

TREASURE is guarded by fairies. It takes the form of silver, gold and jewels. They hide much wealth in their palaces; the walls are of silver and the pavement gold, while the banquet hall is lit by the glimmer of diamonds.[331] All the treasure of wrecked ships is theirs, and all the gold that men have buried in the earth when they were in danger and never retrieved.

Because they live under the earth, or because they are earth ELEMENTALS (*see* GNOMES) fairies are the masters of all that lies under the earth: all the gold of the mines and all the jewels in the rocks belong to them. When miners go beneath the ground, they encounter spirits who may either aid or hinder them. Such spirits include DWARFS, KNOCKERS, RÜBEZAHL, WICHTLEIN, BLACK DWARFS, COBLYNAU, CUTTY SOAMS, KOBOLD and the MINE MONKs. Sometimes fairies will lead humans to hidden treasure, or guide miners to rich seams of ore, but they take a dim view of anyone trying to steal their treasures.

Anyone digging into the fairy MOUNDS (where humans were once buried with grave goods) to loot the gold will be warned by strange voices, sounds and storms and should take heed, or disaster and death will follow. In folklore, there is a general belief that buried treasure is guarded by spirits, either fairies, the ghosts of human DEAD, GIANTS or animals spirits such as DOGS, HORSES or PIGS. At least some of these beliefs may stem from the fact that at one time people or animals were put to death and entombed with buried hoards, so that the spirit might guard the riches.

In Europe, during the Bronze Age and into the Iron Age, large hoards of tools, weapons and decorative objects were buried or thrown into bogs or lakes in Celtic countries. Though some archaeologists think this may have been to safeguard them during raids from opposing tribes, they are often buried in positions where retrieval would have been very difficult if not impossible. It is more likely that there was a magical or religious reason for the burials. Possibly they were offerings to the UNDERWORLD powers and the spirits of water (*see* WATER FAIRIES) to solicit fertility and a good harvest. Thus, these spirits possess a great deal of treasure.

TREE FAIRIES are found in myths the world over. In both the orient and the occident, there are tales of spirits

such as elves and pixies who inhabit trees. According to popular folklore it is bad luck to cut down a tree, particularly those associated with fairies such as hawthorn, oak, birch and rowan. Various types of spirits wander around forests. The Arabian DJINN sometimes live in trees, while in ancient Greece and Rome forests were the home of DRYADS, PAN, and CENTAURS among others. Various NYMPHS were associated with particular trees such as Rhoea with the pomegranate, Daphne with the laurel and Helike with the willow.

In European folklore, witches are said to live in elder trees. In Scandinavia and Germany, the forest spirits are often wild people covered in moss, or MOSS MAIDENS. Other tree fairies include the Burmese NATS, the Thai MOTHER OF THE TREES, the Buddhist DEVAS, the Congolese ELOKO, the KULAK of Burma, the Swedish GROVE FOLK, the Indian SANKCHINNI and the VANDAVATA.

Some fairies are associated with particular types of trees. The Albanian AERICO and the Lithuanian KIRNI guard cherry trees. The English OAKMEN, the Italian SALVANELLI, and the German WOOD-WIVES protect the oak. The ash tree falls under the safekeeping of the Scandinavian ASKAFROA, and the Polish VILE. In Ireland, the LUNANTISHEE guard the blackthorn, in England and Denmark the ELDER MOTHER safeguards the elder, the Russian LESHIE is associated with the birch and in western Slavonic fairies take up their abodes in willows. In Africa, HUNTIN lives in the silk cotton tree, while KAKUA KAMBUZI inhabits incense trees.

Trees were objects of veneration in

ancient times. While the life span of humankind is short, trees can live for many centuries. When all else fades in winter evergreens remain changeless in a changing world, strong enough to resist the death time. Thus, the tree became identified with the power of the deity or was seen as a deity itself. Representations of sacred trees are found in Chaldean and Assyrian temples, and in ancient Egypt several deities inhabited the sacred sycamore fig (*Ficus sycomorus*) which marked the boundary between this world and the OTHERWORLD. In the Old Testament, altars were set up in groves or beneath particular oak trees. The cypress was the symbol of the Persian Ahura Mazda. Similarly, in Greece, Artemis was represented by the willow, Apollo by the bay laurel and Athene by the olive. Sticks or wands were (and still are) carried by elders, kings, heralds and military leaders as a symbol of god-given authority, derived from the sacredness of the tree.

As symbols of the god, or a god in actuality, trees were associated with fertility. At the festival of Dionysus anyone with a tree in the garden would dress it up to represent the god. At various other harvest and fecundity festivals trees would be decorated with wreaths and otherwise honoured. From this connection of the tree deity with virility comes the custom of carrying tree sprigs in a wedding bouquet and such May Day observances such as the leaf-clad Jack in the GREEN dancer. In Scandinavian mythology, Ask and Embla - the first people - originated from trees (ash and rowan or elm). In the *Odyssey,* Homer stated that men originated from the oak.

Many people feel instinctively that a tree has a spirit or consciousness. In the early days of Buddhism, this was a matter of some controversy and it was decided that trees do not have souls like humans, but had certain resident spirits called dewas who spoke from within them. Among the Hindus,

these dewas are gods. Occultists use the term 'devas' to describe the resident spirit of a tree or other plant. We still honour the spirit of the tree when we decorate the evergreen Christmas tree and place the fairy, which represents its living spirit, at the top. *See also* VEGETATION SPIRITS, DEVAS.

TRING is one of the Orkney TROWS.

TRIT-A-TROT is an Irish fairy of the RUMPELSTILTSKIN type, whose NAME has to be guessed.

TRITONIDS are female TRITONS.

TRITONS are sea fairies of Greek myth. The original Triton was a MERMAN, the son of the Greek sea god Poseidon and Amphitrite, half-human and half-fish. He blew his conch shell to summon storms or good weather. Later, there was a race of tritons - sea creatures with hair like marsh FROGs, bodies rough with fine scales, gills under their ears, men's noses, broad mouths and sharp teeth. According to Pausanias, they had blue eyes, fingers and nails like the shells of the murex, and tails like a dolphin. They dwelt alone in sea CAVES and were given to ravishing both women and boys. In addition they raised storms and wrecked ships by sounding conch shells like trumpets.

TROIS MARIES ('Three Maries') are the Swiss FAIRY GODMOTHERS or FATES.

TROLL ('Bewitch') or **Trull** is synonymous with GIANT in the older Norse mythology, though later they are described as DWARF-like. Trolls live alone or in small family groups in remote rocky regions, or in their realm of Útgard. The females are called Troll-wives. In later folklore, Trolls are Scandinavian hill OGRES, who hate noise, church BELLS, people, animals and other fairies. They are large, hairy, and invariably ugly. The males have

humpbacks, large crooked noses and dress in grey coats and RED hats. They are supposed to be very rich and possess much TREASURE in the form of gold and crystal. They lurk about under bridges and on byways, attacking animals and throwing stones at humans, demanding money with menaces. Their children are born without eyes or hearts, which must be taken from human children. They cannot endure sunlight, which turns them to stone, and so they must return home before dawn.

It seems that trolls have diminished even further in number and now dwell almost exclusively inside MOUNDS in gold and crystal palaces. They are sometimes called BJERGFOLK, who are helpful and friendly, but who sometimes steal women, children and goods. They can become invisible, SHAPESHIFT, and predict the future.

TROOPING FAIRIES are the aristocratic fairies of English folklore who gather together to form courts, ruled over by a fairy king and queen. Sometimes, they ride out in formal processions that are occasionally witnessed by humans. The Scottish equivalent is the SEELIE COURT.

TROWLINGS are TROW children.

TROW or Drow (*pl.* Trows) is a term possibly derived from the Scandinavian TROLL. These Shetland fairies, sometimes called Night Stealers or Creepers, come in two varieties; land trows (otherwise called hilltrows) and SEA TROWS. Both have an aversion to daylight. Land trows are squat and misshapen and dress in grey, though they are INVISIBLE to most people. One islander was able to see them dancing on the shore, until his wife took his hand and put her foot on his.

If you see a trow, it will walk backwards as long as you look at it.

Land trows live inside MOUNDS, where they keep their TREASURE, and fly about on *bulwands* (dock stems). They love music, especially fiddle music, and once rewarded a human fiddler who pleased them with the gift of always finding money in his pocket whenever he had need of it. However, when he boasted to others of his good fortune, the gift was withdrawn and he never found a 'trowie-shilling' in his pocket again. Trows can be seen performing a lop sided crouching and hopping dance called *Henking*, especially at YULE when they leave the UNDERWORLD, and at MIDSUMMER which is one of their great festivals. At Yule, the islanders protect their property with crosses of IRON.

Sometimes they invite humans into their mounds, and sometimes steal away women of loose morals to act as wetnurses to trow children, which are called trowlings. They also steal women in childbed, grooms and brides. In the past elaborate rituals would be undertaken before weddings, and women would try to hide the fact that they were pregnant, so the trows would not know. Like other fairies, trows kidnap human children and leave CHANGELINGS in their place, sickly looking trowlings. (Even now, islanders will refer to someone who looks pale and ill as 'trowie'.) To prevent this unbaptised

children were never left alone, with neighbours and relatives taking it in turn to sit by the cradle. However, when Shetland mothers were angry with their children they would sometimes cry: 'Trow take thee!' It is believed that trows are forced to steal human women and children because they can only father male children.

Trows hate anything to be locked, whether house doors, cupboards or boxes. To this day, the islanders leave their houses and possessions unlocked so as not to anger the trows. *See also* KURNAL TROW.

TRUNCHERFACE ('Trencher Face') is one of the Orkney TROWS.

TRWTYN A TRATYN is the Welsh version of TOM TIT TOT, a fairy whose NAME has to be guessed.

TRYAMOUR was a fairy who fell in love with a knight called Launfal or Lanval, according to a thirteenth century tale.[332] She agreed to appear whenever he wished on condition that he must never speak of her or summon her when others were present. Her name means 'test of love'.

TSAI SEN YEH is a Mongolian spirit who appears at the end of the Herdsman's Day festival to distribute gifts to the children. Like YULE, the festival is celebrated at the end of the year.

TSIRK-TSIRK is a German fairy whose name has to be guessed, like RUMPELSTILTSKIN.

TSMOK is a Russian HOUSE FAIRY who appears as a SNAKE and causes lightening.

TUATHA DÉ DANAAN or Tuatha De Danann ('People of the Goddess Danu') were legendary gods who landed in Ireland one BELTANE. According to the *Book of Invasions,* they were descended from Nemed and ruled Ireland after him. They came

from the northern isles of Greece where they learned the arts of MAGIC, bringing with them four magical artefacts, the stone of Fal, the spear of Lugh, the Sword of Nuada, and the CAULDRON of the DAGDA. The Tuatha dé Danaan were tall and fair and had many talents. The *Book of Leinster* described them as 'gods and not gods' but rather 'something in between'. They fought the FORMORIANS and the FIRBOLG, but were eventually conquered in turn by the Milesian Celts.

After this, they retreated to the MOUNDS, each chief being awarded a hollow hill by the DAGDA. Others went beneath the lakes of Ireland, Scotland and Wales. All shrank in size and became invisible to most humans. In this form, they are known as the SIDHE or fairies. Some say they went across the western sea to disappear completely into the sunset. They are often credited with the construction of standing stones and circles. *See also* DANU.

TUEZ ('Killer'?) is a name for Breton fairies who live in bogs, swamps or in stagnant water. They are small, dark and hairy.

TULIPS are sacred to the fairies in England, and it is unlucky to cut them and take them indoors.

TURABUG is the Italian fairy of rue and guardian of REEDS in Tuscany.

TURANNA is the Tuscan queen of the fairies in Italy. The name may be of Etruscan origin.

TÚNRIDUR is a female version of the WILD HUNT in Norse myth.

TUOMETAR is a Finnish cherry TREE FAIRY.

TUREHU are fair-haired Polynesian fairies who occasionally marry humans, but like fairies elsewhere, will return to their own folk if they are abused. A mortal prince called Motaora married the Niwareka, the daughter of the King of the Fairies. They lived happily for several years until he lost his temper and struck her, whereupon she fled back to her father's kingdom. He followed her there and wooed her back with a love song, but as they left, the gatekeeper of FAIRYLAND shut the gate, so that humans can no longer visit.

TUSSE-FOLK is another name for the HULDRE.

TUT/TUT-GUT is a regional English name for a Lincolnshire HOBGOBLIN.

TVESTER is a TROLL that can be controlled once his NAME is guessed.

TWILIGHT is a magical time when fairies are often seen. According to Celtic folklore, this occurs because it is a 'time between times', a THRESHOLD between day and night, when it is easier to pass from the earth to the OTHERWORLD - and vice versa.

TYLWYTH TEG ('Fair Family') are small Welsh fairies who have fair hair, wear WHITE, and live underground or under water. They are ruled by King Gwydion (or Gwyd ap Donn, an ancient Celtic god), whose residence is in the stars. His queen is Queen Gwenhidw, whose name means something like 'white phantom' or WHITE LADY. Small fluffy white clouds are called 'the sheep of Gwenhidw'. Her name is possibly cognate with Gwenhwyvar or GUINEVERE, Arthur's Queen. Some say that the leader of the Welsh fairies is GWYN AP NUDD, an ancient god of the DEAD.

In times past, these fairies were objects of fear and dread, dangerous to be in contact with, and every child was brought up with a healthy fear and respect for them. They like to kidnap babies or older blond children and leave ugly CHANGELINGS called crimbils in their place. Their own

children mature at one hundred years of age when they leave to set up communities of their own. They are fond of singing and dancing in FAIRY RINGS, though a human should be wary of joining them. They are visible only at night. The females are called y mamau, 'the mothers'. They sometimes marry human men. In Carmarthenshire, the fair folk are sometimes called Bendith y Mamau or 'Mother's Blessing'.

The Tylwyth Teg visit human houses after dark, and for this reason people used to tidy up and put fresh coals on the fire before retiring, so that the fairies might make themselves comfortable; if they were pleased they might leave a present for the family, but this would disappear if spoken of. The Fair Family are believed to visit markets and exchange the money in farmer's pockets for their own, which disappears when the farmer gets home or tries to spend it. They may also give favoured humans various fairy gifts.

Edward Davies, writing in 1809, first related the oft-repeated story of a lake near Brecknock associated with the Twyleth Teg. Though an island stood in the middle of the lake it seemed small and undistinguished, but it was observed that no bird would fly over it and sometimes strains of music could be heard, drifting over the water. In ancient times, a door in a nearby rock would open every MAY DAY. Those who entered would find themselves in a passage that led to the small island, where they would be amazed to discover an enchanted garden, full of the choicest fruits and flowers, inhabited by the Twyleth Teg, whose ethereal beauty was only equalled by their courtesy and affability. Each guest would be entertained with delightful music and apprised of such future events as the fairies foresaw. The only rule was that the island was sacred, and nothing must be taken away. One day an ungrateful wretch pocketed a flower he had been

presented with. This did him no good; as soon as he touched the shore the flower vanished and he lost his senses. The Twyleth Teg were extremely angry at this sacrilege, and the door to the island has never opened from that day to this. One man tried to drain the lake to see if he could discover the fairy kingdom, but a horrible figure arose from the lake and commanded him to desist.

The Twyleth Teg, as people of Gwyn ap Nudd, originally referred to spirits in general, particularly ghosts in the UNDERWORLD awaiting rebirth. Titling the females, 'the mothers' has led some authorities to conclude that they are a devolved form of the deities called the *Matres* ('mothers'), a triad of goddesses worshipped during the Roman period by both the Celts and Teutons. They represent a triple aspect of the Mother Goddess.

TYLWYTH TEG Y MWN ('The Fair Folk of the Mine') are Welsh KNOCKERS or mine fairies.

TYLWYTH TEG YN Y COED ('The Fair Family in the Woods') are the Welsh woodland fairies, seen dancing in the moonlight, clad in flowing garments of blue, WHITE, GREEN or RED.

TYRANOE is one of the sisters of MORGAN LE FAY, who dwells with her in AVALON.

TYTON is a fairy mentioned in an old magical manuscript as being one of the treasures of the earth, along with MAB and Florella.[333] The name is possibly an alternative for TITANIA.

TZITSIMINE are Aztec fairies of Central America, the spirits of women who have died in CHILDBIRTH. Out of jealousy, they cause illness in other children. In appearance, they are emaciated, with faces like skulls.

TRYAMOUR

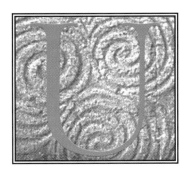

UCAKIJANA or **Hlakanyana** is a southern African DWARF in Zulu and Xhosa folklore. He is mischievous and likes to play tricks. He can disappear at will.

UDELNICY ('Dispensers') are the FAIRY GODMOTHERS of Northern Russia who dispense the fate of a newborn child.

UFOs and their associated literature, with accounts of alien abductions, bear a close resemblance to stories of people kidnapped by fairies and taken to the hollow hills.[334] The themes of amnesia, time loss, lampless lights and seduction are common to both experiences. Perhaps it is a sign of the times, that what was once put down to DEVILS, WITCHES and fairies is now often ascibed to aliens and UFOs. It is curious, too, how the most commonly described aliens – called 'grays' or 'greys' - are also small figures who can seem either friendly or malevolent to humans.

UIIRKSAK is a kind of INCUBUS or male FAIRY LOVER who mates with human women in Innuit myth of the Arctic regions. The female of the kind is called a NULIARKSAK, but the union sometimes produces children who are quite normal.

UILEBHEIST are multi-headed sea monsters that lurk off the coasts of the Shetland and Orkney Islands. They are sometimes called DRAYGANS, which may be a corruption of 'DRAGON'.

UNDERWORLD

ULDRA are Lapland fairies of Sami folklore. They live underground as they are blinded by sunlight. In the long darkness of the far northern winter, they emerge to look after hibernating beasts and have dominion over wild animals including bears, elks and wolves. They are kindly disposed towards human beings but, like other fairies, are easily offended and may take revenge. When pitching a tent on a new spot, the migrant Sami herders check that they are not blocking the access way for the uldra or they may poison their reindeer herds. Alternatively, uldra might steal human babies and leave in their place Umskiptinger, or CHANGELINGS, ugly uldra babies with long teeth and faces covered in black hair. To make a changeling reveal itself, the Lapland Sami would beat it with a burning tree until its real fairy mother, hearing its screams, came to rescue it.

ULK is a male fairy of the Baltic region. The female of the species is called an ulkwife.

UMSKIPTINGER is a fairy baby of the ULDRA left as a CHANGELING.

UN À GAMES-SUK are little spirits of the Native Americans. They inhabit

rocks, trees and streams in the manner of NYMPHS and NATURE FAIRIES.

UNBAPTISED CHILDREN are at risk of being kidnapped by fairies and exchanged for CHANGELINGS. Many fairies are said to be the souls of unbaptised children. These include the Slavonic VILA, the Mexican JIMANINOS, the hounds of the WILD HUNT (such as GABRIEL'S HOUNDS) or the spirits that accompany FRAU HOLDA'S hunt. In Russian folklore, the IGOSHA house fairy is the spirit of an unbaptised child - as are the English PINKET, the Southern Slavonic SAMOVILY, the Scottish SPUNKIES and TARAN and various WILL O'THE WISPS. *See also* DEAD, VAMPIRES, NAME.

UNBORN CHILDREN can be at risk from some evil fairies, such as the Persian AL, who devour their spirits. Other fairies, including the Cambodian PRÃY and the Malaysian BAJANG, are themselves considered to be the spirits of unborn or stillborn children.

UNDERJORDISKE is the Viking term for those TROLLS or fairies that live underground.

UNDERWORLD is the home of many types of fairy. Robert Kirk, an early chronicler of fairies, called all the many races of fairy that live underground 'the Subterraneans'. In Celtic folklore, FAIRYLAND and the underworld land of the DEAD are usually one and the same; or the underworld exists within the boundaries of the Celtic OTHERWORLD. It is accessed through MOUNDS, tors, CAVES, wells or under lakes and pools.

Such entrances were all sites of worship for the early Celts and pre-Celts, who had had no concept of heaven. They believed that all power and fertility, as well as life and death, came from the underworld, which contains the souls of the ancestors, the fairies and the gods. It is also the realm of the HAG goddess, the god of the

Dead, and deep magic.

The Celts held themselves to be descended from the god of the underworld, the Lord of the Dead who came out of the West. The druids postulated that after death a soul departed to the underworld realm, where it dwelled for some time before being reborn. This has led some writers to assume that fairies are nothing more than ancestral spirits (*see* DEAD). The Roman writer Pomponius Mela wrote that the Celts believed that souls were eternal and another life went on in the infernal realms. For this reason, they were buried with things appropriate to them in life. He said that there were even those who would fling themselves on the funeral piles of their relatives in order to share their new life with them.[335] Caesar also commented that the Celts left offerings for the departed. Cups containing MILK and food were left as offerings at wells, groves and sacred stones.[336] The dead were commemorated at Lughnasa and SAMHAIN, when the doors to the Otherworld stood open.

In Welsh folklore, the underworld is called Annwn, ruled over by Arawn, Lord of the Dead, or Gwyn ap Nudd, the king of the fairies. It is a dark realm akin to the Greek Hades, and King Arthur visited it in order to rescue a magical CAULDRON. His party first came to the glass fort Caer Wydyr, then Caer Feddwidd, the Fort of Carousal, also known as Caer Siddi, the Spiral Castle ruled by Arianrhod. Here, a fountain ran with wine and there was no old age, illness or death.

Sometimes, the entrance to the underworld is said to be in the far west, the place of the setting sun. It is here, in ancient myth, that the sun god 'dies' each night, then travels through the realm of the dead throughout the hours of darkness, to be reborn each morning.

UNDINES ('Wave') are ancient Greek sea fairies. There were many reports of sightings in the Aegean Sea, where they appeared as sea horses with human faces. The Romans regarded

them as demi-gods. In Ritual Magic, the Cabala and Sufism, they are regarded as representing the element of water and also, according to Paracelsus, the sixteenth-century scholar (in his 'Treatise on Elemental Sprites'), they are the ELEMENTAL spirits of water.

In popular folklore, they look human and are equal to men and women in every way, except that they lack a SOUL. In one story a young knight called Huldbrand was dared to travel in a haunted wood. Whilst there he met an old man and his adopted daughter Undine and fell in love with the girl. She was a WATER FAIRY and had no soul.

Huldbrand married her and took her home, but water sprang up wherever she went and people began to talk. Ashamed, he began to neglect her in favour of his old sweetheart Bertalda; so the water fairies took revenge by haunting the mortal girl. Undine sealed the fairies inside a well and the couple was reconciled. However, when Undine pulled a coral necklace from the depths of the River Danube to replace a gold chain which the water fairies had snatched from Bertalda, her husband cried that she was still a water fairy and should not walk amongst mankind. Sorrowfully, Undine dissolved into the waters.

Huldbrand and Bertalda decided to marry, but on the morning of the wedding the groom was seen to embrace, as though it were a lover, a misty figure that emerged from the well and then fell down dead.

UNICORN is a fairy beast that dwells in FAIRYLAND. It is seldom seen by humans and its food is spiritual. Generally, it appears as a white horse with a single horn in the centre of its forehead, though single-horned rams, goats, bulls, wild asses, antelopes and rhinos have been known - not to mention the narwhal, and 'one-horned' fishes and snakes.

Unicorns were mentioned by the Greek historian Ctesis of Cnidos. He said that in India, certain wild asses existed, larger than horses, with WHITE bodies, RED heads, blue eyes, and possessing a horn upon their foreheads about 45 cm in length (some eighteen inches). This horn was white at the base, black in the middle and had a red tip. These are the three colours of the moon, associated with the triple MOON Goddess; the white maiden, red mother and black crone. Those who drank from the horn would be protected from disease and poison. In ancient Persia there was a sacred unicorn with six eyes, nine mouths and one horn, made from pure gold. Its touch vanquished all corruption.

Our common image of a unicorn comes from the bestiaries of the Middle Ages. In Christian-based folklore, it represented the purity of Christ, torn apart in willing sacrifice by hunting dogs. The unicorn was too fleet of foot to be captured by huntsmen, and could only be snared by a virgin; attracted by her purity he will come willingly to her and lay his head in her lap. She then breaks its horn and the hunters pounce. This seems to be a story of betrayal, but the symbolism implies a sexual metaphor. She carries a mirror (an ancient representation of female genitalia), while the horn is obvious, there is a flagstaff nearby flying a flag depicting a crescent moon. In the foreground are rabbits, oak and holly leaves.

The horn of the unicorn is called an alicorn, and many noblemen of the renaissance boasted of possessing one. Frequently, they were displayed at banquet as a defence against death by poisoning - which was a definite risk in some circles. The horn was said to sweat in the presence of poison. Such horns were bought and sold for fabulous prices. The poor would beg to be given water into which the horn had been dipped, since this would cure all maladies. *See also* KIRIN and KI-LIN.

UNNERS-BOES-TÖI are Danish fairies of the QUIET FOLK variety.

UNSEELIE COURT ('Unblessed/ Uncanny Court') are malevolent Scottish fairies, sometimes thought to be the SOULS of the damned, which are mostly seen at twilight and are most active from HALLOWEEN to Easter. Those members called 'The Host', the SLUAG, fly through the air at night snatching up any humans in their path, dragging them along and forcing them to commit heinous crimes like throwing ELF BOLTS at human beings and livestock. They live in the UNDERWORLD below the mountains of Scotland. In various localities there are particular monstrosities of the Unseelie Court such as the murderous REDCAPS. Unseelie does not seem to be a Gaelic word but derived from late Saxon *unsele,* meaning 'uncanny'.

UNTÜEG are Danish fairies of the QUIET FOLK variety.

URANIA ('Heavenly') is one of the nine MUSES, the patroness of astronomy. She is depicted with a staff pointing at a celestial globe.

URCHIN is a word that usually refers to a hedgehog, which is called *urcheon* in heraldry. However, the term is sometimes used for any small fairy or, more particularly, the child of a NIXIE. One old Welsh WITCH received payment from the fairies for every human baby she stole and replaced with an 'old urchin.' Hunchbacks were also once called hedgehogs or urchines, since they 'carry their heads in their bosom'[1337] like the curled up hedgehog. This gives us another likely connection with fairy CHANGELINGS, since these were always crooked or deformed. The word is related to the Latin *hirsutes,* meaning 'hairy', a term that is often applied to fairies (*see* HAIR).

An ancient war engine called *ericius* took the form of a beam, studded with iron spikes, and this is the likely source of the word being applied to the hedgehog. The name sea urchin is applied to echinoderms or 'prickly skins' (from the Greek *ekhinos* or 'hedgehog'), and these are likely to be the children of the nixies.

UFO

URD is one of the three NORNS.

URINE is used as a protection against unwanted fairy attentions, according to Irish folklore. It is sprinkled around doorposts and the fairies will not pass by it.

URISK or **Ourisks** are Scottish fairies that haunt pools, waterfalls and woodland. They are very, very ugly with wrinkled skin, misshapen heads, and hairy patches and duck feathers on their backs and necks. Others say that they are half human and half GOAT in appearance, and work like BROWNIES about the house and farm. Yet again, others say that the urisk has yellow hair and a blue bonnet and walks with the aid of a long staff. They look so frightening that some people have been fightened to death by their appearance; and humans generally run from them though urisks would like to be friendly, as they are lonely. What are said to be the footprints of one can be seen in Scotland beside the Inbhirinneoin burn at Glen Lyon, not far from their most famous haunt at Coire nan Irisgean, both in Perthshire.

URSAIE are Romanian FAIRY GODMOTHERS or FATES.

URISNICI or **Uresici/ Urisnica** ('Determining') are Southern Slavonic FAIRY GODMOTHERS or FATES who preordain the fortune of a newborn child.

URSITORY are the gypsy 'fairy godfathers' of Romany folklore. Three of them appear three days after a child's birth to determine its destiny.

URUISG is an unpleasant Scottish fairy that inhabits waterfalls. It has shaggy hair and an uncertain temper.

URVASI is a Hindu NYMPH, one of the APSARAS, who was so beautiful that all the gods wanted to marry her.

ÚTGARD ('The World Outside') is an OTHERWORLD eastern realm in Norse mythology, separate from the world of the gods and the world of men, and inhabited by GIANTS and TROLLS.

UTUKKU or UTTUKU are ancient Babylonian evil fairies of various kinds, including the succubus LILITH. *See also* SUCCUBUS.

VADLEANY ('Forest Girl') is a forest fairy of Hungarian folklore, who appears as a naked girl with hair so long that it sweeps the ground. She likes to seduce young men in order to drain from them their strength. When the forest trees rustle, it tells of her presence.

VAIRIES is the Somerset term for fairies in south-west England. There, fairies dance in high heels on freshly baked cakes, making little pockmarks in them. To prevent this, the cakes should be marked with a cross.

VALA is a Scandinavian female spirit of fate, sometimes synonymous with the VALKYRIE.

VALKYRIES ('Choosers of the Slain') are the SWAN MAIDENS of Norse myth, who choose those slain in battle who are worthy enough to dwell in Valhalla, an OTHERWORLD reserved for the souls of the brave. Thirteen valkyries serve ale in its halls. These spirits are related to the goddesses of FATE. In Scandinavia, a symbol of fate is called the *valknut* or 'knot of Vala', with vala or valkyrie being a female spirit that rules the destiny of humans. Should a man capture the swan robe of a Valkyrie, he can compel her to marry him.

VAMPIRES turn up in folk stories in many parts of the world. In Britain and Ireland, many fairies have vampiristic tendencies and set out to suck the BLOOD of humans. On the ISLE OF MAN, it was believed that if water were not set out for them to drink the fairies would suck the blood of sleepers in the house. They might also bleed them and make a cake with the blood, and if the cake could not be found and eaten by the householders, they would waste away and die.[338] A large number of fairies set out to seduce mortals in order to drain the strength and life force from them, or even suck their blood in the form of a classical vampire. These include ANCHANCHU, AZEMAN, BOABHAN SITH, CHUREL, GELLO, GLAISTIG, HIBLA-BASHI, IELES, LHIANNAN-SHEE, LANGSUIR, LILITH, MAHR, PEY and VADLEANY.

Like some vampires, many fairies are the ghosts of unbaptised children (the VILA, WISHT HOUNDS, SAMOVILY, SPUNKIES, TARAN), murder victims (YARA, BEAN-NIGHE, DRUGGAN HILL BOGGLE, RUSALKI) or women who have died in childbirth (BEAN-NIGHE, CHUREL, ELK, LANGSUIR, PRÄY, TZITSIMINE).

In more modern fiction, the vampire is always a revenant, but it occurs in older myth as a living sorcerer or

WITCH, or as a supernatural DEMON such as LILITH, the first wife of Adam.

Central to the myth of the vampire is the age-old beliefs relating to blood. Many cultures held that blood was the animating spirit or life force (lose a lot of blood and you die) or even that the blood contained the SOUL. Warriors would drink the blood and eat the flesh of their enemies in order to gain their strength. One can see how the idea developed that if a corpse were to gain enough life force from drinking blood, then it could be animated.

Ancient magicians thought that sacrificed blood attracted spirits who would feed on it, and carry out the magician's bidding in return for the gift. It was commonly thought that spirits are jealous of humankind's corporeal nature and always hungry - so that blood could give them strength and form, at least temporarily.

VANADEVATA are Indian DRYADS who preside over the trees in which they make their home. Should the trees be cut down they will punish the aggressor.

VANIR are Norse fertility spirits who once fought a war with the gods, though eventually a truce was called. It may be that the notion of ELVES derived from the Vanir, as they are particularly associated with the god FREY, who is said to dwell with the elves.

VARDÖGL, Vardygr, Vardivil or Vardiel are Icelandic fairies that live in communities beneath MOUNDS. At night, the mounds open and the Vardögls emerge to dance and play fiddles in the moonlight. Should a human approach, they will hurry away and hide. Sometimes, a vardögl may be a FAMILIAR in the manner of a FYLGJA.

VARGAMOR ('Wolf Crones') are HAG fairies that dwell in the Swedish forests and are credited with powers of sorcery and the power of the wolves; they are called 'Wolf Crones'.

VARGAR (s. Varg) ('Wolf' or 'Outlaw') are wolf-like spirits in Norse myth.

VASILY (s. Vazila) ('Basil') are Russian fairies who look after HORSES and have hoofs and horse ears themselves. They are small and come in both male and female varieties. They like to make their homes in stables but are rarely seen by humans, though their presence is sometimes signalled by the sound of sleigh bells.

VATEA is a Polynesian MERMAID, half-human and half-porpoise.

VATTAR are mischievous fairies of the Faroe Isles, akin to the south German WICHTLN.

VATTAREN are Swiss ELVES who dress in brown fur and have long arms and legs, and bulbous bodies. They are mischievous in the extreme and sometimes adopt a house where they will act like poltergeists - unless they are constantly given gifts, when they will perform friendly services and do household chores, like HOUSE FAIRIES.

VED are hairy GIANTS according to Croatian folklore. They might be helpful to humans, or are just as likely to capture and make slaves of people - though they will usually release them in the end. It is said that ved bones have been found on occasion.

VEDENHALTIA is a Finnish WATER FAIRY.

VEGETATION SPIRITS as a concept almost certainly arise from the beliefs of early humans, who were hunter-gatherers. However, during the NEOLITHIC period, our ancestors became food growers, dependant upon the yearly cycle of planting, germination, growth and harvest. In winter, the spirit of vegetation seems to die, to go down as seed into the UNDERWORLD womb of the Mother Earth - until it is resurrected the next spring. Ancient religion was largely concerned with entreating the gods and nature spirits to provide the crops. Many fairies are associated with vegetation, crops and the fertility of the land, with the power of either blessing or blighting.

The German KORNBÖCKE causes the crops to ripen; the Russian POLEVIK grows with the corn and after the harvest shrinks to the size of the stubble. The Russian RUSALKI cause the corn to grow when they move through it. These fairies may be directly related to ancient vegetation spirits.

In Britain, this spirit is still portrayed on MAY DAY by the GREEN MAN. Green, of course, is the colour of growing things. After winter, the spring returns with a flurry of fresh green growth. GREEN is therefore a symbol of regeneration, the spirit of vegetation, hope, beauty, harmony and eternal life. Fairies are very much associated with the colour green. They are often described as wearing green clothes, or as having green skin.

Most fairies haunt wild places, especially ancient woodlands and forests, which they protect. Often it is dangerous for human beings to enter these places and they will be attacked by fairies or be PIXIE LED. Fairies like PUCK and ROBIN GOODFELLOW play tricks on those who enter their domain. In folklore the good fairies like Puck and Robin Goodfellow - who might be seen as representing the powers of summer, growth, and life - retire from sight after SAMHAIN, the start of winter, until spring returns. Evil fairies, representing the powers of blight, winter, and death, such as the Scottish UNSEELIE COURT become very active. They are capable of stealing the spirit of the land, so that ears will not ripen on the corn, or cattle fatten. Good fairies re-appear again with the spring.

Evergreens such as HOLLY and ivy preserve the green vegetation spirit though the winter. In England, there is a saying that 'the little elves fly away on the brown oak leaves' meaning that they disappear for the winter, like the vegetation spirits. ELVES and fairies were both thought to be happy to take part in human family gatherings at Christmas, and greenery was hung at that festival so that the elves could take shelter in it from the wintry weather. This may be directly descended from the druidic custom of hanging up evergreens in the winter as shelter for the vegetation spirits during the dead time of the year.

VERDANI is one of the three NORNS.

VERRY VOLK ('Fairy Folk') is a south Welsh dialect term for 'Fairy Folk' in the Gower district, where the fairies were never called TYLWYTH TEG but referred to as Verry Volk. They appear dressed in bright RED and love music and dancing. They can appear suddenly and disappear just as quickly, no one knows where.

VERVAIN (*Verbena officinalis*) is a herb that protects against fairy enchantments and cures ills caused by fairy spells and ELF BOLTS. The name vervain is derived from the Celtic *Ferfaen; fer* meaning 'to drive away'. Hanging a piece of vervain in the home protects against evil spirits, lightning and storms. Vervain is still called Enchantment Herb, or Wizard's Herb in Wales.

An old Saxon salve against the race of ELVES included female hop, wormwood, bishops wort, lupine, vervain, henbane, harewort, ficus bugloss, sprouts of heathberry, leek, garlic, seeds of cleavers, cockle and fennel. The mixture was boiled in butter, strained through a cloth and the resulting salve smeared on the face and painful areas of the body to release the patient from the pain of illness caused by elves.

VESNA are female fairies of Slovene folklore who live in mountain palaces and influence the fates of both men and crops.

VESTRI ('West') is one of the four DWARFS who hold up the sky, which is formed from the skull of the giant YMIR. The others are Nordri ('North'), Austri ('East') and Sudri ('South').

VETÀLA is a Hindu GOBLIN or GHOUL that haunts graveyards. Sometimes he is viewed as a mischievous prankster, at other times as a more sinister being who possesses corpses. He is recognisable by his backward facing hands and feet.

VETTAR is a Swedish term for spirits, including trolls and fairies.

VETTE is a Danish female woodland fairy.

VIHANS are Gallic fairies, a type of KORRED, who guard standing stones.

VILY, or **Vile** (s. **Vila** or **Veela**) ('Whirlwind') are Slavonic female fairies frequently mentioned in the most ancient writings of the Russians, Southern and Western Slavs. The name is possibly of Indo-European origin and means 'whirlwind', because the fairies appear during storms. The Greek historian Procopius wrote that the ancient Slavs made sacrifices to spirits similar to the Greek NYMPHS. Indeed, until recently all sorts of ceremonies were performed in their honour with people going to the meadows, picking flowers, bouquets and singing songs about the fairies. In Croatia, young girls placed fruits in the fields, while in Bulgaria ribbons were hung on trees and cakes placed besides wells. Like the festivals for the RUSALKI these festivals also honour the DEAD. Each village had its protective Vila, who guarded its crops and fruit trees, protecting against the spirits of rival villages. During the summer hailstorms, they guarded the meadows and crops.

It is said that the Vily once lived in close contact with mankind during a golden age, when peace and harmony reigned over all the earth. It was the fairies who taught humans how to plant crops, how to plough the earth, how to domesticate animals with kindness, and how to bury their dead. However, as the ages passed mankind forsook these gentle ways. The shepherds threw away their flutes, abandoned their songs, and took up whips and goads. People began cursing, swearing and fighting with each other.

Finally, when the first guns were heard and nations went to war, the Vily left their old haunts and went into foreign lands, which is why they are very rarely seen now. Moved by sadness for what humans have done to the Earth, they weep and sing sad songs. They will only return when humans return to the old ways they taught and once again live in harmony with the natural world.

The Vily may transform themselves into HORSES, falcons, SNAKES, wolves or SWANS, though they usually appear as lovely young women, pale and dressed in WHITE gowns or green leaves. They have very long, curly auburn hair and, like the biblical Samson, their strength depends on it. The Southern Slavonic vilys will die should they lose a single hair. Or, according to the Slovenians, a Vila will show her true form to anyone who succeeds in cutting off her hair. Hungarian vilys are darker in appearance, while the Southern Slavonic ones have IRON teeth. They are light as birds and as slender as reeds, occasionally also having invisible wings so that they might fly through the air. Their eyes flash like lightening. Their voices are as lyrical as a nightingale's song and anyone who hears them will never forget. Indeed, a man may be so entranced by their singing that he will listen for many days and nights, forgetting to eat or drink. The fairies sing in a language all their own, and only those who have their friendship will understand it. They dance in circles and any hapless shepherd boy who enters the FAIRY RING is doomed to caper with them until he dies. Any man who once sees a Vila will be so fascinated with her beauty that he will pine away and die with longing. Those born on a Tuesday or Sunday are more likely to be able to see them. While Vily may help humans, or even take mortal men as husbands and lovers, they also may inflict misfortune on humans, wounding them with cruel ELF BOLTS.

Some Vily live in the clouds with the eagles, where they spend their time singing and dancing. These are WEATHER FAIRIES who cause storms and winds. Occasionally, they fly to earth to foretell the future or cure human diseases, as all Vily can. Some live in the stars, on the mountains or in CAVES. Yet others live in the forests and ride about them on horses or on stags, hunting DEER with their ARROWS and herding chamois. Some of the forest Vily are connected with particular trees in the manner of DRYADS and cannot venture far from them. Rare Vily live in FLAX plants. In addition, some of the Vily are WATER FAIRIES, living in streams, lakes or rivers. On moonlit nights, they entice young men into the water and drown them there. Wherever they live, Vily protect the natural world, taking extreme measures to prevent men desecrating it. If anyone should drink from their springs without permission, they will be punished, as the water will turn poisonous. They shout to frighten intruders, and people who hear this call often die of fright. They fire their arrows into people who will then die of a heart attack or a STROKE, or might be buried beneath an avalanche. Minor transgressions might be punished with sunstroke or lumbago.

The Vily are strong and brave. They often fight with each other and when they do the ground shakes. They may KIDNAP human children and leave CHANGELINGS in their place, which are marvellously precocious and knowledgeable. The human children they steal they care for well, feeding them on honey and teaching them all manner of marvellous things, such as healing with herbs and how to bring the dead back to life. They will be returned after THREE, SEVEN, thirteen or twenty-one years as WITCHES called *vileniki* or *vilenaci*, or 'blood sisters' of the Vily.

If a human witch wants to claim this blood sistership with the Vily, she should go into the forest before sunrise on a full moon Sunday. She should then draw a circle around herself with a birch twig bought without bartering. In the middle of the circle, she should place THREE hairs from the mane, head and tail of a HORSE, some manure, a horse's hoof and flesh from under the hoof. Placing her right foot on the hoof she should yell into her folded hands: 'Hu! Hu! Hu!

She then turns the hoof round three times saying:

'Blood sister, Vily!

I look for you over nine fields, nine meadows, nine lakes, nine woods, nine mountains, nine rocky mountain peaks and nine decaying castles, because you want to come to me and be my blood sister'

The fairies will then appear and the witch declares:

'Blood sisters! Vily!

I have found you and I am your beloved sister'

She then asks them to grant her desires and finishes by saying:

'What has belonged to me from the beginning of time must be mine'

They will then grant her wishes.

Some say that Vily are the GHOSTS of dead virgins. The southern Slavonics say that they were once proud maidens who incurred the wrath of God. Among the Slovaks, they are the souls of brides who died before the consummation of the marriage and so wander around frustrated. Others say that they are the spirits of UNBAPTISED CHILDREN. The derivation of the name may be derived from *vel* meaning 'perish' and be cognate with the Lithuanian *veles* meaning 'spirits of the dead'.[339] *See also* WILLI or WILI.

In Southern Slavonic folklore, Vile can be NYMPHS who live in the mountains, hill forests and love singing and dancing. They dress in WHITE and are young and beautiful with long flowing hair. Southern Slavonic vile may appear as with the upper bodies of women, but the lower parts of animals, perhaps with the legs of HORSEs, DEER, GOATs, or cows. They can shapeshift into falcons, wild geese, crows, pigs, wolves and snakes.

The Vile can be seen sitting on ASH trees, singing and conversing with the deer of the forest. They ride through forests on seven-year-old stags, which they bridle with SNAKES, and their cries resemble those of woodpeckers. They often mount up into the air, from where they shoot ARROWS at those who disturb their revels or their particular dance, which is called *kolo*. They are also WEATHER FAIRIES, riding on the wind. The Serbo-Croatian term for the whirlwind means 'dance of the vile'. The summer cumulus clouds are the castles they build in the air. The vile are skilful physicians who will cure wounds for a high price, but if they are offended, they will poison the patient.

It is believed that if, in anger, a mother should consign her child to the DEVIL, the Vile have a right to it. In Dalmatia, they are described as unbaptised, the accursed troop of HERODIAS, the WITCH queen. In Serbia they are called *divna* 'the divine', and it seems likely that they were originally Pagan deities, later associated with witch lore.

VILI CESTITICE is the Istrian version of the VILY.

VILEVRJACI are Slavonic fairies, cognate with the WILY.

VINERI NOAPTE ('Friday Evening') is a Romanian fairy who controls SPINNING. Her goodwill must be ensured by offerings of flour. She is the patron of women's work, MILK and hemp, and also leads the procession of DEAD children's souls.

VÎNTOASELE ('Whirlwind') are Serbo-Croatian WEATHER FAIRIES who appear in storms and are called 'sovereigns of the air' and 'falcons'. They appear as ugly old HAGS.

VIRGINAL is the German Ice Queen who lives in an ice castle. She was once captured by a magician and had to sacrifice one of her ice maidens each day to be consumed by his magic.

VIRIKAS are oriental fairies, OMENS OF DEATH, who gather noisily outside the houses of those doomed to die. In appearance, they are eighteen inches (about 45 cm) tall, RED all over, with pointed, bloodstained teeth. *See also* BANSHEE.

VITRA was a powerful Swedish TROLL-WIFE. She once summoned a human midwife to attend her. The woman was guided to a splendid palace and on a magnificent bed lay the beautiful troll woman. She helped Vitra give birth to a fair girl. The new mother recovered from her ordeal within minutes and fetched all sorts of tempting FAIRY FOOD, which she laid before the midwife. In spite of the troll-wife's persuasions, the woman refused both food and money. As soon as she returned home, she found six silver spoons, the gift of the trolls.[340]

VITTORE is an Albanian HOUSE FAIRY who has the appearance of a small SNAKE. It lives in the walls of the house and whistles to warn the family of both sad and happy events.

VIVANI are Alpine fairies, cognate with the SALVANI and mates of the VIVENE, they protect the lower slopes of the Alps and their trees.

VIVENE are Italian fairies, cognate with the AGUANE and mates of the VIVANI. They protect the lower slopes of the Alps and their meadows.

VIVIENNE or **VIVIAN** is the LADY OF THE LAKE in some Arthurian legends. She was the granddaughter of the goddess of the wood, DIANA. In Breton folklore, she is a woodland spirit who looks after the forest dwellers and their families.

VLKODLAK, **Vukodlak**, **Vrkolák** or **Volkun** is an evil Slavonic spirit, the soul of a DEAD human. Each house has one and it battles with the good fairy of the house, the KRSNIK. The Vlkodlak is sometimes identified as a VAMPIRE who was once a member of the family. A child born feet forward or with teeth may become one, or a person may be turned into one as the result of an evil spell, especially someone on the THRESHOLD of a life change, such as marriage. The Vlkodlak can turn itself into a wolf, a

DOG, a HORSE, COW, CAT or sheep. At night it steals MILK or attacks cattle and human beings, sometimes strangling them to death. It appears during the 'Wolf Nights' of the Twelve Days of Christmas among the Slovenes, while in Croatia it appears at the MIDSUMMER solstice.

VODENI MOZ or **Vodni Moz** ('Water Man') is the Slovenian equivalent of the VODIANOI.

VODIANOI, **Vodayanioi**, **Vodyanik** or **Vodyany** ('Water') (*pl.* **Vodyaniye**) are Russian WATER FAIRIES, the male counterparts of the female RUSALKI. They can SHAPESHIFT and may appear as fat old gentlemen with REED caps, or with red eyes and bloated bodies. In any case, they can be recognised by their GREEN hair, their rush belts and the water dripping from their clothes, especially from the left side of their coats. They live near water mills, in lakes, brooks and the deeper parts of rivers. They may keep herds of cattle, sheep and pigs, letting them out at night to graze.

During the day, they lie hidden in deep water but at night they leap from the water like salmon, clapping their hands. You might see one sitting on the mill wheel, combing his long hair. They become young and voracious at the new moon, but age with the old MOON. Sometimes, they help fishermen, but more often than not they tangle the nets and upset the boats. They pull the spikes out of the mill wheels, divert watercourses, cause floods and drown those who bathe at noon or midnight, or without wearing a cross. They sometimes sit on the riverbank holding a club tied with pretty ribbons; though if a child should try to touch these, the fairy will beat them to death with the club. Should you be unwise enough to venture near their haunts at night, you will be struck down with dropsy or cholera. Sometimes, they disguise themselves as floating logs to snatch unwary travellers and drown them. In Bohemia, they appear as red flowers floating on the water, and if a person tries to gather them they will be sucked under. Try to rescue a drowning man and the fairy will be offended and will take you instead. If you are really unlucky, the vodianoi will eat your body and keep your soul in a jar. For protection, carry a piece of toasted bread or a handful of dry earth.

Though the fairy is very strong in his native water element, as soon as he is on land he becomes very weak. To get about he will have to saddle a HORSE, a bull or a COW and ride it until it falls dead in its traces. He is a Pagan and will not play cards with a deck that has the suit of clubs in it, as the symbol resembles a cross.

Long ago, people used to believe that the only way to keep a water mill safe from the attentions of a vodianoi was to bury a living creature in the foundations such as a cock, a cow or even a human being. When the water spirit awoke hungry in the spring, after his winter hibernation, he would be in a bad mood, and might cause floods. It was necessary to placate him with the sacrifice of a horse, fattened for three days and then smeared in honey, tied with red ribbons, and finally pushed through the ice with two millstones hung round its neck. Fishermen would pour butter and oil into the waters as an offering to him, while millers would kill a black sow, and beekeepers would offer the first swarm of spring. To make a dam safe from his attentions the Ukrainians would bury a horse's head in it.[341]

A vodianoi will either marry a RUSALKA or the spirit of a drowned human girl cursed by her parents. When the rivers flood their banks, he is celebrating his wedding. However, when his wife is about to give birth he will seek the assistance of a human MIDWIFE whom he will reward with gold and silver. He is

usually said to have a hundred and eleven lovely daughters who torment the spirits of the drowned. *See also* DYEDUSKA VODYANOY.

VODNÍ PANNY ('Water Nymphs') or **Bílé Paní** ('White Ladies') are Russian water fairies that appear as tall, pale women dressed in transparent green gowns. They always look mournful. They swing on tree branches, singing sweetly to lure young women into the water. They live in crystal palaces beneath the water, pathed with gold and silver stones. At night, they may venture from their haunts to attend village dances. A clever person may capture a water fairy and these may be set to helping about the house, but like other HOUSE FAIRIES will escape as soon as they are given new CLOTHES. *See also* WHITE LADIES.

VODNÍK is the Bohemian version of the Russian VODIANOI, a WATER FAIRY who appears either as a fish or in human form, but with GREEN hair. He is an evil being who lures humans into the water to drown them. When a child is drowned, a Vodník comes into existence.

VOLOS ('Hair'), **Veles**, **Walgino** or **Vejamat** is a Russian fairy that guards domestic animals. He was the god of the UNDERWORLD, agriculture and fertility. He was sometimes portrayed as a man with a wolf's head or as a water SNAKE. Sacrifices were thrown into the rivers where he dwelled. He was Christianised as St Blaise (Vlas), a shepherd. In his Baltic incarnation, Vejamat, he is the one-eyed god of the DEAD, who leads the WILD HUNT.

VOUGH is an evil Scottish Highland fairy, one of the FUATH.

VUI or WUI are Melanesian spirits. They are invisible and can only be seen by SHAMANS and WITCH doctors. They must be placated to gain their favours. If slighted they will show their anger.

VOUIVRE is a Gascon fairy from south west France, who appears as a SNAKE beside natural fountains. It has a diamond in the middle of its forehead, which is the source of its power. It only lets this out of its sight when it is bathing or drinking. Should a man steal it he will gain that power, while the fairy will fade away and die. The vouivre is sometimes a HOUSE FAIRY.

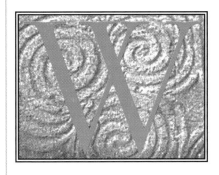

WAALRÜTER is a German NIGHTMARE who sits on the chest of a sleeper and rides him through his dreams.

WAFF is an English FETCH or CO-WALKER, the double of a living human, from Yorkshire. It is an OMEN OF DEATH and may appear to the doomed person or one of their friends. However, if you see it, it may be possible to avert the bad luck by speaking to it boldly and telling it to take itself off.[342]

WAG BY THE WAY is a fairy used to guard the Border highways and byways for the Scots noble families.

WAG-AT-THE-WA' is a grotesque but friendly HOUSE FAIRY or BROWNIE of Lowland Scotland and the Borders. His favourite seat is the empty pothook hanging over the fire. If any servant swings the hook, the brownie will appear. He plagues idle servants but when all is going well and the household is happy, he can be heard laughing. In appearance, he looks like an ugly old man with short crooked legs and a long tail, a red coat and blue breeches and a grey cloak with an old night-cap tied round his face as he is much plagued by toothache. He is a teetaller and gets annoyed if the family drink anything stronger than home-brewed ale.

He can be banished by the sign of the cross.

WALDEMAR is the WILD HUNTSMAN of Denmark, believed to be the Good King Waldemar who, after the death of his beloved wife, sought consolation in hunting in the forests of Gurre night and day. His final words were that God might keep his heaven so long as he was allowed to hunt forever in the forest. He rushes through the forest on a white horse, sometimes with his head under his left arms, preceded by coal BLACK DOGS with fiery tongues.

WALDFRAUEN ('Forest Women') are German forest fairies or WILD WOMEN.

WALDGEISTER ('Forest Spirits') are German woodland fairies that live in the ancient forests, some are kindly, and others ill disposed. They know all the secrets of medicinal plants.

WALDMANN ('Forest Man') is a German forest fairy or a WILD MAN.

WALDWEIBCHEN ('Forest Woman') is a forest fairy or MOSS MAIDEN who weaves the moss that covers the trees. These fairies turn the leaves to gold in the autumn, and can change wood into fairy gold. If they are treated with respect, they may help people who honour the rules of the forest.

WALDZWERGEN (Forest Dwarves) are German forest fairies or a WILD MEN.

WALKING FIRE is another English name for the WILL O'THE WISP.

WALPURGIS NIGHT falls on 30th April (May Eve) in Germany. On this night, WITCHES, fairies, DEMONS

and other spirits hold a festival and meet with the DEVIL. It was formerly a Pagan festival marking the summer, like the Celtic BELTANE, Christianised as St Walburga's Eve, the feast of the eighth-century saint, Walburga.

WÅLRÜDER is a male fairy that presses on the chest of a sleeper to cause NIGHTMARES on the German island of Baltrum.

WANAGEMESWAK are small WATER FAIRIES of the Penobscot Native Americans. They can only be seen when facing you, being so thin that they disappear upon turning sideways.

WANDJINAS are Australian WEATHER FAIRIES. They bring about the change of seasons. Wandjinas dwell beneath the earth or in the mountains.

WARD, THE are a company of benevolent spirits who protect some special places in Western Europe, Scandinavia and Iceland. They gather at dusk at some sacred site, perhaps a special tree, mound (called a Ward Hill), hill, rock, gateway or markstone then each goes to its allotted post. They may protect human settlements, preventing the entry of ill luck, evil spirits and harmful winds.[343]

WÅRIDÈRSKE is a fairy that sits on the chest of a sleeper to cause him NIGHTMARES or temporary paralysis. It is known in the East Friesland region of Germany.

WASHERS AT THE FORD are Scottish HAGs who wash bloody rags when men are about to meet their deaths. The washer is said to be web footed, one nostrilled and to have buckteeth. She is probably a folk memory of the goddess Clota, the 'Divine Cleanser' or 'Divine Washer' after whom the River Clyde was named. *See also* OMEN OF DEATH

WASSERGEISTER ('Water Spirits') are German WATER FAIRIES.

WASSERMÄNNER ('Water Men') (s. **Wassermann**) are male German WATER FAIRIES.

WATER BULL is a form that some fairies will adopt, even though many WATER FAIRIES favour the form of horses. Examples include the TARROO-USHTEY, a water bull that sometimes comes ashore at night to mate with mortal cattle. The resulting offspring will be fat and sleek, and produce copious amounts of milk. In the autumn, when the harvest is completed and the cows are rounded up, they often run about as if mad, though no cause can be discerned. But if you look through a HAG STONE or through the hole in an animal skin made by an ELF BOLT, you will see the fairy bull fighting with the strongest bull in the herd. Yet, before you do this be warned; the eye that sees this will never see again. In Fife, Scotland, a plague of flesh eating water bulls is said to come ashore at HALLOWEEN.

The fairy bull is smaller than an earthly one, mouse-coloured, crop-eared, short-horned, supple, and strong in the body. It appears on the riverbanks where it likes to eat green grass during the hours of darkness.

One farmer had a cow that, every BELTANE, left the herd and walked along the river to a small island, which she swam to. After a while she would return to the pasture. This happened for several years, until she produced a calf that resembled the fairy bull. Then, one Martinmas, the farmer decided to slaughter her for meat. No sooner had he voiced his intention, than she bellowed with rage, gathered all her calves before her and drove them into the water. They were never seen again.

WATER FAIRIES occur in large numbers all around the world. These include the AFRANC, ALVEN, ASRAI, BANNIKS, BÉ FIND, BISIMBI, BLUE MEN OF THE MINCH, BRAGS, CACCE-HALDE, CEASG, DOGIR, DRACAE, DRACS, FUATH, FIN-FOLK, HAVRUE,

HAVMAND, HOTOTS, ITCHETIK, JENNY GREENTEETH, KAPPA, KELPIE, LADY OF THE LAKE, LAKE DEMONS, LORELEY, MEERFRAUN, MERMAIDS, MEERWIPER, MORGENS, MAL DE MER, MUCALINDA, MURDHUACHAS, NÄCKEN, NÄKH, NAVKY, NEGROES OF THE WATER, NEPTUNES, NESSIE, NIX, NIXIE, NOKKE, OISIP, OLD MAN OF THE SEA, PEG O'NELL, PEG PROWLER, PLANT ANNWN, ROANES, RUSALKA, SEA TROWS, SHELLYCOAT, SELKIES, SIRENS, UNDINE, VODIANOI, WANAGEMESWAK, WASSERGEISTER, WASSERMÄNNER, WATER BULL, WATER LEAPERS and WATER NYMPHS.

These fairies are temperamental in character and can either curse with storms or drowning, or bless with TREASURE and the power of healing or MAGIC. The females are generally lovely and seductive, singing bewitching songs in order to lure young men into their clutches. However, their looks are misleading. They often want to drown the young men and steal their souls. Male water fairies are usually bad tempered and ugly with green hair, though there are exceptions.

A 'prototype' of water fairies is the Greek sea god Proteus, known as The Old Man of the Sea who is the most masterful SHAPESHIFTER of all. He is able to assume any shape he desires. Most water fairies are said to be shapeshifters, perhaps because of the fluid and changeable nature of water itself, which is only given shape by the vessel that holds it.

The Celts and other tribes also sacrificed treasure to lakes and river spirits. At the site of Flag Fen in Cambridgeshire, in eastern Engaland, over three hundred bronze artefacts were found. These included PINS and ornaments, rings, a large number of weapons including swords and daggers, and tools such a chisels and awls.[344] The swords were either unsharpened or broken, and there was a pair of bronze shears, which would have been too soft to cut anything, the shields were too thin to be used, and the spears too large, so they were clearly ritual objects.

Human sacrifices may once have been made to the water deities, and this may account for figures such as Peg O'Neill of the River Ribble in Lancashire. She demands sacrifices and will be satisfied with a small animal or bird; but if this is not offered, she will take a human life.

Such sacrificial practices survive in folk tales, like the story of the Scottish guardian water DEMONS. It is said that in older times, when a castle was sacked, a crafty servant might contrive to throw some portion of the family treasure into a nearby pool. On one occasion, a diver was employed to bring the treasure to the surface, but when he dived, he encountered the water guardian of the lake who told him to leave immediately and not come back. However, the diver disobeyed and moments after his second dive his heart and lungs were found floating on the surface of the water, torn out by the demon.[345]

Water has often been considered to be a living thing, or certainly to have the power of sustaining, bestowing and even restoring life. Every ancient society honoured springs, wells and water sources as being sacred. *See also* SNAKES, WATER HORSE.

WATER HORSE is the most common form in which WATER FAIRIES appear. These include the AUGHISKY, CABBYL USHTY, NUEGLE, DECAIR, EACH-UISGE, NOGGLES, EAGER, GLASHTIN, KELPIE, NICKUR and the NUCKELAVEE. These horses often try to trick humans into mounting them, and if they are foolish enough to do so, the water horse will carry them into deep water and drown them. Some water horses will even eat their victims.

WATER LEAPERS or **Llamhigyn y Dwr** are Welsh WATER FAIRIES who prey on fishermen, luring them onto rocks, breaking their lines, dragging the men into the water and drowning them. They also drag sheep into the water in order to kill and eat them. They appear as small TOAD-like creatures with bat wings and tails instead of legs. They bounce along the surface of the sea.[346]

WATER MAID is an alternative term for a MERMAID or WATER FAIRY, usually of the freshwater variety.

WATER NYMPHS inhabit all rivers, streams, pools and lakes in Greek myth. These NYMPHS sometimes marry human men or seduce them into their watery realms. The hero Hylas was just such a victim of water fairies. He beached his ship on the island of Chios and, leaving his companions on the beach, went off alone to find fresh water. Soon, he discovered a lovely woodland spring where water nymphs played and splashed among the rushes and lilies. He was so enchanted that he was unable to tear himself away before the nymphs quickly seized him and pulled him beneath the water. Though his companions sought him, he was never seen again - though his voice was heard, calling plaintively. *See also* WATER FAIRIES.

WATER WRAITH is a Scottish water spirit or WATER FAIRY. She is dressed in GREEN, has a withered appearance and a scowling face.

WATERNÖME is a German sea-woman. *See* MERMAID and WATER FAIRY.

WATER-SHEERIE is an Irish term for the WILL O'THE WISP.

WATERTROLL is another water-dwelling fairy creature. According to the Anglo-Saxon poem *Beowulf,* GRENDEL's mother was a water TROLL.

WAYLAND SMITH is an ELF who lives in Wayland's Smithy, a chambered Neolithic long barrow in Berkshire, southern England. It is said that if a HORSE should be tethered at Wayland's Smithy under a full moon, the owner returning in the morning would find it newly shod. Some say Wayland the SMITH is the King of the ELVES.

Wayland or Volund was originally a Saxon smith god (Witege, Wieland or Voeland). In Anglo-Saxon poetry, a fine piece of smith craft was known as 'the work of Wayland'. Wayland made Beowulf's corselet. He is comparable to the Greek Hephaestos and the Roman Vulcan, both lame like Wayland.

There is another old tradition concerning Wayland. There was once a clever smith who was taken prisoner by a king who deliberately lamed him and forced him to work. One day, the king's sons visited the smith's workshop and he revenged himself by killing them and cutting off their heads. He set their skulls in silver, and made jewellery from their eyeballs. These he sent to the king and queen. Their teeth he made into a brooch for the princess Bothvild. The princes' parents and sister do not seem to have recognised the boys' body parts, since the princess afterwards visited the smith with a ring to mend. He recognised it as one that had been stolen from his wife and, after getting the princess drunk, raped her. When the king came to the smith looking for his sons, the smith told him that he should 'go to the smithy built for Wayland' where he would find the bellows covered in blood. He then went away, still mocking the wicked king.

WEATHER FAIRIES are those who seem to represent spirits, whirlwinds, wind, storm, rain, lightning, sunshine and so forth. The WIND KNOTS or FOLLETTI of Italy ride storms; the GURIUZ bring good weather to farmers; MUNYA is the lightning while her brothers are the two thunders; the SALVANELLI raise storms to ride on the wind; the Swedish SKOSRÅ is a violent whirlwind. Some fairies bring about the change of seasons, such as the Russian FATHER FROST and the Scottish CAILLEACH who bring winter. While good fairies like ROBIN GOODFELLOW are said to be active during the summer months, evil fairies like the PHOOKA are most active during the winter months, suggesting that they may once have represented the opposing powers growth and blight.

A Southern Slavonic song tells how, without a touch of wind, the forest was uprooted by the mere touch of Dragons with long white hair as they passed over the forest in gold chariots, accompanied by their wives, and their children in cradles of gold. The dragons perhaps represent the snowy winter; their wives are the days of summer, which they carry away and the children the days of springtime, which they will bring back.

WEAVER/WEAVING *See* SPINNING.

WECHSELBÄLGE (literally 'Changed Brats') are CHANGELINGS of the German fairies the Stille Volk and Moosweibchen.

WED is the north-east German leader of the WILD HUNT. He is probably derived from the German chief god Woden.

WEDNESDAY is the Sabbath day of the fairies in some stories, not FRIDAY. It is on this day that they have the most power, and are most often up to their tricks.

WEE FOLK is a Scots and Ulster general term for fairies.

WEE WILLY WINKIE is a Scottish fairy that brings sleep, like the SANDMAN, and there is a famous nursery rhyme about his activities.

WEIHNACHTMAN is an Austrian version of FATHER CHRISTMAS.

WEIHNACHSTMAN is a German version of FATHER CHRISTMAS.

WEISSE FRAU ('WHITE LADY') (*pl.* **Weisse Frauen**) is a German fairy who is generally kind and benevolent. She is usually seen in the vicinity of old castles and may give directions to travellers. She particularly likes children and will drown anyone who has abused a child. If she should kiss a child, it will become invulnerable.

WELES are Polish fairies who guard animals.

WELL GUARDIANS are fairy keepers of water sources, taking the form of a salmon, trout, SNAKE, FROG, TOAD or NYMPH, and are particular to the locale. Sometimes, the resident fairies have to be placated with offerings of PINS or coins. If a well guardian should seize you, you will be dragged down into the well and be forced to dwell forever with the fairy.

These legends may derive from the ancient belief that nymphs or goddesses guard wells and other waterways. Such places were holy and veneration of them still persists today. They were believed to have healing or cursing powers, the ability to bestow luck or take it away, and were presided over by Pagan deities, many of whom were later transformed into Christian saints, such as Brighid, or passed into folklore as 'WHITE LADIES' or 'GREEN LADIES'. A well near Penrhos, in Wales, allegedly cured cancer. The sufferer would have to wash in the water, curse the disease, and drop pins into the well.

In the English county of Derbyshire, wells are still dressed with pictures constructed from flowers, seeds and crystalline rocks, which once would have been made to placate the resident spirits. Today, the themes of the pictures are biblical ones, and the wells re-dedicated to Christian saints, usually called Anne (Anu), Mary, Margaret or Brigit (Brighid). Almost every old English town has a well dedicated to some female saint that would once have been sacred to a Pagan goddess. Fairy wells are more common in England, Ireland and Norway than elsewhere.

WENDI are fairies of the Tzeltal Indians of Mexico. They are small and hairy.

WENDIGO or **Windigo** is an OGRE of the Ojibwa and Algonquin people. It haunts the forests of North America, devouring human flesh.

WHISKY JACK is the anglicised name of the Native American MANITOU Wee-sa-kee-jac. He is a trickster with the head of a coyote.

WHITE is often the preferred colour of fairy dress and there are a number of WHITE LADIES in many parts of the world, sometimes appearing as OMENS OF DEATH. White is associated with paleness, bloodlessness, lack of vigour, and death. 'White' is often a constituent part of the name of chthonic fairy kings and deities. The Irish say that fairies have white blood, and want to strengthen it by mating with red-blooded humans. White pebbles were placed in prehistoric graves. In several cultures, the soul is thought to leave the body in the shape of a white BUTTERFLY or a white bird, often a sea bird or dove. Christian ANGELS are depicted as being dressed in white, while GHOSTS are described as emitting a white light. Occultists say that this is because the most visible layer of the aura of an OTHERWORLD being or spirit is white.

White is also associated with the pale light of the MOON and the fierce blaze of the sun. It symbolises light, purity and innocence. The vestal virgins wore white as a symbol of virtue. The Druids sacrificed white bulls in honour of the gods. In general, unblemished white animals were sacrificed to the sky gods, and black animals to the UNDERWORLD gods. Romans wore white when they sacrificed to Jupiter.

WHITE BLOOD runs in the veins of fairies. According to Irish folklore, God is said to have given humans red blood to distinguish them from fairies. If any whitish liquid was seen on the ground, it was said to have been the spilt blood of rival troops of fairies who had fought in the night. It is this white blood that prevents fairies from entering heaven, and this is why they abduct humans and try to interbreed with them. Boys are at particular risk, as males are thought to impart more of their characteristic to their offspring.

WHITE DOBBIE is a fairy who wanders about the coastal villages of Furness, Scotland. It looks like a thin, worn human and is dressed in a dirty white topcoat. It never speaks and is always accompanied by a white HARE with staring, bloodshot eyes. In the north of England, curious 'dobby stones' can be found containing bowl shaped hollows. They were latterly known as 'cats' troughs' since the custom of pouring milk offerings into them carried on long after the original sense of offering milk to the spirits was lost.

WHITE DWARFS dress in WHITE, live beneath the hills in winter and frisk about on summer nights. By day, they can only come out alone, in the form of a bird or BUTTERFLY, according to to the folklore of Rügen in Germany.

WHITE LADIES appear throughout the world, from the African SHAMANTIN to the Irish BANSHEE. A large number of white ladies appear in northern Europe including the SIBELLE, FAINEN, WITTE JUFFERN and WEISSE FRAUEN. In Normandy, they are the fairies of ravines, fords, bridges and other narrow places. They ask passing travellers to dance. If the travellers are polite, all is well; but if they are rude, the fairies toss them into the ditch to learn better manners. They are usually well disposed to humans, and may help travellers find their way, aid women in childbirth, prophesy the future, make cows give milk, show miners rich veins of precious metal, turn pebbles into precious stones and bestow wonderful gifts on their favourites.

A White Lady appears in the Arthurian myths as the Queen, GUINEVERE, which means 'white phantom' (*Gwenhwyvar*). This indicates that she may have been of fairy origin, like the Irish 'white phantom' the BEAN FIONN.[347] It is possible that the White Lady is a GENIUS LOCUS, the spirit of a place. White ladies also manifest near holy wells, streams, borders and bridges, and may once have been the patron deities of the locality - though they have also been associated with the old Pagan priestesses and prophetesses, and are sometimes confused with GHOSTS. Other white ladies include the BOABHAN SITH, FATA, MORGAN LE FAY, ABUNDIA, DAMES BLANCHE and DIRNE-WEIBL. *See also* ANIMA, GENIUS LOCI, and WELL GUARDIANS.

WHITE MERLE is a Basque fairy bird whose singing restores sight to the blind.

WHOOPER, Hooper or Hooter haunted Sennen Cove in Cornwall in the far south west of England. Even when the weather was perfectly clear, a small blanket of mist would form on Cowloe Rock from within which a SWAN would make its whooping cry by day and emit showers of sparks by night. It foretold storms and prevented fishermen going into the open sea when storms threatened. The creature sadly disappeared when two insensitive men, who were determined to go fishing, ignored its warning and beat their way through the misty cloud with a flail. Neither they nor the creature were ever seen again.

WHUPPITY STOORIE is a fairy that helped a farmer's wife near Lanark in Scotland. When she fell on difficult times, after her husband was carried off to the navy by a press gang, her only pig became ill. A fairy HAG appeared and cured the pig, but demanded the woman's only son in payment - unless she could guess the fairy's NAME. By chance, the woman was walking in the woods when she heard a gleeful voice singing:
'Little kens our guid dame at hame
That Whuppity Stoorie is my name'
Thus, when the crone appeared to collect the promised baby, the farmer's wife declared that her name was Whuppity Stoorie; and the disgruntled fairy was forced to flee empty handed.[348]

WICHT is a Scots dialect version of WIGHT. A bad fairy might be referred to as 'the evil wicht' or 'unseelie wicht' ('unblessed wight').[349]

WICHTLEIN ('Little Wight' or 'Little Creature') are South German MINE FAIRIES who warn of miners' deaths by tapping three times. When a disaster looms, they can be heard digging and pounding. If Wichtleins are present in a mine, it means there are rich seams in the vicinity. They look like little old men, with long beards and are 'a quarter of an ell high'. They dress like miners, with WHITE hooded shirts, leather aprons, and carry miniature mallets, lamps and hammers. They require daily presents of food, and once a year the miners must present them with a little RED coat.

WICHTLN are German HOUSE FAIRIES who are small - less than 90 cm (three feet). They have hairy bodies, big heads, long grey beards, spindly legs, big bellies, hooded eyes and deep voices. They dress in brown fur or RED jackets and stockings, and carry a BIRCH walking stick. When they work, they are very industrious, doing housework and jobs around the farm, looking after the children, and protecting the house and family by frightening away tramps and burglars. However, they are mischievous in the extreme and unless they are constantly given gifts, they get up to all sorts of tricks. They pull the blankets off cosy sleepers, steal food, trip up the servants, let the animals out of their pens, hide the children and board up the front door during the night. Sometimes, they live behind the walls and wainscots or they have been known to dwell beneath MOUNDS and tree stumps in the garden. They tap THREE times as an OMEN OF DEATH when the head of the house is doomed.

Occasionally, they fall in love with the maidservants and manifest to declare themselves, but if the girl rejects their advances, they cause havoc about the place. They fear water of any kind and hide when it rains; holy water kills them instantly. Some symbol of water or the sea - such as an anchor - will prevent them entering a house.

WIGHT ('Creature') is a Scandinavian term for DWARFS and fairies or supernatural creatures in general. It is used in Britain as an unspecific term for a preternatural spirit or fairy. In late Saxon, unsele wiht means an uncanny creature (see UNSEELIE COURT). In the Canterbury Tales, Chaucer equated wights with dangerous elves in The Miller's Tale.

WIHWIN is a spirit of Central America that resembles a WATER HORSE. Normally, it lives in the sea, but in the summer it lives in the mountains and roams the forests at night looking for human victims.

WILD EDRIC is a WILD HUNTSMAN who, with his fairy wife, haunts the Welsh border.[350]

WILD HERDSMAN is a character who appears in Celtic tales as the Lord of the Animals and guardian of beasts. Especially associated with the stag, he is described as a black GIANT and is the guardian or GENIUS LOCI of the forest. This mighty woodsman appears in the Mabinogion story of Cynon, who, riding through the forest, came upon a mound in a clearing. On it was sitting a huge black man who had one foot, one eye in the centre of his forehead and a massive iron club. He struck a stag with his club and it set up a cry that called hundreds of wild animals to the clearing. They bowed down their heads and gave him obeisance as to a lord. He has parallels in CERNUNNOS, HERNE THE HUNTER and MERLIN, who lived for a time in the forest and rode on a stag.

WILD HUNT is a terrifying spectral host of hounds and hunters. It appears all over Western Europe and Britain, led variously by Charlemagne, King ARTHUR, Odin, HERNE THE HUNTER and the DEVIL. Various localities have their own version of the WILD HUNTSMAN. In some Norse myths, the riders are women, túnridur or 'HAG Riders', or gandreid 'WITCH Ride'. (The original leader of the wild hunt may well have been the Greek witch goddess Hecate, who led the procession of those who had died before their time, accompanied by her hell hounds.) They emerge from the UNDERWORLD at the CROSSROADS and ride the storm, carrying human souls back with them to hell.

The hunt variously chases the damned, ghostly DEER, other beasts or fairy women. Woden, the Germanic

chief god, hunted the spirits of the DEAD, mounted on a white horse accompanied by a pack of ghostly BLACK DOGS. The appearance of the hunt is a very bad OMEN. Anyone who sees the hunt is doomed to die, though some may hear it with impunity.

WILD HUNTRESS *See* FRAU GODEN.

WILD HUNTSMAN is the leader of the WILD HUNT who appears in many guises and in many lands. Storms in the forest were often attributed to the careering of the huntsman.

A wild huntsman called Le Grand Veneur is said to haunt the forest of Fontainebleau near Paris, and is about when the wind blows through the trees. In Germany, the Wild Huntsman is Hans von Hackelnberg, who refused the last rites after an accident in 1521, but instead prayed that he might hunt forever and this became his doom. He hunts through the forests with his pack of dogs, while a night OWL flies before him. In Westphalia, more especially, he is Hackelbärend who, while alive, hunted even on Sundays and so was cursed in death to hunt forever.

Another tale involves a prince of Saxony who punished his subjects for breaking forest laws. When a boy stripped the bark from a WILLOW to make a whistle the prince had the boy cut open and his entrails twined round the tree (an ancient punishment for destroying a sacred tree). When a peasant shot a stag, he had the unfortunate serf riveted to the stag. At last, the prince broke his own neck by dashing it against a beech tree while hunting and is now doomed to hunt forever. He rides a white horse and is followed by hounds, haunting lonely forests and heaths hunting WITCHES, thieves, murderers and other criminals. He falls down at CROSSROADS and avoids the highways.

In Sweden, and some parts of Britain, the god Odin is the wild hunter and he is heard on his wild career. The windows of sick rooms were once opened so that if the SOUL were ready to depart it could join the hoards.

The wild huntsman is also found in Central Europe, in Carinthia, riding on the wind. To propitiate the wind, peasants would place a wooden bowl full of meat in a tree in front of their houses.

A similar figure ranges the Malay forests, and travels with a pack of ghostly dogs, and whenever he is seen sickness and death follow. Certain night flying birds are believed to be his attendants. When their cry is heard the peasants run out with a knife on a wooden platter and cry 'Great grandfather, bring us their hearts'. The huntsman is fooled into thinking they are his own followers asking for a share of his bag and passes them unharmed.

The Iroquois people of North America know a comparable figure. He is called Heno the Thunder and rides on the clouds, splitting trees with his thunderbolts.

WILD MEN are the male counterparts of WILD WOMEN in Germany, whom they sometimes hunt and kill. Wild Men are found elsewhere, and they have a common origin in the GREEN MEN or nature fairies of the kind sometimes called WOOD WOSES. They are hairy, shaggy creatures.

Wild men also appear in Slavonic folklore, though less often than WILD WOMEN. They live in the forests and their bodies are covered in hair or moss, while a tuft of fern perches on top of their heads. They take human girls as their wives, but if she should try to run away, they will tear her children to pieces. They are fierce creatures, appearing in gusts of winds to frighten or play cruel tricks on human gamekeepers, foresters and woodcutters, imitating the sound or falling trees, or getting them lost by misleading them. They hunt deer and make horrible noises while careering through the forest. The DIVJI MOZ is particularly fierce, while the DIVJE DEVOJKE helps human farmers with the harvest.

WILD MAN OF ORFORD appeared at Orford in Suffolk, in eastern England, in the thirteenth century. A local fisherman captured a strange creature in his nets. It resembled a man with a bald head and a long, shaggy beard. It was handed over to the governor of Orford castle for safekeeping, and became known as The Wild Man of Orford. He would eat only fish and never spoke a word, though he seemed quite content at the castle – until, one day, he went for a swim in the sea and was never seen again.

WILDE FRAUEN/FRÄULEIN ('Wild Women/Maidens') are female German and Austrian woodland fairies of all ages who stand some 1-1.5metres tall (about three to five feet), are slender, blue-eyed, and have long blond hair. They wear CLOTHES in the colours of the season to blend in with their backgrounds (or some say they dress in WHITE) and appear all year round. They live beneath the Wunderberg Mountain, near Salzburg, which is said to be hollow and filled with palaces, gardens, and springs of gold and silver. They share this habitation with other fairies and GIANTS, and the Emperor Charles V who, like the British King ARTHUR, sleeps there with his knights until he is needed once more. The Wild Women are kindly disposed towards children who are given the task of herding animals, and often emerge to feed them. They also help with reaping corn. A powerful queen rules them.

WILDE JAGD (literally 'Wild Hunt') is the German WILD HUNT.

WILDE LEUTE ('Wild Person') is a German nature fairy who is both kind and benevolent.

WILDE MÄNNER (s. **WILD MANN** 'Wild Man') are Tyrolean WILD MEN who chase the benevolent female fairies the SELIGEN FRÄULEIN. Wilde Männer are GIANTS who rage through the forests, uprooting trees and causing storms.

WILKIE is a little Shetland fairy.

WILLIAM WITH THE LITTLE FLAME is another English name for the WILL O'THE WISP.

WILL O'THE WISP is a curious light seen flickering in the distance over swamps and marshes. In many parts of the world, the will o'the wisp is attributed to the bog fairies who appear as balls of light in order to lead travellers astray. Others are said to be fairies who carry lanterns to guide the unwary over cliff tops or into marshland. If a person follows one, he may meet his death in a bog or a deep pool. Some particularly vicious will o'the wisps have chased terrified people through mire and thorns, leaving them stranded amid peals of malicious laughter. However, some lights have proved helpful, and shown travellers to safety.

Some say that the lights are the souls of DEAD children. Others say that will o'the wisps are the SOULS of greedy men with hidden TREASURE, money lenders and swindlers, or people neither good enough for heaven nor evil enough for hell. In Northern Europe, such lights are seen hovering over the tombs or burial mounds of warriors, and are thought to be the souls of the dead, guarding the treasure buried within the grave. In German and Swedish folklore, the lights belong to the souls of those who, in life, disregarded boundary markers and stole a neighbour's land. In Italy they are souls in purgatory. Seeing a will o'the wisp or CORPSE CANDLE may be an OMEN OF DEATH, either for the person who sees it, or someone they love.

Science cannot explain fully these strange lights, though there are various theories. The usual explanation is that decomposing organic matter causes methane gas – marsh damp - that ignites spontaneously to form flames and fireballs. These are then blown about on the breeze. In recent years, however, some scientists have disputed the fact that this could happen. In the UK, Dr Alan Mills at Leicester University's Department of Geology tried to duplicate will o' the wisp type fires, but found he was unable to do so.[351] Nor could he find any natural spark that would ignite the gasses. Such flames would hardly move about and seem to dance, as will o'the wisps have been witnessed to do.

Despite this, such lights continue to appear. Some reserchers, such as Paul Devereux in the UK, have designated them as part of a wider phenomenon termed 'earthlights', arising from electromagnetic anomalies in the earth's crust. Such anomalies are also thought to affect the human brain, so this may link both sightings and consequent behaviour of witnesses.

WILL O'THE WYKES is an English WILL O'THE WISP from Lincolnshire.

WILLI or **Wili** are Polish fairies, the spirits of lovely but frivolous young girls condemned to wander forever between heaven and earth in penance for their vanity while alive. They help those who were kind to them but harm those who affronted them. *See also* VILA.

WILLOW (*Salix sp.*) is a tree associated with MAGIC, the moon, fairies, spirits and WITCHES. There are a number of fairies that live in old willows, and some fairies are willow DRYADS. It was once widely believed that old willows deep in the forest threatened passing mortals with sighs and mutterings, and could even shuffle after them. An old Celtic custom involved tying cloths to the willow trees near wells and sacred fountains so as to honour the guardian spirits within them.

A Western Slavonic tale tells of a willow fairy that married a mortal and they lived happily, until he unwittingly cut down her tree and she died. The sorrowing man made a cradle out of the wood, which rocked their child to sleep.

In ancient times, the willow was associated with HAG or death goddesses, queens of the UNDERWORLD, like Hecate, Circe, PROSERPINA, Cerridwen, MORRIGAN, the CAILLEACH or Old Veiled One and MORGANA LE FAY. It grows on the margins of water, which is the entrance to the underworld. It is also sacred to the moon goddess for many reasons; it is the tree that loves water most, the Moon Goddess is the giver of the dew and moisture, the leaves and bark are effective medicine against rheumatism, thought to be caused by witchcraft.[352] Of course, the willow was also the orginal source of the drug we call aspirin.

The willow is connected with witchcraft and fertility rites throughout Europe, especially on MAY EVE. The word 'witch' is derived from the old English word for willow, *wicce*, which also yields 'wicker'. The witches' besom is made of an ASH stake with BIRCH twigs and an osier or willow binding. The birch is for the expulsion of evil spirits, the ash is the *axis mundi* and the willow used in homage to the hag goddess.[353]

WILLY RUA is a lucky member of the Irish SIDHE who gets the first few drops of each new batch of whiskey.

WINTERKÖLBL ('Winter Kobold') was a German fairy whose NAME had to be guessed.

WISE WOMAN was once a common feature of every village, she who knew the secrets of herbs both to heal and to harm. She was the village MIDWIFE and also knew the ways of the fairies, could break fairy spells and remedy fairy curses. Often, she had learned her magic from the fairies. Other names for her are WITCH or, in Ireland, the FAIRY DOCTOR. Her male equivalent is the CUNNING MAN.

WISH HOUNDS, Wist Hounds or **Wisht Hounds** haunt Wistman's Wood on Dartmoor in south west England. They are a pack of phantom BLACK DOGS who hunt human souls.

WITCHES are often interchangeable with fairies in stories. Some characters will be referred to either as a witch or a fairy, depending on who is telling the tale, for example the Russian BABA YAGA, and the Indian CHUREYL.

Witches and fairies have many things in common: both use ELF-BOLTS; both steal MILK from cattle;

both have magical powers and both use herbs to poison, curse or cure. Both curse or bless crops, are sexually active and free spirited, conjure storms, ride through the air or fly on RAGWORT stalks, and are associated with SPINNING. The CAILLEACH (Hag) is sometimes called a witch, and sometimes a fairy; many witches are associated with nature and the turning of the seasons, regenerating themselves with the seasonal cycles or emerging from tree or stream when they are called or protect streams, rocks, trees, caves and so on. Like fairies, witches can change shape to seduce men, and like many fairies, some fairytale witches, such as Baba Yaga, are said to eat human flesh.

In many instances, witches were said to gain their powers from fairies. In Irish folklore the young girls that fairies carry off for brides grow old and ugly after seven years and are sent back to the human world, but with the knowledge of herbs and philtres and secret spells to give them power over men.[354] The famous Biddy Early (d. 1873) derived her powers from the fairies. She used a blue bottle, given to her by the fairies, for healing and prophecy. At her death it was thrown into a lake. The Romanian *Cullusar* dancers are the followers - or the initiated - of the Fairy Queen, and their dances are thought to be of the Otherworld. Similar Macedonian troops are called *Rusalia* or 'Fairies'. Like fairies, they are responsible for bringing fertility, and mock battles are fought to ensure its success. The Italian carnival society of the Cavallino assembled under the banner of Erodiade, Queen of the Fairies. It is possible that such masked dancers represent the remains of an ancient fertility or archaic witch cult associated with nature spirits, a subject explored by writers such as Margaret Murray and Carlo Ginzburg.

In Ireland, fairies and witches dance together on All Hallows Eve, while during the witch trials in Britain fairies were the familiars of witches or it was

believed that they worked together. In England, James Walsh, a Dorset witch convicted in Exeter in 1566, admitted that he learned how to bewitch people from the fairies. He said he visited them in their MOUNDS and spoke with them between the hours of noon and one, or at midnight. In Scotland, 1613, Isobel Halfdane of Perth was carried from her bed into the fairy hills where she spent three days, learning the secrets of witchcraft. John Stewart was initiated into the magical arts by fairies on the hills above Lanark, and an Orkney witch confessed that she saw fairies rise from Greinfall Hill on their way to a feast at YULE. The famous Scottish witch Isobel Gowdie 'went into the Downie hills: the hill opened and we came to a fair and large braw room in the day time. There are elf bulls routing and skoyling there at the entry, which feared me'.

Anne Jeffries lived at the time of the English Civil War. One day, she was knitting in an arbour when six tiny, handsome men appeared, the finest one with a red feather in his cap. They began to kiss and caress her - and when one touched her eyes, she was transported to FAIRYLAND, where she seemed to be the same size as the other inhabitants. She was courted by all six men, but stole away with her favourite red-feathered beau. The others followed with an angry cloud and then the world turned black and she found herself back in the arbour. She became famous as a clairvoyant and healer until she was arrested as a witch in 1646. She was not fed while in prison but the fairies sustained her. Eventually she was released, but spoke no more about fairyland.[355]

During the witch trials the accused sometimes claimed that they worked with fairies, not devils. In the north of England, a man was accused of witchcraft and trafficking with the devil to gain a medicinal white powder. The man answered that he had the medicine from the fairies. He would go up to the fairy MOUND, knock THREE times and the hill would open. He

would then go inside and confer with the fairies, after which they would give him a white powder with which he was able to cure those who asked his aid. He offered to take the judge and jury to the fairy hill to see for themselves. The judge was unimpressed, but the jury refused to convict him.[356]

According to the old folklore, witches are the only people who can communicate with fairies with impunity. They are on good terms with each other and witches are frequent visitors to the fairy hills; being accused of such visits was enough to secure a conviction as a witch during the persecutions. Witches were also known to grow many of the fairy-plants (such as foxgloves and bluebells) in their gardens or gather them from the wild to attract their fairy friends, or to use them in their spells. At one time, even the presence of such plants in a garden was enough to warrant an accusation of witchcraft.

In Germany, ELVES were said to be the children of witches and the devil. They could appear as caterpillars and butterflies and as they bored into a tree or ate the leaves, so the hearts of people the witches desired to injure were troubled.

WITCH BALL is a round glass ball or fisherman's float hung up at the window to deter evil fairies and bad luck.

WITCH RIDE is another name for the WILD HUNT.

WITTE JUFFERN ('White Ladies') are Dutch fairies who like to live in CAVES close to towns and villages. *See also* WHITE WOMEN.

WITTE WIEVEN or **Witte Wijven** ('White Ladies') are Dutch FAIRY GODMOTHERS who dress in WHITE and roam near swamps and MOUNDS. They can predict the future.

WIVES OF RICA are the Albanian FATES or FAIRY GODMOTHERS.

WOD is a WILD HUNTSMAN who, mounted on a white horse, haunts regions of Germany with his pack of wild hounds. Any traveller abroad at night on the desolate heath, in dark forest or at the CROSSROADS should beware. He spares only those who remain in the middle of the path and show no fear. Though he is cruel and ruthless, he is known to have rewarded those who withstood him with gold and silver. He is probably a folk survival of the god Wotan or Woden.

WODA ('Water') is a Slavonic WATER FAIRY, fond of MUSIC and of drowning travellers.

WODEL is an evil spirit found in water, in the air, or in fire, according to Chermessian folklore.

WODEN'S HUNT is the Scandinavian WILD HUNT led by the god Odin, accompanied by a pack of spectral BLACK DOGS. To see it is an OMEN OF DEATH or disaster.

WÓDJANOJ (from *woda*, meaning 'water') is a male Polish WATER FAIRY equivalent to the Russian VODIANOI.

WODNA ZONA ('Water Woman') is a Polish WATER FAIRY. She lives with her husband the WODNY MUZ or 'Water Man'. She wears RED stockings and sits on the banks bleaching linen or SPINNING. Sometimes she will visit a human market in order to sell butter. If she sells it at a more expensive price than everyone else, then this is a sure sign that the price of butter is about to rise. If she sells it cheap, then this indicates the price will fall.

WODNY MUZ ('Water Man') is a Polish WATER FAIRY who lives in the rivers or lakes. During the first and last quarters of the MOON he sits quietly on the bank where a river is slow and deep. He entices travellers into the water in order to drown them. If a body should be found with blue spots, it is a sure sign that the victim was killed by the Wodny Muz or his wife the Wodna Zona ('Water Woman').

He is very ugly with pale skin and long black hair. His clothes are patchworked from scraps of leather, and he can sometimes be heard counting these aloud. He wears a RED CAP made out of feathers and often a linen jacket, though the hem of this is always wet. Should a man in a damp jacket be spotted in the marketplace this is a cause for concern. If he sells corn at a higher price than other traders, then the price will rise. If he sells it for less, then the price will fall. If anyone interrupts his counting, they will be haunted by the sound of counting and clapping for a good while.

The children of the Water Man frequently associate with humans, falling in love with youths and maids at village dances. However, they can always be recognised by the wet hems on their clothes.

WOKULO are Indonesian fairies of the Bammana of Mali, and are about 7.5 cm tall (some three inches), have big hairy hands and are usually

INVISIBLE. They are ruled by a devil called Dume.

WOLTERKEN ('Little Walter') is a small German HOUSE FAIRY that will help with the housework if he is fed and treated with respect.

WOMAN OF THE MIST is an English HAG fairy who appears in Somerset in the autumn and winter along the hill top road, near Loxley Thorn. She looks like an old woman gathering sticks, then just becomes part of the mist.[357]

WOODFOLK is another name for the south German MOSS MAIDENS.

WOOD-WIVES or **Wish-Wives** are German and Scandinavian fairies that haunt the old forests and sacred groves. Sometimes wood-wives appear to people and ask them to bake a cake for them, or to repair their wheelbarrows. Occasionally, they also ask woodcutters for food, or else help themselves to it. But they always leave a gift in return in the form of wood chips, which turn into gold. Wood wives are very emotional and are known to wail and cry at the drop of a hat; people are often told: 'you cry like a wood-wife'. Wood wives are shaggy in appearance and covered in moss.

It is said that every time the stem of a young tree is twisted until broken off, a wood-wife dies. Woodsmen used to cut three crosses on a part of felled trees to propitiate them. They are hunted by the WILD HUNTSMAN, but can be saved if they can reach a tree with a cross. In Germany, the Devil is said to hunt wood-wives through the forests on Ash WEDNESDAY. Occasionally, a wood-wife is called a wish-wife and her clothes are kept in an OAK tree. There is a story of a poet wandering in the woods on MAY DAY who was guided by a wood wife to the tower of Dame Charity who sent him away laden with TREASURES.

WOODWOSE, Wodewose, Wood Wose or **Woodwouse** is a WILD MAN or GREEN MAN, a forest spirit of Anglo-Saxon folklore. These creatures have a shaggy appearance, are naked and covered only in their own hair. They do not seem to speak. They have been known to carry off women and eat children.

A woodwose may appear like Perceval, the noble savage, ignorant of civilisation, or like Sir Orfeo who had his wife HERODIAS stolen by fairies and went off to live like a beast in the forest, sleeping on the ground, eating nuts and berries, and growing hairy and shaggy. One day he saw the fairies and their king passing and recognised his wife among the throng. He was able to win her back.

Merlin went to dwell in the forest as a wild man, as a punishment for starting a war. St Kentigern of Scotland encountered a wild man, naked and hairy. He was called Lailoken and said he was being punished for his sins by living apart from men. The coats of arms of the earls of Atholl in Scotland feature a wild man in fetters. It is explained that one of their ancestors captured a wild man by giving him athollbrose (honey and whisky) to drink.

The wild man is connected with the green man who personified the life of the VEGETATION SPIRITS, and the unearthly woodman who guards the forest and its inhabitants, like the WILD HERDSMAN. Another type of wild man of the forest is the outlaw, typified by ROBIN HOOD.[358]

WOOSER is another name for the WOODWOSE.

WRAITH is a term for a spirit, usually applied to GHOSTS, but sometimes to fairies.

WRAP-ROUND EARS are fairy GIANTS, 5 metres tall (fifteen feet) and 3 metres wide (ten feet). Their ears are so large they use them as bedclothes, They will lie on one ear and wrap the other around them to keep them snug at night.

WREN (*Troglodytes troglodytes*) is one of the smallest of European birds. On the ISLE OF MAN, it is said that the wren is an evil fairy forced to assume the shape of a bird every Boxing Day (St Stephen's Day). This seems to be an attempt to account for the persecution of the wren. Wren hunting ceremonies were enacted up to the nineteenth century and may well have dated from the Megalithic Age. These ceremonies were conducted around the midwinter solstice, when rituals were performed to chase away the powers of darkness. The wren represented the death and rebirth of the sun. In ogham, its name *druen* is related to *dur* or OAK, ruler of the light half of the year. It was hunted on St. Stephen's Day and carried in procession by the Wren Boys.

WRYNECK is an evil Lancashire fairy, reputed to surpass the devil in wickedness.

WULVER is a Shetland fairy with the head of a wolf and the body of a man. He lives in a CAVE and spends his time fishing. Despite his strange appearance he has a kindly nature, and will leave a fish on the windowsill of a person he knows to be in need.

WYLDAELFEN ('Wild Elves') seem to have lived in trees in the manner of DRYADS.

XANA is a Spanish nature fairy who lives in a CAVE or in the mountains. Xanas appear as small, beautiful women with long hair. Some of them may be enchanted human women.

XIAN are Chinese fairies who were once humans skilled in MAGIC. There are hundreds of them dwelling on the Islands of the Blessed in the Eastern Sea.

XINDHA are female Albanian ELVES.

XINDHI are male Albanian ELVES who are usually kindly disposed towards humans, but may play cruel tricks if the fancy takes them. When a door creaks or a flame flickers, they are approaching.

Y FUWCH FRECH is a freckled fairy COW that lived near Cerrigydrugian in Denbigh, Wales. She supplied the whole neighbourhood with milk, filling any vessel brought to her. Then one day a WITCH tried to milk her into a sieve, and continued to do so until the cow went mad and drowned herself in Llyn Dan Ychen.

Y GWYLLIED COCHION ('The Red Fairies') are Welsh fairies who lived in the forest of Coed y Dugoed Mawr and used stone arrowheads, or ELF BOLTS. They may have died out as Baron Owen hanged many of them in 1534 - though it is said that some survivors revenged themselves on the Baron. The local people place IRON scythes in their chimneys to prevent them from entering their cottages.

Y MAMAU ('The Mothers') are the females of the Welsh fairies, the TYLWYTH TEG.

YAKIRAI are DEMONs or WEATHER FAIRIES of the skies above Papua New Guinea. They cause storms, thunder and lightening.

YAKKUS are North American fairies. They are SHAPESHIFTERS who cause sickness and disease in human beings unless propitiated.

YAKSHAS are nature fairies of the Himalayas, usually associated with particular wells, mountains and other localities as GENIUS LOCI or perhaps NYMPHS. They are ruled by Kubera and guard TREASURE hidden in the earth and under the roots of trees. The females rarely wear clothes, but are adorned with large amounts of jewellery. If one is offended, she might steal and eat a human child, but they are generally benevolent and were once the objects of worship. Kubera lives in a magical kingdom in the Himalayas called Alaka.

YALLERY BROWN ('Yellowy Brown') was a fairy, possibly a YARTHKIN, discovered beneath a stone, cocooned in his own long golden hair and beard. He was so evil that it was dangerous even to earn his gratitude.

A man found the fairy moaning piteously beneath a stone and it offered him gifts, money, a beautiful wife or help in his work in return for freeing it. The man chose help in his work and helped the fairy out from beneath the stone. Yallery Brown was no bigger than a year-old child, but had long, tangled hair and a beard, all twisted round his body so that his clothes could not be seen. The hair was all yellow ('yaller') and shining, silky like a child's, but his face was old, looking as though two hundred years had elapsed since it had been young and smooth; just a heap of wrinkles and two bright black eyes in the middle. His skin was the colour of 'fresh turned earth in the spring, brown as brown could be'.[359]

The man had cause to regret freeing the fairy, for Yallery Brown was the most evil thing that ever lived. All the help the man received caused more harm than good. Misfortune followed him for the rest of his life.

YAMA ENDA is a fairy of Papua New Guinea who appears as a lovely maiden to seduce men. She then devours them like a tigress.

YAMA-UBA is a mountain HAG of Japan. She has hair formed of writhing serpents that catch hold of her human prey for her, and feed them into the mouth on top of her head.

YANN-AN-OD (John of the Dunes) is a fairy known all along the coast of Brittany. He is a shapeshifter, sometimes appearing as a giant, at others as a dwarf. He might dress in a seaman's costume with an oilskin hat and be discovered leaning on an oar; or he might wear a black felt hat. He wanders the shoreline, uttering piercing cries to caution people not to venture out at night. If he finds anyone abroad during the hours of darkness, he will strike them, and admonish them to get safely under cover. He warns mariners of the proximity of the shore when they fail to take notice of the lighthouse beacon or hooting of the foghorn.

YARA is a WATER FAIRY of Papua New Guinea who lures young men into the water with sweet singing. Once she has them in her clutches, she will drown them. Yara was once a mortal girl murdered by her lover and takes her revenge in this way. A man can protect himself from her wiles by wearing a shell into which his sweetheart has sung.

YARTHKIN/YARTHKINS ('Little Earth Men') are English East Anglian EARTH FAIRIES. See TIDDY MUN.

YCHEN BANNOG are the Fairy COWS that were used to haul the dreaded AFRANC from its lair in the River Conway, near Betwys y Coed in Wales. The creature was enticed from its cave by a young girl it had fallen in love with, and though the villagers wrapped it in chains, it escaped, clawing the girl as it did so. The two magical fairy oxen were called in to haul it from its hiding place. They did so, but in the struggle one of them lost its eye. It fell to the ground and became a pool called Pwll Llygad Ych ('The Pool of the Ox's Eye') that can still be seen.

YECK is an Indian fairy SHAPESHIFTER, usually appearing as a little furry creature with a white cap. It is mischievous and likes to lead travellers astray. If a human can steal the white cap and hide it beneath a millstone, the Yeck will be forced to become his servant.

YEFF HOUNDS or Yeth Hounds ('Heath Hounds') is a Somerset name for the hounds of the WILD HUNT or phantom BLACK DOGS. One pack haunts Cleeve Hill, Somerset, England.

YEREN is a creature, found in southern China, similar to SASQUATCH or a WILD MAN in appearance, being tall, hairy and human-like, and covered in shaggy RED HAIR.

YMIR ('Groaner') was the primordial GIANT from whom the world was shaped, in Norse myth. Odin and his brothers killed him. The sea was formed from his blood and the vault of the sky from the skull. His bones became the rocks and his flesh the earth. Maggots emerging from his body were transformed into the ALFAR, or ELVES, which were divided into two types. The Light Elves (LIOSÁLFAR) dwell in the air and are happy and benign; while the Dark Elves (DÖCKÁLFAR), who are possibly identical to DWARFS, live below ground and are generally evil.

YMPE See IMP.

YNIS GWYDRIN ('The Isle of Glass') is a fairy island said to be off the coast of Wales and on which are crystal palaces.

YOSEI are Japanese fairies.

YUKI ONNA is a Japanese HAG fairy who lives in the snowstorm. She delights in making travellers lose their way so that they perish in the cold.

YULE is the Norse and Germanic midwinter festival, the winter solstice, falling on or near 21st December in the Northern Hemisphere. It is the longest night of the year, when the ancients believed that the powers of darkness held sway. Fires were lit as a form of sympathetic magic to encourage the 're-birth' of the sun. In Norse tradition, this was a festival of the dead, with ghosts being free to wander during the long hours of darkness.

Some of the more unpleasant fairies increase their activity around this time. In the Orkney, the Trows leave the Underworld and dance. In England, the Wild Hunt rides out, led by Herne the Hunter.

At Yule, a wide variety of gift giving fairies appear. The Icelandic JOLA SVEINAR, the Danish JULENISSE, the Swedish JULTOMTE and, of course, FATHER CHRISTMAS all deliver gifts. The Icelandic JUBUK visits houses at Christmas. Between Christmas Day and Twelfth Night, the German FRAU HOLDA rides about in a wagon. BERCHTE ('bright one') destroys any spinning left unfinished. The Greek CALLICANTZAROI fairies gather to celebrate the solstice, staring at the sun and vanishing on Twelfth Night. The Italian BEFANA delivers gifts at the Epiphany.

The Twelve Days of Yule, as the newborn sun struggles to grow to manhood, were considered to be a particularly dangerous time, existing as a time of chaos before normal life resumes after Twelfth Night (or the Epiphany).

In many places, the Twelve Days are considered unblessed or 'unbaptised'. They belong to the creatures of the Otherworld, particularly those associated with winter, death and dissolution who might appear as black dogs, human headed chickens, whirlwinds or fire. In the Balkans, they belong to those fairies that are the dead souls of unbaptised children or suicides, to werewolves and demons. The Twelve Days bring storms, hail, cold and Death, who takes away the sick and frail.

YUMBOES are West African fairies from Senegal that are entitled *bakhna rakhna* or 'the good people'. They live beneath the hills where they feast and enjoy dancing. The yumboes are hospitable and have invited many humans to their revels. These are seated at richly furnished tables and served by attendants who are completely INVISIBLE, except for their hands and feet. Yumboes go out at night to the nearby villages and steal the corn that women leave unattended. They are about 60 cm tall (around two feet) with pearly skin and silver hair.

ZAGORKINJA are Balkan mountain fairies who live on mountain tops, hillsides or even in CAVES.

ZALIK ZENE are fairies of the Swiss/southern German SILIGEN type. **ZALTYS** is a strange Lithuanian HOUSE FAIRY that appears as a black SNAKE with a third eye in the middle of its forehead. It protects humans and animals, and if one takes up residence in a property, it is an OMEN of good fortune. Originally, Zaltys was the serpent who coiled around the roots of the World Tree, the enemy of the thunder god Perun, and the target for much of his lightening.

ZÂNA is an Albanian term for fairies in general, originally derived from the name of the goddess DIANA.

ZASHIKI WARISHI is a Japanese BOGGART who disturbs families at night, though his presence is considered lucky. Some say he is the GHOST of a little boy.

ZDUHACZ or **ZDUH** ('Spirit') are southern Slavonic spirits that come in two types, those of the land and those of the sea. The former causes drought, while the latter brings rain. When there is a sudden storm it shows that they have gathered together on mountaintops to fight, and the coming weather depends on who wins. The spirits are the souls of humans and animals which leave their bodies to fly about the countryside while their owners sleep. They are generally considered benevolent, and the winners of their constant battles bring their countrymen good luck and fruitful harvests.

ZENNOR MERMAID appeared at Zennor in Cornwall, in south west England, attracted ashore by the lovely singing of Mathey Trewella in Zennor church. She lured him into the sea and he was never seen again. In the side chapel of Zennor church is the Mermaid Chair, featuring a mediaeval carving of a mermaid with comb and mirror. She may have been the original deity worshipped on the site. Nothing is known about the alleged saint for whom the church is named, save that the feast day is celebrated on Old BELTANE.[360]

ZEPHYRS are the guardians of the winds in popular folklore. In Greek myth, Zephyr was the west wind, son of Aurora, goddess of dawn. He was the lover of Flora, goddess of flowers and together they make the flowers grow in spring.

ZËRA is an Albanian term for fairies in general, derived from DIANA.

ZÎNA is a Romanian term for fairies in general, derived from DIANA.

ZÎNA APEI is a Romanian WATER FAIRY that lives in streams and lakes.

ZÎNA MAGDALINA is a Romanian fairy sitting in the World Tree that supports the earth. She was probably originally a protective fertility goddess.

ZINSELMÄNNCHEN ('Little Luck Bringer') is a small German fairy who is gentle and kindly - unless crossed.

ZIPS are small male fairies that live in Mexico and Central America. They wear little helmets and hold their tiny spears ready for battle. They care for DEER and stags.

ZLATA BABA is a Balkan HAG fairy who appears between Christmas and Twelfth Night, leading a procession of DEAD souls.

ZMAJ is an Indian HOUSE FAIRY who appears as a SNAKE or rooster.

ZRACKE VILE is a Baltic storm fairy who brings bad weather and devastates the cornfields with hailstorms.

ZMEK is an Idrian HOUSE FAIRY that appears in the form of a SNAKE.

ZORYA is the Slavonic equivalent of the FATES, three female spirits who guard the universe and who keep the Doomsday Hound chained up among the stars in the constellation of Ursa Major. If ever it gets free, it will destroy the universe.

The first sister is Dawn, called Zorya Utrenyaya, or Zwezda Dnieca in Polish, Dennitsa in Eastern Slavonic, and Auseklis in Latvian. In the morning, Dawn opens the gates so that the chariot of the sun might ride out. She was a protective warrior spirit, patroness of horses.

The second sister was Dusk or Twilight, called Zorya Vechernyaya or Zwezda Wieczórniaia in Polish. In the evening, Dusk closes the gates after the return of her father's sun chariot. She is a protective mother figure.

The third sister is Midnight, Zwezda Polnica or POLUNOCNICA. She is the HAG, representing death and the UNDERWORLD, witchcraft and MAGIC. Sometimes these three goddesses merge to form one warrior goddess called Zorya who protects warriors with her veil.

ZORYA UTRENYAYA ('Dawn') is the dawn or maiden aspect of the three ZORYA sisters. She opens the Gate of Heaven to let out the sun chariot each morning in Slavonic folklore.

ZRUTY or **Ozruti** are Slovak GIANTS or WILD MEN who live in the wilderness of the Tátra Mountains. **ZTRAZHNIK** is a noisy Slavonic HOUSE FAIRY.

ZUIBOTSCHNIK ('Cradle') is a wood LESHY who gets his name from his peculiar habit of making himself a cradle in the bough of a tree and crying and howling like a baby. He may appear as tall as a tree or as tiny as a leaf. He has goat feet, horns, claws and one eye with no lashes or eyebrow. He has grey skin, is covered in green hair and wears a sheepskin.

ZVORUNA is the Lithuanian equivalent of DIANA, a forest maiden, patroness of the hunt, who roams the forest with her dogs in pursuit of her prey.

ZWART PIET ('Black Peter') is a Dutch fairy, the servant of Sinterklaas or FATHER CHRISTMAS. He looks like a Moorish boy in Arabic dress. He keeps the names of all the naughty children, whom he will punish or stuff in his sack to take them to SPAIN.

ZWERGE ('Dwarf') is a German DWARF who lives beneath the earth in UNDERWORLD chambers filled with gold, jewels and other TREASURE, or in springs, wells, CAVES and ruined castles. These fairies can pass through rocks as a fish swims through water and have the power to become INVISIBLE. Sometimes they will help humans or take them into the hills and give them rich presents, or at other times they may steal corn or damage cattle. *See also* SCHACHT-ZWERGEN.

ZWEZDA POLNICA ('Midnight') is the HAG aspect of the three ZORYA sisters.

ZWEZDA WIECZÓRNIAIA ('Dusk') is the mother aspect of the three ZORYA sisters. She closes the gate of heaven after the return of the sun chariot each evening.

ZORYA

REFERENCES

[1] *Aislinge Oenguso* (The Dream of Aengus), an eighth century text.

[2] Jacob and Wilhelm Grimm, *The Complete Fairy Tales*, Bantam, 1987

[3] Bloom 1998

[4] Geoffrey of Monmouth, [trans. Lewis Thorpe] *The History of the Kings of Britain*, Penguin, 1991

[5] Ruth Tongue, *Somerset Folklore: County Series VIII*, Folk Lore Society, 1965

[6] Steve Wilson, *Robin Hood and the Spirit of the Forest*, Neptune 1993

[7] Tongue 1970

[8] Lady Augusta Gregory, *Visions and Beliefs of the West of Ireland*, Colin Smythe, 1920

[9] Sue Phillips, oral family tradition

[10] Yeats 1888

[11] Or at least she did until a housing estate was built on top of her bower!

[12] Bob Trubshaw, 'Black Dogs in Folklore', *Mercian Mysteries No. 20*, August 1994

[13] Palmer 1976

[14] Henderson 1879

[15] W.W. Gill, *A Manx Scrapbook*, Arrowsmith, 1932

[16] Mackenzie, *Scottish Folklore and Folklife*, 1935

[17] J.F.Campbell, *Clan Traditions and PopularTales*, London, 1895

[18] A. Carmichael, *Carmina Gadelica*, Oliver & Boyd, Edinburgh, 1928

[19] Lady Wilde, *Ancient Legends, Mystic Charms and Superstitions of Ireland*, London, 1878

[20] K.M. Briggs, *The Fairies in Tradition and Literature*, Routledge & Kegan Paul, 1967

[21] W. Henderson, *Notes on the Folk-lore of the Northern Counties of England & the Borders*, Folk Lore Society, 1879

[22] Joseph Campbell, *The Way of Animal Powers*, Times Books, London, 1984

[23] Dáithí Ó Hógáin, *The Sacred Isle*, The Boydell Press, Woodbridge, 1999

[24] Lady Wilde, *Ancient Legends, Mystic Charms and Superstitions of Ireland*, Ward & Downey, London, 1887

[25] Crofton Croker, *Fairy Legends and Traditions of the South of Ireland*, John Murray, London, 1827

[26] W. Bottrell, *Traditions and Hearthside Stories of West Cornwall*, Penzance, 1870

[27] Angela Bourke, *The Burning of Angela Cleary*, Pimlico, 1999

[28] Lady Wilde, *Ancient Legends, Mystic Charms and Superstitions of Ireland*, London, 1878

[29] William Henderson, *Folklore of the Northern Counties*, Folk Lore Society, 1879

[30] Mrs E.M. Wright, *Rustic Speech and Folk Lore*, Oxford University Press, 1913

[31] K.M. Briggs, *The Fairies in Tradition and Literature*, Routledge & Kegan Paul, London, 1967

[32] Tom Chetwynd, *A Dictionary of Sacred Myth*, Mandala Books, London, 1986

[33] J.C. Cooper, *Symbolism - The Universal Language*, The Aquarian Press, Wellingborough, 1982

[34] Crofton Croker, *Fairy Legends and Traditions of the South of Ireland*, John Murray, London, 1827

[35] Wirt Sikes, *British Goblins: The Realm of the Faerie*, 1880; Llanerch facsimile edition 1991

[36] Roy Palmer, *The Folklore of Warwickshire*, Batsford, 1976

[37] W.B.Yeats, *Folk and Fairy Tales of the Irish Peasantry*, 1888

[38] *The Guernsey Magazine*, June 1872

[39] Mike Dixon-Kennedy, *Celtic Myth and Legend A-Z*, Blandford, London, 1997

[40] W.B.Yeats, *Folk and Fairy Tales of the Irish Peasantry*, 1888

[41] Lady Wilde, *Ancient Legends, Mystic Charms and Superstitions of Ireland*, London, 1887

[42] I.D. Bayanov, *In the Steps of the Eastern Slavonic Snowman*, Moscow, 1996

[43] Rev. Edmund Jones given by Crofton Croker

[44] Adapted from Robert Hunt, *Popular Romances of the West of England*, Chatto & Windus, 1930

[45] Dáithí Ó Hógáin, *The Sacred Isle*, The Boydell Press, Woodbridge, 1999

[46] K.M. Briggs, *The Fairies in Tradition and Literature*, Routledge & Kegan Paul, 1967

[47] Evans-Wentz, *The Fairy Faith in Celtic Countries*, 1911

[48] W.C. Hazlitt, *The Romance of King Orfeo*, London, 1875

[49] W. Bottrell, *Traditions and Hearthside Stories of the West of Cornwall*, Penzance, 1870

[50] Grant Allen, Cornhill Magazine No. 43, 1881

[51] Lewis Spence, *British Fairy Origins*, Watts, London, 1946

[52] Jan Máchal, *Slavonic Mythology*, Cooper Square, New York, 1964

[53] Wilhelm and Jacob Grimm, *The German Legends*, [trans. Donald Ward] Philadelphia, 1981

[54] Gillian Edwards, *Hobgoblin and Sweet Puck*, Geoffrey Bles, London, 1974

[55] Hugh Miller, *The Old Red Sandstone*, Edinburgh, 1841

[56] William Bloom, *Working with Angels, Fairies and Nature Spirits*, Piatkus Ltd, 1998

[57] Dorothy Maclean, *To Hear the Angels Sing*, Turnstone Press, 1980

[58] Lady Wilde, *Ancient Legends, Mystic Charms and Superstitions of Ireland*, London, 1887

[59] K.M. Briggs, *The Fairies in Tradition and Literature*, Routledge & Kegan Paul, 1967

[60] Charles G. Leland, *Aradia, Gospel of the Witches*, 1890

[61] Bob Trubshaw, 'Black Dogs, Guardians of the Corpse Ways' in *At The Edge*

[62] Miranda Green, *Animals in Celtic Life and Myth*, Routledge, 1992

[63] Dáithí Ó Hógáin, *The Sacred Isle*, The Boydell Press, Woodbridge, 1999

[64] Robert Kirk, *The Secret Commonwealth of Elves, Fauns and Fairies*, Stirling, 1933 [first pub. 1691]

[65] Gervase of Tilbury, *Otia Imperialia* [1211], Hanover, 1856

[66] W.B.Yeats, *Folk and Fairy Tales of the Irish Peasantry*, 1888

[67] William Henderson, *Folk-Lore of the Northern Counties*, Folk Lore Society, 1879

[68] Snorri Sturluson [trans. Anthony Faulkes], *Snorri Sturluson: Edda*, Dent, London, 1987

[69] Alexander Porteous, *Forest Folklore*, George Allen & Unwin Ltd., London, 1928

[70] Nigel Pennick, Personal Communication

[71] Paul Devereux, *Earth Lights Revelation*, Blandford, London 1989

[72] David Clarke, 'Peakland Spooklights', *At The Edge* No. 10, June 1998

[73] Croften Croker, *Fairy Legends and Traditions of the South of Ireland*, John Murray, London, 1826

[74] Paracelsus [1493-1541], *Liber de nymphis, sylphis, pygmaeis et salamandris et caeteribus spiritibus*

[75] Louis Marie Sinistrari [1622-1701], *Daemonalitas*

[76] Gillian Edwards, *Hobgoblin and Sweet Puck*, Geoffrey Bles, London, 1974

[77] Snorri Sturluson [trans. Anthony Faulkes] *Snorri Sturluson: Edda*, Dent, London, 1987

78 Crofton Croker, *Fairy Legends and Traditions of the South of Ireland*, John Murray, London, 1827

79 Evans-Wentz, *The Fairy Faith in Celtic Countries*, 1911

80 Wirt Sikes, *British Goblins: The Realm of the Faerie*, 1880; Llanerch facsimile edition 1991

81 Adapted from Wirt Sikes, *British Goblins*, 1880; Llanerch facsimile edition 1991

82 Nancy Arrowsmith, *A Field Guide to the Little People*, Macmillan, London, 1977

83 Raven Grimassi, *Italian Witchcraft*, Llewellyn, St. Paul, 2000

84 Lady Augusta Gregory, *Gods and Fighting Men*, Murray, London, 1910

85 Nancy Arrowsmith, *A Field Guide to the Little People*, Macmillan, London, 1977

86 Marie de Garis, *Folklore of Guernsey*, no date

87 Lady Wilde, *Ancient Legends, Mystic Charms and Superstitions of Ireland*, Ward & Downey, London 1887

88 W. Bottrell, *Traditions and Hearthside Stories of West Cornwall*, Penzance 1870

89 Wirt Sikes, *British Goblins: The Realm of the Faerie*, 1880; Llanerch facsimile edition 1991

90 Lady Wilde, *Ancient Legends, Mystic Charms and Superstitions of Ireland*, Ward & Downey, London, 1887

91 Lady Wilde, *Ancient Legends, Mystic Charms and Superstitions of Ireland*, Ward & Downey, London, 1887

92 Robert Kirk, *The Secret Commonwealth of Elves, Fauns and Fairies*, Stirling, 1933 [first pub. 1691]

93 W.W.Gill, *A Manx Scrapbook*, Arrowsmith, 1932

94 Richard Bovet, *Pandaemonium, or the Devil's Cloyster*, 1684

95 Ruth Tongue, *Somerset Folklore: County Series VIII*, Folk Lore Society, 1965

96 Lady Wilde, *Ancient Legends, Mystic Charms and Superstitions of Ireland*, Ward & Downey, London 1887

97 Hugh Miller, *The Old Red Sandstone*, Edinburgh, 1841

98 Hugh Miller, *The Old Red Sandstone*, Edinburgh, 1841

99 A.J. Huxley, 'Trees', *Man Myth and Magic*, part work magazine, no date

100 Evans Wentz, *The Fairy Faith in Celtic Countries*, Oxford University Press, 1911

101 Lady Wilde, *Ancient Legends, Mystic Charms and Superstitions of Ireland*, Ward & Downey, London, 1878

102 Jón Arnason, *Icelandic Legends* [trans. G.E.J. Powell & E. Magnússon], R.Bentley, London, 1864

103 Crofton Croker, *Fairy Legends and Traditions of the South of Ireland*, John Murray, London, 1827

104 W.B.Yeats, *Folk and Fairy Tales of the Irish Peasantry*, 1888

105 Adapted from Lady Wilde, *Ancient Legends, Mystic Charms and Superstitions of Ireland*, Ward & Downey, London 1887

106 Lady Wilde, *Ancient Legends, Mystic Charms and Superstitions of Ireland*, 1887

107 Lewis Spence, *The Fairy Tradition in Britain*, Rider, London, 1948

108 W.B. Yeats, *Irish Fairy and Folk Tales*, 1888

109 Sloane manuscript, 1727, The British Museum

110 Gordon Wasson, *Soma: The Divine Mushroom of Immortality*, Harcourt Brace Jovanovic, 1968

111 Peter Lamborn Wilson, *Irish Soma*; see website: http://www.lycaeum.org/~lux/features/irshsoma.html

112 Peter Lamborn Wilson, *Irish Soma*; as above

113 Carl Ruck, *The Offerings from the Hyperboreans, Persephone's Quest*, Yale, New Haven, 1986

114 Robert Graves, *The White Goddess*, Faber and Faber, London, 1961

115 Dora Broome, *Fairy Tales from the Isle of Man*, Penguin, 1951

116 Nancy Arrowsmith, *A Field Guide to the Little People*, Macmillan, London, 1977

117 Patrick Kennedy, *Legendary Fictions of the Irish Celts*, Macmillan, London, 1866

118 Crofton Croker, *Fairy Legends and Traditions of the South of Ireland*, John Murray, London, 1827

119 Lady Wilde, *Ancient Legends, Mystic Charms and Superstitions of Ireland*, Ward & Downey, London, 1887

120 J.F.Campbell, *Popular Tales of the Western Highlands*, 1890

121 Allan Cunningham, *Lives of Eminent British Painters*, 1876

122 James Bowker, *Goblin Tales of Lancashire*, London, 1883

123 Wirt Sikes, *British Goblins: The Realm of the Faerie*, 1880; Llanerch facsimile edition 1991

124 Nancy Arrowsmith, *A Field Guide to the Little People*, Macmillan, London, 1977

125 Nancy Arrowsmith, *A Field Guide to the Little People*, Macmillan, London, 1977

126 Ruth Tongue, *Somerset Folklore: County Series VIII*, Folk Lore Society, 1965

127 E.M.Wright, *Rustic Speech and Folklore*, Oxford University Press, 1913

128 Osgood MacKenzie, *A Hundred Years in the Highlands*, London, 1921

129 Sir Walter Scott, *The Lay of the Minstrel*, no date

130 Edmund Spenser, *Faerie Queene*, 1590-96

131 W. Bottrell, *Traditions and Hearthside Stories of West Cornwall*, Penzance, 1870

132 Jolande Jacobi, *Paracelsus: Selected Writings*, Routledge, 1951

133 Gillian Edwards, *Hobgoblin and Sweet Puck*, Geoffrey Bles, London, 1974

134 William of Newborough [b.1135] and Ralph of Coggeshall [1207] related this story

135 Wirt Sikes, *British Goblins: The Realm of the Faerie*, 1880; Llanerch facsimile edition 1991

136 Peter Buchan, *Ancient Scottish Tales*, Peterhead, 1908; quoted by K.M. Briggs, *The Fairies in Tradition and Literature*, Routledge & Kegan Paul, London, 1967

137 Ruth Tongue, *Forgotten Folk-tales of the English Counties*, Routledge & Kegan Paul, London, 1970

138 Roy Palmer, *The Folklore of Warwickshire*, Batsford, London, 1976

139 Alexander Porteous, *Forest Folklore*, 1928

140 *The Life of Robin Goodfellow*, 1628

141 John Rhys, *Celtic Folklore: Welsh and Manx*, Oxford University Press, 1901

142 Wirt Sikes, *British Goblins: The Realm of the Faerie*, 1880; Llanerch facsimile edition 1991

143 Wirt Sikes; as above

144 BobTrubshaw, 'Black Dogs in Folklore', *Mercian Mysteries* No. 20, August 1994

145 Tom Chetwynd, *A Dictionary of Sacred Myth*, Mandala Books, 1986

146 J.C.Cooper, *Symbolism*, The Aquarian Press, 1982

147 Kevin Callahan, *Rock Art and Lilliputian Hallucinations*; see website: www.geocities.com/Athens1996

148 Bob Trubshaw, 'Fairies and Their Kin' in *At the Edge* No. 10, June 1998

149 Víga-Glúms Saga [13th century], quoted by Andy Orchard, *Dictionary of Norse Myth*, Cassell, London 1997

150 Marie de Garis, *Guernsey Folklore*, no date

151 Andy Orchard, *Dictionary of Norse Myth and Legend*, Cassell, London, 1997

152 *Ordericus Vitalis*, 1619

153 K.M. Briggs, *The Fairies in Tradition and Literature*, Routledge & Kegan Paul, 1967

154 Walter Map, [Ed. F. Tupper and M.B. Ogle], *De Nugis Curialium*, Chatto & Windus, London, 1924

155 Janet and Stewart Farrar, *The Witches' Goddess*, Hale, London, 1987

156 Charles G. Leland, *Aradia, Gospel of the Witches*, 1890; Phoenix edition, 1990

157 Ruth Tongue, quoted by K.M. Briggs, *The Fairies in Tradition and Literature*, Routledge & Kegan Paul, London, 1967

158 Nancy Arrowsmith, *A Field Guide to the Little People*, Macmillan, London, 1977

159 K.M. Briggs, *The Fairies in Tradition and Literature*, Routledge & Kegan Paul Ltd., London, 1967

160 William Henderson, *Notes on the Folk-Lore of the Northern Counties of England and the Borders*, Folk Lore Society, 1879

161 Sue Phillips, personal communication

162 Margaret Baker, *Folklore and Customs of Rural England*, David & Charles, Newton Abbot, 1974

163 Sue Phillips, *Healing Stones*, Capall Bann, 1998

164 Lady Wilde, *Ancient Legends, Mystic Charms and Superstitions of Ireland*, London, 1878

165 Thomas Keightley, *The Fairy Mythology*, H.G. Bohn, London, 1850

166 Derek Walters, *Chinese Mythology*, Diamond Books, London, 1995

167 Kenneth Radford, *Fire Burn*, Guild, London, 1989

168 Gillian Edwards, *Hobgoblin and Sweet Puck*, Geoffrey Bles, London, 1974

169 Nancy Arrowsmith, *A Field Guide to the Little People*, Macmillan, London, 1977

170 Nancy Arrowsmith, *A Field Guide to the Little People*, Macmillan, London, 1977

171 W.W. Gill, *A Manx Scrapbook*, 1932

172 K.M. Briggs, *The Fairies in Tradition and Literature*, Routledge & Kegan Paul, London, 1967

173 Jan Máchal, *Slavonic Mythology*, Cooper Square, New York, 1964

174 Andy Orchard, *Dictionary of Norse Myth and Legend*, Cassell, London, 1997

175 Douglas Hill, 'Pueblo Indians' in *Man, Myth and Magic* part work magazine, no date

176 J.F.Campbell, *Popular Tales of the Western Highlands Orally Collected*, 1890

177 Thomas Ticknell, *Kensington Gardens*, 1779

178 K.M. Briggs, *The Fairies in Tradition and Literature*, Routledge & Kegan Paul, London, 1967

179 William Henderson, *Notes on the Folk-Lore of the Northern Counties of England and the Borders*, Folk Lore Society, 1879

180 A.Chodsko, *Fairy Tales of the Slav Peasants and Herdsmen* [trans. Emily J. Harding], London, 1896

181 Nancy Arrowsmith [*A Field Guide to the Little People* p.36] gives this variation, which must be regional, but I have so far been unable to place it.

182 Crofton Croker, *Fairy Legends and Traditions of the South of Ireland*, John Murray, London, 1827

183 E.B. Simpson, *Folklore in Lowland Scotland*, Letchworth Press, 1908

184 Adapted from Thomas Keightley, *The Fairy Mythology*, London, H.G. Bohn, 1850

185 John Woodward, *Fossils*, 1728 [quoted by Gillian Edwards, *Hobgoblin and Sweet Puck*, Geoffrey Bles, London, 1974]

186 Arrowsmith, Nancy *A Field Guide to the Little People*, Macmillan, London, 1977

187 Thomas Keightley, *The Fairy Mythology* Whittaker & Treacher, London, 1833

188 Wolfram Von Eschenbach, *Parzival*, [trans A. T. Hatto], Penguin, Harmondsworth, 1980

189 Gnomes: http://www.erols.com/michaelmyrick/history.html

190 Ovid, *Fasti* [trans. J.G. Frazer]

191 Raven Grimassi, *Italian Witchcraft*, Llewellyn, St. Paul, 2000

192 W.B. Yeats, *Folk and Fairy Tales of the Irish Peasantry, 1888*

193 Crofton Croker, *Fairy Legends of the South of Ireland*, 1826

194 Crofton Croker, *Fairy Legends of the South of Ireland*, 1826

195 W.B.Yeats, *Folk and Fairy Tales of the Irish Peasantry*, 1888

196 Peter Berresford Ellis, *Dictionary of Celtic Mythology*, Constable & Co., London, 1992

197 Grimm, W. & J. *Irische Elfenmärche* [trans. by Crofton Croker 1827], Thos. Davidson, Whitefriars, 1827

198 Crofton Croker, *Fairy Legends of the South of Ireland*, 1826

199 Nancy Arrowsmith, *A Field Guide to the Little People*, Macmillan, London, 1977

200 *The Life of Robin Goodfellow*, 1628

201 Trans. Anthony Faulkes, *Snorri Sturluso: Edda*, Dent, London, 1987

202 Sheena McGrath, *The Sun Goddess*, Blandford, London, 1997

203 Sheena McGrath, *The Sun Goddess*, Blandford, London, 1997

204 Lady Wilde, *Ancient Legends, Mystic Charms and Superstitions of Ireland*, Ward and Downey, London, 1878

205 J.F. Campbell, *Popular Tales of the Western Highlands*, 1890

206 Lady Wilde, *Ancient Legends, Mystic Charms and Superstitions of Ireland*, Ward & Downey, London, 1887

207 J.F. Campbell, *Popular Tales of the Western Highlands*, 1890

208 From the ballad '*Lore Lay*' by Clemens Brentano, 1801

209 K.M. Briggs, *The Fairies in Tradition and Literature*, Routledge & Kegan Paul, London, 1967

210 Jan Máchal, *Slavonic Mythology*, Cooper Square, New York, 1964

211 Jan Máchal, *Slavonic Mythology*, Cooper Square, New York, 1964

212 Peter Berresford Ellis, *Dictionary of Celtic Mythology*, Constable, London, 1992

213 Julius Ceasar, *The Conquest of Gaul*

214 Donald MacKenzie, *Scottish Folk-Lore and Folk Life*, Blackie, 1935

215 *The Life of Robin Goodfellow*, 1628

216 G.F. Black, *Country Folklore; Orkney and Shetland Islands*, Folk Lore Society, 1903

217 Crofton Croker, *Fairy Legends and Traditions of the South of Ireland*, John Murray, London, 1827

218 W.B. Yeats, *Folk and Fairy Tales of the Irish Peasantry*, 1888. Variations on this tale are found in British, Irish and Continental folk tale collections.

219 Evans Wentz, *The Fairy Faith in Celtic Countries*, Oxford University Press, 1911

220 John Aubrey, *Miscellanies*, London, 1890

221 Quoted by Gillian Edwards, *Hobgoblin and Sweet Puck*, Geoffrey Bles, London, 1974

222 Thomas Keightley, *The Fairy Mythology*, London, H.G. Bohn, 1850

223 *Larousse Dictionary of World Folklore*, Larousse, Edinburgh, 1995

224 Bottrell, *Traditions and Hearthside Stories of West Cornwall*,

225 W.B. Yeats, *Folk and Fairy Tales of the Irish Peasantry*, 1888

226 K.M. Briggs, *The Fairies in Tradition and Literature*, Routledge & Kegan Paul, London, 1967

227 W.B. Yeats, *Folk and Fairy Tales of the Irish Peasantry*, 1888

228 Morrison, Sophia, *Manx Fairy Tales*, Nutt, London, 1911

229 Berners, *The Boke of Duke Huon of Bordeaux, done into English by Sir John Bourchier, Lord Berners*, Early English Text Society, 1883-7

230 John Rhys, *Celtic Folklore: Welsh and Manx*, Oxford University Press, 1901

231 Thomas Mallory, *Le Morte D'Arthur*, ed. John Matthews, Cassell, London, 2000

232 Ruth L. Tongue, *Forgotten Folk-Tales of the English Counties*, Routledge & Kegan Paul, London, 1970

233 Lewis Spence, *The Minor Traditions of British Mythology*, Benjamen Bloom, 1972

234 David Clarke, *A Guide to Britain's Pagan Heritage,* Hale, London, 1995

235 K.M. Briggs, *The Fairies in Tradition and Literature,* Routledge & Kegan Paul, London, 1967

236 W. Bottrell, *Traditions and Hearthside Stories of West Cornwall,* Penzance, 1870

237 Robert Hunt, *Popular Romances of the West of England,* Chatto & Windus, 1930 [first pub. 1881]

238 Evans Wentz, *The Fairy Faith in Celtic Countries,* 1911

239 Margaret Murray, *The God of the Witches,* Faber & Faber, London, 1931

240 J.C. Lawson, *Modern Greek Folklore and Ancient Greek Religion,* Cambridge, 1910

241 Map, Walter [Ed. F. Tupper and M.B. Ogle], *De Nugis Curialium,* Chatto & Windus, 1924

242 Jacob and Wilhelm Grimm, *The German Legends,* [trans. Donald Ward] Philadelphia, 1981

243 Jon Arnason, *Folktales and Fairy Tales of Iceland,* [trans. Jacqueline Simpson], University of California Press, 1970 [original imprint 1862]

244 Walter Scott, *Letters on Demonology and Witchcraft,* 1830

245 Jacob and Wilhelm Grimm, trans. Donald Ward, *The German Legends,* Philadelphia, ISHI, 1981

246 Evans Wentz, *The Fairy Faith in Celtic Countries,* Oxford University Press, 1911

247 George Douglas, *Scottish Fairy and Other Folk Tales,* Scott Publishing

248 George Douglas, *Scottish Fairy and Other Folk Tales,* Scott Publishing

249 *The Boke of Duke Huon of Bordeux, done into English by Sir John Bourchier, Lord Berners,* Early English Text Society, 1883-7

250 K.M. Briggs, *The Fairies in Tradition and Literature,* Routledge & Kegan Paul, London, 1967

251 K.M.Briggs, *The Fairies in Tradition and Literature,* Routledge & Kegan Paul, 1967

252 Lady Wilde, *Ancient Legends, Mystic Charms and Superstitions of Ireland,* Ward & Downey, London, 1887

253 Derek Walters, *Chinese Mythology,* Diamond Books, London, 1995

254 *The Life of Robin Goodfellow,* 1628

255 Ronan Coghlan, *Handbook of Fairies,* Capall Bann, 1998

256 Adapted from G.F. Black, *Country Folk Lore; Orkney and Shetland Islands,* The Folk Lore Society, London, 1903

257 John Rhys, *Celtic Folklore: Welsh and Manx,* Oxford University Press, 1901

258 Robert Graves, *The Greek Myths,* Penguin, 1955

259 Marie de Garis, *Folklore of Guernsey,* no date

260 W.B. Yeats, *Folk and Fairy Tales of the Irish Peasantry,* 1888

261 Crofton Croker, *Fairy Legends and Traditions of the South of Ireland,* John Murray, London, 1827

262 W.B. Yeats, *Folk and Fairy Tales of the Irish Peasantry,* 1888

263 Adapted from Lady Wilde, *Ancient Legends, Mystic Charms and Superstitions of Ireland,* Ward & Downey, London, 1887

264 David MacRitchie, *Fians, Fairies and Picts,* 1893

265 Alexander Porteous, *Forest Folklore,* George Allen & Unwin, London, 1928

266 *The Life of Robin Goodfellow,* 1628

267 Nigel Pennick, personal communication

268 Robert Hunt, *Popular Romances of the West of England,* Chatto & Windus, 1930 [first pub. 1881]

269 John Rhys, *Celtic Folklore: Welsh and Manx,* Oxford University Press, 1901

270 Michael Drayton, *Nymphidia,* 1627

271 E.M. Wright, *Rustic Speech and Folk-Lore,* Oxford University Press, 1913

272 Gervase of Tilbury, *Otia Imperialia* [1211], Hanover 1856

273 Gillian Edwards, *Hobgoblin and Sweet Puck,* Geoffrey Bles, London, 1974

274 Marie de Garis, *Guernsey Folklore,* no date

275 Spenser, *Faerie Queene,* 1590-96

276 I. & J. Zingerle, *Kinder-und Hausmärchen,* Wagner'schen Buchhandlung, Innsbruck, 1852

277 Wirt Sikes, *British Goblins: The Realm of the Faerie,* 1880; Llanerch facsimile edition 1991

278 Dáithí Ó Hógáin, *The Sacred Isle,* The Collins Press, Cork, 1999

279 Anne Ross, *Pagan Celtic Britain*

280 R. Chambers, *Popular Rhymes of Scotland,* Edinburgh, 1870

281 Lady Wilde, *Ancient Legends, Mystic Charms and Superstitions of Ireland,* Ward & Downey, London 1887

282 Steve Wilson, *Robin Hood, the Spirit of the Forest,* Neptune Press, London, 1993

283 Steve Wilson, *Robin Hood, the Spirit of the Forest,* Neptune Press, London, 1993

284 Lady Wilde, *Ancient Legends, Mystic Charms and Superstitions of Ireland,* Ward & Downey, London, 1887

285 The Brothers Grimm, *The German Legends,* [trans. Donald Ward] Philadelphia, 1981

286 This is a similar charm to the strips of cloth hung on 'cloutie trees' near healing wells and streams in Britain

287 Phillipa Rappaport, *If It Dries Out, It's No Good: Women, Hair and Rusalki Beliefs,* SEEFA Journal, 1999

288 Julius Caesar, *The Conquest of Gaul*

289 Éva Pócs, *Fairies and Witches at the Boundary of South-Eastern and Central Europe,* paper presented at the Finnish Academy of Science and Letters, 7th April 1988, Helsinki, 1989.

290 *King Perceforest,* Paris, 1528

291 Ashmole manuscript 1406, Bodleian Library, Oxford

292 Jan Máchal, *Slavonic Mythology,* Cooper Square, New York, 1964

293 Lady Wilde, *Ancient Legends, Mystic Charms and Superstitions of Ireland,* Ward & Downey, London, 1887

294 W.B. Yeats, *Folk and Fairy Tales of the Irish Peasantry,* 1888

295 Gutch and Peacock, *Country Folk-lore; Lincolnshire,* Folk Lore Society, 1908

296 Crofton Croker, *Fairy Legends and Traditions of the South of Ireland,* John Murray, London, 1827

297 Walter Scott, *Minstrelsy of the Scottish Border,* 1801

298 Evans Wentz, *The Fairy Faith in Celtic Countries,* 1911

299 Crofton Croker, *Fairy Legends and Traditions of the South of Ireland,* John Murray, London, 1827

300 *The Life of Robin Goodfellow,* 1628

301 Crofton Croker in his Dedicatory Letter which prefaces his translation of Grimm's *Irish Elves*

302 John Rhys, *Celtic Folklore: Welsh and Manx,* Oxford University Press, 1901

303 John Rhys, *Celtic Folklore: Welsh and Manx,* Oxford University Press, 1901

304 K.M. Briggs, *The Fairies in Tradition and Literature,* Routledge & Kegan Paul, London, 1967

305 Lady Wilde, *Ancient Legends, Mystic Charms and Superstitions of Ireland,* Ward & Downey, London, 1887

306 John Beaumont, *An Historical, Physiological and Theological Treatice of Spirits,* D. Browne, 1705

307 Jan Máchal *Slavonic Mythology,* Cooper Square, New York, 1964

308 Robert Hunt, *Popular Romances of the West of England,* Chatto & Windus, 1930 [first pub. 1881]

309 Nigel Pennick, personal communication

310 Mircea Eliade, *The Forge and the Crucible,* Rider, 1962

311 Alexander Porteous, *The Lore of the Forest,* no date

312 K.M. Briggs, *The Fairies in Tradition and Literature,* Routledge & Kegan Paul, London, 1967

[313] Robert Hunt, *Popular Romances of the West of England*, Chatto & Windus, 1930 [first pub. 1881]

[314] Robert Hunt, *Popular Romances of the West of England*, Chatto & Windus, 1930 [first pub. 1881]

[315] Gillian Edwards, *Hobgoblin and Sweet Puck,* Geoffrey Bles, London, 1974

[316] J.M. Macpherson, *Primitive Beliefs in the North-East of Scotland,* London, 1929

[317] A fougou is a Neolithic subterranean chamber or tunnel, peculiar to Cornwall. Archeologists have speculated that they may have had a ritual purpose or been used for storage. Naturally, they were associated with fairies and witches, who were said to meet the devil there. Locals noted that hares often took refuge in the fougou, but never came out again...

[318] Adapted from Robert Hunt, *Popular Romances of the West of England,* Chatto & Windus, 1930 [first pub. 1881]

[319] Nigel Pennick, personal communication

[320] J.G. Frazer, *Folklore in the Old Testament,* Vol. 3, Macmillan, London, 1918

[321] William Henderson, *Folk Lore of the Northern Counties,* no date

[322] *The Life of Robin Goodfellow,* 1628

[323] M.C. Balfour, *Legends of the Cars,* 1891

[324] Hartland, 'The Supernatural Lapse of Time in Fairyland', *The Science of Fairytales,* no date

[325] K.M. Briggs, *The Fairies in Tradition and Literature,* Routledge & Kegan Paul, London, 1967

[326] Hugh G. Evelyn-White, *Hesiod, the Homeric Hymns,* London, 1959

[327] E.M. Wright, *Rustic Speech and Folklore,* Oxford University Press, 1913

[328] R. Scot, *Discoverie of Witchcraft,* 1584

[329] Richard Johnson, *Tom Thumb,* 1621

[330] Drayton, *Nymphidia,* 1620

[331] Lady Wilde, *Ancient Legends, Mystic Charms and Superstitions of Ireland,* Ward & Downey, London, 1887

[332] *Lanval, Poësies de Marie de France,* ed. by B. de Roquefort, Paris, 1920

[333] Sloane manuscript, 1727, The British Museum

[334] John Michell & Robert J.M. Rickard, *Phenomena,* Thames & Hudson, London, 1977

[335] Lewis Spence, *The Mysteries of Britain,* no date

[336] Julius Caesar, *The Conquest of Gaul*

[337] Gillian Edwards, *Hobgoblin and Sweet Puck,* Geoffrey Bles, London, 1974

[338] Lady Wilde, *Ancient Legend, Mystic Charms and Superstitions of Ireland,* 1887

[339] Jan Máchal, *The Mythology of all Races - Slavonic Mythology,* Cooper Square, New York, 1964

[340] Edwin Sidney Hartland, *The Science of Fairy Tales,* London, Walter Scott, 1891

[341] Jan Máchal, *Slavonic Mythology,* Cooper Square, New York, 1964

[342] William Henderson, *Folk Lore of the Northern Counties*

[343] Nigel Pennick, *Natural Magick,* Thorsons, London, 2001

[344] Marion K. Pearce, 'Flag Fen Lake Village', *Silver Wheel,* February 1997

[345] Walter Gregor, *Notes on the Folk-Lore of North-East Scotland,* London, 1881

[346] John Rhys, *Celtic Folklore: Welsh and Manx,* Oxford University Press, 1901

[347] Evans Wentz, *The Fairy Faith in Celtic Countries*

[348] Adapted from Robert Chambers, *Popular Rhymes of Scotland,* Edinburgh, 1858

[349] K.M. Briggs, *The Fairies in Tradition and Literature,* Routledge & Kegan Paul, London, 1967

[350] C. Burne and G. Jackson, *Shropshire Folk-Lore,* London, 1883

[351] A.A. Mills, 'Will o'the Wisp', *Chemistry in Britain* No. 16, 1980

[352] Robert Graves, *The White Goddess*

[353] Robert Graves, *The White Goddess*

[354] Lady Wilde, *Ancient Legends, Mystic Charms and Superstitions of Ireland,* Ward & Downey, London, 1887

[355] Robert Hunt, *Popular Romances of the West of England,* Chatto & Windus, 1930 [first pub. 1881]

[356] Durant Hotham, *Life of Jacob Behmen,* 1654

[357] Ruth Tongue, quoted by Briggs, 1959

[358] Richard Cavendish, 'The Wildwood' in *Man Myth and Magic* partwork magazine, no date

[359] M.C. Balfour, *Legends of the Cars,* 1891

[360] Ian Cooke, *Mermaid to Merrymaid,* Men an Tol Studio, Penzance, 1987

SELECT BIBLIOGRAPHY

Addy, S.O., *Household Tales with Other Traditional Remains,* Nutt, 1895

Allies, Jabez, *Ignis Fatuus, or Will o'the Wisp and the Fairies,* Worcester, 1840

Anderson, Hans Christian, *Fairy Tales,* Edmund Ward, 1958

Anderson, William, *Green Man,* Harper Collins, 1990

Ariosto, Ludovico, *Orlando Furioso,* University Press, London, 1974

Arnason, Jón, *Icelandic Legends* [trans. G.E.J. Powell & E. Magnússon], R.Bentley, London, 1864

Arrowsmith, Nancy *A Field Guide to the Little People,* Macmillan, London, 1977

Atkinson, J.C., *Forty Years in a Moorland Parish,* 1891

Aubrey, John, *Miscellanies* [1696], Reeves & Turner, London, 1890

Baker, Margaret, *Folklore and Customs of Rural England,* David & Charles, Newton Abbot, 1974

Balfour, M.C., *Legends of the Cars,* Folk-Lore II, 1891

Beaumont, John, *An Historical, Physiological & Theological Treatice of Spirits,* D. Browne, London, 1705

Berners, *The Boke of Duke Huon of Bordeaux, done into English by Sir John Bourchier, Lord Berners,*1601. First published 1548, Early English Text Society, 1893-7

Billson, Charles, *County Folk-lore I: Leicestershire and Rutland,* Folk Lore Society, 1895

Black, G.F., *County Folk-lore III: Orkney & Shetland Islands,* Folk Lore Society, 1903

Blakeborough, R., *Wit, Character, Folklore and Customs of the North Riding of Yorkshire,* 1898

Blamires, Steve, *The Irish Celtic Magical Tradition,* Aquarian, London, 1992

Bloom, William, *Working with Angels, Fairies and Nature Spirits,* Piatkus, London, 1998

Bord, Janet and Colin, *The Secret Country,* Paladin, London, 1978

Bottrell, W., *Traditions and Hearthside Stories of West Cornwall,* Penzance, 1870-80

Bourke, Angela, *The Burning of Angela Cleary,* Pimlico, 1999

Bowker, James, *Goblin Tales of Lancashire,* Swan Sonnenschien, London, 1883

Branston, Brian, *The Lost Gods of England,* Thames & Hudson, London, 1957

Bray, A.E., *Traditions, Legends, Superstitions and Sketches of Devonshire on the Borders of the Tamar and the Tavy,* London, 1838

Brewer, E., *Dictionary of Phrase and Fable*, Cassell, London, 1885

Briggs, K.M., *The Anatomy of Puck*, Routledge & Kegan Paul, 1959

Briggs, K.M., *The Fairies in Tradition and Literature*, Routledge & Kegan Paul, 1967

Broome, Dora, *Fairy Tales from the Isle of Man*, Penguin, 1951

Buchan, Peter, *Ancient Scottish Tales*, Peterhead, 1908

Burne, C., and Jackson, G., *Shropshire Folk-lore*, London, 1883

Campbell, Archibald, *Waifs and Strays of Celtic Tradition from Argyllshire*, Nutt, 1889

Campbell, J.F., *Popular Tales of the Western Highlands Orally Collected*, 1890

Campbell, J.G., *Superstitions of the Highlands and Islands of Scotland*, MacLehose, Glasgow, 1902

Campbell, Joseph, *The Way of Animals Powers*, Times Books, London, 1984

Carmichael, Alexander, *Carmina Gadelica*, Oliver & Boyd, Edinburgh, 1928

Chambers, R., *Popular Rhymes of Scotland*, W. & R. Chambers, Edinburgh, 1870

Child, F.J., *The English and Scottish Popular Ballads*, 1882

Clodd, Edward, *Tom Tit Tot*, London, 1898

Cooke, Ian, *Journey to the Stones*, Men-an-Tol Studio 1987

Cooper, Joe, *The Case of the Cottingley Fairies*, London 1990

Courtney, Margaret, *Cornish Feasts and Folklore*, 1890

Croker, T. Crofton, *Fairy Legends and Traditions of the South of Ireland*, John Murray, London, 1826

Crossing, William, *Tales of Dartmoor Pixies*, W. H. Wood, London, 1890

Cunningham, Allan, *Traditional Tales of English and Scottish Peasantry*, 1874

Curtin, Jeremiah, *Irish Folk-Tales* 1835-1906, [ed. S. O. Duilearga], Talbot Press, Dublin, 1960

Deeney, D., *Peasant Lore from Gaelic Ireland*, London 1901

Devereux, Paul, *Earth Lights Revelation - UFOs and Mystery Lightform Phenomena*, Blandford, 1989

Dillon, M., *Early Irish Literature*, Chicago, 1948

Dineen, Patric, *Irish English Dictionary*, P. Shalom, New York

Dorson, Richard, *The British Folklorists*, Routledge & Kegan Paul, London, 1968

Douglas, George, *Scottish Fairy and Other Folk Tales*, Scott Publishing, 1893

Edwards, Gillian, *Hobgoblin and Sweet Puck*, Geoffrey Bles, London, 1974

Frazer, James, *The Golden Bough*, Macmillan, 1976 [First published 1922]

Garis, Marie de, *Guernsey Folklore*, no date

Geoffrey of Monmouth [trans. Lewis Thorpe], *The History of the Kings of Britain*, Penguin, 1991

Geoffrey of Monmouth, *Vita Merlini*, University of Wales Press, 1973

Gill, W.W., *A Manx Scrapbook*, Arrowsmith, 1932

Gill, W.W., *A Second Manx Scrapbook*, Arrowsmith, 1932

Giraldus Cambrensis, *The Historical Works*, [ed. Thomas Wright], Bohn, 1863

Gordon Wasson, *Soma: The Divine Mushroom of Immortality*, Harcourt Brace Jovanovic, 1968

Grant, Mrs., *Myth, Tradition and Story from Western Argyll*, no date

Graves, Robert, *The Greek Myths*, Penguin, London, 1955

Graves, Robert, *The White Goddess*, Faber & Faber, London, 1961

Green, M., *Gods of the Celts*, Allan Sutton, Gloucester, 1986

Green, Miranda, *Animals in Celtic Life and Myth*, Routledge, 1992

Gregory, Lady Augusta Persse, *Visions and Beliefs in the West of Ireland* Colin Smythe, 1920

Grimm, Jacob and Wilhelm, *The Complete Fairy Tales of the Brothers Grimm*, Bantam, 1987

Grimm, Wilhelm and Jacob, *The German Legends*, [trans. Donald Ward] Philadelphia, 1981

Guest, Charlotte, & Jones, J. [trans.], *Mabinogion*, University of Wales Press, 1977

Harland, J., & Wilkinson, T.T., *Lancashire Folklore*, London, 1882

Harrison, W., *Mona Miscellany*, Douglas, 1869

Hartland, E.S., *County Folk-Lore I. Gloucestershire*, Folk Lore Society, 1895

Hazlitt, W.C., *The Romance of King Orfeo*, London, 1875

Henderson, George, *Survivals in Belief among the Celts*, MacLehose, 1911

Henderson, William, *Notes on the Folk-Lore of the Northern Counties of England and the Borders*, Folk Lore Society 1879

Hodson, Geoffrey, *Fairies at Work and Play*, Theosophical Publishing House, 1925

Holt, J.C., *Robin Hood*, Thames & Hudson, London, 1991

Hunt, Robert, *Popular Romances of the West of England* [1881] Chatto & Windus, 1923

Hyde, Douglas, *Beside the Fire*, Nutt, London, 1890

Hyde, Douglas, *Legends, Tales and Stories of Ireland*, Dublin, 1887

Jacobs, J., *English Fairy Tales*, David Nutt, 1890

Jacobs, Joseph, *Celtic Fairy Tales* David Nutt, 1894

Keightley, Thomas, *The Fairy Mythology* Whittaker, Treacher, London, 1833

Kirk, Robert, *The Secret Commonwealth of Elves, Fauns and Fairies* [1691] The Folklore Society, London, 1976

Lawson, J.C., *Modern Greek Folklore and Ancient Greek Religion*, Cambridge, 1910

MacDonald, George, *Dealings With Fairies*, London, 1867

Máchal, Jan, *The Mythology of all Races - Slavic Mythology*, Cooper Square, New York, 1964

MacKenzie, Donald, *Scottish Folk-Lore and Folk Life*, Blackie, 1935

MacKenzie, Osgood, *A Hundred Years in the Highlands*, 1956

Maclean, Dorothy, *To Hear the Angels Sing*, Turnstone Press, 1980

MacManus, D.A., *The Middle Kingdom*, Max Parrish, 1959

MacNeill, Marion, *The Silver Bough*, Maclellan, 1957

MacRitchie, David, *Fians, Fairies and Picts* London 1893

Malory, Thomas, *Le Morte D'Arthur*, Penguin, 1969

Manning-Sanders, R., *Scottish Folk Tales*, Methuen, London, 1976

Map, Walter [ed. F. Tupper and M.B. Ogle], *De Nugis Curialium*, Chatto and Windus, London, 1924

Marie de France, *Poèsies de Marie de France* [ed. B. de Roquefort], Paris, 1920

McGrath, Sheena, *The Sun Goddess*, Blandford, London, 1997

McPherson, J.M., *Primitive Beliefs in the North-east of Scotland*, Longmans, London, 1929

Miller, Hugh, *Scenes and Legends of the North of Scotland*, Edinburgh, 1857

Miller, Hugh, *The Old Red Sandstone*, Edinburgh, 1841

Moore, A.W., *Manx Folklore*, Douglas, 1899

Morrison, Sophia, *Manx Fairy Tales*, Nutt, London, 1911

Murray, Margaret, *Witch Cult in Western Europe*, Oxford University Press, Oxford, 1921

Naddair, Kaledon, *Keltic Folk and Faerie Tales*, Century, 1987

Nennius [ed. J.Morris], *Historia Britonum*, Phillmore, Chichester, 1980

Nichols, Ross, *The Book of Druidry*, Aquarian, London, 1990

Ó Hógáin, Dáithí, *The Sacred Isle*, The Boydell Press, Woodbridge, 1999

O'Grady, S.H., *The Silva Gadelica*, William & Norgate, London, 1892

Palmer, Roy, *The Folklore of Warwickshire*, Batsford, 1976

Perrault, *Popular Tales*, ed. Andrew Lang, Oxford, 1888

Porteous, Alexander, *Forest Folklore*, George Allen & Unwin, London, 1928

Priest, Harold, *The Faerie Queene, Spencer*, Coles Notes, London, 1968

Rhys, John, *Celtic Folklore: Welsh and Manx*, Oxford, 1901

Robertson, R. Macdonald, *Selected Highland Folktales*, Oliver and Boyd, 1964

Ruck, Carl, *The Offerings from the Hyperboreans*, *Persephone's Quest*, Yale, New Haven, 1986

Scott, Sir Walter, *Letters on Demonology and Witchcraft*, John Murray, 1830

Scott, Sir Walter, *Minstrelsy of the Scottish Border* [1801], Oliver & Boyd, Edinburgh, 1932

Sikes, Wirt *British Goblins: The Realm of the Faerie*, 1880; Llanerch facsimile edition 1991

Simpkins, J.E., *County Folk-Lore VII: Fife*, Folk Lore Society, 1914

Simpson, E.B., *Lore in Lowland Scotland*, Dent, London, 1908

Spence, John, *Shetland Folk-Lore*, Lerwick, 1899

Spence, Lewis, *The Fairy Tradition in Britain*, Rider, London, 1948

Stewart, R. Grant, *The Popular Superstitions of the Highlands*, Archibald Constable, 1823

Sturluson, Snorri [trans. Anthony Faulkes] *Snorri Sturluson: Edda*, Dent, London, 1987

Tongue, R.L., *Somerset Folklore: County Series VIII*, Folk Lore Society, 1965

Tongue, Ruth, *Forgotten Folk Tales of the English Counties*, Routledge & Kegan Paul, 1970

Von Eschenbach, Wolfram, *Parzival*, [trans At. Hatto], Penguin, Harmondsworth, 1980

Wentz, Evans, *The Fairy Faith in Celtic Countries*, Oxford University Press, 1911

Wilde, Lady, *Ancient Legends, Mystic Charms and Superstitions of Ireland*, Ward and Downey, London 1878

Wilson, Steve, *Robin Hood the Spirit of the Forest*, Neptune, London, 1993

Wood-Martin, W.G., *Traces of the Elder Faiths of Ireland*, Longman, London, 1902

Wright, E.M., *Rustic Speech and Folk-Lore*, Oxford University Press, 1913

Wright, Thomas, *Essays on Subjects Connected with Popular Superstitions*, Smith, London, 1846

Yeats, W.B., *Folk and Fairy Tales of the Irish Peasantry*, 1888

Yeats, W.B., *The Celtic Twilight*, London, 1893

PERIODICALS

Pete Jennings, *Gippeswic* No. 9, June 1994 [quoting Sir Walter Scott]

Bob Trubshaw, 'Black Dogs in Folklore' in *Mercian Mysteries* No. 20, August 1994

The Guernsey Magazine, June 1872

Grant Allen, *Cornhill Magazine* No. 43, 1881

Bob Trubshaw, 'Black Dogs, Guardians of the Corpse Ways' in *At The Edge*

David Clarke, 'Peakland Spooklights' in *At The Edge* No. 10, June 1998

Bob Trubshaw, 'Fairies and Their Kin' in *At the Edge* No. 10, June 1998

Man, Myth and Magic, partwork magazine, no date

Seán Russell Friend, 'Banshee: Herald of Death' in *Silver Wheel Magazine*, May 1999

Phillipa Rappaport, University of Virginia, 'If It Dries Out, It's No Good: Women, Hair and Rusalki Beliefs', *SEEFA Journal*, Vol. 4, No. 1, 1999

INTERNET SITES

Peter Lamborn Wilson, *Irish Soma*: http://www.lycaeum.org/~lux/features/irshsoma.html

Kevin Callahan Rockart: http://zzyx.ucsc.edu/comp/Bill/naral.html

Gnomes: http://www.erols.com/michaelmyrick/history.html

ILLUSTRATIONS

The colour illustrations were created by Paul Mason, many incorporating his own special photography. Additional special photography by the author Anna Franklin is also incorporated within the following: *AMORTAS; BOGINKI; BUTTERFLY; BELTANE; ELF; FINVARRA; GRIG; LADY OF THE LAKE; PERI*

The black & white/tinted illustrations were created for the book by Helen Field.

The model for *DAVY JONES* courtesy of the Bill Brookman Foundation; the fairy chimneys photograph in PERI by Kathy Cocks

Some of the illustrations have appeared previously. They other are reproduced here with grateful thanks to the original publishers for permission to use, as follows:

The Sacred Circle Tarot Anna Franklin & Paul Mason, Llewellyn 1998 *AMFORTAS; FATE; GREEN MAN; LABYRINTH; MEDB; MOON; UNDERWORLD*

The Fairy Ring Anna Franklin & Paul Mason, Llewellyn 2001 *BANSHEES; BELTANE; FACHAN; HALLOWEEN; KNOCKER; ROBIN GOODFELLOW; SPRITE; TRYAMOUR*

The Wellspring Anna Franklin & Pamela Harvey, Capall Bann 1997 *EGGSHELLS; WILD HUNT*

Magical Beasts Nigel Pennick, Capall Bann 2002 *BOLLA; BRIGHID; CAT; CLIONA; DEVANA; DIWICA; FRAU HOLDA*

The Goddess Year Nigel Pennick & Helen Field, Capell Bann, 1996 *RHIANNON; UNICORN; WITCH*

The God Year Nigel Pennick & Helen Field, Capall Bann, 1998 *HERNE; PROTEUS/OLD MAN OF THE SEA*

How to Meet Fairies Sheila Jeffreys, Capall Bann 2002 *ELF*

Magical Gardens P. Heston, Capall Bann 1999 *DRYAD*